Artemisia Gentileschi and the Business of Art

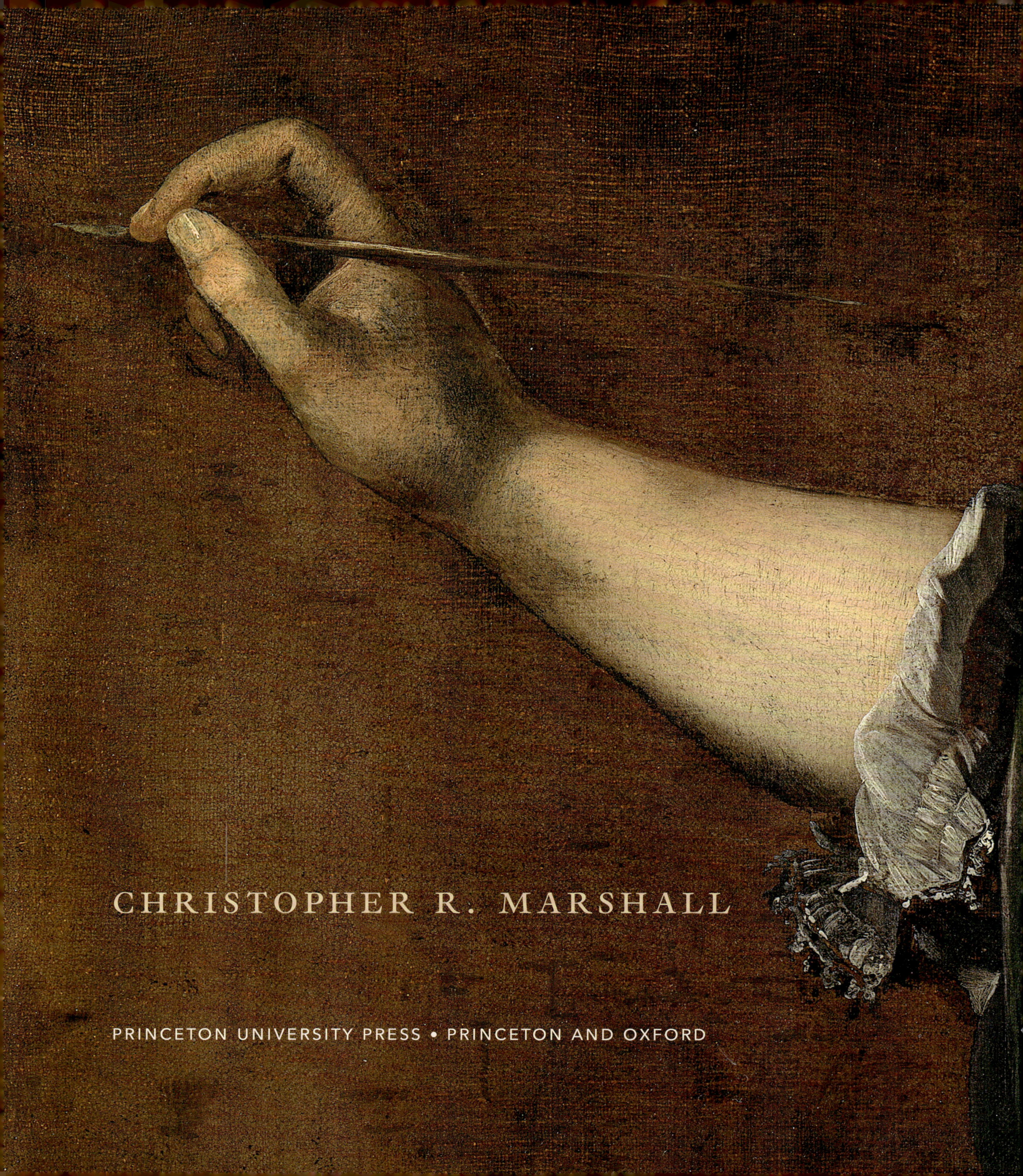

CHRISTOPHER R. MARSHALL

PRINCETON UNIVERSITY PRESS • PRINCETON AND OXFORD

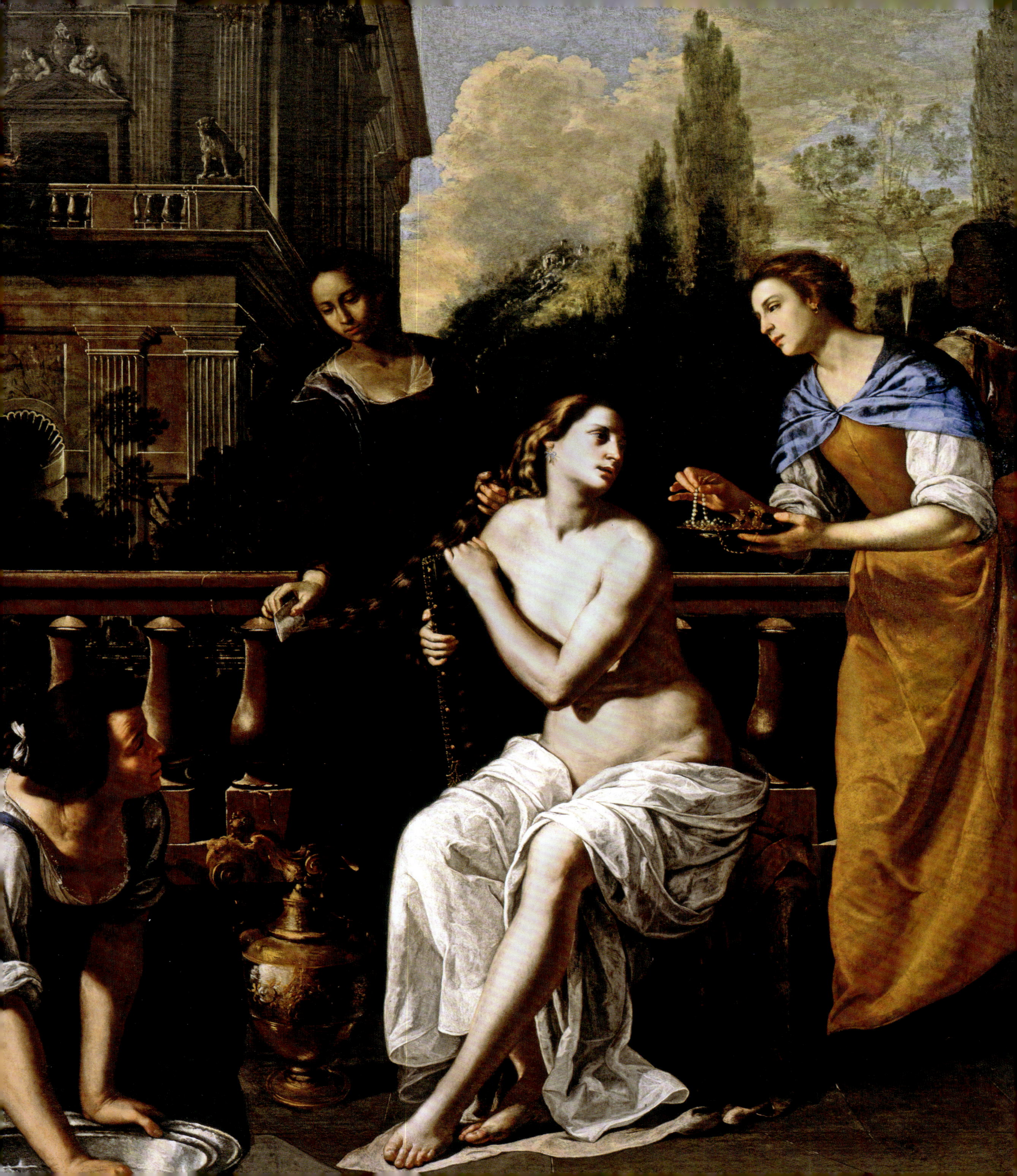

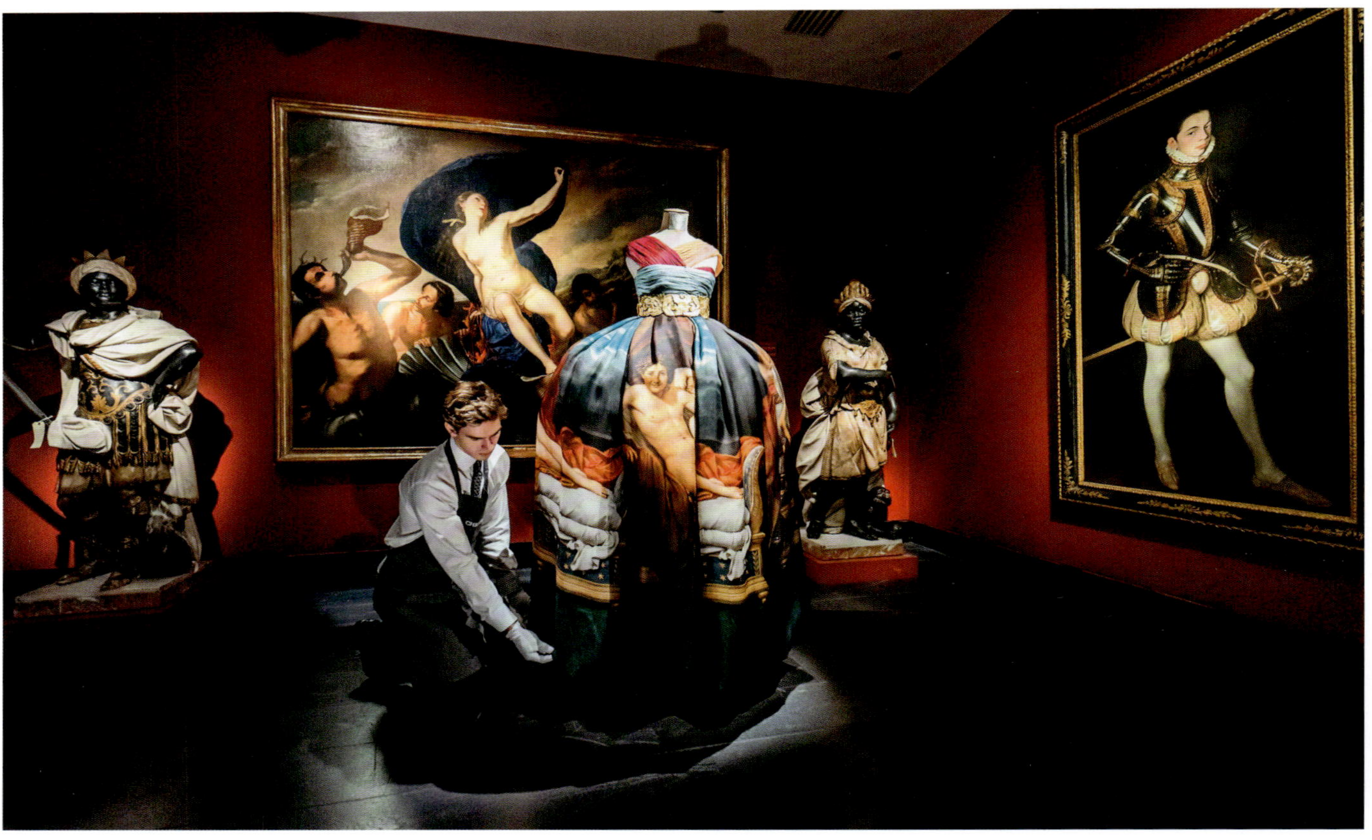

1 *Art Adorned* exhibition, Christie's, London, November 2019

been auctioned at Christie's, New York, early that year under an attribution to the Neapolitan Baroque painter Bernardo Cavallino (1616–1656), an artist whose oeuvre is as distinguished as it is little known beyond specialist circles. The lot had, nonetheless, achieved a creditable hammer price of US$550,000, rising to a final figure of $656,000 with the addition of Christie's customary buyer's premium and fees.[2] Within a few short years, this attribution had been revised upwards as a number of scholars sought to identify the painting as one of the last works produced in Naples by Artemisia Gentileschi, with the probable assistance of a junior collaborator by the name of Onofrio Palumbo.[3] The new attribution was helped along by virtue of the work's appearance in a number of exhibitions dedicated to Gentileschi, including one in Milan in 2011 and another in Rome in 2016.[4] Now it was for sale again in London, 'price on request'. *Vogue UK* accordingly encouraged its readers to consider taking the painting home as an attractive investment item: '*The Triumph of Galatea*, therefore, makes for an interesting conversation piece . . . And with the first major exhibition of Artemisia Gentileschi's work going on display at the National Gallery in spring 2020, now's the time to invest – your hand-painted corset dress, after all, deserves better than a mere handbag as a companion piece.'[5]

As *Vogue* correctly underscored, the Christie's exhibition of the *Triumph of Galatea* was timed to coincide with the increased publicity attendant on a forthcoming Gentileschi retrospective that was scheduled to open at the National Gallery, London, in April 2020 (although subsequently postponed until October 2020 as a result of the Coronavirus pandemic). The London exhibition included another recent art-market discovery. For decades, Gentileschi's *Self-portrait as St Catherine of Alexandria* had languished unnoticed in a French private collection before appearing for auction with a new attribution to Artemisia at the Hôtel Drouot, Paris, on 19 December 2017 (fig. 35). The painting had sold on that occasion for the then record price of €2,400,000 (US$2,832,960), including premium and fees, before being sold the following year to the National Gallery, London, for £3,600,000 (US$4,750,000). This made the *St Catherine* the first painting by a woman artist to be acquired by the National Gallery since 1991 and one of a mere twenty-one artworks by women in the gallery's collection.[6] In the space of three short years, then, the *St Catherine* had progressed from being an unknown entity to becoming a canonical addition to the oeuvre of one of the most important artists of the seventeenth century. Its acquisition, moreover, had helped redress the critical imbalance of women in one of the world's most important museums. It, accordingly, figured prominently in the media commentary surrounding the 2020 Gentileschi exhibition – which also turned out to be the first major exhibition to be dedicated to a female artist in the gallery's 196-year history.[7]

The Triumph of Galatea remained unsold following the conclusion of Christie's *Art Adorned* exhibition in December 2019. Yet the initiative had benefited the auction house's longer-term strategy of building publicity for the canvas among its global network of clients. The painting was thus able to take advantage of an increased visibility and momentum when it was subsequently included in the Christie's, New York, auction of 15 October 2020 (two weeks after the opening of the London Gentileschi retrospective, as it transpired). On this occasion, the painting was attributed to Artemisia Gentileschi 'and associate' and placed with an estimate of one to one and a half million dollars. This time the painting did sell: for US$2,130,000, a significant price increase that represented a more than threefold return on its owner's initial investment over the space of thirteen years. Its new owner was the Lucas Museum of Narrative Art in Los Angeles. The canvas was thus now also transitioning from the relative anonymity of a private collection to the increased public visibility and recognition attendant upon its new home in an American museum devoted to a multi-disciplinary investigation of the historical and contemporary processes of visual story-telling and myth-making.[8]

Yet neither the *Galatea* nor the *St Catherine of Alexandria* can claim the title of the world's most expensive painting attributed to Gentileschi to be sold at auction. That distinction goes, instead, to a third 'sleeper' canvas discovered in a private Lyonese collection, where it had remained unnoticed since the 1980s. This work was sold at the Paris auction house Artcurial on 13 November 2019, with an estimate of €600–800,000 (US$600,240–880,320) (fig. 77). Depicting the ancient Roman heroine *Lucretia* and probably datable to Gentileschi's Venetian period of 1627–30, the painting exceeded its estimate by a considerable amount. In fact, it achieved a new record for the artist of €4,777,000 (US$5,200,000), including buyer's premium and fees. It also passed from private to public ownership, being acquired by the J. Paul Getty Museum, Los Angeles. The steeply rising prices and increased public visibility attendant upon these three paintings over such a short period highlight the degree to which Artemisia Gentileschi's work is currently moving into a new phase of increased institutional and art-market-based recognition. This will inevitably drive the prices for her work yet higher, so that a new series of auction records will no doubt soon come to replace those cited here.

What would Gentileschi have made of this? One wonders whether the artist might have felt a certain sense of pique, in fact, at the prospect of commercial firms and private collectors benefiting from the resale of her works on the secondary market while she – the individual who created them – was unable to profit from the sales herself. Neither auctions nor museums, moreover, were as prominent in Baroque Italy as they are today. Gentileschi's career was dominated, rather, by the primary market, with its persistent stream of patrons, agents, artists, dealers and all the other individuals with whom artists needed to remain on good terms in order to maintain an edge in a highly competitive art world.

Many other aspects of the above-mentioned transactions would have, nonetheless, struck an immediate chord of familiarity with Gentileschi. Christie's emphasis on the exclusivity of luxury as a branding strategy, for example, was something with which she was very familiar. She deployed a similar strategy in attempting to create a unique brand for herself based on the glamour and distinctiveness of her own appearance and persona, as we shall see. Being able to cultivate and then mobilize a global network of influential friends, allies and supporters was also something on which Gentileschi expended a great deal of energy throughout her career. This was particularly important for her given her concern to move beyond the pre-existing boundaries of the complex geographic and political landscape that defined Rome and its surrounds, for example, as a country entirely foreign to Naples. Gentileschi's constant attempts to expand her network to a truly international level further reflected her ceaseless drive to bring her work to the attention of a wide range of powerful individuals throughout Europe, from Messina to London and beyond.

The decisive role played by timing and momentum in making or breaking an artist's career was something that Gentileschi would have well understood as a result of the many ups and downs of her own long and storied career. She had seen for herself the way in which the tipping point of success in an art world will often hinge upon a sudden convergence of factors. Artists lucky enough to experience success of this kind may suddenly notice themselves becoming the focus of sustained and co-ordinated art-world attention, to the extent that a synergy may become evident, as, for example, between the business activities of Christie's in New York and the art-historical, canon-building efforts of the National Gallery in London. Good timing of this sort, however, is an elusive quality that can often seem to remain frustratingly just beyond an artist's reach. Gentileschi also experienced the significance of timing – both good and bad – during her own career. In 1620, circumstances impelled her to leave Florence hurriedly, before being able to capitalise on the growing interest in a particular kind of female-oriented imagery for which she had been carefully building momentum during the previous years. Conversely, and at the other end of her career, during the early 1630s, a more favourable convergence of factors enabled her to enjoy a brief moment of heightened financial and professional recognition in Naples, following her relocation there at the behest of the viceroy.

This is a book about these kinds of professional and business concerns as they apply to one of the most fascinating and topical artists of the early modern era. It will consider the life, art and afterlife of Artemisia Gentileschi (1593–*c.*1656) from the point of view of the business considerations that informed her career and legacy and that have helped to shape her audiences' responses to her work and reputation from her own time to the present. It will consider Gentileschi's continual quest for recognition as an enterprising businesswoman seeking to make her way in a male-dominated art world. The kinds of questions that it will accordingly pose include the following: How did Gentileschi negotiate with patrons to receive fair recompense for her work? What strategies did she employ to keep herself in demand over the space of forty years and in the face of a series of newly ascendant, fashionable styles that soon came to eclipse the popularity of her initial training in Caravaggism? How did she exploit her international fame in order to promote herself in ways that manipulated her own image as part of the allure of what was being sold? Which different versions of Gentileschi are presented to us in more recent exhibitions and what do they have to tell us about the ongoing role of the museum in conferring posthumous validation on the historical status of a select few canonical artists?

In pursuing these considerations, I draw inspiration from the emerging field of studies of the Italian Baroque art market and economic analyses of Italian Baroque art more generally.[9] I am thus concerned to articulate such directly economic and art-market-oriented issues as Gentileschi's pricing strategies, productivity and the market dimensions of the different levels of her workshop output. But I seek also to interpret the topic of the business of art in a broader sense in order to gain insight into how Gentileschi promoted and marketed both herself and her artworks in a varied series of artistic centres throughout Baroque Europe. The ensuing study interprets Gentileschi's art not so much from the point of view of a self-contained aesthetic oeuvre, but rather from the perspective of a dynamically evolving career responding strategically to a series of external challenges and opportunities that presented themselves to her in multiple settings over the space of more than forty years.

This book hinges on the premise that the business of art involves much more than the literal sale of art. For every dollar expended on an artwork – or ducat or florin or scudo in Gentileschi's case – a vast amount of work will have already gone on in the background to build up a credible infrastructure of meaning and critical value that can be used to support and enhance the claims that are encapsulated within that sale. A successful transaction of this kind will rest on the ability of both the artwork and its creator to 'sell' to the audience a complex array of signifiers of artistic value.[10] These work together to communicate an abstracted form of value to the buyer: what might even be described as a convincingly interwoven fiction of value. This understanding of value seeks to bolster the artwork's authority with reference to such notions as reputational prestige, originality, inventiveness, glamour, luxury, exclusivity and so on. Understanding the business of art in this broader sense will also lead us to consider the influence of the different sectors of the art world in advancing Gentileschi's reputation, both during her career and following her death. This ranges from the earliest art criticism written during her own lifetime to the fundamental role played by the contemporary museum in promoting varying interpretations of her art on the global stage.

In researching this book, I have been constantly reminded of the degree to which Gentileschi has attracted some of the greatest writers on the Italian Baroque, from Roberto Longhi to today. Within the resulting text I have, therefore, sought to highlight my deep indebtedness to the rich tradition of Gentileschian scholarship, an indebtedness that extends even to my sequencing of chapter titles.[11] I also acknowledge the ongoing debt incurred by scholars in following the vital contribution made by feminist scholarship to the study of Gentileschi, both in the context of her own time and in terms of the issues that she continues to raise in relation to more contemporary considerations. This book aims to provide a useful complementary framework to the collective insights of these analyses, drawing as they do on the fundamental contribution of Mary D. Garrard, from her early articles published in advance of her landmark monograph of 1989 to her more focused account of 2001, leading in turn to her most recent study of 2020.[12]

Gender and feminist readings will continue to inform many of the topics to be addressed within these pages. In terms of the previous discussion of Gentileschi's auction prices, for example, they can help to remind us of the obvious structural discrimination that persists in undercutting the relative earning capacities of female versus male artists in an art world that perpetuates many of the inequities that were a fact of life during Gentileschi's day. Gentileschi may have achieved a high of US$5,200,000 at auction, but this pales in comparison with the prices achieved by her father's work. The reputation of Orazio Gentileschi (1563–1639) was ultimately overshadowed during his own lifetime by that of his daughter. Yet the current record for prices obtained for his work exceeds those for Artemisia's by a factor of six to one. His *Danaë* was acquired by the J. Paul Getty Museum at Sotheby's, New York, on 28 January 2016 for a hammer price of $27,000,000, or US$30,500,000, including premium and fees.[13] His second most expensive painting is *The Finding of Moses*, which was acquired in 2019 by the National Gallery, London, for £22,000,000 (US$29,000,000). This is more than six times the amount paid by the same organisation, we recall, for Artemisia's admittedly rather smaller *Self-portrait as St Catherine of Alexandria*.

This economic disparity between otherwise directly comparable male and female artists becomes more evident still when Artemisia's prices are viewed in relation to other, supposedly more 'mainstream' Baroque artists. Rubens's *Massacre of the Innocents*, for example, was sold at Sotheby's, London, on 10 July 2002 for £49,000,000 (US$76,700,000). Caravaggio's paintings remain today almost entirely locked up in museum collections and thus hardly ever appear on the market. In 2019, a painting attributed to Caravaggio of *Judith and Holofernes* was, nevertheless, put to auction with an estimate of US$113 to $170 million. It was privately acquired for an undisclosed sum just prior to auction, and so, presumably, was sold for a figure within that range.[14] It seems that the Guerrilla Girls had it right all those years ago, then, when they sought to shame collectors into recognising the obvious disparities of gender and race informing the financial dimensions of their collections (fig. 2). This they did by highlighting the relative affordability of Gentileschi and other female artists in comparison with the 'mega-bucks' required to purchase a work by the leading male artists of the day. In the late 1980s, this equated to an artist like Jasper Johns; today, we might want to exchange Johns's name for that of Jeff Koons. That should remind us, in turn, of the mind-boggling sum of US$91,000,000 that was

WHEN RACISM & SEXISM ARE NO LONGER FASHIONABLE, WHAT WILL YOUR ART COLLECTION BE WORTH?

The art market won't bestow mega-buck prices on the work of a few white males forever. For the 17.7 million you just spent on a single Jasper Johns painting, you could have bought at least one work by all of these women and artists of color.

Bernice Abbott
Anni Albers
Sofonisba Anguisolla
Diane Arbus
Vanessa Bell
Isabel Bishop
Rosa Bonheur
Elizabeth Bougereau
Margaret Bourke-White
Romaine Brooks
Julia Margaret Cameron
Emily Carr
Rosalba Carriera
Mary Cassatt
Constance Marie Charpentier
Imogen Cunningham
Sonia Delaunay
Elaine de Kooning
Lavinia Fontana
Meta Warwick Fuller
Artemisia Gentileschi
Marguérite Gérard
Natalia Goncharova
Kate Greenaway
Barbara Hepworth
Eva Hesse
Hannah Hoch
Anna Huntingdon
May Howard Jackson
Frida Kahlo
Angelica Kauffmann
Hilma of Klimt
Kathe Kollwitz
Lee Krasner
Dorothea Lange
Marie Laurencin
Edmonia Lewis
Judith Leyster
Barbara Longhi
Dora Maar
Lee Miller
Lisette Model
Paula Modersohn-Becker
Tina Modotti
Berthe Morisot
Grandma Moses
Gabriele Münter
Alice Neel
Louise Nevelson
Georgia O'Keeffe
Meret Oppenheim
Sarah Peale
Ljubova Popova
Olga Rosanova
Nellie Mae Rowe
Rachel Ruysch
Kay Sage
Augusta Savage
Vavara Stepanova
Florine Stettheimer
Sophie Taeuber-Arp
Alma Thomas
Marietta Robusti Tintoretto
Suzanne Valadon
Remedios Varo
Elizabeth Vigée Le Brun
Laura Wheeling Waring

Please send $ and comments to:
Box 1056 Cooper Sta. NY, NY 10276 GUERRILLA GIRLS CONSCIENCE OF THE ART WORLD

2 Guerrilla Girls, *When Racism and Sexism Are No Longer Fashionable, How Much Will Your Art Collection Be Worth?*, 1989, screen-print on paper, 43.5 × 55.5 cm

realised for Koons's *Rabbit* at a Christie's, New York, auction of 15 May 2019, making it the world's most expensive artwork by a living artist (a record that will no doubt be surpassed in the not-too-distant future).[15]

Research into Artemisia Gentileschi constitutes one of the most active and hotly debated areas of art history. The image of the artist that we are presented with today is complicated and enlivened by a raft of new ideas, challenges and hypotheses. These render her, in many respects, a radically different proposition from the image that was presented some twenty years ago, when several key studies were published. Another motivation in writing this book has, therefore, been to create an updated monograph for a fresh generation of readers, one that takes into account the many recent developments in the field. The new findings that this book incorporates within its analysis include an additional twelve paintings with credible attributions to Artemisia that have been discovered since the time of the landmark catalogue raisonné produced by R. Ward Bissell in 1999.[16] Other key new findings of the past few years include the earliest recorded biography of the artist, which came to light in 2018;[17] a trove of more than thirty letters, written by the artist and her husband, which was discovered in a private Florentine archive in 2011;[18] the previously noted documentation regarding the workshop assistance of the Neapolitan painter Onofrio Palumbo in Naples during the 1650s;[19] and the discovery of two sonnets written by Gentileschi in the mid-1620s, a research finding that confirms the artist's 'attainment of a gloss of the poetic skills that were the delightful currency of polite society in Italy', as Sheila Barker has underscored.[20]

Given all that has been written and contended about Artemisia Gentileschi over the years, it is my hope that the framework here adopted might offer readers an opportunity to reconsider her art and life from a fresh perspective. This should be nowhere more so than in the account of her origins and early works. Previous studies have stressed the significance for understanding Gentileschi of the trial brought by her father in February 1612 against his former close associate and colleague Agostino Tassi (1578–1644). The ensuing case – which caused a major scandal among the tightly knit networks of the Roman art world – hinged on the charge of *stuprum*. This term is often loosely translated today as rape and is also thus referenced in these pages for the sake of convenience. Yet the term was understood rather differently during its own day. In a legal sense, it denoted the concept of forcible defloration, and its litigation depended upon Baroque notions of family honour and paternal property rights – emphases that seem worlds removed from today's concentration on the intrinsically harmful legacy and impact of the violent crime of rape.[21] The event occurred on 6 May 1611. Gentileschi was aged seventeen; Tassi was thirty-two. In the pages that follow, the trial proceedings are analysed not so much for their insights into the traumatic nature of Gentileschi's early biography, fundamentally distressing though that experience can only have been;[22] rather, the rich documentation of the trial proceedings is used as the basis for an attempt to discern the nature of Gentileschi's artistic training and first steps as an independent artist. It is to be hoped that a less familiar picture of Gentileschi's early years might emerge from this focus, one that begins by highlighting the restricted and demanding nature of her initial training and early workshop employment within the hardscrabble environment of the artists' district of Baroque Rome.

PAGE 11 Artemisia Gentileschi, *Allegory of Inclination* (detail of fig. 4)

— PART I —

Becoming Artemisia

ROME, 1606–1613

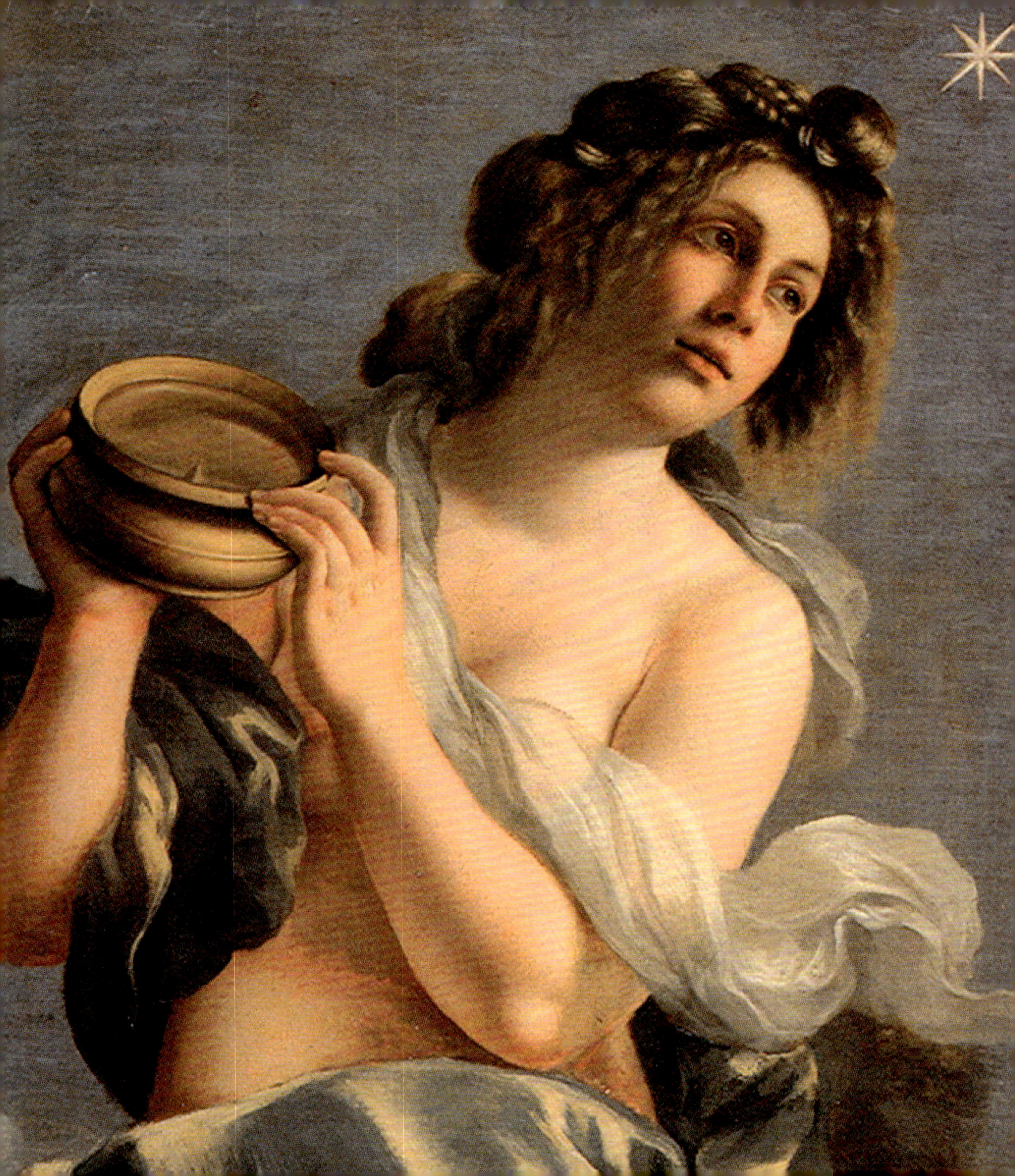

I

In her Master's House

GENTILESCHI'S ARTISTIC TRAINING IN THE ARTISTS' DISTRICT OF BAROQUE ROME

INTRODUCTION
IN THE NAME OF THE FATHER: ARTEMISIA AND THE MYTHOLOGY OF ORIGINS

Nothing conveys the impression of fame quite so well as a good origin myth. Giorgio Vasari certainly knew this. As the critic responsible for establishing an artist's biography as one of the fundamental reference points of art history, Vasari was keenly aware of the power of suitably embroidered origin stories to set a golden seal on artistic fame. Instances include his vivid image of Cimabue observing the youthful Giotto scratching pictures onto rocks with a sharpened stone while tending to his flock. Or, Verrocchio returning one afternoon to his *Baptism of Christ* altarpiece, only to discover that his young apprentice, Leonardo, had effortlessly surpassed him by painting an angel that was judged to be 'much better than the figures painted by Andrea' (fig. 3).[1] In these and other instances, Vasari underscored the mythic dimensions of his most famous protagonists by stressing their prodigious origins, together with their youthful, self-absorbed ability to follow their own inspiration while exceeding the best efforts of their peers.[2]

Michelangelo took this process one step further. Not content with Vasari's attempts to write a flattering life story on his behalf, he sought to shape his own origin myth by producing the world's first ghost-written artist's biography.[3] This, in combination with

FACING PAGE Jan van der Straet (Johannes Stradanus), *Color Olivi/Oil Paint* (detail of fig. 9)

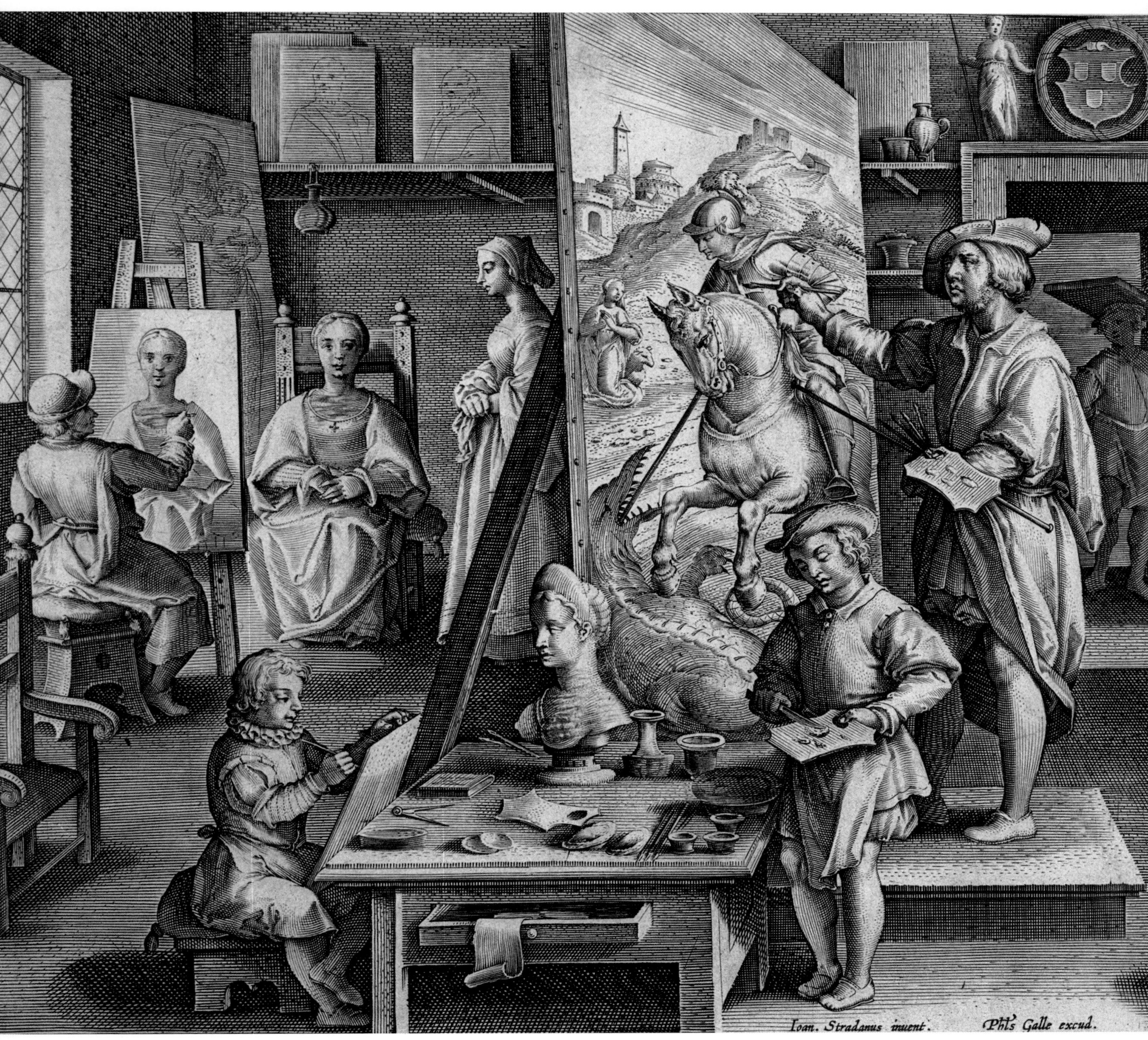
Ioan. Stradanus inuent.
Phls Galle excud.

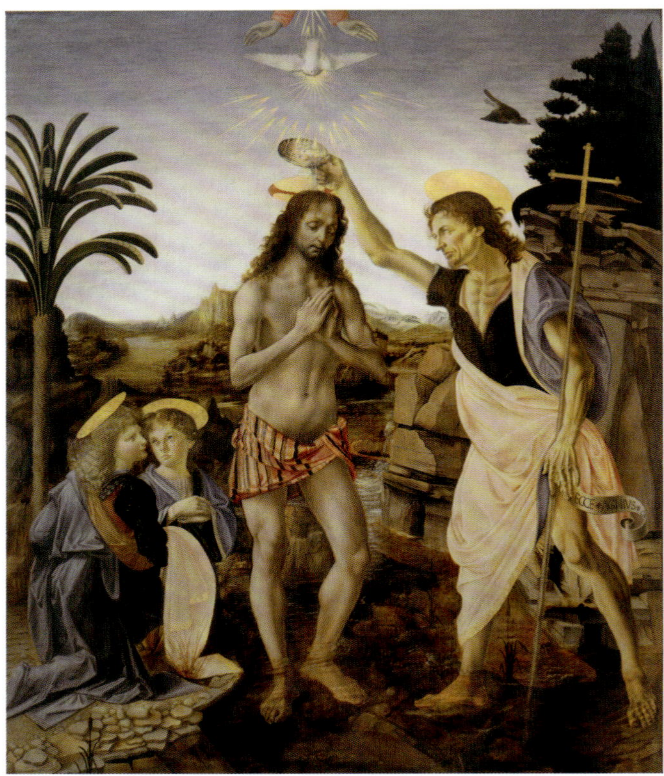

3 Andrea Verrocchio and Leonardo da Vinci, *The Baptism of Christ*, c.1470–75, tempera and oil on panel, 177 × 151 cm, Galleria degli Uffizi Florence

all the other retellings of his life, established an archetypal format for an authoritative, early-life story, characterised by precocious pre-eminence shot through with intimations of immortality. In Michelangelo's case, the story involves such elements as his family's initial hostility to his innate artistic calling, his subsequent apprenticeship to a jealous master – who taught him nothing, or so we are told – the early recognition and encouragement given to the young prodigy by the greatest of all of Florence's enlightened patrons who invited him to improve himself on his own terms by studying in the garden of San Marco, where he, nonetheless, attracted the enmity of yet more rivals, one of whom broke his nose in a fit of jealous rage. And so on.

In 1615, Artemisia Gentileschi contributed to this process of artistic myth-making. In that year, she was selected by the great-nephew of Michelangelo to paint one of the key canvases for the Casa Buonarroti's innovative iconographic programme, which extolled his forebear's legacy for a seventeenth-century audience. Her work depicts a personification of the artistic quality of natural inclination, an important dimension of Michelangelo's mythic characterisation, since it glorifies his natural propensity towards art, his sense of inner calling and his commitment to follow that calling towards the heights of greatness, regardless of the consequences (fig. 4).[4] Although only twenty-two and still very much at the beginning of her career, Gentileschi demonstrated a certain level of audacity in her contribution to this cycle. She sought to link herself with Michelangelo and with the quality of artistic inclination that he personified by incorporating an idealized self-portrait of herself onto the semi-naked allegory of Inclination. The direct connection between art and life that she created, however, proved a little too unexpurgated for the Casa Buonarroti's subsequent owners. One of them eventually asked the painter Volterrano to add heavy green drapery over the figure's lap and right arm in order to conceal its nudity.[5]

Gentileschi turns out to have been considering origin myths quite deeply during the time that she painted this work while residing in Florence. This has now become evident thanks to a brief manuscript biography of her early life that was first published in 2018. This biography was ostensibly written – although never published – by Cristofano di Ottaviano Bronzini (*c.*1580–1633), a prelate attached to the household of Cardinal Carlo de' Medici. Sheila Barker, who made the discovery, has credibly argued that Bronzini's account should be understood as being essentially attributable to Gentileschi herself, with Bronzini acting as a kind of amanuensis to the artist's musings, in much the same way that Condivi had acted as a medium for Michelangelo some seventy years earlier.[6] The biography makes fascinating reading, not simply for what it communicates about Gentileschi's early years; it is equally revealing about the many aspects of her early life that it chooses not to mention, elements that tend to be taken for granted today as fundamental to the artist's identity and reputation:

> There lives today (and may she live many centuries!) Mizia, of Florentine ancestry but born in Rome, who, one

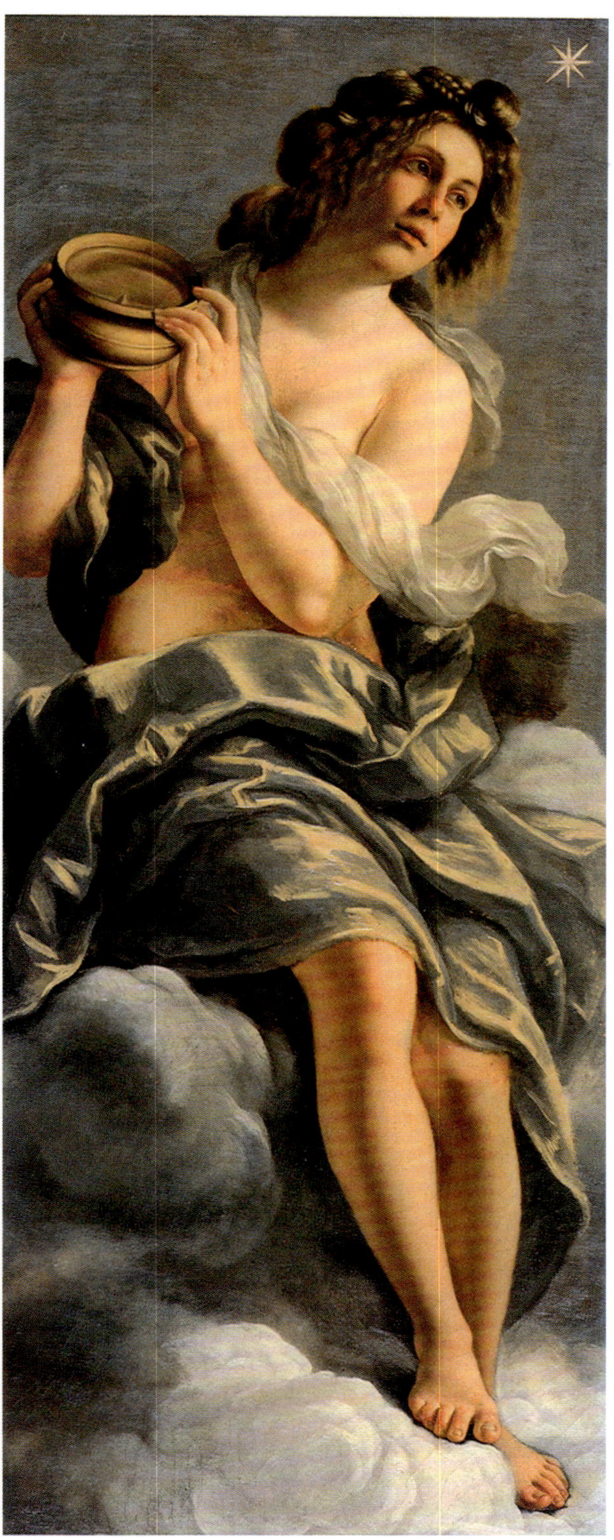

day, when she was about twelve years old, wanted to wear a skirt that her mother had made for her a few years earlier. Finding the skirt now to be by far too short, she decided to lengthen it by herself, and when she did this, she added a little something of her own imagination, adding an embroidery design that she had invented. It happened that this skirt was seen by experts in the realms of design and painting, and they were convinced by what they saw the young girl had a potential for great achievement in these arts.

They spoke with her father and strongly encouraged him to let his daughter study painting, but he would have none of it. Not only did he refuse to teach her, but he also tried to prevent her from becoming an artist by sending her to the convent of Sant'Apollonia in Trastevere for her education. Here in the convent, however, she felt more strongly inclined than ever to become a professional painter, and she begged the abbess to let her study in secret the good painting of a worthy master. The abbess brought her several paintings, including a Susanna by Caravaggio, an artist once judged to be the greatest painter alive. The copies that Artemisia made of these paintings came out so well (especially one of the Susanna) that everyone was amazed, and none more so than her own father.

When Orazio saw the copies and was assured that they were done by his daughter, he was stunned with disbelief and exceedingly impressed. Still not convinced, he sent his daughter additional paintings to copy, this time quite large ones, all by Caravaggio (whose style she always tried to imitate as the one that pleased her most). After she completed the copies with a masterful finish, some were sold, attaining prices of 300, 500, and even 600 and more, even though these were among her very first paintings. She then married and was brought by her husband to Florence, his native city. The paintings and portraits she made here were as admired no less than the

4 Artemisia Gentileschi, *Allegory of Inclination*, 1615–16, oil on canvas, 152 × 61 cm, Casa Buonarroti, Florence

> ones made by the above-mentioned Lalla Cizicena [Iaia of Cyzicus, an ancient woman artist discussed by Pliny], and they adorned and still adorn the rooms of the most prominent and respected gentlemen, and the halls of the most illustrious and exalted princes living in Florence today.[7]

This clearly fabricated account projects a fascinating alternative reality for Gentileschi's early life and career that seems, on first reading, to bear no relationship to what is known about her formative years. It is possible, nonetheless, to discern, embedded within the roots of the narrative, the following essentially accurate biographical details about Artemisia Gentileschi's early years: she grew up in Rome, the daughter of a painter and with a mother – Prudenzia di Ottaviano Montoni – who was already absent by her teens (her mother had died in 1605, when Gentileschi was twelve). She had not one but two father figures: an actual father, with whom she clashed, and an artistic father figure, with whom she identified strongly. The youthful Gentileschi carefully studied and copied Caravaggio's works, culminating in an early version of *Susanna and the Elders* (fig. 13). This constituted a milestone in her early development and attracted particular attention. She married soon thereafter and transferred to Florence, where financial success and critical applause awaited.

In seeking to stress the astronomically high prices that she supposedly received for her work, Gentileschi evidently wished to highlight for the reader a direct correlation between her purported financial success and the intrinsic artistic value of her early paintings. The quoted prices of '600 [florins] or more' were meant to attest to her extraordinary artistic success up to that point. And yet, as with so much else in this obviously self-serving construct, Gentileschi's claim to have received this much money for her paintings at this early stage of her career is in no way supported by the documentary record. This is made clear in a list of recorded payments awarded to her during her lifetime that is discussed in greater detail in Chapter 11 (see also table 1, pp. 256–57) . As the documents show, Gentileschi might conceivably have received a handful of high payments from the Medici by this point in her career for one or other unusually large paintings of Hercules, Pluto and Persephone or Judith and Holofernes, but these payments were atypical in relation to the majority of her earnings and were unlikely, in any event, to have exceeded 200 florins. Smaller amounts seem to have been much more the norm: 10 florins for a privately commissioned *Judith*, for example, or 34 florins for the *Allegory of Inclination* (and even here, the price recorded for the *Allegory* is itself inflated, since it included an unspecified amount that was advanced to Gentileschi and her husband as an additional loan to be used for other purposes). Thus, the idea that Gentileschi might have routinely received '300, 500 and even 600 and more' florins, scudi or ducats for her paintings constituted an inflated rhetorical claim, which served the purpose of reinforcing an idealized image of her as an outstandingly successful practitioner whose works were in keen demand from the most exalted patrons of the day.

The biography is noteworthy also for the degree to which it seems to depart from many of the standard emphases of the modern literature on the artist. This extends even to Gentileschi's name. Artemisia, we note, has not yet been coined as a virtual trademark, designating the artist's brand. Instead, we are presented with Mizia, a diminutive that, as Sheila Barker notes, goes back to her teenage years in Rome.[8] Yet the single most glaring omission from this early authorised account is any reference to her father's association with the villain of her early years. Bronzini's biography omits any reference to the painter Agostino Tassi and the rape accusation made by Orazio Gentileschi (1563–1639) against him in February 1612. The subsequent trial caused a major scandal within the tightly knit Roman art world. Dragging on from March to October 1612, it resulted eventually in the judges' ruling in favour of Orazio and his daughter on 28 November 1612. This resolution, however, brought the family little satisfaction. Tassi's career went from strength to strength – made possible by a combination of his inherent audacity and the influential support provided by a network of powerful Roman patrons. For Artemisia, on the other hand, the trial constituted an ordeal and an early reputational crisis that required careful management by her father. On 11 August 1612, a marriage was negotiated with a twenty-seven-year-old Florentine apothecary by the name of Pierantonio Stiattesi, the brother of the Roman notary Giovanni Battista Stiattesi, who had acted as a supporter, legal adviser and witness for the Gentileschis during the trial.[9] On 29 November 1612, immediately following the trial's conclusion, Artemisia and Stiattesi married in Rome and then relocated to Florence soon thereafter.[10]

The addition of this early biography into the literature on the artist finally puts paid to the notion that Gentileschi might have sought to benefit from the notoriety attracted by the trial, an argument based on the assumption that 'no publicity is bad publicity'. Such an argument suggests that Gentileschi might have decided that there were benefits to be gained from the frisson associated with a sex scandal attached to her name and used it strategically to catch the attention of would-be patrons.[11] Instead, we now learn, the opposite was the case. In common with so many other survivors of sexual violence, Gentileschi wished not to be defined by this youthful trauma, preferring to move on from the memory altogether – at least, in so far as that was possible in a public context – and to redefine herself in other, more socially advantageous ways. This, then, is the first of many challenges to the received truths that have come to surround Gentileschi's reputation that need to be taken into account when considering her early career.

YOUNG ARTEMISIA IN THE ARTISTS' DISTRICT OF ROME

For the first seventeen years of her life, Artemisia Gentileschi and her family resided within a thin wedge of about half a square kilometre in the artists' quarter of Rome. This subdivision of the larger district of Campio Marzio constituted a densely inhabited pocket in the north-west of the city, stretching from the Piazza di Spagna down the via del Babuino (then known as the via Paolina) to the Porta del Popolo and the Church of Santa Maria del Popolo, with its famous paintings by Caravaggio and his contemporary and rival Annibale Carracci. If that suggests a certain degree of domestic stability and continuity during the artist's early years, then that impression would be mistaken. In fact, the family changed its place of residence no fewer than five times during this period, sometimes settling in one location for as little as three months before moving on to another temporary abode. This was not in itself unprecedented – the cost of workshops and living quarters in Rome being beyond the reach of all but the most successful artists of the day.[12] Nevertheless, the documents describing the Gentileschis' successive residences and material circumstances during this period convey an overwhelming impression of a not especially successful, struggling household and professional artistic practice.

Small and densely populated, the artists' quarter of Baroque Rome constituted a veritable microcosm, providing artists with ready access to everything they needed to complete their work, together with much that would distract them from it as well. This included local shops and itinerant salespeople trading in all types of artists' materials and supplies. The neighbourhood was also home to a highly diverse labour force comprising artists and artisans of all ranks, from fully matriculated, independent masters to their most struggling apprentices. Models and independent academies were on hand, offering basic training for young artists, together with a burgeoning field of second-hand traders and professional art dealers to sell their work in both the primary and secondary markets. The area offered also a hospital and a series of churches and religious associations catering to the artists' physical and spiritual needs. In addition, there was a honeycombed network of taverns, brothels, gambling dens, sex workers, gang members, criminality in all its stripes and a barely controlled culture of street violence that combined one with the other to create a combustible blend of illicit attractions catering to the less sanctioned dimensions of the artistic lifestyle.[13] The neighbourhood's cheapness as a place in which to live added further to its overall impression of a zone set aside for a thronging mass of relatively modest souls, all leading an intensely day-to-day existence. Accordingly, successive waves of foreigners arriving at the Porta del Popolo chose to live there in preference to other, more well-to-do – and therefore more expensive – districts.[14]

The Gentileschi family's various apartment residences within this neighbourhood all followed the same basic sequence of amenities. Their lodging in 1611, in via Margutta, for example, is described as comprising a ground-floor entrance hallway with a small laundry/storage room off to the left overlooking a courtyard with tubs and a well. Stairs led to two rooms above. The first of these was a kitchen and dining area. The other, with two windows overlooking the street, was Orazio's workshop. Stairs then led to a further two rooms for the entire family to sleep in – at that stage comprising Orazio and his three sons in one room and the seventeen-year-old Artemisia in another.[15] A fourteen-year-old nephew of Orazio lodged there also and briefly worked as an apprentice before Orazio threw him out, reputedly, for suggesting that Artemisia had been acting improperly by standing for too long at a window.[16] Shortly thereafter, the family moved again, this time around the corner to via della Croce. On this occasion, they sought an additional two rooms that were to be taken up by a neighbour from the earlier apartment – Tuzia Medaglia, her husband and two daughters would temporarily become part of the family operation. They were hired, in effect, to look after Artemisia while Orazio was away on some increasingly time-consuming commissions on the Quirinal Hill on the other side of the city. They also helped to defray the household expenses by acting as sub-tenants, paying Orazio a rent of 12 scudi a year, Orazio being described in other respects as not especially wealthy and too poor to employ a servant.[17] Soon after moving into this apartment, however, on 6 May 1611, Artemisia was raped by Agostino Tassi. Tassi, Orazio's friend and business associate, had, supposedly, been contracted to teach Artemisia perspective. She was two months shy of her eighteenth birthday. He was thirty-two.

BAROQUE SWEAT SHOP: ARTEMISIA'S EARLY TRAINING WITHIN THE WORKSHOP OF ORAZIO GENTILESCHI

Perched on the infinitely more salubrious slopes of the Pincian Hill and overlooking the endless comings and goings of the artists' quarter, is the Palazzo Zuccari. This, the Roman residence of the Zuccaro family of painters, represented the apogee of solidly genteel success and ennobled bearing towards which the struggling Roman painters down below aspired. Its expansive hallways and quietly echoing corridors – presided over today, fittingly enough, by an art-historical institute – remain worlds removed from the pinched reality of Orazio's cramped rental accommodations and semi-itinerant lifestyle. Nevertheless, the Zuccaro family's recently deceased head, Federico Zuccaro (*c.*1540/41–1609), had been intensely concerned for the care and well-being of the city's aspiring painters. As the first Principe or Rector of the painters' association of Rome, the Accademia di San Luca, he had developed a comprehensive programme for reorganising the education of the city's artists. Zuccaro's plans, although not fully implemented during his lifetime, are significant for helping to articulate the preferred expectations of professional training practices against which the more humble artistic education of Artemisia should be measured.

Central to the training programme of the Accademia di San Luca was an *accademia del nudo*, or life-drawing class, that was to be held for three hours every second Sunday.[18] The opportunity to draw from the male nude model, fundamental to the development of an artist, was meant to be provided during the summer months, and to make anatomical studies from dissected cadavers, together with additional studies from posed clay and wax models, during colder periods.[19] Such classes were held sporadically during the opening decades of the seventeenth century, but the academy seems not to have really gotten off the ground until 1628, when its members voted to allocate a monthly allowance of 12 giulij (1.2 scudi) to pay the life model.[20] Under Zuccaro's guidance, the academy was, nevertheless, influential as an ideal, encouraging the development elsewhere in Rome of an alternative network of more or less informal academic sessions, described by Peter Lukehart as 'pop up academies'. These ranged from the relatively elevated and aristocratically oriented dilettante academy held periodically in the Palazzo Crescenzi, through to sessions hosted by some of the city's more established artists, such as Girolamo Muziano. They included also more informal arrangements made by groups of junior artists banding together to share resources in one or other rented property.[21] The independent academies of Domenichino and Andrea Sacchi, for example, would come to play an influential role a decade or so later in providing training opportunities for the next generation of artists, such as Nicolas Poussin and Gaspard Dughet.[22]

These opportunities would have been comprehensively barred to Artemisia Gentileschi on account of her gender. So, too, would the other major avenue for artistic self-improvement then open to young artists. Whatever their material circumstances, aspiring male artists still at least had the freedom of physical mobility to roam the city, seeking out its many ancient and modern examples of artistic excellence to study, be it the Laocoön on the Vatican Hill or Michelangelo's tomb for Julius II in the Church of San Pietro in Vincoli. Copies after these sources would then form part of an artist's stock-in-trade, a repository to dip into for inspiration during the years to come.[23] The importance of this informal educational programme is vividly underscored by Federico Zuccaro in a series of allegorical drawings documenting the early trials and tribulations of his older brother, Taddeo, as a youthful, aspiring painter wandering the streets of Rome searching for lodgings and inspiration. These drawings constituted another version of an artistic origin myth. Federico probably planned to use them for frescoes in the Palazzo Zuccari, which he intended to have converted after his death into a *foresteria* or hostel for foreign artists seeking accommodation in the city.[24] A particularly touching scene from the series, whose imagery would have offered encouragement to student artists, depicts the young Taddeo copying Raphael's frescoes in the Villa Farnesina before falling exhaustedly asleep by the light of the moon in the very loggia in which he sketched (fig. 5).[25]

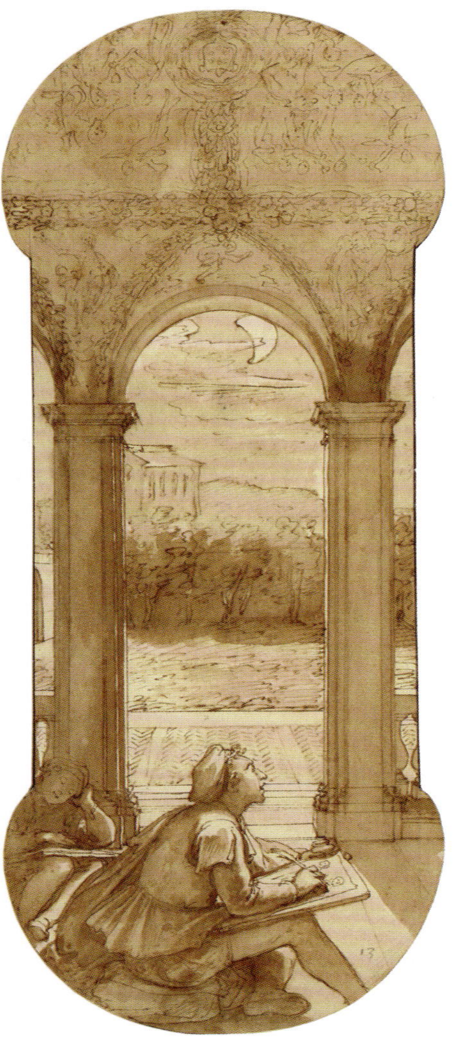

5 Federico Zuccaro, *Taddeo Zuccaro Copying Raphael's Frescoes in the Loggia of the Villa Farnesina, Where He is also Represented Asleep*, c.1595, pen and brown ink, brush with brown wash, over black chalk and touches of red chalk, 42.4 × 17.5 cm, The J. Paul Getty Museum, Los Angeles, 99.GA.6.13

Artemisia had no such freedom of movement. She was severely constrained and was allowed to leave the house only under certain conditions, such as attending Mass or on specially arranged outings, and always only in the company of a chaperone. More specifically still, and as Patrizia Cavazzini and others have noted, she was further hemmed in by perceptions of propriety, even within the supposed security of her own home. These demanded that she keep constantly on guard against allowing herself to be seen in the company of male strangers visiting the master in his workshop to inspect work, deliver materials, negotiate contracts and so on. In this respect, it is significant that none of the witnesses in the rape trial ever mentioned having seen Artemisia assisting Orazio in the room in which he maintained his workshop.

This does not mean, of course, that Artemisia did not work alongside her father when there were no outsiders present. The task of keeping to herself within the house was probably made easier by Orazio's naturally unsociable manner. He is described in the rape-trial documents as 'quasi sempre solo' ('almost always alone') when seen in public, and the Roman Ambassador to Florence described him in 1615 yet more unsparingly as having 'such strange manners and way of life and such temper that one can neither get on nor deal with him'.[26] The painter and art historian Giovanni Baglione (1566–1643), who was also Orazio Gentileschi's former rival and the enemy of Caravaggio, describes Orazio as an intensely difficult character. He considered him to be 'more bestial than human . . . he kept to his opinions, and with his satirical tongue offended everyone'.[27]

Even the most closed workshop, however, needed to maintain at least some connection with the outside world. Artemisia would, therefore, have needed another room – her bedroom obviously, since that was the only other space available to her – in which to carve out a modest zone of retreat and an additional workspace to undertake her artistic training. Artemisia's own deposition at the trial describes her as painting a portrait of Tuzia's son at the entrance to her bedroom. One imagines from this a landing at the top of the stairs leading to her bedroom, or some other form of basic antechamber communicating with the bedroom. It was at the threshold leading from this space into her bedroom that Agostino Tassi encountered Artemisia on the afternoon of 6 May 1611 before making up his mind to force her into her room to rape her.[28]

The previously outlined microcosm of the artists' district, therefore, with all its possibilities both benevolent and malign, reduced down in Artemisia's case to a professional universe of just two rooms: her father's workshop, whenever it was available to her, and her own bedroom or the landing outside it. Here it was that the young Artemisia underwent the most basic and time-honoured form of professional, trade-oriented education. Here she remained bound to the experience of working day in and day out as an apprentice to a master who also happened to be her father. In his often-quoted letter of 3 July 1612, extolling Artemisia's abilities to the Medici Dowager Grand Duchess of Tuscany, Christine de Lorraine, Orazio dates this process as having begun three years earlier, in 1609. However, given that Artemisia was the oldest by four years of the family's four children (with two sons having died earlier – one, born in 1594, died in 1601, and another, in 1603), it seems more probable that she would have become an apprentice several years earlier. On 8 July 1606, six months after her mother's death (on 26 December 1605[29]), Artemisia turned thirteen, the customary age for apprentices to commence their training. This date thus offers a reasonable *terminus post quem* for Artemisia to have begun assisting her father in initially basic and menial tasks, gradually progressing to an advanced level of aptitude, such as would enable her to produce finished works in her own right.[30] She evidently soon became the most valued member of the family team, too useful, in any event, to be granted a formal education. By the time of the trial of 1612, she was an outstandingly promising young painter with the beginnings of an independent career already in the offing. And yet she declared herself at the same time as being unable to write and able to read 'only a little'.[31]

EARNING ONE'S KEEP: ARTEMISIA'S WORKSHOP EDUCATION AND THE TRANSITION FROM APPRENTICE TO ASSISTANT

What, then, did the process of learning by assisting the master actually entail in Orazio Gentileschi's workshop? The rape-trial documents are highly revealing on this point. They identify two other apprentices as having recently passed through Gentileschi's workshop. One of them – 'Giovanni Battista' – is mentioned only briefly and indirectly as having entered the workshop sometime in 1610. He is the same individual who was thrown out a few months later for suggesting that Artemisia had spent too long being seen at a window.[32] Of greater significance for the trial as a whole was the testimony of Nicolò Bedino. Although aged only about fifteen or sixteen, Bedino was pressured into acting as a central witness for Tassi's defence. His testimony was potentially the most damaging to Gentileschi's case, since it involved accusations of impropriety on Artemisia's part towards various men – Tassi's defence consisting of the age-old tactic of attempting to refute a charge of sexual violence by smearing the reputation of the victim.[33] Leaving aside the more contentious aspects of Bedino's testimony, this young apprentice is, nonetheless, quite specific about what the process of training in Gentileschi's workshop entailed. He states (as recounted back by the court notary) that 'Orazio asked him to move in with him, and offered to teach him to draw, and [to give him] food and drink as well, in exchange for work at his house.' This was then corroborated by the other witnesses, who observed that 'Orazio took in a young man named Nicolo, who helped him with house chores, and came to learn to draw' (testimony of Caterina Zuccarini), and that 'a young man, thirteen or fourteen years old, [who was] there a few times. He was learning to draw' (testimony of Bernardino de Franceschi); and then again that 'Orazio had taken a young man to do chores around the house. Later he saw the young man there; he was learning to draw' (testimony of Pietro Hernandes, a neighbour, who must have been on good terms with the Gentileschis since he identifies Artemisia as the godmother of his son). What is striking about the testimony is the repeated phraseology adopted by all the witnesses that Gentileschi's apprentices were being taught by 'learning to draw'. In keeping with the long-established traditions of Central Italian workshop practice, the methodology for learning how to paint in Gentileschi's workshop was clearly based on the study of the process of drawing.[34]

It is easy to underestimate the emphasis on draughtsmanship in Orazio's workshop, given the revolutionary nature of his simultaneous adoption of Caravaggio's method of painting directly from life. Yet it was an emphasis that derived naturally from Orazio's own cultural background and his training in the artistic practice and theory of late sixteenth-century Central Italy. The stress on the importance of repeated drawing exercises is equally evident in Romano Alberti's *Origine, et progresso dell'Accademia del Dissegno* [sic.], *de pittori, scultori, ed architetti di Roma* of 1604. As Peter Lukehart and others have noted, this publication essentially summarises and codifies Zuccaro's educational programme, then under consideration at the Accademia di San Luca. According to Alberti, the process of learning to paint consisted of three stages of training, which were based, in turn, on sequential processes of sustained draughtsmanship. First came *copiare*, the imitation or copying of a master's work. This was followed by *ritrarre*, the creation of credible representations of observed things and based particularly on the study of life models. Finally, *disegnare*, which consolidated all that had been learned previously into the composition of a *disegno di'invenzione*, or drawing of an original subject.[35]

This process would have begun with the young apprentice copying repeatedly from the prints of individual features of the body – eyes, hands, feet, faces – that were included in art-training manuals or primers and were compiled for this purpose by such painters as Agostino Carracci (1557–1602) and Jusepe de Ribera (1591–1652) (fig. 6).[36] In fact, it is possible to detect echoes of the repertory of features and poses contained in these primers appearing as a kind of continued muscle memory in a number of Artemisia's compositions. The semaphore-like, spread-out fingers of Susanna's left hand in the *Susanna and the Elders* of 1610, for example, appear to have benefited from the lessons outlined in Luca Ciamberlano's engravings of anatomical details after drawings by Agostino Carracci (figs 6 and 7). The distinctive 'pinching' gesture of the hand in the upper right of the same print seems equally to have informed the framing of the Magdalene's left hand as she turns away from earthly temptations in the *Conversion of the Magdalene* of around 1614–15 (fig. 8).

The exercise of copying from precisely this kind of art primer is shown in the figure of the teenage boy who is depicted seated on a stool at the right of an engraving by Stradanus (Jan van der Straet; 1523–1605) of the invention of oil painting (fig. 9). Stradanus produced this print during the latter stages of a decades-long residence in Florence working for the Medici.[37] Although intended as an idealized depiction of Jan van Eyck's workshop in early fifteenth-century Bruges, the print also reads as a remarkably informative visual summary of Central Italian workshop practice at that time. It depicts, in addition, the second stage of Alberti's educative process – *ritrarre* – or learning to render accurately objects in three dimensions. This is shown in the figure of the slightly older apprentice seated to the left who is busily copying a female bust. Orazio's workshop would have presumably included some examples of this kind of standard studio prop, be it a reduced-scale fragment after the antique, an anatomical model of a part of the body and/or a statuette. Such basic tools of workshop training often appear in contemporary scenes of informal academies (fig. 10), and a number are included propped up above the doorway of Stradanus's print. Orazio Gentileschi's contemporaries are known to have possessed them: Orazio Borgianni, for example, owned a collection of twenty plaster casts of parts of the body in various postures which he donated to the Accademia di San Luca; another early Caravaggesque painter, Mao Salini, is also known to have used casts of this kind, including one of his hands in prayer.[38]

One senses, nonetheless, that the collection of prints and drawings that Orazio must have kept in his workshop was of overriding importance for Artemisia's early training and for the operations of his workshop more generally. This type of visual

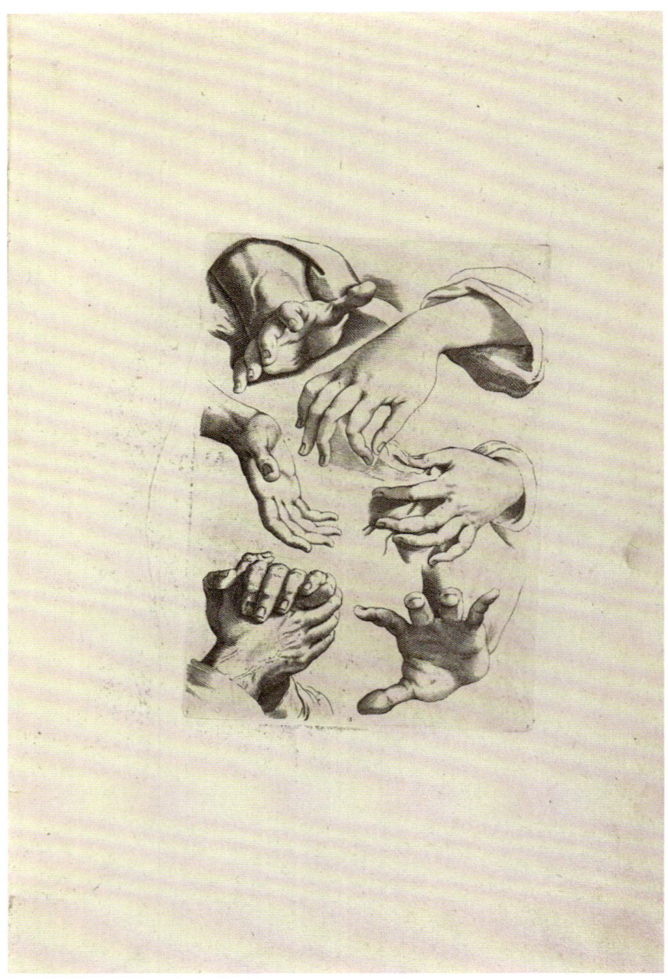

6 Luca Ciamberlano after Agostino Carracci, *Study of Hands*, c.1600, engraving, 15.4 × 11.9 cm, from *Scuola perfetta per imparare a disegnare tutto il corpo humano*, Getty Research Institute, Los Angeles

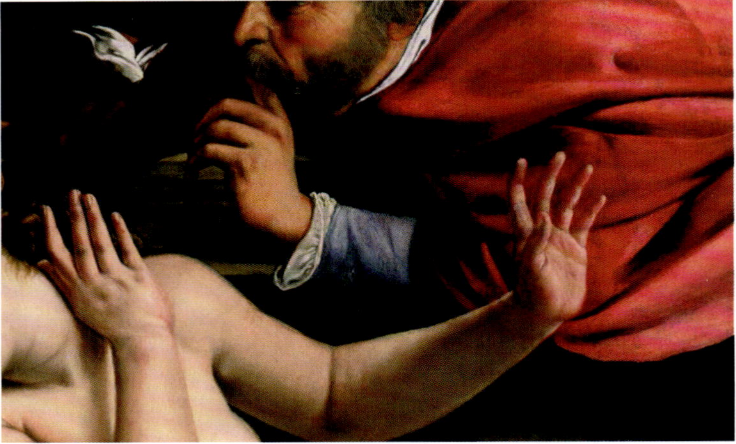

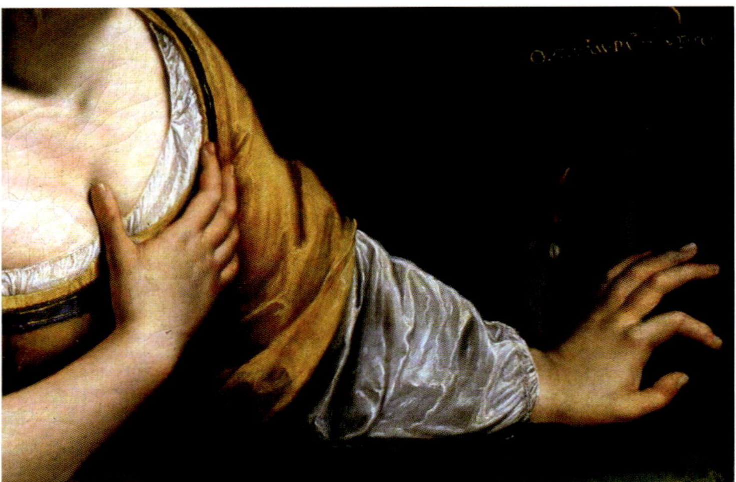

7 (TOP) Artemisia Gentileschi, *Susanna and the Elders* (detail of fig. 13)

8 (ABOVE) Artemisia Gentileschi, *Conversion of the Magdalene* (detail of fig. 40)

resource must have been particularly important in Artemisia's case, given her inability to move freely beyond the four walls of the family's apartment. Prints, accordingly, exert a persistent influence on nearly all of Artemisia's earliest canvases. R. Ward Bissell noted the importance of a print by the school of Raimondi, for example, for the Galleria Spada *Madonna and Child*, which I would follow Mary Garrard among others in positioning as one of the earliest extant works by Gentileschi's hand (fig. 11).[39] The Michelangelesque pose of the baby in this painting must also derive from another as yet unidentified printed source, since it is clearly not a pose that a baby could hold for any length of time. The serpentine, twisting pose of the figure of Susanna in the 1610 canvas of that subject is likewise taken from a print after Michelangelo's *Expulsion of Adam and Eve from the Garden of Eden*. Similarly, the pose of Cleopatra and of Danäe in the early versions of these respective compositions, which are attributed to both Artemisia and Orazio, must have derived from a print of the Ariadne in

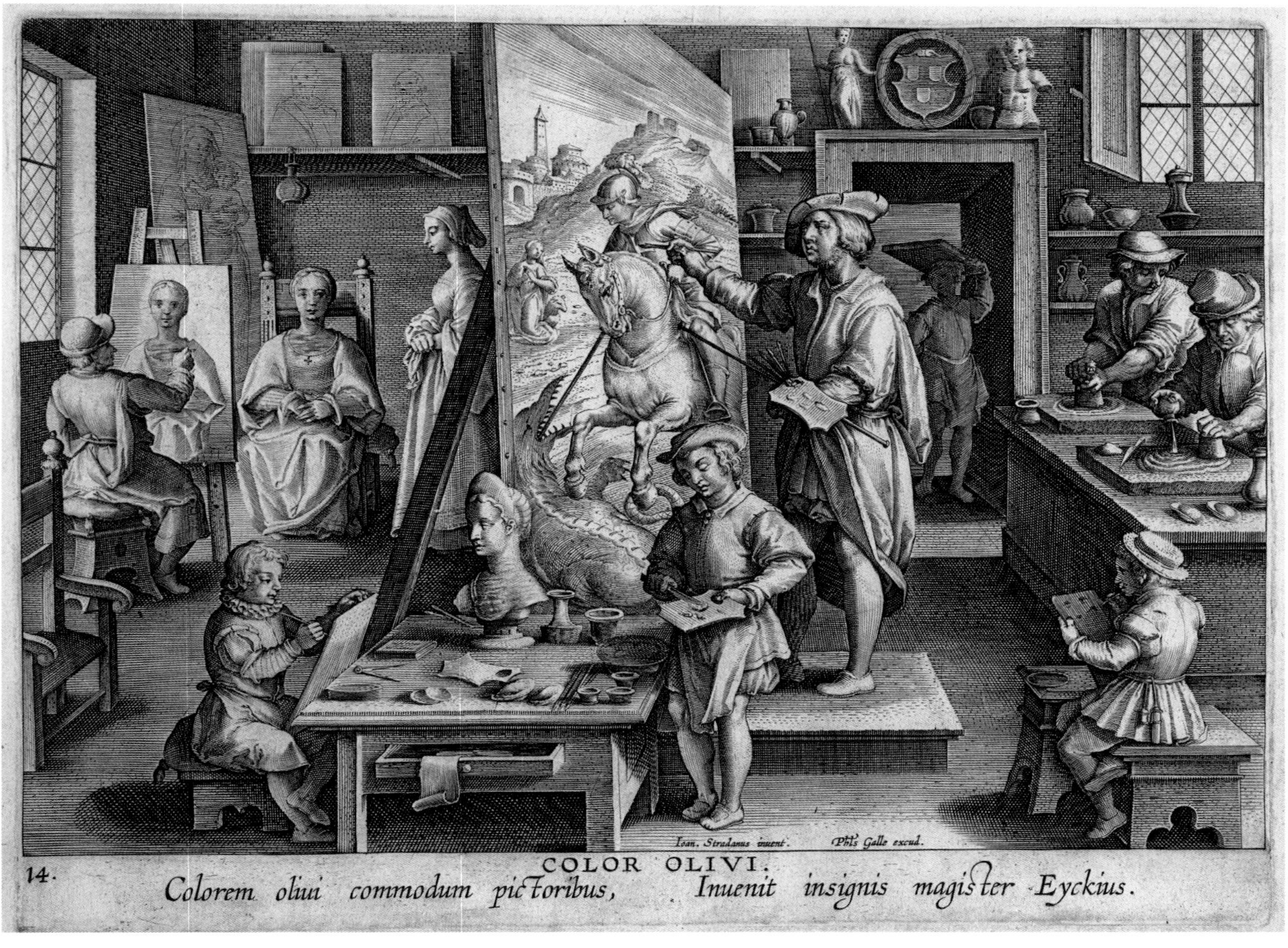

9 Jan van der Straet (Johannes Stradanus), *Color Olivi/Oil Paint*, c.1591, engraving, 20.4 × 27.1 cm, from *Nova Reperta*, British Museum, London

the Vatican Belvedere rather than the sculpture itself, since Artemisia would never have been allowed to see the work in situ (figs 21 and 22). Prints remain fundamental to Artemisia, in fact, throughout her career and remain important reference points for a number of her later works as well.[40] During her early training, then, although physically constrained within the confines of her father's workshop, it seems that the young Artemisia was, nevertheless, allowed to roam free at least in her mind while poring over her father's collection of works on paper as she dreamed up ideas for her earliest independent creations.

Returning to Stradanus's print, we note the presence in the centre of the composition of a yet more mature teenage boy who assists the master by spreading his colours onto the palette from one of the ready-loaded shells that have been handed to him by the middle-aged workmen grinding and mixing pigments at the back of the workshop. Unlike the two younger boys on either side, this youth has evidently progressed up the hierarchy of shop-floor responsibilities to the point at which he is now assuming a more significant role in closer working proximity to the master himself. This individual is no longer a raw apprentice and odd-job *garzone* (boy);

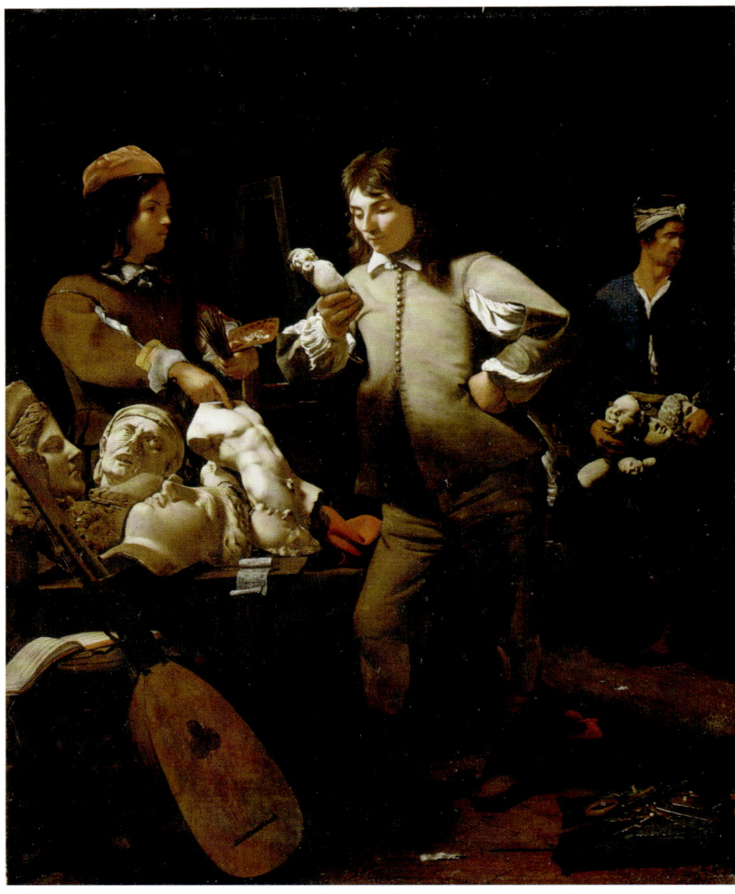

10 Michael Sweerts, *In the Studio*, signed and dated 1652, oil on canvas, 73.5 × 58.8 cm, Detroit Institute of Arts, City of Detroit Purchase, 30.297

he is, rather, progressing towards being recognised as a valued assistant to the master. This yet further stage of artistic and professional development is indicated, in turn, by the obviously much older assistant, who is shown seated at the back left of the composition. Unlike the youngsters in the foreground, this figure has clearly completed his training and has been granted a certain degree of responsibility and autonomy within the workshop. He has been given the right to work alongside the master on independent portrait commissions, thereby gaining additional revenue for the business as a whole, while leaving the master free to concentrate on his major commissioned work.

The rape-trial documentation makes clear that Artemisia had also moved up this four-step ladder of artistic and professional development by the time she was seventeen. Nicolò Bedino's testimony confirms this when he notes (again, via the court notary) that 'Nicolo [Bedino] ground the colours and mixed them with oil for Artemisia, who used them to paint her canvases, not for the father.'[41] This statement was not made in relation to any of the contentious aspects of Bedino's testimony – it was not made, for example, as part of some accusation directed against Artemisia's propriety. Accordingly, there seems no reason to doubt its veracity. It is, in any event, directly corroborated by the independent statement of the Spaniard Pietro Hernandes, whose testimony stated that he saw Bedino in the Gentileschis' apartment in S. Spirito, where they resided from around the middle of 1611 until the time of the rape trial in mid- to late 1612: 'he was learning to draw, and Artemisia also taught him to paint'.[42]

Artemisia was thus now not only assisting Orazio in the workshop, but also teaching his apprentice 'how to paint'. This was undoubtedly useful to Orazio, who had an increasing workload during this period as a result of his collaboration with Agostino Tassi. Since early 1611, he had been working with Tassi on an important sequence of frescoes, first in the Sala del Concistoro in the Quirinal Palace, and then at the garden casino of Cardinal Scipione Borghese, also on the Quirinal Hill.[43] For his part, Bedino would have prepared Artemisia's materials and mixed her colours while observing her paint and receiving a certain degree of training in return. There is also reference to Artemisia's working during these months on an independently commissioned portrait – just like the assistant seated at the left of Stradanus's print. This was a portrait of a papal steward by the name of 'Artigenio'. Although less well appreciated today than are other aspects of her work, Gentileschi's portraits would go on to constitute one of the most popular aspects of her later production.

Nothing more is known about the subject of Artemisia's portrait, unfortunately, other than that his name would subsequently be dragged into the mud as part of the wider strategy of the Tassi camp to counter the charges against him by impugning Artemisia's honour.[44] Like so many other peripheral figures caught momentarily in the spotlight of the rape-trial

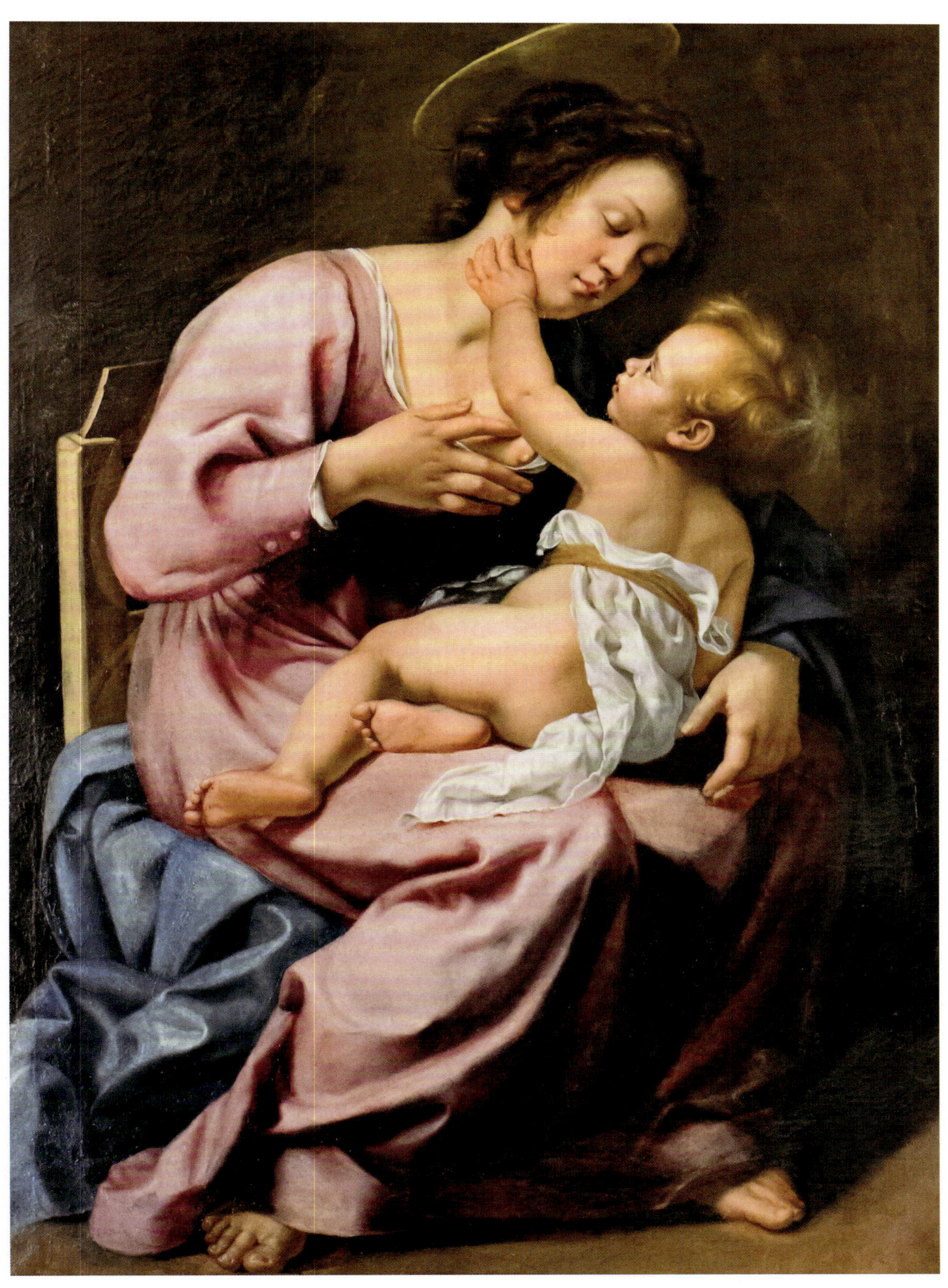

11 Artemisia Gentileschi, *Madonna and Child*, *c.*1608–10, oil on canvas, 116.5 × 86.5 cm, Galleria Spada, Rome

proceedings, this character appears briefly in the legal records before exiting the stage in order to make way for the oncoming cataclysm of the rape and its aftermath. The rape itself and the wider repercussions of betrayal and disruption that it set off would soon also come violently to overturn the natural course that Artemisia's personal and professional development might otherwise have been expected to follow. Yet these years of seismic disturbances would also prove uniquely formative as Orazio sought to train his daughter in relation to the innovative model provided by the work of Caravaggio. This model would impel both father and daughter to develop novel methods of production that, in turn, would have a fundamental impact on both their later lives and careers in ways that they could never have anticipated when they first began to consider the possibilities opened up by this new technique. The resulting works would include some of their most famous. Yet the intricately interconnected nature of their production during this period would result also in a number of canvases that remain among the most hotly debated of their respective oeuvres.

FACING PAGE Artemisia Gentileschi, *Madonna and Child* (detail of fig. 11)

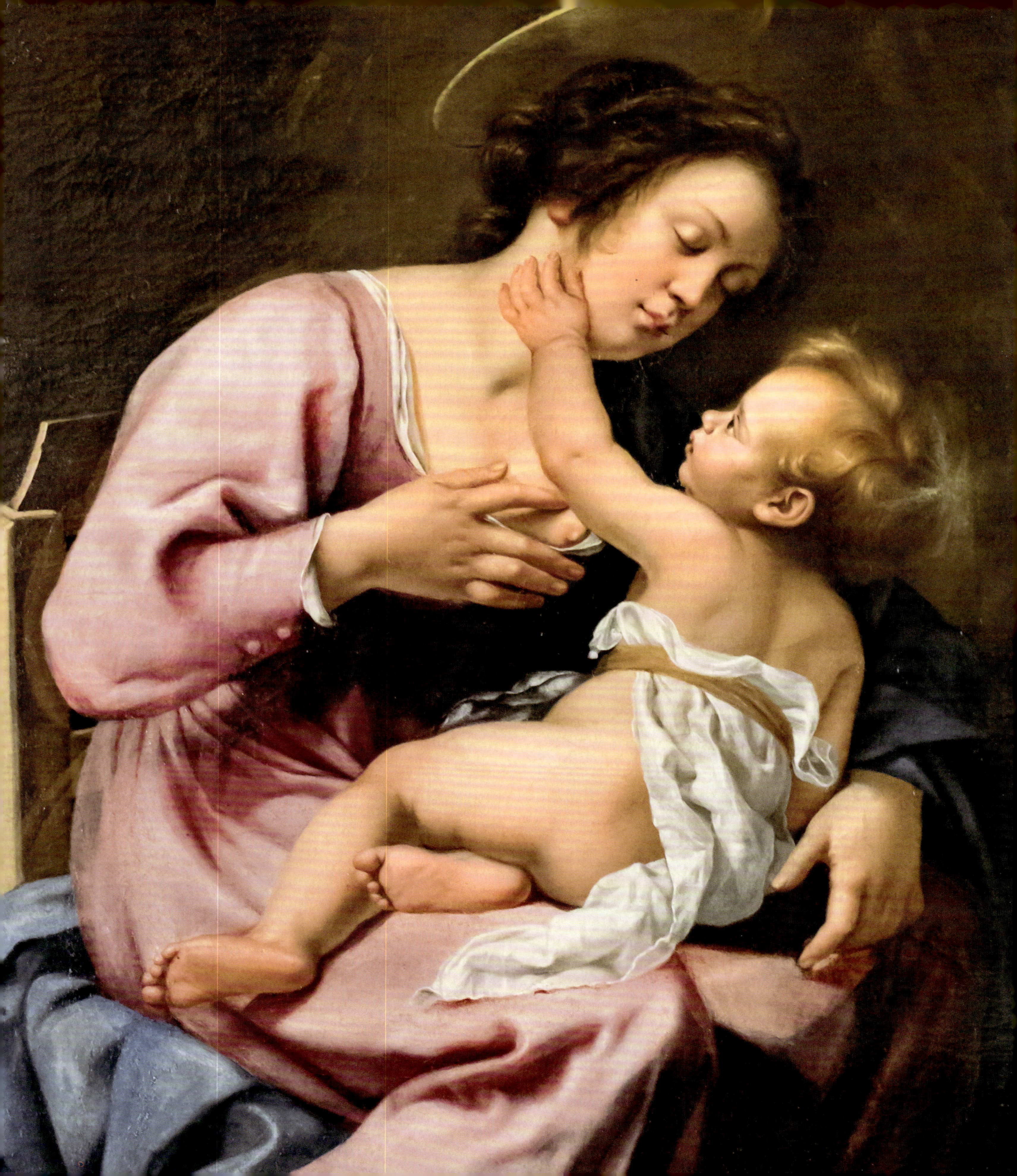

2

'Ritratto nudo'

GENTILESCHI'S FIRST PAINTINGS IN THE WORKSHOP OF ORAZIO GENTILESCHI

INTRODUCTION

SUSANNA AND THE ELDERS AND THE MODEL OF CARAVAGGIO

Orazio's training provided Artemisia with a range of fundamental skills and frames of reference to enable her to advance towards a stage of independent mastery. Yet it also resulted in the creation of an aspiring painter who remained deficient throughout her career in a number of key professional indices. Artemisia had no facility with the medium of fresco painting, for example, an ability judged integral to Central Italian practice of the period and the medium in which Orazio had been principally employed since his transferral to Rome in the 1570s.[1] More significantly still, her lack of access to life drawing and the other educational opportunities afforded her male peers meant that she lacked a fully developed awareness of many basic areas such as anatomy, foreshortening and the correct disposition of figures in perspectivally credible landscape and urban settings. The fact that Orazio supposedly contracted Agostino Tassi to teach her perspective strongly suggests his awareness of the need to supplement Artemisia's training in this respect, although, if so, it was a decision that he soon had cause to regret. More specifically still, the intensive Accademia degli Incamminati (for 'those who are making progress'), promoted by the Carracci in Bologna during these years was just then

FACING PAGE Artemisia Gentileschi, *Susanna and the Elders* (detail of fig. 13)

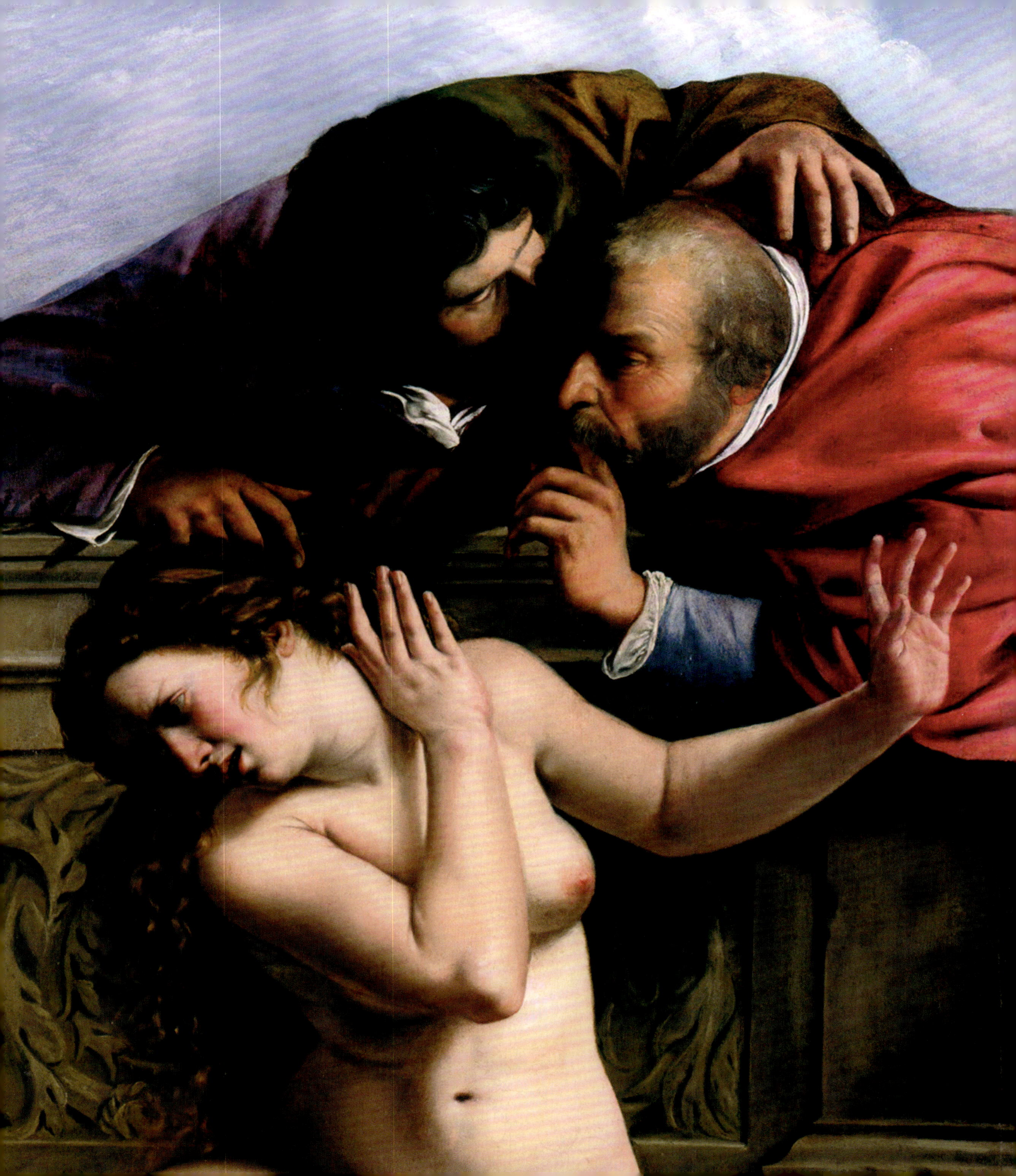

beginning to produce a crop of highly talented graduates, such as Domenichino (1581–1641), Guido Reni (1575–1642) and Giovanni Lanfranco (1582–1647) among others. These artists were just then commencing their own careers, armed with the benefit of a formidable array of artistic skills. Their rigorous educational background provided them with the capacity to work across a range of artistic media, from paintings on canvas, to fresco and prints, even architecture on occasion. They were also able to create complex, multi-figure compositions in three-dimensional settings that often went well beyond the technical capabilities of anything Artemisia was able to produce at that stage, or indeed at any other point of her career (fig. 12).

And yet, Artemisia learned to work with her limitations. In fact, one might say that she learned to turn them to her advantage: to make them positive enablers of what was most distinctive about her art rather than technical deficiencies holding it back. An analogy might be drawn in this respect with those rare musicians who are able to compensate for their lack of formal training in the more advanced aspects of technique by approaching composition from another angle altogether, thus creating a more lateral and original artistic expression as a result. In her own case, Artemisia had two fundamental points of innovation to bring to the task of painting. First, she possessed an independent and unique perspective as an emerging and talented young woman artist hemmed in on all sides by a challenging professional and personal environment dominated by men. And second, she was one of the first to be privy to the secrets of Caravaggio's radically new approach to painting.

The dynamic impact of Caravaggio's new methodology is powerfully apparent in Gentileschi's *Susanna and the Elders* of 1610 (fig. 13). The *Susanna* continues many of the previously noted features underpinning her early training programme. This includes the reliance on prints, with its prominent reference to Michelangelo in the figure of Susanna, together with additional derivations from a range of sources, such as a print by Annibale Carracci and a fresco by Baldassare Croce in the Church of Santa Susanna in Rome.[2] Yet the *Susanna* goes far beyond these reference points in its ability to project itself as a powerful and accomplished statement of artistic difference as based on a sustained observation of precisely modelled, naturalistic form. This is evident as much in the painting's smallest details as in its most prominent features. It can be observed, for example, in the crisp white cuff of the younger elder's right arm, which projects its own jagged shadow over the entablature of the wall upon which the two elders rest. The sculptural play of the drapery folded over Susanna's thigh is rendered equally vividly. It emphasises the exposed vulnerability of Susanna's pale flesh, as she perches precariously on the cold, chipped stone seat. Susanna's face and torso are framed equally emphatically by the cascading curls of her long golden hair

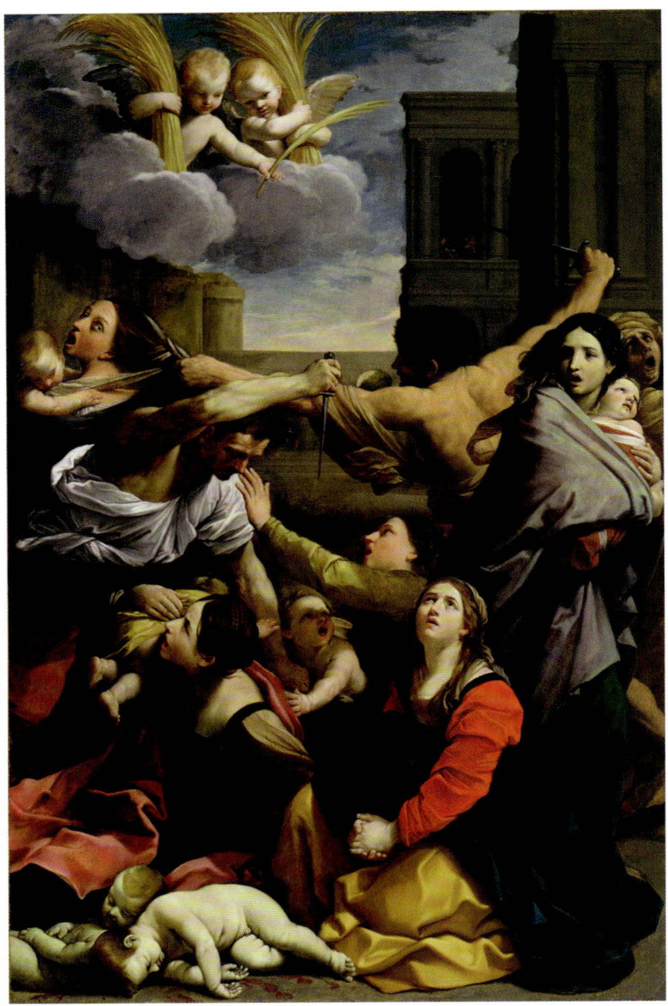

12 Guido Reni, *Massacre of the Innocents*, c.1610–11, oil on canvas, 268 × 170 cm, Pinacoteca Nazionale di Bologna

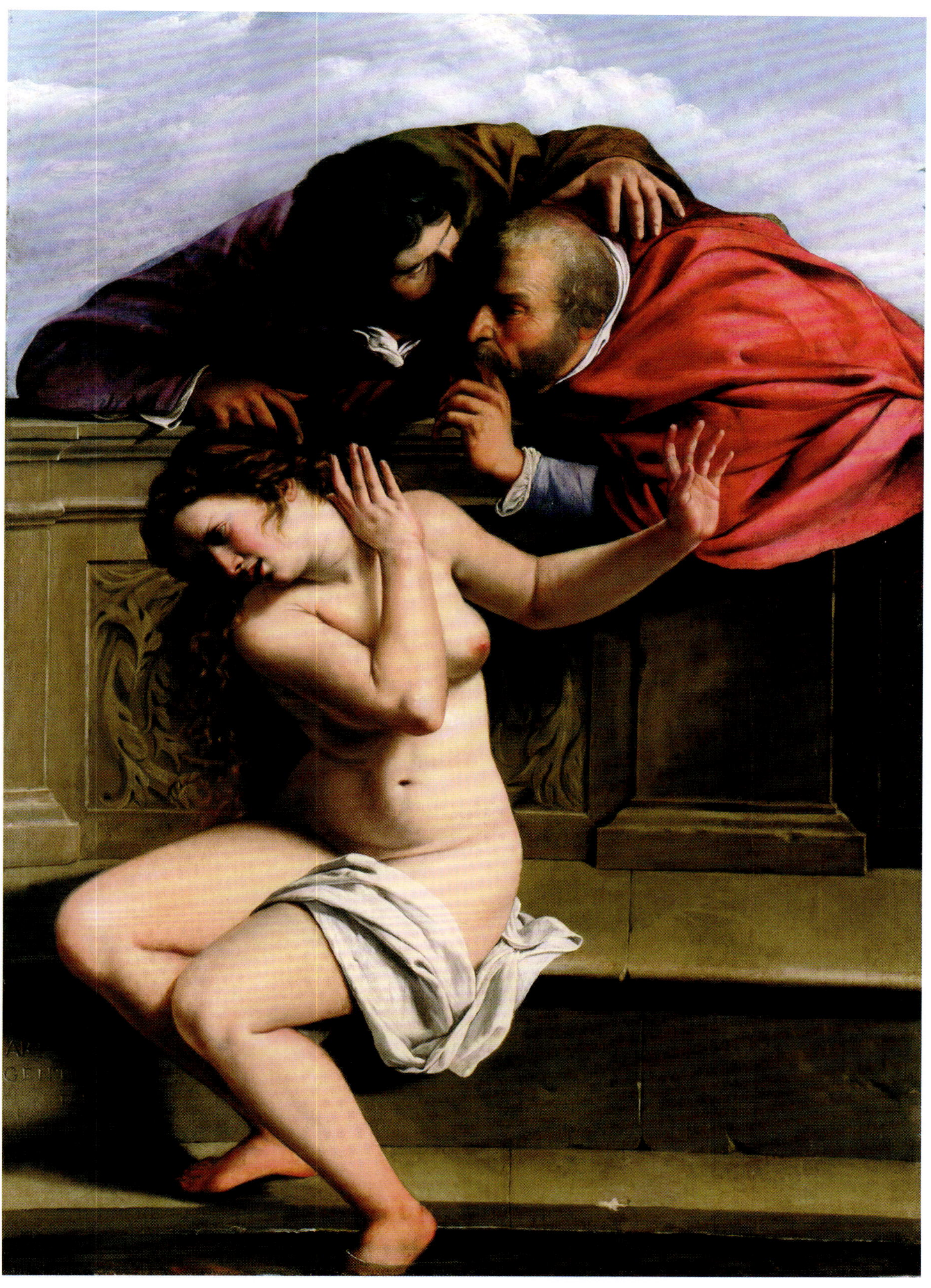

13 Artemisia Gentileschi, *Susanna and the Elders*, signed and dated 1610, oil on canvas, 170 × 119 cm, Schloss Weißenstein, Pommersfelden

that almost grazes against the elder's right hand as he leans forward to whisper conspiratorially in his colleague's ear.

Artemisia's treatment of Susanna's body lies at the heart of the painting's continued ability to capture the attention of contemporary viewers. Mary Garrard's description vividly conveys Artemisia's originality in this respect:

> Susanna's body is persuasively composed of flesh; it is articulated by specific realist touches that are unflattering by conventional standards of beauty, such as the groin wrinkle, the crow's foot wrinkles at the top of her right arm, and the lines in her neck. The naturalistically pendant breast, the recognisably feminine abdomen, and the awkwardly proportioned legs further attest that this figure was closely studied from life.[3]

Here, then, is the moment when Artemisia, following her father's lead in his own early Caravaggesque paintings from the same period (fig. 14), picks up on the potential of the new Caravaggesque mode to offer a radical alternative to the rhetorical artificiality of paintings composed solely on the basis of then current academic practices. This new approach gave Caravaggio's earliest followers the opportunity to highlight the physically projective presence of their works by supplementing the initial design process of drawings with a final stage of painting directly from the posed model. Yet this was a technique that involved certain risks. As Giulio Mancini, the physician and writer, observed, Caravaggio's approach was positive in so far as it could create vivid and effective single-figure compositions. Yet, on the other hand, it showed its inherent deficiencies when applied to multi-figure paintings, since,

> in narrative compositions and in the interpretation of feelings, which are based on imagination and not direct observation of things, mere copying does not seem to me to be satisfactory, since it is impossible to put in one room a multitude of people acting out the story, with that light coming in from a single window, having to laugh or cry or pretending to walk while having to stay still in order to be copied.[4]

Mancini may have had a point, as Caravaggio himself discovered in the difficulties he experienced working up the challengingly complex and monumental composition that was required for the *Martyrdom of St Matthew* in the Church of San Luigi dei Francesi in Rome.[5] Yet, for the *Susanna* at least, the reverse is the case. In a classic example of less is more, the composition sets itself apart from its contemporaries by distilling the narrative elements of the story down to their bare essentials. The result is a composition of almost poster-like clarity, concision and projection. It was a lesson that Artemisia would follow keenly in her future trajectory, most particularly in the forthcoming *Judith Slaying Holofernes*.

Of all the many potential sources cited for this work it seems strange that Caravaggio's name has never been put forward other than as an overall influence. Yet Caravaggio's model seems especially important given the prominent emphasis accorded to him and to the subject of Susanna in Bronzini's biography, discussed in Chapter 1, in which it is noted that 'she begged the abbess to let her study in secret the good painting of a worthy master. The abbess brought her several paintings, including a Susanna by Caravaggio, an artist once judged to be the greatest painter alive. The copies that Artemisia made of these paintings came out so well (especially one of the Susanna) that everyone was amazed, and none more so than her own father.'

In mentioning a work of this subject by Caravaggio, Artemisia must, in fact, have been referring to a now-lost canvas of *Susanna* that Caravaggio is known to have painted for the poet Giambattista Marino (1569–1625) immediately prior to the departure from Rome of both painter and patron in the years 1606 and 1608 respectively.[6] In Marino's absence, the painting was kept in the palace of Marino's Roman protector, the dilettante painter, architect and early promoter of Caravaggesque still-life painting, the Marchese Giovanni Battista Crescenzi.[7] The Crescenzi family palace was situated close by the Pantheon and has been mentioned in the previous chapter as the setting for one of the informal 'pop-up' academies that were popular during the period. Its relative openness to the comings and goings of painters may thus have facilitated the production of one or more copies of the *Susanna* that might, in turn, have come to the attention of Orazio and Artemisia. Alternatively, it might also be relevant to cite in this context the large, unattributed painting of Susanna that is listed in

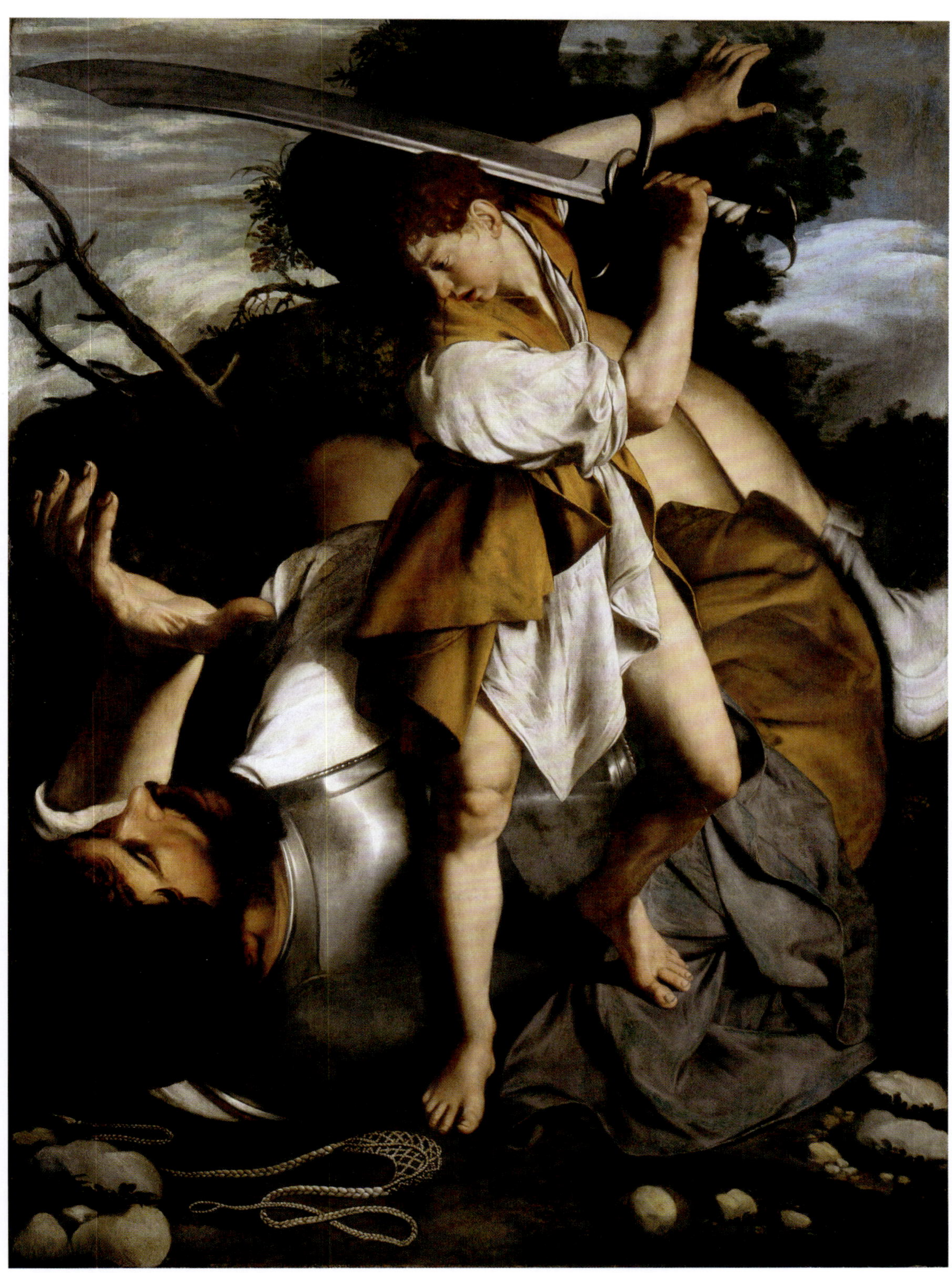

14 Orazio Gentileschi, *David Slaying Goliath*, c.1607–9, oil on canvas, 186 × 135 cm, National Gallery of Ireland, Dublin

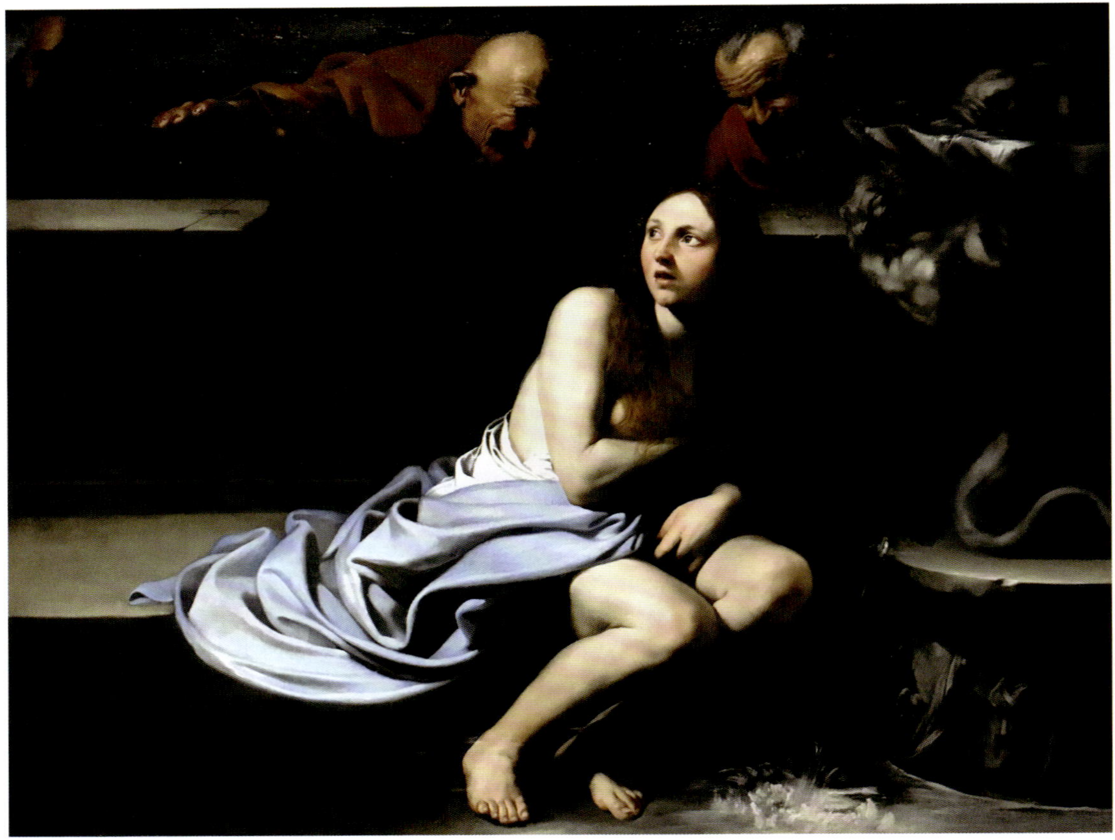

15 Jusepe de Ribera, *Susanna and the Elders*, c.1615, oil on canvas, 138.5 × 179 cm, The San Diego Museum of Art: Museum Purchase

the 1612 inventory of the papal steward Cosimo Quorli (an associate of Orazio and Artemisia who was also mentioned in the rape trial).[8] Quorli is known to have associated with Caravaggio – having assisted Caravaggio in another court proceeding in 1605 – so Artemisia may have had access to Caravaggio's composition by means of a work in Quorli's collection that was possibly a copy.

It has been suggested elsewhere that an early version of *Susanna and the Elders* by Jusepe de Ribera might provide an indication of the original appearance of Caravaggio's lost work (fig. 15).[9] The probability that Ribera's version might preserve at least some aspects of Caravaggio's composition is strengthened by the fact that this subject is otherwise atypical for this artist. Ribera tended to favour more religiously devout subjects, in keeping with his youthful background in early seventeenth-century Valencia – and subsequently reconfirmed once he relocated to the comparably devout culture of Baroque Naples. The numerous compositional features that are common to both Ribera's and Artemisia's versions are thus highly suggestive in this respect: both depict Susanna dipping her feet into a band of water that runs parallel to the painting's edge, with Ribera's Susanna forming a kind of mirror image to the Michelangelesque pose of Artemisia's figure. For his part, Ribera might have come across Caravaggio's treatment of the subject, either in the original or in a copy, sometime during his youth, which was spent maintaining a similarly itinerant lifestyle in the artists' quarter of Rome (in between time spent also in Parma and elsewhere) from around 1608 (when he was himself aged seventeen), prior to his eventual relocation to Naples in 1616.[10]

PAINTING FROM THE MODEL IN THE GENTILESCHI WORKSHOP

The documents from the rape trial of 1612 make clear the Gentileschi workshop's reliance on models during this period. The family's washerwoman, Margerita Agostino, for example, lists four local residents – all men – whom she knew to have been working as regular models for Orazio: 'She knew that he used them as models because he showed her the paintings for which they had posed.'[11] Among them was Orazio's barber, together with a seventy-three-year-old pilgrim from Palermo, Giovanni Molli. Molli was subsequently brought in for questioning. His description to the Curial court is particularly revealing of Orazio's working procedures during this period. He noted that he posed 'for some heads as well as for a whole figure of St Jerome, for which he was asked to undress from the waist up'.[12] This latter painting has been identified as the version of this subject now in Turin (fig. 16).[13] The process of posing was evidently intensive, since Molli notes of Orazio that 'He kept me in the house all during Lent, and three or four days a week I had to go to his house. Some days I would go and stay from morning to night, and I ate and drank in his house, and he paid me by the day, and I returned to my own house to sleep.'[14]

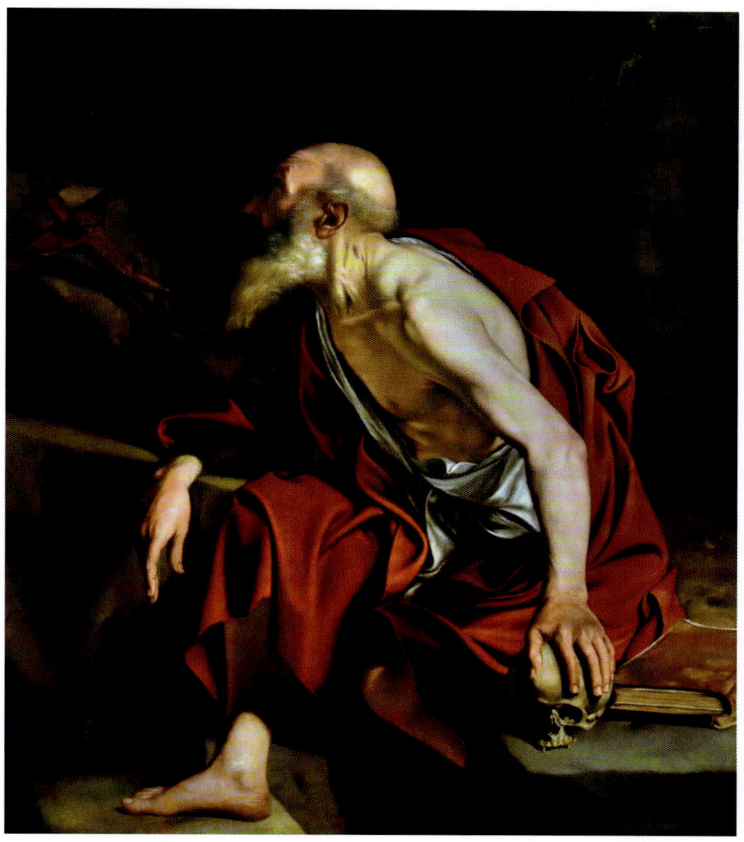

16 Orazio Gentileschi, *St Jerome*, 1610–11, oil on canvas, 153 × 128 cm, Museo Civico d'Arte Antica e Palazzo Madama, Turin

Molli would have regularly posed for Orazio for a full six weeks, therefore, and so for something like twenty sittings, simply to complete this single full-length figure.[15] The new practice of painting directly from the model after the manner of Caravaggio was thus an extremely laborious process. It was also quite expensive. The standard day rate for labourers during this period was around 0.3 of a scudo, which was the amount paid, for example, to Mario Trotta – also interviewed at the trial – for his work as an assistant to Gentileschi and Tassi while they were working on the frescoes on the Quirinal Hill.[16] Exactly the same amount was paid to the model for the life-drawing classes at the Accademia di San Luca. If we presume equivalent rates for Molli's work, then this means that Orazio would have had to pay something like 6 scudi in life-modelling fees for this figure alone – a substantial overhead to factor into the expenses required for completing an easel painting of this kind.

Of course, and as Artemisia's 1610 *Susanna* so vividly demonstrates, both daughter and father had ready and free access to the use of Artemisia's own body as a model (for Artemisia's possible access to a full-length mirror, see below, p. 43). Yet this was a venture that also carried certain risks. It may strike us as hypocritical today when considering a city so awash with displays of public carnality, either for sale on the street or rendered up more privately to suit other contexts, but the idea of 'wanton' nudity and the supposedly unbridled sexuality that it might encourage were still considered a shocking prospect in Counter-Reformation Rome. When it came to nude life-drawing classes, for example, the deliberations of the Accademia di San Luca reveal a strong desire on the organisation's part to regulate the practice as far as possible. The 1596 statutes prohibited students from arranging life-drawing meetings of their own accord without first obtaining a license from the Principe, while the 1607 statutes barred members from holding an academy without first informing the Principe of their plans.[17] The Academy was evidently concerned to exert control over this practice, not only for legislative purposes but also for fear of the 'many scandals that arise from these particular meetings'.[18]

The idea of women posing nude was yet more contentious. Thus, again in 1607, the Academy prohibited its members from engaging in the use of women for life modelling – on pain of a fine of 10 scudi.[19] This was a powerful disincentive to the practice, encouraging Italian Baroque artists to avoid using female life models (certainly unclothed ones) for their compositions, whether painted or drawn, wherever possible. Only very occasionally does one hear about artists resorting to direct life modelling of the female nude in the privacy of their own home with an especially trusted family member: Giovanni Battista Passeri mentions Francesco Albani's using his wife and children as nude models for his mythological paintings, for example.[20] The Neapolitan biographer Bernardo de' Dominici (1683– 1759) disapprovingly noted that Luca Giordano used his own wife as the model for his *Sleeping Venus with Cupid and Satyr* of 1663 (fig. 17). Giordano is in other respects presented as the hero of De' Dominici's *Vite de' pittori, scultori ed architetti napoletani* (1742–45), so it was evidently a major criticism on the author's part to express an admiration tinged with discomfort in relation to this activity: 'on this occasion Luca used his own wife as a model, who was tall, well proportioned and very beautiful, without looking for others [i.e., other models], and perhaps he did this scandalously'.[21] One has to look as far afield as the workshop of Rembrandt to encounter seventeenth-century life drawings that display signs of being based on female nude models.[22]

Italian Baroque artists who were required to depict a female nude from classical mythology and the like tended to follow the time-honoured technique of posing male models and then 'converting' them into females after the fact. As Carl Goldstein has noted in the context of a study of the Carracci's drawings, this resulted in a situation whereby, 'When the female is studied . . . a decidedly masculine physique takes shape.' Thus, one of the female attendants in Annibale Carracci's *Triumph of Bacchus and Ariadne* from the Farnese Gallery derives from a study after a life model who clearly betrays the more muscular physique of one of Annibale's male assistants (fig. 18).[23] In a similar respect, Carlo Cesare Malvasia's Life of Annibale includes the revealing observation that the fleshy appearance of the back of Venus in Annibale's *Venus, a Satyr and Two Cupids*, now in the Uffizi (fig. 19), derives from Annibale's use of his own cousin, Ludovico Carracci, as a model for her form. This resulted in a rendition of the goddess that, while more decorous, was less anatomically credible than Giordano's.[24] Peter Paul Rubens (1577–1640) clearly also took the path of least resistance when it came to modelling the body of Susanna in his version of the subject in the Borghese collection which is often cited in connection to Artemisia's painting of the same subject (fig. 20).[25] As this comparison makes clear, Rubens's and Artemisia's depictions of Susanna could not be more dissimilar in positing diametrically opposed understandings of

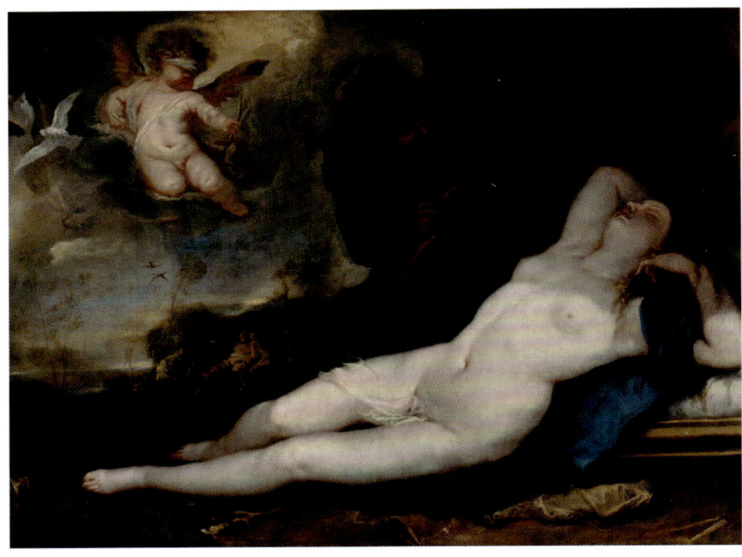

17 Luca Giordano, *Sleeping Venus with Cupid and Satyr*, signed and dated 1663, oil on canvas, 137 × 190 cm, Museo e Real Bosco di Capodimonte, Naples

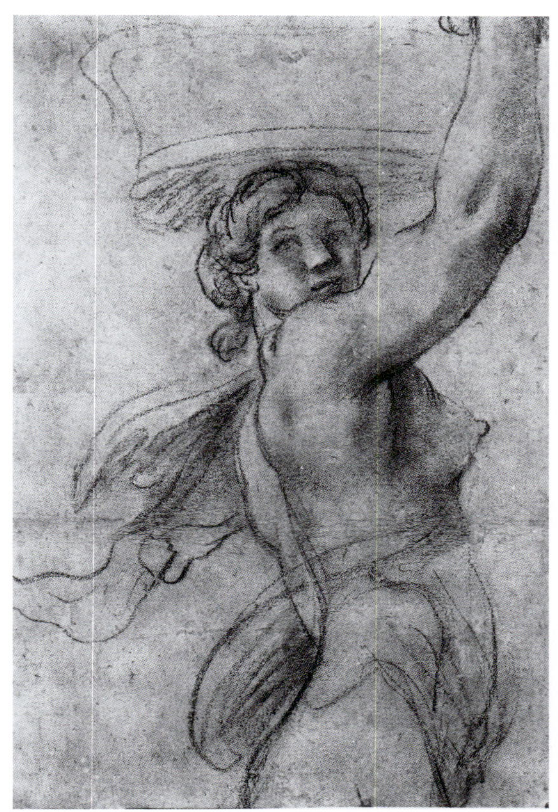

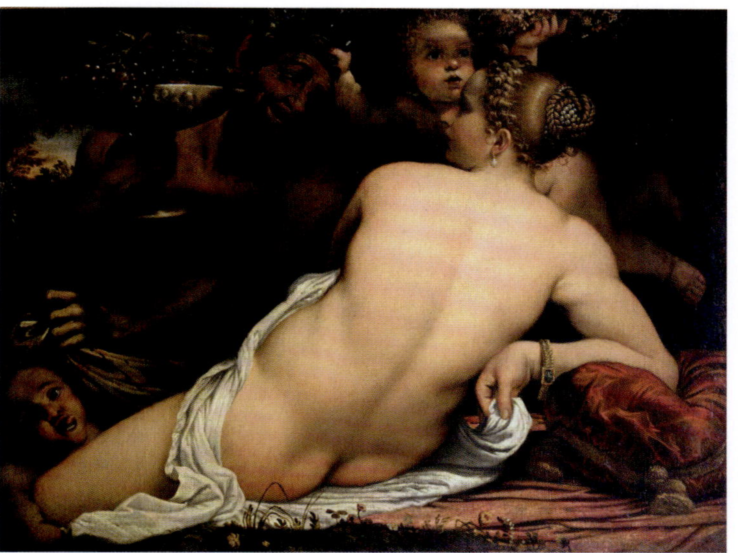

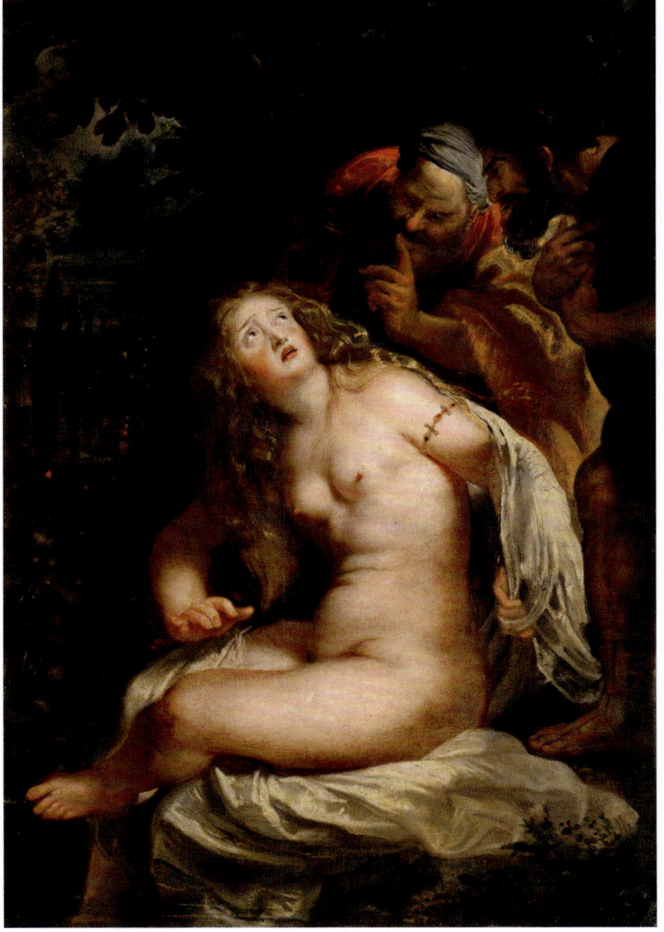

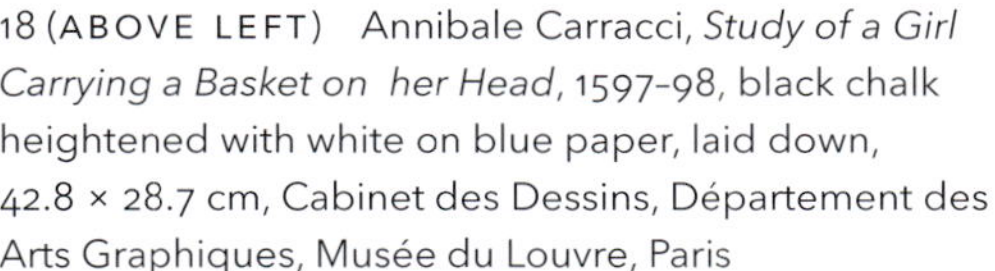

18 (ABOVE LEFT) Annibale Carracci, *Study of a Girl Carrying a Basket on her Head*, 1597–98, black chalk heightened with white on blue paper, laid down, 42.8 × 28.7 cm, Cabinet des Dessins, Département des Arts Graphiques, Musée du Louvre, Paris

19 (ABOVE RIGHT) Annibale Carracci, *Venus, a Satyr and Two Cupids*, c.1588–90, oil on canvas, 112 × 142 cm, Galleria degli Uffizi, Florence

20 (RIGHT) Peter Paul Rubens, *Susanna and the Elders*, 1607, oil on canvas, 94 × 65 cm, Galleria Borghese, Rome

the female form – one idealized and abstracted, the other shockingly palpable and specific. This distinction, with its clear breaking, on Artemisia's part, of the Baroque taboo against the depiction of unidealized female nakedness, would have been immediately evident to contemporary viewers, setting Gentileschi's *Susanna* radically apart from the work of her male competitors.

The proceedings of the rape trial also highlight that for a woman to pose nude could do damage to her honour. Particularly revealing in this context is the testimony of Martino Coppino, a thirty-four-year-old supplier of artistic materials. This witness described himself as a 'maker of the colour of ultramarine' – that is, one who prepares ultramarine by grinding it and mixing it with pigments – a comment that further attests to the high degree of professional specialisation then on offer in the artists' quarter of Rome. Coppino claimed that he had heard it said in the workshop of a certain sculptor that 'there was a beautiful young woman . . . her father did not want her to marry, and that when he was producing a nude he had her strip naked and would portray her thus ['quando faceva qualche ritratto nudo la faceva spogliar nuda e la ritraheva'] and that [he had heard] he liked it when people came to see it'.[26]

The tendency in the literature for many years has been to dismiss this comment as a scurrilous slander – as indeed it clearly is on one level – concocted by the Tassi faction in order to smear Artemisia's honour and thus her credibility as a witness.[27] And yet, in another sense, it tallies with the anatomical specificity of the depiction of the female form in the *Susanna* and the other early paintings, such as the *Cleopatra/Danaë* pair discussed below. It also strikes one, moreover, as a rumour that would be difficult to invent out of thin air without its first having some basis in fact – or, at least, some basis in the 'fact' of its already existing as a rumour. It has the ring, in other words, of constituting on Coppino's part a genuinely unsolicited and independent observation that he had picked up during the course of his daily interactions as he moved among the local workshops. If it were something that Coppino had been told in advance to say by Tassi, then one could assume that Tassi himself would have also used it as further ammunition to add to the litany of sordid accusations and insinuations that he levelled against Artemisia as part of his own defence. The fact that no other member of the Tassi defence team made any attempt to exploit this particular line of attack strongly suggests, therefore, that there was indeed a rumour to this effect circulating around the Roman workshops and that Coppino independently raised it in response to the court's questioning.

GENTILESCHI INCORPORATED: NUDITY AND THE ISSUE OF ARTISTIC DIFFERENTIATION IN THE MASTER'S WORKSHOP

The likelihood that this rumour was not simply something that Coppino had made up to smear Gentileschi's reputation during the trial and that it did reflect the working practices of the Gentileschi workshop during this period is further suggested by two closely related paintings of *Cleopatra* and *Danaë* that have been the focus of considerable debate over the years (figs 21 and 22). The *Cleopatra* is a large painting on canvas that is first mentioned in an eighteenth-century Genoese guidebook as a work by Orazio and as being in the collection of Pietro Maria III Gentile. An earlier provenance has also been suggested for the work: that it probably derives from the collection of Gentile's forebear and a major patron of Orazio, Pietro Maria I Gentile, to whom Orazio is likely to have sold the canvas during his stay in Genoa in 1621–22.[28] The *Danaë*, on the other hand, is a small painting on copper that first appeared at auction in the 1980s with no early provenance.

The extremely close relationship between the two works has encouraged a range of arguments in favour of their attribution to either one or other artist.[29] Further compounding the attributional complexity is a related discussion concerning the authorship of the 1610 *Susanna and the Elders*. The Pommersfelden *Susanna* was for many years accepted as the definitive point of reference for Artemisia's early development, a secure status that seemed further cemented by its conspicuous signature and date. In a review of the 1991 Casa Buonarroti exhibition devoted to Artemisia Gentileschi, John T. Spike initiated a counter-argument when he observed that the overall accomplishment and obviously heavy indebtedness of the *Susanna* to Orazio's compositions and technique meant that the work,

FACING PAGE Artemisia Gentileschi, *Danaë* (detail of fig. 22)

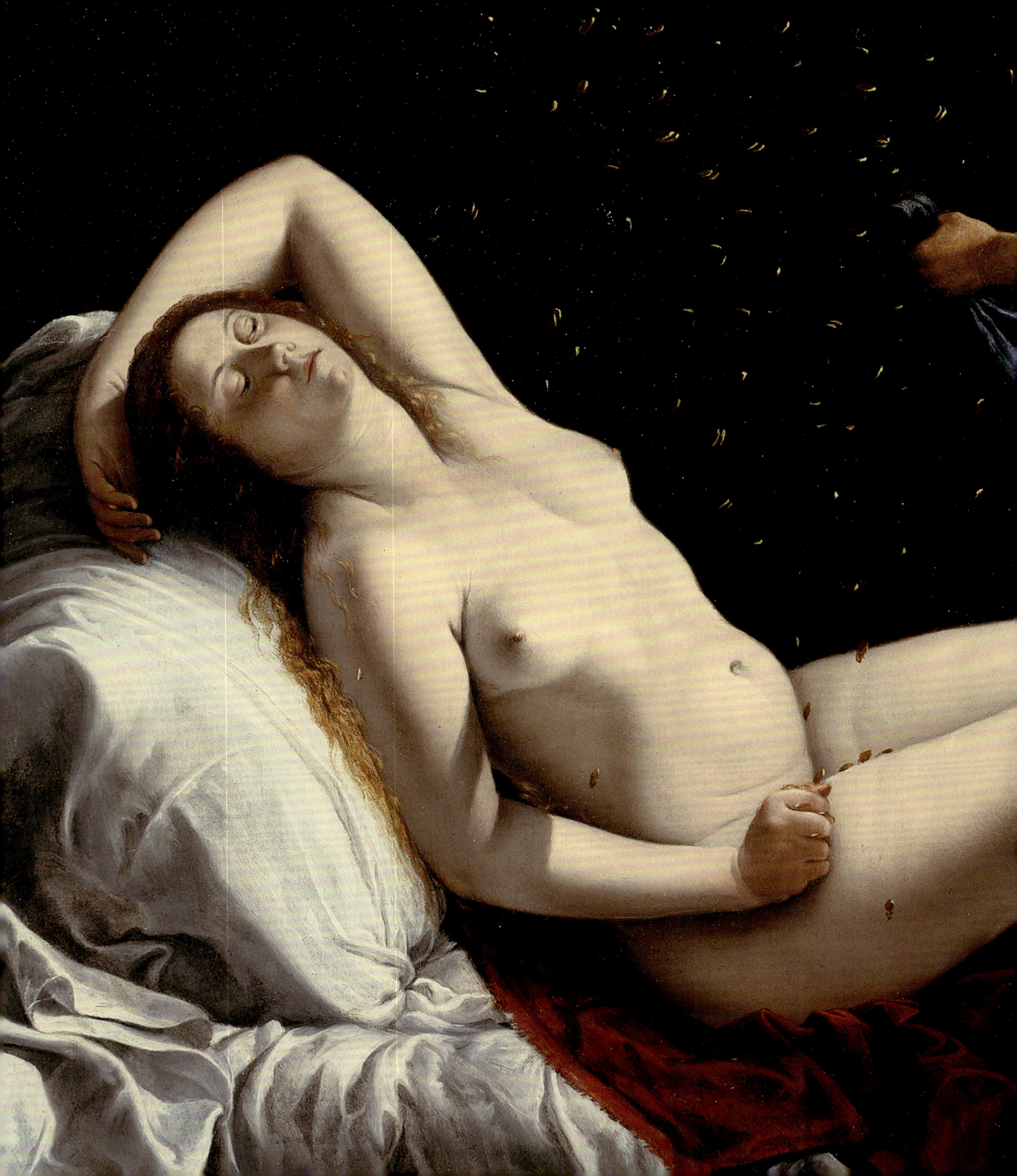

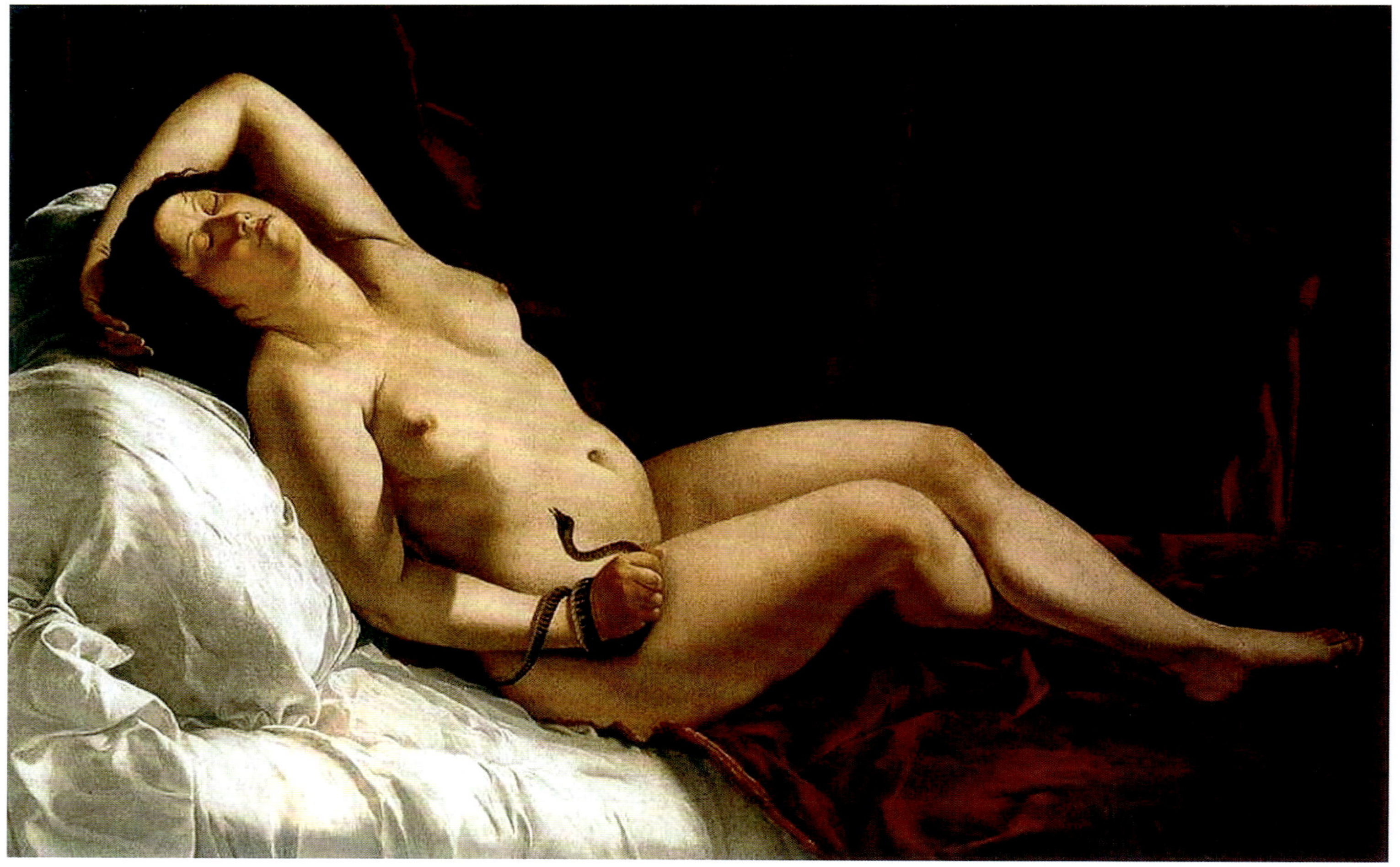

21 Orazio Gentileschi, *Cleopatra*, c.1610–12, oil on canvas, 118 × 181 cm, Etro Collection

although signed by Artemisia, should, nonetheless, be seen as essentially Orazio's creation. He remarked, 'I believe that this fascinating picture is best seen as a collaboration directed by Orazio, who, in an understandable reversal of workshop tradition, proudly encouraged his daughter-assistant to take the credit.'[30] To this opinion was added the subsequent agreement of R. Ward Bissell, the author of the standard catalogues raisonnés of both artists. Reversing his earlier acceptance of the attribution of the 1610 *Susanna* to Artemisia, Bissell subsequently revised his opinion in favour of the assertion that 'as an advertising ploy Orazio allowed Artemisia to sign a picture for the conception and execution of which he had primarily been responsible'.[31] Since then, the debate has continued, although a swing in favour of reasserting Artemisia's sole authorship of the painting has become apparent. An assessment by Gianni Papi, Nina Gram Bischoff and Thierry Ford in 2019, for example, concludes that 'the [1610 Pommersfelden] painting differs markedly from those painted by Orazio at this time, and is the work of a different, more brilliant personality, better able to handle the placing of figures within the compositional space as well as their anatomical resolution'.[32]

I should like to address this issue from a slightly different perspective. I suggest the importance, instead, of considering it from the point of view of the working practices of the

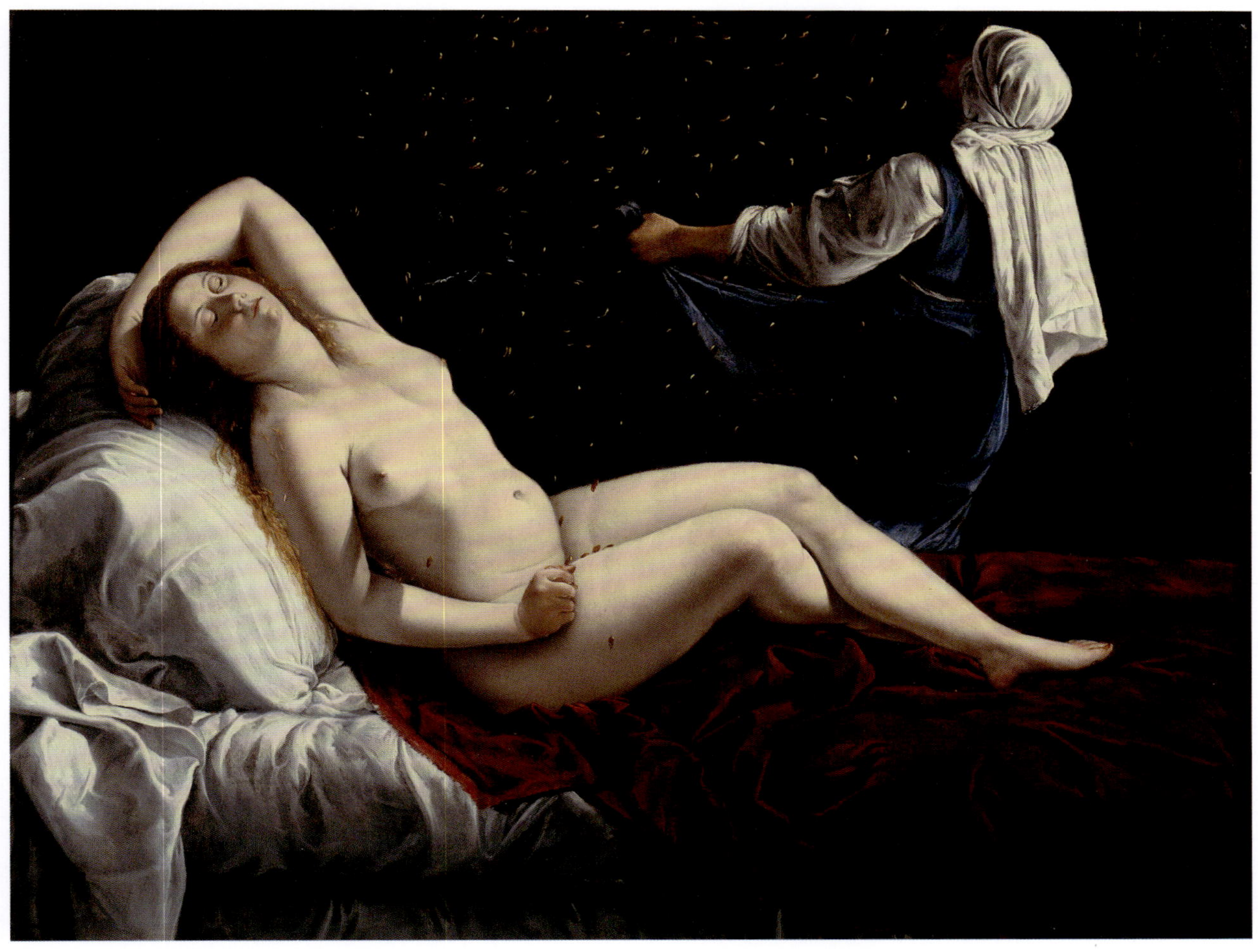

22 Artemisia Gentileschi, *Danaë*, oil on copper, c.1610–12, 41.3 × 52.7 cm, The Saint Louis Art Museum, Saint Louis

Gentileschis during this period and Orazio Gentileschi's likely motivations, as head of the workshop, in choosing to present his daughter's work in this way.

In considering these circumstances, it might be helpful to remind ourselves of an obvious but nevertheless fundamental truth: our wish today to frame the issue in attributional terms is readily understandable, but it would have been perceived very differently in its own day. Orazio was the head of the workshop, and Artemisia was his assistant. Everything they produced was, accordingly, considered to be the work of a single mind – and hand – and this is what constituted the 'product' of the workshop as presided over by the master. All of the workshop's output, therefore, whether by Artemisia or Orazio, was, also by definition, Orazio's alone and so belonged to him on both an intellectual or conceptual level and in a physical, commercial and legal sense.

It goes without saying that, in teaching Artemisia how to paint, Orazio also taught her to paint in his style. The idea that obvious stylistic distinctions might be apparent between the two artists' work at this stage would have been considered bizarrely anachronistic from the point of view of Renaissance and Baroque workshop practice. It was not the way that workshops were meant to operate. In this sense, Vasari's anecdote, referred to above, about the young Leonardo upstaging his master by adding a yet more beautiful angel to Verrocchio's *Baptism of Christ* was clearly meant to be read as an exception that proves the rule. Leonardo might have been able to get away with such anomalous practice because he was, after all, Leonardo. By the time of Vasari's writing, moreover, the anecdote had become codified and mythologised to the extent of its becoming part of Leonardo's origin myth. For others, however, the idea of an assistant departing from the master's style to such an extent that his handiwork stood out from the rest of the painting would have been anathema.

An early viewer of a Renaissance or Baroque master painting should not have been able to discern the presence of different hands at work. The entire point of Renaissance and Baroque workshop practice was to achieve the opposite effect and so to produce a pleasingly unified and consistent product in which all the various elements were aesthetically integrated into a harmonious composition attributable to a single artistic identity. The skill of an assistant thus lay not so much in their ability to stand out as, rather, precisely in the degree to which they were able to blend their work with the master's. Time and time again, therefore, the early sources accordingly stress the talent of one or other young assistant in relation to a more famous master as being evident in their ability to produce works that – with only a few retouchings – could be sold as originals by the master's hand.[33]

A study undertaken by Keith Christiansen in 2004 highlighted the extent to which this stylistic harmony within the Gentileschi workshop functioned at the most microscopic level of technical detail. With access to a series of X-radiographs representing a large corpus of works by both Orazio and Artemisia, Christiansen was able to discern a wealth of revealing information about the Gentileschis' working practices, including their use of incisions, tracings and cartoons and the process of working from the model. At the same time, he was also able to see evidence of the beginnings of a technical distinction between father and daughter. Orazio's canvases are said to reveal a higher degree of care and methodical forethought in the development of compositions prior to the application of paint to canvas. Artemisia's canvases, by contrast, betray a slightly looser and freer emphasis: 'As X-radiographs show, contours in Artemisia's paintings are important but rarely emphatic, and she tends not to distribute her lights and shadows with the same clarity and tidiness of her father.'[34]

These distinctions, however, become apparent only over time and are particularly difficult to discern in the early works produced by the two artists working together. Thus, Christiansen notes, in support of attributing the *Cleopatra* to Orazio, that 'We find Orazio's emphasis on a strong silhouette, with the figure drawn onto the canvas and the forms worked up in a fashion that leaves distinct edges between them.'[35] For Judith Mann, Curator of Early European Art at the St Louis Art Museum, on the other hand, the same evidence gives rise to an opposing point of view: both the *Cleopatra* and the *Danaë* are by Artemisia, in her opinion. Arguing against interpreting the characteristic technical signs of Orazio's hand in the *Cleopatra* as indicating Orazio's authorship of the work, she instead suggests that these signs should be read as demonstrating Artemisia's ability to imitate effectively the master's style. Mann accordingly notes that 'Christiansen, based on x rays made at the Metropolitan Museum at the time of the 2002 Gentileschi exhibition, has argued that the manner in which Cleopatra's body has been laid onto the canvas and then built up into a finished figure conforms to Orazio's process. However, given that Artemisia was initially trained to paint exactly like her father, it is not surprising to see her mimicking his process in her earliest pictures.'[36]

All of this suggests the usefulness of considering the two paintings as simultaneous products of the workshop of Orazio Gentileschi. One of the most striking features of the pair, in this sense, is that it demonstrates the workshop's ability to create two different, saleable products from a single pose. The compositions of the *Cleopatra* and *Danaë* are almost identical, being based on a repeated template, even down to the arrangement of pillows and drapery on the bed. And yet, with just a few deft changes, a study of the same model viewed from the same position has been presented as two completely different subjects: the death of Cleopatra by the asp and the seduction of Danaë by the shower of gold. By exploiting the inherent ambiguity of this identically posed figure, the Gentileschi workshop has thus managed to invoke both death and ecstasy from the same pose.

Is this innovation attributable to Artemisia? Or to Orazio? Or to the artists working collaboratively? We have no way of knowing for sure other than perhaps to concur with Elizabeth Cropper's conclusion that Artemisia was most likely the enabler of this development: 'The new direction in the Gentileschi studio around 1610 involved the bodily presence of Artemisia as both model and painter.'[37] Beyond this, the understandably closed and secretive nature of the Gentileschis' activities in this regard means that we have no more precise way of knowing just how this new practice might have been carried out. When considering the mechanics of reproducing such poses, for example, Patrizia Cavazzini has suggested that Artemisia might have been able to use herself as a model by gaining access to a full-length mirror, such as that owned by the previously mentioned Cosimo Quorli which is documented in his inventory of 1612.[38] Ann Sutherland Harris, on the other hand, highlights the physical difficulties involved in painting oneself while lying down.[39] She asserts, instead, that the painting would have been produced by Artemisia using another woman as a model. Yet this would have been even more risky and, therefore, in my opinion, less likely to have been the case. My own suggestion on the basis of all of the above is to posit the greater likelihood that the near identical figures of Cleopatra and Danaë were painted in the first instance by Orazio, using Artemisia as a model.

Perhaps it would be best, therefore, to conclude this brief consideration of the vexed issue of the conjoined nature of the Gentileschi workshop by noting that our continued difficulties in differentiating between the two artists' creations at this stage represent an accurate reflection of the no doubt highly secretive manner in which Orazio and Artemisia were required to evolve this new manner of treating the nude behind the veil of privacy provided by the workshop in its most 'closed' aspect. Perhaps we should identify both the *Cleopatra* and the *Danaë*, in this respect, as works 'by the hand of Orazio' in the Renaissance and Baroque sense of the term rather than with the more granular emphasis of modern attributional connoisseurship to which we are accustomed today. Both paintings were created during a period in which Orazio acted as the head of the workshop, while Artemisia functioned as a more or less entirely unknown junior assistant. Both works would have thus been perceived – in their own time at least – as by Orazio. This is not to say that the smaller painting on copper might not have been painted by Artemisia as a reduced-scale variant upon Orazio's *Cleopatra*. If so, and to make things yet more complicated, then she would have been copying a composition that had probably been based in turn on a study by her father, possibly using her own nude body modelled from life.

Where should we draw the line then, when considering the issue of where one artist stops and another artist begins in the context of a tightly interlocking workshop? It may well suit today's 'masterpiece mentality' to prefer the relative clarity and museological authority of assigning the two works to two distinct artistic identities – for example, the *Cleopatra* to Orazio, and the *Danaë* to Artemisia. Yet this would be to deny the subtle connections and multiple points of overlap articulated above. The Gentileschi workshop constituted an inherently conjoined enterprise that was, in a literal sense, patriarchal, and Artemisia's individuality and identity – even as it applied to her own body – were thus subsumed into the corporate identity of the workshop. There were, nonetheless, signs during this period that she was given greater latitude to express herself on a more individualised standing, as a semi-independent creator of new categories of art that would enhance the novelty and marketability of the output of the Gentileschi workshop. This shift in direction would be signalled, above all, by the first two masterpieces of her early career, *Susanna and the Elders* of 1610 and *Judith Slaying Holofernes* of 1612–13.

3

‘Without peer’

THE BEGINNINGS OF GENTILESCHI’S CAREER AS AN INDEPENDENT SPECIALIST

INTRODUCTION
ARTEMISIA AND THE PROGRESSION FROM WORKSHOP ASSISTANT TO INDEPENDENT MASTER

Susanna and the Elders stands out as a very different proposition from the *Cleopatra* and the *Danaë*. In the *Susanna*, there is a prominent declaration of authorship that has been added in highlighted capital letters to the painted entablature at bottom left of the canvas: ‘ARTIMITIA/GENTILESCHI F [fecit = made this]/1610’. John T. Spike’s explanation for this, as we saw, was that the painting was produced for the most part by Orazio but that he then allowed his daughter to sign it in ‘an understandable reversal of workshop tradition’, in order proudly to encourage ‘his daughter-assistant to take the credit’. Yet the harshly constrained circumstances of Artemisia’s early years would seem to indicate that there was very little latitude in the Gentileschi household for such an altruistic act of paternal indulgence. The working procedures of the Gentileschi workshop suggest a very different reality: namely, that Orazio considered Artemisia as part of his workshop collateral. It seems scarcely credible that he would have allowed her to sign a work had it not accorded with his sense that, in so doing, she might be able to contribute materially to the fortunes of the Gentileschi family enterprise.

FACING PAGE Artemisia Gentileschi, *Judith Slaying Holofernes* (detail of fig. 29)

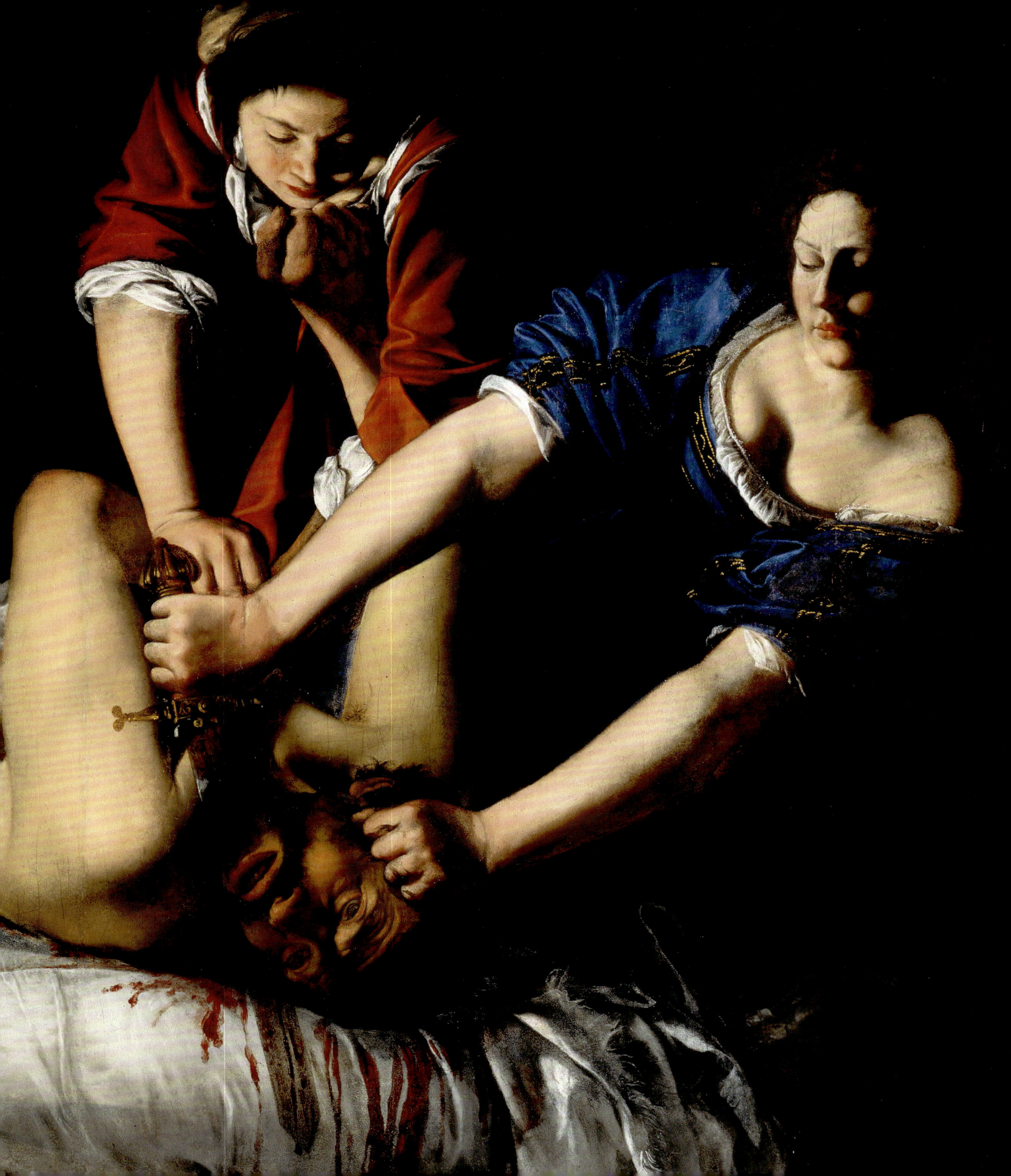

It is worthwhile considering, therefore, just what Orazio might have been seeking to achieve in encouraging his daughter to sign the *Susanna*. I suggest that he did so as a marketing ploy to announce his daughter's ability to maintain a subsidiary specialisation of independently produced canvases within the workshop. Artemisia was to be considered from this point forward, in effect, as a specialist assistant capable of producing autonomous work, such as portraiture and history painting – albeit with the proviso that all proceeds from this activity would naturally flow to Orazio. (Alternatively, we might perhaps imagine Orazio setting aside part of the proceeds from the sale of these works to build up a dowry for his daughter, although there is no information to suggest anything more specific on this score.)

Of course, it is likely – almost certain – that Orazio would have assisted Artemisia as part of this process. This would have involved his adding the necessary 'retouchings', part of his customary duties as head of the workshop, which was entirely in line with standard Baroque workshop practice. Yet, the act of allowing Artemisia to sign her own work was clearly intended to function as a significant and meaningful statement on the part of both Orazio and Artemisia. It marks the *Susanna* out as a public declaration of Orazio's recognition of Artemisia's ability and authority to complete works in her own name while, nonetheless, continuing to work in a business venture presided over by the master. In allowing her to sign it thus, Orazio formally endorsed Artemisia's ability to function within the workshop at that level from now on. As Judith Mann has also noted, Orazio did this only because he saw this as a realistic possibility that would bring benefits to the workshop, since he would not 'benefit from promising talents that she did not in fact possess. Rather, his interests were served by a painting that was a true testament to Artemisia's abilities and that established her abilities as a reputable artist, a master of the human figure who could attract commissions.'[1]

The biblical subject matter and large-scale figures of the *Susanna and the Elders* add a further level of significance to the painting's intended message. As Patrizia Cavazzini and others have noted, the shift from Artemisia's smaller *Madonna and Child* to this grand-manner figure painting represented an audacious and virtually unprecedented step up by both Artemisia and Orazio. It deliberately sought to reposition Artemisia's work beyond the recognised genres of 'female-appropriate' painterly production as they were then understood. According to the norms of the day, if women were to be countenanced as artists, and only very few ever actually were, then they would be generally expected to restrict themselves to smaller-scale work executed with subject matter and in genres of painting that were supposedly less 'demanding', such as devotional imagery, still life and portraiture.[2] History painting, on the other hand, was ranked well above these genres at the apex of the artistic hierarchy. This was because it was understood as being based not on observation alone, but rather on the careful application of the highest degree of abstract intellectual thought, or *invenzione*. This was a quality that was generally considered to be beyond the capabilities of women. Michelangelo gave voice to this widely held prejudice in his now notorious comment that the superficial realism and direct observation found in Flemish landscape painting meant that it was a genre that should appeal only 'to women, especially very old and very young women, and also to monks and nuns and to certain noblemen who have no sense of true harmony'.[3] Thus, the key features of narrative, scale and genre in the *Susanna* become gendered issues. Artemisia – and her father – were wilfully transgressing the traditional bias against female proficiency by proclaiming Artemisia's skill as a monumental figure painter with the ability to produce history paintings on a level directly comparable with that achieved by her male peers.

Another significant factor is the audaciously young age at which Artemisia was being encouraged to make this shift. She was seventeen – or perhaps still sixteen, if the *Susanna* were completed prior to her seventeenth birthday on 8 July 1610. It would seem, therefore, that Orazio was intending to frame his daughter as a precociously talented young female artist. These qualities correspond precisely with those that he chose to stress in the letter, cited in chapter 1, that he composed on 3 July 1612, in the immediate context of the still unresolved rape trial. In the letter, he recommended Artemisia to Christine de Lorraine, the Dowager Grand Duchess of Tuscany and mother of the reigning Grand Duke, Cosimo II (1590–1621). The letter particularly emphasises the fact that Artemisia had attained a prodigiously high level of artistic progress at a tender age: 'this girl [*femina*], it has pleased God, having been trained in the profession of painting, has in three years become so skilled that I can venture to say today she is without peer, indeed, she has produced works which demonstrate a level of understanding that perhaps even the principal masters of the profession have not attained, as I will show Your Very Serene Highness at the proper time and place'.[4]

Orazio appears to have been intentionally exaggerating the rapidity of his daughter's artistic progression, claiming that Artemisia's training had begun only three years earlier. This is understandable as an attempt on his part to convey an impression of the young Artemisia as a child prodigy. That she was female, of course, only added to the sense of this teenage painter's phenomenal exceptionality. In this respect, then, I would also propose that the 1610 *Susanna* should be regarded as a kind of visual proclamation attesting to Artemisia's talents as an uncommonly youthful female practitioner of the otherwise male-dominated genre of history painting. In so doing, Orazio was setting Artemisia up as a 'virtuosa' artist, a model of female artistic virtuosity that was only just then emerging as a form of creative practice.[5]

LAVINIA FONTANA AND THE NEW MODEL OF THE *VIRTUOSA* ARTIST

The theoretical basis underpinning this new understanding of female artistic accomplishment derived from the broader literary tradition of the so-called *querelle des dammes* – literally, the argument about women.[6] The term has been used to designate the substantial body of literature arguing in favour of according a greater level of recognition to women's rights and achievements that stems back to the writings of Christine de Pizan (1364–*c.*1430) and Boccaccio (1313–1375) among others.[7] Artemisia's engagement with this tradition is documented at least from the time of her inclusion in Cristofano Bronzini's manuscript biography, which stems directly from this tradition.[8] This new appreciation of the roles of women in at least some sections of society was beginning to manifest itself also on a professional and artistic level. The first examples of successful women artists were just beginning to make their way into positions of, at times, considerable public recognition. The two most prominent recent examples were the Lombard painter Sofonisba Anguissola (*c.*1535–1625) and Lavinia Fontana (1552–1614) from Bologna. Anguissola had been able to draw on her family's aristocratic and diplomatic connections to garner early interest in her work from a series of influential and high-ranking connoisseurs. This success culminated in an invitation in 1559 to serve as a lady-in-waiting at the Spanish royal court.[9] Her artworks elicited positive comments even from the likes of Michelangelo and served as a basis for one of Caravaggio's most innovative early compositions.[10]

Lavinia Fontana seems to have been a yet more directly relevant role model for Artemisia – but would also have been of interest to Orazio, in terms of how he might best draw attention to his daughter's talents.[11] Fontana was also the daughter of a well-known painter: her father, Prospero Fontana (1512–1597), had pursued a successful career, first in Rome and then Bologna, before opening a school that trained many of the key artists of the next generation, such as Ludovico and Agostino Carracci. Lavinia, like Artemisia, learned her trade by her father's side before developing a prosperous livelihood on her own terms with particular specialisations in devotional paintings and in portraiture, interests shared by the young Artemisia, as we have seen.[12] In Rome, Orazio and Artemisia were given an opportunity to familiarise themselves with Fontana's work as a result of her relocation to the papal city in 1604, at the age of fifty-two. Here, she came to enjoy the patronage of a network of powerful clerics, including Cardinal Girolamo Bernerio, who secured an altarpiece commission for her in Santa Sabina, as well as Pope Clement VIII Aldobrandini (r. 1592–1605) and Cardinal Camillo Borghese, the former papal legate to Bologna and soon to succeed Aldobrandini as Pope Paul V Borghese (r. 1605–21). Borghese had acted as godfather to Lavinia's son in Bologna in 1592 and was thus a committed patron, both commissioning work from her as well as promoting and supporting her career more generally. The timing of Fontana's residence in Rome and her patronage by the Borghese family is probably significant, since Orazio was attempting to gain Borghese's patronage at precisely the same period in which the *Susanna* was being completed.[13] Fontana was also recognised on an institutional level around this time.

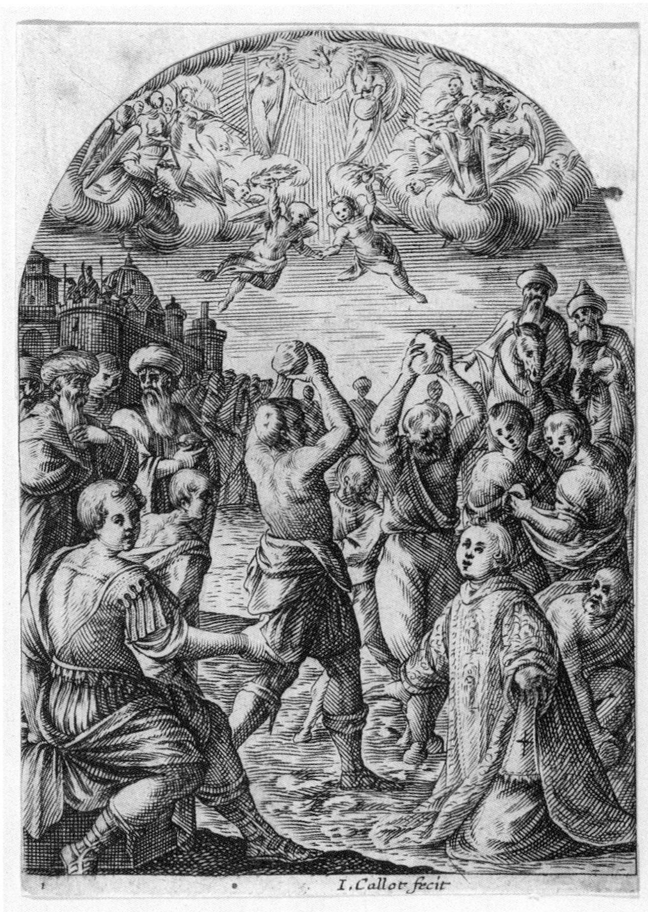

23 Jacques Callot after Lavinia Fontana, *The Martyrdom of St Stephen*, 1607–11, engraving, 11.3 × 7.8 cm, from *Les Tableaux de Rome, Les Eglises Jubilaires* (*The Paintings of Rome, The Churches Jubilee*), plate 1, The Metropolitan Museum of Art, New York, The Elisha Whittelsey Collection, The Elisha Whittelsey Fund, 59.569.2

She was one of the first women to be admitted into the Accademia di San Luca, at some point between 1607 (when the rules were changed to allow women to become members, while still barring them from attending meetings and life classes) and her death in 1614.[14]

In 1603, Fontana had completed a major altarpiece, *The Stoning of St Stephen*, for the Roman basilica of San Paolo Fuori le Mura. This painting was situated just across the transept, as it transpired, from one of Orazio's own altarpieces, produced for the church in 1596.[15] Both works were destroyed by fire in 1823, but a visual record of Fontana's altarpiece is preserved in an early reproductive print (fig. 23). Artemisia must have known this painting, since the proceedings of the rape trial mention a family excursion to this very church, where one can imagine Fontana's monumentally scaled altarpiece making a powerful impression on the young aspiring artist.

Finally, around the time that Artemisia was working on the *Susanna*, Fontana had created for herself a new area of specialisation: subtly erotic depictions of Venus and other classically inspired female nudes. These were avidly sought after by collectors in both Bologna and Rome, including the Cardinal-Nephew, Scipione Borghese (1577–1633), who commissioned one of Fontana's last paintings of this kind (fig. 24). It may well be that the *Susanna* was conceived by Orazio to act as a demonstration of the prodigious skills of his young daughter and her ability to create nude figures on a grand scale and of a type that could withstand comparison with the work of any artist, male or female, including that of Lavinia Fontana, the most prestigious and highly acclaimed woman artist of the day.

If this is an accurate reconstruction of Orazio's probable thinking, then it must be said that the ploy seems to have backfired. The 1610 *Susanna* is sometimes proposed as a commission from the Ludovisi family, since a 'Susanna with the Elders . . . by the hand of artimitia' is listed in a Ludovisi inventory of 1623. This reference, however, is more likely to refer to Gentileschi's later, 1622 painting of the same subject now at Burghley House (discussed below in Chapter 7).[16] If so, then the 1610 *Susanna* remains without provenance until the eighteenth century. Orazio's aspiration to launch Artemisia's parallel specialisation in history paintings incorporating female nudes may have been frustrated by the unanticipated negative attention generated by the trial. In which case, Orazio's workshop stock of such paintings would have likely become unsaleable. Works that would have been affected by this negative perception include the 1610 *Susanna*, the copper *Danaë*, the canvas *Cleopatra* and any other workshop productions based on studies of Artemisia's nude body of which we remain unaware. Orazio would have had to hold onto his stock of this kind of imagery until the passage of time and perhaps also geographic distance had helped to erase whatever reputational taint might

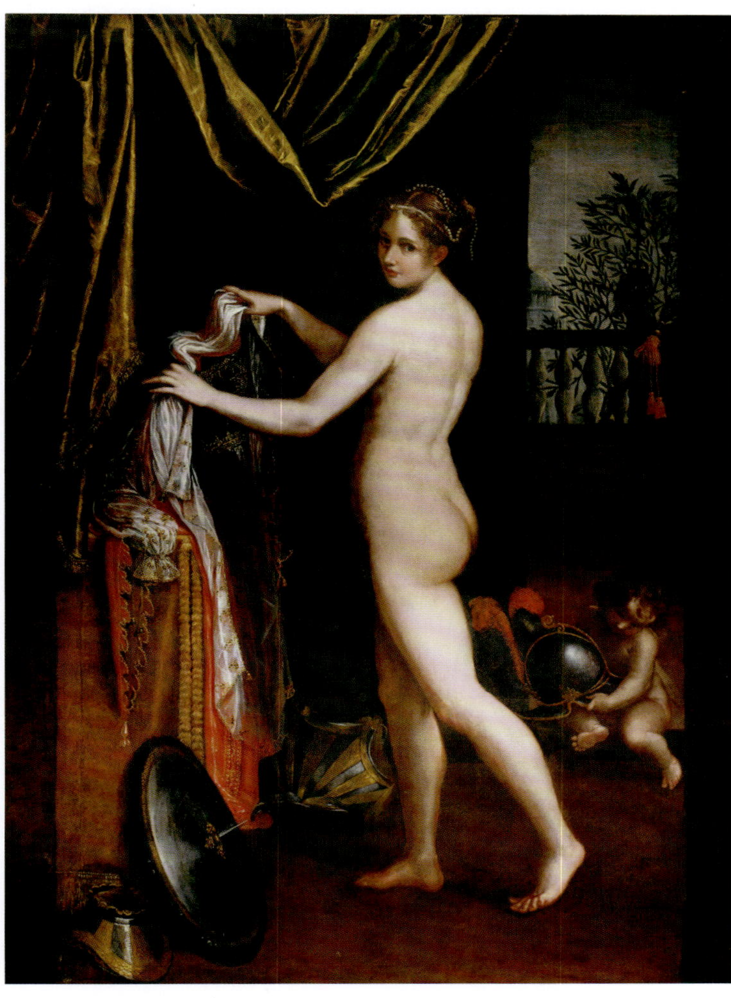

24 Lavinia Fontana, *Minerva Dressing*, dated 1613, oil on canvas, 260 × 90 cm, Galleria Borghese, Rome

have been associated with these works in Rome following the trial. Only some years later, then, would he have been able judiciously to offload his paintings of this kind to more sympathetic – or perhaps unknowing? – patrons, such collectors as Pietro Maria I Gentile, for example, to whom, as noted above, Orazio appears to have sold the *Danaë* in Genoa in 1621–22.

ARTEMISIA'S EARLY *JUDITHS*: FROM IMITATION TO INNOVATION

In following the new model set by Caravaggio of producing easel paintings for independent sale to private collectors, Orazio's imagination appears to have been particularly captured by the subject of the triumphant head-hunter.[17] He returned to this imagery frequently during the first two decades of the century, producing multiple versions of David and Goliath and Judith and Holofernes, as well as a signed canvas of an executioner holding the severed head of St John the Baptist, all highly dramatic subjects first painted by Caravaggio.

This focus seems, nonetheless, counter-intuitive given Orazio's tendency to avoid depictions of overt violence and the kinds of extreme physical activity that one might have otherwise expected as mandatory for subjects of this kind. From time to time, because of the particular requirements of one or other commission, he was compelled to represent subjects incorporating such action and/or violence, yet, as R. Ward Bissell has pointed out, 'These attempts at portraying vehement physical activity seem to have convinced him that his real talents lay toward the opposite end of the range of expression.'[18] Orazio thus developed a particular propensity for capturing lyrically pensive and introspective moments that lie at the edges of narrative exposition. When treating violent subjects similar to or the same as those painted by Caravaggio, Orazio's predilection led him to focus on the frozen aftermath of violence: David leans wearily on his sword, gazing meditatively upon Goliath's head; Judith and her maidservant wait tensely in the shadows as they listen for the sounds of the guards; the executioner holds up the head of the Baptist like a slice of meat to be sold at market. Even in those very few instances where Orazio does depict the vigorous denouement of the story, as in the version of *David Slaying Goliath* now in Dublin (fig. 14), there is a strangely stilled and silent feel about the composition. Whether consciously formulated or intuitively arrived at over time, this approach constituted one of Orazio's most distinctive features and it resulted in some of the most original expressions of the Caravaggesque mode.

One of the key paintings demonstrating Orazio's early emphasis on this stilled vision of Caravaggesque violence also appears as a central piece of evidence in the rape-trial proceedings. As was noted in Chapter 2, Orazio's case against Tassi was not solely based on the accusation of *stuprum* – one that was at that time legally defined as the act of forcible defloration rather than as rape as it is understood today.[19] It included the additional charge that, at some point in the months leading up to or around the time of the rape, Tassi and his associates had robbed Orazio of a painting. This had been achieved – as further spelt out in witness statements – by their inducing or somehow tricking Artemisia into handing over a painting of *Judith* through the machinations of Tassi's associate, Cosimo Quorli, the papal steward and an associate of Caravaggio during these years, who seems to have forged a document to encourage Artemisia to give them the painting.[20]

As was also noted above, Orazio did not specify whether the stolen *Judith* was by him or Artemisia, an omission that has led to many works being proffered as potential candidates for the purloined painting over the years, including some suggestions that it may have been Artemisia's own first version of *Judith Slaying Holofernes*, her signature masterpiece now in Naples (fig. 29). Alexandra Lapierre (following an initial proposal by Stephen Pepper in 1984) was the first to confirm, however, the presence of an inscription reading: 'HORAZIO GENTILESCHI A° 1612 Pizz' that appears on the back of a version of *Judith and her Maidservant with the Head of Holofernes* that has been attributed by all commentators to Orazio, and which was formerly at Colnaghi's and then at Sotheby's, New York, in 1993 before being acquired for the Museo de Bellas Artes, Bilbao (fig. 25). The inscription turns out to have been written in reference to the notary Tranquillo Pizzuti, within whose premises the painting was sequestered during the trial proceedings, while the status of its ownership was being clarified.[21] This, then, confirms that the painting stolen from the Gentileschi workshop while in Artemisia's keeping was Orazio Gentileschi's Bilbao *Judith*.[22]

Orazio, it will be remembered, was called away from the workshop on a daily basis during this period as a result of his ongoing commitments to on-site work with Tassi on the frescoes on the Quirinal Hill. Why would he, so it seems, leave one of his versions of *Judith* in Artemisia's particular care while he was away? Bissell is one of the few commentators to directly address this issue. He speculates that Orazio might have left it with Artemisia as 'a teaching tool or guide'.[23] Yet this cannot be so, since, as the previous analysis has clarified, Artemisia had progressed far beyond the level of a mere apprentice by this stage. She was, instead, a senior assistant who was expected to work with a degree of independent autonomy within the workshop. She would thus have been expected to earn her keep as a key contributor assisting with the task of keeping the workshop running in the master's absence. A much more likely answer to the question of why Orazio left the painting with Artemisia during this period was thus for her to produce a copy of it for him to sell – following retouchings by the master, of course – as an original by his hand.

Mary Garrard, in fact, reached a similar conclusion. In her 1989 monograph, she suggested that: 'A possible explanation for the ambiguity of authorship in the trial records is that the *Judith* given by Artemisia to Tassi was a copy by her of a work of her father – a copy that may even have been destined for sale *as* an Orazio'.[24] Garrard was, however, writing prior to Lapierre's discovery of the true candidate for the *Judith* referred to in the trial proceedings. She was also arguing on the basis of a different hypothetical reading of the evidence. This included a suggestion that the painting stolen by Tassi and his entourage may have been a copy by Artemisia rather than (as we know now to have been the case) an original by Orazio. The painting that she proposed as a potential candidate for this stolen copy was, moreover, a copy in the Vatican after an entirely different version of *Judith and her Maidservant* by Orazio, now at the Wadsworth Atheneum in Hartford, Connecticut, that is generally dated later than this period. This proposal has also been rejected by subsequent authors including Bissell, Papi and Christiansen, the latter of whom has asserted that 'the Vatican picture is a fine workshop replica based on a tracing of the Hartford painting and has no special claim to being by Artemisia; it certainly has nothing to do with the painting mentioned in the rape trial'.[25]

I would argue in favour of the essential soundness of Garrard's hypothesis while recognising its basis in an inaccurate sequence of works. If, as seems likely, Artemisia was making a copy after the Bilbao *Judith*, we need to look elsewhere for a potential candidate. Another, closely related version of

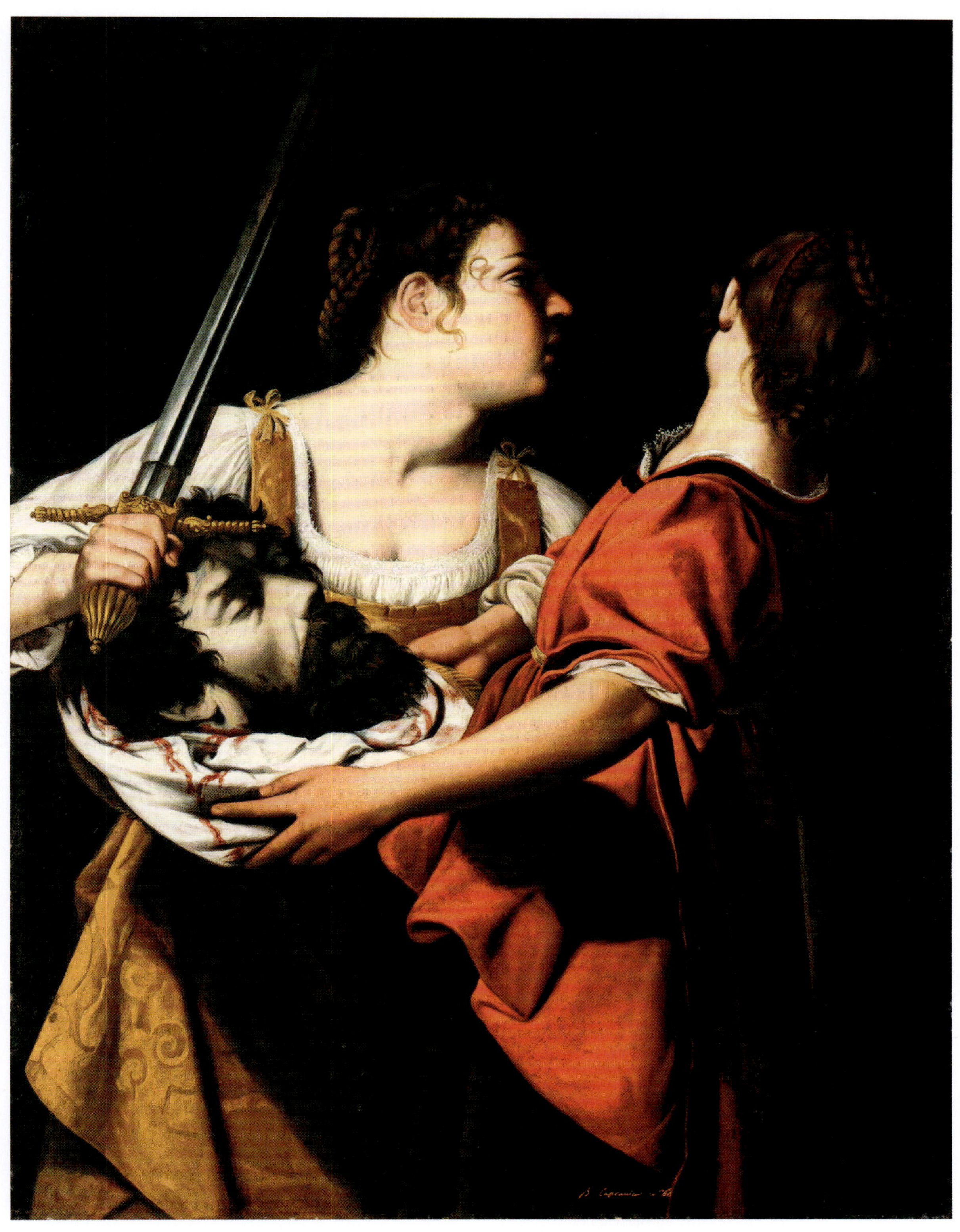

25 Orazio Gentileschi, *Judith and her Maidservant with the Head of Holofernes*, c.1610–11, oil on canvas, 131 × 101 cm, Museo de Bellas Artes de Bilbao, Donated by Óscar Alzaga Villaamil in 2021, inv. no. 21/83

Orazio's painting does exist and may fit the bill. This painting, in the Nasjonaalmuseet, Oslo, has a provenance stretching back only as far as the early nineteenth century, where it first appears as a work attributed to Caravaggio (fig. 26). Most modern scholars, from Longhi onwards, have attributed it to Orazio, although some have expressed reservations about this attribution. Bissell, for example, attributed the painting to Orazio in 1981, while noting the presence of 'certain features here that are unusual in the art of [Orazio] Gentileschi'.[26] In 1991, Gianni Papi readdressed the issue by exhibiting the canvas as 'Orazio (or Artemisia) Gentileschi' in the landmark exhibition dedicated to Artemisia's work held at the Casa Buonarroti.[27] Papi has also subsequently argued in favour of the painting's re-attribution to Artemisia in an article co-authored with Nina Gram Bischoff and Thierry Ford in 2019.[28]

While clearly based on Orazio's Bilbao *Judith*, the Oslo *Judith* is more accurately an elaboration upon Orazio's model rather than a strict copy. The position of Judith's right arm has been changed, as has the pose of the maidservant. Holofernes' head has also been shifted from a profile view to one facing out towards the viewer. This significantly alters the psychology of the second version. In the first painting, the two figures face inwards into the darkness in order to listen for a perceived danger emanating from outside. In the Oslo composition, by contrast, Judith places her left hand on Abra's shoulder in a calming gesture as if to urge her towards a yet greater stillness while the two protagonists take in the threat of danger from outside. As many commentators have noted, the Oslo canvas is also distinguished by a greater emphasis on building up details, including the refined costumes of the protagonists and, in particular, a considerably more elaborate rendition of jewellery. As Papi and others have noted, this last feature is more characteristic of Artemisia than Orazio. Papi, Bischoff and Ford's proposal to view this canvas as Artemisia's workshop copy after Orazio's stolen painting should thus be considered an intriguing proposal that, however, awaits further testing against a broader range of other scholarly opinions.[29]

ATROCITY EXHIBITION: *JUDITH SLAYING HOLOFERNES* AS A VIRTUOSO DEMONSTRATION OF THE PROJECTIVE POWER OF VIOLENCE

Another argument in favour of Artemisia's involvement in the creation of the Oslo *Judith* is the painting's much more graphic rendition of violence than in the Bilbao *Judith*. In the Bilbao canvas, Holofernes' ashen face is flecked with a subtly applied mist of dots of blood (fig. 27). Blood also stains the white cloth that surrounds his head in a network of trickles and smears. The overall effect is, nonetheless, one of understatement and an implicit rather than explicit violence, an emphasis which is entirely in keeping with Orazio's predisposition towards stillness and subtlety.

The Oslo *Judith*'s handkerchief, by contrast, is saturated with a patchwork of ugly, bruise-like smudges, while the blood positively gushes through the gaps in the open-weave basket held by the maidservant. From there it pools and puddles into a cascade of free-running rivulets (fig. 28). The intensity of this visceral outpouring is so strong that it conveys an uncanny suggestion that Holofernes' head is continuing to pump blood from the severed gash of his neck even after death. Indeed, the flow of blood is so extreme that it has begun to ooze out of the general's ear. This intense focus on the specificity of violence is utterly unlike Orazio.[30] It is the strongest argument, in my opinion, in favour of apportioning a major contribution by Artemisia to the Oslo *Judith*. The same emphasis on vividly dripping blood will reappear in Artemisia's own re-adaptation of this composition in her version of the subject produced some years later in Florence (fig. 52).

Artemisia's emphasis on extreme violence would reach its apogee in the culminating point of her early development and the last major work produced during her initial years in Rome.[31] Any analysis of the first version of the *Judith Slaying Holofernes*, now in Naples (fig. 29), should, nevertheless, begin with a recognition of its significantly compromised technical condition, as well as its having been cut down along the top and on the left side by what appears to have been a substantial amount. On the topic of its dating, moreover, the Naples *Judith* was for many years believed to post-date the Uffizi version. In 1989, however, Garrard published the X-radiographs

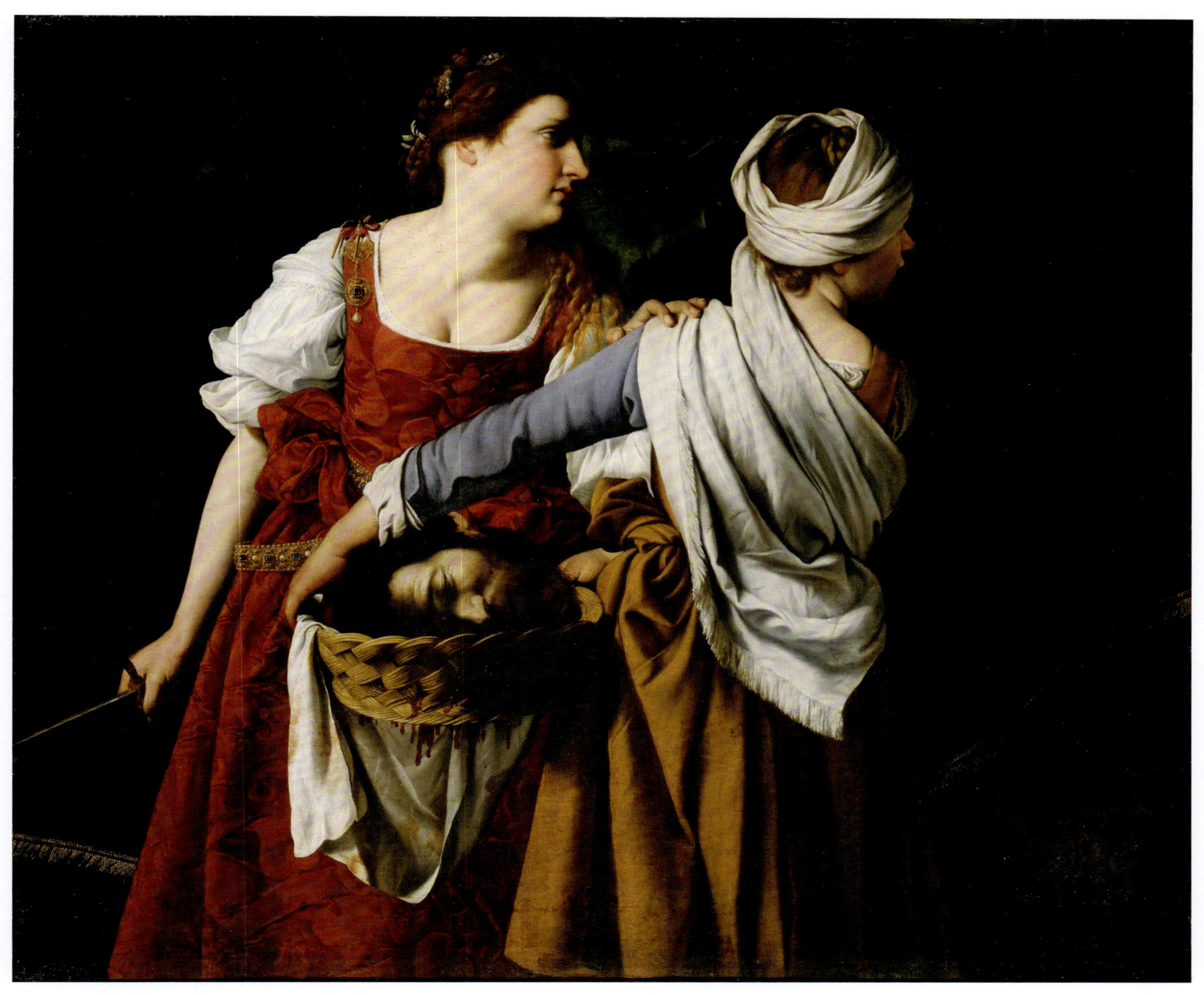

26 Here attributed to Artemisia Gentileschi after Orazio Gentileschi, *Judith and her Maidservant with the Head of Holofernes*, c.1611–12, oil on canvas, 136 × 159 cm, The National Museum of Art, Architecture and Design, Oslo

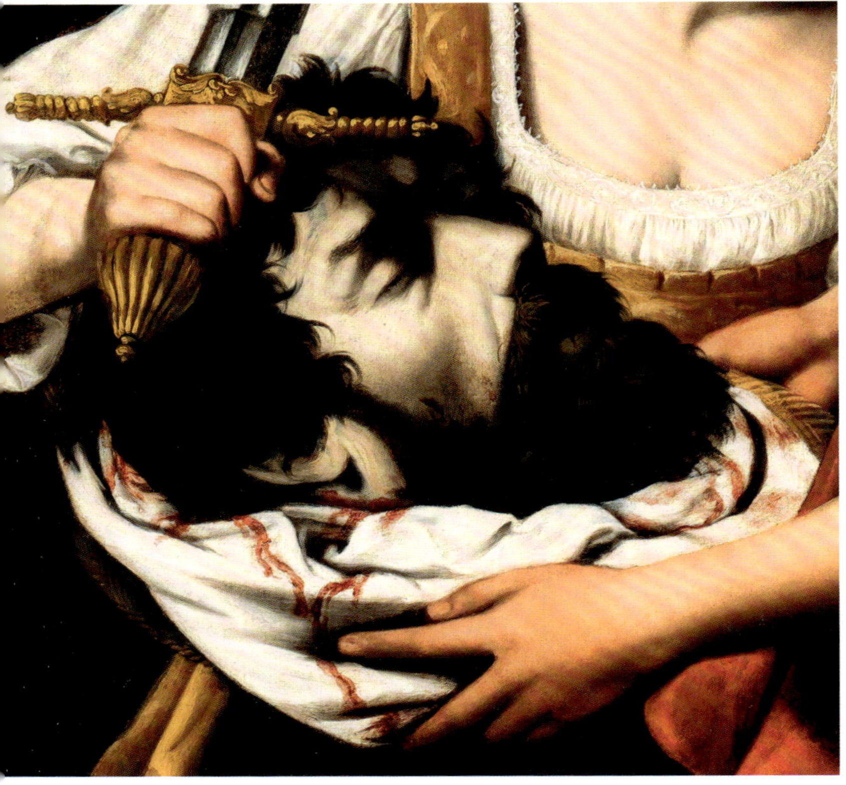

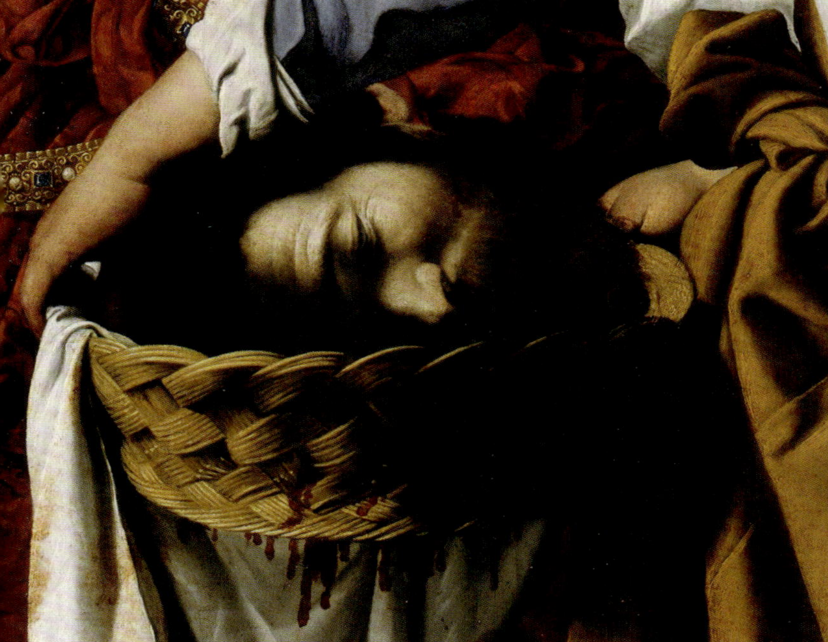

establishing the pentimenti evident in the Naples version and thus its status as the prime canvas on which the Uffizi version was subsequently based.[32] Its dating is now, accordingly, generally agreed upon as around 1612–13, placing it immediately in the aftermath of the rape trial just prior to Artemisia's relocation to Florence.[33]

In terms of the workshop practices here discussed, the Naples *Judith Slaying Holofernes* constitutes another example of a virtuoso composition of great novelty on a par with the 1610 *Susanna and the Elders*. Its conception should, therefore, be read as being based on a similar strategic motivation as that previously outlined for the *Susanna*. Both paintings seek to stand out as tour de force statements of Artemisia's growing confidence as an independent painter of powerful and dramatic narrative figure paintings on a monumental scale that could withstand comparison with any composition produced by her counterparts, be they male or female. The Naples *Judith*, nonetheless, represents a yet more audacious statement along these lines. It achieves this by exchanging the *Susanna's* emphasis on sex with a dramatically heightened focus on the projective power of violence. In so doing, it develops a new specialisation on Artemisia's part involving a shockingly direct concentration on the realistic rendition of extreme brutality that shows her beginning to step out from under the shadow of her father's influence.

The change in direction represented by the Naples *Judith* begins from the reference point of Caravaggio's *Judith Slaying Holofernes* painted in about 1600 for Ottavio Costa, a Genoese banker resident in Rome (fig. 30).[34] Artemisia's *Judith* takes many elements from this source including the right-to-left composition, the claustrophobically reduced background, the stiff-armed pose of Judith, and so on. And yet, Gentileschi has simultaneously transformed these borrowings to an extent that constitutes a radical revision of her source.

Caravaggio's *Judith* maintains an expressively extreme, practically caricatural emphasis that grows out of a Leonardesque/Lombard tradition of graphic physiognomic expressiveness.[35] It is evident in Caravaggio's painting in the almost grotesquely distorted grimace and exaggerated ugliness of the old crone holding the sack. It is also present in the theatricality of

27 (TOP) Orazio Gentileschi, *Judith and her Maidservant with the Head of Holofernes* (detail of fig. 25)

28 Here attributed to Artemisia Gentileschi after Orazio Gentileschi, *Judith and her Maidservant with the Head of Holofernes* (detail of fig. 26)

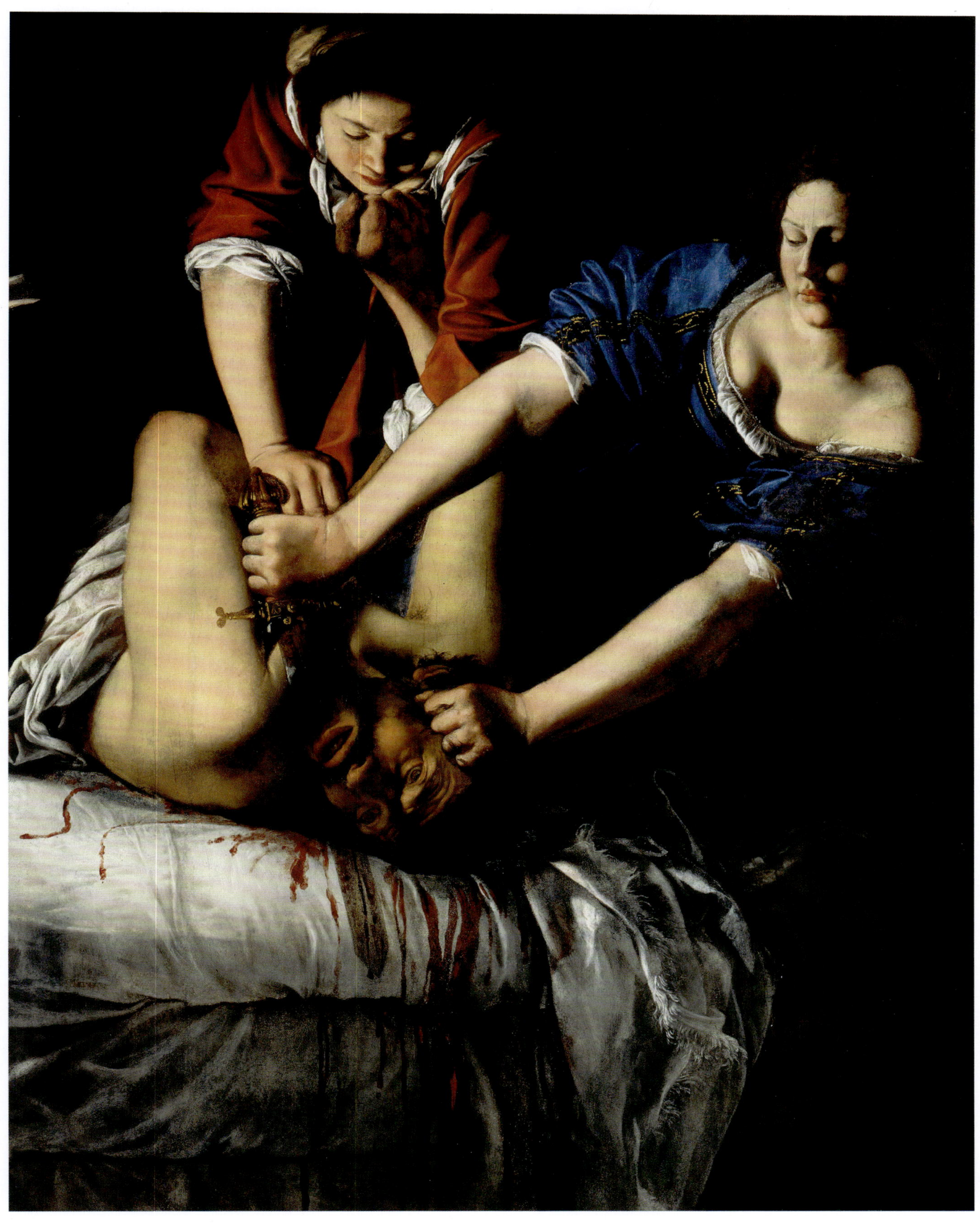

29 Artemisia Gentileschi, *Judith Slaying Holofernes*, *c.*1612–13, oil on canvas, 158.8 × 125.5 cm, Museo e Real Bosco di Capodimonte, Naples

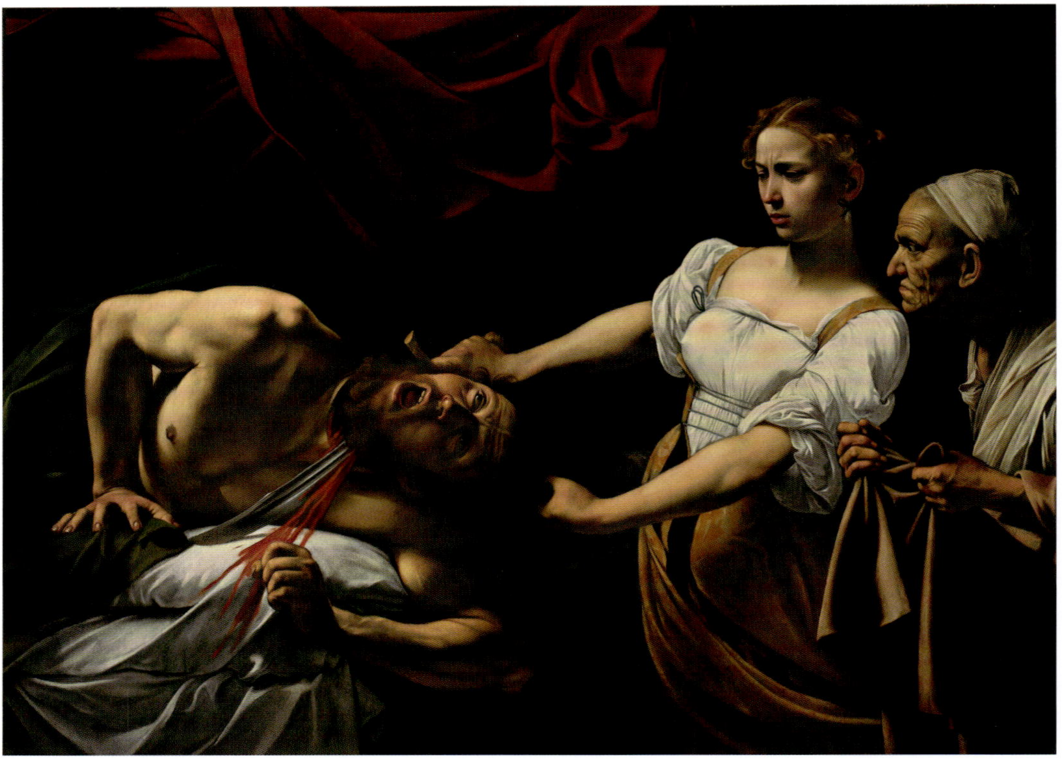

30 Michelangelo Merisi da Caravaggio, *Judith and Holofernes*, c.1600, oil on canvas, 145 × 195 cm, Galleria Nazionale d'Arte Antica di Palazzo Barberini, Rome, inv. 2533

Holofernes' screaming mouth as he wakes from his drunken slumber to discover that his worst dreams have come true. In Gentileschi's rendition, on the other hand, the female protagonists dispatch the general with a determined discipline that eschews any sense of the exaggerated drama of Caravaggio's source. The mugging for the camera present in Caravaggio's prototype has been systematically removed. Gentileschi's Judith maintains, instead, an implacable resolve that is mediated only by the merest hint of an inwardly focused smile as she recognises with grim satisfaction that her plan to kill Holofernes is going to succeed. Likewise, Caravaggio's elderly crone/procuress has been replaced in Gentileschi's composition with a youthful servant who joins forces with Judith in order to respond directly to the drama. No longer a mere bystander, Abra has been recast as an active co-conspirator to the deed. She bears down on Holofernes from above, deflecting the final spasm of his last impotent fist pump while pinning him to the bed to clear a path for Judith's righteous blade.

Gentileschi has chosen to downplay sex in this painting in favour of a rendition of extreme violence. This is understandable, given the scandal and unwelcome profile created by the recently concluded trial. As further comparison with her source makes clear, this violence is articulated with an intensity of physical brutality that has been counterbalanced with a precise, almost clinically detached study of the mechanics of killing. The blood that gushes from Holofernes' half-severed neck, for example, looks about as plausible in Caravaggio's version as a hastily assembled prop for a primary-school play. As Judith Mann has noted, 'Artemisia's painting, by contrast, is a visualisation of how such a grisly deed could actually be accomplished.'[36] Francesca Whitlum-Cooper has similarly highlighted the contrast between the two compositions, remarking, 'What Artemisia brings to her composition is a sense of the reality of such an act: of exactly the kind of brute force that would be required for two women to overpower a man of Holofernes' size.'[37] This results in a minutely observed rendition that has been modelled in full awareness of the many ways in which blood can actually fall, run, spurt, drip and otherwise disrupt the order of everyday life. The treatment of blood in this painting manifests a startling diversity, from the mottled smears on the sheet covering Holofernes' body to the erratically twisting dribbles at the left of his shoulder, and from thence onwards to the smudged blotches beneath his neck and the coagulating clots at the lower reaches of the bed.

This, however, constitutes no more than a prelude for the yet more radical manner in which Artemisia has transformed Caravaggio's depiction of the act of decapitation itself. In Caravaggio's painting, Judith's pose, though rhetorically effective and aesthetically elegant, is scarcely credible on a physical and practical level. Caravaggio's Judith pushes down with her right arm fully extended. This will leave her with no power to slice through Holofernes neck. Gentileschi, by contrast, has conceived a cutting action that has been carefully thought through to the extent of its being physically modelled, one can imagine, as part of a readily achievable sequence of body movements. In so doing, she effectively corrects the weaknesses of Caravaggio's original pose. Her Judith's cutting technique incorporates an efficient, scissor-like motion that functions on the principle of the increased force that one can attain by pushing and pulling on an object from two opposing directions simultaneously. Thus, with her left arm, Judith pushes diagonally down on the general's head from right to left, while her right arm slices in an opposing direction from left to right. This creates a highly effective reverse-action cut that is depicted in the very middle of its path through the general's neck. Trapped in the midst of this carnage, Gentileschi's Holofernes utters no stage-like cry of horror as does Caravaggio's: he remains transfixed, in a state of drugged somnambulance. Caught midway between the animated wakefulness of life and the eternal sleep of death, he gazes beseechingly into space with one still just animate eye. Yet his brain is shutting down, and his other eye is clouding over with the milky-white pallor of death. So it is that Gentileschi has managed to surpass all other treatments – including even the master's – and thus to create in this canvas a perpetually vivid rendition of the stark reality of violent death that continues to shock and enthral viewers to this day.

CONCLUSION: RAGGED ENDINGS, FRESH BEGINNINGS

With the *Judith Slaying Holofernes* just completed and the trial reaching its resolution, there was little that remained for Artemisia in Rome. On 29 November 1612, two days after the trial's conclusion, a wedding ceremony was held to consecrate Gentileschi's marriage vows with Pierantonio Stiattesi.[38] She and her husband would depart for Florence by the end of the year and would be documented in their new home by 11 January 1613.[39]

The judges found Tassi guilty and banished him to exile. Yet it was a hollow victory, since the condemned artist was as well-connected as he was unrepentant. He seems never to have served his sentence, and, with the support of powerful patrons working behind the scenes, he was soon busy on a host of new commissions. Tassi first presided over a series of frescoes at the fabled Villa Lante at Bagnaia. These were produced for Cardinal Alessandro Peretti-Damasceni, also known as Cardinal Montalto (1571–1623), the great-nephew of Pope Sixtus V and one of the leading patrons of early seventeenth-century Rome. Then, in 1616, Tassi was back at the Quirinal in charge of a large team entrusted with yet further prestigious and extensive fresco commissions for Pope Paul V.[40]

Tassi's professional star was very much on the rise. His specialisation in architectural perspective painting, or *quadratura*, was considered very novel and thus attractive to a wide range of patrons. He managed to make this specialisation yet more fashionable by combining it with influences and entrepreneurial collaborations that reflected the latest developments in landscape and view painting, another emerging area of specialisation previously monopolised by northern European painters.[41] Tassi had thus managed to hit upon a winning formula just as it was growing in popularity among patrons and collectors, and he would go on to enjoy a prosperous and highly productive career. In fact, Tassi's career trajectory was not so different from that of the other great model of productive criminality: Caravaggio himself. As is well known, Caravaggio was a career miscreant. And yet he enjoyed the backing of powerful patrons, who were all quick to extricate him from his frequent misadventures in a manner that kept him at liberty to produce, right until his death. In this way the patrons and collectors of the Roman Baroque showed themselves to be much more interested in enjoying the immediate benefits of all that their money and power could acquire than overly concerned with the messy details arising from the legal complications and ethical issues created by the artists in their employ.[42]

This rendered Orazio all too expendable. In terms of his collaboration with Tassi, it meant that there were any number of other figure painters who could take his place. So it was that Orazio wrote his letter of recommendation to the Dowager Grand Duchess of Tuscany, Christine de Lorraine, and helped arrange the newly married couple's impending departure for Florence. Archival findings have suggested that he may have been planning to relocate with Artemisia and her husband to Florence.[43] This may have been a factor in determining the unusually generous dowry of 1,000 ducats that he gave to Artemisia, although it seems that at least part of this dowry came in the form of family assets – such as rental property – that originated from the Lomi inheritance in Pisa (Orazio's father was the struggling goldsmith Giovanni Battista Lomi and had hailed from Pisa, the base of operations for a number of subsequent family members, including Orazio's older brother, Aurelio Lomi, who was also a painter and who would support Artemisia following her relocation to Florence). These plans, however, came to nothing, and Orazio seems, instead, to have increasingly sought work opportunities outside Rome. In particular, he seems to have concentrated on an extensive series of altarpieces and frescoes that he painted for a range of ecclesiastical locations in far-off Fabriano, in the Marches. These called him away from Rome for progressively extended periods from the end of 1613 onwards.[44] From 1621 to 1624, he quit Rome altogether in favour of Genoa, followed by a brief stint in Paris, before ultimately travelling all the way to London, where he would spend his last years painting at the court of Charles I until his death in 1639.

In 1615–16, Marcantonio Bassetti, a young painter from Verona, visited the workshops of Rome where two paintings in Orazio's workshop caught his eye. He copied them down as pen-and-ink sketches to remind himself of their innovative compositions. One was Orazio Gentileschi's recently completed *Conversion of the Magdalene*, now in Munich, and the other was the Naples version of Artemisia's *Judith Slaying Holofernes*. To Christiansen and Bissell, these drawings indicate the continued presence of Artemisia's *Judith* in Orazio's workshop following her departure for Florence (although Patrizia Cavazzini has suggested an alternative reading of the evidence).[45] Christiansen notes that Bassetti may not have been aware of Artemisia's authorship of the *Judith*, or, even if he had been informed of it, might not have cared to register the distinction. Artemisia's painting had reverted, in the absence of the artist herself, to the status of being part of the stock of Orazio's workshop. It was thus now consigned as merchandise to be sold by the master for whatever price he could achieve.

In relocating to Florence, Artemisia had to start again from scratch. Still a teenager, she had to set up house for the first time with her new husband, while at the same time cobbling together the wherewithal to maintain a workshop of her own. Although not in possession of any of her previously produced paintings, she, at least, still had access to their compositions via a series of tracings that she would have created prior to leaving. These had probably been made on semi-transparent sheets of paper, known as *lucidi*, such as are documented in the workshop of Mao Salini, one of Caravaggio's earliest followers.[46] These would become her stock-in-trade: a visual repertory that she would use in conjunction with whatever else she might have received from her father – possibly some prints and drawings – as resources to help launch her career in a new city.

In looking back over the previous years, there must have been much that Artemisia Gentileschi would rather have forgotten. This is evident, as we have seen, in the wish-fulfilling biography that she helped to construct once she had settled in Florence. At the same time, she could not deny that she had received an intensive induction into the Roman Baroque workshop system. Here she had been trained in a revolutionary new style and given the capacity to develop a series of specialisations that would stand her in good stead for the rest of her career, from copies and adaptations after the master, to small-scale devotional images, to portraits and on to grand, signature statements of nascent artistic independence.

All of this had occurred, nonetheless, within the framework of an unremitting system that sought to mould her into an image of the master. And her father was a harsh taskmaster. He effectively left her in a state of semi-isolation for days on end under lock and key to work intensively on whatever tasks he assigned her. One gains the impression, in fact, of a kind of 'hot housing' going on during these years. Orazio evidently performed the role of an over-bearing father-cum-foreman-cum-coach, drilling his daughter to produce work at his behest while she remained in a state of semi-servitude, working in conditions that we would recognise today as constituting a form of 'sweat shop'. A certain degree of subsequent resentment on her part and animosity between them both – as alluded to in Bronzini's biography and documented more clearly in Artemisia's letters[47] – seems natural, given the circumstances. However skilled Artemisia might have become as a semi-independent painter working under Orazio's control, one can imagine that she would have experienced significant difficulties in attempting to get herself recognised as anything other than a junior member of the family firm. Perhaps she might have attained a comparable position to that occupied by Marietta Tintoretto in Venice. The early sources mention this dutiful daughter of a much better-known artistic father as having worked faithfully to support the master's legacy, while never seeking to rise beyond it.[48]

Now, however, circumstances dictated an altogether different path for Artemisia. This would involve her in making a definitive break from her father and setting out on her own. In Florence, moreover, she would be given the opportunity to start again, while taking all that she had previously learned and using it as the basis for a new career conducted on her own terms. In Florence, she would soon come to attain, in fact, a notable degree of public recognition. Yet in attempting to make this transition, she would also come to experience hardships that would require her to refocus her energies onto the one thing that she could consistently control – the image of herself as reflected back to her in the mirror. This she would refashion into a durable and yet also highly flexible brand that would become the major emphasis, in turn, of her next stage of independent artistic production.

PAGE 61 Artemisia Gentileschi, *Self-portrait as St Catherine of Alexandria* (detail of fig. 35)

— PART II —

Announcing Artemisia

FLORENCE 1613–1620

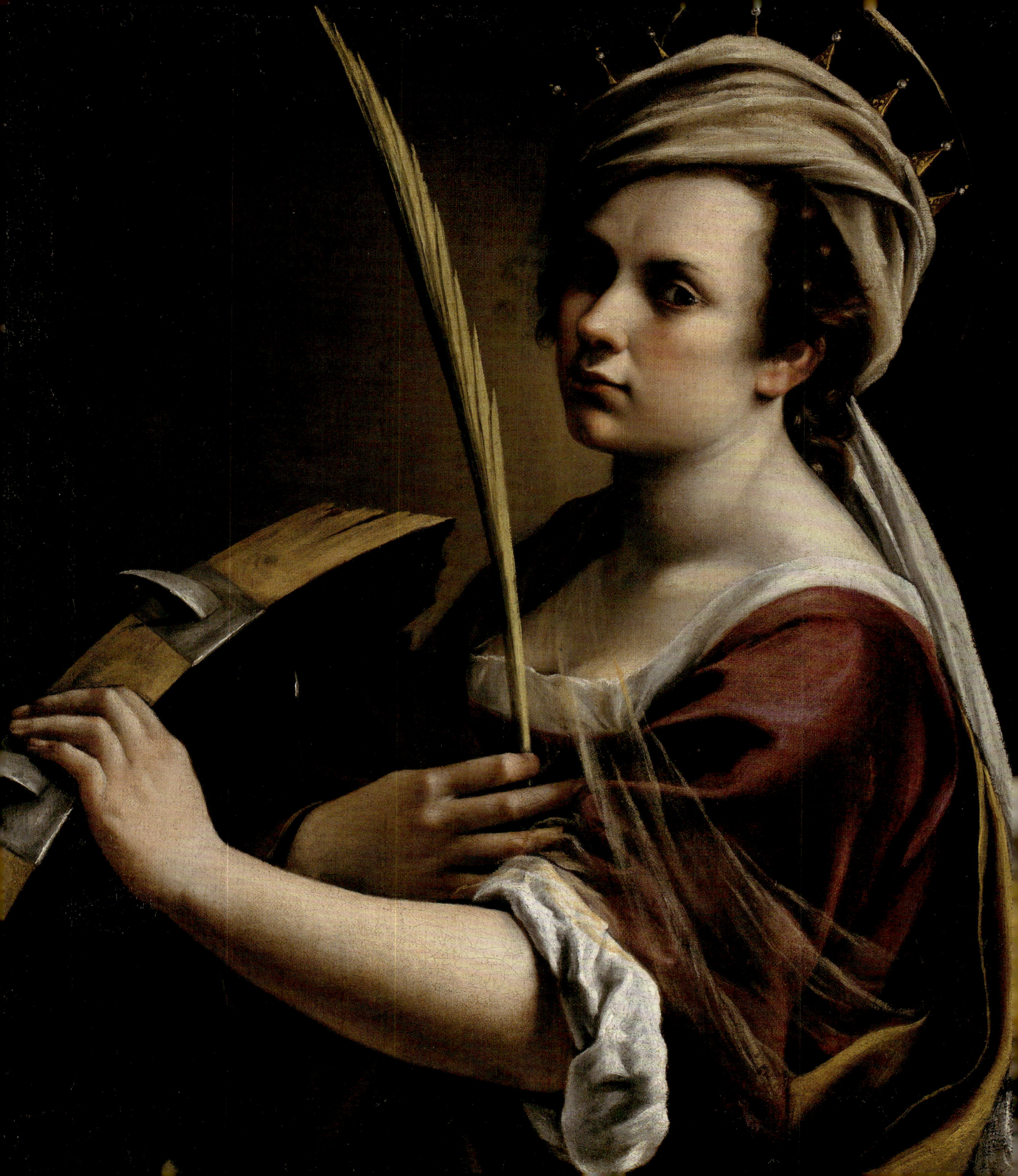

4

Birth, Death, Rebirth

GENTILESCHI LAUNCHES HERSELF AS AN INDEPENDENT PAINTER IN BAROQUE FLORENCE

INTRODUCTION
TRIUMPH AND TRAVAIL ON THE BANKS OF THE ARNO

Florence proved to be the making of Gentileschi, while also almost the source of her undoing. When she traded the banks of the Tiber for those of the Arno, in January 1613, she was still, despite all the hard-earned lessons of her previous years, very much an ingénue, professionally speaking. But, by the time of her return to Rome seven years later, there could be no doubting her transformation into a fully formed and even acclaimed independent master. Gentileschi accomplished many things in Florence that she could not have achieved in Rome. She upgraded her literacy and educational competencies to levels that would allow her to interact successfully with a wide range of patrons, academicians, collectors and other highly ranked individuals.[1] She broadened her understanding of other artistic traditions through reference to the extremely rich Florentine collections, as well as through her relations with other artists and collectors. And she developed effective networking skills to help sway those who might advance her interests in the years to come.

Gentileschi's perspicacity during this period has been highlighted above, in Chapter 1, in reference to the 1615–16 *Allegory of Inclination* commission for Michelangelo

FACING PAGE Artemisia Gentileschi, *Self-portrait as St Catherine of Alexandria* (detail of fig. 39)

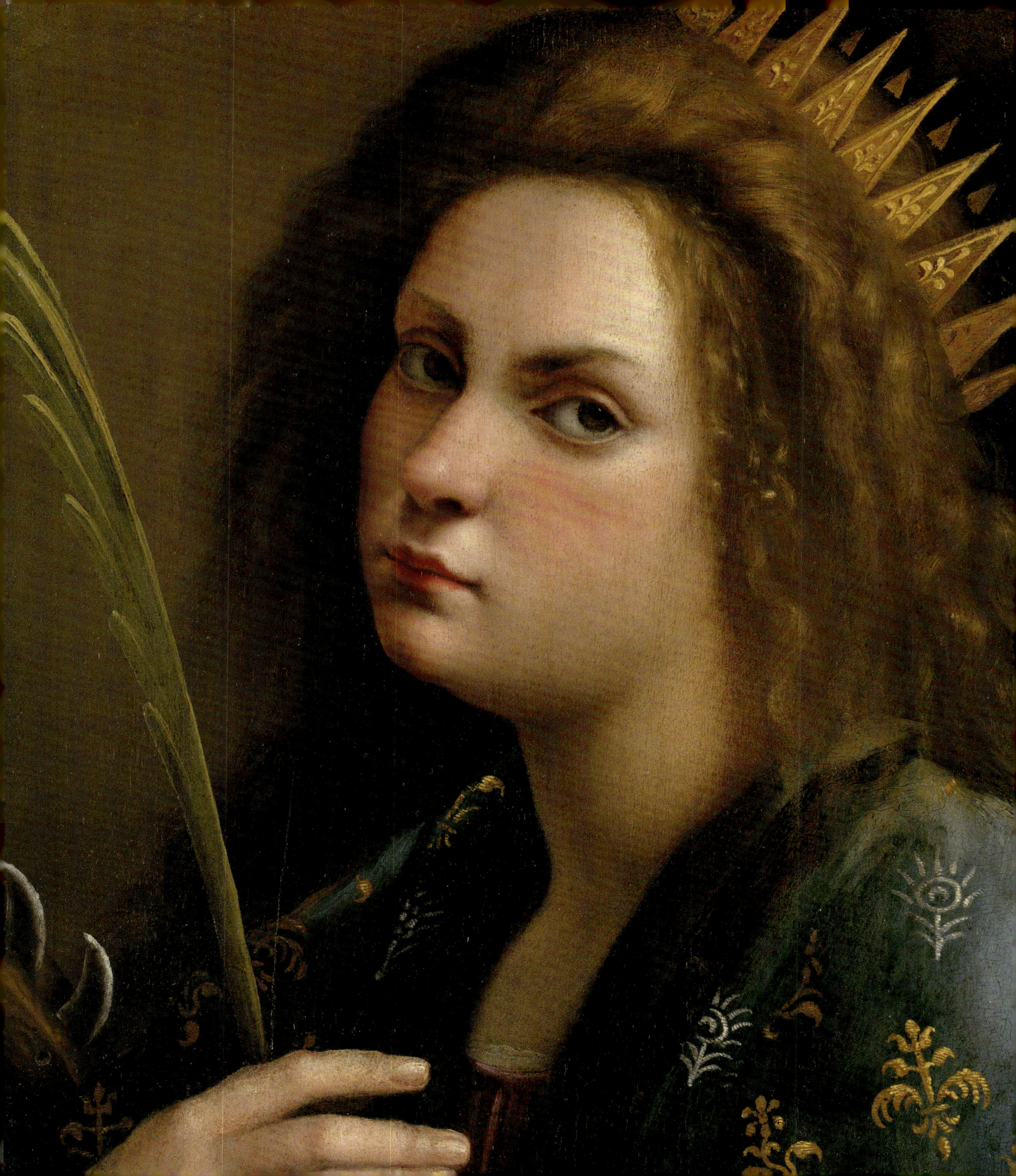

Buonarroti the Younger. Here, within the space of two years of her arrival, she was able to insert herself into one of the city's most innovative artistic projects – and likewise into one of its most influential networks of artists, connoisseurs and literati (including Galileo, who would go on to become one of her principal supporters in Tuscany).[2] By October 1614, she was already working on her first major Medici commission for no fewer than three large paintings for Cosimo II.[3] By March of the following year, she was being referred to as a well-known artist by Cosimo's Secretary of State, Andrea Cioli, who would also become one of her longest-standing supporters.[4] Her absence from records of the Medici payroll suggests that Orazio's letter to Christine de Lorraine of 3 July 1612 had failed in its immediate objective of having her taken under the Medici's wing.[5] Perhaps this lack of officially recognised Medici support – which would have entailed her receiving a monthly salary of between twelve and eighteen scudi in return for a commitment on her part to work more or less exclusively for her patrons – can be seen to have worked ultimately in her favour. It afforded her the freedom to develop her own artistic identity and to pursue independent work in a manner that would have been rendered more difficult, no doubt, had she been retained by the Medici in a more formal manner.[6] Nevertheless, and as the documents and the comment by Cioli indicate, she had no difficulty bringing herself favourably to the Medici's attention and would go on to produce more than half a dozen works for various family members as well as to contribute to the life of the court more generally. Moreover, she received a professional accolade comparable with that achieved by her Roman role model, Lavinia Fontana: on 19 July 1616, she became one of the first women artists to be formally matriculated into the Accademia del Disegno in Florence (although, perhaps characteristically, she seems never to have paid her membership fees).[7]

The Florentine years, however, took their toll on a more personal level. Gentileschi gave birth to five children in the space of five years, between September 1613 and October 1618. Only two survived their early years to be present at the time of her relocation to Rome, with another son dying soon after the family's transfer to Rome.[8] Financial difficulties also plagued the household in a manner that would come to characterise her career. A series of increasingly debilitating debts were run up during these years not just by Gentileschi, but also by her husband, of whose activities as both a painter and apothecary – his stated professions – there is no evidence in the documentation relating to her life and career at this stage.[9] Mounting debts seem to have been a major contributor to the family's semi-peripatetic lifestyle. This was not so dissimilar, in fact, from what she had experienced growing up in Rome. As her father had done earlier, so too now did Artemisia's household move to four different parishes during their stay in the city.[10] An impassioned affair with a scion of one of the city's leading families would also complicate Gentileschi's personal situation, creating a *ménage à trois* that, while socially advantageous to her on one level, was also a source of danger and potential reputational disaster as a result of the intricately interconnected politics of the Medicean court in Florence.[11]

CARAVAGGISM IN FLORENCE AND THE CITY'S EARLY HOLDINGS OF CARAVAGGIO'S PAINTINGS

Gianni Papi has characterised Gentileschi's arrival in the Tuscan capital as the single most important episode in the history of the transmission of the Caravaggesque style into Florence.[12] As voracious collectors of all forms of contemporary painting, both Cosimo II and his successor, Ferdinando II, were naturally keen to secure key examples of the latest trends in Caravaggesque art, acquiring works by Bartolomeo Manfredi, Gerrit van Honthorst, Bartolomeo Cavarozzi and others.[13] Yet Artemisia was the first and most significant early Caravaggesque painter to relocate to the city for any length of time (although she would soon be followed by two other Caravaggesque specialists: the Neapolitan, Giovanni Battista Caracciolo, in 1618, and the Fleming resident in Rome, Theodor Rombouts, from around 1621 to 1624).[14]

Florence gave back to Gentileschi all that she was able to offer. One should not underestimate, in this respect, the high levels of cultural attainment and awareness of current artistic developments that characterised the extremely well-informed Florentine art world at this time. In terms of Caravaggio, for example, this meant that, by the beginning of the seventeenth century, the Medici already owned two outstanding examples

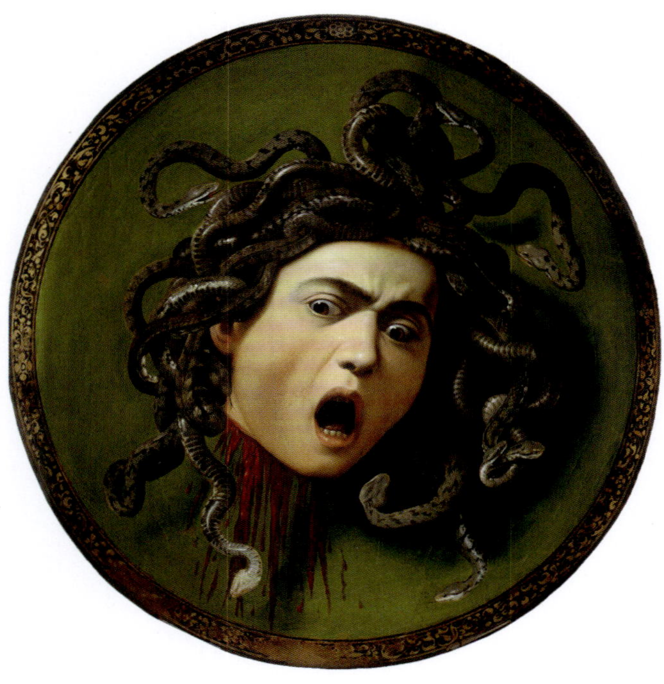

31 Michelangelo Merisi da Caravaggio, *Head of the Medusa*, c.1597, oil on canvas applied onto a poplar wooden shield, 60 × 55 cm, Galleria degli Uffizi, Florence

from the artist's early Roman years. These were Caravaggio's enigmatic *Bacchus*, together with the tour-de-force demonstration of his most theatrically violent manner, the *Head of the Medusa* (fig. 31).[15] Both had been produced around 1597–98, during Caravaggio's stay with the Florentine Ambassador to Rome, Cardinal Francesco Maria del Monte (1549–1627), who subsequently forwarded them to Florence as diplomatic gifts to the Medici.

The *Head of the Medusa* would have been relatively accessible to Gentileschi during her Florentine residency, although it was not, strictly speaking, displayed as a work of art – rather, it was installed in the Uffizi's armoury.[16] There, it formed the centrepiece of a strikingly theatrical, three-dimensional tableau dominated by two figures on horseback. A mannequin presented as a mounted knight dressed for the joust was placed symbolically opposite another mannequin, dressed as a fully armed Turk, likewise seated on horseback. Representing the arch-nemesis of the Christian faith, this latter figure held a scimitar in one hand and Caravaggio's *Head of the Medusa*, applied to a wooden shield, in the other. It was a fittingly bizarre display, attesting to the artwork's wondrously fantastic appearance as well as to its power to inspire both horror and delight in the mind of the viewer. Caravaggio's *Bacchus*, on the other hand, is documented from 1609 in the Medicean Villa 'La Ferdinanda', in the village of Artimino in the Tuscan hills west of Florence. This was the same location as that chosen by the Medici for the original display of many of Artemisia's Florentine works, including her *Conversion of the Magdalene*, *St Catherine of Alexandria* and her *Self-portrait as a Lute Player* which, as discussed below, are all documented at being at 'La Ferdinanda' from 1615 onwards.

Caravaggio's style had undergone a radical evolution since his youthful days with Del Monte. By the time of his late canvases, produced on the run in Malta and southern Italy prior to his death in 1610, he had jettisoned the detailed realism of the early Roman works in favour of an increasingly schematic approach that better suited his peripatetic lifestyle. Such was the Florentine awareness of current artistic developments that at least two of these late paintings had also made their way to the Tuscan capital by the time of Gentileschi's arrival. Caravaggio's *Portrait of a Knight of Malta* of 1608–9 had probably been installed in the Palazzo Martelli from as early as 1609.[17] The *Sleeping Cupid* was likewise dispatched from Malta to the Palazzo Antella in Piazza Santa Croce in the same year. Here Michelangelo Buonarroti the Younger was able to admire it along with other Florentine art lovers of the day.[18]

Had she had the chance to study these last two works, Gentileschi would have had much to ponder in terms of how an artist's late style can evolve into something rich and strange in relation to their earlier output, an issue that would subsequently prove relevant to her own oeuvre. In the meantime, though, the *Head of the Medusa* and possibly also the, admittedly less accessible, *Bacchus* must have seemed extremely suggestive in terms of the artistic ideas that she was just then developing into fundamental themes of her Florentine period. In particular, they convey vividly the essential novelty of Caravaggio's early approach as explained in Baglione's now famous observation that, soon after his arrival in Rome, Caravaggio 'painted some portraits of himself in the mirror. The first was a Bacchus with different bunches of grapes, painted with great care though a bit dry in style. He also painted a boy bitten by a lizard emerging from flowers and fruits; you could almost hear the boy scream, and it was all done meticulously.'[19] Baglione's words vividly convey the striking impression created by these early views through the looking glass. These two paintings would have reinforced for Artemisia the power of the mirror as a means of projecting herself into her compositions in a manner that lent them a new dramatic forcefulness of portrait-like realism.

CRISTOFANO ALLORI AND THE DISGUISED SELF-PORTRAIT

Gentileschi was not alone in making such connections during these years. Many painters travelling between Rome and Florence were likewise hard at work unlocking the secrets of Caravaggio's revolutionary approach.[20] Foremost among these was Cristofano Allori (1577–1621), whom Gentileschi seems to have met as a result of her association with the circle of artists and intellectuals gravitating around the patronage of Michelangelo Buonarroti the Younger. Gentileschi was able to form a particularly close relationship with Allori during this period, with the latter serving as godfather to her son, Cristofano, born on 9 November 1615.[21] This friendship would have been advantageous to her, given Allori's prominence within the cultural life of the city as an artist, poet, musician and well-connected bon vivant. Gentileschi's ability to forge positive connections with a senior artist who could help introduce her to local patrons and other useful contacts while facilitating her integration within the local artistic scene would be subsequently repeated in her close relationship with Massimo Stanzione (1585–1656) during the early years of her Neapolitan residency during the 1630s.[22]

Besides Caravaggio's *Bacchus* and *Medusa*, Cristofano Allori's *Judith with the Head of Holofernes* is also to be ranked as a fundamental challenge to and point of reference for Gentileschi's art in her Florentine years. Begun in 1610, the composition is known through multiple versions, the earliest for the Gonzaga being dated 1613 and the last produced for the Medici in 1620 and today in the Uffizi (fig. 32).[23] Artemisia probably came to

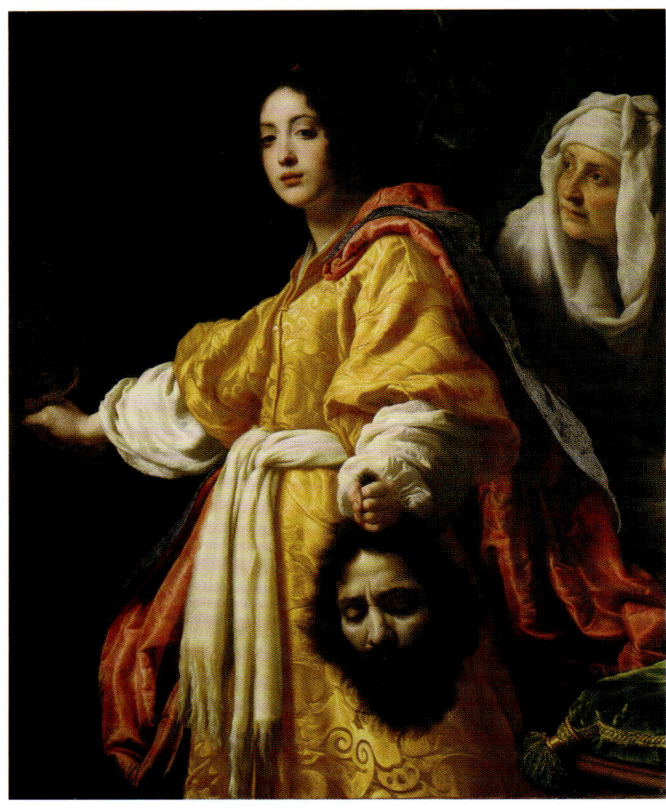

32 Cristofano Allori, *Judith with the Head of Holofernes*, 1620, oil on canvas, 139 × 116 cm, Galleria Palatina, Palazzo Pitti, Florence

know the work through a version produced for a Roman patron but kept at the Casa Buonarroti for most of 1615–16, while Allori agonised over its completion. An overnight success, the composition was serially copied and became one of the most widely admired artworks of its day. Filippo Baldinucci noted that 'all the artists judged it to be of unequalled quality', while Giambattista Marino professed his devotion to it in 1620 on the basis of mediocre copies then circulating in Paris.[24] The painting's obvious relevance to Artemisia's abiding interest in the subject of Judith would have marked it out as being of intense significance for her, as Keith Christiansen has also observed.[25] Its fame, moreover, must have acted as a powerful source of inspiration, as well as a goad to her own aspirations.

The novelty of Allori's *Judith* lay in its transposition of Caravaggesque realism into a vivid grouping of portrait-like characterisations that connect the subject's religious narrative with the artist's personal preoccupations. The painting depicts 'Mazzafirra', Allori's then lover and a celebrated Florentine courtesan. She is depicted in the role of Judith, holding in her left hand the severed head of Holofernes, which is, in fact, a portrait of the artist. The maidservant at the right bears the features of Mazzafirra's mother. Besides Caravaggio's version of the subject painted in Rome (Gentileschi's reference for her own version, as discussed above), commentators have cited additional precedents for Allori's *Judith* as being Caravaggio's subsequently more anguished self-portrait as the severed head of Goliath in the *David and Goliath* in the Borghese Gallery, as well as Titian's depiction of himself as the severed head of John the Baptist in a canvas owned by the Doria Pamphilj in Rome.[26]

The widespread acclaim accorded to Allori's *Judith with the Head of Holofernes* must have stolen Artemisia's thunder in certain respects. It certainly would have given her pause for thought when considering how to follow up on her earlier, violent interpretation of the subject of Judith that she had produced in Rome. Allori's *Judith*, by contrast, manages to touch on the brutality that resides at the subject's core while at the same time appearing both more elegant and more wittily self-assured than Artemisia's first *Judith*. The luxuriant and frankly beautiful manner in which it dwells on surfaces – above all on the brilliant golden yellow of Judith's dress – begins the process of heralding in a new taste towards a more elegant and refined, 'ennobled' version of the Caravaggesque style that has its roots in the *bella e leggiadra maniera* of Allori's master, Ludovico Cigoli.

CONCLUSION: ARTEMISIA GENTILESCHI AND THE HISTORIATED PORTRAIT

So, Gentileschi went back to the drawing board, or, rather, back to the mirror, since it was fundamentally by means of the mirror that she was able to consolidate on Caravaggio's inspirational method of using vividly observed realism to establish a direct link between viewer and artist. The answer lay in exploiting further the expressive potential of the historiated-portrait approach that constitutes such a defining feature of Caravaggio's *Medusa* and *Bacchus* and Allori's *Judith*.[27] Artemisia's innovative reinterpretation of this highly specialised form of imagery led her to develop a new form of self-referential painting that would redefine the expressive possibilities of Baroque self-portraiture, while offering her an important new avenue for marketing herself directly to her audience as a witty and distinguished creative practitioner.

The self-reflexive dimensions of Caravaggio's paintings and Allori's *Judith* all hinged on notions of violence and new understandings of the artist as a purveyor of bohemian excess. The undeniable novelty of these highly experimental essays in artistic self-awareness resulted in the spectacle of Caravaggio's dissolute Bacchus, together with his yet more bizarre self-transformation into the decapitated head of the Medusa.[28] This was followed by Allori's recasting of the biblical story of Judith into a profane love triangle involving his self-projection as the severed head of Holofernes held aloft by his mistress. Gentileschi was herself no stranger to the use of violence to create a shockingly powerful form of self-promotional imagery. The Naples *Judith Slaying Holofernes* drew on this approach, as we saw. She would employ this methodology also for her Florentine versions of the subject. But a different strategy would be required for her Florentine paintings, which would be based on her own image. Let the men pursue their preoccupations with anguish, torment and violence. For her own self-imagery, by contrast, Gentileschi chose to fashion a new form of portrait-like painting in which she cast herself in the role of an actor performing a dazzling array of roles: St Catherine, the Mary Magdalene, a gypsy minstrel and even a knightly warrior. Thus was born a uniquely distinctive approach to reinterpreting the power of the mirror to act as a gateway to both that which seems real in its portrait-like intensity and that which operates on the level of a theatrical, witty, self-promotional image of the artist as an instantly recognisable, celebrity figure.

5

Selling the Self

SELF-PORTRAITURE AND THE INVENTION OF 'ARTEMISIA'

INTRODUCTION
THE MIRROR AND THE GAZE

The previous chapter highlighted the importance for Gentileschi's Florentine years of an innovative trio of self-referential Baroque paintings that were just then attracting attention among the city's art lovers. It also began to note the markedly different path chosen by Gentileschi to fashion her own brand of self-referential imagery. Violence and torment were a natural fit for male artists seeking eye-catching subjects of this kind. Caravaggio's dramatic tenebrism, moreover, lent itself to such an approach (although it should also be recognised that the tradition of violently moody self-portrayals stretches far beyond the immediate context of Caravaggio and his followers[1]). The issue of gender, on the other hand, significantly complicated Gentileschi's options for proceeding along a comparable avenue of vividly projective, self-expressive imagery.

Early modern women had been taught for centuries to distrust the mirror's seductive return of their gaze.[2] A rich tradition of vanitas imagery had reinforced for them the sinful dangers of pride, vanity and falsehood that were supposedly lying in wait for them were they ever to peer into the looking glass too ardently or for too long. Gentileschi would have been well aware, in this context, of the accompanying visual tradition of vanitas imagery that reinforced these messages in distinctly gendered

FACING PAGE Artemisia Gentileschi, *Conversion of the Magdalene* (detail of fig. 40)

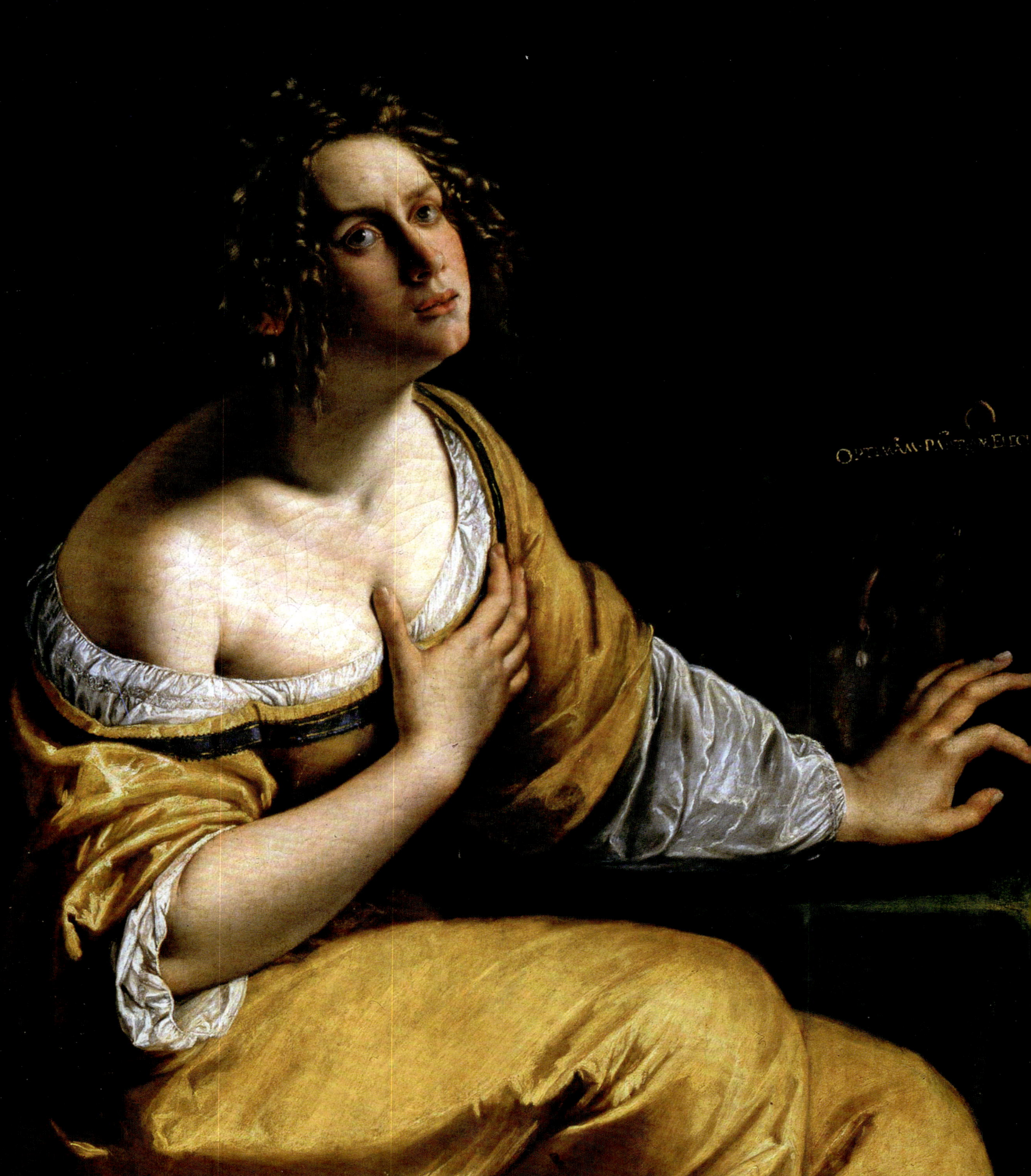

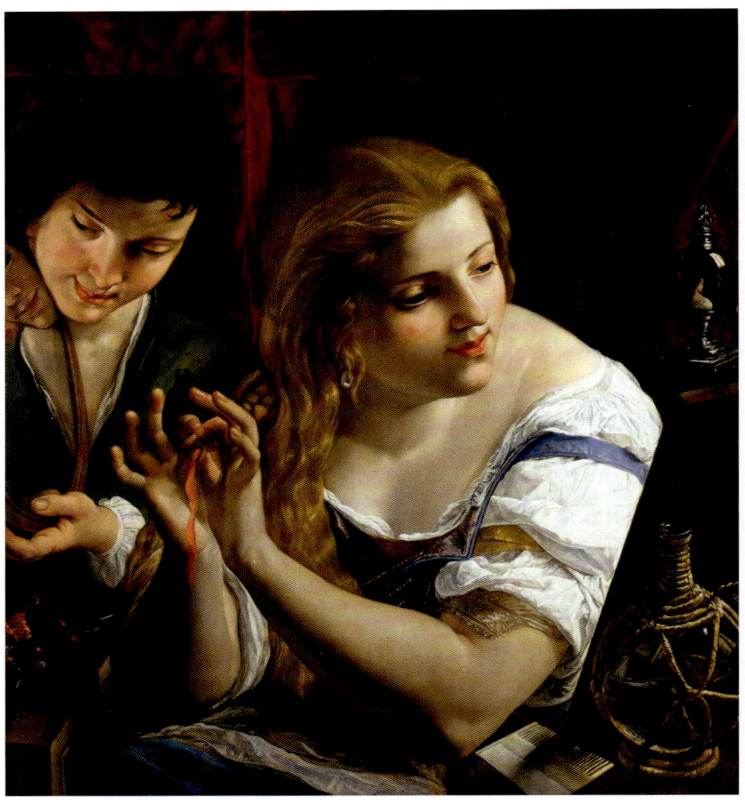

33 Angelo Caroselli, *Vanitas*, *c.*1608–12, oil on wood, 66 × 61 cm, Fondazione di Studi di Storia dell'Arte Roberto Longhi, Florence

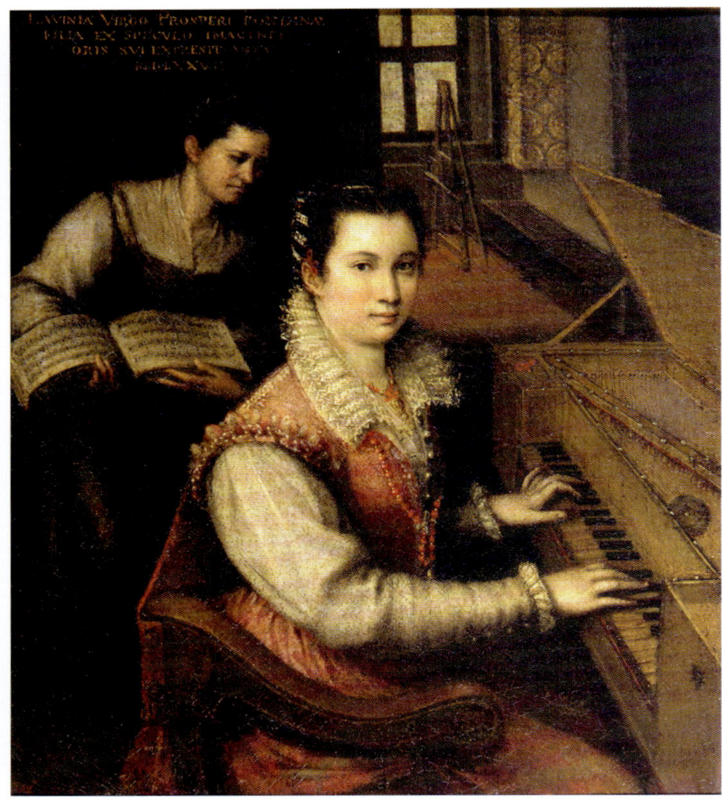

34 Lavinia Fontana, *Self-portrait at the Spinet*, 1577, oil on canvas, 27 × 24 cm, Accademia Nazionale di San Luca, Rome

terms. A contemporary vanitas painting by Angelo Caroselli (1585–1652), for example, seems especially relevant in this context, given this artist's similar position as one of the first-wave Roman Caravaggisti and given, further, the more than passing resemblance of this painting's female protagonist to those found in Gentileschi's canvases (fig. 33).[3]

Sofonisba Anguissola and Lavinia Fontana had already demonstrated their ability to negotiate a successful path through these complex issues. As Joanna Woods-Marsden and Faye Tudor have noted, these artists managed to avoid the potentially negative associations involved in looking into the mirror by stressing their own 'moral goodness' and thus their ability to see beyond the potential falsehood of the mirror's seductive surface.[4] Both artists were accordingly careful in their numerous self-portraits always to counter-balance the potentially negative effects of the mirror focus by depicting themselves surrounded by virtuously appropriate objects and activities. Thus, Anguissola shows herself demurely dressed while playing the spinet or prominently displaying a prayer book. Fontana similarly depicts herself in the guise of a well-educated and devout young woman who is shown either playing the spinet (fig. 34) or surrounded by books and other symbols of learning.[5] In presenting themselves as well-brought-up, pious young ladies of dignity and bearing, these artists were, further, seeking to align their public image with the new understanding of the female *virtuosa* as being not only morally virtuous in terms of their artistic accomplishments but also unassailably pure and unblemished in their own personal demeanour and bearing. Physical beauty, or at least a comely and attractive appearance as defined by the conventional requirements of the male gaze, was a key element of this ideal. This beauty, nonetheless, had to manifest itself as being 'pure' and thus also *graziosa*: gracious, modest and demure rather than threateningly seductive.[6]

GENTILESCHI'S EARLY FLORENTINE DISGUISED SELF-PORTRAITS

Gentileschi's Florentine self-portraits comprise a closely related series of around a half dozen works that develop a strikingly original response to these issues. Three, in particular, share similar formats and dimensions to the extent that they resemble a series of playing cards in different suits. Each of the canvases originally measured around 77 by 70 cm (there are now slight variations in dimensions as a result of their being trimmed or otherwise slightly altered over time). They share also a half-length format and all portray Gentileschi against a dark background and leaning diagonally into the picture plane, so that the left side of her face and body is illuminated while her right remains hidden in the shadows. Two depict her as *St Catherine of Alexandria* and the third captures her assuming the role of a lute player (figs 35–37). Closely related, albeit in a reduced format, is a bust-length painting, formerly with Newhouse Galleries, New York. This frames Gentileschi's face from the neck upwards, while depicting her as a more generic virgin saint, with the palm branch that signifies the triumph of faith over flesh and wearing a garland of roses that reference the purity of the Virgin (fig. 38).[7] Two further variants of this composition exist. These have been relatively inaccessible to scholars in the past and have often been identified as copies rather than as fully accepted autograph works. One, formerly in the Zeri collection, Mentana, depicts Artemisia garlanded with flowers, and so possibly as the Sicilian martyr saint Rosalia of Palermo.[8] The second – formerly in a private collection in Pisa and currently on loan to the National Museum of Art, Architecture and Design, Oslo – is perhaps the most convincing in terms of its possible autograph status (fig. 39).[9]

Scholars have long puzzled over the precise status of these and other paintings from the period that appear to draw on the same facial type and features. Are they to be read as self-portraits? Or should they be seen, instead, as more generalised devotional or subject pictures that utilise Gentileschi's features in a more incidental manner as the basis for the figure depicted in the painting?[10] In 2010, a major breakthrough in the interpretation of this issue was achieved when Nadia Bastogi published a series of inventory references listing the original locations of these works in various Medici properties. A subsequent article by Bastogi in 2021 added important documentation regarding the transfer of four of the paintings to a Medicean villa on the outskirts of Florence in July 1615, together with further references from a 1775 inventory that also identify a number of them as self-portraits.[11] As Gianni Papi correspondingly noted, these early archival references are highly significant in confirming for the first time not only the original location of the works but also the fact that at least four of them were originally regarded as being based on Gentileschi's own features.[12] (The documentation is also significant for the dating of the works and indicates a slightly earlier date than has often been posited for them in the past.[13])

Before analysing these paintings further, it might be useful, therefore, briefly to review this archival information, given that these findings have not been fully disseminated throughout the literature.

On 8 July 1615, four paintings – initially unattributed but cross-referable with the subsequent documentation discussed below – were transferred from Cosimo II's department of the Guardaroba generale to the Villa Ferdinanda at Artimino. They are described as 'a painting on canvas measuring one and a half arms high and one a quarter arms in width [*c.*87 × 72 cm[14]] within which there is painted a St Catherine martyr with a black adornment [on the frame] interlaced with gold', 'a similar painting with a similar adornment within which there is painted a young woman playing a lute somewhat larger', 'a similar painting within which there is painted a Bradamante one and three quarter arms high and one a half arms in width [*c.*101 × 87 cm]' and 'a similar painting within which there is painted a St Mary Magdalene two and three quarters arms high and two and one quarter arms in width [*c.*159 × 130 cms.]'.[15]

From this group we can discern an early reference to the *Self-portrait as a Lute Player* now at the Wadsworth Atheneum, Hartford (fig. 37). This painting was initially described in 1615 as 'a young woman playing a lute' before being referred

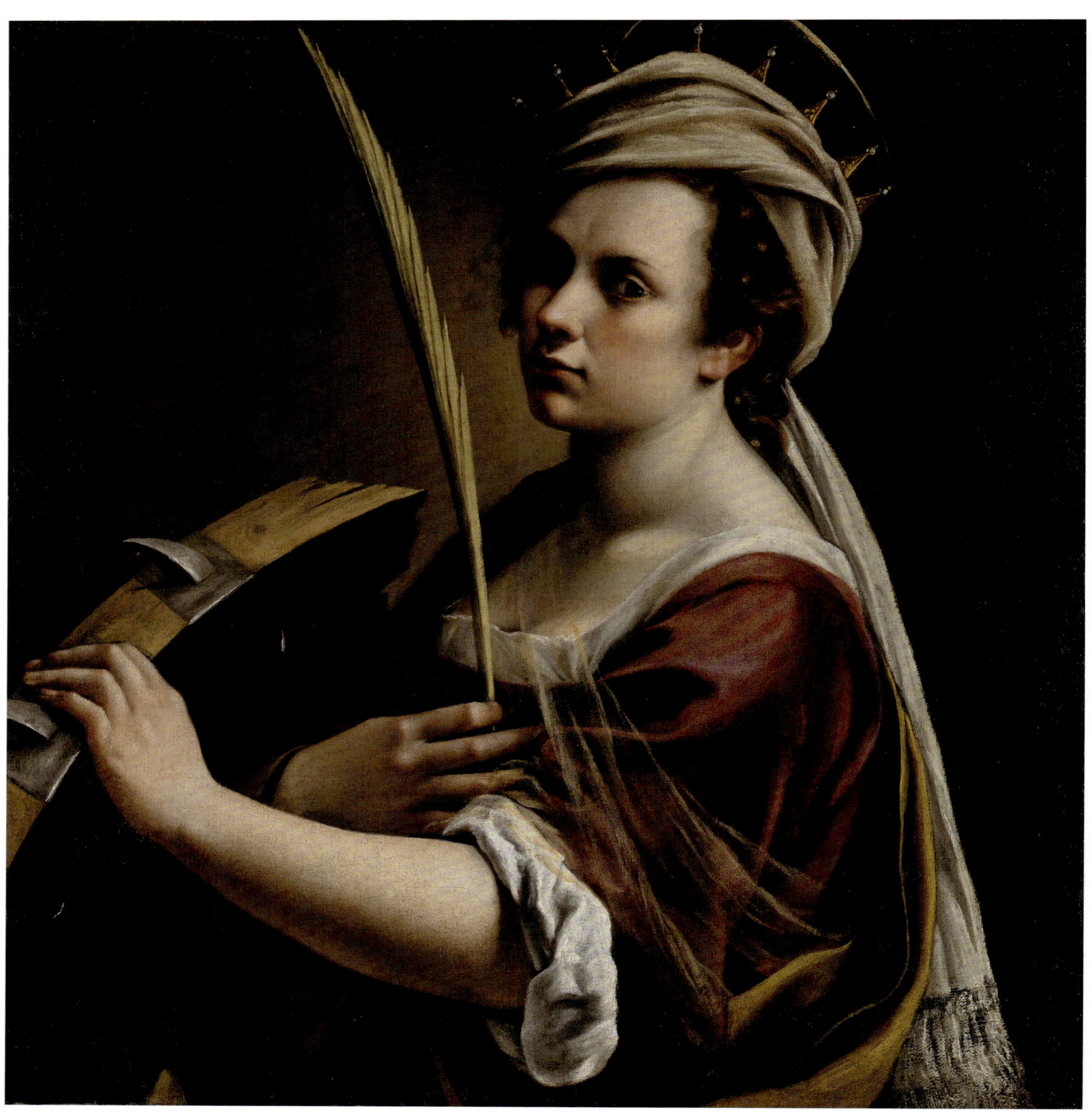

35 Artemisia Gentileschi, *Self-portrait as St Catherine of Alexandria*, c.1615–17, oil on canvas, 71.4 × 69 cm, National Gallery, London, NG6671

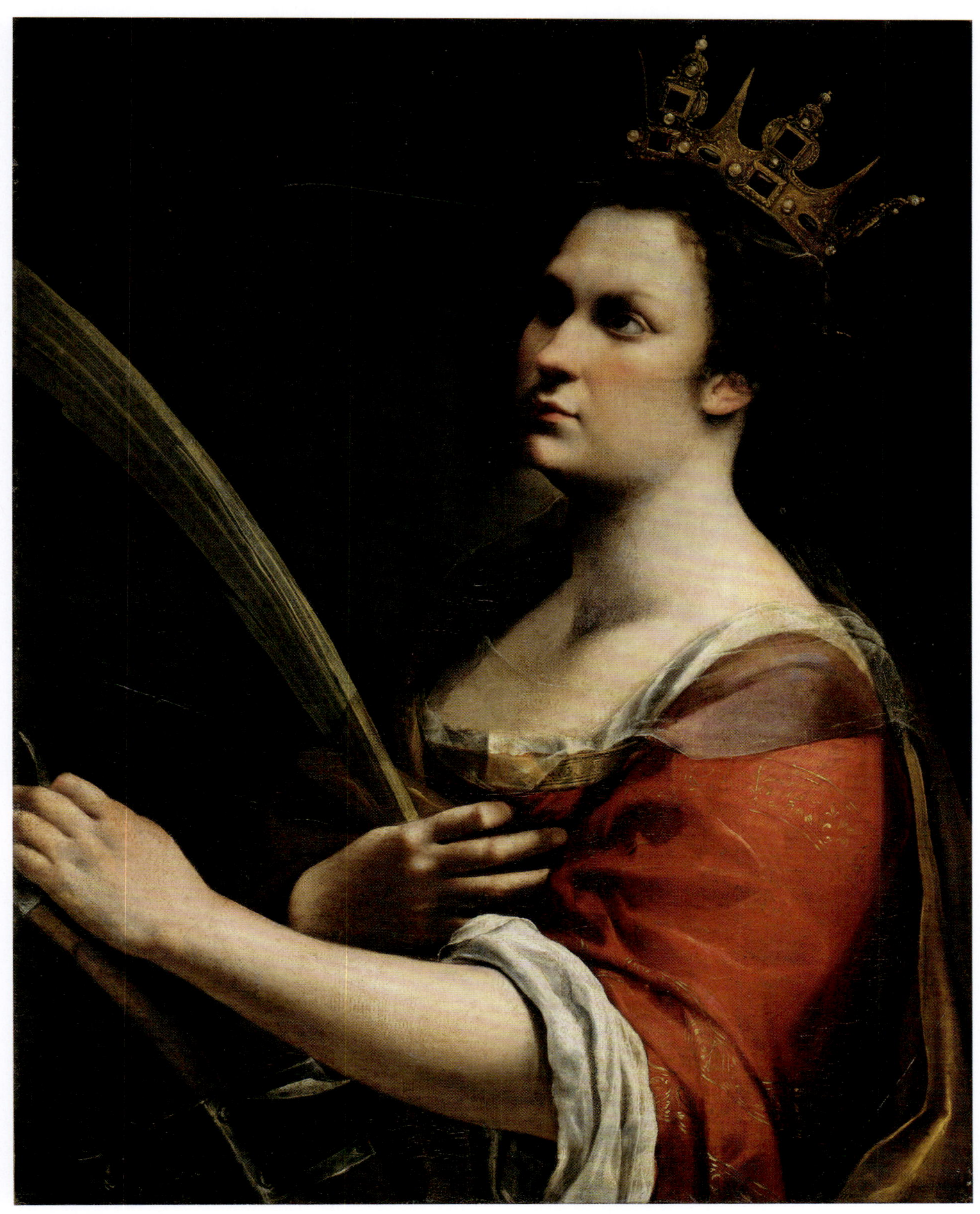

36 Artemisia Gentileschi, *St Catherine of Alexandria*, c.1614–15, oil on canvas, 77 × 62 cm, Galleria degli Uffizi, Florence, inv. 1890 no. 8032

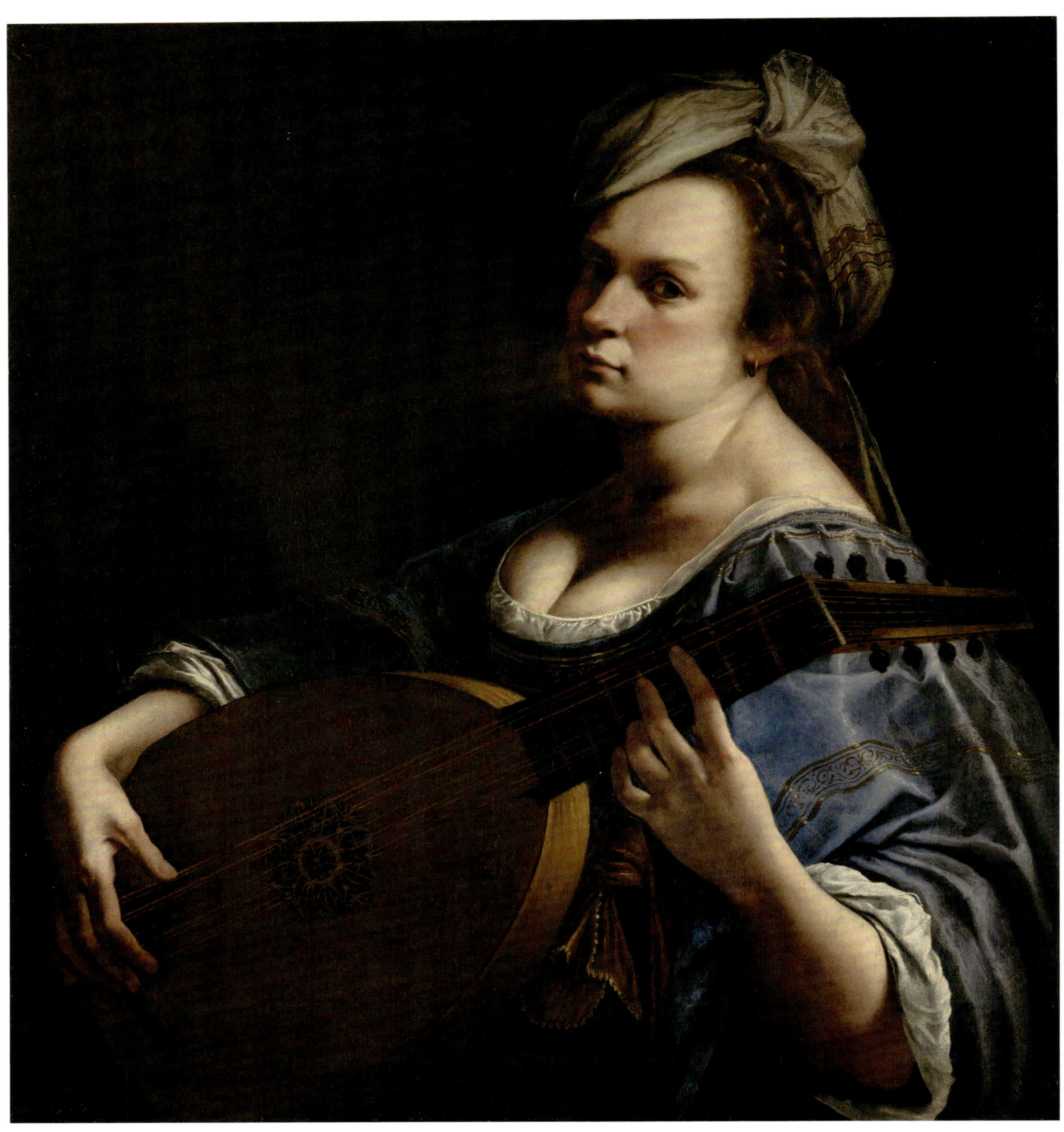

37 Artemisia Gentileschi, *Self-portrait as a Lute Player*, c.1614–15, oil on canvas, 77.5 × 71.8 cm, Wadsworth Atheneum Museum of Art, Hartford, Conn., Charles H. Schwartz Endowment Fund 2014.4.1

to in a 1638 inventory of the Villa Ferdinanda as 'a portrait of Artemisia by her hand playing the lute'[16].

The 'St Catherine martyr' cited in the 1615 document is identifiable with the *St Catherine of Alexandria* in the Uffizi (fig. 36). In 1620, it was paired in the Villa Ferdinanda with a painting of a female warrior and described thus: 'Two paintings on canvas with black and gold frames 1¾ braccia high by 1⅓ braccia wide [*c.*100 × 76 cm] in one there is St Catherine of the Wheel and in the other a woman with a morion [helmet] holding a sword in her hand. no. 2.'[17] A 1638 inventory provides some further information on the second, lost painting of this pair, identifying it for the first time as a self-portrait of Artemisia as an 'Amazon': 'a painting measuring 1¾ braccia high by 1½ braccia wide [*c.*100 × 87 cm] with a black frame with gold detailing in which there is painted the painter Artemisia in the dress of an Amazon with sword, shield and morion [helmet]'.[18] In 2021, Bastogi added to this a newly discovered reference from a Medicean inventory of 1775 that also describes this lost painting as a self-portrait of Artemisia and provides some further information on its original appearance: 'shown from the waist upwards the Portrait of the painter Artemisia Lomi clothed as an amazon with sword in her right [hand], bare left arm, crest with feathers on her head, yellow cloak on her right arm'.[19]

As noted, the first document in the sequence dating from 1615 designates this Amazonian self-portrait as 'Bradamante'. This new information allows us to identify this lost work as not simply depicting a generic Amazon warrior but rather as a self-portrait of Artemisia as Bradamante, the legendary knight of Charlemagne, sister of Rinaldo and beloved of the Saracen Ruggiero whose heroic exploits form one of the major strands of Ludovico Ariosto's epic poem *Orlando Furioso*.[20] Given that the 1638 and 1775 inventories also explicitly identify the *Bradamante* as a self-portrait, and given, further, that the *St Catherine of Alexandria* was originally paired with the *Bradamante* in the Villa Ferdinanda, both Papi and Bastogi have suggested that the works were originally perceived as self-portraits and that it was for this reason that they were hung together as a pair in 1620. This hypothesis was further strengthened in 2021 with the publication of an additional reference from the 1775 inventory likewise identifying the Uffizi *St Catherine of Alexandria* as a self-portrait and describing the composition as showing: 'from the waist upwards the Portrait of Artemisia Lomi representing St Catherine of the Wheel'.[21]

Finally, and perhaps most surprisingly from our perspective today, the *Conversion of the Magdalene* now in the Pitti Palace in Florence (fig. 40) is also identified as a self-portrait in the 1638 inventory. This inventory describes the painting as 'a similar [painting] in which there is painted Artemisia Lomi after the Holy Mary Magdalene with a yellow dress [and] with a skull and mirror in front'.[22] An additional reference from the 1775 inventory, published in 2021, also identifies the painting as a self-portrait and describes it as 'a seated full-length figure [showing] the portrait made by her hand of Artemisia Lomi, representing St Mary Magdalene in distress, [wearing a] yellow dress, right [hand] on her chest and left on the table, on which there is a skull'.[23] Bastogi and Papi have, therefore, both confirmed that the Palazzo Pitti painting was also originally regarded as a self-portrait of Gentileschi in the role of the Magdalene, a reading that has been accepted also by Francesca Baldassari in her discussion of the work in 2016.[24] The canvas should thus be understood as depicting Gentileschi acting out the conversion of the Magdalene in the same way that the Grand Duchess Maria Magdalena of Austria, the consort of Cosimo II and the daughter-in-law of Christine de Lorraine, commissioned Justus Sustermans to paint her portrait in an historiated-portrait mode as the Penitent Magdalene only a few years after Gentileschi's painting (fig. 41).[25]

A FRESH DECLARATION OF IDENTITY: THE LONDON *SELF-PORTRAIT AS ST CATHERINE OF ALEXANDRIA* AND THE PITTI *CONVERSION OF THE MAGDALENE* AS TRANSFORMATIONAL SELF-PORTRAITS

We may designate these canvases as self-portraits today and this new information confirms that they were identified as such during their own time. However, they go far beyond the relatively straightforwardly representational directness of the self-portraits by Anguissola and Fontana. In deciding to explore the much less common visual tradition of the disguised 'portrait historié' – as inspired by Caravaggio and

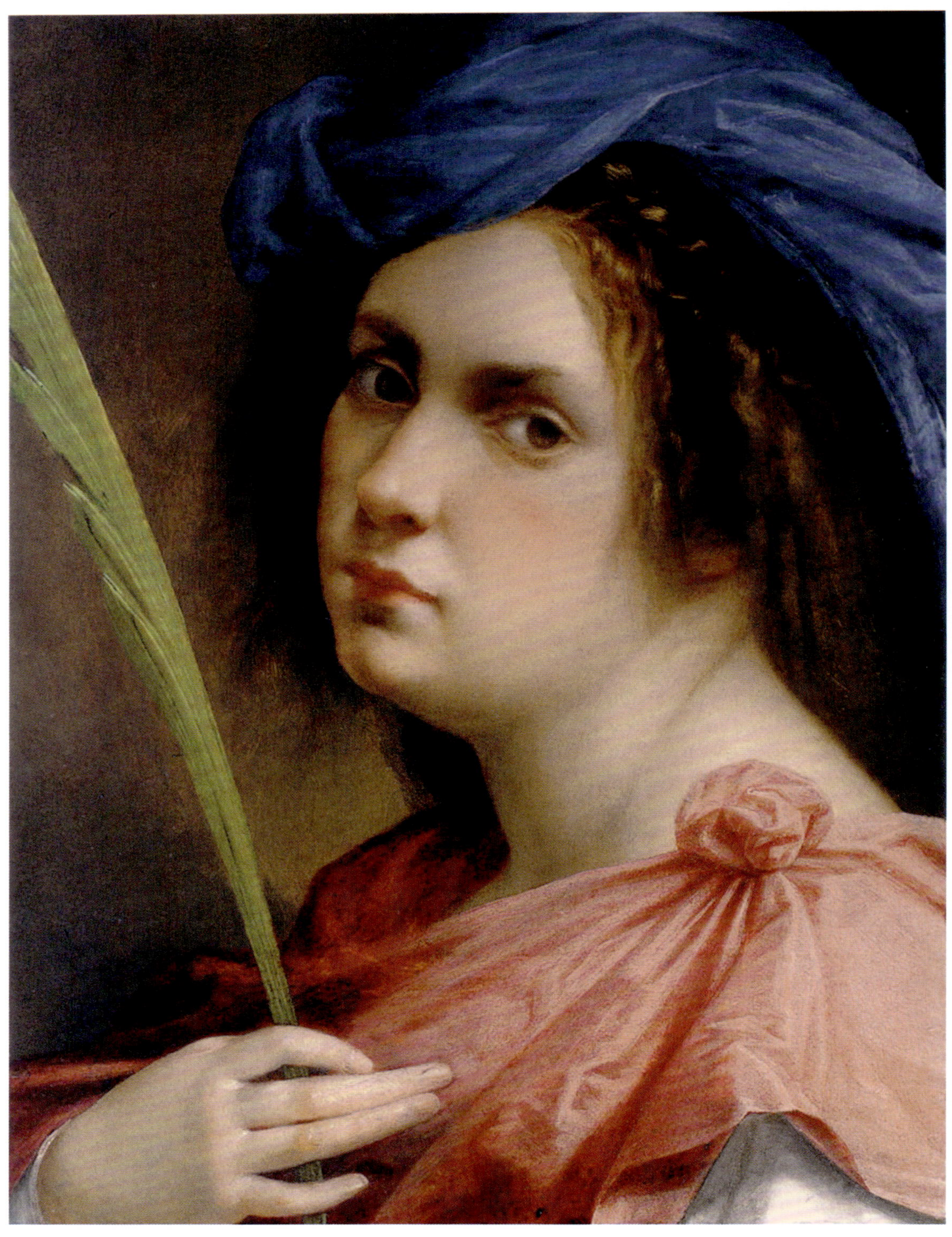

38 Artemisia Gentileschi, *Self-portrait as a Female Martyr*, *c.*1613–15, oil on panel, 31.75 × 24.76 cm, private collection, USA

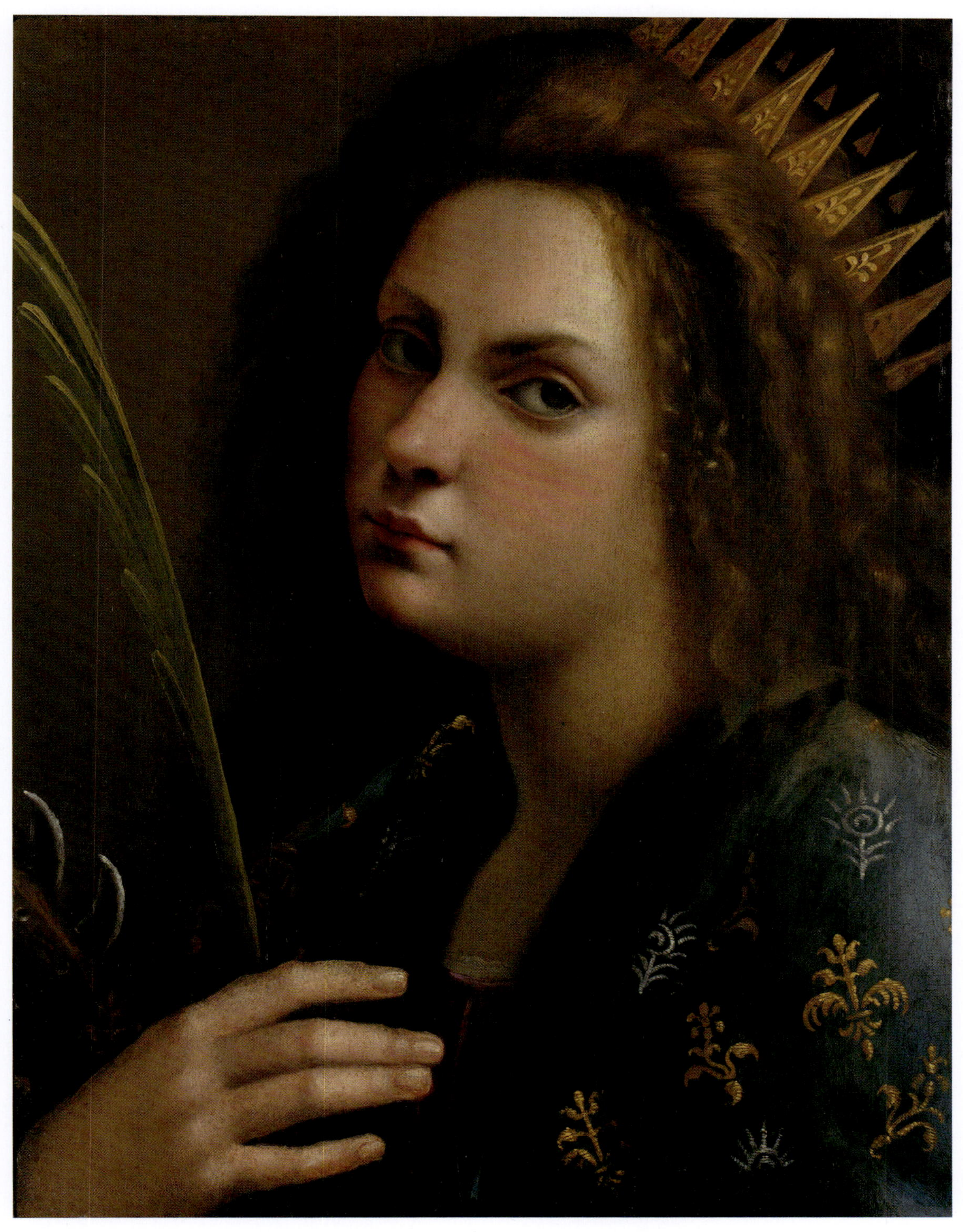

39 Attributed to Artemisia Gentileschi, *Self-portrait as St Catherine of Alexandria*, *c.*1613–15, oil on panel, 32.7 × 32.1 cm, The National Museum of Art, Architecture and Design, Oslo, on loan from a private collection

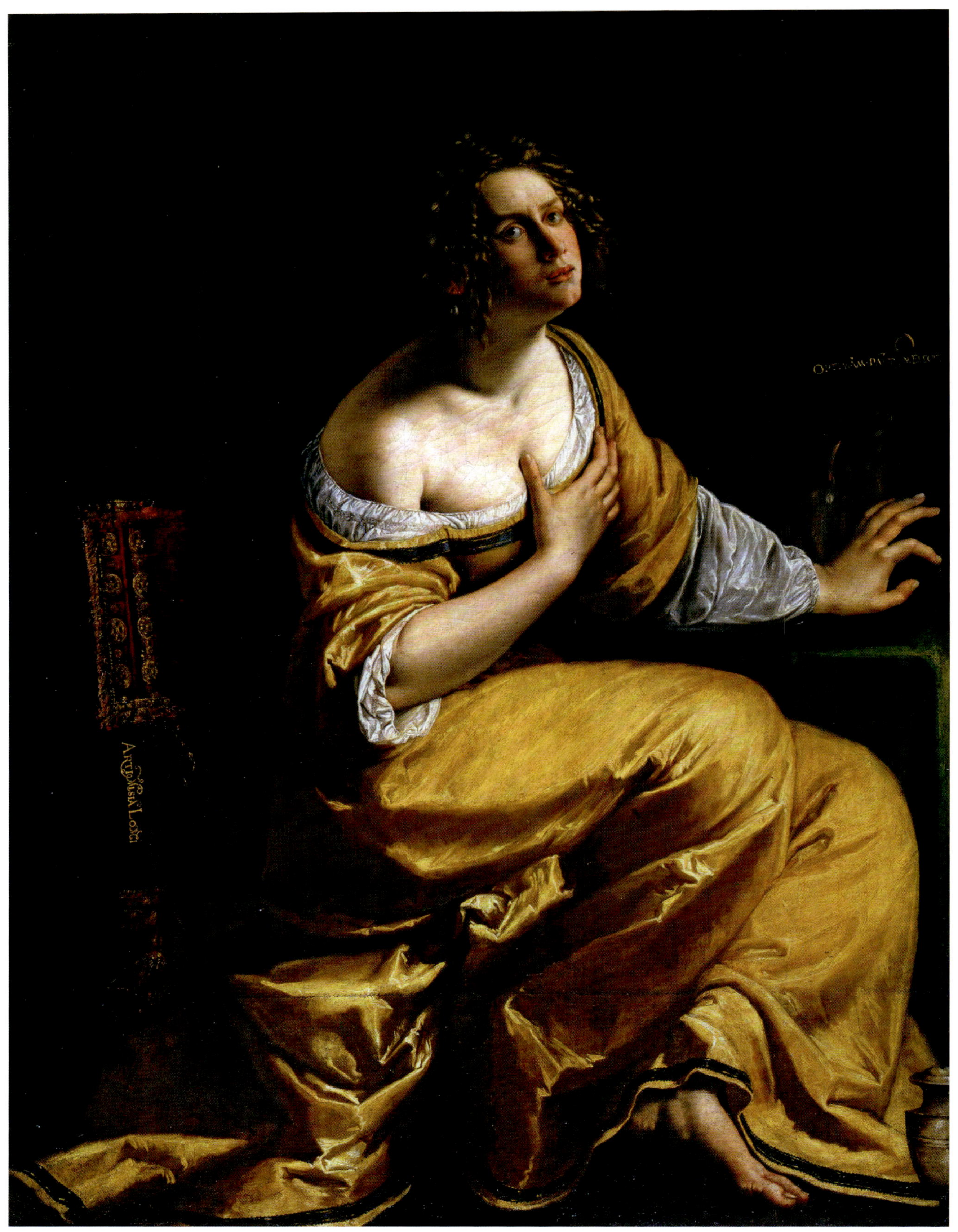

40 Artemisia Gentileschi, *Conversion of the Magdalene*, c.1614–15, oil on canvas, 146.5 × 108 cm, Galleria Palatina, Palazzo Pitti, Florence

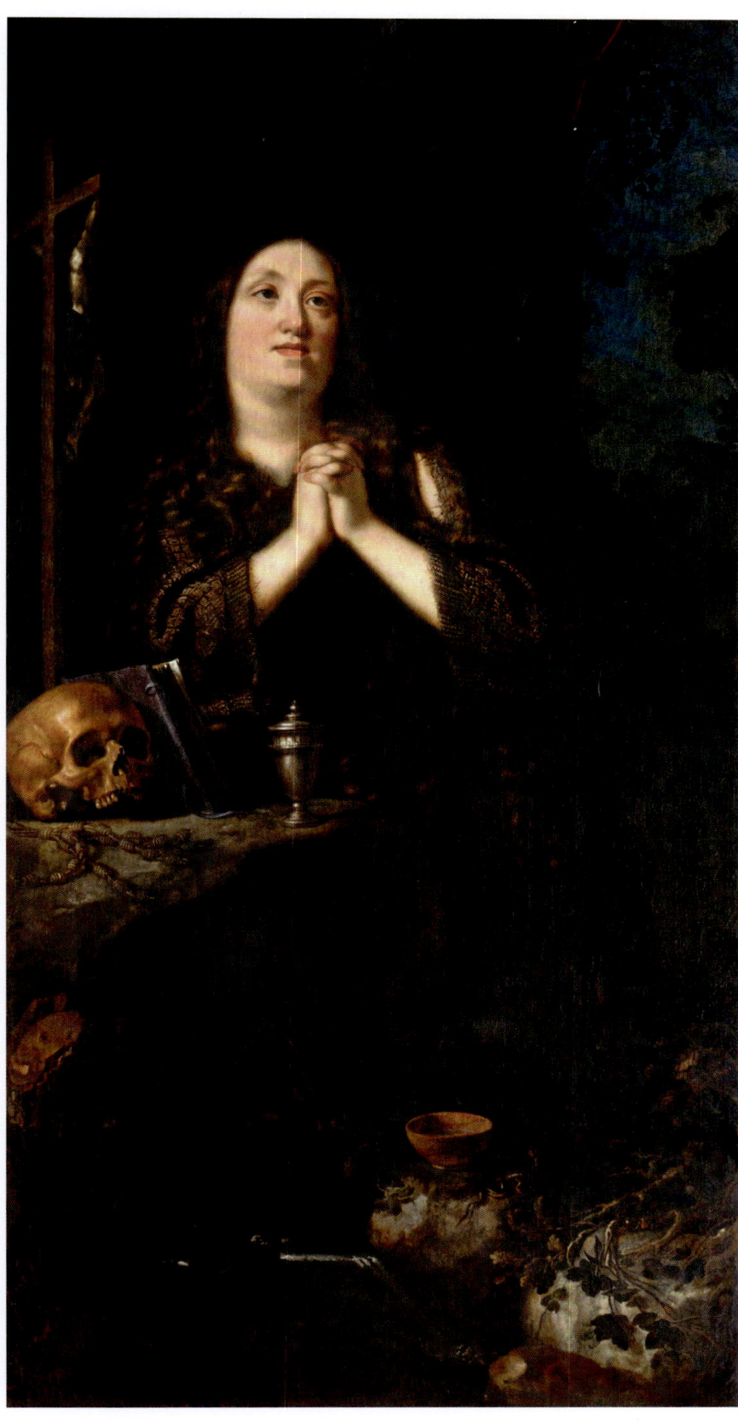

41 Justus Sustermans, *Maria Maddalena of Austria as St Mary Magdalene*, c.1625–30, oil on canvas, 168 × 90 cm, Galleria Palatina, Palazzo Pitti, Florence, inv. 1890, n. 563

as further revived more recently by Allori, as we have seen – Gentileschi seeks in her paintings, instead, to highlight two seemingly contradictory features of portraiture. On the one hand, they celebrate her ability to render her recognisable features so vividly present to the viewer as to allow the painting to function as a kind of stand-in or emissary for the artist herself. Yet this impression of tangible reality is juxtaposed with an equal emphasis on role-playing fantasy and theatricality. The artist operates in this sense as being akin to an actor on the stage. Her paintings manifest her power to evoke proxy phantasms that maintain a vivid presence in the here and now of the viewing moment while simultaneously stressing their provisional status as temporarily staged identities that might equally transform themselves into yet another shape-shifting character at a moment's notice.

The safest roles for Gentileschi to perform within the context of the culture of the Florentine court were, understandably enough, those holy women whose lives and legends aligned most closely to the *virtuosa*'s need to be both distinguished and decorous at the same time. The aspirational story of St Catherine of Alexandria must have been especially attractive in this respect. Only a few years younger than Gentileschi at the time of her death, St Catherine was a princess, the purist of virgins and a scholar of such erudition as to be able to defeat all the philosophers ranged against her by order of Emperor Maxentius. Gentileschi's depiction of herself in this role in the canvas now at the National Gallery, London, emphasises the saint's stoic readiness to embrace martyrdom.[26] Her crossed arms form an X-pattern that is mirrored by the positioning of her hands. One hand grasps the wheel of torture while the other cradles the martyr's palm (fig. 35). This acts as a powerful visual metaphor for the process of martyrdom itself, suggesting that the martyr must first embrace the torment of martyrdom before receiving Heaven's just rewards.

At the same time, however, Gentileschi has allowed a certain degree of calculated artlessness to enter into the composition. This acts to blur the boundaries between devotional image and self-portrait. We note, for example, the simple and unadorned manner in which Gentileschi has chosen to render her costume in comparison with her other depictions of the subject, particularly the Uffizi *St Catherine of Alexandria*, which,

I would argue, indicates a later and more formal re-elaboration of the subject.[27] The deliberate artlessness is especially evident in the tossed-on turban worn by Gentileschi in the London *St Catherine*. This is presumably intended to refer to the iconography of the sybil and thus to convey the saint's historic and exotic sense of intellectual attainment in far-off Alexandria.[28] Yet the informality of Gentileschi's attire undercuts this pious devotional association. It creates a countervailing sense of the artist's apparently showing herself to the viewer in the act of playing dress-up before our eyes.

Gentileschi draws us into the painting through her gaze. This direct eye contact highlights the overall tone of playful self-consciousness that the figure of Gentileschi/St Catherine maintains with the viewer. Elizabeth Cropper has highlighted the viewing dynamics that arise as a result of this self-representational emphasis. In establishing a direct gaze between the viewer and the artist, she notes, Gentileschi follows a long-standing visual convention that seeks to 'render the artist visible within his works'. One of the most important features of this device is to create 'a sort of "pact" between painter and viewer'.[29] The direct gaze brings us into the painting as a friend, confidante and co-conspirator, sharing the moment with the artist who seems, in this instance, to be celebrating her status as being akin to St Catherine while, at the same time, conveying the idea that she is also just an artist playing a role.

The Uffizi *St Catherine*, by contrast, posits a more formalised treatment of the subject that significantly heightens the devotional cues that are in other respects more subtly expressed in the London composition.[30] Thus the Uffizi figure does not look directly at the viewer; instead, she casts her gaze piously heavenwards. She has also taken greater care to dress appropriately. She wears a demonstrably more lavish costume (note the elaborate gold detailing on the sleeve of her red dress, for example) and is more modestly attired (as evident in the gauze fabric across the top of her bodice). Finally, she wears an altogether more convincingly elaborate, bejewelled crown. As Letizia Treves has noted, this crown is reminiscent of the magnificently ornate crown created for Ferdinand I de' Medici (1549–1609) by the goldsmith father of Giovanni Bilivert, a painter whom Gentileschi would have known and whose work is often associated with hers.[31] It seems, therefore, on this basis, that the Uffizi *St Catherine* should be designated as a subsequent and more 'official', formal Medicean commission, quite possibly for Christine de Lorraine (as is discussed below).

The essential distinction between the London and the Uffizi *St Catherine* is that of temporarily assuming a role, in the first instance, and inhabiting it in a more fully engaged and embodied sense, in the second. This process is heightened yet further in Gentileschi's full-length portrayal of herself as the Magdalene in the Palazzo Pitti *Conversion of the Magdalene* (fig. 40). No mere dress rehearsal, this painting constitutes the artist's most forthright expression of her claim towards inhabiting a position of devout nobility as a means of gaining recognition at the Medici court. As such, it has been consistently and appropriately identified in the literature as almost certainly constituting a major commission produced as a highly self-conscious homage to the Magdalene's namesake, the Grand Duchess Maria Magdalena of Austria.[32]

Orazio Gentileschi's earlier rendition of this subject had followed Caravaggio's lead in depicting the Magdalene in the company of Martha. In these earlier versions, Martha maintains the moral high ground by remonstrating with her sister in order to convince her of the error of her ways (fig. 42).[33] Artemisia, however, edits Martha out of the composition altogether, thereby claiming for herself the ability to enact her own self-conversion through sheer force of will. Her Magdalene is, moreover, clad in a silken dress of spectacular luxuriance. It has been clearly inspired by Allori's signature yellow dress in the *Judith*, but it arguably goes one better in managing to convey a striking impression of visual opulence not by mere surface patterning – as Allori had done – but rather in the fleeting play of light that catches its folds as the Magdalene shifts in her chair. Thus, Gentileschi creates a tour-de-force demonstration of the ability of the painter's brush to evoke a dazzling impression of lavish sumptuousness.[34]

The brilliant duality of Gentileschi's *Conversion of the Magdalene* lies in its ability to proclaim the Magdalene's triumphant renunciation of the temptations of the flesh within the context of a composition which remains, in other respects, fixated on the beauty of lavishly adorned surfaces. This is nowhere more evident than in the decisive gesture made by Artemisia/

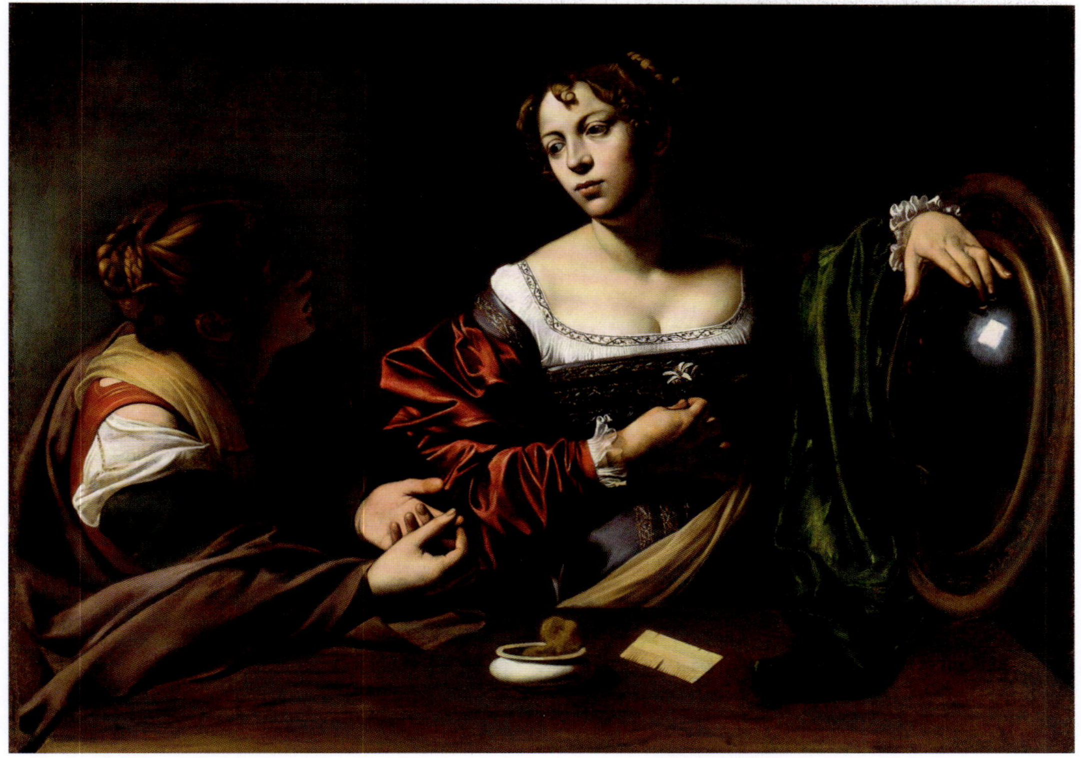

42 Michelangelo Merisi da Caravaggio, *Martha and Mary Magdalene*, c.1598–99, oil and tempera on canvas, 97.8 × 32.7 cm, Detroit Institute of Arts, Gift of the Kresge Foundation and Mrs. Edsel B. Ford, 73.268

Mary as she turns dramatically away from the mirror to gaze heavenwards for strength. In so doing, she creates an odd visual effect as the left side of her head is caught momentarily at an oblique angle in the mirror. This reveals to the viewer the reflected details of the golden ringlets of her hair and her left ear, with its prominent drop pearl earring. These oddly striking details would not be otherwise visible within the picture. This demonstration of the power of painting to reveal multiple points of view within a single image seems directly inspired by those expositions of painterly prowess found in images associated with the paragone debate (on the respective merits of painting and sculpture), such as we see in Giovanni Bellini's attempt to counter the inherent three-dimensional advantage of sculpture by inserting a mirror into the back of his painting, thereby revealing the front and back of his subject's head and left arm simultaneously (fig. 43).[35]

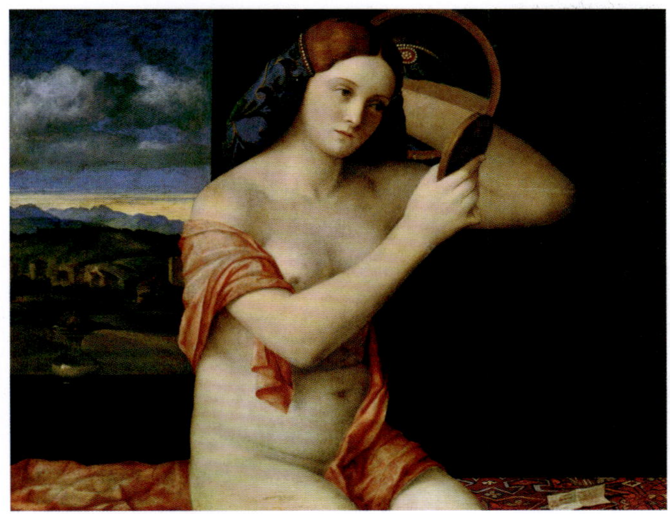

43 Giovanni Bellini, *Woman with a Mirror*, signed and dated 1515, oil on poplar wood, 62.9 × 78.3 cm, Kunsthistorisches Museum, Vienna

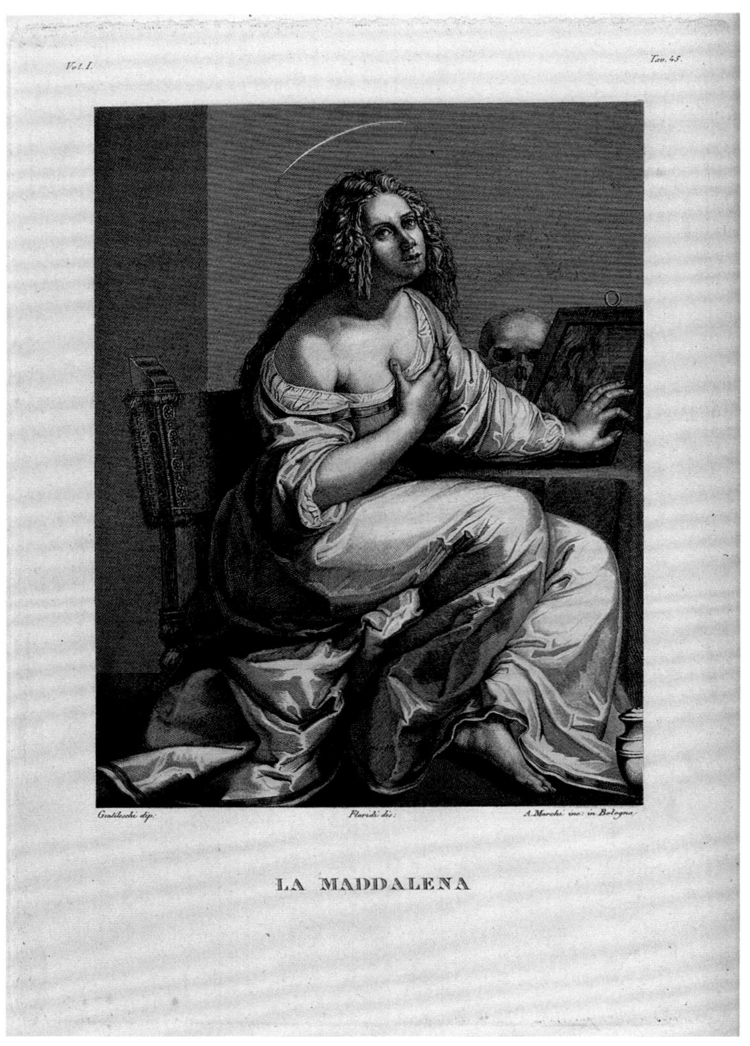

44 Antonio Marchi and Francesco Floridi after Artemisia Gentileschi, *Conversion of the Magdalene*, 1837, engraving on paper, from Luigi Bardi, *L'Imperiale e Reale Galleria Pitti illustrata per cura di Luigi Bardi*, Florence

If we look again at the painting, we can see that the reflection of the Magdalene's partially revealed head in the mirror is framed directly beside a depiction of a skull. This key compositional element has deteriorated over time to the extent of its becoming now almost illegible. (A nineteenth-century reproductive print shows it more clearly; fig. 44).[36] While hardly commented on in the literature, the skull should be recognised as performing an important moralising role within the composition. The Magdalene looks away, while the mirror that should receive the full gaze of the viewer of the painting is able only to catch the side of her head. It thus remains for the skull to project itself into the beholder's consciousness as the only visage within the painting to address the viewer directly. The skull assumes the role of interlocutor that was performed by the artist in the other self-portraits here discussed. Peeking out from behind the mirror, the skull catches our eye conspiratorially in the midst of our observation of the Magdalene's dramatic performance of conversion. It, accordingly, reminds us once more of the Gospel's moral resolution in the path towards total physical abnegation that the Magdalene will pursue from this point onwards. The work thus stresses the power of painting to signal the transformation of its own surface appearances over time. Artemisia/Mary may look like a stunning beauty now, but before too long, and as a result of her decision to convert, her body will be transformed into an emaciated husk of its former self. This process of extreme self-mortification will ultimately bring her into visual alignment with the alternative iconographic tradition of the emaciated Magdalene, a tradition most famously embodied in the irremediable gauntness of Donatello's renowned wooden sculpture of the Magdalene then on prominent display in the Florence's Baptistry (fig. 45).[37]

The painting's decorative inscriptions provide an additional level of commentary on this tour-de-force demonstration of Gentileschi's identity and painterly skills. A signature, 'Artemisia Lomi', has been carefully stencilled in gold on the side of the Magdalene's chair.[38] This is only the second known instance of a signature in Gentileschi's oeuvre. It thus clearly marks the work out as another major statement on the artist's part, in much the same way as was previously noted in the case of the 1610 *Susanna and the Elders*. Ann Sutherland Harris has commented on the script's resemblance to that found in Baroque calligraphic manuals. She interprets the signature in this sense as a proclamation of Gentileschi's new-found literacy and ability to project herself within the Florentine literary ambience.[39] Judith Mann, similarly, describes this feature as 'one of the most elaborate signatures we have in the seventeenth century'.[40] She reads the signature as an allusion to the intricate goldwork for which Orazio's father was known and

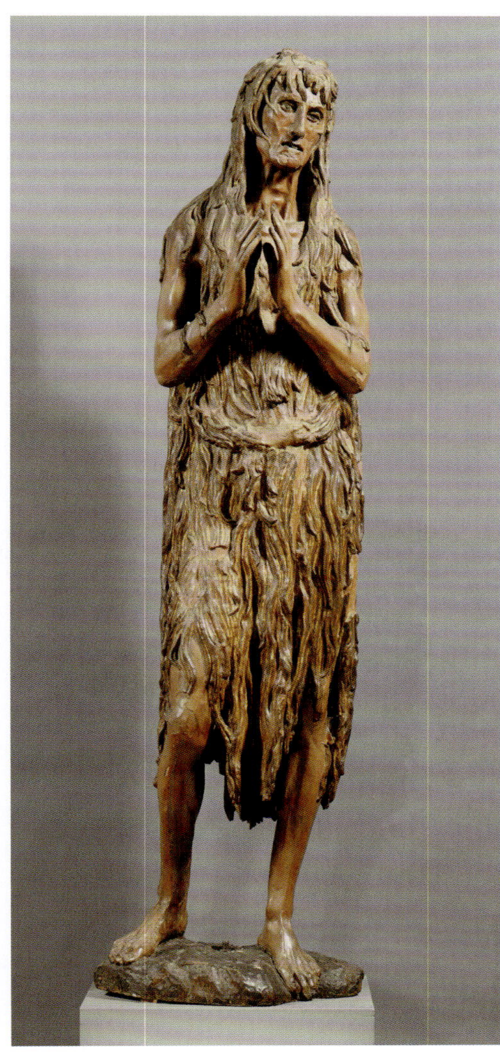

45 Donatello, *Penitent Magdalene*, c.1450, wood with gilding and polychromy, 185 × 51 × 45 cm, Museo dell'Opera del Duomo, Florence

which she perceives Gentileschi drawing upon in order to link herself 'inextricably in the eyes of her public with this Florentine tradition, still a popular component of Florentine art'.[41]

The wording of the signature is also significant, as much in terms of what it refers to as for what it chooses to leave out. Here, Artemisia highlights the Tuscan form of her own surname – Lomi (reflecting the adopted surnames of her grandfather and uncle from Pisa) – above that of her husband, a connection that she would have been otherwise required to acknowledge in a more strictly legal context. She also cancels out any identification with her father's surname (Orazio had chosen at an early stage in his career to identify himself by the Gentileschi part of the family name, omitting Lomi from his surname, once he had moved to Rome from Pisa[42]). The signature should thus be read as a self-conscious declaration of Artemisia's ability at this particular moment of her career to define herself on her own terms and in line with a new identity that proclaims itself to be independent of both her husband and her father's legacy. From this point onwards, this projected painterly identity will become associated with Artemisia's own unique and independent brand.

This reading is further strengthened by the secondary inscription that has been written into the mirror's frame. This quotes the Latin of Luke's Gospel (10:42): 'she hath chosen that good part'. The text records the first half of Christ's response to Martha's complaint that her sister had not been assisting her in making preparations for the feast. In his reply, Christ reminded Martha that the Magdalene had chosen the higher path. Moreover, and as the second half of the quotation made yet more clear (and as all contemporary viewers would have been able to complete in their own minds), the Magdalene's resolve to renounce her former identity in order to follow Christ constituted a decision that 'shall not be taken from her'. Artemisia's use of this quotation in this context, in the same elegant gold calligraphic script that she had used to sign her own name, thus seeks to establish a link between Christ's pronouncement and the declaration of independence encoded in her signature. It proclaims Gentileschi's belief in the righteousness of her decision to leave her Roman upbringing behind and so to reinvent herself with a new identity as an outstandingly successful *virtuosa* at the Florentine court. Her relocation to Florence has now brought her to a position of being able to insert herself into an important commission for the Grand Duchess that she chooses to frame in moral and theological terms as being as unassailably pure as the Magdalene's own decision to convert to Christ.

LOVE, WAR AND DEVOTION: FURTHER TRANSFORMATIONS OF THE DISGUISED SELF-PORTRAIT IN THE *SELF-PORTRAIT AS A LUTE PLAYER*

The early documentation for the *Conversion of the Magdalene* lists it as hanging in the Villa Ferdinanda at Artimino from 1615 onwards, as noted above. At that stage, the painting was situated only a couple of rooms away from what might at first appear to have been an incongruous pairing. This juxtaposed the *St Catherine of Alexandria* (fig. 36) with a now lost painting of the same dimensions displaying 'a woman with a morion [helmet] holding a sword in her hand'. As we have seen, this painting was subsequently identified as a self-portrait in 1638 and 1775 and as a depiction of *Bradamante* – the legendary knightly heroine of Ludovico Ariosto's *Orlando Furioso* – in 1615.

Nadia Bastogi has interpreted these early displays as constituting a carefully curated *galleria* of Gentileschian self-portraits that had been assembled by the Medici for this bucolic location, situated in the Tuscan hills some twenty-five kilometres west of the city (fig. 46).[43] She further notes the original presence of the pairing of the *Bradamante* and the *St Catherine* in the apartment within the villa that was allocated to Christine de Lorraine, the Dowager Grand Duchess of Tuscany and the intended recipient of Orazio Gentileschi's letter of 3 July 1612. Although Orazio's plan to secure Medici support for his daughter appeared not to have been successful, Artemisia, as noted, nonetheless managed to attract the patronage of Cosimo II, Maria Magdalena of Austria and Christine de Lorraine on her own initiative within a very short period of time. Bastogi has further speculated that the otherwise seemingly strange juxtaposition of the Amazonian *Bradamante* with St Catherine of Alexandria might originally have held a personal significance for its original patron, reading Gentileschi's *St Catherine*, in the sense of the pairing, as a homage to Queen Catherine de' Medici (1519–1589), a much-revered Medicean ancestor, who had been Christine de Lorraine's tutor. (Mary Garrard and Letizia Treves, on the other hand, view the painting as an idealized portrait of another Medicean namesake – Christine de Lorraine's daughter, Caterina de' Medici (1593–1629).[44]) Bastogi interprets the second canvas, again in this sense, as a tribute to Christine de Lorraine herself. Here the association would be to de Lorraine's own chivalric and Amazonian qualities, which were frequently commented upon in the context of the Grand Duchess' predilection for hunting in the woods surrounding the villa in which the paintings were displayed.

46 Bernardo Buontalenti, Villa Ferdinanda di Artimino, Carmignano (Prato), 1596

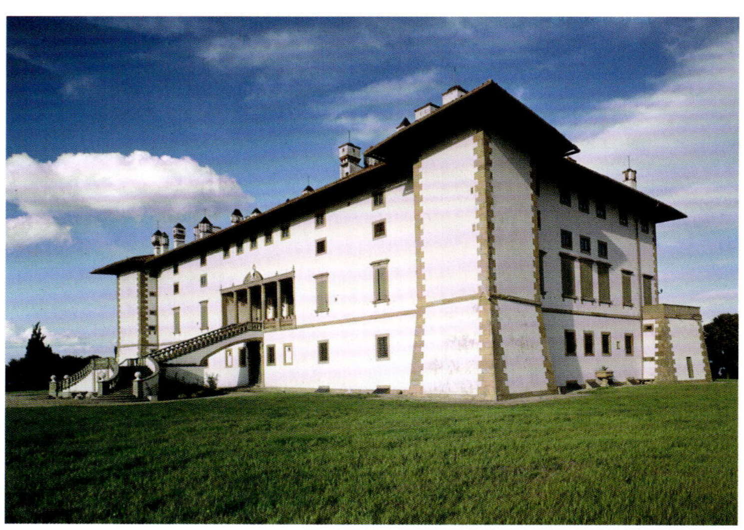

The bucolic setting and relaxed villa atmosphere that was reserved for the paintings' display would seem to constitute an important early viewing context for these works. It seems to have encouraged a series of more intimate and personal readings than might otherwise have been possible in the more formal reception rooms in the Palazzo Pitti or other more public or ceremonial spaces within the city itself. The more relaxed and informal environment in which to view the pictures seems especially important for our interpretation of one of the most enigmatic works in the entire series. The 1615 transfer document mentions a 'a young woman playing a lute', which the 1638 inventory for the Villa Ferdinanda then describes more specifically as 'a portrait of Artemisia by her hand playing the lute'. These references have been accepted by all scholars as documenting the early provenance of a painting that first appeared on the art market in 1998 and that is now in the Wadsworth Atheneum, Hartford (fig. 37).[45]

This canvas constitutes the most daring and experimental work of the entire series in one sense, even more than is indicated by her portrayal of herself as a female warrior in the *Bradamante* painting. Unlike the previously discussed canvases, it deliberately flouts the decorum and modesty that were the required attributes of the *virtuosa*. Gentileschi depicts herself playing a musical instrument; yet, in contrast to the works of Sofonisba Anguissola and Lavinia Fontana discussed above, she makes no attempt to stress the virginal, chaste or otherwise devout aspects of her musicianship. Instead, she evokes the age-old association between music and profane love (a tradition revived most recently, once again, by Caravaggio, but deriving from an earlier iconography that was at that time particularly associated with Venetian Renaissance painting).[46] Elizabeth Cropper's observation concerning the 'sort of "pact" between painter and viewer' that was noted above in relation to Gentileschi's direct gaze towards the viewer renders this canvas even more charged in its associations than the others. By making eye contact with us while playing the lute, she solicits us, in effect, to join with her in song so that we might thus become united with her in the eternal music of love.

At its most extreme, this would seem to suggest an invitation by the artist for the viewer to enjoy with her the sweet pact of erotic intimacy initiated between two lovers, a commonplace reading of works within this tradition.[47] Indeed, Francesco Solinas has interpreted the painting in light of one of Gentileschi's letters to her lover, Francesco Maria Maringhi (1593–1653), composed shortly after Gentileschi's departure from Florence in early 1620. In this correspondence, she refers to another, now lost portrait that she had painted for Maringhi and left behind for him in Florence. With reference to this portrait (which Solinas surmises might have originally been a half-length figure or reclining nude[48]) she notes, in a passage of extraordinary frankness, 'I would beg you with all my heart concerning my portrait, that you do not do what you should not and that you promised me not to do, that thing that perhaps Your Lordship is doing. I remind you that it is a great sin, and I would have you remember that I love your soul as well as your body.'[49]

We are, perhaps, doing the artist a disservice here by removing these comments from behind the veil of confidentiality

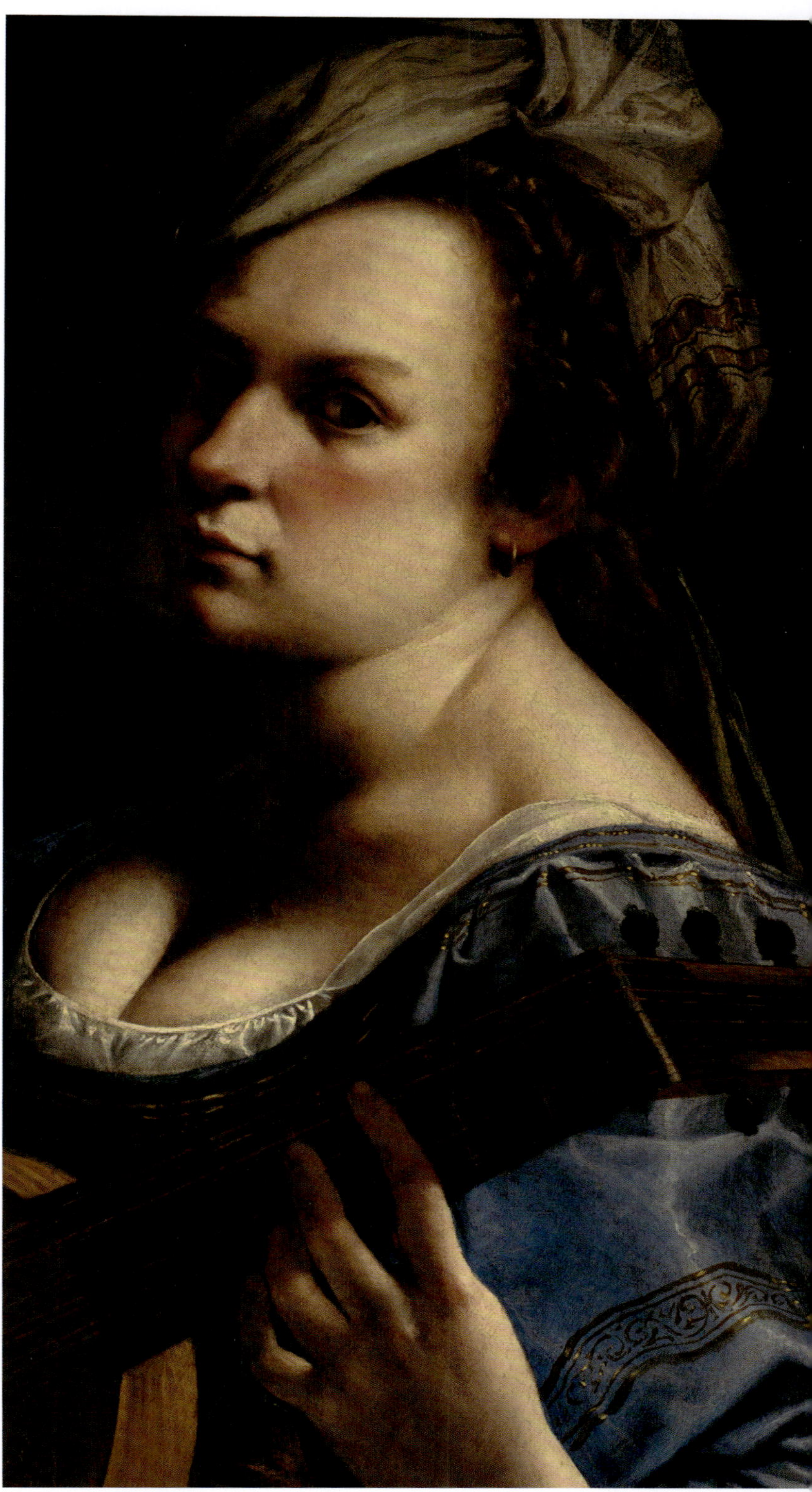

Artemisia Gentileschi, *Self-portrait as a Lute Player* (detail of fig. 37)

that would have been otherwise enjoyed between two lovers conversing freely in the midst of an intimate affair. In addition, and as Elizabeth Cohen has underscored, Gentileschi's words may be more conventional than might be evident today. They can be traced back to a well-worn Renaissance literary trope of lovers addressing portraits of their absent beloved as if they were the lovers themselves.[50] The *Self-portrait as a Lute Player* seems, moreover, to communicate to the viewer on an altogether more public and formal level than the very private and self-consciously intimate format adopted in the letter. Yet Gentileschi's extraordinarily frank comments, made as they were in the context of a direct reference to a now lost self-portrait, are useful in reminding us of the artist's evidently strong belief in the ability of her paintings to render themselves powerfully present within the viewer's consciousness as vividly personified emissaries of the absent artist herself.

Jesse Locker has analysed the *Self-portrait as a Lute Player* within the context of a broader study of the self-portraits and related works from this period. His interpretation, which builds, in turn, on a proposal originally advanced by Mary Garrard, is to suggest that the painting might be best understood as a visual documentation of an actual performance held at the Palazzo Pitti in 1615. A highlight of this Medicean court spectacle was a rendition of a *ballo delle zingare* (Dance of the Gipsy Women), in which six male and six female performers acted out the parts of various gypsies, bedecked in elaborate costumes. One of these performers is listed as a 'Signora Artimisia', a reference identified by Garrard and others as possibly identifiable with Gentileschi. This possibility seems strengthened by Gentileschi's association with Cristofano Allori, Michelangelo Buonarroti and other individuals during this period who are known to have been involved in court performances of this type.[51] Locker's reading is certainly useful in helping to shed light on the broader context within which the painting may have been understood in its own day. Yet it is, arguably, too literal an interpretation for such a deliberately ambiguous and open-ended painting. As Locker himself notes, the painting 'takes its own theatricality as the subject, purposely blurring the distinction between part and actor, and in no way concealing the fact that it depicts Artemisia *pretending* to be the ostensible subject'.[52]

GENTILESCHI'S 'SELF-PORTRAITS' AND THE ICONOGRAPHY OF BRAND 'ARTEMISIA'

Another way of perceiving this and the other paintings that make up this group is to understand them as part of a broader strategy on Gentileschi's part to manipulate the traditions of portraiture in order to patent her own image as an instantly recognisable artist of renown. The obvious precedent for such an undertaking, and something to which Gentileschi must have soon become habituated while living in Florence, was the 'official' or state portrait. Frequently copied and displayed in multiple public locations, these portraits have come to constitute a ubiquitous feature of the urban fabric of Florence to this day.[53] Medici portraits follow the conventions of other official images of dynastic rulers in fixing each family member's image into a standard repertory of tightly defined formats and viewpoints. This formulaic approach enabled them to be repeated on many occasions across a broad range of contexts. The vast majority of Cosimo II's portraits, for example, depict him at a slight diagonal angle so that he is viewed from the left and the right side of his face remains hidden from view. Like a Hollywood star portrayed from the 'right profile', this carefully stage-managed appearance seems to have been favoured as his 'official' pose.

Besides their careful framing of the sitter, official portraits also tend to fix the physiognomic features of the ruler into a typology of easily recognisable and reproducible signs. In the case of Cosimo II, for example, his identifying features constitute a high brow, a wispy moustache and an unmistakably Habsburg nose (fig. 47).[54] All of this seems to have been highly suggestive to Gentileschi when she was searching for a comparable iconography of facial features to assign to her own physical appearance. But perhaps, when speaking of a typology of facial features that could be converted into a series of easily recognisable and reproducible signs, the still more obvious precedent for Gentileschi would have been the physiognomic iconography of the archetypal Tuscan artist, Michelangelo himself (fig. 48).[55] In this context, we will recall that Artemisia's closest Florentine patron, besides the Medici, was none other than Michelangelo's great-nephew, Michelangelo Buonarroti the Younger, for whose *galleria* Gentileschi contrib-

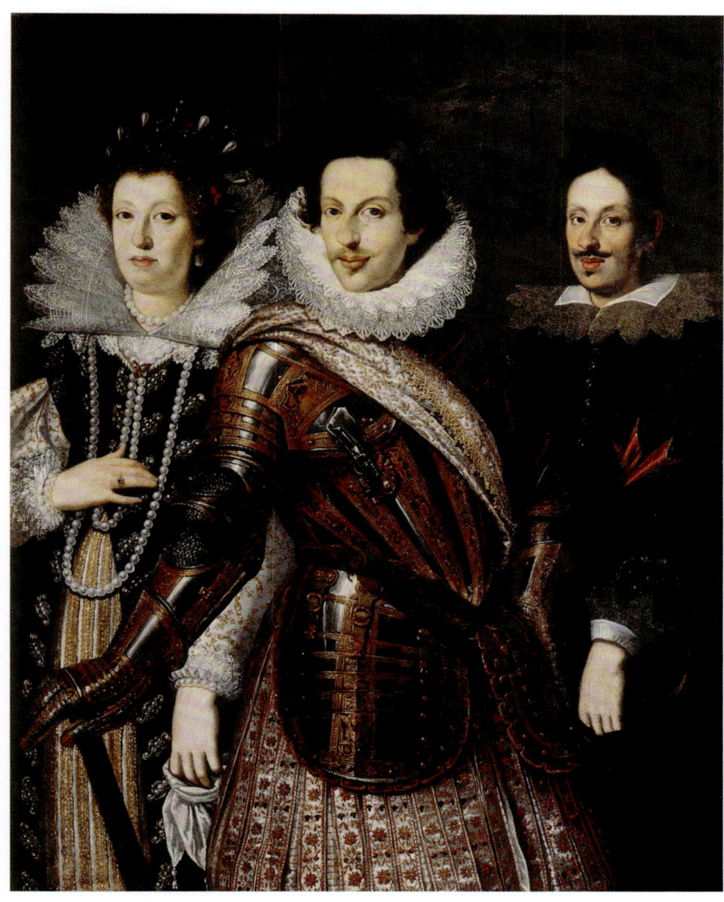

47 Justus Sustermans, *Portrait of Marie Madeleine of Austria, Cosimo II and Ferdinand II de' Medici*, c.1640, oil on canvas, 158 × 12.5 cm, Galleria degli Uffizi, Florence, inv. 1890 n. 2402

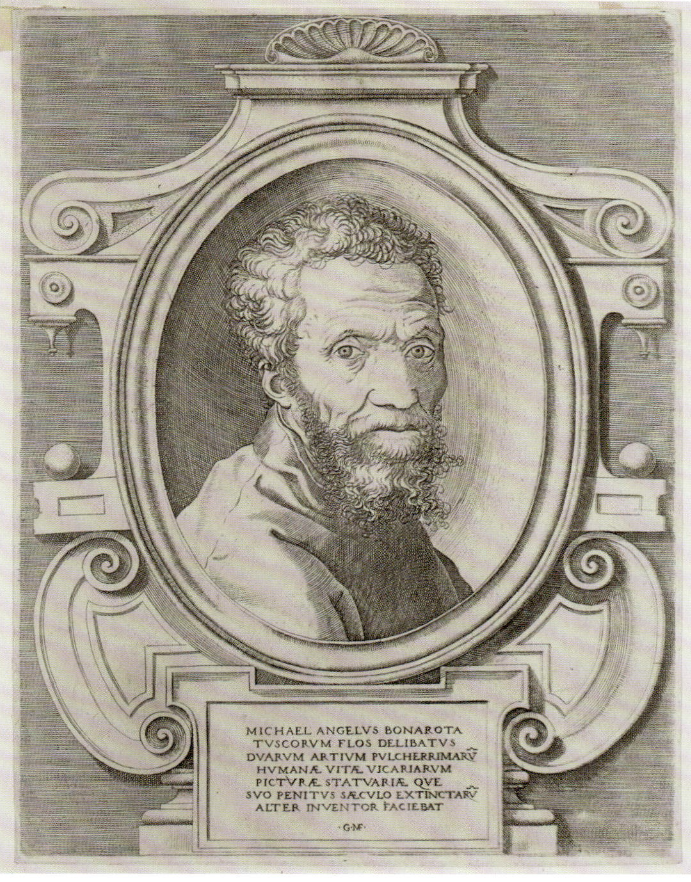

48 Giorgio Ghisi after Marcello Venusti, *Michelangelo*, c.1565, engraving printed in black ink on laid paper, 26.8 × 20.1 cm, Detroit Institute of Arts, Gift of Mrs. James E. Scripps, 09.1S520

uted her own image as an allegory of Inclination. Michelangelo represented a ubiquitous presence in Renaissance and Baroque Florence. When visiting the Casa Buonarroti, or when attending meetings at the Florentine Accademia del Disegno, or even while leafing through the pages of Vasari's *Lives*, Gentileschi would have been constantly reminded of the image of Michelangelo glaring balefully out of the picture plane, each repetition of the artist's image building on the last in terms of its cumulative reinforcement of the indexical recognisability of Michelangelo's distinctive physiognomic characteristics: the broken nose, the creased forehead, the long beard, the dark, hooded eyes and so on.[56]

Gentileschi was no official ruler. Neither was she a majestically imperious, alpha male, 'superhero' artist, standing at the very apex of the artistic hierarchy. She was thus far from being able to present herself as a fixed and inviolate point of reference before which all other artists and patrons must respectfully defer. She was, rather, an artist in fluid formation: a brilliantly mercurial work in progress. In this sense, the disguised self-portraits of Gentileschi's Florentine years help to advance an image of her as an infinitely flexible and aspirationally ascendant female artist of brilliant potential and increasing renown. They function, from this point of view, as a self-promotional advertising strategy that enabled her to maintain her public's interest in her evolving imagery by re-presenting herself across a range of inventively varied roles. She thus presents herself in these images as more than just a painter, but as an equally versatile actor who is able to hold the audience's attention through her ability convincingly to assume many different roles. It is also striking to note how carefully she tailored each of these roles to suit the differing viewing contexts in which they appeared. Gentileschi was thus careful to frame herself as a devout Magdalene for the more intimate Medicean setting of the Villa Ferdinanda at Artimino, as opposed to the more daring portrayal of herself as a semi-naked personification of Inclination for the sophisticated dilettante audiences of the Casa Buonarroti. These modulated instances of self-projection even came to include an intimate and erotic work, as we learned from her letter to her Florentine lover, that she sent as a keepsake for his eyes only.

What, however, remained unwaveringly consistent within all these constantly varied self-transformations, and what Artemisia seems to have absorbed from the twin sources of official Medicean portraiture and the imagery of Michelangelo, is the constant stress upon the distinctiveness of her own physiognomic iconography. Gentileschi's identifying features have been listed and commented on by numerous authors. A definition of Gentileschi's personal iconography would, accordingly, highlight the following commonly noted characteristics that appear throughout her oeuvre: a full face, long nose with a slightly raised sharp tip; full, fleshy or pursed lips (that are defined in particular by the prominent wave-like undulations of the cupid's bow of Artemisia's upper lip); a dimpled chin (also described occasionally as a 'double chin'); a long slender neck (that is sometimes also described as a 'strong' neck) and prominent, shoulder-length, wavy chestnut hair (that is sometimes also described as 'unruly' or 'unkempt' in appearance).[57] There is also a tendency in the literature to describe Artemisia's clothing and personal styling as forming an additional part of this 'signature look' – with her drop-pearl earrings, in particular, attracting comments along these lines.[58] It is noteworthy, moreover, that commentators have consistently sought to identify these features as being present not solely in the disguised self-portraits of her Florentine years, but also, more broadly, in the female protagonists depicted throughout Gentileschi's entire oeuvre. This includes the common tendency to recognise Gentileschi's features as being present in subject paintings that one would not usually consider as containing either portraits or self-portraits.[59] All of this attests to Artemisia's success in propagating her features throughout her work, to the extent that they have now become synonymous with her output in general.

Other artists, of course, have pushed the boundaries of self-portraiture from time to time, including the occasional practice of inserting their own features or those of their associates into their work – and in unexpected contexts, such as that created by Allori's use of his lover, 'Mazzafirra,' as a model for depictions of Judith as well as the Magdalene during this period. Simon Vouet (1590–1649) also used his wife as the model for depictions of the Magdalene in Rome in the 1620s (his model, Virginia da Vezzo (1600–1638) being herself an accomplished painter).[60] Yet none of these artists exploited *their own features* for such deliberately self-referential purposes and over the space of such a concentrated series of works. Caravaggio represents an important precedent in this respect, as noted. Yet his increasingly tormented depictions of himself as violently anti-heroic sinners, villains and the like represent a distinctly masculine take on the notion of artistic self-identity, one that Gentileschi significantly chose to bypass. Instead, she generated a series of much more playful images, all of which hinge upon the idea of role-playing self-presentation that additionally blurs the boundaries between Gentileschi's 'actual' self-portraits (the *Self-portrait as a Lute Player*) and narrative or devotional paintings that incorporate quasi- or transformational self-projections (*The Conversion of the Magdalene*). This innovative emphasis would not become a major focus again until the works of Rembrandt from the late 1620s onwards.[61] In terms of subsequent artists, we do not encounter a comparable emphasis in the work of a woman artist until that of such Modernist and contemporary artists as Frida Kahlo, Claude Cahun and Cindy Sherman, among others.[62]

In the Baroque period one other example of an artist developing a similar interest in stretching the possibilities of self-portraiture can be cited. This occurs in the work of Salvator Rosa (1615–1673) in Florence in the early 1640s. Rosa offers an interesting point of comparison with Gentileschi more

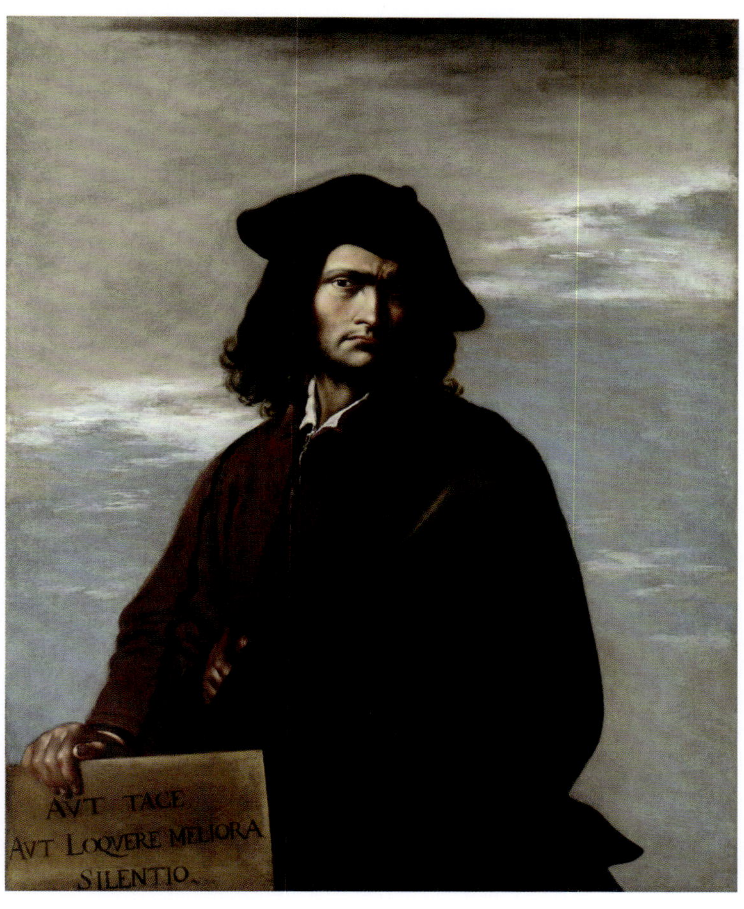

49 Salvator Rosa, *Philosophy*, c.1645, oil on canvas, 116.3 × 94 cm, National Gallery, London, inv. NG4680

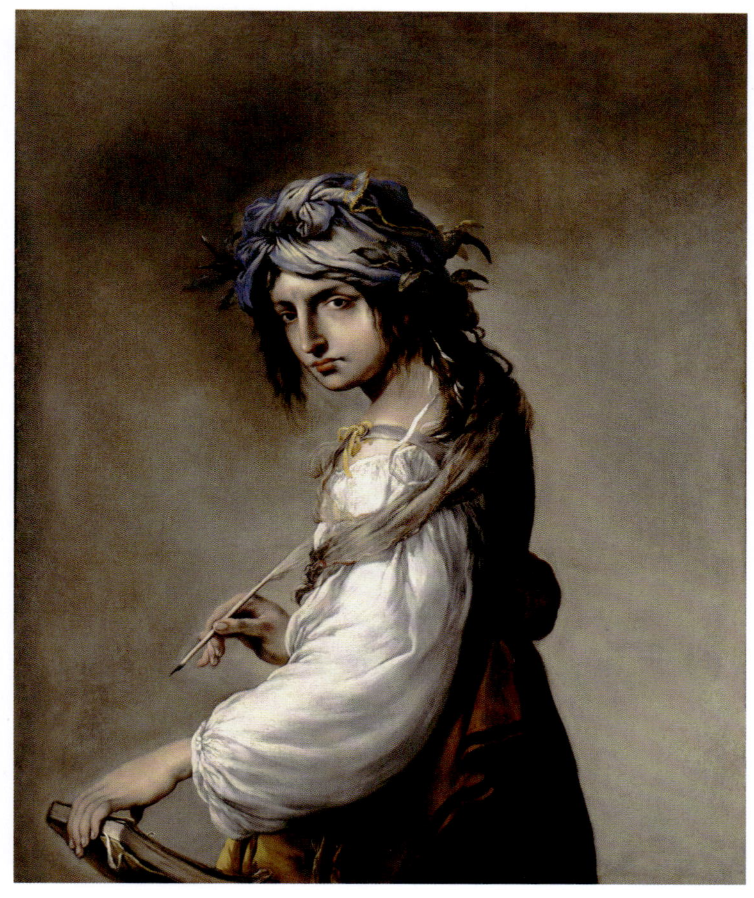

50 Salvator Rosa, *Lucrezia as Poetry*, c.1641, 116.2 × 94.6 cm, Wadsworth Atheneum Museum of Art, Hartford , Conn., The Ella Gallup Sumner and Mary Catlin Sumner Collection Fund, 1956.159

generally. He, too, stands as a self-consciously independent, outsider figure who experienced difficulties in conforming to the conventional expectations of Baroque artistic practice. His difficulties in fitting in, however, did not result from his gender but from his proto-Romantic understanding of the role of the artist, combined with his frustrated desire to be recognised not so much for his landscape paintings – for which he was successful – as for his history paintings – for which he was not.[63]

Unsatisfied with his initial career in Naples in the early 1630s, Rosa relocated to Rome, where he was subsequently forced to depart for Florence as a result of a theatrical performance in the summer of 1639 in which he seriously offended Bernini and his entourage.[64] In Florence, he was able to realise his aspirations to present himself as an artist of significant intellectual ambition. This he achieved particularly as a result of his involvement in a number of the private intellectual academies of the day. Encouraged by these higher-order associations, Rosa then created a number of disguised portraits, in which he proclaimed his new identity as an innovative philosopher artist. In one of them, he addresses the viewer as a personification of the very essence of Philosophy, complete with a mildly threatening sign displaying the pithy Pythagorean aphorism 'Keep silent, unless your speech is better than silence' (fig. 49).[65] In a related work, he depicted his mistress, Lucrezia, as the muse of poetry (fig. 50). The latter image seems especially close to Gentileschi's Florentine self-portraits, as

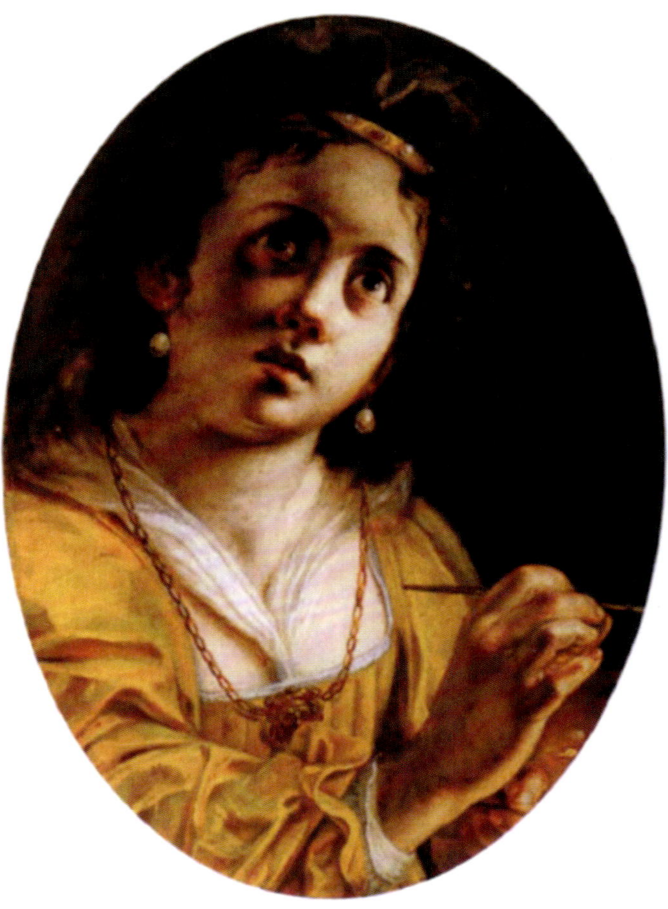

51 ?Artemisia Gentileschi, *Allegory of Painting*, c.1610–17, oil on panel, 33.9 × 24.3 cm, current whereabouts unknown

well as to her depictions of herself as the personification of Painting (discussed further in Chapter 11), even down to its mirroring of the iconography of the unruly freedom of Gentileschi's hair.

One other image should be cited here in the context of this consideration of Gentileschi's development of a personal iconography. This is an enigmatic and little-studied painting, at one stage in a private Brazilian collection but whose current whereabouts are unknown. It depicts an allegory of Painting whose features seem, once again, very reminiscent of those of Gentileschi (fig. 51). Two suggestions have been put forward to account for this work. One is that the painting may be a very early Roman-period self-portrait by Gentileschi that is possibly identifiable with a work mentioned in an early inventory reference that was published in 1992 by Maria Lucrezia Vicini. This inventory lists twelve artworks owned by a certain Alessandro Biffi in Rome that Biffi transferred to the Veralli family in 1637 to liquidate a debt on his rented accommodation. The works then passed into the Spada collection through the marriage of Marchesa Maria Veralli to Orazio Spada. In this way, the collections of the Galleria Spada in Rome came to be enriched by the addition of Orazio Gentileschi's *David Contemplating the Head of Goliath*, together with two paintings by Artemisia: the *Madonna and Child* of 1608–10 (fig. 11) and a *St Cecilia*, dated variously to Artemisia's early Roman years or to her subsequent Florentine period.[66] Biffi's list of artworks transferred to the Veralli also contains a reference to 'Two small ovals with two heads depicting Painting and Poetry by the hand of Artemisia.' Patrizia Cavazzini and Judith Mann, among others, have tentatively associated this citation with the *Allegory of Painting* – although, if so, the provenance sequence outlining how this painting passed from the Spada collection to the Brazilian collection and its current location-unknown status remains to be clarified.[67]

If this latter hypothesis is correct, then this painting should probably be dated as a very early production executed prior to Gentileschi's relocation to Florence in 1613. This would make it a forerunner, then, to the more fully developed Florentine works discussed in this chapter. An alternative suggestion has also been advanced, however, that the painting may have been conceived as a homage to Artemisia by another artist during a later period. If this were so, then the painting may instead be identified as one of the earliest instances of the dissemination of her image by artists other than herself. Most recent commentators have tended to favour the first hypothesis. I would, nonetheless, argue tentatively in favour of the second, at least until such time as the painting comes to light in order for it to be studied in greater depth.[68] Both Garrard and R. Ward Bissell have also rejected the attribution of this painting to Gentileschi (with Ann Sutherland Harris additionally expressing doubts[69]). The first two authors have further suggested the possibility that the panel might be attributable instead to an admittedly little-known artist named Giovanni Battista Guidoni, who worked on the Casa Buonarroti commission alongside Gentileschi (although Garrard adds yet further to this the possibility that it might alternatively have been by Sigismondo Coccopani). Either way, the painting represents another piece of the puzzle that reinforces the highly experimental nature of Gentileschi's production of self-referential paintings during this period.

CONCLUSION: FROM THE MIRROR TO THE BLADE

Gentileschi's radical reimagining of herself as a series of role-playing characters boldly acting out new identities within the reflected microcosm of her own paintings represented only part of the picture of what made her Florentine years so successful in professional terms. In Rome, she and her father had attempted to launch her as an independent artist on the basis of her ability to invent tour-de-force expressions of intensely dramatic history paintings. Allori's *Judith* may have led her, in the years that followed, down other avenues of self-expression. Yet the central challenge remained of how best to consolidate her reputation as a history painter now that she had made the transition in Florence into being recognised as an increasingly successful independent painter on her own terms.

It was inevitable, therefore, that Gentileschi would revisit the subject of Judith as part of her search for a signature *istoria* on which further to stake her claims to artistic distinction. This theme had already offered her a fundamentally important framework for working through her father's influence by first copying and then creatively adapting his workshop model. This had led her, in turn, to the creation of independently realised compositions that were every bit the equal of both his work as well as that of her other, artistic father figure, Caravaggio. It was natural, therefore, that Artemisia would now turn, during the remainder of her Florentine residence, to reconceptualise the subject of Judith and Holofernes into one of the most distinctive subject specialisations of her career.

6

'No little horror'

REINVENTING *JUDITH AND HOLOFERNES* FOR THE MEDICI

INTRODUCTION
ARTEMISIA'S FLORENTINE *JUDITHS*: A RETURN TO THE SCENE OF THE CRIME

Much of Gentileschi's Florentine output awaits further research and discovery. A Medici inventory of 1619, for example, refers to a 'Bath of Diana with various nymphs and nudes, life size, by Artemisia Lomi painter'. This may well have been the largest and most ambitious painting of Gentileschi's career up to that point. It is said to have measured 5 by 4 1/3 braccia – and thus around 3 metres high by 2.5 metres across – and is also described in a subsequent inventory as including no fewer than eight figures.[1] Even at this early stage of her career, then, Gentileschi was already on the way to establishing her reputation as a specialist in monumental history paintings featuring prominent female nudes and on such subjects as *Susanna and the Elders*, the *Bath of Bathsheba* and *Galatea*, with all of which she would become closely associated in the 1630s and 1640s.

More unexpected is Filippo Baldinucci's claim towards the end of the century to have seen a painting by her in the Palazzo Pitti which he describes as 'a very large work [representing] the Rape of Persephone with a great number of figures made in very good style'.[2] In October 1614, Gentileschi had received an ounce of ultramarine from the Medici payroll which was said to be for three unspecified paintings.[3] One wonders if

FACING PAGE Artemisia Gentileschi, *Judith Slaying Holofernes* (detail of fig. 56)

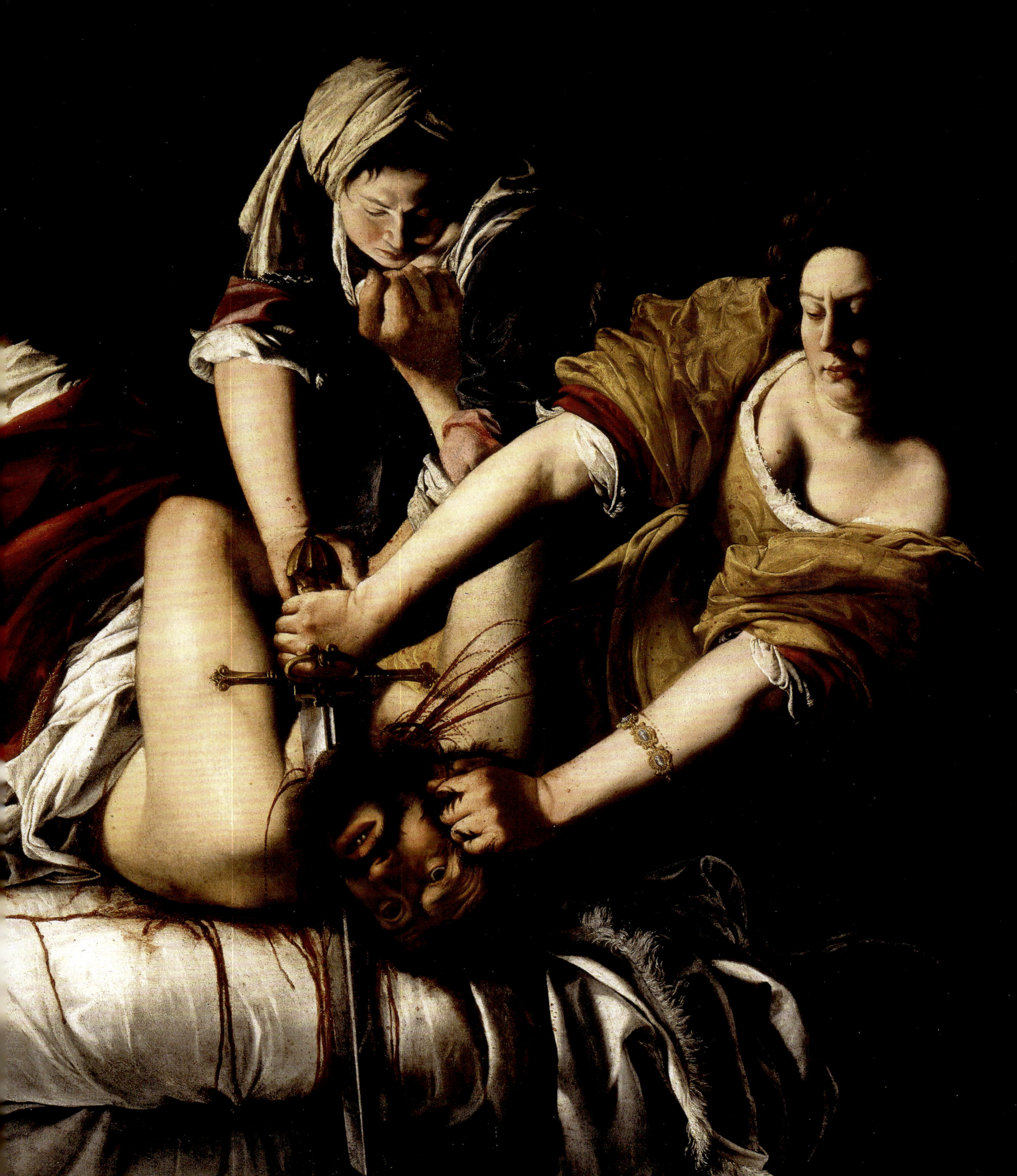

the *Bath of Diana* and *Rape of Persephone* might have constituted two of those three works. If so, it seems reasonable to connect these two paintings, in turn, with a further outlay of one and a half ounces of ultramarine that Gentileschi received from the Medici in January 1620. This disbursement is identified as being for a painting of Hercules.[4] Yet this painting seems not to have been completed in Florence, since it is likely the one referred to in a letter of 10 February 1620, in which Gentileschi informed the Grand Duke of her decision to relocate to Rome while promising to complete the one outstanding painting that she still had on the books. She promised to send this work from Rome within two months of her departure (although whether she ever actually completed the job remains uncertain).[5]

In later years, Gentileschi would receive two separate commissions for large paintings of *Hercules and Omphale*. Given her tendency throughout her career to repeat and adapt her earlier compositions, it seems highly probable that the Medici commission of January 1620 would have also been for a *Hercules and Omphale*.[6] Such a subject would have fitted in perfectly, moreover, with the previously mentioned paintings of the *Bath of Diana* (that is, *Diana and Actaeon*), and the *Rape of Persephone*. It seems reasonable to regard the *Hercules and Omphale*, therefore, as the last instalment in a series of three grand, mythological paintings devoted to the eternal battle between the sexes. If so, this would also provide further confirmation of Gentileschi's early specialisation in *series* of works dedicated to heroic and/or mythological female protagonists, something that she would also become better known for during the 1630s and 1640s. Finally, and at the other end of the spectrum, a small work on copper of *St Apollonia* is listed in the Medici Villa del Poggio Imperiale in 1625.[7] This seems likely to have been yet another version of the disguised self-portrait paintings discussed in the previous chapter.

JUDITH WITH HER MAIDSERVANT

In Florence, Gentileschi decided to rework some of the key compositions that she had helped to produce during her years in Rome. Among these was a refashioning of her earlier workshop copy after Orazio's *Judith with her Maidservant* in a manner that liberated it from its earlier dependence upon Orazio's model and made it synonymous with her own increasingly distinctive manner.

The prototype for the new *Judith with her Maidservant* in the Palazzo Pitti (fig. 52) is the painting in the National Museum of Art, Architecture and Design, Oslo (fig. 26), usually attributed to Orazio. In the discussion in Chapter 3 (p. 52), I followed Papi's lead in tentatively reassigning the canvas as Artemisia's workshop copy after another painting by Orazio of the same subject that had, itself, become embroiled in the allegations made during the course of the rape trial in 1612 (fig. 25). In considering the differences between Orazio's prototype and Artemisia's version now in Oslo, I concluded that Artemisia's painting should be more correctly identified as a creative adaptation of her father's original rather than a mere, slavish copy.

This process is continued in the Pitti canvas, a comparison of which with the Oslo prototype makes it clear that, in the Pitti painting, Artemisia sought to improve upon the minor shortcomings in the earlier composition which were the result of her relative inexperience at that stage of her career. One of the problems with the Oslo *Judith*, for example, is the slight sense of spatial awkwardness and vacuity that seems attributable to the process involved in copying across the portrait-format composition of Orazio's *Judith* into a landscape format (see figs 25 and 26). The figures in the Oslo painting appear too small for the expanded space in which they have been placed. By contrast, the Pitti composition returns the picture to its original portrait format, while cropping the image yet further. This tightens the focus and intensifies the painting's overriding impression of claustrophobic drama. The walls seem now literally to have closed in on the beleaguered duo of Judith and Abra.[8]

Judith and Abra's spatial relationship to each other has also been improved upon in the Palazzo Pitti canvas. The Oslo composition positions the two figures in a bas relief arrangement so that both remain more or less parallel to the picture plane. The Pitti canvas, by contrast, adds a heightened degree of swing and torsion into the composition. Abra now pivots her head and right shoulder outwards towards the threat emanating from beyond the visual field, while the lower part of

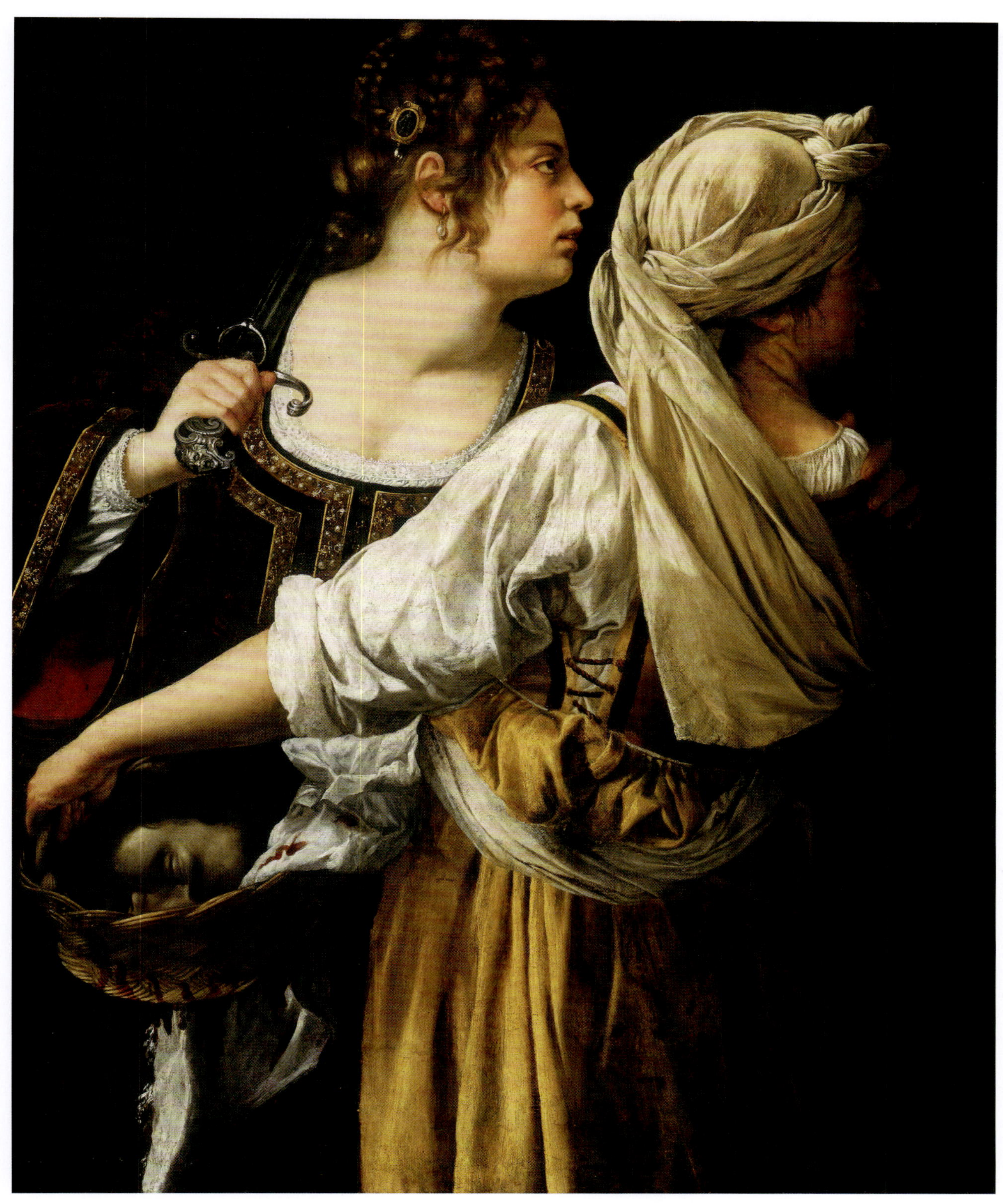

52 Artemisia Gentileschi, *Judith and her Maidservant with the Head of Holofernes*, c.1618–19, oil on canvas, 114 × 93.5 cm, Galleria Palatina, Palazzo Pitti, Florence

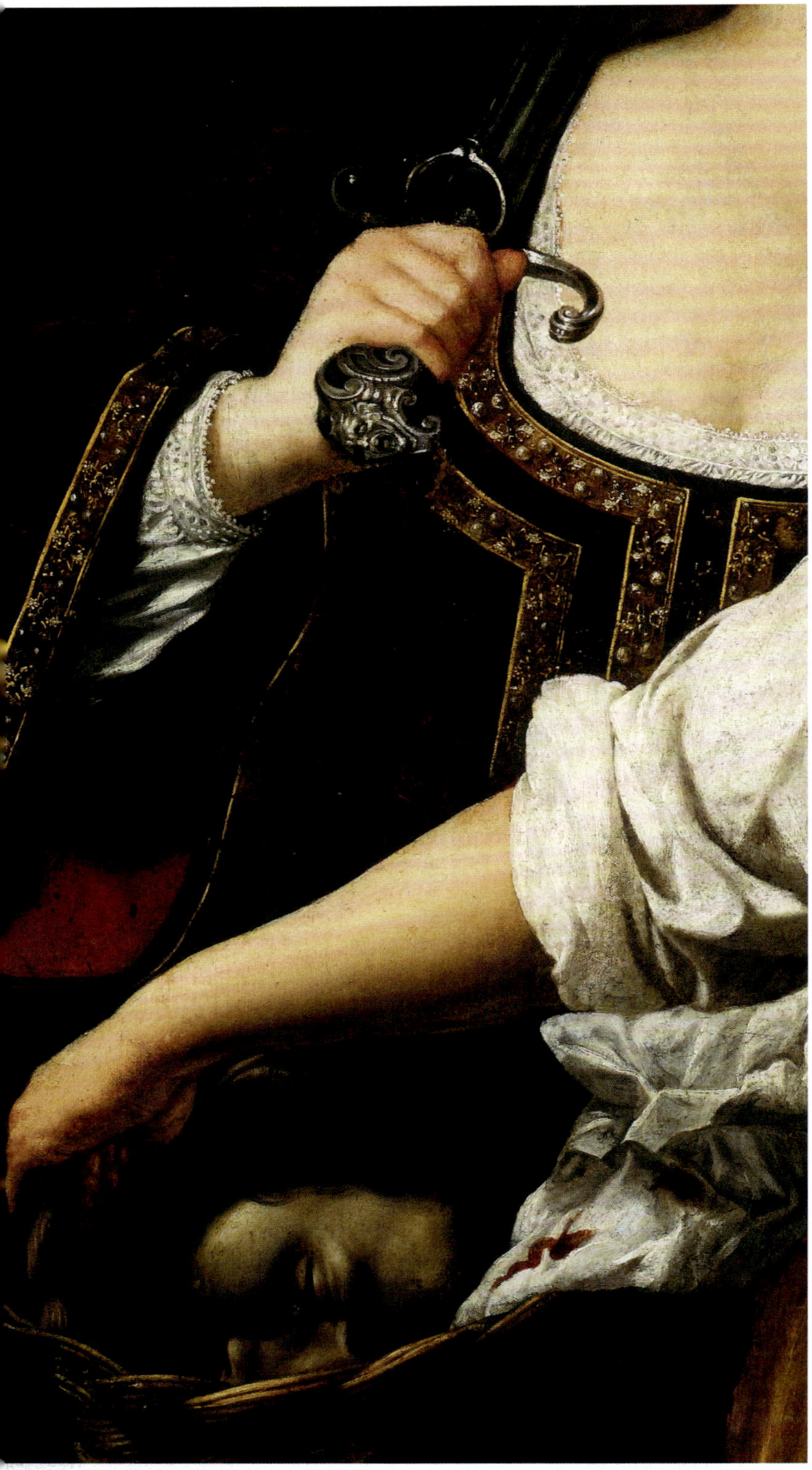

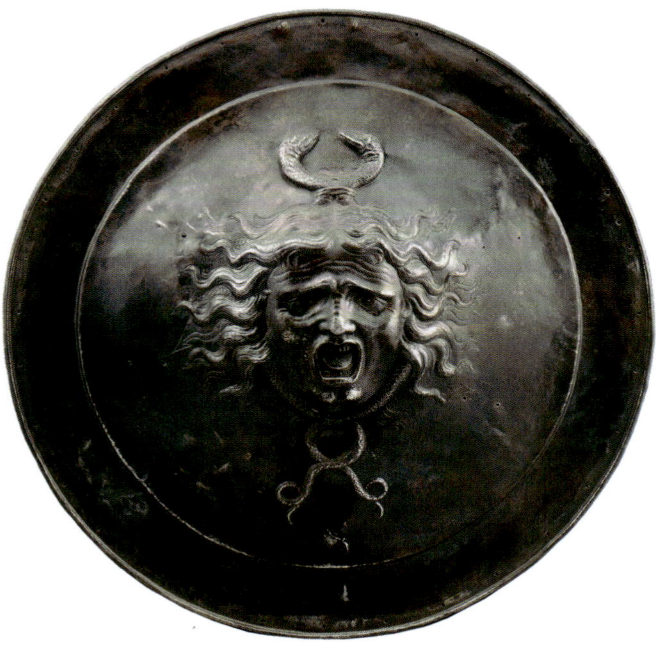

53 Milanese workshop, *Shield with the Head of the Medusa*, 1570–80, embossed, carved and chiselled steel, 60 cm diameter, Museo Nazionale del Bargello, Florence (formerly Medici armoury)

her body bends in the opposite direction to take the weight of Holofernes' head. Judith, likewise, no longer stands passively gazing into space; instead, she leans forward intently, while at the same time holding Abra back – an entirely different gesture than in the Oslo prototype. The two figures now mirror each other's gaze as, alone within the Assyrian camp and yet united together in their continued resolve, they choose to confront their enemies head on.

The Pitti canvas also highlights the intense concentration on the violence of Holofernes' decapitation that was noted above as an innovative feature of the Oslo *Judith*, intended by Artemisia to increase its dramatic impact and to create a point of divergence from the workshop model of Orazio's *Judith*. The Pitti *Judith* takes this approach further. It manifests an even greater emphasis on the blood oozing through the wickerwork basket and onto the white sheet cradling Holofernes' head.

The composition's mood of dramatic horror has also been heightened with the addition of a telling detail in the form

Artemisia Gentileschi, *Judith and her Maidservant with the Head of Holofernes* (detail of fig. 52)

of a screaming grotesque head that has been etched into the steel of the pommel of Judith's sword. This face seems to be gazing directly at Holofernes, thus setting up a contrast between the extreme animation of the figure's expression and the eternally mute silence of the head. It also provides another local point of reference to the above-mentioned Medici armoury in the Uffizi, since it quotes the screaming head in Caravaggio's *Head of the Medusa* shield (fig. 31), as well as the armorial tradition upon which Caravaggio drew when devising his shield.[9] This tradition – examples of which featured prominently in the Medici collection – constituted a highly fashionable trend in late sixteenth-century luxury armour production. The Negroli family workshop in Milan was especially renowned for its ornamental, circular parade shields, which were often surmounted with depictions of the severed head of Medusa in order to increase their visual impact and impress a sense of terror on the enemy (fig. 53).[10]

The small, grotesque face of the Pitti *Judith*, with its multi-layered references to the splendours of the Medici armoury, helps to lift the painting from its original dependence upon Orazio's model and from the Roman Caravaggesque context more broadly. It inclines the canvas yet more specifically towards the sophisticated, courtly atmosphere of the Florentine Baroque. So, too, does the more opulent costume worn by Judith. More specifically still, Judith's elaborately braided hair, decorated luxuriously with jewels, links itself to the Florentine visual tradition of depictions of refined female figures adorned with richly embellished hairstyles that constitute a hallmark feature of Tuscan Mannerism, from Michelangelo's *Ideal Heads* to Bronzino's Chapel of Eleonora in the Palazzo Vecchio. The Pitti *Judith*'s ability to rearticulate this prominent stream of sixteenth-century Florentine imagery would have immediately registered with contemporary viewers.

The Pitti *Judith* bears eloquent testimony, then, to Gentileschi's ability to reinvent her earlier compositions in order to suit new cultural contexts. The results speak for themselves. While not reaching the heights of universal acclaim enjoyed by Allori's *Judith and Holofernes*, the immediate popularity of her Pitti *Judith* is attested to by the presence of numerous copies circulating on the art market and in various public and private collections. In 1991, Roberto Contini was able to point to seven of these, while Bissell added around a half dozen more – an impressive indication of the growing esteem for Gentileschi's increasingly recognisable trademark style.[11]

JUDITH SLAYING HOLOFERNES

It was inevitable that Gentileschi would return to the unfinished business of the fundamental achievement of her Roman years, the *Judith Slaying Holofernes* now in Naples (fig. 29), notwithstanding the significant acclaim already awarded to Allori's *Judith*. Forced to leave this painting behind in her father's workshop when she left Rome at the beginning of 1613, Artemisia was deprived of the opportunity to receive any recognition (or financial recompense) for what she can only have considered to have been one of the major achievements of her career. It makes sense, therefore, that she would have at some stage considered it strategically advantageous to rework this composition afresh for a Florentine audience. The revised version that she produced for the Medici is probably identifiable with a reference in an inventory of 1638 to a painting of this subject at the Palazzo Pitti that was transferred to the Uffizi in 1774 (fig. 56).[12] It has been dated by scholars variously from early in her Florentine career to the suggestion that it was still to be produced at the time of her departure for Rome in 1620. Bissell, Cropper and Garrard's consensus that the canvas is to be situated among the last works executed in Florence for the Medici seems the most reasonable proposal, despite the tendency towards an earlier dating that has made its way into the literature more recently.[13]

The discussion in Chapter 3 (pp. 52–57) of the first version of the *Judith Slaying Holofernes* underscored its compromised technical condition and the fact of its having been cut down at some stage along the top and on the left-hand side by what appears to have been a substantial margin. An early copy after the *Judith Slaying Holofernes* in Milan is helpful to consider in this context (fig. 54).[14] It might document the original appearance of the first *Judith*, since it includes on its left side the additional elements of a candle and a bedside table that are absent from both the Naples and Florence *Judiths*. If these details do confirm the original appearance of the Naples *Judith* prior to its being cut down on the left, then this suggests that

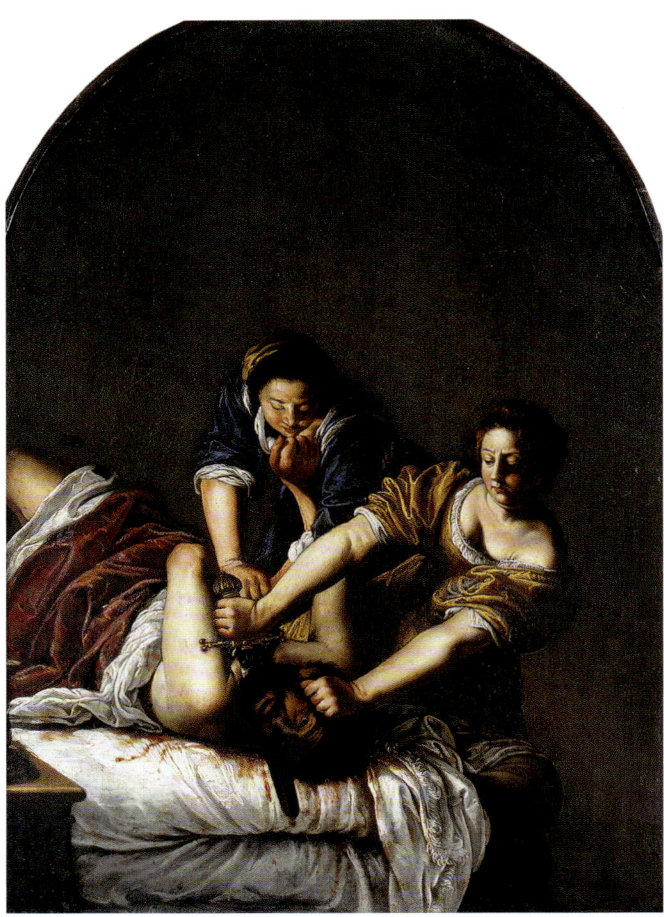

54 After Artemisia Gentileschi, *Judith Slaying Holofernes*, oil on slate, 32 × 22 cm, Quadreria dell'Arcivescovado, Milan, before 1650

Gentileschi made substantial modifications to the second version of the *Judith* when she came to rework the composition in Florence, and that, in adapting the prototype across to its new Florentine context, she decided to edit these details out of the new version. In so doing, she improved upon the original, since she reduced its essential elements down to a more clear and concise composition.

The Uffizi *Judith* now reads as a giant, compressed W radiating out from the central column created by Holofernes' and Abra's interlinked bodies, with Holofernes' legs and Judith's body forming two diagonal spokes branching outwards from either side. The compositional simplification and the better state of preservation of the Uffizi *Judith* – relative to her first treatment of the subject now in Naples – enable the figures to project themselves more forcefully out of the foreground plane, almost as if they were a singular organism emerging out of a tangled snarl of arms, legs and hands. This more overt focusing on the piling up of the protagonists' intertwined bodies parallel to the picture plane once again brings to mind the local traditions of Tuscan Mannerism. In particular, Rosso Fiorentino's *Moses Defends the Daughters of Jethro* (fig. 55), formerly belonging to the French king Francis I but owned by the Medici in the seventeenth century, shares with the Uffizi *Judith* an emphasis upon a comparably entwined combination of writhing figures, the inspiration for which goes back ultimately to Michelangelo's *Battle of Cascina*.[15]

55 Rosso Fiorentino, *Moses Defends the Daughters of Jethro*, 1523–27, oil on canvas, 160 × 117 cm, Galleria degli Uffizi, Florence

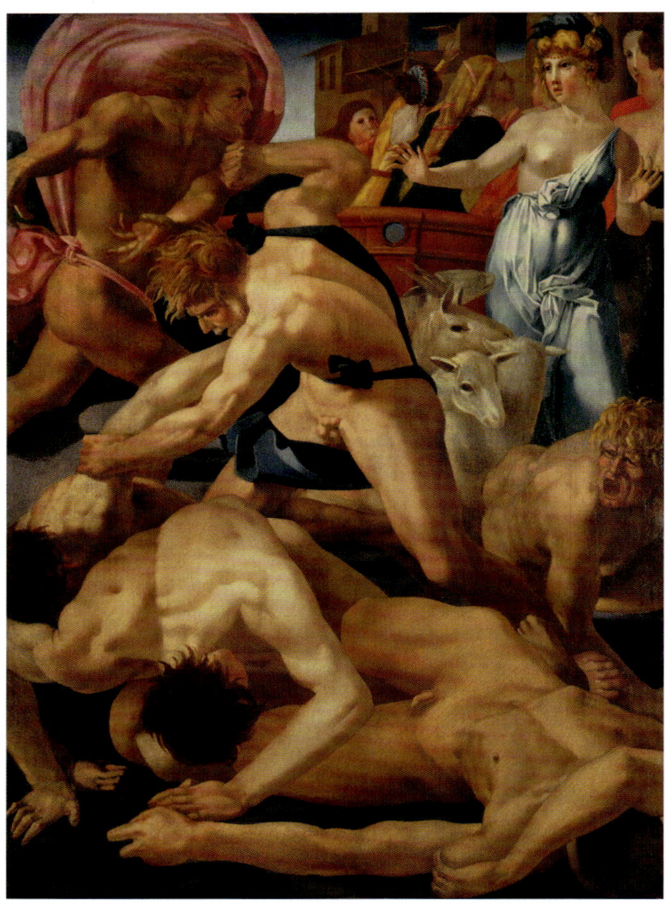

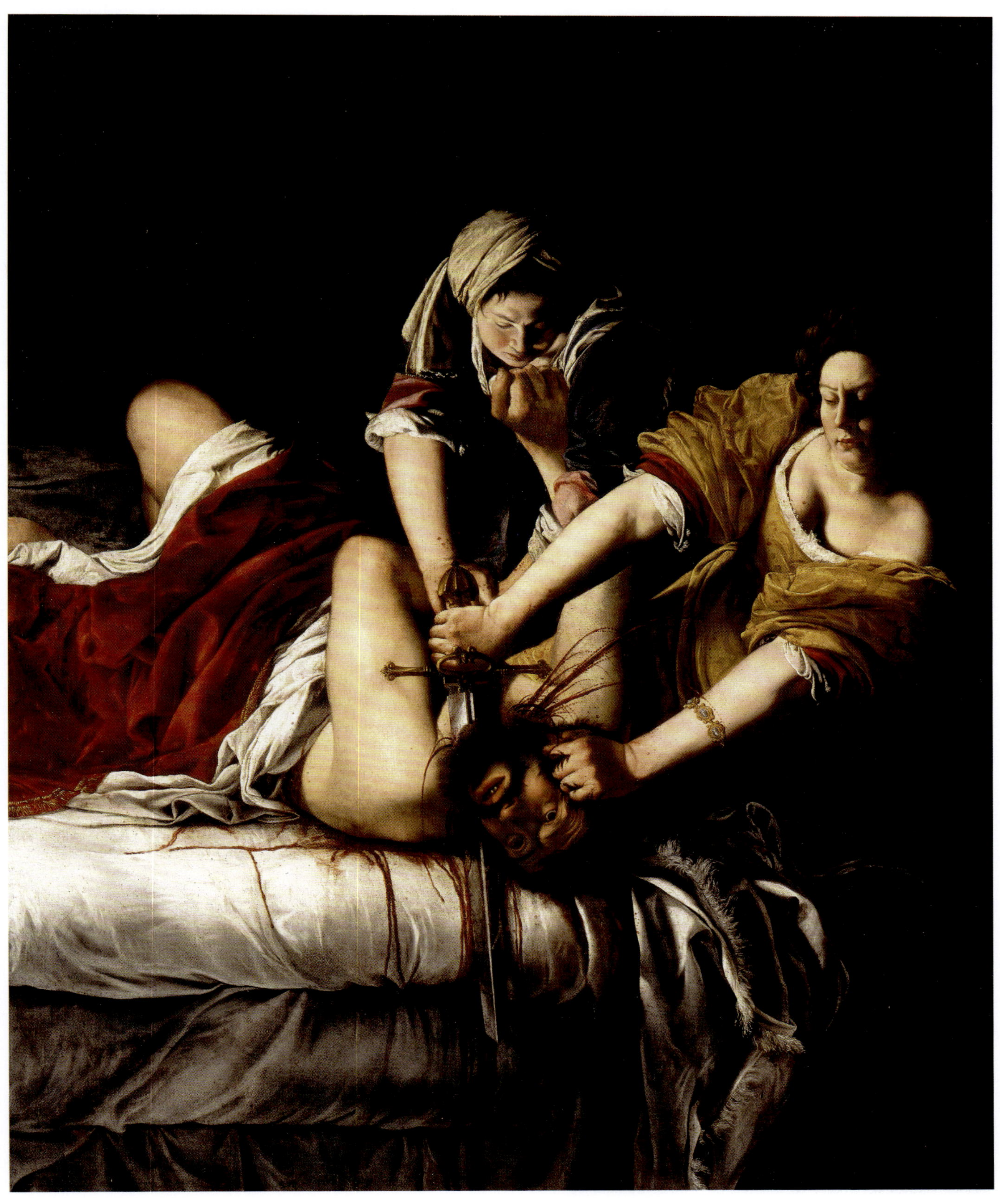

56 Artemisia Gentileschi, *Judith Slaying Holofernes*, signed on the bed at bottom right, *c.*1620, oil on canvas, 198 × 160 cm, Galleria degli Uffizi, Florence

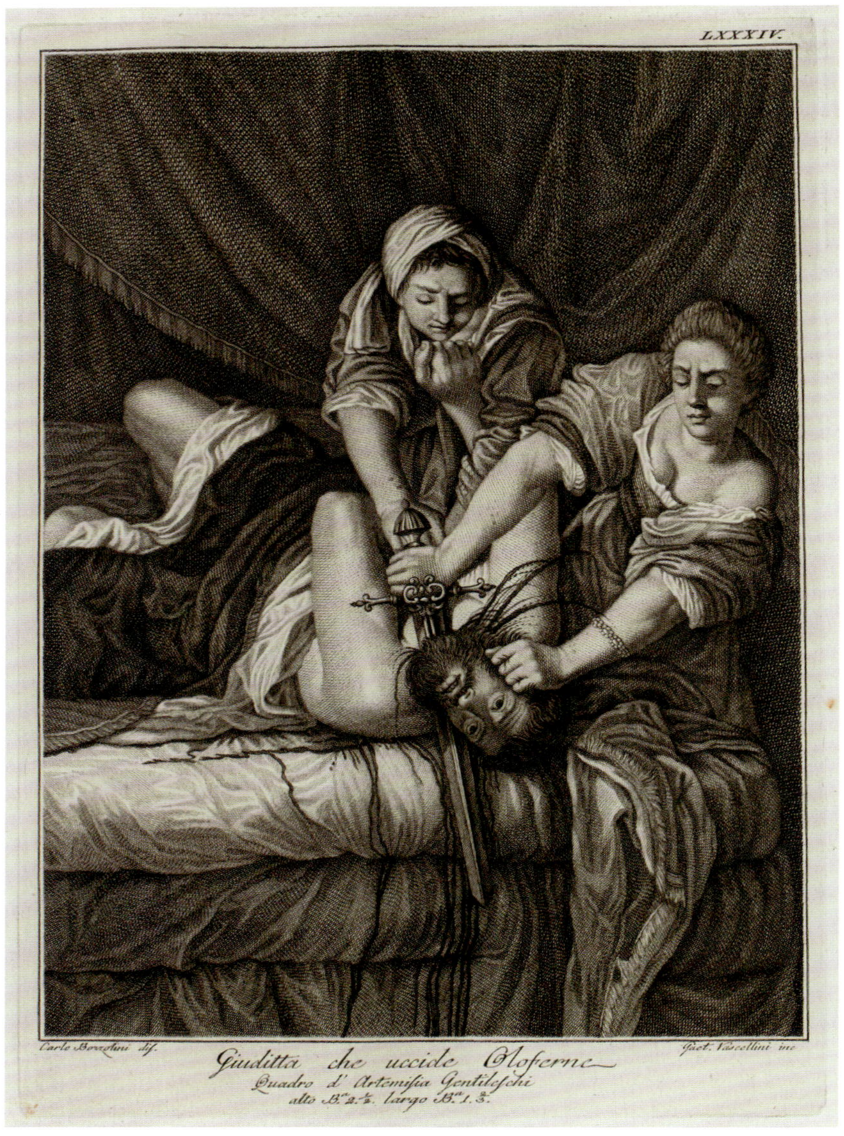

57 Carlo Bozzolini and Gaetano Vascellini after Artemisia Gentileschi, *Judith Slaying Holofernes*, 1791, engraving and etching in black on blue laid paper. 35.8 × 25.4 cm, from Marco Lastri, *Etruria Pittrice*, Florence

Rosso's foreground figures crumple up against the picture plane. Gentileschi's figures, by contrast, dynamically project out of it. It is hard to appreciate this aspect of the painting today as a result of the deterioration of its background over time. The work's original appearance can be seen more clearly in an eighteenth-century reproductive print (fig. 57). Like some hapless fish flopping off a fishmonger's stall, Holofernes would originally have appeared to be almost sliding off the bed and onto our laps in his impotent struggle to resist the blade.

The comparison between the Naples and Florence *Judiths* has not proved entirely satisfying to all commentators. In particular, John T. Spike, in a review of the 1991 exhibition at the

Casa Buonarroti, Florence, devoted to Artemisia, expressed his concerns about the way in which the second, Uffizi version of the subject seemed, in his opinion, to 'misinterpret' the distinctive features of the original composition. The broader argument that followed from this was his assertion that Orazio was, in fact, largely responsible for the first *Judith* while the Uffizi version was to be seen as a pallid misrepresentation by Artemisia of the 'original' principles of Orazio's invented composition:

> the second, Uffizi, version of the Judith is not merely a reprise in fancy dress: it is the Naples composition seen through the wrong end of a telescope. The Capodimonte Judith confronts us with an urgency, a terribilità, and an obtrusive physicality that are worthy of Caravaggio; its inky shadows are a metaphor for premeditated murder. There is no need to detail the contrasting effect of the Uffizi repetition in which the gratuitous spatterings of red paint look like special effects, not blood . . . Perhaps the chief merit of this exhibition is that it has made it possible for the first time to compare the Capodimonte and Uffizi Judiths side-by-side. Is it possible that Artemisia's removal from Rome to Florence rendered her incapable of understanding her previous work?[16]

These comments formed part of the author's more general attempt to reassign authorship of the 1610 *Susanna and the Elders* to Orazio rather than to Artemisia. This, then, represents a further manifestation of the same critically revisionist process of depriving Artemisia of the authorship of another of her most renowned and iconic compositions and reallocating it to her father, on the basis that Artemsia was 'too young' and too immature to be able to produce such accomplished works.

This argument has not been generally well received by commentators. It has been, for the most part, ignored in the subsequent literature and is not even mentioned, for example, as a live issue requiring notice in the catalogue entries written for both works on the occasion of the exhibition of Artemisia's work at the National Gallery in London in 2020.[17] It is, nonetheless, important to remind ourselves of this viewpoint, since it speaks to a general mindset – still evident in the literature today – that finds commentators struggling at times to reconcile the stylistic shifts made by Artemisia at various stages of her career (an issue to be addressed more directly in relation to the later, Neapolitan paintings). More specifically, it reflects the common perception – dare I say prejudice? – that only Artemisia's first, intensely Caravaggesque paintings are to be considered worthy of being judged as the true masterpieces of her career.

The current study seeks, instead, to project a renewed emphasis on the continued *evolution* of Gentileschi's style throughout her career, as she sought to adapt herself and her art strategically, in response to the changing tastes, fashions and cultural traditions with which she came into contact. In terms of the two versions of *Judith Slaying Holofernes*, I would, accordingly, assert that the substantial differences between them do not need to be explained away by the extreme and unnecessary proposal of interpreting them as the work of two hands. Their differences grow, instead, out of a natural process of continuous artistic revision and critical reassessment that characterises Gentileschi's career as a whole. At this stage, she was concerned to demonstrate to her new Florentine public her transformation from her initially raw, first-wave Roman Caravaggesque style to a much more subtle, and supple, blend of influences. In this sense, the Uffizi *Judith* stands out as a forthright declaration of Gentileschi's intention to present herself now as a celebrated exponent of the most sophisticated and up-to-date trends of the Florentine Baroque.

'WITHOUT POLLUTION': RUBENS'S BLOOD AND HOLOFERNES' LUST IN THE UFFIZI *JUDITH SLAYING HOLOFERNES*

Returning to the issue of the differences between the depiction of blood in the Naples and Uffizi *Judith*s, I would contend that the Uffizi *Judith*'s increased emphasis on the outpouring of blood represents much more than mere 'gratuitous spatterings of red paint', as suggested by Spike. Rather, I would read this element as forming a vital component of Gentileschi's radical rethinking of the composition more generally.

Cornelis Galle I's *Great Judith* engraving of around 1616 after Rubens's *Judith Beheading Holofernes* seems to have provided the impetus for Gentileschi's startling reconceptualisation of the depiction of blood in the second *Judith* (fig. 58).[18] The print influenced Gentileschi's composition on a number of levels, including, for example, the motif of Holofernes' outstretched arm becoming interlaced between Judith's and Abra's arms, a detail that is not otherwise encountered in Caravaggio's model. One cannot also fail to note Rubens's highly distinctive motif of the jets of Holofernes' blood. In choosing to accentuate this spectacular visual effect in the second, Uffizi version, Gentileschi radically alters the depiction of violence within the subject as a whole and in a manner that adds further nuance to the painting's multiple levels of meaning and association.

In the first *Judith*, the copious outpouring of Holofernes' blood is confined to his body and the sheets beneath. A barely perceptible stain has started to spread to the left and so has just begun the process of smudging the bed's top sheet. In other respects, though, the blood remains localised in the Naples version, to the extent that the rest of the composition appears strangely untouched by the violence that otherwise pervades it so forcefully. The Uffizi *Judith*, by contrast, rectifies what, with hindsight, must have seemed an obvious omission in the original treatment. Not only does the blood ooze and spread with all the insect-trail-like variation of the first version, it now also spurts forth and cascades outwards with spectacular vigour. This increases the visceral impact of the central motif of the blade itself. One can now apprehend the vitality of the blood gushing freely out of Holofernes' freshly cut veins following the blade's path from left to right. This is contrasted, in turn, with the progressively less intense dribble of spent blood passing from right to left. This contrast in the intensity of the blood flow registers the extent to which the blood is already beginning to empty out of Holofernes' stiffening body as the blade slices its way through his arteries while cleaving towards the right side of his neck.

In the Book of Judith, before leaving Bethulia for the Assyrian camp, Judith had prayerfully entreated the Lord to deliver her from 'strangers who had defiled by their uncleanliness' (9:2). Once back in the city, she proclaimed her victory with a similar metaphor, declaring, 'the Lord hath not suffered me his handmaid to be defiled, but hath brought me back to you without pollution of sin' (13:20). Gentileschi's Uffizi Judith may thus be without sin, yet her body has become literally polluted by Holofernes' profuse bodily outpourings. These have contaminated her otherwise unblemished form – to the extent of spattering her bodice and the exposed top of her right breast. This transferral of blood from one opened-up body to another that remains righteously closed sets up an obvious analogy to the 'uncleanliness' of Holofernes' lustful sexuality. Indeed, there is something especially ejaculatory, it must be said, about the spatter and dribble of the rich, beading claret of Holofernes' blood as it strikes Judith's stomach and runs down her dress.

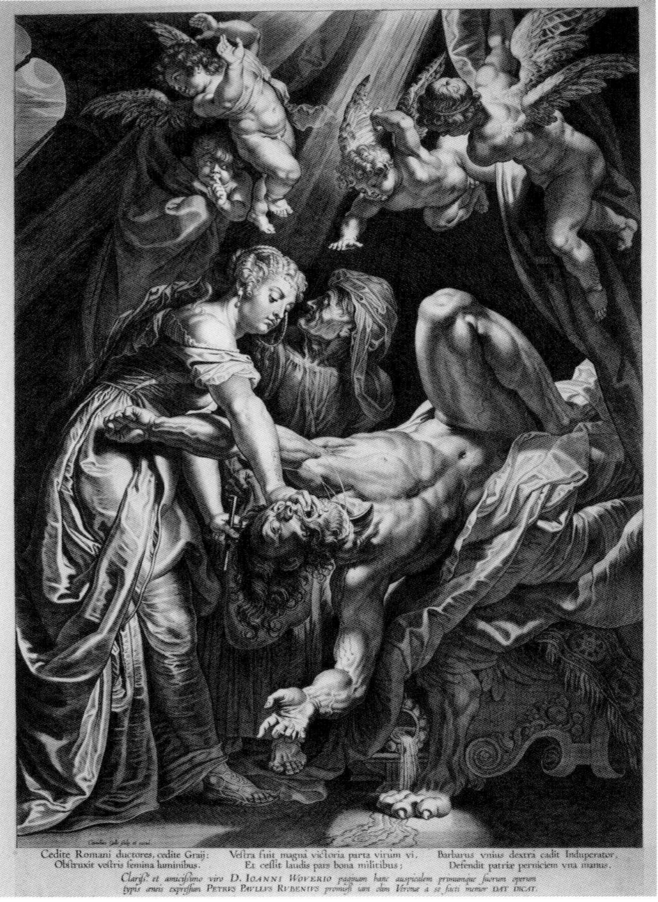

58 Cornelis Galle I after Peter Paul Rubens, *Judith Beheading Holofernes*, c.1616, engraving, 55.2 × 37.9 cm, The Metropolitan Museum of Art, New York, The Elisha Whittelsely Collection, The Elisha Whittelsey Fund, 1951

And yet all this inter-bodily contamination causes no let-up in Judith's resolve. Grimly undaunted, she continues with the blade, while ensuring that she remains as physically distant as possible from the bodily emission to stop herself from either slipping in its wash or from becoming blinded by its spray. This creates an entirely new meaning for Judith's backward leaning pose that Gentileschi had initially extracted from Caravaggio's prototype. Now, rather than merely flinching, as had Caravaggio's Judith, Gentileschi's Judith chooses more mindfully to swerve her body to the right in order to avoid Holofernes' polluted outpourings of death. Gentileschi's critical reinterpretation of this pose in this second version of the subject thus provides further evidence of her ability to rework her earlier compositions in new and critically inventive ways.

One particularly ingenious interpretation of the arcs of blood in the Uffizi *Judith* reads them as a demonstration of Galileo's theory of the parabolic law of projectiles, at that stage not yet published but potentially accessible to Artemisia through his manuscripts – or even from his own conversations with her, given their friendship during this period.[19] Yet such a complex explanation seems unnecessary for a visual effect that appears, in rudimentary form, in the print after Rubens. Moreover, this parabolic effect could have been much more easily observed simply by noting the fiery trails made by the arching flames of fireworks shooting across the night sky, then, as now, a popular feature of Florentine festival culture (fig. 59).

The original slaughter shown in the first version of *Judith Slaying Holofernes* has thus been transformed in the process of its being recast for a new, Florentine audience. Yet it has lost none of its original power in the translation. Instead, it has been successfully transposed to the more elaborate and expanded stage of a festive Medicean courtly setting. To behold the second Uffizi version of *Judith* in this sense is an entirely different viewing experience from the first version. To view the first *Judith* is to witness a foul murder carried out in a Roman basement. To take in the second version, by contrast, is to enjoy an elegant opera set against the glistening backdrop of a nocturnal firework display on the Arno. The result is a painting that manages to be both horrifying and delightful at the same time – a novel and invigorating combination of

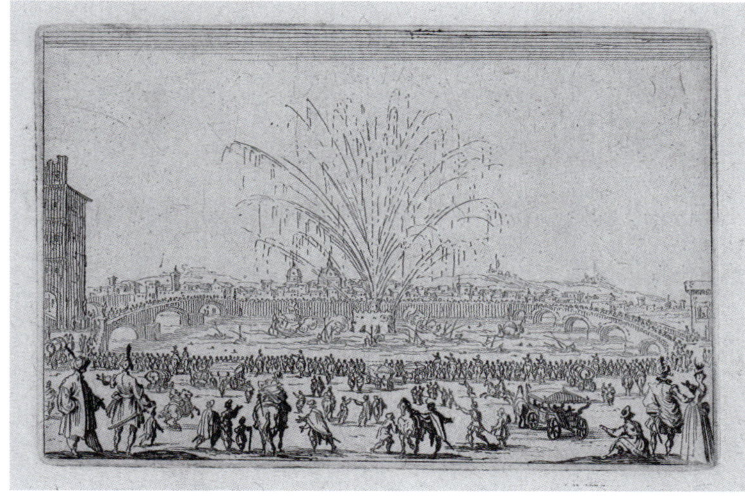

59 Jacques Callot, *Le Feu d'Artifice sur l'Arno (Fireworks on the Arno)*, 1617–20, from *Les Caprices* Series B, The Nancy Set, etching, 5.3 × 7.8 cm, The Metropolitan Museum of Art, New York, Bequest of Edwin De T. Bechtel, 1957

qualities that prompted Baldinucci's observation that 'it merits such worthiness and is so well thought out and so vividly expressed that merely a glance at this painting will incite no little horror'.[20]

CONCLUSION: A RETURN TO ROME, AND THEN BEYOND

Sheila Barker has analysed Gentileschi's recourse, during her Florentine years, to building up extensive lines of credit when acquiring clothing and other household requirements. This forms part of a deeper investigation into the circumstances leading to the artist's hasty departure from the city on 11 February 1620. Barker's broader argument is to rebut the standard account of Gentileschi's withdrawal from Florence as a case of the artist's fleeing impending financial ruin. Instead, Barker stresses the importance of viewing 'Artemisia's financial strategies during the crucial first years of her business . . . in a new light . . . [so that] even her debts, previously interpreted as unambiguous indicators of economic crisis, can now be recognised as signs of her familiarity with vital entrepreneurial tools, and perhaps even as signs of her financial success.'[21]

The resulting analysis offers a useful corrective to the common perception of the artist as a chronically impecunious, economic mis-manager. It helps us to understand, instead, the extent to which she drew on the then widespread credit-culture of Renaissance and Baroque Italy as a basis for developing an economically independent career of her own.

Yet no amount of sugar-coating can hide the precipitous collapse of Gentileschi's reputation and professional situation in early 1620. At this stage, faced with numerous creditors beating on her door, she found herself confronted with the additional threat of a dangerous rumour that was just then beginning to circulate regarding her illicit affair with Maringhi.[22] Her decisive next steps render clear her own feelings regarding how best to respond to these challenges. A day after informing Cosimo II of her intention to leave, she was gone. In her absence, all her remaining goods, including her workshop collateral and personal effects, were sequestered by the officers of the Medici Guardaroba who kept them under lock and key until Maringhi, acting as her Florentine procurator, was eventually required to pay them off on his own credit to the substantial tune of 165 ducats.[23] Artemisia was thus revealed as a chronic defaulter to both the Medici and to the Florentine Accademia del Disegno, who had for some time been arbitrating a growing number of claims surrounding her mounting debts. This would have represented a considerable loss of face, and Gentileschi can only have found the experience deeply humiliating on both a personal and a professional level.

It was an abrupt and calamitous end to what had been building into a highly successful stage of her career.[24] It is striking to note, in this respect, the extent to which Gentileschian elements would become staple features in the visual vernacular of Florentine Baroque painting more generally from the late 1620s onwards. Roberto Contini stresses this point when he notes, 'We do not know of images of Madonnas, saints, half-length, three quarter length or even full length heroines (Magdalene) expressed with parallel pride, a sculptural body and veiledly self-referred in Florence, at least during this period. To be able to see similar paintings we will have to wait until the 1630s, with the work of artists such as Furini, Cesare Dandini and Ficherelli'.[25] A painting such as Francesco Furini's

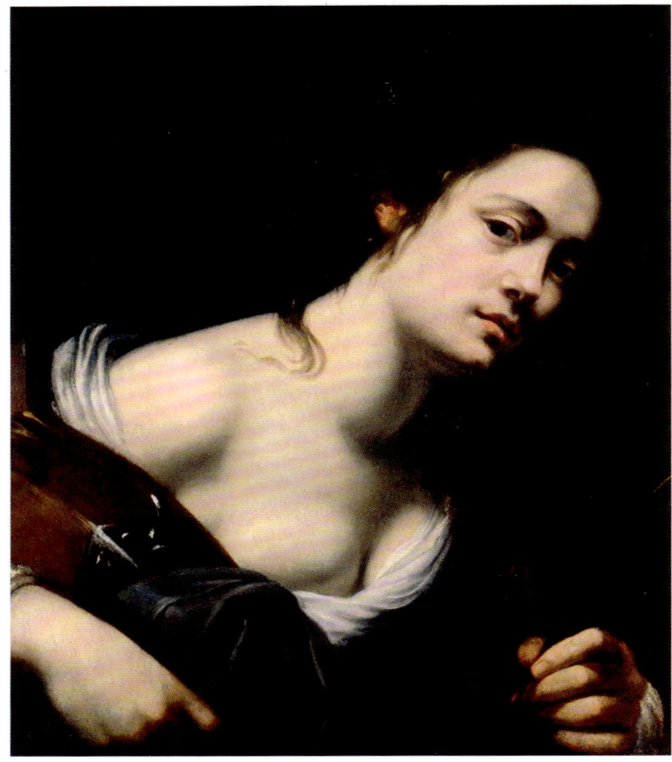

60 Francesco Furini, *St Catherine of Alexandria*, c.1625–30, oil on canvas, 50 × 40 cm, Galleria degli Uffizi, Florence

St Catherine of Alexandria, for example, is unthinkable without the model of Gentileschi's paintings of this subject; so much so, in fact, that it is easy to understand why this canvas was mistakenly attributed to her in the past (fig. 60).[26] The same is true of Cesare Dandini's palpably Gentileschian *Rinaldo and Armida* from the 1630s (fig. 61).[27]

And yet, by the time that these and other paintings can be seen to register the consolidation of the Florentine taste for luxurious renditions of female-orientated themes and protagonists, the artist who had done more than any other to spearhead this taste – to the extent of embodying it in her physical presence as well as in her paintings – was no longer resident in the city. She had returned to Rome in the first instance, then made a trip to Venice and thence, ultimately, to Naples, where she would stay for the remainder of her career, save for a brief journey to assist her father in London in 1639.

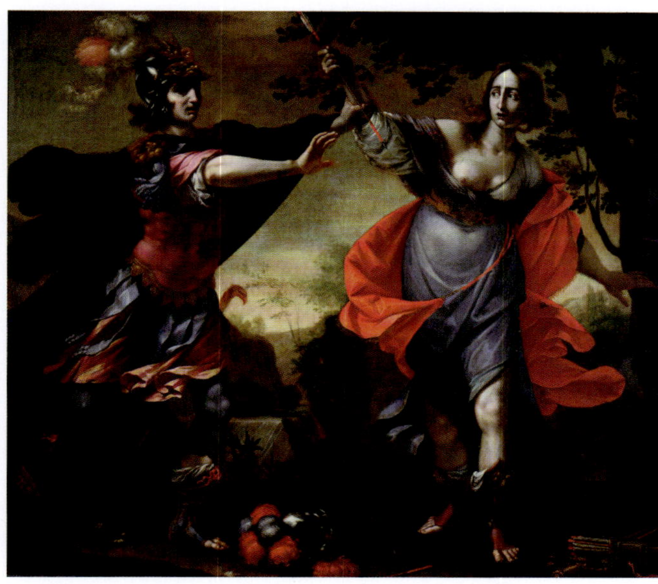

61 Cesare Dandini, *Rinaldo and Armida*, 1635, oil on canvas, 185 × 203 cm, Galleria degli Uffizi, Florence

Another example, then, of bad luck and bad timing in a career that had its fair share of both. It is all too easy, however, to anatomise an artist's career with the benefit of hindsight. Perhaps the move back to Rome and then beyond did Artemisia a service in the long run. It certainly saved her from the danger of becoming complacent within the narrow confines of a more or less static provincial setting, no matter how dazzlingly sophisticated and stimulating this ambience might have been. Instead, the move reinforced a certain restlessness within Gentileschi's persona as well as in her art. Gentileschi would operate from this point on as an artist who was active within a particular artistic scene but, at the same time and in a certain sense, above it. The Artemisia that we shall encounter henceforth, while perfectly ready to identify herself with her native Rome by changing her surname back from Lomi to Gentileschi when it suited her, was, at the same time, increasingly preoccupied with cultivating a perception of herself as functioning on a level that was more akin to that of other, more internationally renowned artists. Aided by her association with influential individuals and with literary academies and other value-adding cultural institutions, she would disseminate this new persona during the next stage of her career in Rome, transforming her personal iconography from the experimental permutations of her Florentine years to a more consistent 'official' image of herself as an internationally orientated, celebrity artist.

PAGE 107 Simon Vouet, *Portrait of Artemisia Gentileschi* (detail of fig. 76)

— PART III —

Acclaiming Artemisia

ROME AND VENICE 1620–1629

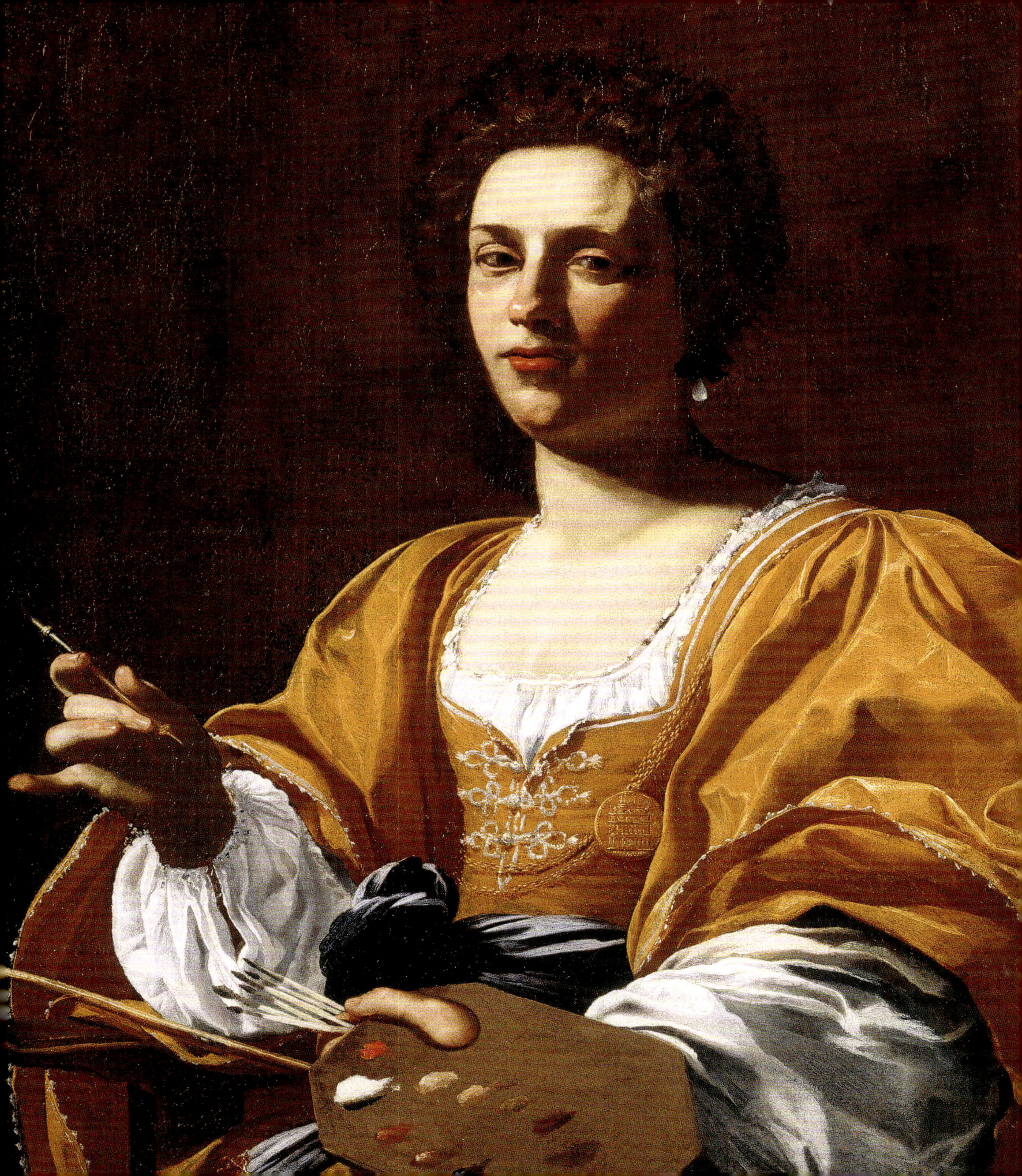

7

Rome, 1620–1627

TRANSFORMING OLD SUBJECTS AND THE CHALLENGE OF PATRONAGE

INTRODUCTION
FROM MARTYR'S PALM TO BABY'S RATTLE, ARTEMISIA GENTILESCHI AND THE UNOFFICIAL PORTRAIT

A shaft of light pierces the shuttered gloom of one of the modest workshop residences of the artists' quarter of Rome. A young painter falls out of bed and crawls over to the breakfast table in an attempt to clear his head of the night before. He can't quite face the mirror yet, so he has the idea instead of fixing onto paper a series of rapid pencil characterisations of the other members of the merry company with whom he had been partying the night before. He dashes off a series of seven informal, half-length portraits that present a vivid snapshot of a closely knit group of foreign artists resident in Rome. These include the Dutch and Flemish Caravaggisti Nicolas Régnier, Dirck van Baburen and Gerrit van Honthorst, and the French landscape painter Claude Lorrain. To each he gives a mildly parodic, caricatural treatment, together with an attribute to help tell them apart. Régnier is a besotted lover clutching a flower to his breast; Claude is a serious drinker examining a frothy glass of beer (fig. 62); Baburen brandishes a flute, thus resembling one of his own paintings of Bacchic revellers.

FACING PAGE Artemisia Gentileschi, *Judith and her Maidservant with the Head of Holofernes* (detail of fig. 69)

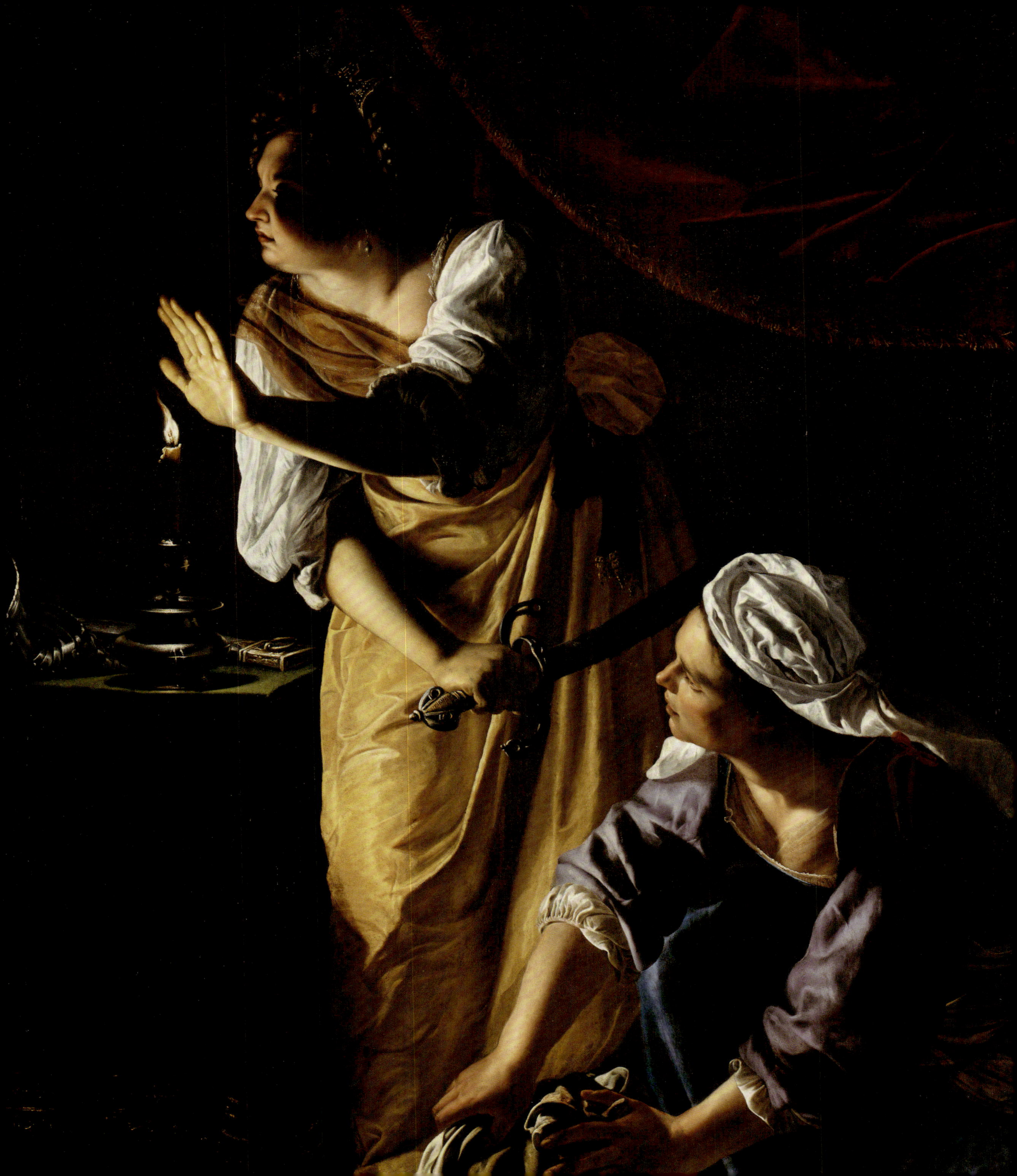

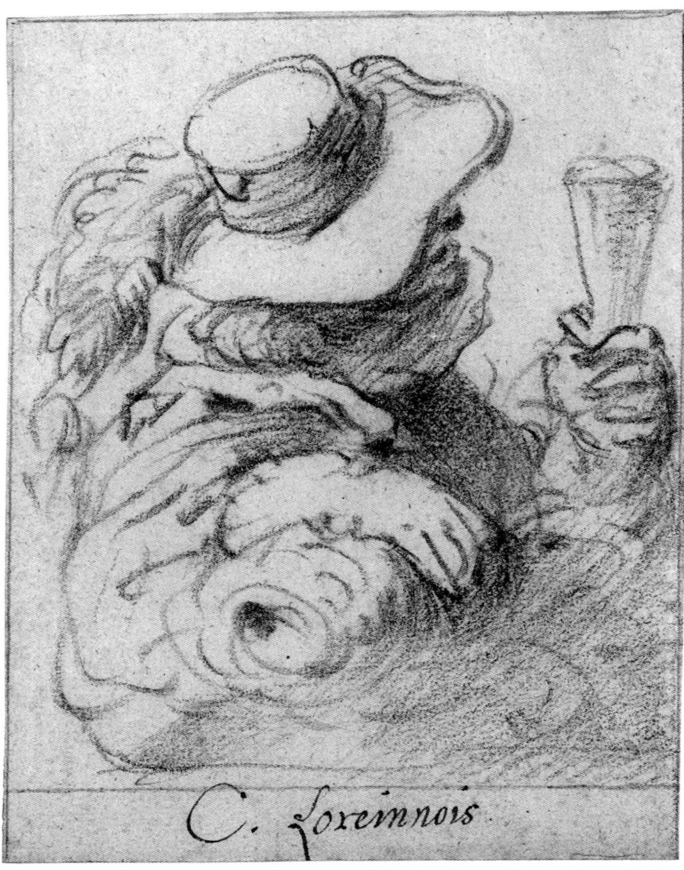

62 Leonard Bramer, *Portrait of Claude Lorrain*, 1620, black chalk on paper, 13.4 × 10.1 cm, Musées Royaux des Beaux-Arts de Belgique, Brussels

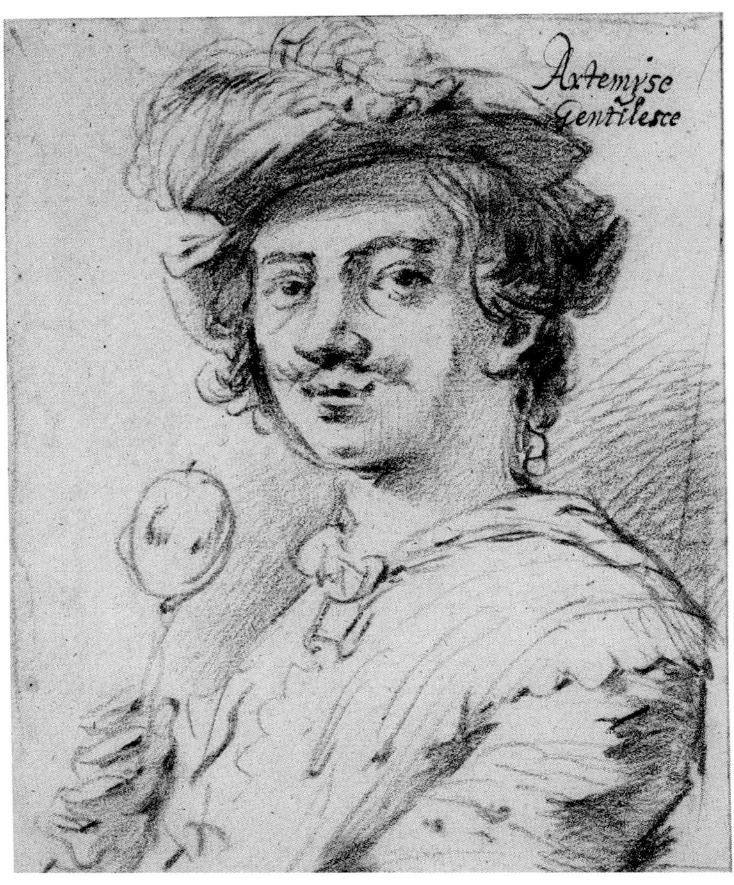

63 Leonard Bramer, *Portrait of Artemisia Gentileschi*, 1620, black chalk on paper, 14.1 × 11.2 cm, Musées Royaux des Beaux-Arts de Belgique, Brussels

The drawings reinforce the jocular insularity of this band of Northern brothers as further reinforced by their semi-secret and ludicrous nicknames. Leonard Bramer, the creator of the portraits, was known as *Nestelghat* or 'buttonhole', for example, while Van Baburen was *Biervliech* or 'fly in the beer'. The group's clannishness was also expressed through their regular meetings as part of the self-consciously bohemian cultural/professional association known as the Bentvueghels or 'birds of a feather', also the *Schildersbent*, literally meaning 'painters' clique'.[1]

All of this would usually merit discussion only in the context of an assessment of the drawings' significance in documenting the activities of the Northern colony of artists in Rome. Together with other related comic sketches, paintings and prints of carousing figures, they have been interpreted, in this respect, as demonstrating this group's perception of itself as a kind of anti-classical alternative to the stuffed-shirt officialdom of the Roman Accademia di San Luca.[2] Their bacchic revels and rituals helped to set them apart from the Accademia, with which they were beginning to clash over their professional rights and prerogatives. But what seems more surprising about these drawings for our present purposes is that the seventh member of this bacchic gang of revellers was none other than Artemisia Gentileschi (fig. 63).

Bramer depicts Gentileschi playing the role of a man, complete with clipped moustache, masculine figure and jaunty hat.

Indeed, were it not for the identifying inscription, there would be virtually no way of telling that the figure was female. The feminising give-away comes in the identifying attribute that s/he holds. Previous commentators have identified this object as either a mirror or a candied apple.[3] Yet it seems quite clear that it should be identified instead as a baby's rattle.[4] The image thus sets up an ironic contrast between Gentileschi's status as a rabble-rousing member of this gang of boys on the tiles and her responsibilities as a mother. In Florence, Gentileschi identified herself with a range of attributes including the martyr's palm. Here, in a decidedly bohemian and anti-academic twist to the notion, discussed above, of the authorised or 'official' portrait of the Medici or Michelangelo, these more artistically conventional signifiers have been replaced with a decidedly more prosaic object. The resulting image hinges on the ironic play that this sets up between the public-facing persona of the 'masculine' Gentileschi versus the supposedly more inward and private focus of the domestic, female sphere within which the contemporary viewer might have expected her to confine herself. Sexist as this conventional gender opposition may have been, it seeks, nonetheless, to celebrate, in its own way, Gentileschi's extraordinary ability to bypass such restrictions. Here we see a successful woman artist entering into the exclusively male, clubbish domain of the hard-drinking Roman Baroque art world and getting away with it. The drawing thus attests to Gentileschi's uncanny knack of successfully negotiating the often byzantine byways of the Roman art world to form strategically advantageous friendships and alliances within a very short period of time (the image being dateable to within six months of her arrival in the city, in early 1620).[5]

So much had clearly changed for Gentileschi since her hurried departure from Rome after the rape trial in 1613. By the middle of 1620, following some initial short-term rentals near the Chiesa Nuova, she was back in the heart of the artists' quarter, literally a block away from the apartment in which she had been born – and only a stone's throw from the residences of her new drinking partners, Bramer and Régnier. She had travelled light years, however, in terms of her career. No longer sequestered within the confines of her father's workshop, Artemisia now had the freedom to move through the city. She had also managed to accumulate the trappings of success. She was the professional head of a household of her own with two servants (two more than her father had ever been able to maintain, or so she must have reflected).[6] And the city, for its part, seemed to be beating a path to her door.

Gentileschi's husband was still at her side – at least for now. By 1623, however, Pierantonio Stiattesi would be gone. During this last period of their cohabitation, Stiattesi acted as a kind of business manager, talking Gentileschi up to his contacts while assisting her in her dealings with patrons and with contracts and the like. His correspondence with Gentileschi's lover and protector back in Florence confirms his sense of the sea change in their fortunes, brought about by the evident bankability of his wife's name in Rome. On 20 March 1620, he noted, 'she is gaining great credit among the princes', while, on 30 May, he informed Maringhi, 'she has so much to do and so much work, and so many cardinals and leading men seek her out that our house is always so full that she has no chance to put hand to mouth'.[7]

Gentileschi's first year back in Rome would, nonetheless, be marred by continued personal setbacks and family conflict. Her four-year-old son, Cristofano, would die in April 1620, leaving her with only one surviving daughter.[8] In the meantime, inter-familial friction still threatened the equilibrium of her family life: Orazio blamed Artemisia for squandering her dowry and for compromising the family's reputation, and, as a result, he seems to have refused to pay the second instalment of the dowry. His animosity may have derived in part from the fact that his daughter's reputation was now beginning to eclipse his own, a factor that might have also encouraged his definitive departure from the city in 1621. Before that moment, though, Artemisia's and Pierantonio's letters from this period highlight an ongoing series of chaotic and acrimonious family confrontations, recriminations, moments of litigation and even flashpoints of domestic violence.[9]

THE ROMAN PAINTINGS OF THE 1620S: MAKING OLD SUBJECTS NEW AGAIN

The 1622 *Susanna and the Elders*

The works produced during Artemisia's second Roman period of the 1620s attest to the increasing consolidation of her reputation, while reinforcing her flexibility in modifying her work to suit differing contexts of market demand. They also signal the challenges that she faced as a result of her patrons' expectations, both in terms of the work they wanted from her and also in regard to the roles and projects for which they evidently did not consider her.

In 1622, Gentileschi signed and dated a second version of *Susanna and the Elders* that reprises many of the elements from the 1610 composition, including its similar portrait format and closely matching dimensions (fig. 64). At the same time, a number of supposedly 'uncharacteristic' elements within the composition has led to its being treated as a problematic work by R. Ward Bissell and Mary Garrard. Their concerns were based, in part, on the unusual form of the signature, which combines both of Artemisia's surnames: 'ARTEMISIA GENTILESCHI LOMI FACIEBAT'. However, as Judith Mann and others have pointed out, there is no real consistency in Gentileschi's signatures, and there are other instances during the artist's second Roman period of her using both surnames.[10] Moreover, a technical analysis undertaken at the Indianapolis Museum of Art in 1995 found the signature to be consistent with the rest of the painting.[11]

Garrard and Bissell also questioned Gentileschi's authorship on the more fundamental grounds of the painting's stylistic features and compositional elements. Garrard's approving characterisation of the aggressively realist and Caravaggesque treatment of Susanna's body in the 1610 *Susanna* was noted above (p. 32); in the 1622 painting, by contrast, Susanna's body has been smoothed over and idealized, and her gaze directed towards heaven in a manner that conveys a more conventional reaction to the elders' lecherous advances. In addition, the elaborate fountain and, most tellingly of all perhaps, the landscape that patently owes a great deal to those by Guercino (1591–1666) are worlds removed from the bare-bones Caravaggesque realism of the earlier version.

All of this led Bissell and Garrard to question the work's attribution, with Bissell remarking, 'when the work is evaluated against our current understanding of Artemisia's development, the *Susanna* cannot be made to fit at any stage'.[12] In 1989, Garrard went further still, observing that 'the nature of [the painting's] expression is sharply out of character for the artist',[13] while noting, 'this English *Susanna* shows no interpretive continuity with the Schönborn picture [the 1610 *Susanna*], but reverts instead to the Carracci and Domenichino prototypes, reintroducing a seductive, Venus pudica pose and upturned eyes, and an environment swelling with cupids and spurting fountains'.[14] In 2001, Garrard presented a yet more complex argument to account for the painting's supposedly problematic features, proposing that Gentileschi had indeed painted the work, but that her initial composition must have been substantially revised without her permission by a later artist. This artist had converted Gentileschi's original composition into the more conventional, Bolognese-inspired work that we see today, while, at the same time, modifying the signature to make it more saleable: 'The alteration of the Burghley *Susanna* must have been motivated by the desire to make the artist as well as the picture more attractive. It is not coincidental that the person who transformed Artemisia's original Susanna into a more glamorous and conventional heroine in a more bland and supportive setting also insistently identified the picture with Artemisia through the new inscription.'[15]

These hypotheses have not been supported by technical analysis undertaken by the Paintings Conservation Department of the Metropolitan Museum of Art. Instead, as Keith Christiansen noted in 2004, the technical examination revealed that changes to the composition were 'made at a very early stage in painting the picture . . . and there is no evidence for Garrard's thesis that Artemisia's original figures were repainted by another artist . . . and there is no reason to doubt the ascription or the authenticity of the signature'.[16] Since then, the attribution to Gentileschi has been consistently accepted, to the extent that it has been catalogued as a secure work in both the 2001–2 Metropolitan Museum and the 2020 National Gallery, London, exhibition catalogues. It has also been attributed to Gentileschi without qualification in a number of other contexts, including Sheila Barker's monograph of

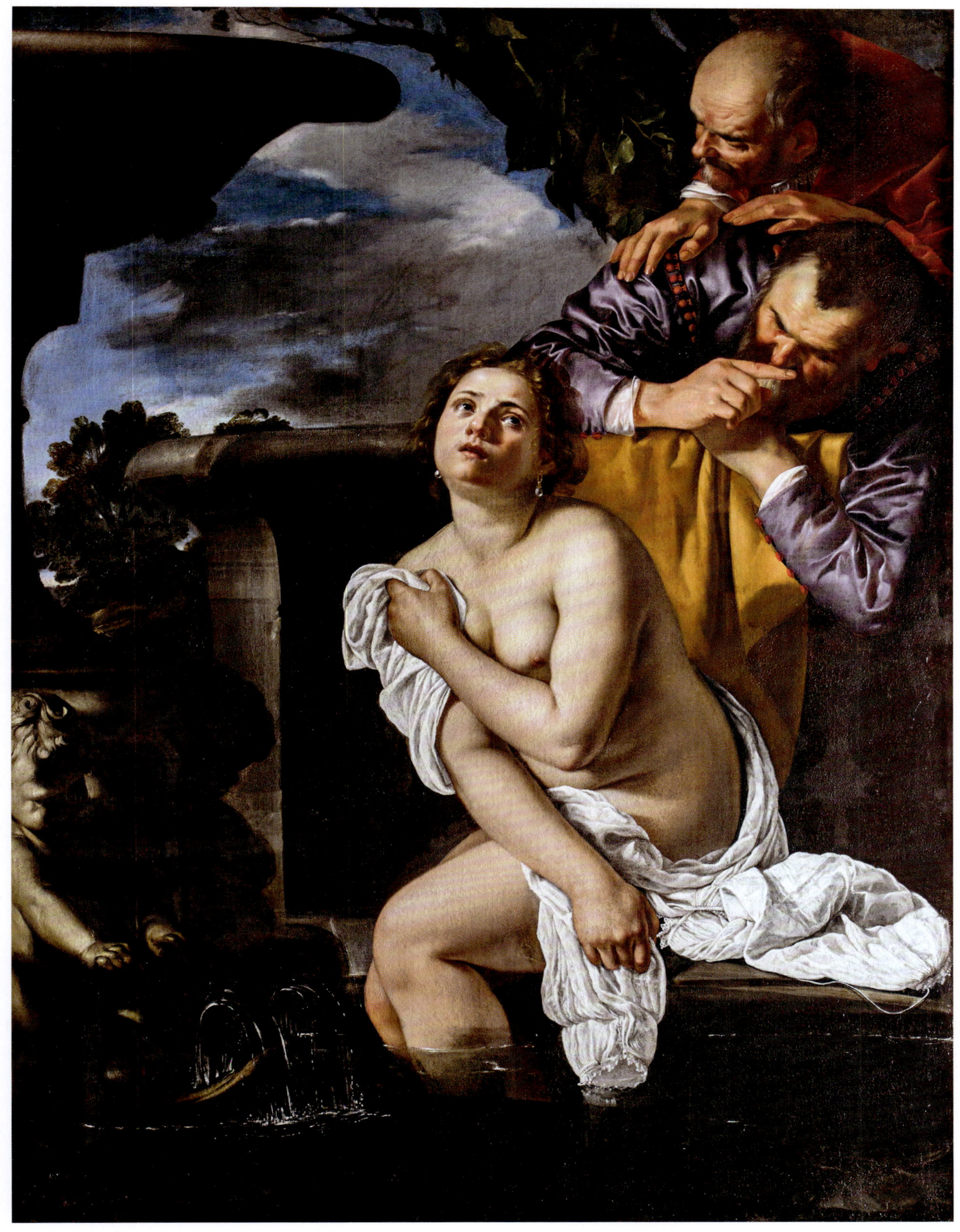

64 Artemisia Gentileschi, *Susanna and the Elders*, signed and dated 1622, oil on canvas, 161.5 × 123 cm, Burghley House Collection

2022.[17] Meanwhile, Garrard has revised her position further, conceding that, 'in retrospect I would acknowledge the possibility that Artemisia might have reconceived the picture for a prospective patron, modifying her style accordingly'.[18]

With all of this in mind, we are perhaps now in a better position to appreciate the positive achievement registered by Gentileschi's ability to modulate her style to suit the tastes of the painting's probable patron, Ludovico Ludovisi, who was the nephew of Pope Gregory XV, the former Archbishop of Bologna and Pope from 9 February 1621 to 8 July 1623. Ludovico Ludovisi's art collection was housed in the palace and casino of the Vigna di Porta Pinciana on the Pincian Hill that he had purchased as recently as June 1621 from Cardinal Francesco Maria del Monte (who had given Caravaggio's *Bacchus* and *Head of Medusa* to the Medici). Ludovisi had immediately set about contracting Guercino to fresco the ceiling of the Casino di Villa Ludovisi – Guercino himself having only just arrived in Rome from Bologna a month previously. The resulting fresco of *Aurora* was completed before the year's end and prefigured the coming craze for spectacular illusionistic ceilings that formed one of the central elements of the new High Baroque style. The other artist responsible for this modish statement of emerging taste was none other than the arch-nemesis of the Gentileschis, Agostino Tassi, whose high profile and thriving professional fortunes must have constituted a persistent source of aggravation for Artemisia.

Cardinal Ludovisi's art collection comprised some three hundred paintings, of which nearly ninety were by artists from Bologna and Emilia Romagna.[19] It also featured a number of paintings of Susanna and the Elders, including a version produced by Guercino in Bologna in 1617.[20] Had she had the opportunity to view this painting, then Gentileschi would certainly have gained a clear sense of the winds of change in favour of the new Bolognese style that were just then beginning to make an impact on the Roman art scene. This change in taste would evolve yet further towards more complex syntheses of post-Caravaggesque trends that would particularly become a feature of the artists promoted by the Barberini family during the papacy of Urban VIII from August 1623 onwards.

The 1622 *Susanna and the Elders* suggests that Gentileschi closely studied Guercino's new manner. In fact, what is perhaps most surprising about this painting is not so much that it shows Gentileschi modulating her style to fit in with a newly ascendant Bolognese taste, but that, given the thoroughness of its absorption of Bolognese influences, it begs the question of whether it would have been possible for Gentileschi to achieve such an in-depth understanding of this complex artistic tradition within such a short space of time. Mann has noted, in this respect, that the painting demonstrates the extent to which Gentileschi 'is in fact a gifted mimic who is able to adapt the styles of others as she deems necessary'.[21] While certainly agreeing with the sentiment, I would, nonetheless, propose instead that the depth of understanding of the new style evident in this work might suggest that it should be classified as a collaborative work between Gentileschi and Guercino himself.

The landscape background of the *Susanna*, in particular, is striking for the degree to which it expertly captures the silvery-blue tonalities and the brown, at times almost opaque, sketched-in trees that constitute hallmark features of Guercino's early landscape style. This approach to rendering the landscape grows out of Guercino's immersion in the sixteenth-century Ferrarese landscape tradition of Scarsellino, Dosso Dossi and others.[22] One may well ask, therefore, whether it would be conceivable for Gentileschi to have acquired the ability to absorb this tradition and then imitate this new manner so quickly and adroitly, given that Guercino had been resident in the city only from the middle of the previous year. The alternative, and much more likely hypothesis in my opinion, is to suggest that Guercino might himself, in fact, have collaborated on the work.

This possibility has already been suggested in passing by Christiansen. He allowed that, in the case of this painting, 'perhaps, from the outset, a second hand may have been involved'.[23] In 2001, Garrard also entertained this possibility, advancing the idea that Gentileschi and Guercino might have collaborated on the commission before concluding, 'It remains unclear, however, why Guercino would have been willing to collaborate in a work for which he took no credit.'[24] Yet it is conceivable that Guercino did, in fact, originally receive credit for his contribution, but that the record of this might have subsequently been lost. That the painting is attributed to 'Artemisia' alone in the 1623 Ludovisi inventory, moreover, means nothing in itself.[25] Inventories are, by their nature, a more or less shorthand and not particularly systematic compilation of essential data. Many of the paintings listed in the 1623 inventory have no attributions assigned to them at all.

All of this would seem to indicate that the 1622 *Susanna and the Elders* should be identified as an early example of Gentileschi's subsequently common practice of sub-contracting the landscape and other elements of her work to other specialists. The landscape background in the *Sleeping Venus* of the late 1620s, now in the Barbara Piasecka Johnson Foundation, Princeton, New Jersey, for example, has also been identified on technical grounds as having been produced by another hand.[26] This would become a standard feature of Gentileschi's work during her later, Neapolitan years. Either way, the painting again attests to Gentileschi's extraordinary ability strategically to reframe her output in relation to a broad range of fashionable artistic trends. In this instance, we have to imagine her coming to hear of Guercino, then seeking him out in his studio and befriending him to the extent of being able to study his paintings and/or collaborate with him on a major commission – all of this within a year and a half of her arrival in the city. No mean feat and further testament to Gentileschi's impressive networking abilities in the otherwise internecine and competitive art world of Baroque Rome.

The *Penitent Magdalene* and *Magdalene in Ecstasy*

Gentileschi's ability to adapt her sources during these years is also evident in her revisiting of the subject of the Magdalene. Her *Penitent Magdalene* in Seville cathedral (fig. 65) has been linked to a reference in a 1630s inventory to a painting of this subject exported to Seville from the collection of Fernando Enrìquez Afán de Ribera, Duke of Alcalá, the Spanish Ambassador to the Holy See in Rome from 1625 to 1626 and the Viceroy of Naples from 1629 to 1631.[27] (The presence of a more recently discovered version in a private US collection has raised the issue of whether or not this one is to be considered the original version.[28]) Alcalá, a key figure in the story of Gentileschi's late patrons, almost certainly acquired Gentileschi's *Penitent Magdalene* in Rome, while serving as ambassador there, thus helping to provide the painting with a relatively secure dating to the mid-1620s.[29]

Once again, Caravaggio provides the model for Gentileschi. His version of the subject, now at the Palazzo Doria Pamphilj (fig. 66), would become the focus of a famous anecdote by Giovanni Pietro Bellori. In his *Lives of the Modern Painters, Sculptors and Architects* (1672), Bellori describes the painting as originating in an informal life study taken directly from the model to which Caravaggio then added various attributes – not entirely convincingly in Bellori's estimation – in order to convert it into a subject painting: 'He painted a girl drying her hair, seated on a little chair with her hands in her lap. He portrayed her in a room, adding a small ointment jar, jewels, and gems on the floor, pretending that she is the Magdalene.'[30] As Bellori's words attest, the underlying surprise informing Caravaggio's artistic approach here lay in his refusal adequately to idealize the image in order to elevate it sufficiently above the prosaic reality of an unadorned scene of everyday life. The resulting painting purported to be a history painting depicting the biblical narrative of the conversion of the Magdalene but was, in Bellori's opinion, nothing of the sort. In reality, it was no more than a genre painting – or scene of everyday life – which depicted a commoplace girl drying her hair while 'pretending that she is the Magdalene'. The last phrase is particularly evocative, since it could very well be applied to the subsequent process adopted by Gentileschi of 'pretending' that she was the Magdalene in the Pitti *Conversion of the Magdalene* of 1617–18 (fig. 40) and other paintings of the period.

In the *Penitent Magdalene*, Gentileschi retains Caravaggio's sense of genre-like immediacy, while adding to it a greater monumentality and decorum, which have been combined, in turn, with an increased emphasis on emotional intensity. Her Magdalene, too, appears as a vividly down-to-earth, contemporary figure. Her dress is deliberately plain – worlds removed from the spectacular finery of the Pitti *Conversion of the Magdalene*. Her hair is depicted in an extreme state of disarray – again, completely unlike the carefully oiled, corkscrew curls and scented locks of the Pitti *Magdalene*. Her bent head and almost closed eyes are obvious derivations from Caravaggio's model. But here, too, Gentileschi has transformed her source: with her puffy eyes, tear-stained face and reddened nose, this Magdalene reveals herself as having been recently consumed by an episode of emotional upheaval. She now lies back in

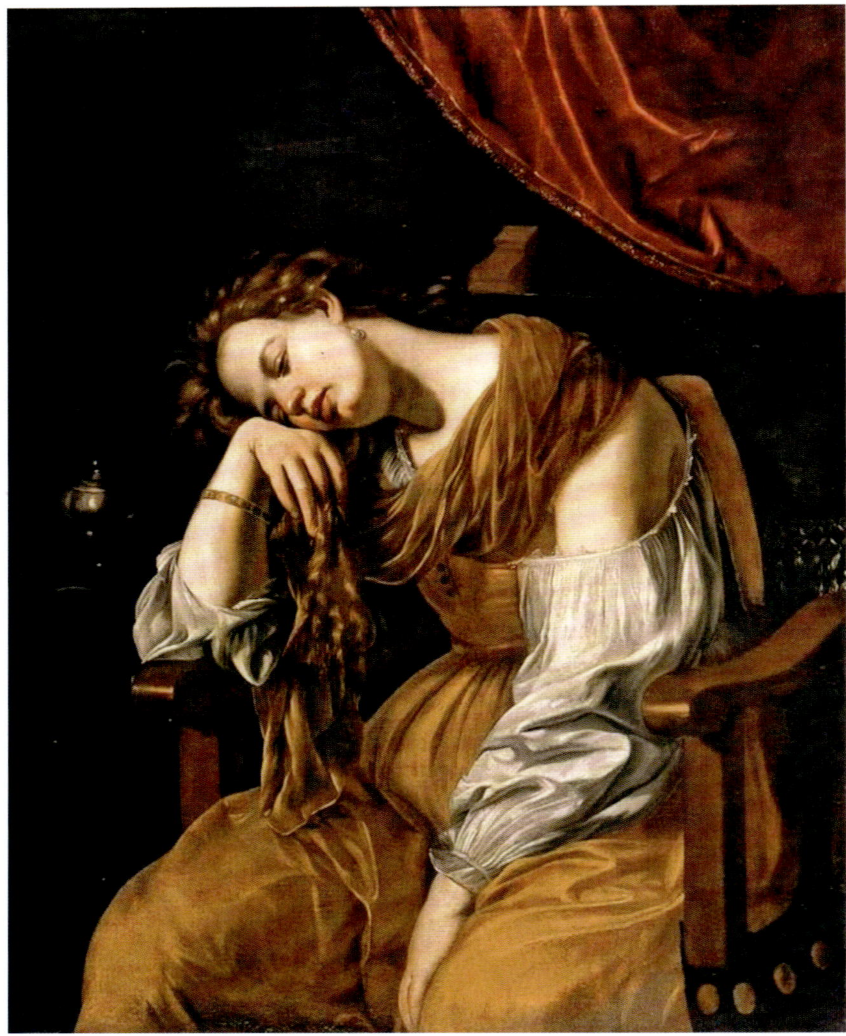

65 Attributed to Artemisia Gentileschi, *Penitent Magdalene*, *c.*1625–26, oil on canvas, 122 × 97 cm, Catedral de Santa María de la Sede, Seville

a state of swooning semi-consciousness, cast adrift within a tearful and melancholic reverie.

It feels almost voyeuristic to observe Gentileschi's *Magdalene* in the midst of such a heightened state of emotional disequilibrium. Yet here again, Gentileschi has made sure to 'improve' on Caravaggio's prototype by counterbalancing what might, in other respects, appear indecorously extreme. She achieves this by framing the Magdalene within a dignified and sober composition, with the figure placed front on and in a centralised position relative to the picture plane. She has also brought the subject's religious dimension more clearly to the fore by placing the Magdalene's jar of ointment by her right elbow. In relation to the 1610 *Susanna and the Elders*, I noted Gentileschi's ability to distil the narrative elements of the story down to their bare essentials, without any extraneous background or ancillary details. Here Gentileschi applies the same principles to the story of the Madgalene in order to maximise its devotional impact. The image was evidently

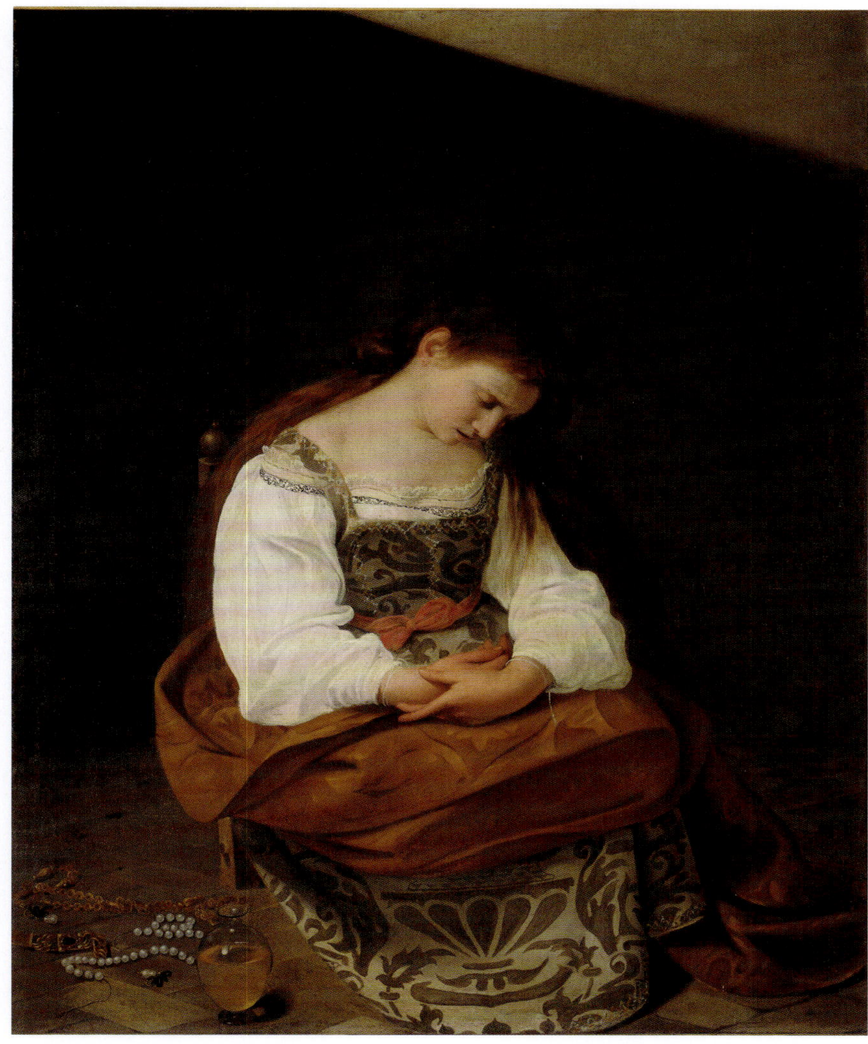

66 Michelangelo Merisi da Caravaggio, *Penitent Magdalene*, c.1598, oil on canvas, 123 × 98.5 cm, Galleria Doria Pamphilj, Rome

highly successful in this regard. An indication of this lies in the decision by the duke's heirs to remove the canvas from the family palace and to donate it, instead, to Seville cathedral. This facilitated the painting's transition from its original aristocratic and secular gallery setting to a more public and devotional, institutional environment, to which, in truth, it seems better suited.

Another version of the *Magdalene* appeared on the art market in 2014 (fig. 67). Its attribution to Gentileschi has since gained widespread acceptance among scholars, an otherwise rare point of consensus in the literature on the artist.[31] This canvas is based on yet another Caravaggesque prototype – a later version of the subject painted by Caravaggio while he was en route to Naples that is known through multiple copies, including one by Louis Finson (fig. 68).[32] Caravaggio's composition functions almost as a counterpoint to the negative critique subsequently aired by Bellori in his *Lives*: it presents a more clearly delineated Magdalene, complete with

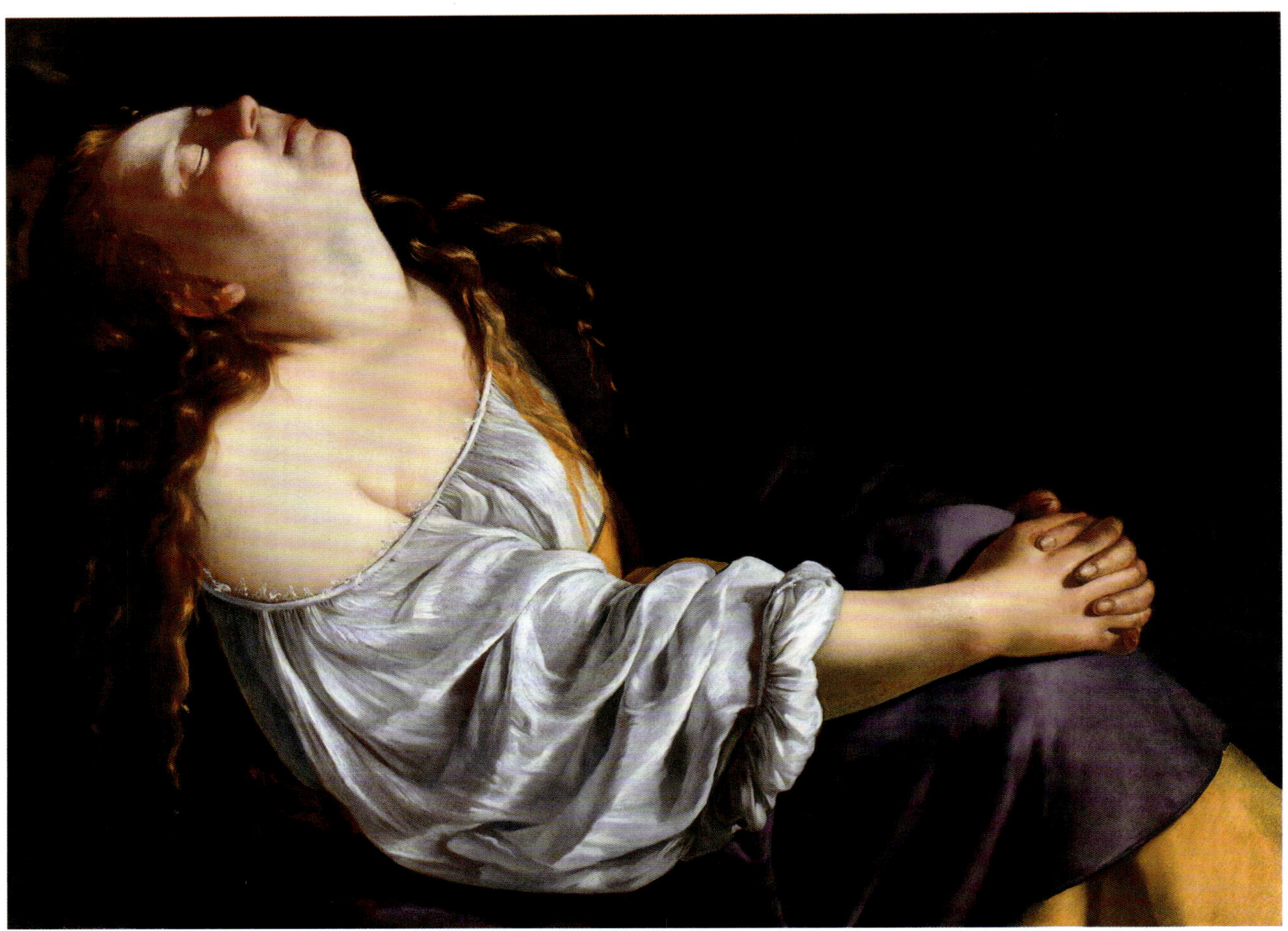

67 Artemisia Gentileschi, *Mary Magdalene in Ecstasy*, c.1623–25, oil on canvas, 81 × 105 cm, Fondazione Musei Civici, Palazzo Ducale, Venice, on long-term loan from a private collection

the traditional attributes of a cross and skull. To this, the artist has added a considerably heightened sense of emotion. Caravaggio's second Magdalene literally drops her head backwards onto her shoulder in a swooning state of ecstasy.

Gentileschi has taken this prototype and used it as the basis for a second and yet more systematically 'deconstructed' Magdalene. She has forced her Magdalene into an almost awkwardly extreme position hard up against the picture plane, while also creating a composition that is almost entirely devoid of any background contextualisation (although the bare traces of a cave-like interior can just be made out in the enveloping gloom). The painting seems conspicuously lacking in adornment, to the extent of its appearing almost as if it were an entirely 'subject-less' life study of a model 'pretending that she is the Magdalene', as per Bellori's estimation. An intensely Baroque religious aura is, nonetheless, present. This is attributable primarily to the figure's emotional state, which Gianni Papi has described as 'a sort of hypnotic catalepsy'.[33] The result is a strikingly original adaptation of a Caravaggesque model that remains utterly dissimilar to other, more conventional depictions. It is unfortunate, therefore, that nothing is currently known about the early provenance or the circumstances surrounding the patronage of this extraordinary canvas. In the absence of further information, one can imagine that this second version of the *Magdalene* was painted for a collector with slightly more experimental tastes than the more conventionally pious and devotionally 'correct' tastes of the Duke of Alcalá which had been influenced by the Spanish Counter-Reformation. It provides another strong indication of Gentileschi's flexibility in being able to produce two such radically different treatments of the same subject during the same period.

The Detroit *Judith and her Maidservant with the Head of Holofernes*

Gentileschi's flexibility during this period is further demonstrated by her ability to produce works in a more unalloyed Caravaggesque style on occasion. This is particularly evident in a composition that has been identified as among the major achievements of her second Roman period. *Judith and her Maidservant with the Head of Holofernes*, now in the Detroit Institute of Arts (fig. 69)[34] stands fourth in line in the sequence of her known treatments of this subject. These can be traced back, as has been shown, to the prototype of Orazio Gentileschi's painting of the same subject of 1610–11 (fig. 25). From there, the sequence progresses to the modified copy now in Oslo (fig. 26). The composition was then further modified in Florence (fig. 52). Gentileschi's rapidly evolving artistic development during these years is rendered yet more apparent when the version created in Rome in the 1620s is viewed in relation to its predecessors.

The Pitti canvas provides an initial point of meditation on the moment when Judith and Abra begin to turn their attention away from the act of assassination towards the next challenge – their projected escape through the enemy camp (fig. 52). The Detroit composition builds on this by adding further indications of the protagonists' motivations and resolve. The empty scabbard on the table top, for example, highlights Judith's extraordinary achievement in successfully turning Holofernes' own weapon against him. Yet the empty gauntlet – facing outwards in the direction of their gaze – points to the extreme threat that they now face as they find themselves isolated and alone at the very epicentre of the enemy camp.

In the Pitti *Judith*, Judith and Abra anxiously scan the darkness in order to discern the danger that lies just beyond their vision. The Detroit canvas, by contrast, stretches the narrative in more complex ways and for greater dramatic effect. Abra attempts to cover Holofernes' head in a sheet, while pushing it hurriedly into a sack. But a noise has disturbed her, so she freezes, craning to hear what is moving outside in the dark. The sound has also rendered Judith immobile, although her more active pose denotes her greater level of resolve and her in-command role. She instinctively confronts the enemy lurking beyond her vision by executing a deft counter-pivot with her body. One arm brings the falchion down and back to conclude the earlier action of dispatching the general, while the other swings forwards and upwards to mask the candlelight.

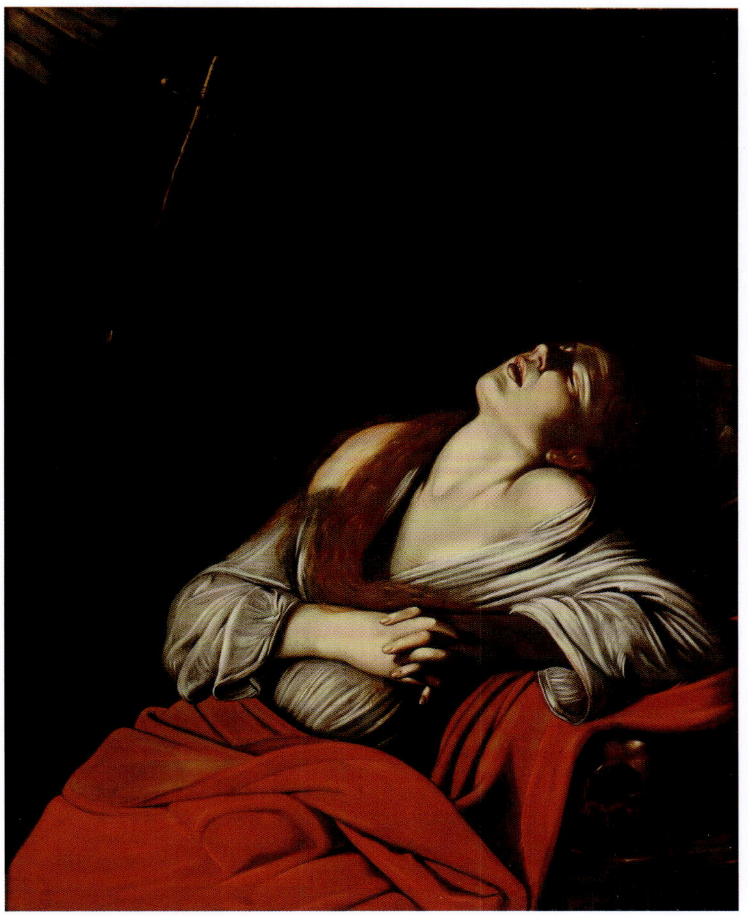

68 Louis Finson after Michelangelo Merisi da Caravaggio, *Mary Magdalene in Ecstasy*, 1612, oil on canvas, 120 × 100 cm, Musée des Beaux-Arts de Marseille

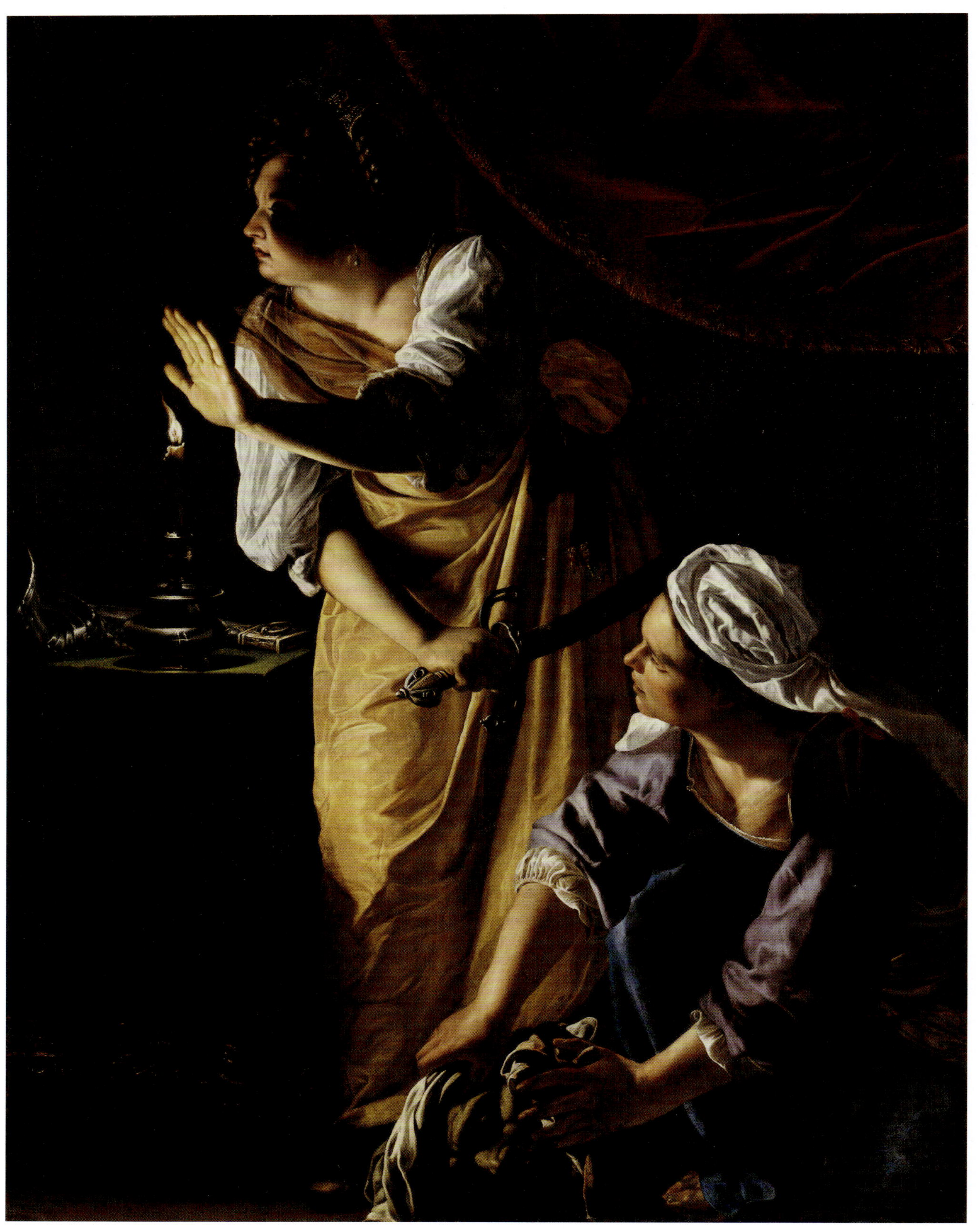

69 Artemisia Gentileschi, *Judith and her Maidservant with the Head of Holofernes*, c.1623–25, oil on canvas, 187.2 × 142 cm, Detroit Institute of Arts, Gift of Mr. Leslie H. Green, 52.253

This last gesture constitutes a brilliant visual device that enables the viewer to 'see' the process of Judith's attempting to penetrate the blackness of the tent's wall in order to discern the lurking menace beyond their vision in the dark.

As Richard Spear and others have noted, the motif of the candle derives from the model of Gerrit van Honthorst.[35] This artist's novel ability to combine the already established Caravaggesque chiaroscuro approach with the yet more spectacular lighting effects provided by nocturnal torchlit and candlelit scenes earned him considerable success and the nickname of Gherardo delle Notti (Gerard of the Nights).[36] Gentileschi's familiarity with Honthorst's work is confirmed by her participation in the drinking parties held by Honthorst, Bramer, Régnier and their other friends from the Northern Caravaggesque community. The Detroit *Judith* thus demonstrates her ability to revise her own, first-wave Caravaggesque training with reference to the more fashionable and up-to-date developments of the Northern torchlight masters (as also seen in works from this period by Trophime Bigot, Carlo Saraceni and others).

In the Detroit canvas, Gentileschi also draws on the candlelit motif as a means of increasing the composition's suspense-filled tension. This is evident in the open palm of Judith's right hand as it remains dramatically framed in the candle's glare. The longer that she remains frozen in that position, the more will her hand absorb the heat of the rising flame. This evokes an obvious reference, in turn, to the famous embodiment of ancient Roman bravery, Mucius Scaevola, a subject treated also by the Caravaggesque torchlight specialists on occasion (fig. 70).[37] The story of Mucius Scaevola, as recounted in Livy's *History of Rome*, in fact, bears many parallels with that of Judith. Like Judith, Scaevola was a heroic, would-be assassin. He was tasked with a deadly mission to infiltrate an invading enemy's camp in order to kill their leader. Unlike Judith, however, he failed in his goal and was captured by the Etruscans, who were thus poised to defeat the weakened Romans. Yet Scaevola remained unbowed. He demonstrated his continued resolve by plunging his hand into the fire in front of his captors. This act of unquestioning bravery and willingness to sacrifice himself for his country caused the Etruscan king to set him free and to sue the Romans unexpectedly for peace. Gentileschi's quotation of this famous gesture of Roman heroism recasts her Judith as a female Mucius Scaevola. Her *Judith* stands resolute, even in the midst of the pain that we can feel mounting, as we, too, crane to see what lies in wait for the two protagonists, just beyond our vision. This painting offers yet another example, then, of Gentileschi's ability to revisit and recast her themes in order to tailor them to suit the artistic and cultural background of her changing audiences.

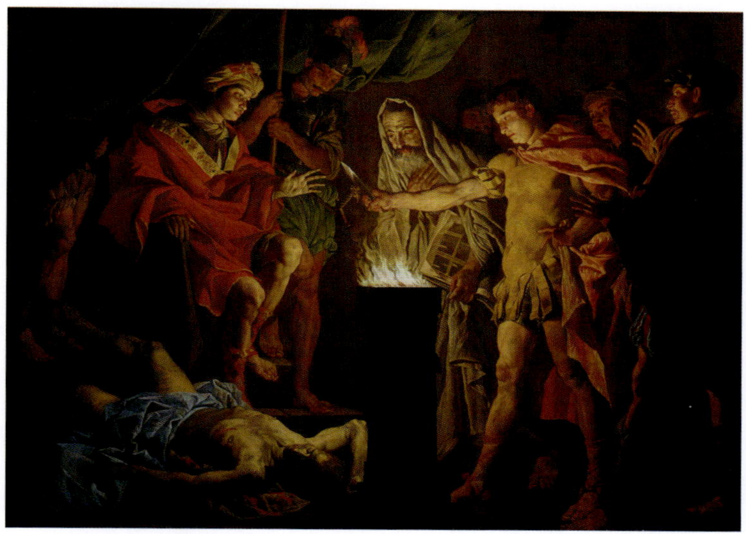

70 Matthias Stomer, *Mucius Scaevola in the Presence of Lars Porsena*, early 1640s, oil on canvas, 152.6 × 205.7 cm, Art Gallery of New South Wales, Sydney

8

A Business Evaluation of Gentileschi's Career in the 1620s

PRODUCTIVITY, SPECIALISATION AND THE PROBLEM OF TYPECASTING

INTRODUCTION
ARTEMISIA IN THE EARLY TO MID-1620S

If we were to ask a Roman connoisseur of the mid-1620s their opinion of Artemisia Gentileschi's paintings, we might be surprised by their response. The first thing that they might highlight – on the basis of what appears in early sources at least – would be her reputation as a portraitist. This emphasis occurs in the earliest published biographical commentary on Artemisia, a brief note composed by Giovanni Baglione, Orazio Gentileschi's former rival. In his *Vite de' Pittori Scultori et Architetti* of 1642, Baglione inserts a four-line reference to Artemisia at the end of his two-page biography of Orazio. In it, he mentions her fame in Naples at that stage and the fact that she was a specialist in portraiture.[1] Joachim von Sandrart's *Teutsche Academie* elaborates marginally on this account. This German compilation of artists' biographies was not published until 1675 but was based on a visit by the author to Artemisia's Neapolitan workshop in 1631. Sandrart does mention a single subject painting – *David with the Head of Goliath* – a reference that has been associated with two closely related, variant compositions, one signed

FACING PAGE Artemisia Gentileschi, *Mary Magdalene in Ecstasy* (detail of fig. 67)

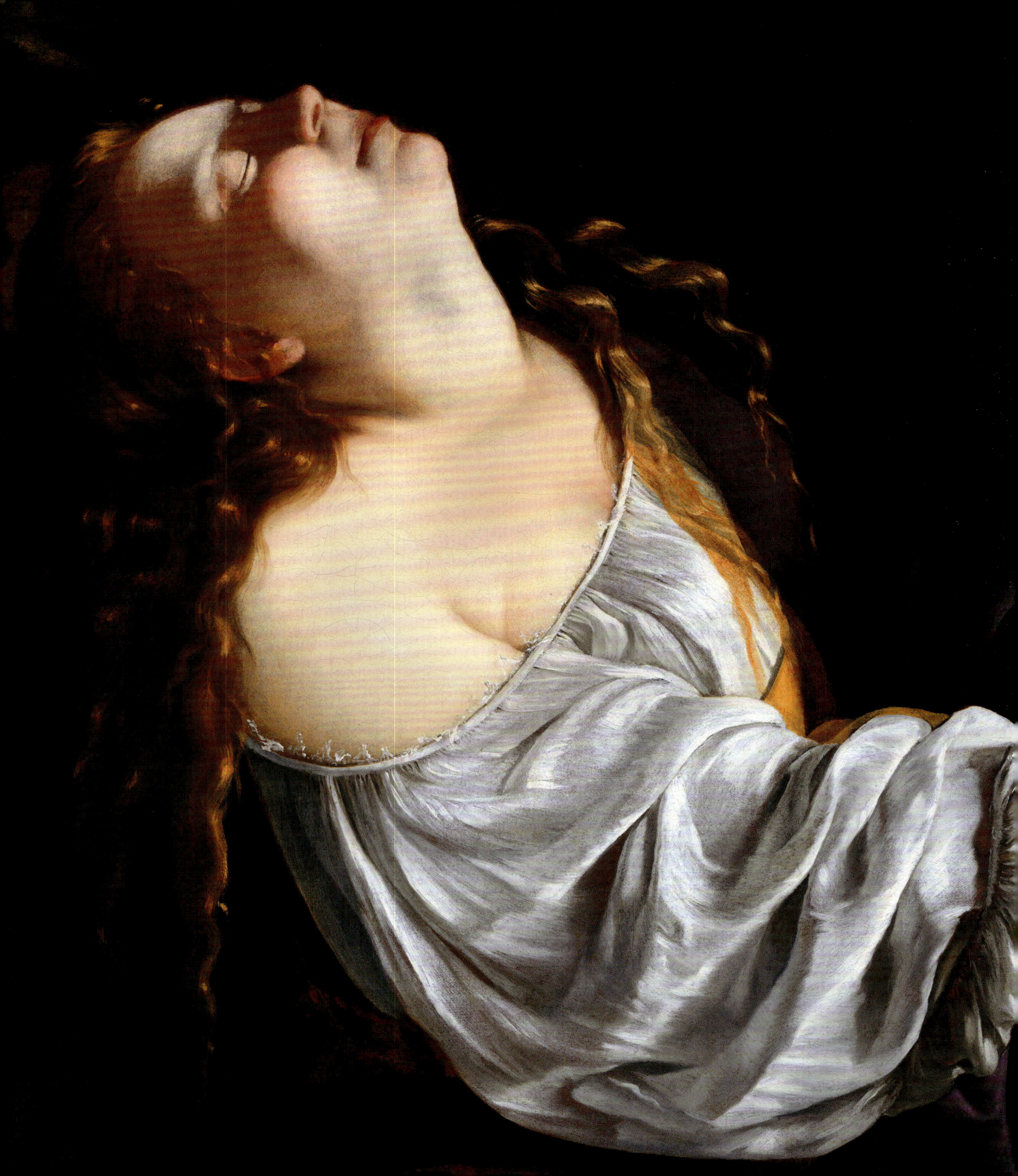

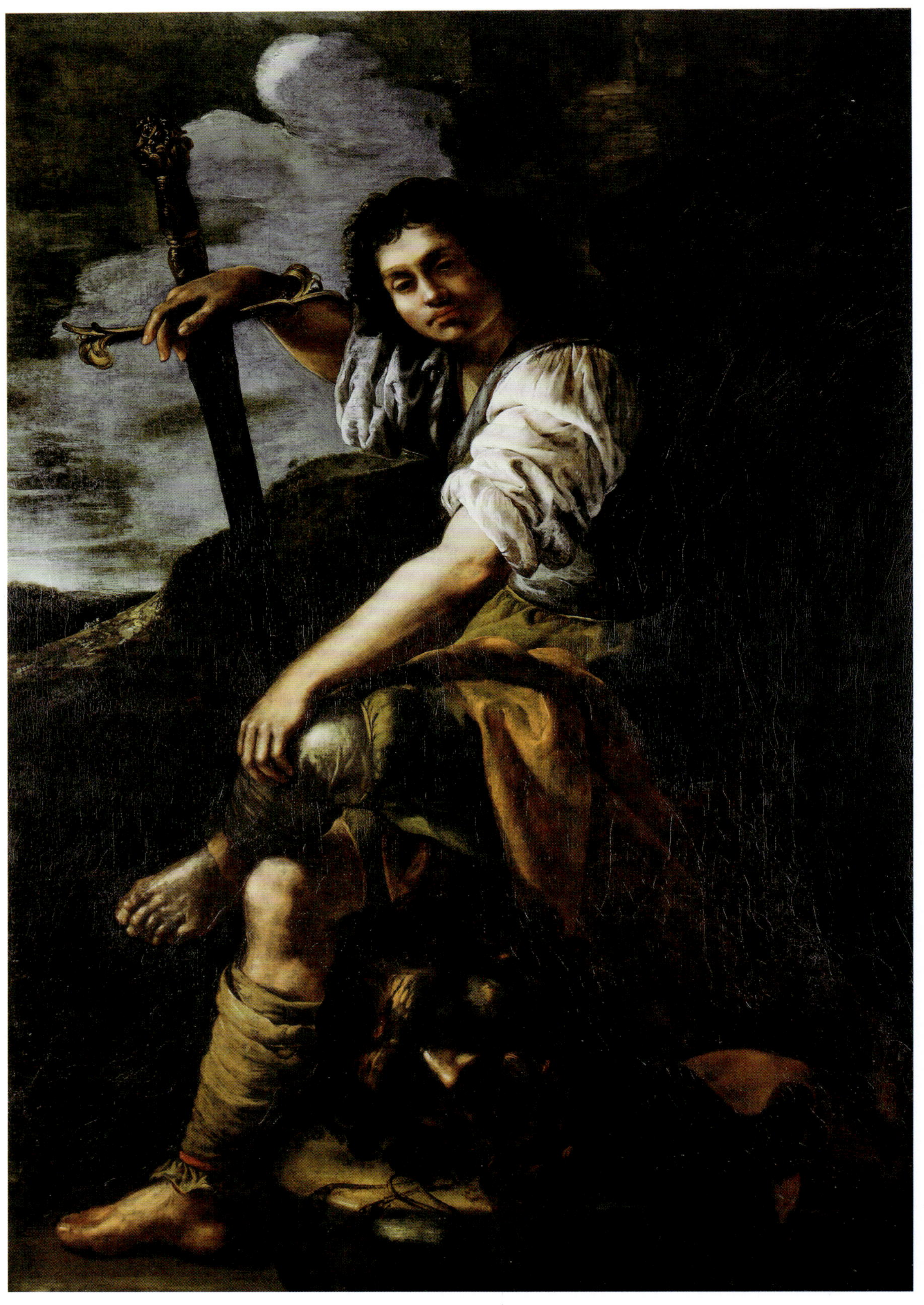

71 Artemisia Gentileschi, *David with the Head of Goliath*, signed and illegibly dated, *c.*1631, oil on canvas, 203.5 × 152 cm, private collection

and illegibly dated (fig. 71).[2] The only other paintings he mentions, however, are her 'excellent portraits', which, he notes, were a major contributing factor to her Neapolitan fame.[3]

A good example of Gentileschi's mid-career expertise in portraiture comes down to us in a portrait of an as yet unidentified papal standard-bearer that is signed and dated 1622 (fig. 72).[4] It adheres more closely to portraiture's essential requirement – that it remain true to life – than was the case for the more evidently idealized figures of the *Susanna and the Elders* from the same year (fig. 64). In this respect, Gentileschi's attentiveness to the sitter's stray locks of hair springing from his thinning temple, the sheen of the cross on his breastplate, the golden brocade on his shoulder, the varying levels of shadow on his elaborate ruff and so on are all noteworthy realistic details.

To describe an artist as an excellent portraitist was, nonetheless, something of a backhanded compliment, since portraiture's supposedly imitative and mechanical qualities placed it among the lowest ranked of the artistic genres.[5] The leading patron of Caravaggesque painting, Vincenzo Giustiniani, for example, positioned portraiture as the fourth-lowest form of artistic expression in an ascending scale stretching eight levels higher to the twelfth or most advanced level of artistic attainment.[6] In Giustiniani's estimation, portraits were next in line after the purely transcription-based processes of tracing designs by other artists (level 1), copying works by eye (level 2) and drawing from nature (level 3; although Giustiniani qualified this point by noting that the method was particularly effective when it involved 'copying antique statues, or good modern ones or paintings by worthy masters'). Portraits were even more imitative, in this respect, than still-life painting (level 5). Giustiniani placed still life above portraiture, since he believed that a good still life required 'great patience' to produce (revealing himself to be more progressive than many of his contemporaries in his estimation of the critical status of this emerging, so-called 'minor' genre[7]).

At the uppermost level of the scale were the works of 'world famous painters of the highest rank'. These combined the best aspects of the observation of nature with the most advanced facility in applying the creative powers of *invenzione*. Although he did not spell out the basis for this understanding, what Giustiniani clearly had in mind when alluding to works at the top of the artistic hierarchy were history paintings by Guido Reni and the like. History painting purportedly represented the most intellectually demanding and therefore the 'noblest' challenge that could be given to a painter.[8] It was precisely the fact that portraiture and still life were supposedly so imitative

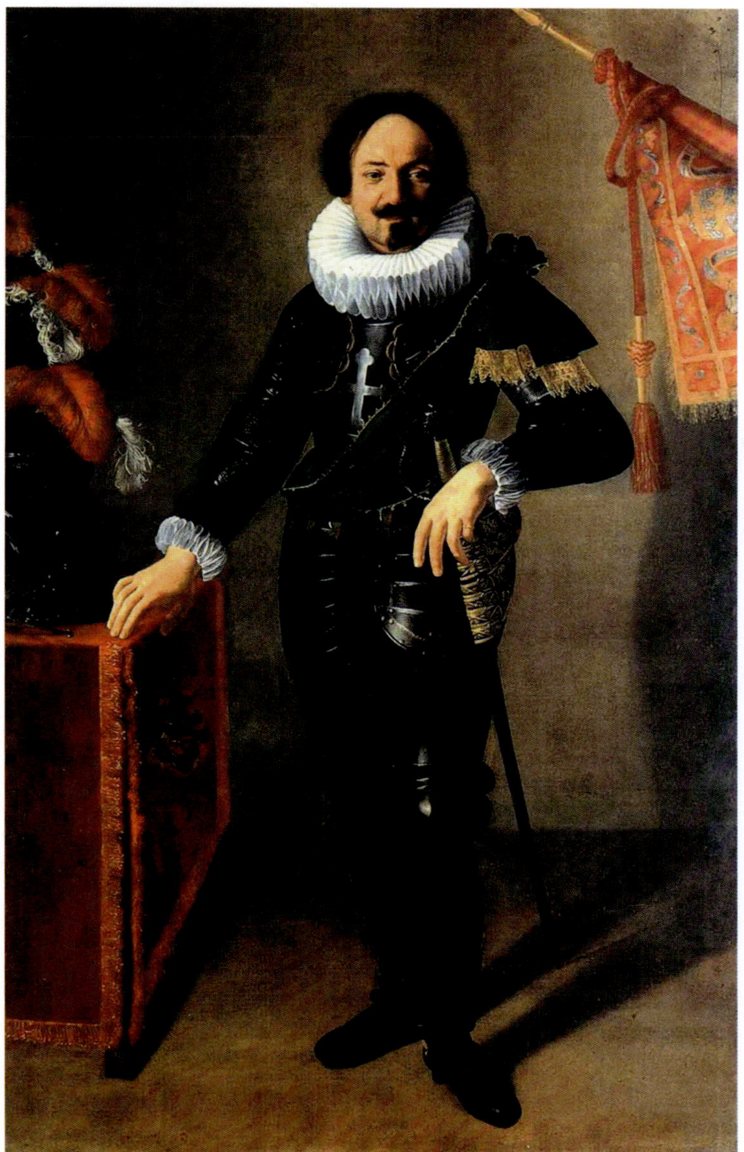

72 Artemisia Gentileschi, *Portrait of a Gonfaloniere*, signed and dated 1622, oil on canvas, 208.4 × 128.4 cm, Collezioni Comunali d'Arte Bologna

and thus so lowly ranked in relation to history painting that they were often explicitly identified as the kinds of specialisations that were appropriate for women artists.[9]

Even the most exalted of history painters, nevertheless, tended to produce portraits from time to time, including such pre-eminent artists as Raphael, Caravaggio and Reni. The distinction between these artists and Gentileschi, however, is that they were defined as history painters who occasionally dabbled in portraiture, rather than the other way around. An early critic would have never made the mistake of describing Raphael as a portrait painter who occasionally painted history paintings. Yet this is exactly how Artemisia was being constructed on a critical level in early writings on contemporary art, and despite Artemisia's – and her father's – best efforts to have her recognised as a history painter, first and foremost, from the time of her earliest signed work.

THE PROBLEM OF TYPECASTING AND THE ISSUE OF GENTILESCHI'S PUBLIC VISIBILITY IN ROME

Another problem experienced by Gentileschi in relation to her audience's perceptions during the 1620s was that she was becoming increasingly boxed into a narrow band of subject specialisations. For every ambitious work that she produced with an unusual or complex subject – such as the *Pluto and Persephone* listed in the Medici collections (see pp. 92 and 94) – one could cite three or four references to a limited repertory of more standardised compositions. These frequently requested subjects included paintings of Susanna, Lucretia, Judith and the Magdalene – to which one might add David and Bathsheba and the Death of Cleopatra, both subjects that would become especially popular during the latter stages of her career. From relatively early on in her career, Gentileschi was effectively typecast as a woman artist from whom her predominantly male patrons would go to acquire a limited range of subjects depicting female protagonists.

Of equal concern to Gentileschi would have been the only very limited opportunities that existed during this period for Roman audiences to view her works in settings more public than those offered by private collections. The importance of publicly accessible display contexts for spreading awareness of Italian Renaissance and Baroque painters to a wider audience should not be underestimated.[10] Time and time again, be it in Vasari or Baglione or in the comments of some other biographer, the early sources all stress the importance of ecclesiastical commissions for making and breaking artists' reputations. A church altarpiece or fresco commission provided artists with a degree of public visibility that no amount of private patronage could match. Gentileschi's lack of training in fresco automatically put her at a disadvantage in this respect. Still, this should not have precluded her from attracting at least some commissions for altarpieces, lateral canvases or other paintings for church interiors.

The glaring nature of this omission from Gentileschi's career seems especially pronounced in a city like Rome, home of the Vatican and, at that stage, the engine house of the Counter-Reformation. Rome was in the midst of a boom in ecclesiastical artistic patronage that had been stimulated by the emergence of a host of new religious orders responding to the dictates of the Council of Trent. These new orders prompted, in turn, a competition with the more established orders, all of whom were seeking fresh ways of maintaining their relevance by increasing the numbers and dedication of their congregations. Much of the ensuing energy focused on the development of well-springs of popular devotion – such as the Dominican Rosary – or the formulation of entirely new areas of iconography relating to recently created saints that were just then springing up throughout the city.[11] In the year 1622 alone, the canonisation of five new saints took place – Ignatius of Loyola and St Francis Xavier (Jesuits), Philip Neri (Oratorians), Teresa of Avila (Discalced Carmelites) and St Isidore the Farmer.

It is striking to note in this context the absence of any reference to altarpiece commissions being awarded to Gentileschi during all her years in Rome. A church like San Lorenzo in Lucina, for example, contains a particular concentration of altarpieces that were commissioned during the 1610s and 1620s, making it a snapshot of the Roman art scene throughout the period of Gentileschi's second residence there. She would have known this church very well, since it was one of the main parish churches for her local community and was the very church in which she had been baptised in 1593.[12] How galling it must have been, therefore, to observe a number of her fellow Caravaggisti contributing to this church's renovation during these years, while she herself remained shut out from any comparable contracts. These artists included Carlo Saraceni, Tommaso Salini, Alessandro Turchi, Simon Vouet and – possibly – Massimo Stanzione (although Stanzione's involvement at San Lorenzo has also been dated to the early 1650s).[13] Some of them could be said to be favourably connected and in particular demand during these years: Vouet, for example, a close friend of Artemisia, was popular with many of the leading Roman patrons and was Principe of the Accademia di San Luca from 1624 to 1627. Tommaso Salini, by contrast, was not especially pre-eminent in relation to Gentileschi; yet he was profitably employed at San Lorenzo de Lucina while she was excluded, as she was likewise overlooked for any other religious commissions during this period, as far as can be presently determined.

GENTILESCHI'S PRODUCTIVITY

All of this might not have mattered had Gentileschi been able to maintain a different type of workshop organisation that focused on maximising her productivity within the market for the specific types of paintings upon which her reputation was based. Yet Gentileschi was never a prolific artist. Her oeuvre pales – at least in terms of its physical output – in comparison with that of other, more established artists. D. Stephen Pepper's catalogue raisonné of Reni, for example, lists 215 works (not including variants), while Nicholas Turner and Luigi Salerno's catalogue of Guercino lists 364 secure works.[14] In terms of her subsequent Neapolitan colleagues, Jusepe de Ribera's catalogue lists some 300 prime autograph compositions for this artist, not including variants. Likewise, the standard catalogue for Stanzione records 230 works, similarly not including variants.[15] Even Carlo Dolci (1616–1687), whose reputation for slowness during his own lifetime was proverbial, has an oeuvre that takes in 162 secure paintings, as outlined in his standard catalogue.[16] By contrast, Bissell's comprehensive catalogue of Gentileschi's oeuvre stretches to only 58 paintings.[17] To this number, one could add around a dozen additional works that have been either re-attributed to Artemisia more securely since Bissell's catalogue or else that have come to light since then, while also managing to attain a certain level of critical consensus among scholars.[18]

An oeuvre of around seventy works remains a very small number when judged by any standard of the day. By contrast, for example, in Bologna, Elisabetta Sirani (1638–1665) was able to note down the much more substantial figure of 195 works in a list that she maintained of her own production dating from a mere decade of her career, 1655–65. As Raffaella Morselli has highlighted, this document omits a number of works that Sirani identified as being not noteworthy enough to warrant mentioning on either artistic or social grounds. The final list would thus be more like 300, an unusually productive average of around 30 paintings per year that, in fact, exceeds the average of fifteen to twenty canvases produced by Guercino during his peak years of productivity.[19] Unlike Gentileschi, however, Sirani never married and thus remained unburdened by the all-consuming preoccupations of motherhood. Neither was she forced to uproot her base of operations as a result of financial exigencies or other pressures. Instead, she remained more or less fully supported within her father's prosperous Bolognese workshop until her untimely death in 1665, aged just twenty-seven.

The nexus between Gentileschi's output and her personal circumstances indicates a very different trajectory from that of Sirani. The output of Gentileschi's Florentine years, for example, must have been significantly affected by her near-constant cycle of pregnancies followed by periods of mourning that resulted from the high mortality rate of her children (five births, three deaths, and with a second son dying shortly after the family's relocation to Rome in 1620).

The inventory of Gentileschi's workshop holdings seized by the grand-ducal authorities at the time of her departure from Florence in early 1620 reinforces this picture by suggesting a workshop operation with a very modest turnover of saleable output, at least when judged against other workshops of the day.[20] The document outlining her sequestered goods should not, of course, be viewed as comparable with a standard inventory, such as would customarily be compiled at the time of an artist's death. Artemisia must have taken some materials and unfinished works with her when she left for Rome, and she may also have asked Maringhi or some other trusted associate to look after some of her belongings in order to keep them from her creditors. Nonetheless, the urgency with which she was compelled to leave the city, together with the constant stream of letters sent back to Maringhi in Florence, asking him to forward materials that she needed to restart her operations in Rome, tend to suggest that Gentileschi was not able to take much with her and that the inventory of her sequestered possessions does, in fact, represent a more or less accurate snapshot of the main body of her workshop productivity at that time.

If so, then it needs to be recognised that Gentileschi maintained a remarkably modest business operation in relation to what might otherwise have been expected of an artist operating at her level of reputation. She possessed only three easels, for example (with a fourth missing the 'board[s] to be put crosswise on the easels' that she presumably kept as a spare). The inventory of her confiscated possessions, moreover, lists a total of only eight paintings. One almost finished 'portrait of a woman', was already framed. This might have been a personal item (a self-portrait kept on display for visitors to admire, perhaps?). Alternatively, it could have been awaiting collection. The document also mentions '1 large canvas, half painted'. This could conceivably have been the missing *Hercules* for the Medici (see p. 94), although one very much doubts that she would have left behind such an important work. There is also a painting of the *Magdalene*, measuring around 115 cm high, which is described as 'just begun'. Then there are two nearly complete paintings, albeit unframed, that might have been pendants: depicting the *Madonna* and the *Magdalene*, these measured around 115 cm high. Finally, there are 'three small paintings on copper', attesting to her facility in a medium that is otherwise hardly documented in her oeuvre.

It seems reasonable to assume that the eight unfinished paintings represent the sum of Gentileschi's work in hand, which she decided to leave behind on the grounds that they would not be of much use to her when setting up a new base of activity in Rome. If so, then it must be said that this represents a remarkably meagre output of works to have on the go at any one time. It contrasts, for example, with the dozens of unfinished works and/or unframed paintings that are listed among the two-hundred-odd canvases that make up the 1644 inventory of Onofrio de Anfora, a Neapolitan painter operating at a much lower level of the market than Gentileschi. He, nonetheless, managed to maintain a higher level of workshop productivity than was the case in Gentileschi's evidently 'boutique' Florentine operation.[21] Such a comparison is seen also in relation to the inventory of the possessions of the fifty-year-old Roman painter Tommaso Salini, a pupil of Baglione and an early practitioner of Caravaggesque still-life painting. Salini's 1625 inventory lists over two hundred paintings that are stacked in various states of production in his upstairs workshop and downstairs basement storage space and that are often described as either 'sketched' (*sbozzata*) or 'unfinished' (*non feniti*).[22]

The Florentine documentation also contains the first notice of Gentileschi's dilatoriness as a painter. Documents discussed by Elena Fumagalli and subsequently brought together and published more fully by Sheila Barker record a disputed commission that seems to have been left incomplete at the time of Gentileschi's relocation to Rome in February 1620.[23] The timeline for this commission can be reconstructed on the basis of the documents as follows: on 4 June 1618, a certain Simone Carducci (whom Barker identifies as a silk merchant in regular contact with the Medici) disbursed to Gentileschi and her husband an unspecified payment of ten scudi.[24] One and a half years later, on 1 January 1620, the widow Margherita Benvenuti presented a testimony to the Florentine Accademia del Disegno, whose members, as mentioned above, were adjudicating a number of the artist's debts. In it, she notes that she had given Gentileschi a down payment of ten scudi for a painting of the Madonna, for which she was still waiting. She also notes that she had gone to see Artemisia to enquire about the painting in Carducci's company. Carducci should, therefore, probably be identified as a merchant-agent who was acting on Benvenuti's behalf in this matter.[25] An additional, undated testimony by this same creditor from the same period notes that she had gone to Gentileschi's house on more than one occasion to ask after her painting.[26] Another document, dated 3 January 1620, adds to this the testimony of a certain Domenico d'Ottavio Boscoli. Boscoli notes that he had been in the workshop of Tomaso del Salvatico (known as Masino *merciaio*) on several occasions when Carducci had visited and asked if the Madonna was finished. His answer to Carducci was that the painting was well underway.[27] Del Salvatico was a shopkeeper who acted as a business agent, in turn, for Gentileschi during this period. His assistance was necessary when, during periods of her husband's absence, Gentileschi needed a trusted male legal witness to act as a proxy in her financial dealings.[28] So, in this instance we must imagine Carducci impatiently visiting del Salvatico in order to put further pressure on Gentileschi to honour her contract. Barker identifies Boscoli as Gentileschi's workshop assistant, which may be so, although he may equally have been an assistant to del Salvatico who had been observing Gentileschi's progress on the commission.

Down payments were customarily made to artists in instalments, leading up to the *saldo* or final payment made on completion of an account following delivery of a finished painting. A down payment of ten scudi would have typically represented around half the final fee for a painting of this type, which would have been made in two instalments: half at the initial agreement and half again on delivery. We can, accordingly, deduce that the finished painting of the *Madonna* for Carducci and the widow Benvenuti would have probably cost around twenty scudi or thereabouts, an amount (actually paid in the smaller denomination of 140 lire) was exactly the same as that received by Gentileschi in July 1617 from another Florentine patron, Laura Corsini, for an otherwise unidentified painting of *Judith*.[29] On the basis of other payments that will be discussed in Chapter 11, we can further deduce that both these payments would have been for mid-level commissions rather than for major gallery paintings, such as the *Pluto and Persephone*, since these would have cost considerably more. Twenty scudi represented a price that would, instead, have been customarily paid for small to medium-sized works, comprising either one full-length or two half-length figures.

The documents relating to the unfinished *Madonna* commission of 1618–20 would seem to indicate that Gentileschi experienced difficulties in finishing a mid-range commission for a single-figure painting for which she was given a full one and a half years to complete. Of course, Gentileschi can hardly be said to be the world's first dilatory artist. As Rudolf Wittkower and others have noted, patrons were becoming increasingly accustomed during this period to having to wait often long periods before receiving completed work, particularly from painters who were especially in demand.[30] There is thus nothing exceptional in itself about Gentileschi leaving an unfinished commission behind her when suddenly having to leave her base of operations. Nevertheless, the fact that the long-delayed, unfinished commission was not for a major work, in combination with the relatively limited range and scope of Gentileschi's oeuvre relative to other painters, does begin to suggest an apparent issue of productivity on Gentileschi's part during these years. It highlights the possibility that, for whatever reasons, Gentileschi may have been unable to maintain a well-oiled and highly productive workshop enterprise during this early to mid-period stage of her career, an issue to which I shall return in Chapter 12.

CONCLUSION: GENTILESCHI'S PAINTINGS IN EARLY ROMAN COLLECTIONS AND HER DEPARTURE FOR VENICE

The previous analysis has suggested that Artemisia Gentileschi's earning capacity during the 1610s and mid-1620s was restricted on two counts: first, she was limited by being typecast in terms of the narrow range of subjects that her patrons tended to want from her; second, she was restricted by the nature of her workshop operation, a 'boutique' enterprise that was markedly different from the more productive and successful workshops of the day.

Another factor that must have also acted as a drag upon Gentileschi's ability to achieve real success within the insular Roman art world of the 1620s is the lack of any clear indication that her work was being collected in depth during this period. As Richard Spear has observed, the consistent pattern that emerges during these years is of the major Roman collectors of the day all maintaining an only marginal interest in Gentileschi's work.[31] Having gone to the trouble of commissioning Gentileschi's 1622 *Susanna and the Elders*, for example, the Ludovisi family do not appear to have taken the next step of acquiring any further paintings by her. Likewise, Vincenzo Giustiniani seems to have been the intended recipient of Gentileschi's *David with the Head of Goliath*, seen by Sandrart in 1631, yet this commission does not appear to have inspired Giustiniani to order anything more. (By contrast, and as an example of the kind of in-depth collecting that she seems to have largely missed out on, Gentileschi's colleague Nicolas Régnier was heavily patronised by Giustiniani, employing him as an official artist-in-residence in his family palace and owning no fewer than nine of his paintings.[32])

There must have been some exceptions to this prevailing trend, but documentary evidence of the collecting of Gentileschi's paintings while she was in Rome remains frustratingly opaque at this stage of our understanding. In a letter of 1635, she refers to 'the happy memory of His Eminence Cardinal d'Este, whose generosity I greatly enjoyed'.[33] This might indicate an interest in her work on the part of Cardinal Alessandro d'Este (1568–1624), the celebrated patron of the Villa d'Este at Tivoli. Yet the subsequent documentation following the transferral of the cardinal's collection from Rome to Modena contains no reference to her work.[34] In 1620, the Stiattesi/Gentileschi/Maringhi correspondence makes tantalising reference to Gentileschi's working on a commission for Cardinal Alessandro Peretti Montalto (1571–1623), the great-nephew of the former pope, Sixtus V, and likewise one of the leading patrons in early seventeenth-century Rome (also, incidentally, a patron of Agostino Tassi, as mentioned above). But, here again, no record of her work appears in the publications on Montalto's collecting activities.[35] This makes the documentation surrounding the collection of Alessandro Biffi especially significant. This important Roman collector bequeathed a dozen paintings to the Veralli family in the 1630s that were subsequently integrated into the Spada collection by marriage (see p. 90). These included Orazio Gentileschi's *David Contemplating the Head of Goliath*, together with four paintings by Artemisia, a *Madonna and Child* (fig. 11), a *St Cecilia* and two small oval paintings depicting personifications of Painting and Poetry. The relative obscurity of this early collector in comparison with the more high-profile individuals mentioned above is probably significant in itself, as is the collector's initial interest in the work of Orazio rather than that of Artemisia. Yet more important were the religious paintings acquired in the mid-1620s by the Duke of Alcalá during his tenure as the Spanish Ambassador to the Holy See. The exceptional nature of this collector's interest in Gentileschi's work seems to have been a major factor encouraging her move to Naples in the 1630s (see pp. 145–46).

This pattern holds true even for a patron like Cassiano dal Pozzo. Dal Pozzo was a key ally of Gentileschi's Roman years. He subsequently owned a self-portrait by her as well as Vouet's *Portrait of Artemisia Gentileschi*, an important visual document of Artemisia's growing celebrity status during the 1620s (fig. 76).[36] Yet Dal Pozzo does not appear to have collected her works to any great extent. He was also largely unsuccessful in bringing Gentileschi to the attention of his masters and patrons, the Barberini, who would soon come to dominate the local scene as arbiters of taste and leaders of cultural policy more generally during the papacy of Urban VIII (1623–44). The Barberini seem to have been only marginally interested in collecting Gentileschi's work. A 1644 inventory of the collection of Cardinal Antonio Barberini, for example, lists a single painting by Gentileschi of a 'woman with a cupid'.[37] Scholars have associated this reference with Gentileschi's *Sleeping Venus* now in the Barbara Piasecka Johnson Foundation, Princeton, New Jersey (see p. 115).[38] If commissioned sometime during the mid-1620s in Rome, as one would expect, the *Sleeping Venus* seems not to have been delivered to the cardinal until the mid-1630s, some years after Gentileschi's departure from Rome. The evidence for this comes in one of her letters to Dal Pozzo, written in Naples in 1635, in which she mentions sending her brother to Rome to deliver a painting to Cardinal Antonio Barberini.[39] She asks Dal Pozzo to take charge of presenting her brother to the cardinal and to look after the details – presumably to make sure he gets paid and then sent promptly on his way. The long delay involved in taking possession of this work may well have constituted one reason for the Barberini's lack of any apparent interest in commissioning further paintings by Gentileschi.

The leading Roman connoisseurs of the late 1620s and 1630s preferred instead to focus on more recently emerging talents, such as Nicolas Poussin, Andrea Sacchi, Guercino, Lanfranco, Valentin de Boulogne and the new star on the scene, Pietro da Cortona.[40] Gentileschi may have been enjoying a certain kind of fame by this period, as discussed below, but, if so, it was one that appears not to have been based on any particular increase in the collecting of her work by the local connoisseurs. She would, therefore, have had reason to feel increasingly marginalised in Rome during the late 1620s.

These factors seem to have encouraged Gentileschi to take the otherwise unexpected step of uprooting her base of operations once more and making another move, this time to Venice, in search of improved circumstances. This trip, however, also met with mixed results. It certainly helped to raise Gentileschi's profile to a yet higher level of international acclaim, but this, too, appears not to have translated into a comparable strengthening of her popularity among a solid collector base, leading to a further relocation, after just three years in Venice, to Naples.

9

Venice, 1627–1629

FROM REALISM TO REFINEMENT AND THE CREATION OF A CELEBRITY BRAND

INTRODUCTION
ARTEMISIA AMONG THE ACADEMICIANS

The previous discussion sought to shed light on the broader career considerations informing Gentileschi's decision to leave Rome in favour of an extended period of residence in Venice from either late 1626 or early 1627 to 1629. A further impetus for her reasoning may have been that a number of Artemisia's Roman colleagues made a similar journey during this same period. Simon Vouet also travelled to Venice in the same year, although in his case he was visiting the city en route to Paris to take up the position of Premier Peintre du Roi. Gentileschi might, in addition, have received positive reports on the Venetian scene from another recently departed colleague: in 1626, Nicolas Régnier, her drinking partner from among the Northern Caravaggisti, had left the papal city for Venice, where he subsequently came to enjoy success as a painter and art dealer.[1]

Jesse Locker has added to our knowledge of Gentileschi's Venetian sojourn by investigating the artistic culture and patronal networks underpinning a series of poems, songs, dedicatory inscriptions and letters that were written in praise of the artist by a group of Venetian academicians between 1627 and 1630. These demonstrate that Gentileschi's Venetian relocation was highly successful – at least, in terms of promoting her reputation

FACING PAGE Artemisia Gentileschi, *Lucretia* (detail of fig. 77)

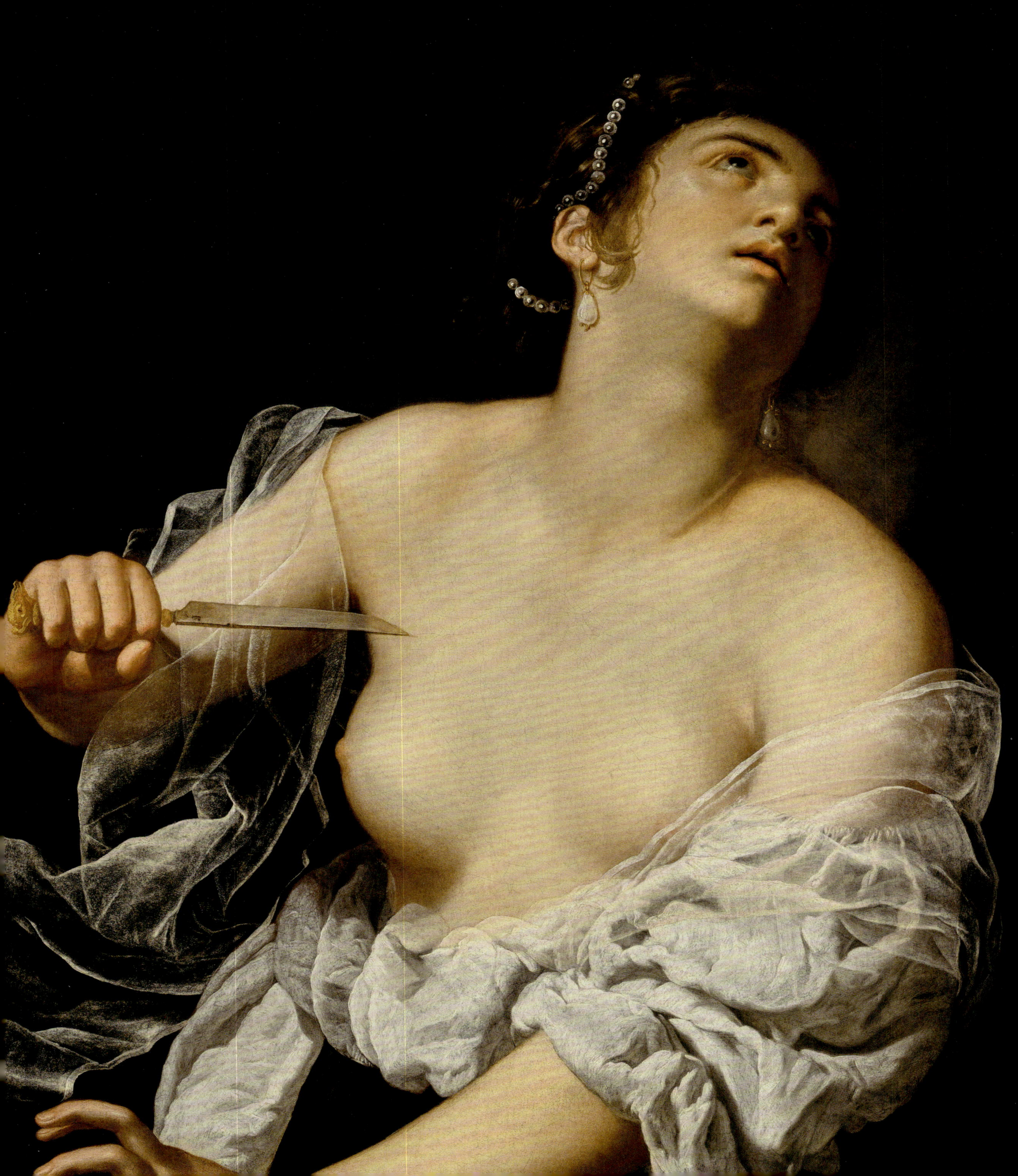

within a more international arena than had hitherto been possible.[2] Seven poems dedicated to Artemisia and her paintings appear in a manuscript of 1627 in the Barberini archives;[3] two letters containing further poems, as well as madrigals and inscriptions in her honour, appear in the correspondence of the writer and academician Antonino Collurafi which was published in 1628.[4] The members of the group of writers responsible for these pieces were all closely related – Collurafi, for example, was the childhood tutor of Giovan Francesco Loredan, who was the Principe of the Venetian Accademia dei Desiosi, of which Gentileschi was also a member, and so on.

Three of the poems from 1627 describe a painting of *Lucretia*, one each describe paintings of *Susanna* and a *Sleeping Cupid* and two more were penned in honour of self-portraits of Artemisia. They all grow out of an explicitly Marinesque literary tradition that had sprung up in the wake of the international renown enjoyed by Giambattista Marino's series of ekphrastic poems about paintings and sculptures entitled *La Galeria*, of 1619–20 (an anthology that includes poems dedicated to Caravaggio's *Head of the Medusa* and Cristofano Allori's *Judith with the Head of Holofernes*, among others; see pp. 65–66).[5] The Marinesque literary style tends to refer to paintings only indirectly, using them as reference points for often wilfully extravagant meditations on the interplay between artifice and reality. It is, accordingly, often problematic to conclude with certainty which painting is being referred to in a poem said to be about a painting by a particular artist on a particular subject, and, therefore, difficult to be absolutely confident, for example, whether the two poems in praise of Gentileschi's self-portraits were based on completed portraits, or merely the idea of them, as it were. Be that as it may, a print by Jérôme David after a lost self-portrait of Gentileschi that also dates to this period should certainly be seen as part of this broader process of reputation-building (fig. 73). It may even be more specifically identifiable with one or other of the two self-portraits mentioned in the poems.[6]

JÉRÔME DAVID'S *PORTRAIT OF ARTEMISIA* AND THE SHIFT FROM THE DISGUISED SELF-PORTRAIT TO THE OFFICIAL CELEBRITY PORTRAIT

The discussion of Gentileschi's Florentine self-portraits above (pp. 86–88) interpreted them as part of a self-promotional strategy to develop an instantly recognisable branded imagery of herself as an alluring and inventive female artist of renown. Like the official portraits of the Medici or of Michelangelo, they were intended to distil her features into a fixed typology that could then be converted into a series of easily distinguishable and reproducible signs: a physiognomic iconography constituting a celebrity artist's signature look.

In David's print, we witness this typology being taken up by another artist and then converted by way of the engraving process into an image of yet greater clarity, crispness and mass-reproducibility (fig. 73). Gentileschi's trademark features are once again to the fore: the full face; the long nose with a slightly raised sharp tip; the pursed lips that highlight the clearly defined undulations of the cupid's bow of Artemisia's upper lip; the dimpled chin; the long, slender neck; the drop-pearl earrings; and the prominent, cropped, wavy chestnut hair. This hair has even been parted in the middle: a direct match with Gentileschi's hairstyle in *The Conversion of the Magdalene* (fig. 40). The only new element that has been added to this anthology of Gentileschian physiognomic identifiers is a quizzically raised eyebrow. This conveys the impression that Artemisia is sizing us up at just the same time as we are visually appraising her.

What is distinctive about this printed portrait, then, as well as the poems and other items associated with this mid- to late-1620s reputational push, is the way in which they take the strategy of self-promotional imagery and transfer it from Artemisia's looking at herself in the mirror to the acclamation of the celebrated image of Artemisia by writers and other artists. In so doing, the more experimental self-portraits of the Florentine period are resolved in these later examples into a more iconographically stable series of official portraits in their own right. Artemisia's self-promotional strategy has now evolved from her promoting herself to others promoting her. She has successfully transformed herself into something that

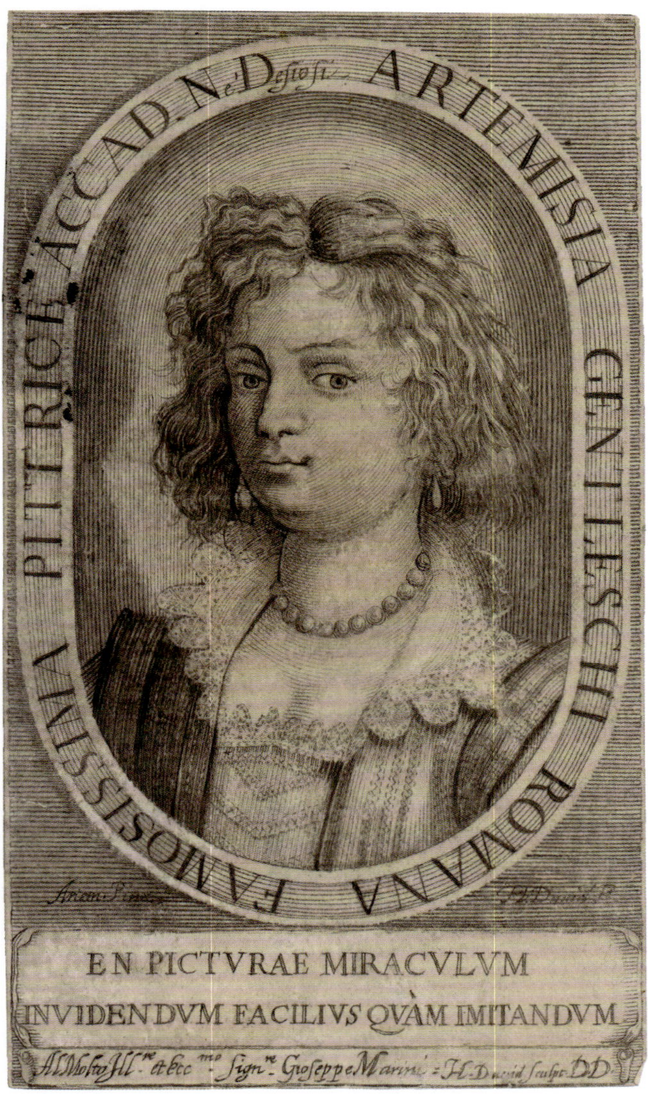

73 Jérôme David after Artemisia Gentileschi, *Portrait of Artemisia Gentileschi (after her Self-portrait)*, c.1627–28, engraving, 14.1 × 8 cm, British Museum, London

she had long since wished to become – a celebrity in her own right, with a trademark self-image of instantly recognisable visual identifiers. These are capable of being taken up by other artists and then translated across a range of media, including painting, poetry and engraving.

The inscriptions that accompany David's print provide further, textual corroboration of the portrait's claims to Artemisia's fame. The one along the bottom extols Gentileschi as 'a marvel in the art of painting/more easily envied than imitated'. It is based on an epigram describing the greatness of Zeuxis and Apollodorus, thus creating the allusion that Artemisia's stature is comparable with that of the most renowned ancient artists.[7] Indeed, one of the above-mentioned poems goes further still, to claim that Artemisia's greatness actually eclipses that of both Zeuxis and Apelles.[8] The inscription around the portrait identifies Artemisia as 'a very famous painter, academician in the Desiosi'. Thus, the young woman who declared during the rape trial, 'I cannot write and can read very little',[9] has progressed within the space of fifteen years to the extent of becoming a celebrated member of one of the most learned and clubbish societies of the Venetian patrician literati. Once again, and as was noted earlier in the context of Leonard Bramer's caricatures, one is struck by the rapidity with which Gentileschi has been able to cultivate strategically advantageous associations in a new city in order to set up effective networks with leading groups of cultural brokers and other influential figures active on the scene.

These activities formed part of a concerted effort to promote Gentileschi's image that, in fact, slightly predated the artist's relocation to Venice. A one-sided, commemorative portrait medallion is probably to be dated just prior to her departure for Venice. It adopts a profile view of the artist that includes all the elements of David's print but adds to it a classicising mantle worn around Gentileschi's shoulders. This reinforces the image's associations with the ancient Roman medallion format adopted for emperors, famous generals, poets and the like (fig. 74).[10] A curious drawing by Pierre Dumonstier, a Parisian artist resident in Rome, takes as its subject a painstakingly transcribed portrait of Gentileschi's right hand, created, as the accompanying inscription notes, on 31 December 1625 in the presence of the artist, who is described as both 'excellent and learned' (fig. 75).[11] The drawing's reverse includes a poetic inscription comparing her beauty and artistic accomplishments with those of Aurora, the goddess of dawn: 'The hands of Aurora are praised and renowned for their rare beauty. But this one is a thousand times more worthy for knowing how to make marvels that send the most judicious eyes into rapture.'

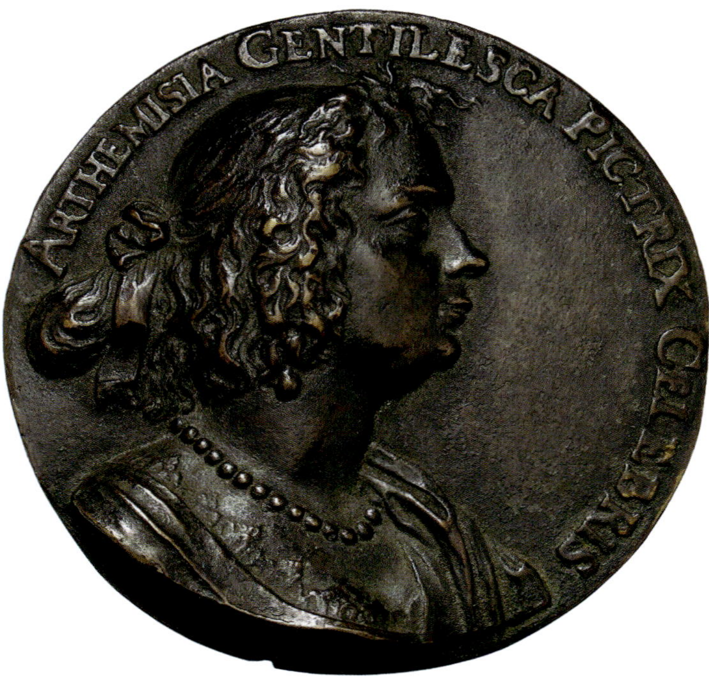

74 Unknown artist active in Rome in the 1620s, *Portrait of Artemisia Gentileschi*, *c.*1625, bronze, diam. 5.4 cm, Münzkabinett (Numismatic Collection), Staatliche Museen zu Berlin (reproduced larger than actual size)

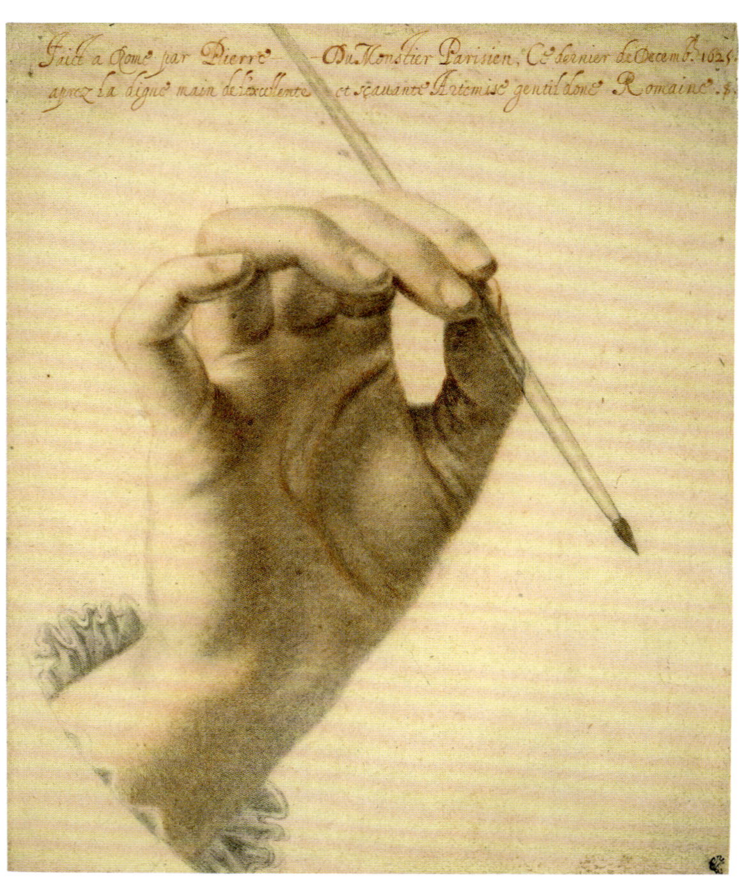

75 Pierre Dumonstier II, also known as Dumonstier le Neveu, *The Right Hand of Artemisia Gentileschi Holding a Brush*, signed and dated 1625, black and red chalk on paper, 21.9 × 18 cm, British Museum, London

Dumonstier's reference to Gentileschi's beauty and her ability to provoke a sense of rapture in the viewer grows out of the broader, conventional tendency to associate female intellectual accomplishment with physical beauty.[12] This star-struck, fetishisation of Artemisia's hand is directly comparable with the campaign to praise Artemisia's physical attributes that forms a notable feature of the Venetian poems and letters. The leader of this circle of authors and Principe of the Accademia dei Desiosi, for example, the Venetian senator referred to above (p. 134), Giovanni Francesco Loredan (1607–1661), was effusive in his admiration of Gentileschi's physical attributes. This is notable in a letter written for circulation prior to its being eventually and posthumously published in 1673. Loredan's hyperbolic flattery may well strike a discordant note in relation to today's cultural values, but it conforms to the standard conventions of Baroque panegyric rhetoric and so provides important additional documentation of Gentileschi's renown in Venice during this period. In the letter, Loredan describes her as having 'a superhuman beauty', stating, further, that 'my heart has become subject to the power of the beauty of your face'. It concludes by declaring with yet greater specificity that 'the richness of Love can do no more than to trade in your breast, your eyes and your hair'.[13]

SIMON VOUET'S *PORTRAIT OF ARTEMISIA GENTILESCHI*

At some stage before her relocation to Venice, Artemisia sat for a portrait painted by Simon Vouet in a yet further indication of her increasing fame. The painting was discovered by

Roberto Contini in 2001 but not integrated into the wider literature on Artemisia Gentileschi until 2011 (fig. 76). Still relatively little studied, it constitutes a crucial addition to the iconography of Artemisia.[14]

The composition reveals one painter posing for another while assuming a carefully staged role of pre-eminent artistic authority and renown. In her pose and demeanour, Artemisia shows herself to be 'bold and self-confident, ironic and playful, a professional artist in possession of herself and her technical tools', as Mary Garrard has noted.[15] Garrard and others have also underscored the painting's numerous visual references to Artemisia's high degree of success and artistic proficiency. The pencil, multiple brushes and range of colours shown on her palette, for example, all proclaim her skills not only as a colourist but also in terms of the more intellectual and theoretically demanding academic requirements of the art of *disegno*.[16]

Even more overt in terms of its allusion to the properties of fame is the gold medallion that has been pinned to Artemisia's bodice. As Contini and others have noted, this medallion bears a miniaturised image of the legendary Mausoleum of Halicarnassus.[17] It associates Gentileschi with her legendary namesake, Queen Artemisia II of Caria, who was buried in the Mausoleum with her brother-husband, Mausolus, and whose name was often invoked in the literature on *donne forti* (strong women) as a 'lasting example of chaste widowhood and of the purest and rarest form of love'.[18] One might also be justified in seeing the motif as a specific allusion to Queen Artemisia's fame not only as an embodiment of female virtue but also as the creative 'inventor' of the Mausoleum itself, a structure renowned for eternity as one of the seven wonders of the ancient world. In support of this reading, it should be noted that the same association was made by the academician Collurafi, who observed, in one of his letters published in 1628, that Gentileschi had attained greater renown for her creations than had Queen Artemisia herself.[19] The ancient queen and the modern painter are thus linked together in Vouet's composition as famous artistic and creative representatives of the *donne forti* tradition.

To whom should the iconography of this symbolically allusive painting be assigned? This is an important question, bearing in mind, of course, that it relates to a portrait of Gentileschi rather than a portrait by her. Garrard has suggested that the painting should be viewed as 'a collaboration, in which the sitter provides the psychological complement to the painter's brush'. For Francesco Solinas, on the other hand, Vouet is to be attributed with much of the painting's *concetto* (conceit). He, accordingly, characterises the inclusion of the medallion as 'a clever and amusing puzzle devised by the French master to indicate the name of his friend'. An alternative reading can, nonetheless, be proposed, one that rests on a more direct and, in a sense, more straightforward observation concerning the medallion and its iconography. The specificity of the medallion's depiction suggests that it may have been a decorative feature actually worn by Artemisia while sitting for the portrait in order to highlight her status and fame.

In support of this reading, I would note that there is something very particular about the way that this medallion and chain have been so purposefully arranged upon Artemisia's dress and body. We observe, for example, the manner in which the chain drapes elegantly down the side and middle of her bodice, while the medallion has been highlighted – just so – in order to rest on a clear area of her dress immediately to the right of the elaborately embroidered buttons that would otherwise dominate her front and detract from the medallion's visual impact. None of this is possible in a natural sense – particularly if one imagines the sitter moving about – bending forward to paint, for example, while turning to listen to her interlocutor. Any movement at all, in fact, would disturb the precise equilibrium created by the careful placement of this elegant – and obviously highly significant – piece of formal attire.

Clearly, then, the medallion and chain must have been affixed precisely with pins in order to rest in just this way against the sitter's bodice. And it makes logical sense to assign agency for this creative act of self-adornment to the person responsible for dressing herself – that is, of course, to Artemisia rather than to Vouet. Once we have attributed the medallion's presence in the painting to Gentileschi herself – to grant her the agency, in other words, of having owned it and brought it with her to the sitting – it then follows that the chain from which the medallion hangs might also be of personal significance. Notable, in this respect, is the very particular way that this chain has been pinned around the sitter's bodice in a manner that accords it a visual prominence within the composition that is equal to that of the medallion itself.

The chain should thus be understood as performing the same rhetorical function as the gold chain worn subsequently by Artemisia as La Pittura in the *Self-portrait as the Allegory of Painting (La Pittura)*, executed in London around fifteen years later (fig. 103).[20] Here, in Vouet's earlier portrait, the chain and medallion work together as a unit. They were probably an honorific gift presented to the artist sometime in the past and now worn proudly by her in order to proclaim her status as a decorated painter. In so doing, Artemisia rehearses a role in Rome in the mid-1620s that she will reprise at the end of the 1630s, when she reuses the motif of the gold chain to refer to La Pittura as well as to the gold honorific chain presented to the most renowned artists of the day.

Gold chains could be conferred on artists only by pre-eminent patrons. Titian, for example, depicted himself wearing a chain that had been given to him by Charles V in 1533, on the occasion of the artist's elevation to noble rank.[21] One can only speculate as to who might have given Artemisia her chain. Fernando Enrìquez Afán de Ribera, the Duke of Alcalá, represents a strong candidate for someone who might have made such a learned and munificent gesture. As noted in the previous chapter, the Duke of Alcalá acted as one of Artemisia's most enthusiastic patrons during this period, while serving as the Spanish Ambassador to the Holy See. He was also a scholar of some erudition and lover of complex allegories, as attested by the extensive library and elaborately symbolic decorative scheme in his palace in Seville. He would also go on to act as one of Artemisia's principal sponsors during her early years in Naples, in his capacity as Neapolitan viceroy from 1629 to 1631.

A second possibility derives from the portrait's original context. As Contini's archival research has established, the picture was painted to form part of Cassiano dal Pozzo's collection of portraits of illustrious personages. With its erudite references to ancient medallions and antique iconography, it seems eminently reasonable to proffer Dal Pozzo as a potential contender for the bestower of this original gift. If so, then Artemisia would be depicted here returning the compliment by posing for a painting for Dal Pozzo while wearing the very medal and chain that he had given her. Whatever the truth, and the point must remain speculative at this stage of our knowledge, it is, at least, certain that the presence of the chain and medallion in Vouet's painting would have done much to magnify and emblazon the associations of fame attached to the commissioning of this portrait and its subsequent installation in Dal Pozzo's collection of *uomini famosi* (portraits of famous men) that formed part of the decoration of his library during the period just before Artemisia's departure for Venice.[22]

GENTILESCHI'S VENETIAN PAINTINGS: *LUCRETIA* AND *ESTHER AND AHASEURUS* AND THE TRANSITION FROM REALISM TO REFINEMENT

The Venetian poems and letters provide some of the only indications on record for the work produced by Artemisia during her Venetian period. The references found in the group of seven poems from 1627 were to a *Susanna*, a *Sleeping Cupid*, one or two self-portraits and a *Lucretia*. A possible candidate for the last cited work appeared in 2019 on the Paris art market before being acquired by the J. Paul Getty Museum (fig. 77).[23] This significant addition to Gentileschi's oeuvre is noteworthy for demonstrating the artist's first-hand knowledge of sixteenth-century Venetian painting. Lucretia's creamy white sleeves, for example, draw upon the luxurious rendition of fabrics that is found in paintings of courtesans and the like by Titian and others.[24] This contrasts with the harsher and less idealized treatment of drapery encountered in an earlier version of *Lucretia* that has been placed as either among Gentileschi's earliest works or else to the beginning of the 1620s (the later dating being preferrable in my opinion) (fig. 78).[25] This earlier version of the subject maintains a relatively unconstrained Caravaggesque approach that relates it back to the directly observed modelling from life that was a defining feature of the 1610 *Susanna and the Elders* (fig. 13).

Gentileschi's attentiveness towards modelling the body from life remains as a kind of muscle memory in the Getty *Lucretia*. We note, in this respect, the projective clarity of the rendition of Lucretia's right fist, or the sheen of sweat running along the ridge of her cheek bone. Yet this approach has been

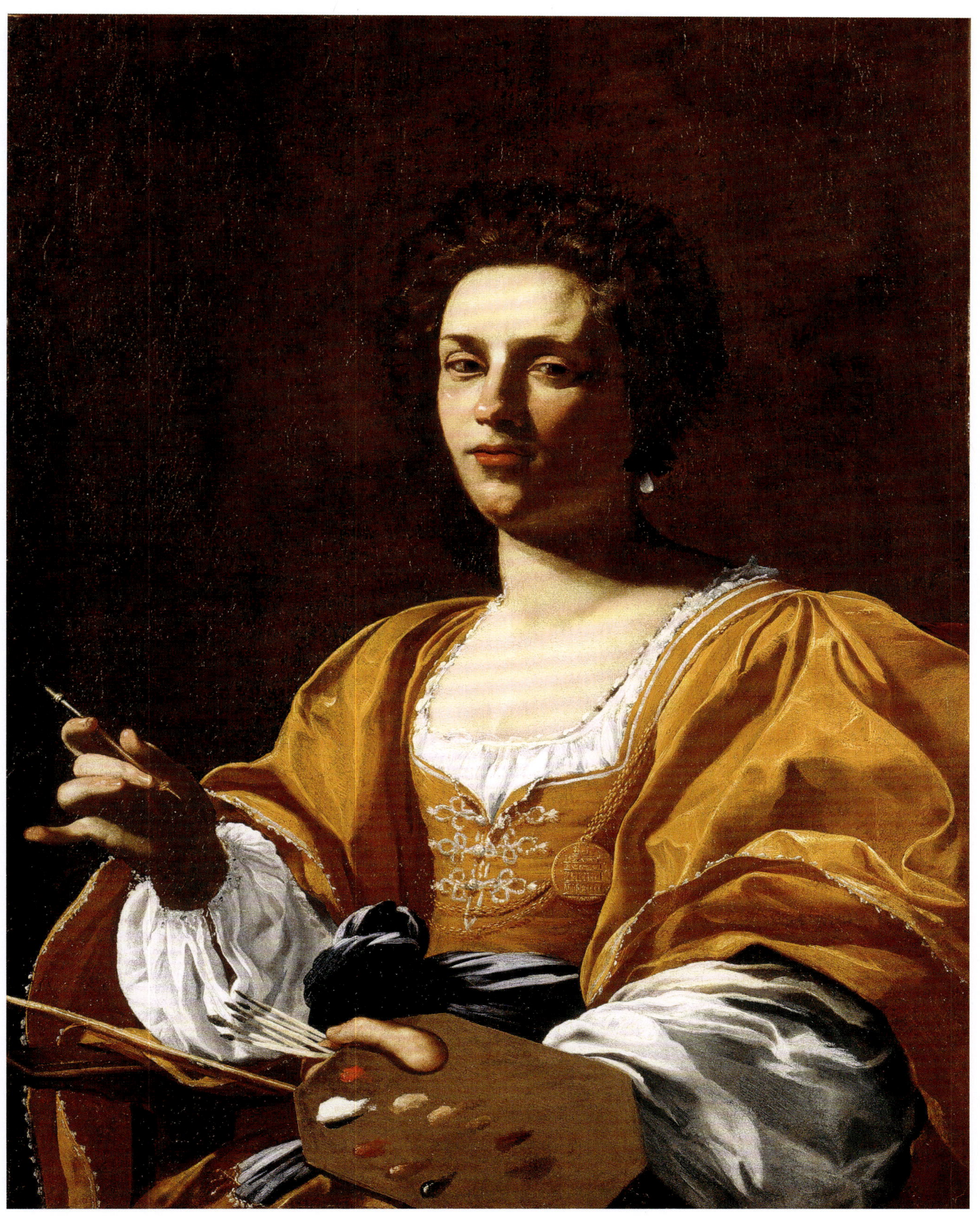

76 Simon Vouet, *Portrait of Artemisia Gentileschi*, *c.*1623–26, oil on canvas, 90 × 71 cm, Palazzo Blu, Pisa, Property of the Fondazione Pisa

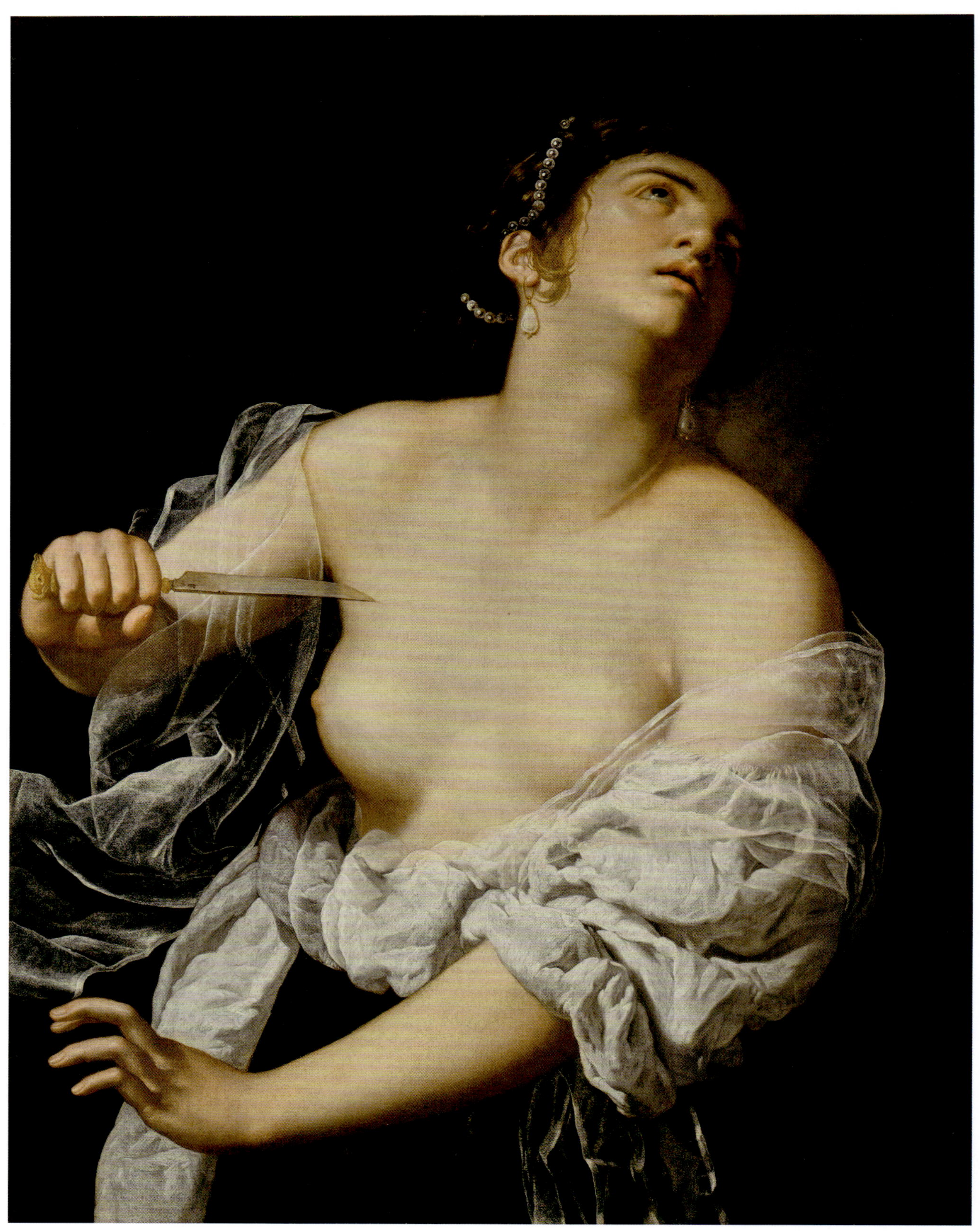

77 Artemisia Gentileschi, *Lucretia*, c.1627, oil on canvas, 92.9 × 72.7 cm, The J. Paul Getty Museum, Los Angeles

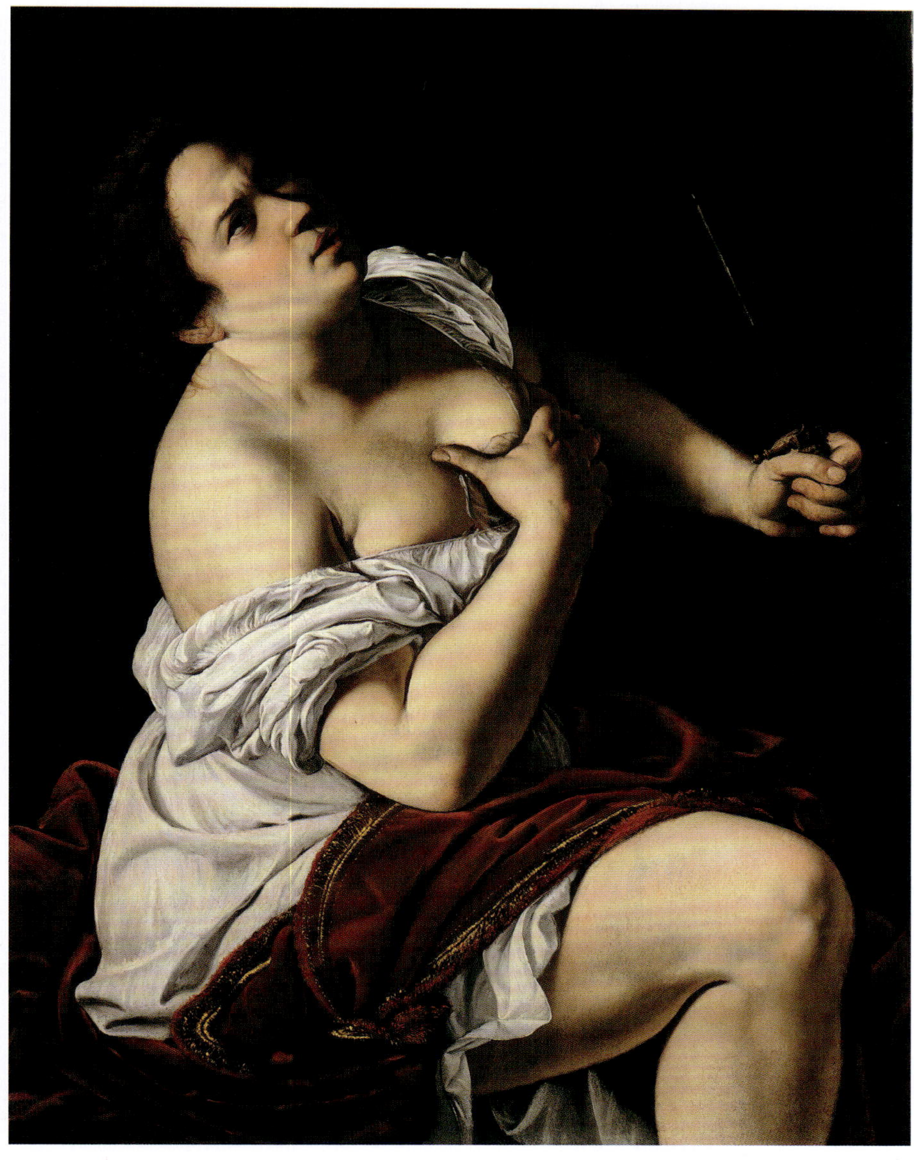

78 Artemisia Gentileschi, *Lucretia*, early 1620s, oil on canvas, 100 × 77 cm, Etro Collection

reconfigured by transforming Lucretia's body into an elegant arabesque of ornamentally frozen motion. The contrast with the dramatic realism of the first version of *Lucretia* could not be greater. The first Lucretia literally grasps her breast with her free hand in a gesture of almost shocking physicality. The second Lucretia, however, uses her free hand to swivel downwards and across in an elegant counter-motion that recalls the sweeping gesture in the Detroit *Judith and her Maidservant* (fig. 69). Lucretia's left hand remains frozen in an almost abstract, wave-like gesture of supplication. This acts as a pleading counterpoint to the clenched-fist certainty of her right hand as it grasps the blade from above.

A bravura display of transparent chiffon drapery swirls around Lucretia's body, acting as a kind of external manifestation of the inner turbulence of her thoughts. She looks towards the heavens for guidance as she weighs up the consequences of her fateful decision to free herself of the guilt created by her rape at the hands of Tarquin. Knowing the story's conclusion, as would have been expected of seventeenth-century viewers, we can see that she has already resolved to carry out the ultimate act of ritualised self-sacrifice in order to regain her honour and virtue. The work's emphasis on rape and self-imposed honour-killing also carries with it some potentially uncomfortable associations with the artist's experience of rape some fifteen years earlier. And yet the viewer, in this instance, is not left with any sense of raw unresolvedness lurking beneath the painting's surface. Instead, the painting projects an overwhelming sense of the triumph of the artist's evident desire to subsume her personal experience within a refined and discerning visual language. This maintains all the power of her earlier treatments of Susanna, Judith and other historically wronged women but adds a new confidence and bravura based on an increased focus on the artistic qualities of refinement, concision and poise.

After being endorsed by Mauro Natale and Jesse Locker, the *Lucretia* was acquired in 2021 by the Getty Museum and featured in Sheila Barker's monograph of the following year.[26] The rapid acceptance of this painting as an autograph work renders it especially significant as one of the few works with clear links to Gentileschi's Venetian years.[27] One canvas with which it does demonstrate close stylistic connections and which has for many years been associated with Gentileschi's Venetian period is the *Esther and Ahaseurus* now at the Metropolitan Museum of Art (fig 79).[28] As Locker and Natale have observed, the lost-profile facial type in the Getty *Lucretia* relates closely to that of Esther in the Metropolitan painting, to which one can add the luxurious treatment of draperies, such as the translucent chiffon that again appears in the headdress worn by the maidservant to the left of Esther. The *Esther and Ahaseurus* is, moreover, a palpably Venetian work. It is based on a painting of this subject by Veronese, the popularity of which as a source is confirmed by another, closely related adaptation by a Paduan contemporary of Gentileschi, Alessandro Varotari called Padovanino (1588–1649), whose work also bears a number of other points of contact with her art of this period.[29]

At nearly three metres across, *Esther and Ahaseurus* is directly comparable with the imposing dimensions of Gentileschi's lost Medicean canvases of *The Bath of Diana* and *Pluto and Persephone*. It ranks as the first extant work by her to demonstrate of what she was capable when given the opportunity to work at the maximum scale of the grandest of history paintings produced for a (still-to-be-identified) palatial setting. While all commentators have noted its obviously neo-Venetian manner, some have, nonetheless, also sought to date it on stylistic grounds to the first years of her Neapolitan residence, from 1630 onwards.[30] The painting can, therefore, be perceived as a transitional work pointing the way forwards to Gentileschi's Neapolitan period, as much as it also looks back to encapsulate her progression from Rome to Venice during the late 1620s. It certainly represents an excellent summation of the kind of sweeping luxuriousness that she was able to offer her new Neapolitan client base upon her arrival in the administrative centre of the Spanish viceregal Kingdom of Naples in 1630, a sprawlingly vast region that, at that time, took in the entire sweep of southern Italy, from the border of the Papal States in the Roman Campania to the heel of Messina, and beyond to the island of Sicily.

GENTILESCHI FINDS A DEDICATED SOURCE OF PATRONAGE AND SHIFTS HER POWER BASE ONCE MORE

So why would Gentileschi take it upon herself to move her base of operations yet again, this time to southern Italy, given the increase in reputational cachet that she had just been able to achieve in Venice? It is sometimes suggested that she might have fled Venice in advance of a devastating plague that ravaged the city during the summer of 1630, ultimately claiming the lives of as much as thirty per cent of the city's population.[31] Yet, if so, Gentileschi did not choose to return to Venice following the plague's cessation. Furthermore, and as Bissell and others have argued, the chronology of her movements between cities during this period render it more likely that she had already left Venice sometime earlier, in 1629, before the plague broke, .[32] In attempting to account for her reasoning, we need to consider once again her probable professional concerns as

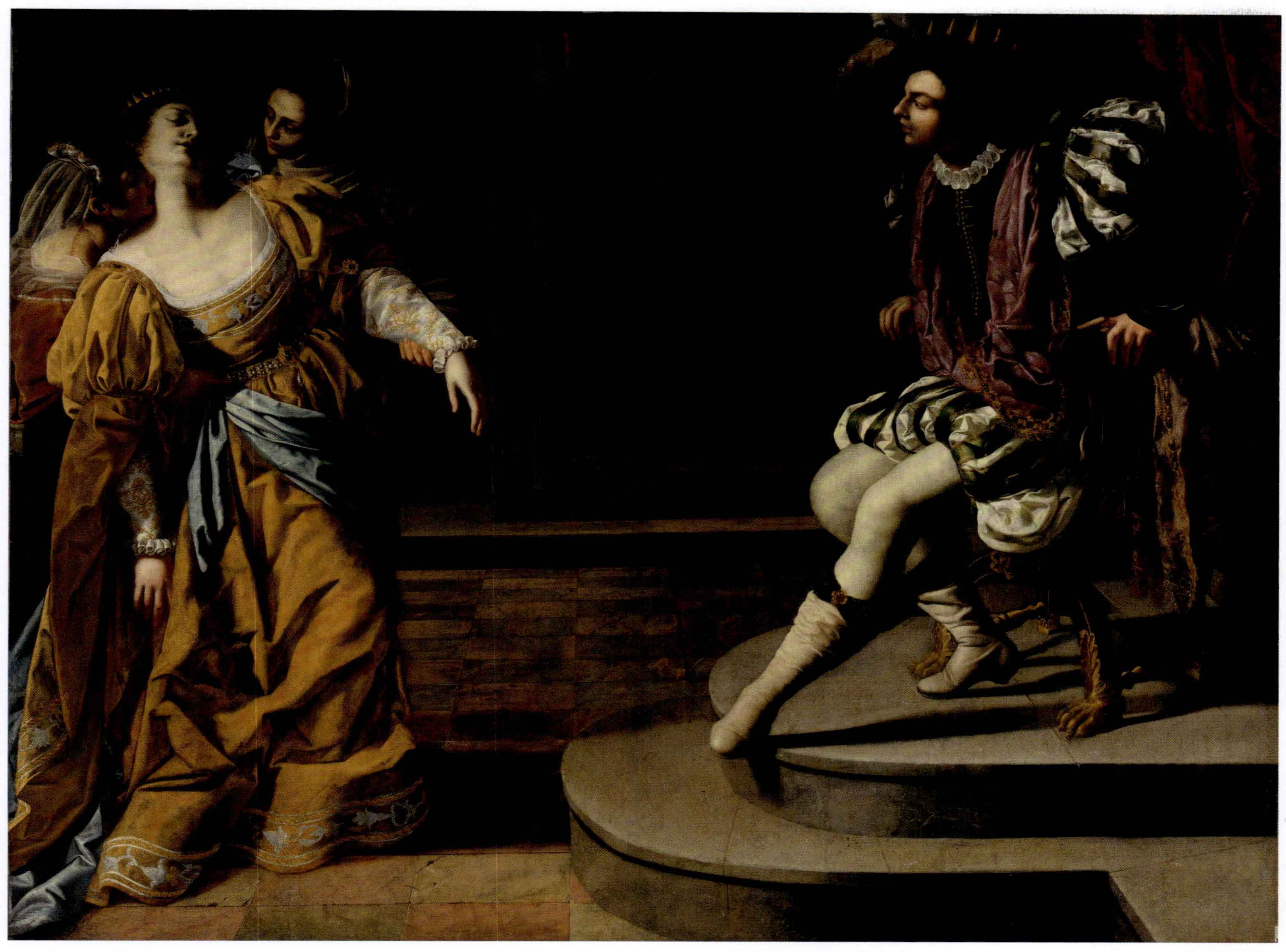

79 Artemisia Gentileschi, *Esther and Ahaseurus*, c.1628–30, oil on canvas, 208.3 × 273.7 cm, The Metropolitan Museum of Art, New York

she sought to consolidate her reputation in ways that brought her adequate financial recompense in addition to the more abstract benefits of her increasing international fame.

By the late 1620s, Gentileschi had clearly attracted significant international renown among a broad range of influential admirers and institutions based in cities throughout the Italian peninsula. In Florence, it had been the Medici, together with the Accademia del Disegno and the circle of associates surrounding Michelangelo Buonarroti the Younger, who had helped to push her reputation to another level. In Venice she captivated the academicians associated with Giovan Loredan and his entourage. In Rome, we have already noted the commemorative medallion, the drawing of Gentileschi's hand and Vouet's portrait of Gentileschi for Cassiano dal Pozzo's gallery of *uomini famosi*, all attesting to her international prominence during the 1620s.

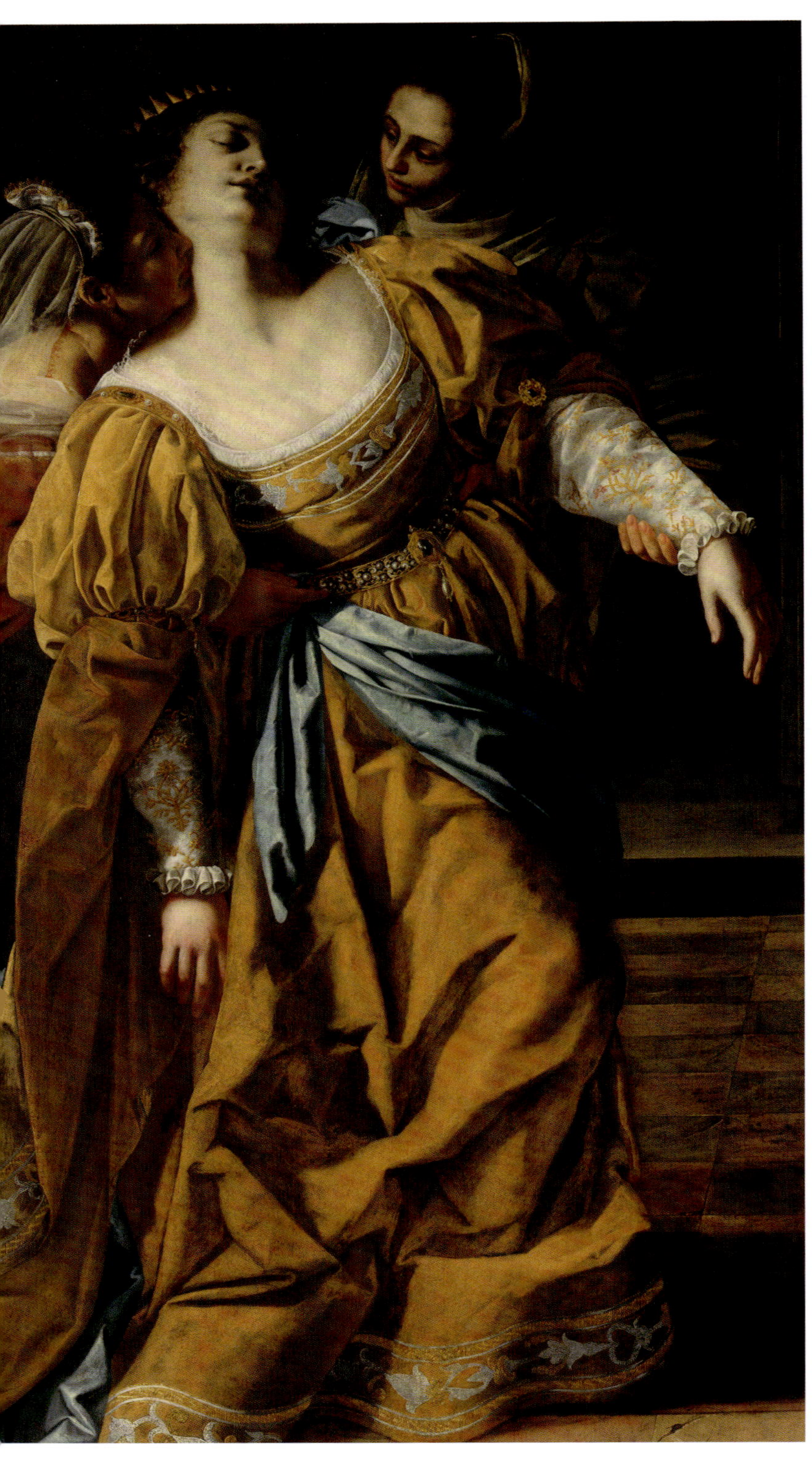

Artemisia Gentileschi, *Esther and Ahaseurus* (detail of fig. 79)

A further indication of the Roman art world's fascination with Gentileschi's celebrity status during these years comes in a tantalising reference contained in a document in the archives of the Accademia di San Luca.[33] This occurs in the context of a general meeting of the Academy that was held on 29 June 1627 and that coincided with the announcement of Vouet's stepping down as Principe and his replacement by Ottavio Leoni, a painter and printmaker best known for his portraits of Caravaggio and other protagonists of the Roman Baroque.[34] The minutes of the meeting record six artworks that are listed as being in the possession of various individuals but that are identified as needing to be returned to the Academy as part of the general administrative settling of accounts that accompanied Vouet's departure. Among these are a 'portrait of Raphael of Urbino and the portrait of Artemisia' that were then in the safekeeping of another academician, the Sienese painter Michelangelo Guidi.[35]

The timing of this reference coincides more or less exactly with the production of Vouet's previously discussed portrait of Gentileschi for Cassiano dal Pozzo. One wonders, therefore, whether there might originally have been some link between the portrait belonging to the Academy and Vouet's painting. Perhaps it was a second version of Vouet's portrait for Dal Pozzo that Vouet had produced as a copy for the Academy while working on Dal Pozzo's commission. The Academy's portraits, however, tend to be more regular in format and less elaborate than Vouet's painting. The 'portrait of Artemisia' mentioned in the document thus appears more likely to have been an independently produced work that had been acquired by the Academy at some point in the past. This would not have been without precedent. The Academy is known to have owned other portraits of distinguished non-members, including a portrait of Sofonisba Anguissola, which is listed as being in their possession by 1633.[36] Whatever the case may have been, the presence of this portrait in the collection of the Accademia di San Luca during the late 1620s attests further to Gentileschi's standing in the papal city as a figure of considerable renown both institutionally and on an individual level, despite the fact that she never appears to have been a fully fledged member of the Academy.[37]

None of this, however, seems to have fundamentally altered the underlying structural problems that were noted above in the context of Gentileschi's career during this period. She was now a celebrity. This constituted a major career accomplishment. Yet for all its undoubted significance on a reputational level, this enhanced status does not appear to have created any significant additional demand for her work or to have led to any other more material benefits. Artemisia had become famous, in effect, for being famous. She was celebrated as a *stupor mundi*, a *virtuosa*, an exceptional woman: all of which rendered her as an object of powerful curiosity and respectful admiration among her male colleagues. Yet it did not make her famous on the more fundamental level of receiving greater recognition for her intrinsic artistic capabilities. Her fame did not principally reside, in short, in her ability to maintain an independently successful career as an artist.

All the medallions, portraits, panegyrics and other trumpets of renown, it seems, could do nothing substantially to improve Gentileschi's career prospects by the end of the 1620s. Significant ecclesiastical commissions continued to elude her. Furthermore, and as far as can be determined on the basis of the available evidence, this situation had not been greatly ameliorated as a result of her recent Venetian sojourn. The paucity of documentation for her Venetian period is probably significant in itself. It suggests that, for all her reputational cachet among the academicians, Gentileschi's Venetian years did not pay any major dividends in the more tangible areas of any increase in the collecting and commissioning of her work. The only early biographical source that relates specifically to Gentileschi's Venetian period, in fact, seems remarkably poorly informed in this respect. This source – a paragraph about Gentileschi written in 1649 by a certain Girolamo Gualdo in a manuscript describing the artworks to be seen in his Vicentine collection – contains no new information about her. The only specific work that it does mention is a commission from the Barberini in Rome, but Gualdo seems to have confused Gentileschi with another contemporary woman artist, the still-life painter Giovanna Garzoni (1600–1670), whose career and movements between different Italian cities mirror Gentileschi's to a certain degree.[38]

Gentileschi had thus won the first stage of the battle for recognition. Yet she had still fallen short of the next career goal of achieving a more substantial level of material prosperity and ongoing professional success. As a result, it seems that the more concerted patronage that was offered to her during this period by the Duke of Alcalá and his high-ranking Spanish colleagues played a decisive role in encouraging her relocation to Naples.

One of the most discerning Spanish connoisseurs of the period, the Duke of Alcalá had already distinguished himself, before arriving in Italy, by virtue of his early collecting and academic activities in his native Seville. Here, he had maintained one of the most important libraries and collections of antiquities in Spain. He had also commissioned works from the young Velázquez, as well as an elaborate allegory of the *Triumph of Hercules* for the ceiling of his palace by the painter and theoretician Francisco Pacheco.[39] In July 1625, Alcalá arrived in Rome to serve as the Spanish Ambassador to the Holy See. In the space of just a few months, he appears to have become a dedicated admirer of Gentileschi's work, commissioning no fewer than five canvases from her in rapid succession.

Alcalá's collection of Gentileschis included the *Penitent Magdalene* (fig. 65) and a now-lost painting of *David with his Harp*.[40] In Naples, as viceroy, he acquired two self-portraits by Gentileschi, also now lost.[41] Finally, and perhaps most significantly in terms of what it adds to our understanding of her oeuvre today, his inventory, compiled in Seville between 1632 and 1636, refers to a copy after a painting by Gentileschi of *Christ Blessing the Children*. This inventory reference was connected in 2012 with a painting formerly in the collection of the Metropolitan Museum of Art and now in the Basilica of Santi Ambrogio e Carlo al Corso in Rome (fig. 80).[42]

For the first time since the days of the Medici in Florence, there is evidence of a concerted effort by a prominent and distinguished aristocratic collector to collect in depth paintings by Gentileschi. The range of works, moreover, is significant. Alcalá's collection of Gentileschis went well beyond the artist's fairly narrow range of standard subjects. Instead, it comprised a cultivated and adventurous selection of subject matter with a particular emphasis on Gentileschi's religious and devotional

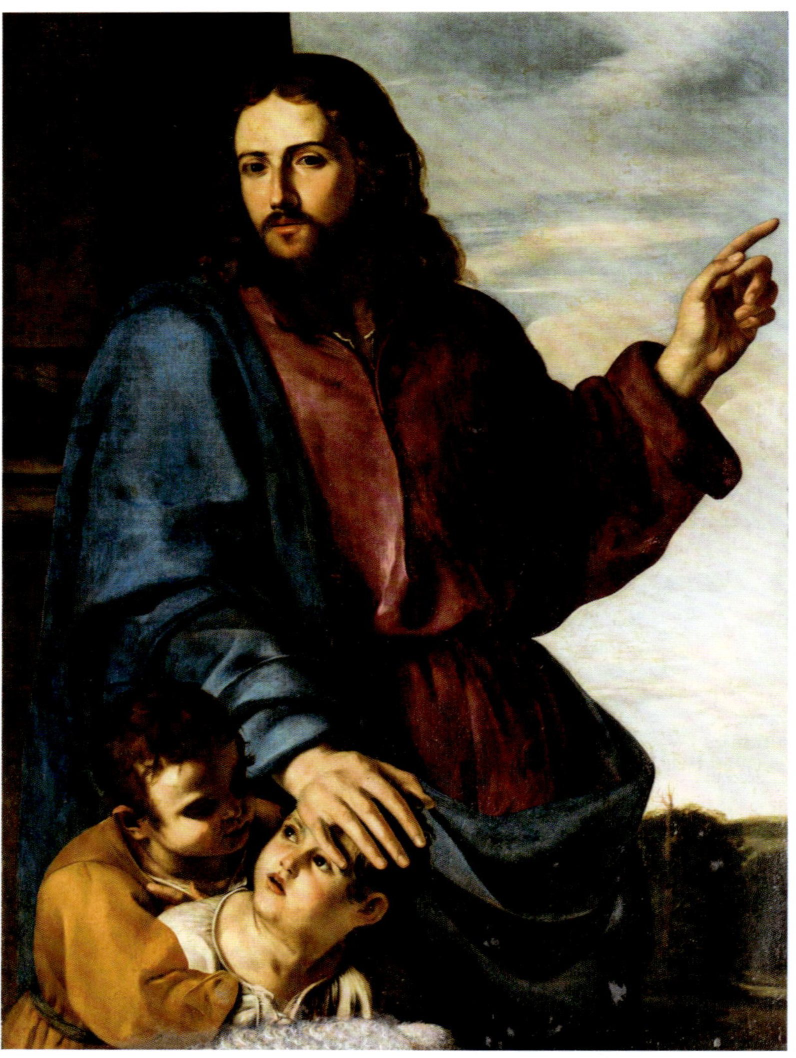

80 Artemisia Gentileschi, *Christ Blessing the Children* (*Sinite Parvulos*), inscribed on the reverse of the canvas: 'Artimizia Gentileschi Roma 1626', oil on canvas, 135 × 98.5 cm, Basilica dei Santi Ambrogio e Carlo al Corso, La Venerabile Arciconfraternita dei Santi Ambrogio e Carlo, Rome

imagery. This constituted an area of subject specialisation that, as we have seen, seems otherwise to have largely eluded Gentileschi during these years. That Alcalá's personal interest and input was a major factor encouraging Gentileschi to develop her work along these lines is reinforced by his equally discerning patronage of Jusepe de Ribera during these years. In Naples, Alcalá became one of Ribera's most dedicated supporters, eliciting from him some of the most distinctive and innovative works of his career, including a group of *Four Philosophers* and the celebrated portrait of Magdalena Ventura.[43]

A final and probably equally significant factor that seems to have motivated Gentileschi to follow Alcalá to Naples is her increasing involvement with high-ranking Spanish patrons more generally from this time onwards. Alcalá's successor as Spanish Ambassador to the Holy See was Íñigo Vélez de Guevara, the 8th conde de Oñate, likewise a cultivated art connoisseur who would go on to serve as the Viceroy of Naples from 1648 to 1653.[44] A list of payments made during Oñate's embassy in Rome, from 1626 to 1628, records an outlay of 1,467 giulij and 14 baiocchi (equivalent to 147 scudi) as having been paid to Gentileschi for a painting of *Hercules and Omphale*.[45] It is unfortunate that this work (which was probably a reworking of her earlier *Hercules* for the Medici) was destroyed in a fire of 1734, since this commission seems to have constituted one of the most important works of her career.

The *Hercules* was commissioned as part of an extensive programme to decorate the recently constructed Salon Nuevo of the Alcázar palace in Madrid. Other painters involved in this prestigious project included Rubens and Anthony van Dyck (1599–1641), together with Domenichino – who contributed two works, *The Sacrifice of Isaac* (fig. 97) and *Solomon and the Queen of Sheba*. The original commission was also meant to include one of Guido Reni's most celebrated paintings, *The Abduction of Helen*, although complex politico-cultural circumstances ultimately prevented this painting from reaching Madrid.[46] The conde de Oñate's commission, therefore, represented a major breakthrough for Gentileschi. It presented her with her first opportunity to have her work exhibited in a truly international setting and in the company of the leading international history painters of the day.

CONCLUSION: GENTILESCHI'S RELOCATION TO NAPLES

Gentileschi must have received the impression from Alcalá that, in following him to Naples, where he was to take up the position of viceroy, the best was yet to come. She was not wrong. Within five years of her arrival, her name would be extolled even more ardently throughout the city, not just by the poets and academicians as before, but as the result of a series of increasingly important, high-profile public and private commissions. This culminated in an order for three monumental altarpieces for the cathedral of Pozzuoli, a venerated site in southern Italy. The transition from celebrated anomaly to one of the most prestigious and in-demand painters of the day would force Gentileschi to restructure her workshop from the ground up. Its previously boutique, cottage-industry character would be reconfigured in Naples into a much more efficient and multi-dimensional enterprise. This process, however, would create new challenges. These would include the issues of workshop integration and long-term career viability that have created problems for the reception of her oeuvre that persist to this day. Finally, Gentileschi would also be called upon to continue the never-ending struggle for the maintenance of profile and relevancy in a constantly evolving art world that was every bit as competitive and faction-ridden in Naples as in any other city in which she had operated hitherto. The onset of old age, moreover, would exact a further toll, while, at the same time, spurring her on to produce some of the most fascinating and complex works of her career.

PAGE 149 Artemisia Gentileschi, *The Birth of Saint John the Baptist* (detail of fig. 86)

— PART IV —

Selling Artemisia

NAPLES AND LONDON, 1630–c.1656

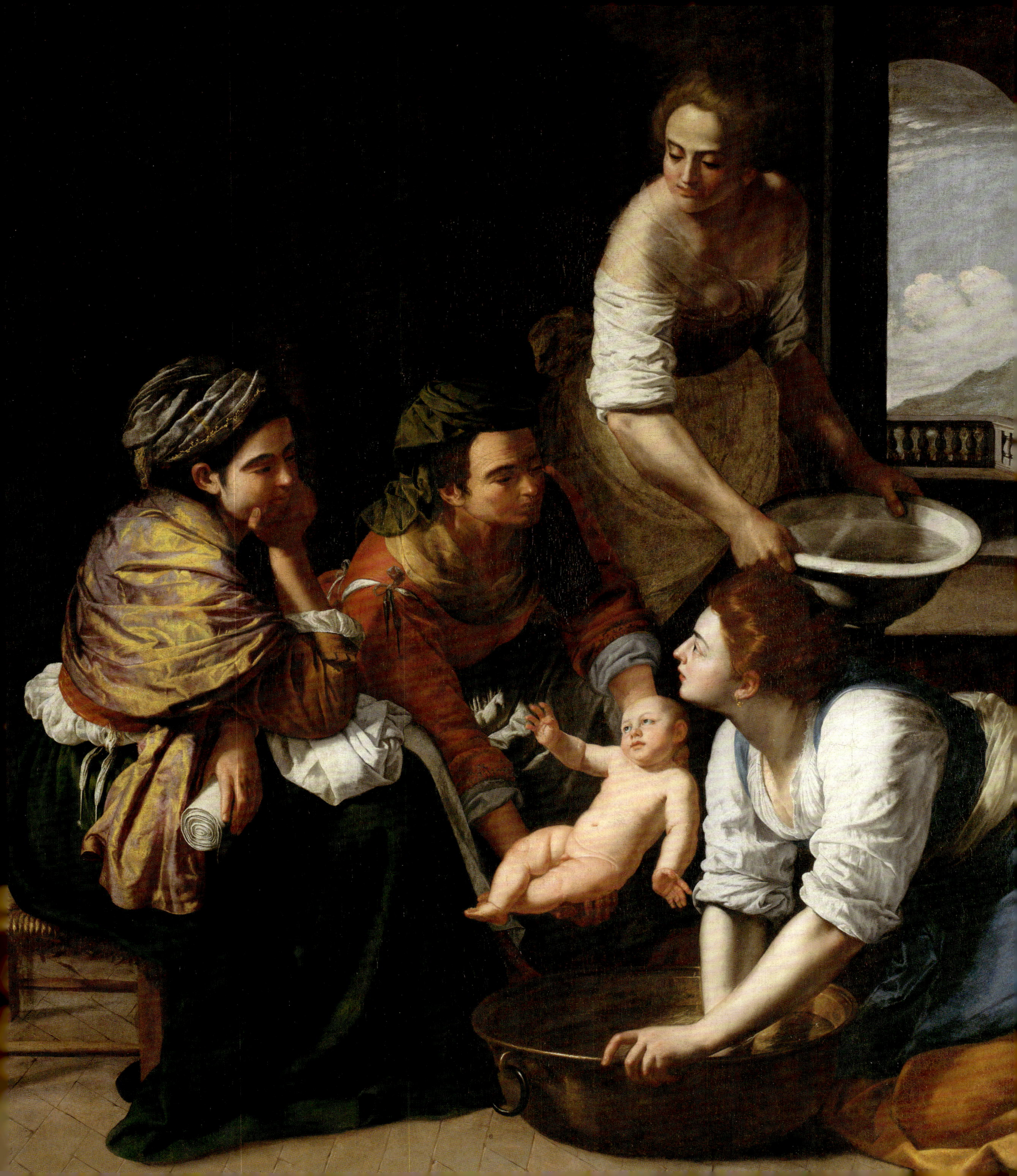

10

'A great cry spread throughout the city'

GENTILESCHI'S NEAPOLITAN SUCCESS IN THE 1630S

INTRODUCTION
ARTEMISIA COMES TO REST IN A CITY OF MIRACLES, AND DISASTERS

At the heart of the second of the three cataclysmic disasters that convulsed the city of Naples during Gentileschi's stay there lies an upturned basket of figs. The Revolt of Masaniello, as it came to be known, should have been foreseen by the Spanish viceroys who ruled the Kingdom of Naples on behalf of the Spanish Crown. For decades, they had been acceding to Madrid's demands to tax the kingdom mercilessly in order to provide revenue for the cash-strapped finances of the Spanish Empire.[1] On 7 July 1647, the breaking point finally came when the stallholders in the central marketplace rose in violent opposition to agents collecting the hated tax on fruit. A collaborative canvas by the architectural painter Viviano Codazzi (1604–1670) and the figure painter Michelangelo Cerquozzi (1602–1660) records the fateful moment when the tax agents were chased out of the market in a hail of fruit and vegetables (fig. 81).[2] Advancing behind them like a diminutive general on a rearing horse is Masaniello, a humble fisherman from Amalfi who would lead the revolution for a week until he was assassinated on 16 July. The revolt would then spread throughout the southern peninsula in a confusing series of attempts by warring factions to wrest control from the Spanish. Finally, in April 1648,

FACING PAGE Artemisia Gentileschi, *St Januarius in the Amphitheatre at Pozzuoli* (detail of fig. 88)

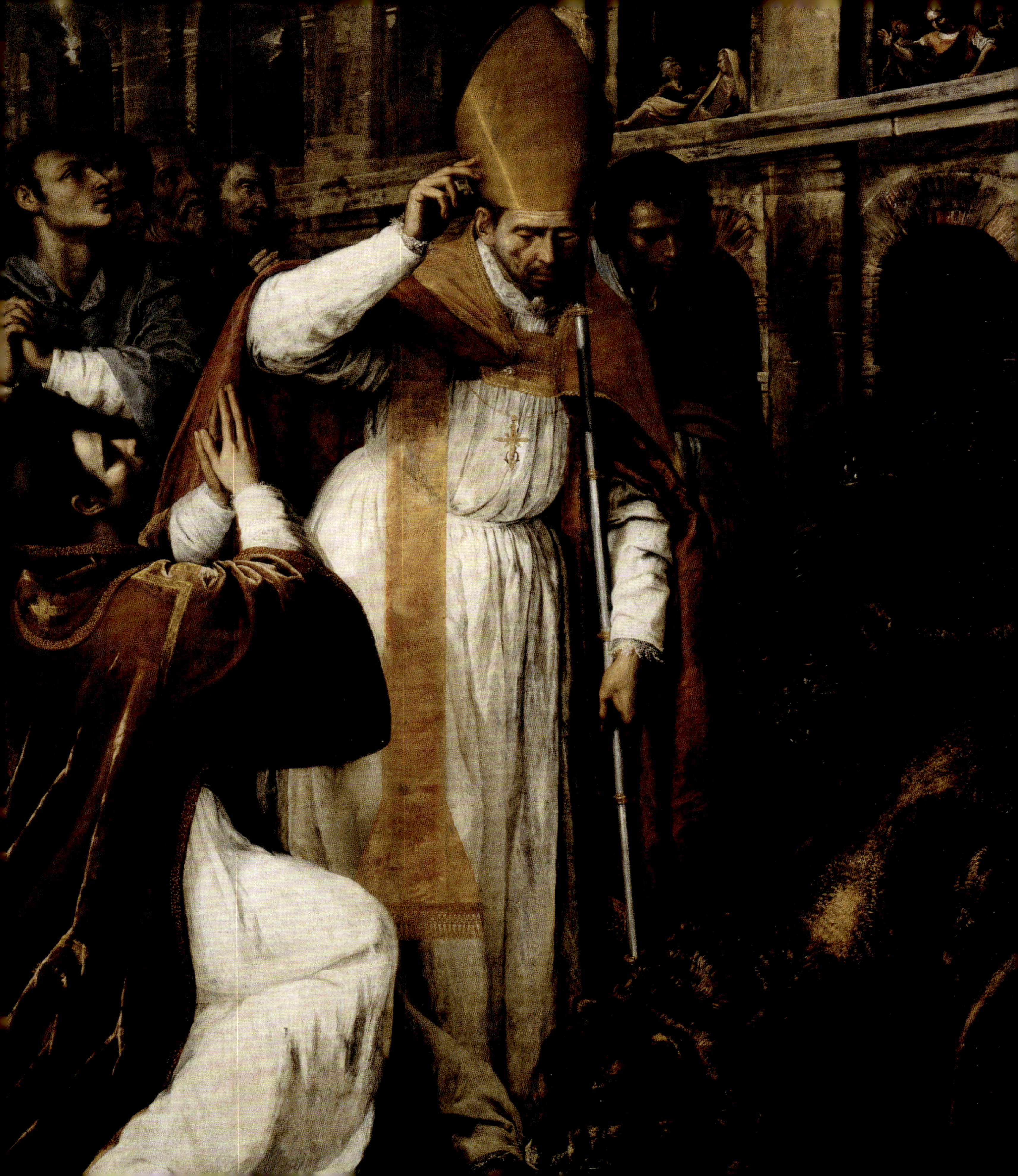

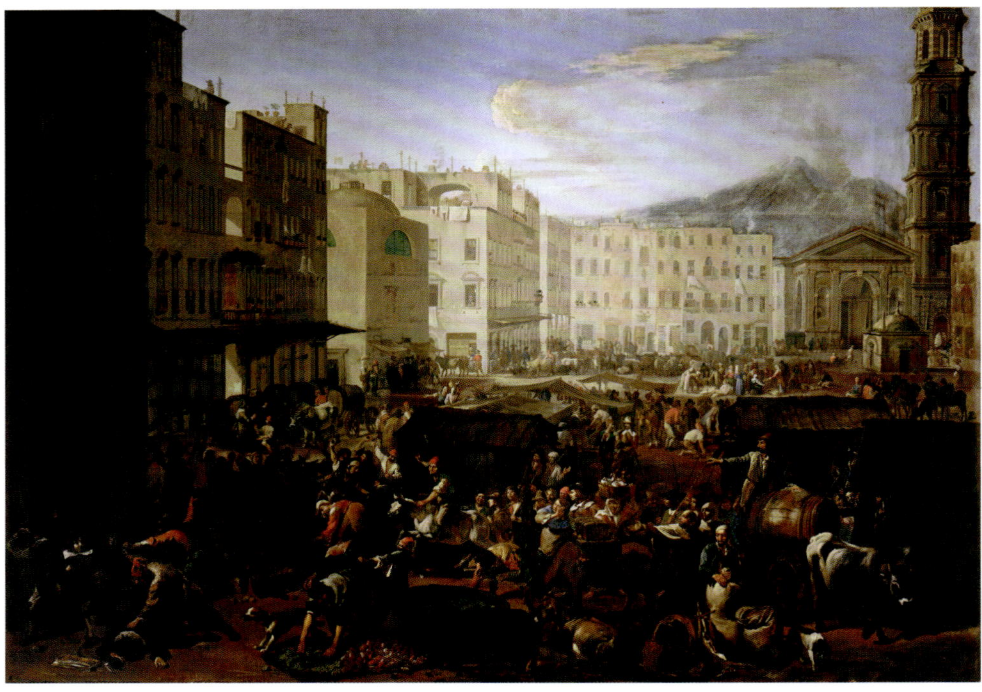

81 Viviano Codazzi and Michelangelo Cerquozzi, *The Revolt of Masaniello*, late 1647–early 1648, oil on canvas, 96 × 134 cm, Galleria Spada, Rome

it was ruthlessly put down by an expeditionary force sent from Madrid and led by the king's illegitimate son, Don Juan of Austria.[3]

Gentileschi may have formed part of the Spanish party seeking refuge from the disturbances in the impregnable bastion of the Castel Sant'Elmo, high on the Vomero Hill overlooking the city. A contingency plan would have been prudent, given the widespread destruction of property carried out by the revolutionaries and given the number of her patrons specifically targeted by Masaniello and his followers. Such was the case, for example, for Don Giuseppe Carafa dei duchi di Maddaloni. This scion of one of the leading Neapolitan aristocratic families was also one of the city's most distinguished collectors. His palace was filled with canvases by contemporary Neapolitan artists, including dozens by local practitioners of the new specialisations of landscape and still life. He was also a devotee of Baroque violence. He owned paintings of the suicides of *Lucretia* and *Cleopatra*, together with a depiction of the decollation of the patron saint of Naples, the early Christian martyr and Bishop of Benevento, St Januarius, a figure whom Gentileschi would also paint during this period.[4] Perhaps most intriguingly, he owned also a version of Gentileschi's *Judith Slaying Holofernes* (which is identified in the inventories only as a 'Judith', but which probably depicted the death of Holofernes, on account of its larger scale). He matched this canvas with a canvas of *Herod with the Severed Head of John the Baptist* by the little-known Neapolitan female painter Annella de Rosa (1602–1643).

How grimly ironic, then, that this connoisseur of artistic gore was himself beheaded in retribution for his involvement in a failed counter-insurgency mounted against Masaniello and his followers on 10 July 1647. A painting by Gentileschi's sometime collaborator Domenico Gargiulo (*c.*1609/10–1675) documents the event in unstinting detail (fig. 82).[5] It depicts a group of figures who rush into view carrying the heads of Carafa's followers. A partly dismembered corpse lies on the ground beside another, depicted at the very instant of dismemberment. One figure lunges forward, severing his head

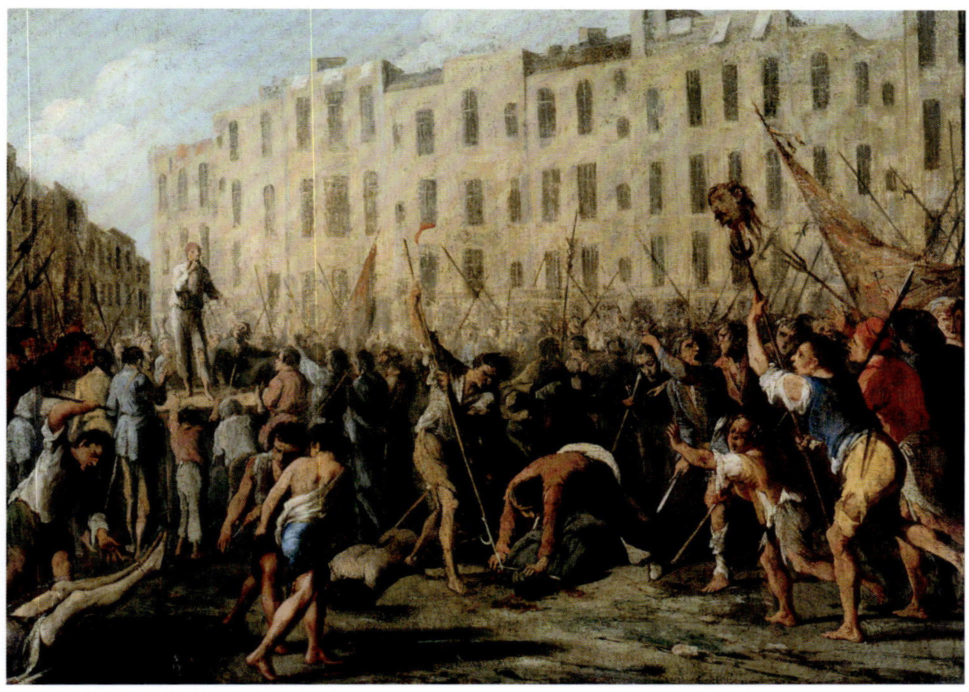

82 Domenico Gargiulo, *The Execution of Don Giuseppe Carafa*, c.early 1650s, oil on canvas, 29 × 38 cm, Museo Nazionale di San Martino, Naples

with a knife, while another prepares to impale it on a pike. A group of children come into view dragging Carafa's almost naked corpse, beating it as they go. At the back of the composition, Masaniello stands on a stage haranguing the crowd.[6]

Gentileschi successfully withstood this disaster, as she did its crippling economic after-shock. So, too, had she endured an earlier Neapolitan catastrophe that had also nearly destroyed the city shortly after her arrival. In December 1631, the long dormant volcano of Mount Vesuvius, which overlooks the Bay of Naples, awoke from centuries of slumber and threatened to engulf the city in a flood of lava and deadly ash of an intensity equal to that which had buried Pompeii and Herculaneum in 79 C.E. The flow of lava changed direction just short of the city's gate, however, thus sparing the city from annihilation in a miraculous deliverance that was attributed to the intervention of St Januarius. The city's dedication to the promulgation of the cult of St Januarius formed part of a wider pattern, in turn, of continuous religious renewal in Naples during this period. 'La fedelissima', or 'the most faithful city', as it was termed, was, at that stage, enjoying a building boom that had been facilitated by virtue of its status as the most fertile centre for the renewed energies of the Counter-Reformation. As a result, dozens of churches, convents, monasteries and hospices were either substantially renovated during this period or built anew to provide operational bases for such recently arrived orders as the Jesuits, Theatines and Oratorians or for previously established orders like the Carthusians, who completely rebuilt and extended their ancient charterhouse overlooking the Bay of Naples.[7]

Yet all the prayers and lamentations throughout the length and breadth of the kingdom could not save Gentileschi – or the hundreds of thousands of other sufferers who perished with her – during the course of the third and final cataclysm in this trilogy of Neapolitan Baroque disasters. In spring 1656, the plague made its way into Naples via the port. In the months that followed, it would rage out of control through the city's streets, progressively reducing the population by as much as half of its 400–450,000 inhabitants. Most of the plague's victims had to be gathered up as cadavers lining the streets and buried hurriedly in mass graves on the city's periphery.[8] Many of the city's artists were among the dead. These included Gentileschi's friend and associate Massimo Stanzione, her sometime collaborator Bernardo Cavallino and, it seems, Gentileschi herself, two years shy of her sixty-fifth birthday and two years since the last record of her in the city, in early 1654.[9] Gentileschi had long since wanted to leave Naples. In her correspondence with her friends, associates and would-be patrons she had frequently complained about its many inconveniences and its overall harshness as a place in which to live. In the end, however, and despite her best efforts to find better employment elsewhere, Naples kept her close and then finally claimed her as one of its own.

THE 1630 *ANNUNCIATION* ALTARPIECE AND GENTILESCHI'S GROWING RECOGNITION IN THE EARLY TO MID-1630S

For all its challenges as a place in which to live, Naples offered Gentileschi a series of significant opportunities for renewal on both a personal and professional level.[10] Two letters written in 1630 to Cassiano dal Pozzo in Rome vividly convey the transformation of Gentileschi's professional circumstances during these years. In the first, she informed Dal Pozzo that she was much too busy even to think about commencing work on a self-portrait that she had previously promised him. Her excuse is a pressing commitment that she has recently incurred from 'the Empress'. This comment has been taken as referring to an impending commission from the Spanish Infanta, Maria Anna of Spain (1606–1646), who was just then temporarily residing in Naples while on her way to Vienna to meet her promised spouse, Ferdinand Ernest, Archduke of Austria and King of Hungary and Bohemia (and, from 1637, the future Holy Roman Emperor).[11] The Duke of Alcalá must have facilitated Gentileschi's introduction to the Infanta, who was travelling in the company of none other than Velázquez. Bernardo de' Dominici – the Neapolitan Vasari of the early eighteenth century whose comments constitute a fundamental early source of information on Gentileschi – is thus no doubt correct in stressing the extent to which Gentileschi's initial Neapolitan reception was facilitated by a series of letters of introduction and recommendation that prompted 'a great cry [that] spread throughout the city about her works and in particular her portraits of high ranking personages'.[12]

Gentileschi's initial focus on her specialisation as a portraitist is also emphasised in her follow-up letter to Dal Pozzo of December 1630. In it, she informs him that she had only just returned to Naples following a period away from the city working on a portrait of a duchess.[13] Although she does not provide any further details about this commission, we can speculate that she might have already made contact with the distinguished regional court of Count Giangirolamo II Acquaviva d'Aragona and his consort Isabella Acquaviva (née Filomarino) in Conversano, Bari (Isabella Filomarino being the niece, in turn, of one of Gentileschi's most important patrons and contacts back in Rome, Ascanio Filomarino, the future Archbishop of Naples).[14] Gentileschi's work for the court of Conversano includes a *Roman Charity* that has been identified with a painting formerly in the Castello di Conversano (fig. 83).[15] The letter attests once more to Gentileschi's impressive networking skills. Within just a few short months of her arrival in a new city, she had been able to cultivate a series of fruitful associations with influential figures active across a wide range of fields. In this instance, the influencers whose protection and assistance she was able to draw on can be seen to have covered the local art scene, as well as its aristocratic, administrative and academic spheres.[16]

The date 1630 is found also on an *Annunciation* that was acquired in Naples in 1815 for the Real Museo Borbonico, the forerunner to today's Museo di Capodimonte (fig. 84).[17] Many of the paintings sold to the Neapolitan state during these years came from recently suppressed churches that had had their property confiscated during the Napoleonic occupation of the Kingdom of Naples from 1806 to 1815.[18] The subject, treatment and dimensions of Gentileschi's *Annunciation* make it almost certain to have formed part of this group and thus to have been originally conceived as a major altarpiece for an ecclesiastical setting. The dimensions suggest, moreover, that it was originally painted for a significant urban ecclesiastical setting and is comparable, for example, to Domenico Fiasella's *Crucifixion* altarpiece, a work of similar dimensions that is

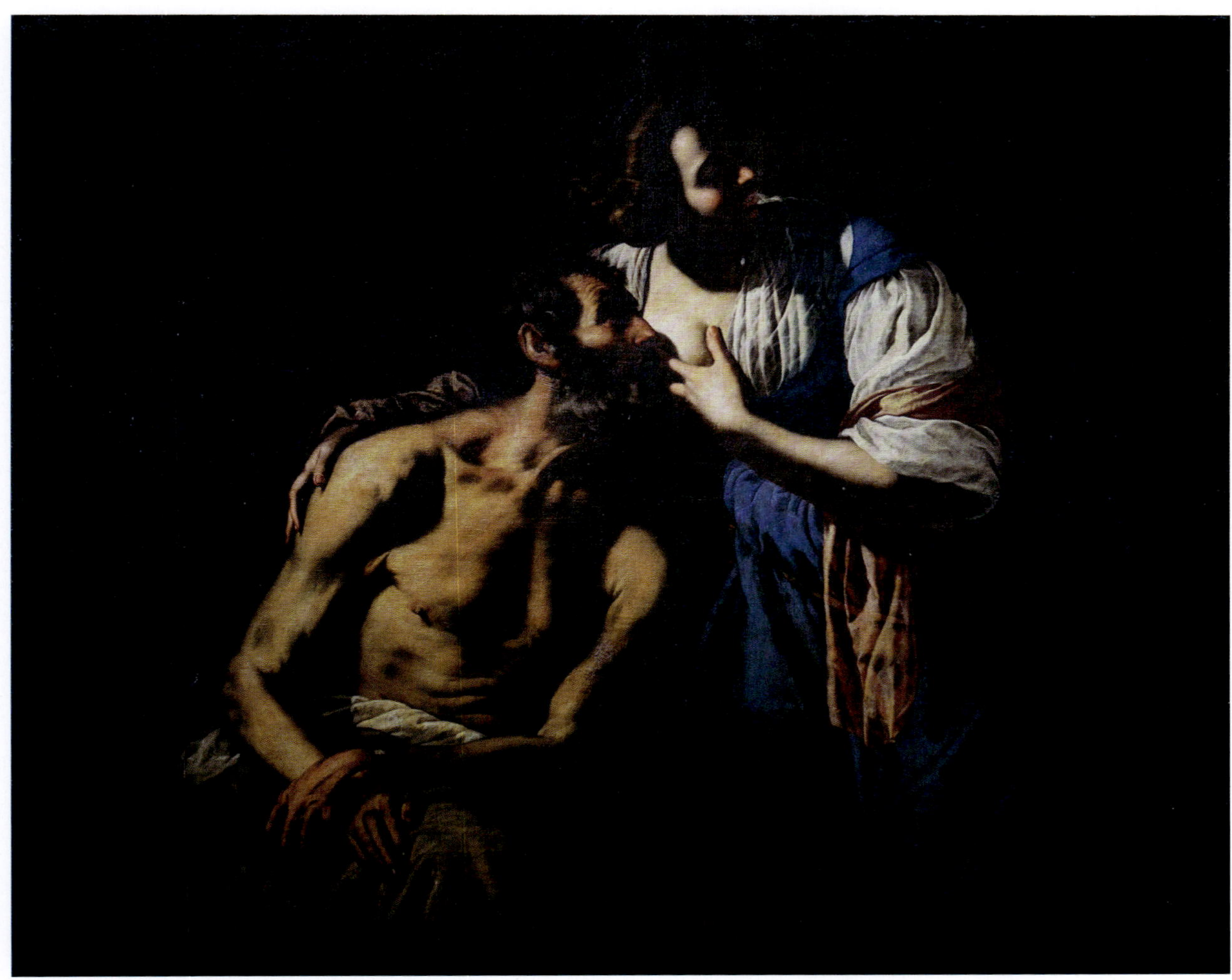

83 Artemisia Gentileschi, *Roman Charity (Cimone and Pero)*, c.1640–45, oil on canvas, 121 × 147 cm, on deposit at the Comando Carabinieri per la Tutela del Patrimonio Culturale, Bari, 2023 (photo taken before 2018 restoration)

often connected to the *Annunciation* and that was originally painted for one of the nave chapels of San Giorgio dei Genovesi.[19] Within a year of her arrival in Naples, then, it seems that Gentileschi had at last realised her long-frustrated ambition of securing significant ecclesiastical patronage on a scale commensurate with that achieved by her father and Lavinia Fontana for their altarpieces at San Paolo Fuori le Mura, Rome, the site of an inspirational outing she had made nearly twenty years earlier (see p. 48).

GENTILESCHI'S NEAPOLITAN ALLIANCES

The post of Neapolitan viceroy represented something of a poisoned chalice for its successive Spanish grandee recipients. The Duke of Alcalá, for one, was not able to withstand its many challenges and found himself recalled to Madrid in 1631, after only two years in the position. One might have anticipated that the sudden removal from the scene of Gentileschi's principal Neapolitan protector would act as a significant setback to her Neapolitan career, but she seems to have taken this in her stride and to have lost no time in forming an equally

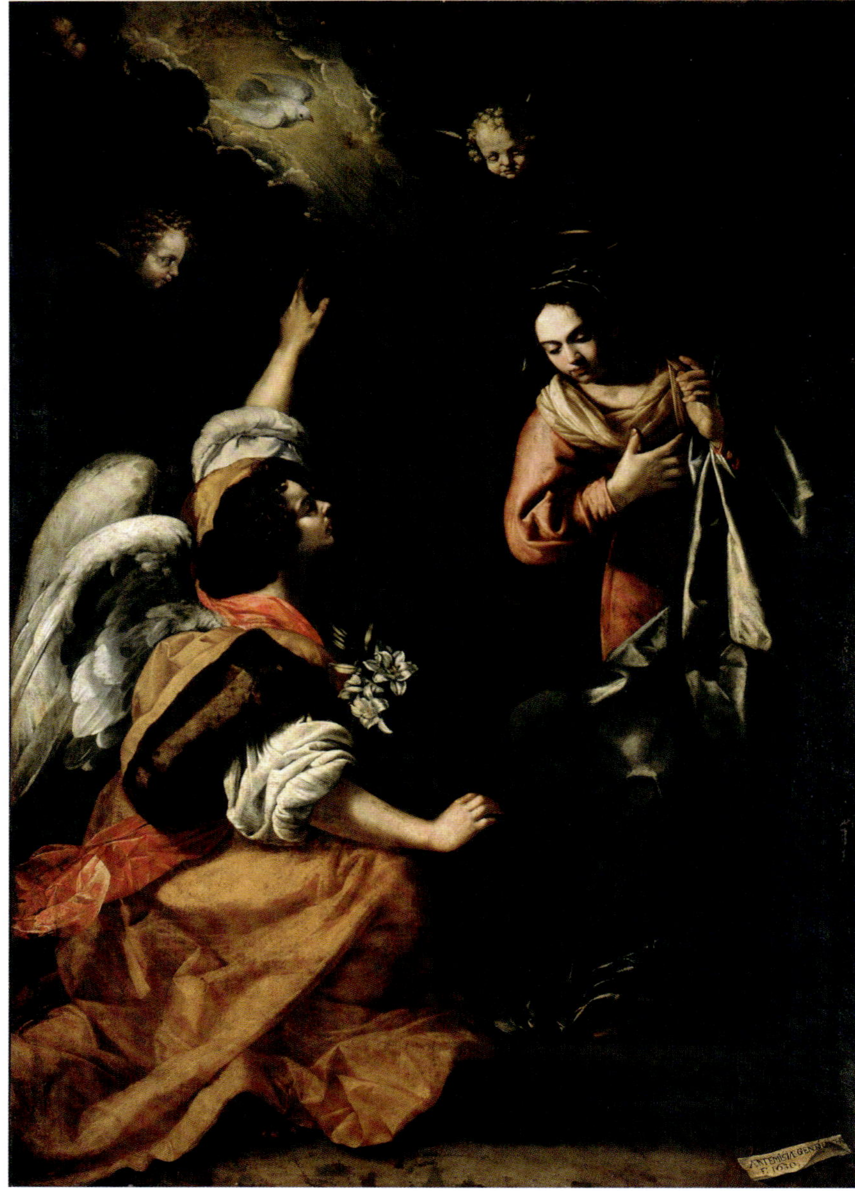

84 Artemisia Gentileschi, *Annunciation*, signed and dated 1630, oil on canvas, 257 × 179 cm, Museo e Real Bosco di Capodimonte, Naples

advantageous relationship with the duke's successor as viceroy from 1631 to 1637, Manuel de Acevedo y Zúñiga, the 6th Count of Monterrey.[20]

The Count of Monterrey entertained aspirations for the viceregency in the area of cultural diplomacy that were yet more ambitious than Alcalá's. In particular, he presided over a series of major artistic commissions for cycles of paintings that were contracted in Italy and then shipped back to decorate the new Buen Retiro palace that was nearing completion on the outskirts of Madrid. One of the first of these was a

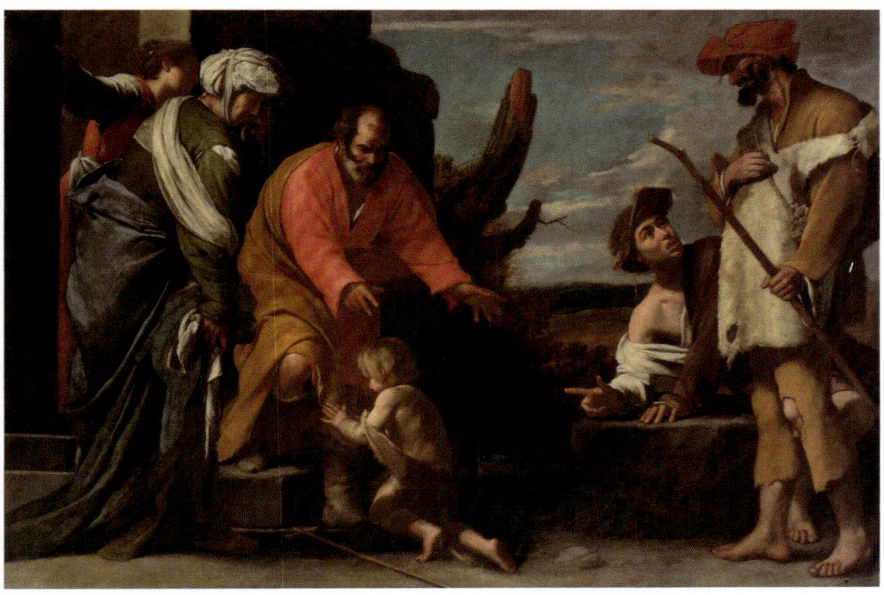

85 Massimo Stanzione, *St John the Baptist Taking Leave of his Parents*, signed, c.1633–35, oil on canvas, 181 × 263 cm, Museo Nacional del Prado, Madrid, P000291

group of six large canvases dedicated to the life of the Baptist which are generally identified as having been commissioned for the official residence at the Buen Retiro that was reserved for the use of Monterrey's brother-in-law, the all-powerful Count-Duke of Olivares.[21] This commission constituted the first ensemble exhibition of contemporary Neapolitan painting then to be seen outside Naples and included four works by Massimo Stanzione (fig. 85), together with one each by Paolo Finoglio (*c.*1590–1645) and Gentileschi (fig. 86).[22]

The project leader for this landmark commission was Stanzione, himself recently arrived in Naples from Rome. Stanzione's growing influence within the Neapolitan art world made him a particularly important ally for Gentileschi. Their acquaintance probably dated back to the early to mid-1620s, when both artists had moved in the same circles among the Northern Caravaggisti resident in the papal city, as well as among the Barberini and their entourage, whose patronage Stanzione was also cultivating during the same period. Now, in Naples, Stanzione was rapidly gaining prominence as one of the city's two most successful local painters. His principal competitor during this period, Jusepe de Ribera, had been ascendant for more than a decade, following his own arrival in Naples from Rome in 1616. Ribera represented the other major dominant local tradition of Neapolitan Caravaggesque painting. Yet even his unique blend of vividly intense Caravaggesque realism was evolving in complex new directions at this time, as Neapolitan artists and collectors alike were opening themselves up to a diverse range of external artistic influences that coincided with a particularly dynamic moment in the evolution of Neapolitan artistic taste.

Prominently situated within the cathedral of Naples, the Cappella del Tesoro di San Gennaro (Chapel of the Treasury of St Januarius) remains one of the city's most venerated sites. In 1620, the administrators of the newly redesigned chapel had taken the contentious decision to award the contract for its decoration to the Bolognese Guido Reni. News of the decision aroused intense resentment in Naples and triggered clamorous anti-foreign-labour agitation on the part of the local painters. The locals' campaign to oust the foreigners from this prime contract was so effective that Reni was impelled to flee the city shortly after his arrival. A decade later, Domenichino made his way down from Bologna to the southern capital as Reni's replacement, lured by some of the most attractive rates of pay then on offer. Yet he would soon come to complain about his own harassment at the hands of the local artists, to the extent of also having to retreat from the city in fear of his life, in 1634. Compelled to return a short while later, Domenichino grudgingly recommenced work on the project before eventually dying in 1641, still some years prior to its completion. For many years afterwards, his widow continued to accuse the Neapolitans of having poisoned him.[23]

Gentileschi, by contrast, does not appear to have suffered any particular antagonism from the local painters, and Stanzione's support seems to have played a major role in this regard. Unlike Reni or Domenichino, Stanzione had the major advantage of being a Neapolitan by birth and the previous twenty years, moving between Naples and Rome, had given him ample opportunity to pay his dues while familiarising himself with the local bedrock traditions of Neapolitan Caravaggesque realism. At the same time, however, he was also able to use his travels as a basis on which to supplement his Neapolitan background with an awareness of more up-to-date influences emanating from the new and fashionable traditions of the Bolognese school combined with the yet more contemporary trends of Poussin and the tempered classicism of such artists as Claude Mellan and Simon Vouet. This earned him the nickname of the 'Neapolitan Guido Reni' and served as the basis for his growing prominence within the Neapolitan art world during the 1630s – a critical period that coincides with Gentileschi's arrival and increasing prominence in the city.

Gentileschi's complex artistic background paralleled Stanzione's in many respects. Her professional career and artistic evolution embodied precisely the kinds of artistic transformations that Stanzione was seeking to achieve in his own work. Her initial involvement in first-wave Caravaggism had been tempered, as we saw, through her exposure to the urbanely sophisticated works of Cristofano Allori and the courtly expressions of the Florentine Baroque. These influences had been rendered more complex, in turn, with reference to the even more sophisticated manifestations of so-called ennobled Roman Caravaggism, evident in the works of the second-wave Northern Caravaggesque painters like Gerrit van Honthorst and Simon Vouet. This was then combined with the emerging tastes for classicism and the Bolognese Baroque style that she had encountered gaining ground among the Roman connoisseurs and in key Roman artistic commissions during the 1620s. Finally, Gentileschi was able to add to this a renewed emphasis on the painterly and chromatic aspects of Venetian Cinquecento painting with which she had been able to reacquaint herself as a result of her recent residence in Venice. This uniquely complex and well-travelled combination of artistic knowledge and experience would serve Gentileschi well during her Neapolitan years, constituting one of the prime reasons for her significant success and influence among the local artists and patrons.

IN THE RIGHT PLACE AT THE RIGHT TIME: THE MADRID *BIRTH OF ST JOHN THE BAPTIST* AND GENTILESCHI'S WINNING COMBINATION OF STYLES IN THE EARLY TO MID-1630S

Gentileschi's ability to reclaim for herself a sense of modish popularity during these years was based directly on her capacity to evolve beyond the relatively raw and unconstrained Caravaggesque realism of her early works. In truth, Caravaggism was not an especially valuable commodity in which to trade during the 1630s. In Rome, it was regarded as an outmoded and increasingly unfashionable style that had been long since superseded, first by the advent of Bolognese classicism and then by the coming of the High Baroque style of Pietro da Cortona and his followers. In Naples, by contrast, Caravaggism was still a commonplace feature within a city that constituted the only Italian Baroque centre to have embraced Caravaggio's style wholeheartedly as the mainstream of its artistic traditions. But this created the corresponding problem of a lack of competitive advantage for any artist practising Caravaggism in a city that was already saturated with artworks produced in this style.

What made Gentileschi's work of the 1630s stand out from that of other Neapolitan artists and what constituted its point of market distinction and source of attraction to both painters and collectors alike was its manifestation of a novel fusion of styles during a particularly important moment in the evolution of Neapolitan Baroque painting. Gentileschi's work of the

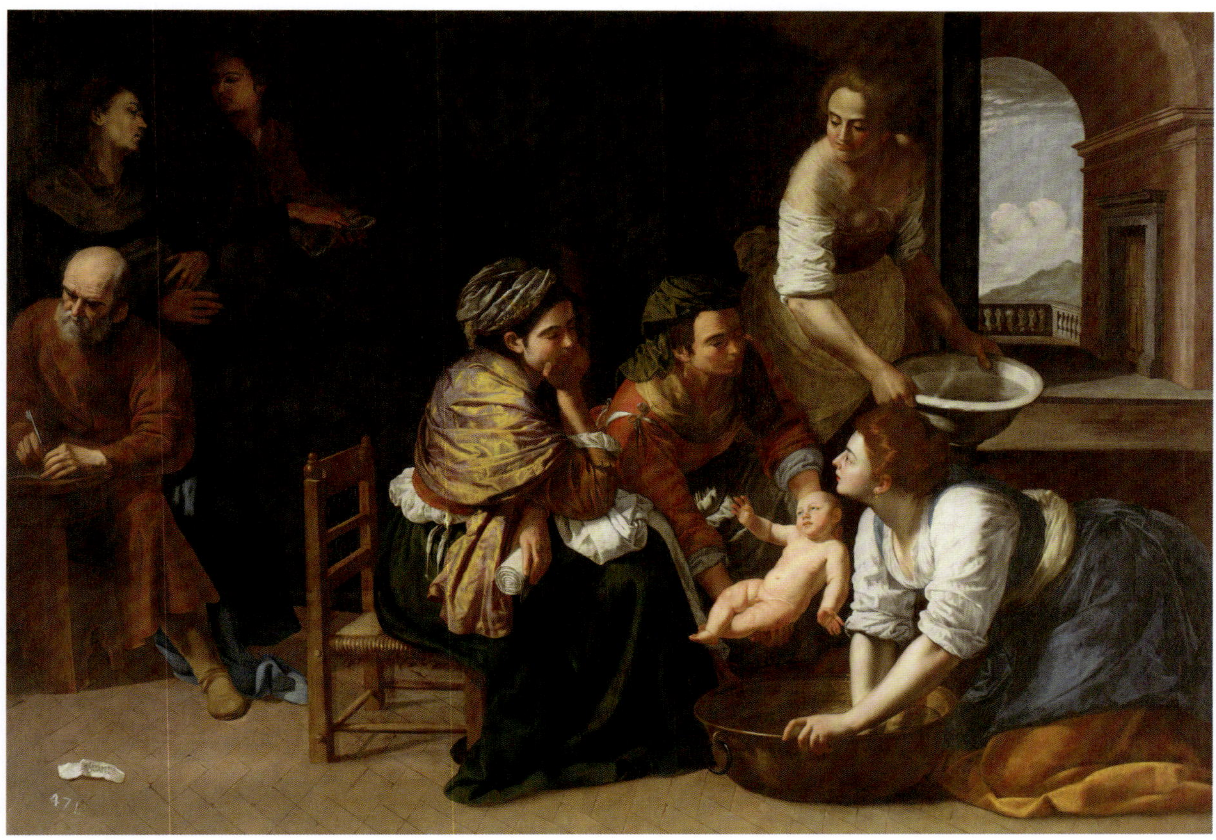

86 Artemisia Gentileschi, *The Birth of Saint John the Baptist*, signed, *c.*1633–35, oil on canvas, 184 × 258 cm, Museo Nacional del Prado, Madrid, P000149

1630s offered the Neapolitans one of the most sophisticated syntheses of the dominant mode of Caravaggism tempered and rendered yet more attractive with reference to other, supposedly more progressive and fashionable contemporary styles. For the first time, and in strategic alliance with Stanzione, who was spearheading a comparably 'progressive' synthesis of a similar range of styles at exactly the same time, Gentileschi was able to reinvent herself as an artist in touch with the most up-to-date trends of the day.

Gentileschi's *Birth of St John the Baptist* demonstrates not only the artist's close knowledge of recent developments in grand-manner, Roman history painting, from Raphael to Vouet, but also a particular facility with the rendition of luxurious, polychrome fabrics that had been re-energised by her recent engagement with Venetian painting (fig. 86). The painting also relates to the local traditions of Caravaggesque realism, as well as to the more specifically Hispanic naturalism of Velázquez, whom she may have met when he was passing through Naples in 1630, in the company of the Spanish Infanta (see p. 154). As such, the painting exerted a powerful influence on a number of other artists, despite the fact that it remained in Naples for only a brief period before being shipped, as noted above, to the Buen Retiro in Madrid. Francesco Guarino's *Birth of the Virgin* (fig. 87), for example, is unthinkable without the model of the rich garments and meditative solemnity of the female figures in Gentileschi's *Birth of St John the Baptist*.[24] The young Bernardo Cavallino was also struck by the painting, as were Aniello Falcone (1607–1656) and Ribera's still-shadowy pupil, the Master of the Annunciation to the Shepherds.[25]

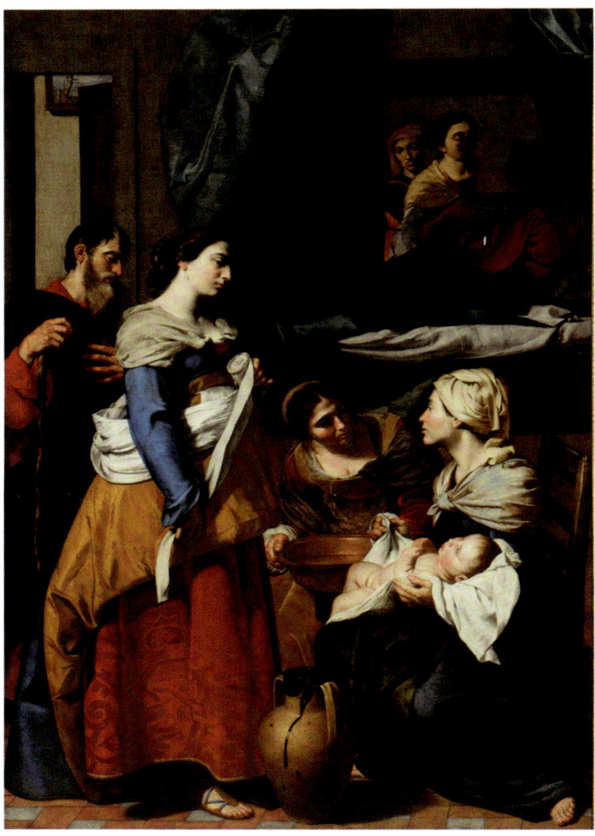

87 Francesco Guarino, *Birth of the Virgin*, *c.*1645, oil on canvas, 170 × 118 cm, Catello collection, Naples

GENTILESCHI AT POZZUOLI CATHEDRAL: REVERENCE AND REALISM

Of yet greater prominence and influence on the development of Neapolitan Baroque painting during this period were Gentileschi's three monumental altarpieces produced between 1635 and 1637 for the newly reconstructed cathedral of Pozzuoli on the outskirts of Naples: *St Januarius in the Amphitheatre*, the *Adoration of the Magi* and *Sts Proculus and Nicea*.[26] Gentileschi's involvement in this highly prestigious commission was, once again, probably facilitated by the recommendation of Stanzione and/or the Count of Monterrey.[27] Yet the confidence with which Gentileschi responded to the specific requirements of this major undertaking demonstrates her ability to stand firmly on her own two feet at this stage of her career, without the need of any excessive degree of outside intervention to prop her up or advance her interests. In fact, Gentileschi's services were especially singled out in this instance. Entrusted with the contract for not one but three major canvases, the commission represented both a significant honour and also a vote of confidence in her ability to undertake large-scale, public religious commissions that was otherwise given only to Giovanni Lanfranco, also recently arrived in Naples from Rome to undertake a series of frescoes at the Gesù Nuovo, followed by work at the Certosa di San Martino and the Theatine Church of Santi Apostoli.[28]

The task of producing three major works measuring three meters high and two meters across clearly added an extra degree of pressure and accountability to Gentileschi's characteristic rates of productivity and workshop output. The project, accordingly, forced her to rethink her workshop arrangements and to sub-contract parts of the work to specialist collaborators (see Chapter 12). Fortunately for her, the ultra-competitive nature of the Neapolitan art world, coupled with her undoubted celebrity and her standing as a prestigious foreign artist resident in the city, meant that many of the local painters were only too willing to assist. This enabled her to add to these works landscape backgrounds by the local specialist Domenico Gargiulo and architectural components by the architectural painter Viviano Codazzi, the co-author of the *Revolt of Masaniello* (fig. 81) and himself only recently arrived in Naples from Rome.

Gentileschi's Pozzuoli altarpieces have long been recognised as constituting a pivotal moment in the development of Neapolitan Baroque painting.[29] Bissell has, nonetheless, added a dissenting voice, judging them to be conventional and 'without much expressive passion'.[30] Yet this arguably misses the point of the brief to which Gentileschi was responding. This is particularly evident in the *St Januarius in the Amphitheatre at Pozzuoli*, which recounts the episode in 305 C.E. when the saint and his five companions were thrown to the beasts at Pozzuoli amphitheatre by order of the local prefect (fig. 88).[31] Gentileschi depicts the subsequent moment when the animals refused to attack the Christians, abasing themselves before the startled party and even licking the bishop's feet in recognition of his sanctity.

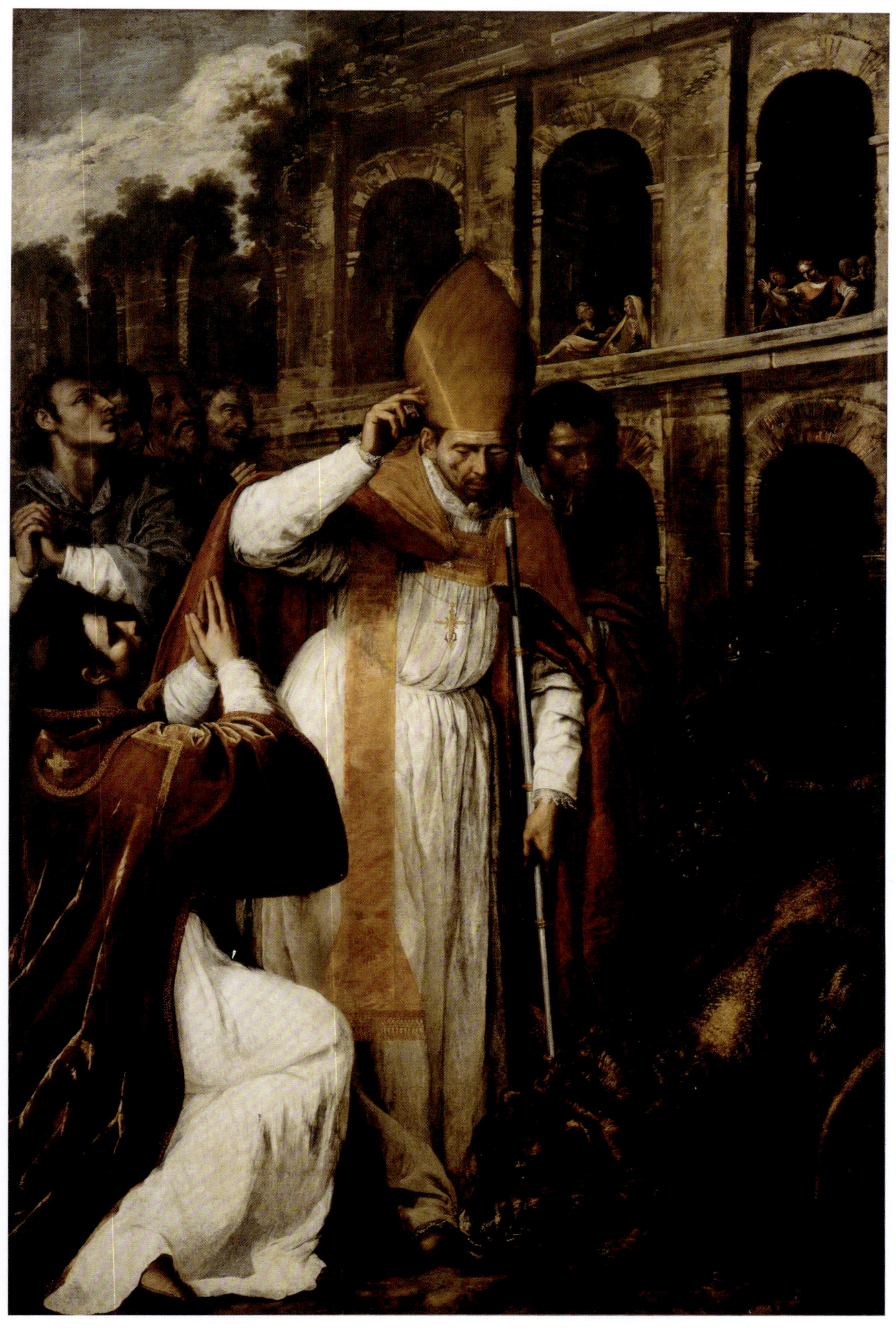

88 Artemisia Gentileschi, *St Januarius in the Amphitheatre at Pozzuoli*, signed, c.1635–37, oil on canvas, 308 × 200 cm, Cathedral Basilica San Procolo martire, Diocese of Pozzuoli, Naples

Gentileschi has reduced the composition down to its primary visual focus: the dense repetition of forms that has been created by the bishop's centrally positioned head alongside those of his followers. The figures are then enfolded within the compact, planar composition, which is dominated by the two opposing diagonals formed by the deacon at the left and the wild beasts to the right. This creates an inverted triangle of interlinked faces and gestures, all rotating around the central figure of the saint and each expressing differing responses to the unfolding miracle. The tightly controlled composition returns Gentileschi once again to the fundamental principles of clarity, concision and projection that were noted as defining aspects of her art as far back as the *Susanna and the Elders* of 1610. Indeed, the positioning of the amphitheatre as a kind of screen, which has the effect of removing the visual distraction of ancillary details in the background, performs a similar role to that of the high stone wall in the background of the *Susanna and the Elders*.

With its compressed background and concise figuration, the *St Januarius* projects a hieratic and concentrated monumentality that renders the process of viewing it almost akin to observing a painted version of monumental sculpture. This is appropriate to the ancient Roman associations of the story as well as the site itself, since Pozzuoli cathedral was built upon the foundations of a Roman temple dedicated to Augustus. The overriding impression of a poised, sculpture-like monumentality adds further to the dignified and measured bearing of the saint and his companions. Time seems suspended in this painting as, under the harsh glare of a southern sun, St Januarius stands exposed in the arena. The viewer is then invited to bear witness to the miraculous moment of deliverance as the saint bends slowly forward, almost as if in a trance, while leaning on his crozier for support. He raises his right hand to bless the lion at his feet, thereby creating a frozen instant of eternal benediction that is echoed, in turn, by the deacons' gestures of prayerful thanks.

All of this would have been enough to create a work of considerable devotional power. Yet Gentileschi has also been careful to counterbalance the painting's dominant mood of hieratic poise and solemnity with a renewed emphasis on a pungently incisive Caravaggesque realism. This is nowhere more evident than in the figure of St Januarius himself. The saint projects into our space with a startling physicality that is heightened by virtue of his almost portrait-like physiognomy. A sense of how fresh and contemporary this portrait-like appearance must have appeared in its own day can be gained if we compare Gentileschi's highly particularised rendition of the saint with the bland conventionality of Domenichino's more comprehensively idealized rendition in his contemporaneous treatment of the same subject for the Chapel of the Treasury in the cathedral at Naples (fig. 89).[32] Gentileschi's St Januarius, by contrast, appears drawn and lined; his prominent five o'clock shadow bears significant points of contact, in fact, with the comparably earthy characterisation of sanctity that is found in Ribera's representations of St Januarius from the same period.[33]

The previous analysis highlights Gentileschi's attentiveness to a wide array of contemporary and historical artistic trends, as well as to the continued importance of life modelling as a still-significant counterpoint to her concern for constructing compositions of increasing idealization, clarity and poise. This is further reinforced by the tour-de-force treatment of the varied surfaces of the saint's vestments: the crisp white lace at his wrists; the highlighted sheen running along the edge of his mitre; and, perhaps most prominent of all, the iridescent salmon pink stole that creates a visually oscillating effect with the white alb beneath and that contrasts in turn with the deep crimson of the bishop's cape.

Here, then, is the true source of Gentileschi's moment of in-demand prosperity during the 1630s. She was able to offer artists and patrons alike a compelling vision of a 'third' way of artistic productivity that enabled her to reinvent herself to a new audience as neither a retardataire Caravaggesque nor as a bloodless classicist. Instead, she opened up another chapter in her evolving career as a uniquely free agent operating in an innovative space of artistic fusion between and beyond these polarities.

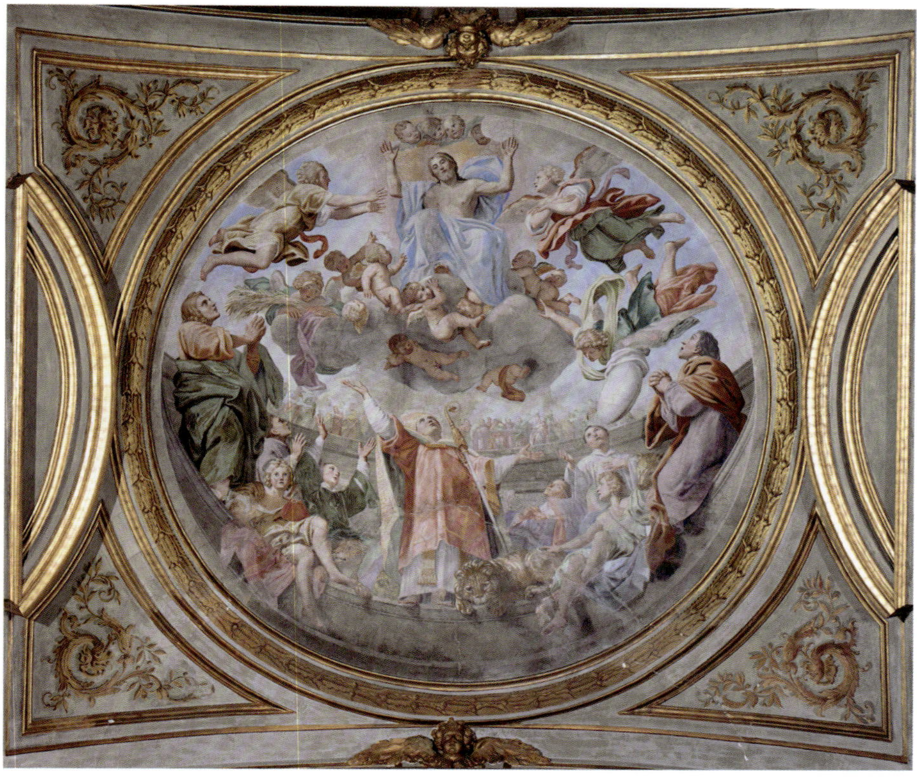

89 Domenichino, *The Attempted Martyrdom of St Januarius and his Companions at Pozzuoli*, 1637–38, fresco, Cappella del Tesoro di San Gennaro, Cathedral of Santa Maria Assunta, Naples

MASTERS AND DISCIPLES: THE REINVENTION OF GENTILESCHI AS A FEMALE GUIDO RENI

The foregoing analysis should help to explain what might have otherwise appeared as a puzzling emphasis in Bernardo de' Dominici's *Vite de' pittori, scultori ed architetti napoletani* (*Lives of the Neapolitan Painters, Sculptors and Architects*) of 1742–45. De' Dominici's *Vite* constitutes the first comprehensive series of biographical lives of the Neapolitan school of artists and as such remains fundamental to our knowledge of Neapolitan Baroque painting to this day.

Like Vasari, De' Dominici promoted the idea of art history as a series of extended family trees of masters and pupils. De' Dominici's *Vite* follow Vasari's in structuring the history of Neapolitan Renaissance and Baroque art around a series of great chains of artistic lineage that were forged over the course of generations by means of the deep continuities of the workshop tradition. These chains stretched from one master artist down to his pupil (the word used being *discepolo*, 'disciple' in Italian) and onwards from that master's pupil to the next and on through the ages. In Vasari's original template, Perugino had trained Raphael, who then acted as a master for Perino del Vaga and so on. Vasari frames these schools of artistic workshops as operating in dynamic emulation and/or competition with other master-pupil lineages – Raphael's school, for example, is shown to have clashed with that of Michelangelo over the competition for the contract for the Sala di Costantino in the Vatican.[34]

De' Dominici adopted this methodology in the context of his wider concern to trace the evolution of two contrasting approaches to Neapolitan art, each in opposition to the other, across the course of the seventeenth century. One was formed by the dominant school of Caravaggio, as embodied most powerfully by the works of Ribera and his followers. This was, however, increasingly challenged by the growing Neapolitan presence of the Bolognese school of Annibale Carracci and his heirs. While De' Dominici admired many aspects of Caravaggesque painting, he was, nonetheless, concerned to advocate for the ultimate ascendancy of the more idealized and noble tradition of the classical/Bolognese school. The result is the creation within the *Vite* of an overarching narrative of a clash of artistic traditions that would lead to the contemporaneous struggle between these two traditions in the work of the artists of his own day.

We might be surprised today to find that De' Dominici situates Gentileschi as a pivotal figure within the classical/Bolognese tradition, rather than with the Caravaggisti, with whom she is now more closely associated. De' Dominici was writing from a specifically Neapolitan rather than a Roman or even Florentine perspective. He thus remained unaware of (or perhaps chose not to emphasise) Gentileschi's initial training under Orazio Gentileschi and her early career as one of the leading, first-wave Caravaggisti. It was on the basis, instead, of her Neapolitan works of the 1630s to 1650s that he sought to characterise her as a former pupil of Guido Reni, an artist with whom we might not otherwise associate her.[35] This was important, in turn, to De' Dominici's broader narrative of a Neapolitan Bolognese/Guido Renian inheritance that he could posit in artistic opposition to Ribera and the Neapolitan Caravaggesque tradition. De' Dominici correctly understood the central significance of Stanzione within this countervailing tradition. The problem was, though, that he needed a master artist to act as a source for Stanzione's understanding of Guido Reni's art. De' Dominici had been explicitly informed that Stanzione had arrived in Rome too late to have been directly taught by Reni. So, Gentileschi was brought in to play this role instead.

Stanzione is described by De' Dominici as having undertaken an informal apprenticeship with Gentileschi in Naples, watching her paint every day until 'his genius was so satisfied with the freshness of her beautiful colors, that he proposed to imitate her: and with good reason, since she was said to have applied herself diligently in order to acquire the beautiful colours employed by her master Guido while he painted in Rome for Pope Paul V'.[36] De' Dominici also mentions a number of other artists who are said to have come under the sway of Gentileschi's Renian influence during these years. One is Bernardo Cavallino, a former pupil of Ribera who is said to have been particularly struck by 'the delicacy of her colours'. The other, a pupil of Giovanni Battista Caracciolo named Onofrio Palumbo (1606–1656), is said to have become similarly inspired by Gentileschi's style during this period. Caracciolo was one of the first Neapolitan followers of Caravaggio. He has been mentioned already in relation to a trip that he undertook in 1618 to Florence where he was able to present himself to the Medici as one of the most up-to-date protagonists of the new Caravaggesque style (see p. 64). Palumbo's crossing over to the other side, as it were, is thus framed by Bernardo de' Dominici as an example of a significant defection of a former Neapolitan Caravaggesque over to 'the sweetness of Gentileschi', as he puts it.[37] These otherwise brief references to Gentileschi's Neapolitan followers are significant in constituting the first biographical writing linking Gentileschi's Neapolitan oeuvre to these two artists, an influence that has been frequently commented on in the case of Cavallino but that was documented only in 2005 for Palumbo, as is discussed below (pp. 219–20).

CONCLUSION: GENTILESCHI'S COMPETING FATHER FIGURES

At the beginning of this study, I remarked upon Gentileschi's attempts in the Florentine biography supposedly written by Cristofano di Ottaviano Bronzini to create an early account of her life that sought to downplay the significance of her father's formative role as her first master. Instead, she replaced Orazio's name with that of Caravaggio, whom she posited as her preferred 'artistic' father figure. A little over a hundred years later, the same process was repeated by De' Dominici. This time, however, both Orazio's and Caravaggio's names have been substituted with that of Guido Reni, who thus assumes the role, in turn, of a more 'progressive' artistic father figure for Gentileschi. As with Gentileschi's first biography, De' Dominici's account has been constructed to serve a rhetorical purpose. It should not, therefore, be understood as being literally true. Gentileschi and Stanzione were contemporaries rather than master and pupil, and the chronology is also out by several decades. It's also likely – as Jesse Locker has noted – that De' Dominici's suggestion that Gentileschi was Reni's pupil was the result of a confused reference on his part to the literature on Elisabetta Sirani, since the Bolognese art historian Carlo Cesare Malvasia (1616–1693) discusses Sirani in this context – but not Gentileschi.[38] Yet the point here is not so much the accuracy or otherwise of De' Dominici's account, as the deeper 'truth' of the argument that he was seeking to advance regarding Gentileschi's pivotal role within his more comprehensive narrative of the evolution of Neapolitan Baroque painting.

The association of Gentileschi with Reni remained, in any event, a remarkably widespread perception in the subsequent literature on the artist. In 1792, for example, both Luigi Lanzi and Averardo de' Medici identified Reni as a major influence on Gentileschi's Neapolitan paintings.[39] To this can be added an intriguing reference in a late eighteenth-century sales catalogue announcing a sale of work from the Earl of Spencer's collection that was about to be held in London in 1796. This catalogue describes a painting of the *Toilet of Bathsheba* that sounds highly reminiscent, in fact, of Gentileschi's late Neapolitan versions of this subject (discussed below, pp. 196 and 213). Its brief reference contains the assertion that the painting is attributed to Reni but that it should be re-attributed to Gentileschi: 'this beautiful picture belonged to Lord Spencer, and was always attributed to Guido, but it is in reality the most valuable work of Gentileschi'.[40]

Gentileschi's paintings of the 1630s demonstrate once again the artist's ability to reinvent herself in ways that enabled her to be appreciated by a new audience and in an entirely new light. It also brought her substantial financial rewards. In 1636, for example, she received the princely sum of six hundred ducats for a set of three very large gallery paintings depicting *Susanna*, *Lucretia* and *Bathsheba*, the latter of which would have formed a close match to the painting described in the sales catalogue referred to above. Gentileschi was, therefore, able successfully to relaunch her career during the 1630s within the new and unfamiliar artistic environment of Naples at the uppermost levels of its pay scales as well as within its most exalted patronage structures. There is more involved in this evaluation, however, than simply the amount of money paid to Gentileschi. The price of six hundred ducats needs to be understood in relation to the broader system of pricing and the economic rates of comparison, judgement and reputation that formed the basis for these payments. Gentileschi's 1636 commission also raises the issue of just how a major work of this kind was evaluated – and paid for – in comparison with other categories of her artistic production during this period. Finally, the payments she received raise again the issue of Gentileschi's productivity and workshop output during her time in Naples. Having established the nature of Gentileschi's late-career success in the city, therefore, it is appropriate that attention is now turned to the issue of just how this success was mediated within the context of Gentileschi's financial arrangements and the complex workings of the Neapolitan art market.

II

'Sold by her hand'

SETTING PRICES AND GETTING PAID IN BAROQUE NAPLES

INTRODUCTION

The previous chapter highlighted the increased levels of success enjoyed by Gentileschi in Naples during the 1630s, as she cultivated fruitful associations with such pre-eminent individuals as the Spanish Infanta, the Count of Monterrey and the Bishop of Benevento. These assisted her, in turn, to secure a range of significant public commissions, including the 1630 *Annunciation* altarpiece, the *Birth of St John the Baptist* for Madrid and the three monumental canvases for Pozzuoli cathedral: *St Januarius in the Amphitheatre*, the *Adoration of the Magi* and *Sts Proculus and Nicea*. All of this resulted in a significant mid-career elevation of Gentileschi's public profile that would be reflected at the beginning of the next century by De' Dominici's decision to frame her – memorably, if not entirely accurately, as we saw – as one of the major protagonists of the classical/Bolognese tradition, standing in creative opposition to the bedrock realism of Caravaggio and his Neapolitan heirs.

Running alongside these defining moments of wider public and critical endorsement was a series of privately conducted sales and commissions. The works that Gentileschi produced for the Neapolitan private sector ranged from some of the largest and most ambitious of her career to more workaday, half-length and single-figure compositions painted for a diverse range of clients. Naples offered a perfect base for the consolidation

FACING PAGE Artemisia Gentileschi, *Samson and Delilah* (detail of fig. 99)

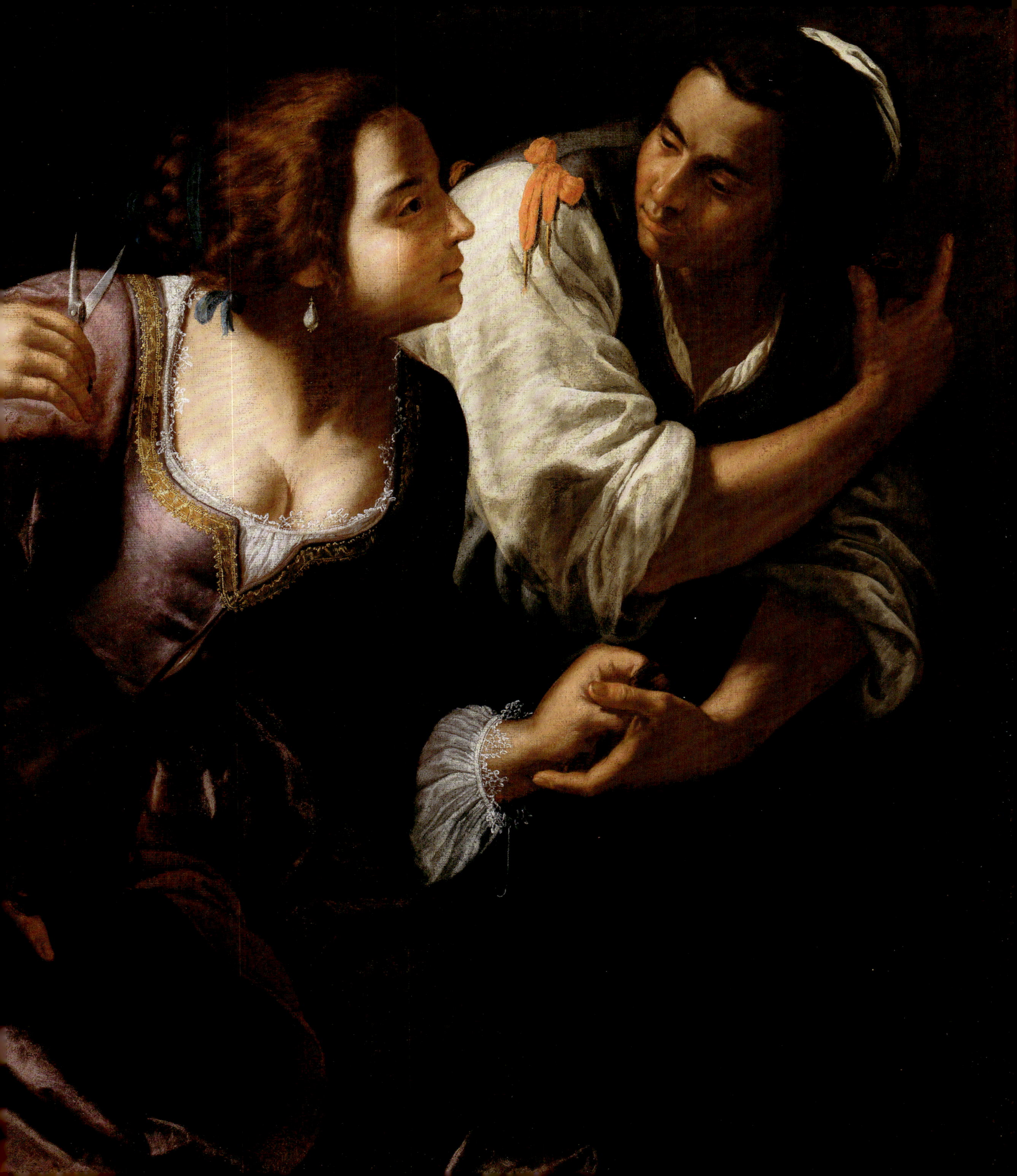

of this dimension of her career. The city's population of almost 300,000 inhabitants outstripped Rome's by almost three to one and Venice's by more than 100,000 (Florence's population of 72,000, by contrast, put it far behind the other urban metropolises in this respect).[1]

Naples also offered significant commercial and entrepreneurial opportunities by virtue of its prime position as a major port acting as a commercial and administrative entrepôt for the entire reach of southern Italy as well as for the Italian interests of the vast Habsburg chain of empire stretching from Seville to Santiago. A vivid sense of the significant benefits that Gentileschi was able to gain from this lively and dynamic situation can be found in the archival holdings of the city's public banks. These preserve the records of a number of Gentileschi's financial interactions with a broad range of private collectors, from the city's most venerable aristocratic families to the leading protagonists of the emerging professional classes. They also provide insight into the cut-and-thrust tactics involved in negotiating sales, as well as into the financial and business pressures that Gentileschi and her associates experienced as they sought to advance their interests in this most auspicious yet also pressure-ridden city. A document of 1636 provides a particularly useful point of entry into the complex processes underpinning Neapolitan transactions of these kinds.

GENTILESCHI, 1636: PURVEYOR OF LUXURY ART FOR AN INTERNATIONAL CLIENTELE

On 5 May 1636, Lorenzo Cambi and Simone Verzone paid a visit to Gentileschi's Neapolitan workshop. In the course of their appointment, they jotted down a summary of their dealings with the artist, while also arranging to pay her for her work. The resulting document, known as a *fede di credito*, functioned as a circulating cheque or bill of exchange that was fundamental to the workings of the Neapolitan Baroque economy. In the absence of such a thing as paper money prior to the nineteenth century, the *fede di credito* (credit statement, or *polizza*/bill) allowed Neapolitans to conduct financial transactions that were endorsed by the bank and also acted as a form of legally binding contract outlining the agreed-upon terms that needed to be satisfied before a matter could be said to be resolved.[2] Much is thus to be gleaned from the necessarily dry and notarial language contained in documents of this kind:

> To Lorenzo Cambi and Simone Verzone 250 ducats and through them to Artemisia Gentileschi that are said to amount to 300 ducats, the other fifty having been received in cash. These are said to be on account of 600 ducats which are given to her by order of the most excellent prince Carlo de Loctenten [and that are] paid to her for the value of three paintings which consist of a Bathsheba, a Susanna and a Lucretia each of which is to be 11.5 palms high [about 303 cm] to give and consign in every particular [of this agreement]. And through her to the standard bearer Costantino del Cunto for other things.[3]

The highly specific nature of the information captured in these documents means that there is still much about them that remains inaccessible to us today. One would like to know more, for example, about the standard bearer, Costantino del Cunto, to whom Artemisia transferred the 250 ducats after receiving it from her visitors. He remains no more than a name at present. What can be gleaned from the document is, nonetheless, illuminating in opening a window onto Gentileschi's business practices during this felicitous stage of her late career. It confirms, for example, that her visitors were not acting as patrons in the traditional sense; rather, they were operating as commissioning agents working, in effect, as talent scouts ordering works in Naples by prestigious artists on behalf of their evidently very wealthy foreign client. This individual can be identified, in turn, as Prince Karl Eusebius von Liechtenstein (1611–1684), son of the dynasty's founder and one of the most distinguished collectors in the history of the Princely House of Liechtenstein.[4] Karl Eusebius, who had become prince at the young age of sixteen, was just then commissioning dozens of artworks to decorate the family residence in Valtice, in what is now the Czech Republic.[5]

Cambi and Verzone's association with Von Liechtenstein would have formed part of their wider activities as international merchant/financiers operating out of the port of Naples. Lorenzo Cambi seems to have been an especially important figure in this regard. He belonged to the Neapolitan branch of a venerable Florentine family of merchant bankers who maintained agencies throughout Europe and whose success remained contingent on their long-standing loyalty to the Medici.[6] They were also significant patrons of the arts. In 1529, Lorenzo's forebear and namesake, Lorenzo di Giovanni Cambi (1479–1553), had commissioned an important altarpiece from Bronzino for the Cambi family chapel in Florence's Santa Trinita.[7] The Neapolitan branch of the Cambi family is likewise documented as including important collectors of ancient sculpture during the late sixteenth century.[8] While less documentation exists for Simone Verzone, we do at least know that he hailed from Prato, was a member of the local community of Tuscans resident in Naples and was on close, personal terms with another prominent member of the local community, Cosimo del Sera, the Neapolitan agent of the Grand Duchy of Tuscany, an important early patron of Ribera and a godfather to Verzone's son in 1633.[9]

It was, presumably, on the basis of Cambi and Verzone's recommendation that Gentileschi would have been referred to Von Liechtenstein, who would then have authorised the commission. But if Von Liechtenstein thought he was receiving a truly independent assessment on their part, he would have been mistaken. In fact, Gentileschi had longstanding links with the Cambi family. In 1620, Lorenzo Cambi's Florentine relative Francesco Cambi had acted as one of the signatories on the document that was drawn up to allow Gentileschi's lover, Francesco Maringhi, to take possession of the sequestered collateral and personal effects left behind by Gentileschi following her hurried departure from Florence (see pp. 104 and 127).[10] As is often the case with complex business dealings, therefore, the 1636 transaction between Gentileschi and Cambi and Verzone on behalf of Von Liechtenstein grows out of a network of associations stretching back more than a decade and attesting once more to the strength of Gentileschi's long-term cultivation of connections from Naples to Florence and beyond.

Cambi and Verzone represent a new breed of art-world intermediaries who were just then emerging as increasingly active players on the local scene. Cultivated and well-connected, mercantile entrepreneurs were optimally placed to export Neapolitan paintings to leading international collectors in the early stages of the growing internationalisation of Neapolitan art.[11] The key figure in this process was another merchant resident in the city, Gaspar Roomer (*c.*1596/1606–1674). Originally from Antwerp, Roomer was engaged in building up a vast business empire that would make him proverbially rich and one of the most influential back-room brokers in the entire Kingdom of Naples. Roomer maintained a fleet of ships operating out of the city's port which he used to run a series of increasingly complex ventures, incorporating international freight, loans and insurance, arms dealing and naval outfitting, shipping and financing of all kinds, much of it conducted in the service of the insatiable administrative enterprise of the Spanish Habsburgs and the Neapolitan viceregency.

Roomer was also one of the city's leading art dealers, a practice that he combined with parallel activities as one of Naples' most distinguished collectors. His collection numbered some 1,500 paintings and was said to be worth as much as 80,000 ducats at the time of his death.[12] He was a prodigious and omnivorous collector, manifesting a particular love of early Caravaggesque painting, among numerous other genres that demonstrated, as Francis Haskell has observed, a particular 'taste for the grotesque, the dark and the cruel'.[13] One might, therefore, have expected him to have commissioned work from Gentileschi during this period – a Neapolitan version of her signature composition of *Judith Slaying Holofernes*, for example (fig. 90).[14] Yet we cannot be certain of this, since a full inventory of Roomer's collection was not drawn up during his lifetime. His collection is known only from a series of scattered references and descriptions. Roomer, nevertheless, gave or sold large portions of his collection to favoured business associates, a number of whom are also known to have owned work by Gentileschi. A version of Gentileschi's *Judith* documented in the Venetian collection of the prosperous international financier Giovanni Andrea Lumaga might thus have originally belonged to Roomer. So, too, might a *Judith Slaying Holofernes* attributed to Orazio Gentileschi – but identified by some commentators as a work by Artemisia – which is cited in an early inventory of the collection of the son of Roomer's business partner, Ferdinand Vandeneynden.[15]

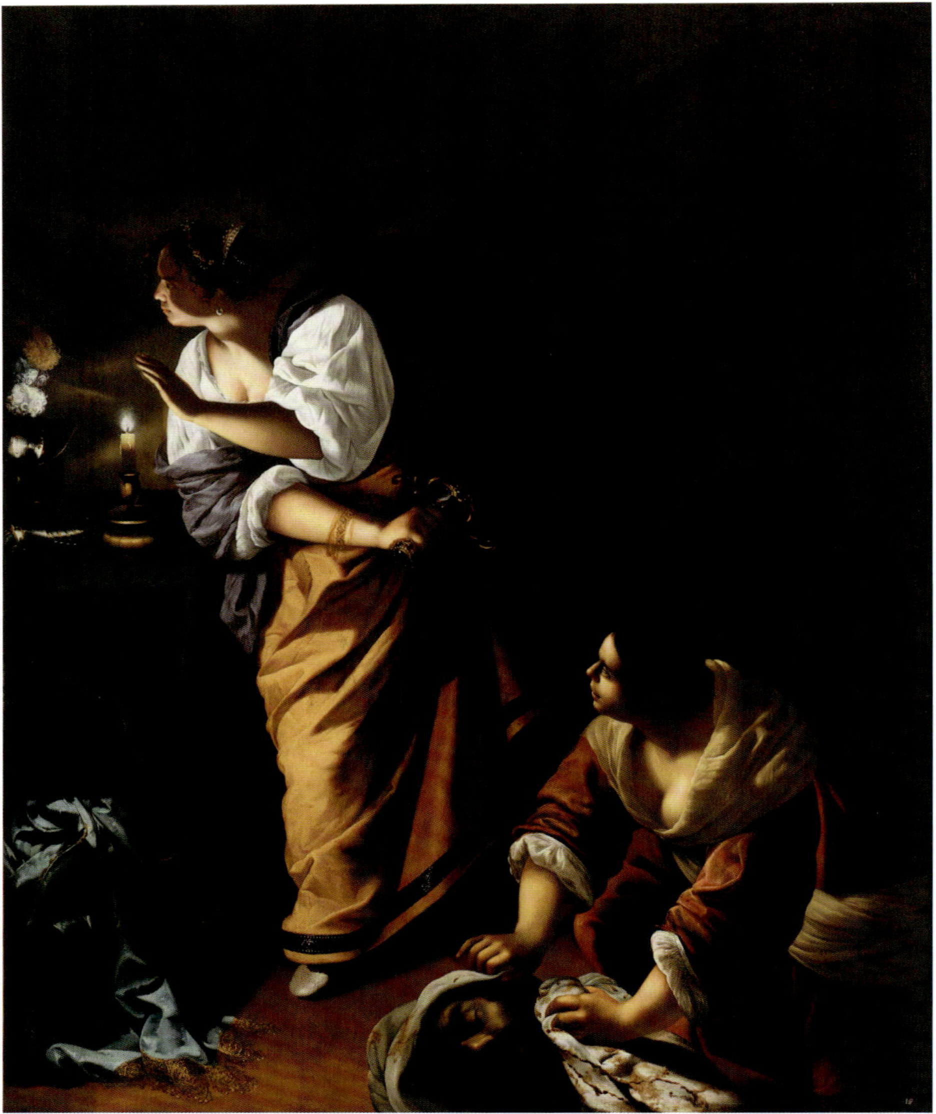

90 Attributed to Artemisia Gentileschi, *Judith and her Maidservant with the Head of Holofernes*, c.1648–50, oil on canvas, 272 × 221 cm, Museo e Real Bosco di Capodimonte, Naples

MANAGING LUXURY: NEGOTIATING PRIVATE PAINTING COMMISSIONS IN BAROQUE NAPLES

The prestigious nature of the 1636 Cambi/Verzone art-buying venture is underscored by the fact that the two merchants also contracted work from Ribera for the same international collector only two days after visiting Gentileschi:

To Lorenzo Cambi and Simone Verzone 100 ducats and through them to Giuseppe de Ribera that are said to be paid by order of Count Carlo Felesbergh and they are on account of 500 ducats for the value of twelve paintings 5 palms high and 4 palms wide [about 132 × 105 cm] in each one of which there is to be painted a philosopher by his own hand which is to be done to serve Don Carlo

> Felsbergh and these [paintings] must be delivered to them within six months and failing this he will be required to return all the money at their pleasure.[16]

The 1636 Ribera document sheds further light on the negotiating process informing high-level commissions of this kind. It shows that, in this case at least, Cambi and Verzone were evidently not as confident of their dealings with Ribera as they had been with Gentileschi. They, therefore, felt the need to insert more stringent terms into the agreement in order to keep this leading artist on track to complete the commission satisfactorily and in a timely manner, setting a six-month time limit on the contract, with the proviso that Ribera would have to return the money if he did not complete the contract by then. Even so, Ribera had finished only six of the twelve paintings by the following year. A follow-up payment of fifty ducats made on 20 April 1637 accordingly notes that Ribera had at that stage received a cumulative total of 250 ducats on account for six of the twelve canvases. As for the remaining six: 'he will have to consign them to them [that is, to the merchants] at their pleasure'.[17]

Ribera appears to have left the commission in limbo at that stage and never did produce further works for Von Liechtenstein. This early sign of Ribera's own productivity problems chimes with a number of other documented instances during this period.[18] On 7 August 1632, for example, he had been required to return a *caparra*, or initial downpayment, of one hundred ducats to the high-ranking aristocrat and administrative functionary Giovanni d'Avalos. Ribera had received the payment for a painting of *St Lawrence*, but, the document notes, 'not having been able to complete the work, he is sending back the sum [of money]'.[19] Gentileschi, by contrast, seems to have had no difficulties in completing her work for the same family, most probably for the same patron, during this period. This can be determined on the basis of a painting by her of the *Sleeping Venus* that is listed in a 1739 inventory of the D'Avalos family collection (see below, pp. 194 and 196).[20]

It is striking to note the significantly improved rates of productivity that Gentileschi seems to have been able to maintain as a result of her move to Naples. I noted above the difficulties that she had experienced in honouring a contract for a privately commissioned *Madonna* during her earlier years in Florence. Gentileschi had still not completed this relatively straightforward contract for a single-figure composition some two years after its initial commissioning in 1618. To this might be added the other examples of unfinished commissions: the self-portrait for Dal Pozzo in 1630 and her delayed *Venus* for the Barberini. Now, however, in Naples, during the mid- to late 1630s Gentileschi had no such problems in successfully juggling numerous contracts. These included the three large paintings for Von Liechtenstein, as well as the commission for three monumental altarpieces for Pozzuoli cathedral.

Cambi and Verzone's evident trust in Gentileschi's abilities to manage her complex professional obligations during this period is indicated also by the sequence and the amounts of money that they paid her. They had given her an initial downpayment of fifty ducats at some earlier stage to get the commission underway. Then, on 5 May 1636, they returned to review the work and were evidently happy with the results. They, accordingly, paid her a second instalment of 250 ducats, a large amount of money that, presumably, indicated their satisfaction that Gentileschi had successfully passed the commission's halfway mark. She must, therefore, have finished and delivered one of the three paintings and been able to show them a second canvas underway.

In their contract with Ribera, Cambi and Verzone inserted a clause requiring the artist to produce the paintings 'by his own hand' ('di sua mano') – something that they did not, by contrast, feel the need to stipulate in Gentileschi's contract. 'Di sua mano' constituted a conventional phrase that patrons customarily inserted into contracts to encourage the maximum amount of personal responsibility and obligation on an artist's part.[21] The two merchants were evidently worried that Ribera might not be able to give the commission his full attention. This was an understandable concern, given that he was, at that time, preoccupied with numerous high-profile, private and public commissions, including a number of major paintings for the King of Spain as well as for both the present and former viceroys of Naples. The six paintings that Ribera did complete for Von Liechtenstein are, nonetheless, some of his best productions of this type (fig. 91).[22] It was Gentileschi, rather, who appears to have felt the need to

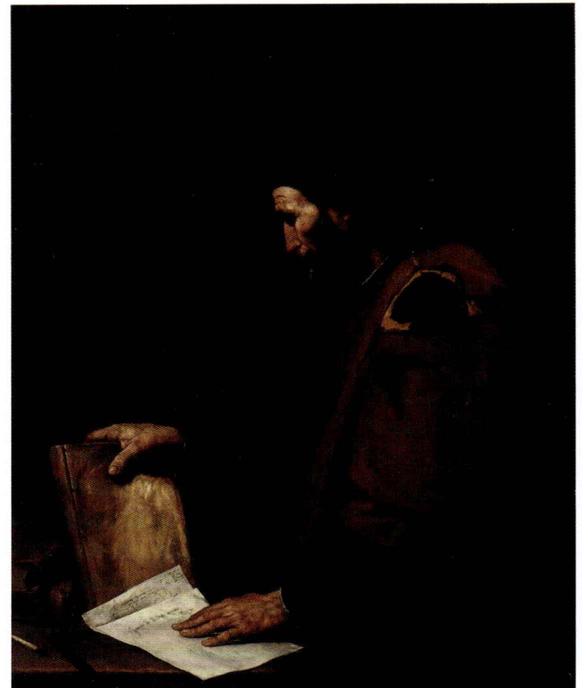

91 (ABOVE LEFT) Jusepe de Ribera, *Aristotle*, signed and dated 1637, oil on canvas, 124 × 99 cm, Indianapolis Museum of Art, the Clowes Fund Collection

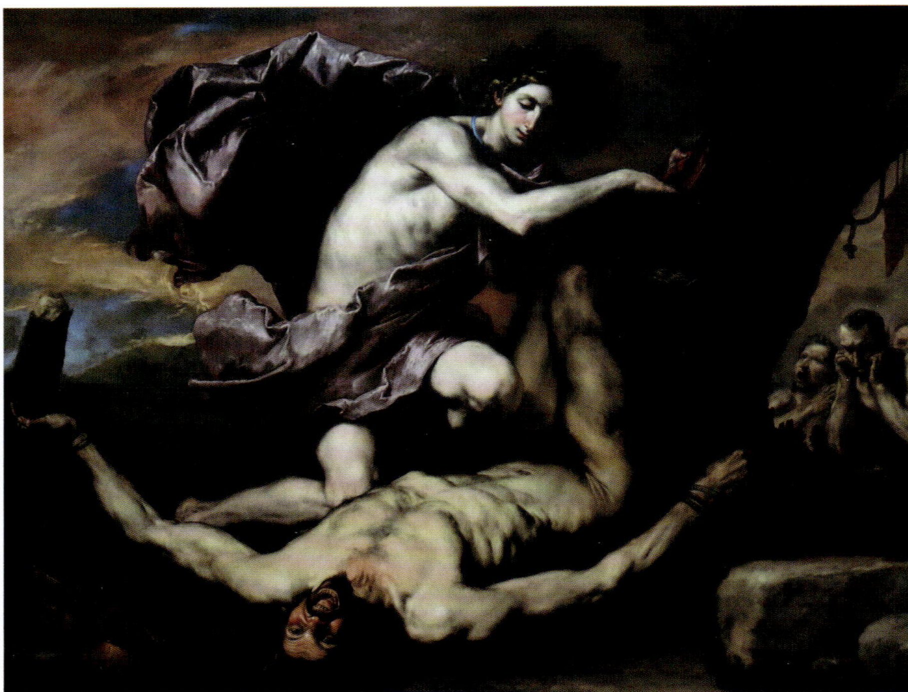

92 (ABOVE RIGHT) Jusepe de Ribera, *Apollo and Marsyas*, signed and dated 1637, oil on canvas, 182 × 232 cm, Museo e Real Bosco di Capodimonte, Naples

augment her workshop during this period and bring in external specialists to assist her with her work. The version of *David and Bathsheba* now in the Columbus Museum of Art is sometimes identified as one of the three paintings she produced for Von Liechtenstein (fig. 93), although it may equally have originally formed part of another series from the same period seen by De' Dominici in the collection of Dr Luigi Romeo in Naples.[23] Modern scholars have identified the input of a number of collaborators within this painting, including an architectural background by Viviano Codazzi, landscape elements by Domenico Gargiulo and two of the maidservants by Bernardo Cavallino.[24] This aspect of Gentileschi's Neapolitan production will be discussed further in the next chapter.

At two hundred ducats apiece, Gentileschi's three paintings of *Bathsheba*, *Susanna* and *Lucretia* would have constituted some of the most expensive privately commissioned Neapolitan paintings of the day. The same amount, for example, was paid to Ribera in 1645 for his *Apollo and Marsyas*, a work that corresponds closely with Gentileschi's three paintings for Von Liechtenstein in terms of its overall size, format and number of figures (fig. 92).[25] How, then, would Cambi, Verzone and Gentileschi have arrived at a price for commissions of this kind?

The number of figures depicted within a work is often cited as a determinant in arriving at the fee for more exclusive commissions at this level.[26] This form of price structuring remained an option for those particularly fortunate painters active in other cities who operated at the highest reaches of the art market. Guercino, for example, was well known for being able to set a benchmark of one hundred ducats per figure and so to be able to command prices for paintings that could at times push well beyond the usual limit of two hundred scudi or ducats.[27] Gentileschi would clearly have liked to do the same, judging by the wish-fulfilling comment contained in her

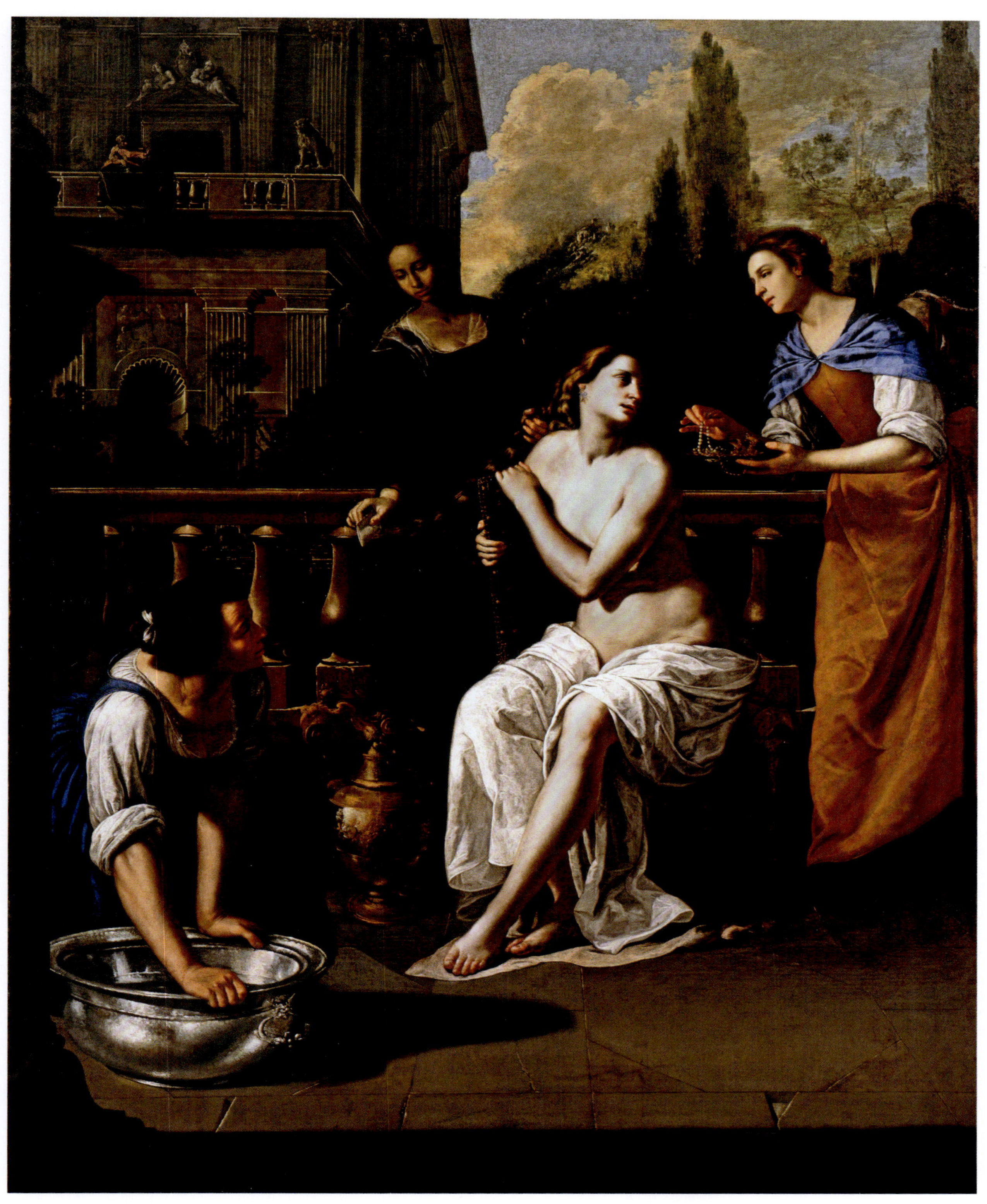

93 Artemisia Gentileschi, *David and Bathsheba*, c.1636–38, oil on canvas, 265.4 × 209.5 cm, Columbus Museum of Art, Ohio, Museum Purchase, Schumacher Fund, acc. no. 1967.006

ghost-written Florentine biography, that her earliest paintings had 'attain[ed] prices of 300, 500, and even 600 and more'. She also referenced the practice of payment by the number of figures in a letter of 1649 to her patron Don Antonio Ruffo of Messina (1610/11–1678). In it she notes, 'In fact, if it were not for your Most Illustrious Lordship, of whom I am so affectionate a servant, I would not have been induced to give it [the painting] for 160, because everywhere else I have been paid 100 scudi per figure. And this was in Florence, as well as Venice and Rome and even in Naples when there was more money'.[28]

The slightly pleading undercurrent to Gentileschi's tone should alert us to the fact that her observation in this instance represented an ambit claim on her part rather than a reflection of her actual experience. In reality, figures in Neapolitan paintings were only ever counted and used as the basis for computing costs in the very rare cases of exceptionally complex and/or prestigious public commissions. One of the few examples of this – and the precedent that Gentileschi probably had in mind when making this claim – is the commission for the Chapel of the Treasury of Saint Januarius in Naples cathedral (see pp. 157–58). As noted, this commission constituted one of the city's most high-profile public art projects. In 1620, Guido Reni had set the bar high on the cost of art in Naples when he successfully negotiated a price of one hundred Roman scudi per figure to induce him to come down to the city to work on the project. This was payable, moreover, at the unfavourable local exchange rate of 130 Neapolitan ducats per 100 Roman scudi, since Naples was at that stage in the grip of a major economic crisis. Reni was, however, unable to profit from this lucrative arrangement, being instead obliged to flee the city before completing any work.[29] It was Domenichino who ultimately reaped the benefits of this agreement when he relocated to Naples in 1630 to take up the contract, although only at a considerable cost to his own physical and mental well-being. The figures in his *Martyrdom of St Januarius*, for example, were painstakingly itemised by the Chapel's deputies and financially accounted for one by one (fig. 94). This included the computation of the number of 'equivalent' figures, with one figure being deemed equivalent, for example, to 'five [heads of] seraphims' in his painting, or to the three heads formed by 'the other saint who is being pulled by the hair by a scoundrel [and] with the soldier with the silver [helmet behind him]').[30] With so many elements to add up within the painting's crowded composition, it is no wonder that Domenichino's altarpiece ended up costing 1,400 ducats, making it one of the most expensive paintings of the day.

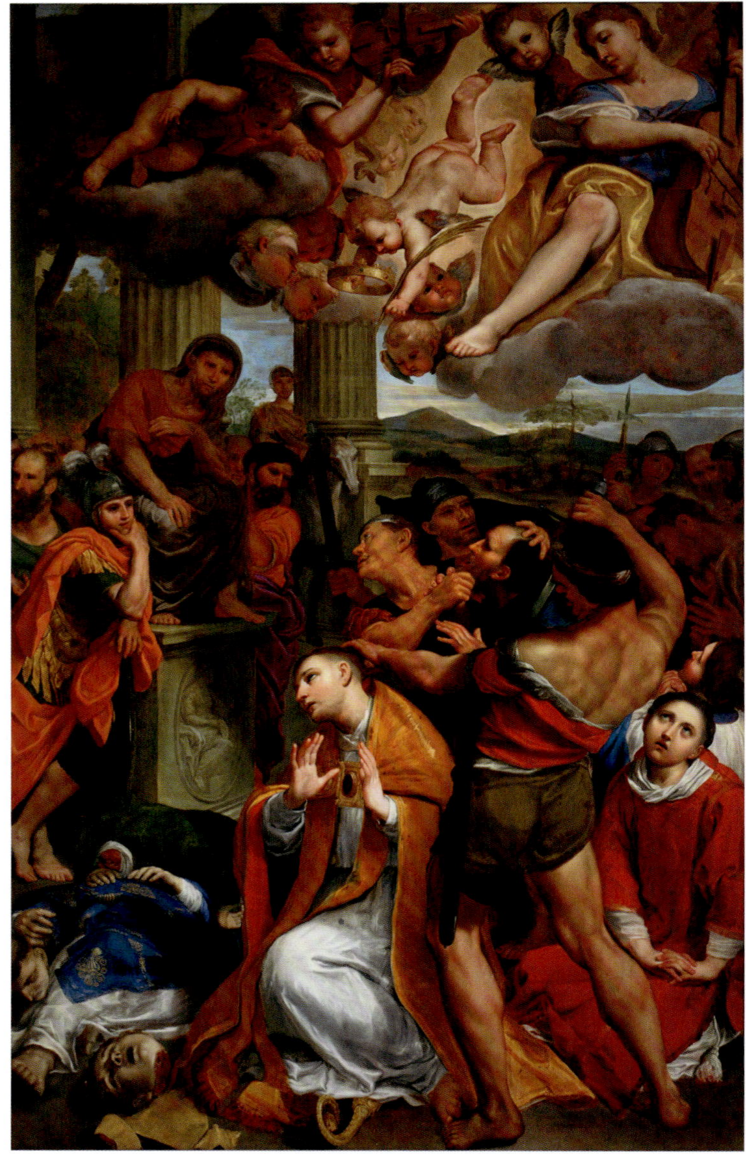

94 Domenichino, *The Martyrdom of St Januarius*, 1639-40, oil on copper, 355 × 220 cm, Cappella del Tesoro di San Gennaro, Cathedral of Santa Maria Assunta, Naples

Private Neapolitan secular commissions, by contrast, were not subject to such stringent itemisation and were never anywhere near as expensive. This was one of a number of factors keeping the prices of Neapolitan paintings down in relation to the costs of comparable artistic production elsewhere. In 1631, for example, Guercino received four hundred scudi for his *Death of Dido*, commissioned by the papal legate in Bologna, Cardinal Bernardino Spada, and intended for the Queen Mother, Marie de Medici.[31] Likewise, in 1645, he received 750 scudi for his *Intervention of the Sabine Women*, painted for the Hôtel de la Vrillière in Paris.[32] Guido Reni, likewise, received very significant compensation for his work throughout his career, including the truly exceptional fee of 250 ducatoni/1,000 scudi for each of his four canvases of *The Labours of Hercules*, painted for the Duke of Mantua between 1617 and 1621.[33] In Naples, by contrast, privately commissioned work only very rarely exceeded the two hundred ducat mark, a factor strongly suggesting that this amount constituted a kind of 'glass ceiling' and represented a generally agreed-upon uppermost limit for the more expensive – and thus most prestigious – privately commissioned gallery paintings of the day.[34]

Gentileschi alludes to this Neapolitan reality when she qualifies, in her letter to Ruffo, her claim to have received one hundred scudi per figure as being predominantly for work undertaken in other cities. She had received comparable rates in Naples, as she puts it, only 'when there was more money'. Here she is undoubtedly alluding to the continued social and economic crises buffeting the Kingdom of Naples from the time of the financial crash of the early 1620s and continuing thereafter up to and beyond the trilogy of Neapolitan disasters – the eruption of Vesuvius in 1631, the Revolt of Masaniello of 1647–48 and the plague of 1656. Each of these major disturbances added to a prevailing impression that Naples was labouring under a significant burden of social and economic disadvantages.[35]

GENTILESCHI'S PAYMENTS AND NEAPOLITAN WORKSHOP OUTPUT: GENDER BIAS, PRICE SCALING AND PRODUCT DIFFERENTIATION

In fact, the documentation suggests that Gentileschi very rarely, if ever, received rates of payment at the uppermost level of the scale at any stage of her career (table 1, pp. 256–57). The only known substantial payments dating before her Neapolitan years are an unspecified Medici payment of 150 scudi in March 1619 and the 1626 commission for a *Hercules and Omphale* for the Alcázar palace in Madrid from the conde de Oñate which amounted to the equivalent of 146 scudi.[36] The Medici payment is stated as being a 'saldo', or settlement payment, whose purpose is, however, unspecified.[37] Although we have no way of knowing for sure, it seems reasonable to interpret it as a final payment for one of Gentileschi's major Medici commissions. Stretching this speculative point a little further, we might interpret the document as a settlement for the second Florentine version of the *Judith Slaying Holofernes* (fig. 56). If so, then this might possibly represent the kernel of truth out of which Gentileschi's claim to have received one hundred scudi per figure grew. If Gentileschi received an initial down-payment from the Medici of fifty scudi for this painting, then the second payment might have followed on from this as the final payment, bringing the total to two hundred scudi for the Florentine *Judith Slaying Holofernes*, a composition containing the equivalent, we might say, of two full-length figures.

The 1626 *Hercules and Omphale* commission for the Alcázar palace in Madrid, by contrast, cannot be read in support of Gentileschi's claim to have received one hundred ducats per figure, no matter how we interpret the documents. Gentileschi received the equivalent of 146 scudi for this commission, a by no means munificent amount for a work of this kind. The Alcázar *Hercules* remains untraced, having been probably destroyed in an eighteenth-century fire in the palace. But some further information about it can be gleaned from two Neapolitan versions of the same subject dating to the 1630s and 1640s. One of these is by Artemisia's early Neapolitan collaborator Bernardo Cavallino and is almost certainly heavily influenced by Gentileschi, given that it was produced during the period of his close association with her and given further that it is

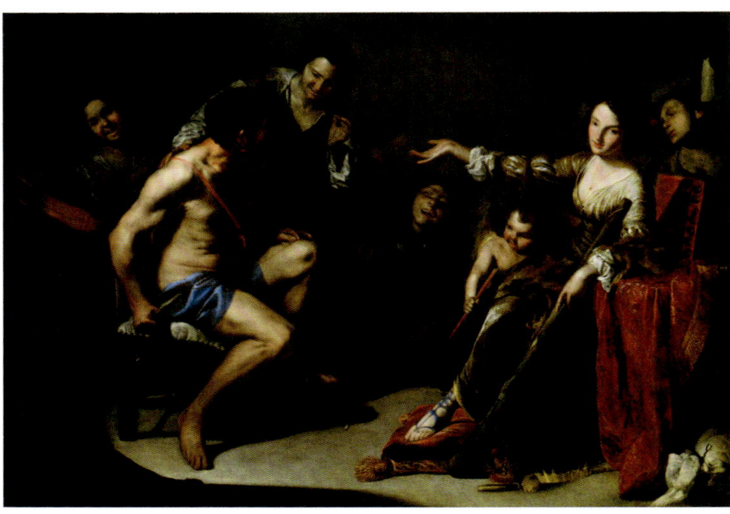

95 Bernardo Cavallino, *Hercules and Omphale*, *c.*1640, oil on canvas, 128 × 187 cm, The National Museum of Western Art, Tokyo

utterly unlike anything else in this artist's oeuvre at this point of his career (fig. 95). The other canvas, from a private Beirut collection and in a tragically parlous state of preservation, was first brought to the attention of Gentileschi scholars by Gregory Buchakjian in 2020 (fig. 96). Buchakjian identified it as being by Artemisia and proposed it as being possibly identifiable with a work attributed to Artemisia in the 1699 inventory of Carlo de Cardenas, a collector belonging to a Neapolitan family of some significance (see p. 179).[38]

Both the Beirut canvas and Cavallino's *Hercules and Omphale* contain the equivalent of around four figures. If we apply this number to Gentileschi's payment from the conde de Oñate, we arrive at an average of around thirty-six ducats or scudi per figure. The degree to which this falls far short of the highest rates attained by the most successful artists operating in other cities can be judged, once again, by comparing this payment

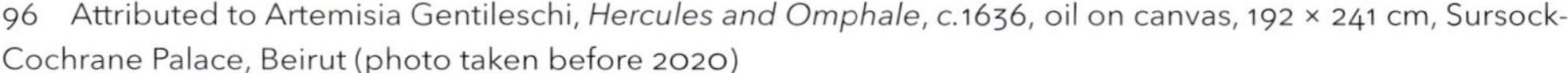

96 Attributed to Artemisia Gentileschi, *Hercules and Omphale*, *c.*1636, oil on canvas, 192 × 241 cm, Sursock-Cochrane Palace, Beirut (photo taken before 2020)

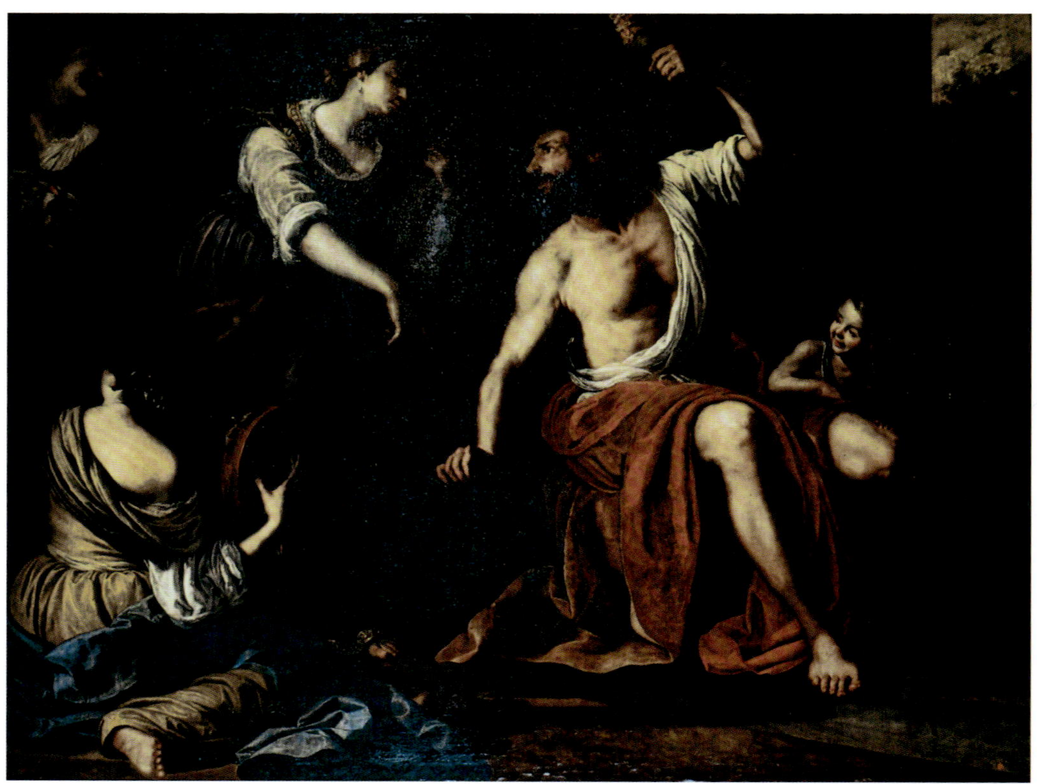

with the amount paid by Oñate to Domenichino for his work on the same commission during the same period. In 1627–28, Oñate paid Domenichino 10,000 giulii, equivalent to 1,000 scudi, for two paintings for the Alcázar: *Solomon and the Queen of Sheba* (now lost) and *The Sacrifice of Isaac*, now in the Prado (fig. 97).[39] *Solomon and the Queen of Sheba* would have been the costliest of the two, given that its subject would have required a more complex composition and a greater number of figures. Still, and however we notionally divide the amounts apportioned between the two works (perhaps 600 for the *Solomon* and 400 for the *Isaac*?), there is no doubting the much more generous rates afforded to Domenichino by this same patron, a point also underscored by Richard Spear in his analysis of the earnings of Orazio and Artemisia Gentileschi.[40] This discrepancy between the different levels of payment made by the same patron to Gentileschi and Domenichino for otherwise directly comparable work is especially evident given that Domenichino's *Sacrifice of Isaac* also contains a total of only three figures.

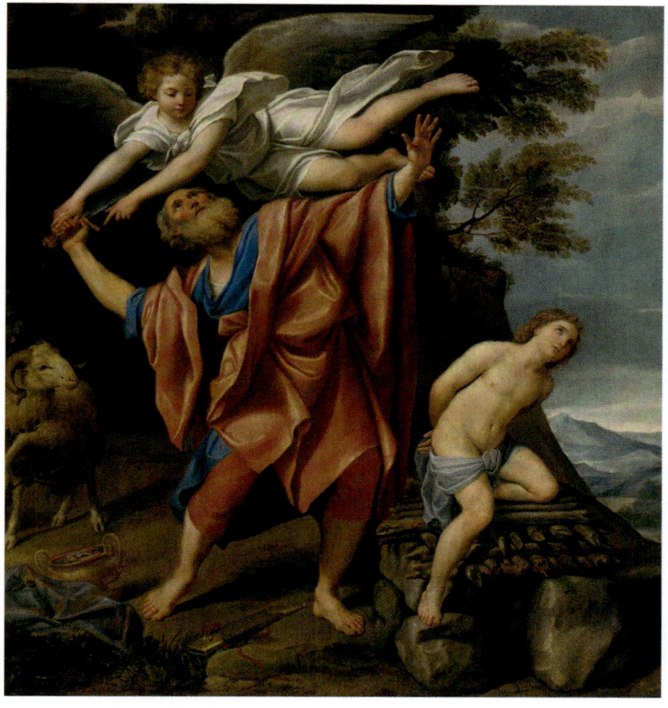

97 Domenichino, *The Sacrifice of Isaac*, c.1627–28, oil on canvas, 147 × 140 cm, Museo Nacional del Prado, Madrid, P000131

Gentileschi's claim to have received one hundred scudi per figure in this correspondence was made in the context of her ongoing negotiations with Ruffo over the cost of a large painting of *Galatea* that measured around 211 by 264 cm and that included the equivalent of around seven figures. Gentileschi had nearly completed the canvas, but Ruffo now wanted to beat her down on its price. The letter records Gentileschi haggling with him over the fee before eventually settling on a final price of 160 ducats for the finished work. Undeterred by this experience, Gentileschi then went on to produce a companion piece for this same patron in the following year. This painting depicted *Diana and Actaeon* and is described in the inventories as also incorporating seven figures – plus two dogs. For this she received 230 ducats.

These payments were among the highest prices of Gentileschi's career. Yet they were, however, slightly lower than the money paid by this same patron to Gentileschi's male colleagues during the same period. In 1651, Ruffo paid Stanzione three hundred ducats for a painting of *The Judgement of Paris* – likewise measuring around 211 by 264 cm and including four figures and two dogs. This represented a rate of around sixty ducats per figure, as opposed to the twenty-three ducats per figure paid by Ruffo for Gentileschi's *Galatea*. Ruffo also commissioned a large *Pietà* from Ribera during the same period for which he eventually paid out 270 ducats plus a 'gift' of finely worked fabric from Messina.[41] This was an outlay of around fifty-four ducats per figure, as opposed to the thirty-two ducats per figure – or thereabouts – paid to Gentileschi for her *Diana and Actaeon*.

Given the picture here presented of Gentileschi and her male colleagues producing otherwise directly comparable work for the same patrons during the same period, and in the absence of any further documentary evidence to the contrary, one can only conclude that an inherent gender bias was at play during the financial negotiations undertaken by Gentileschi with these and other male patrons. As Caroline Murphy has pointed out, within the context of a study of the economic considerations informing female artistic practice more broadly, when it came to conducting financial negotiations, Renaissance and Baroque women artists were at a significant disadvantage relative to their male peers. Sofonisba Anguissola, Lavinia

Fontana, Elisabetta Sirani and their other female colleagues were required to interact with their male customers in ways that took them far beyond the established norms of female social interaction: the processes of 'soliciting clients, establishing prices, and bartering and brokering deals . . . involved levels of aggressive behaviour that certainly did not appear in the literature for ideal female comportment'.[42]

Gentileschi was at a particular disadvantage in this regard. She maintained a fully independent business operation from 1613 onwards – and even more independent from the 1620s, following her split from her husband, Pierrantonio Stiattesi. In this, she differed significantly from the more conventional business and domestic arrangements entered into by Anguissola, Fontana and Sirani. Anguissola was promoted and supported by her father, the Cremonese nobleman Amilcare Anguissola. Fontana was sustained in her business dealings first by her father, the painter Prospero Fontana, and thereafter by the greater social respectability provided by her marriage to a member of the lesser nobility of Imola. Sirani remained unmarried but similarly flourished – before her untimely death aged twenty-seven in 1665 – as the highly talented daughter operating out of the workshop of one of Guido Reni's favoured pupils in Bologna. Gentileschi, by contrast, maintained her full independence and was evidently at pains to distance herself from her father's control from the moment of her transfer to Florence in 1613. From that time on, she sought to rely solely on the financial proceeds generated by her own labour. She thus represented a double anomaly in Baroque Italy: a woman professional who was also independent of male guardianship, from either a father or husband.

I have noted her recourse in Florence to a male legal witness – Masino *merciaio* – to act as a proxy on her behalf to sign and witness documents (pp. 128–29).[43] This individual's presence – and that of other male advocates on whose assistance she must have drawn from time to time – would have constituted an unavoidable necessity during a period in which women were significantly restricted in their legal ability to act on their own behalf in signing agreements, entering into contracts, taking on financial liability and so on.[44] Yet, from the late 1620s, in Rome, Venice and Naples, Gentileschi appears to have sought to act in her own capacity wherever possible. Certainly, her numerous letters from this period to her extensive network of friends, supporters and prospective clients never make any reference to her deferring her business considerations to a male agent. Little wonder, then, that this resulted in her encountering frequent instances of gender bias in her dealings with clients and that this involved her in a concomitant struggle at times to attain parity with her male peers. Yet Gentileschi seems to have become accustomed to this and to have evolved strategies in response that enabled her to turn the tables on her clients' prejudices.

Gentileschi's letters include frequent reference to the common perception of women as 'the weaker sex', a concept that she ingeniously recasts to her own advantage. Towards the end of her letter to Ruffo of 30 January 1649, for example, she remarks in a tone that is mock defiant as well as ironically deferential, 'You think me pitiful, because a woman's name raises doubts until her work is seen.' Later in the year, she informs Ruffo that she 'will say no more, except what I have on my mind, that I think your Most Illustrious Lordship will not suffer any loss with me, and that you will find the spirit of Caesar in this soul of a woman'.[45] This last comment constitutes an especially powerful inversion of gender norms. Here, Gentileschi is presenting herself to her all-powerful male patron as embodying the conventionally 'softer' qualities of feminine comportment – 'a woman's soul'. But, in the same breath, she combines this acceptably feminine attribute with the military and strategic acumen of Caesar himself. In this way, Ruffo learnt the fundamental lesson of never underestimating this fiercely proactive and independent individual.

The list of Gentileschi's payments (see table 1, pp. 256–57) is revealing for the indications that it provides about the various pricing options that she was able to offer her clients, depending on the format produced by her workshop. Single-figure works, for example, were considerably cheaper than the two-hundred-ducat gallery paintings situated at the top of the scale. A case in point is the fifty ducats paid in 1630 for a painting of the Franciscan saint *St Elisabeth of Hungary*. This was a commission for a private chapel in the small regional town of Pisticci, in the province of Matera, Apulia. The commission was orchestrated through the agency of Don Geronimo de Cardenas. As Riccardo Lattuada has pointed out, this individual belonged to the venerable aristocratic De Cardenas family of mixed Neapolitan and Spanish heritage whose considerable holdings of fiefdoms and territories, including that of Pisticci, derived from their time spent in the service of the fifteenth-century Aragonese rulers of Naples.[46] As a member of this influential, 'old moneyed' family of Naples, Geronimo would have been related to the Bishop of Pozzuoli, Martín de León y Cárdenas, who was the commissioner of Gentileschi's three monumental Pozzuoli altarpieces. Geronimo de Cardenas is also to be counted as the probable patron of the *Hercules and Omphale* (fig. 96), since the 1699 inventory in which the painting appears belonged to another, subsequent family member, Carlo de Cardenas, conte di Acerra and marchese di Laino. Gérard Labrot has pointed out, in relation to this collection, that the absence of late seventeenth-century paintings within it suggests that it must have been assembled by an earlier family member, rather than by Carlo de Cardenas himself.[47] If so, then Geronimo de Cardenas, as one of Gentileschi's earliest and most important aristocratic Neapolitan patrons, would be the prime candidate for performing this role. Once again, then, we find a chain of connections between Gentileschi and her patrons and supporters stretching, in this instance, from the bustling Florentine-Neapolitan mercantile associations of Lorenzo Cambi and Simone Verzone to the long-standing Spanish-Neapolitan affiliations of one of the oldest and most accredited aristocratic families of the Kingdom of Naples.

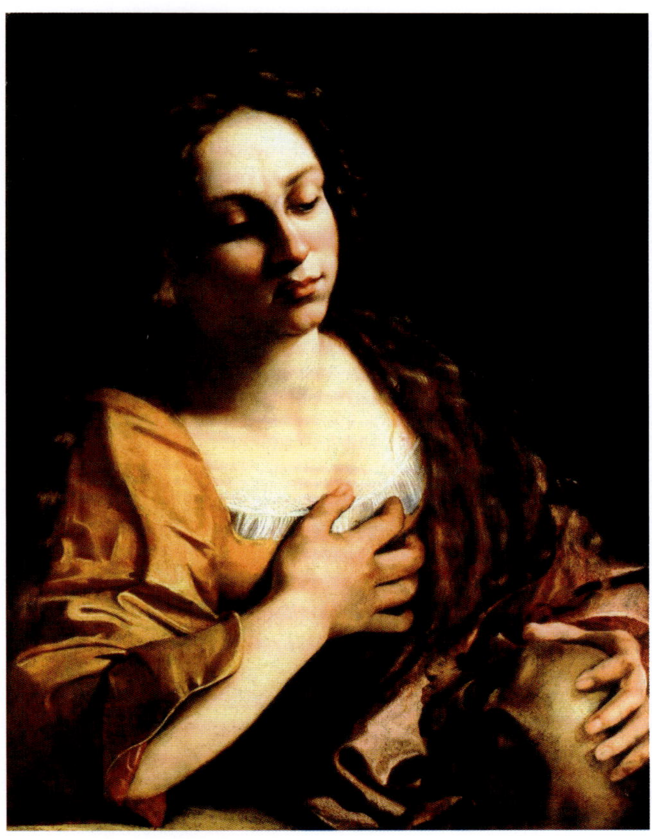

98 Artemisia Gentileschi, *Penitent Magdalene*, *c.*early to mid-1630s, oil on canvas, 65.7 × 50.8, Rita R. R. and Marc A. Seidner Collection, Los Angeles

There are some further documentary indications of the ways in which Gentileschi graded her workshop output in order to introduce pricing levels for her customers. The 1659 inventory of Ettore Capecelatro, marchese di Torella, includes a reference to a 'Madalena di Artemisia di 4 e 5' ('Magdalene by Artemisia measuring around 105 by 132 cm'), which is valued at twenty-six ducats.[48] Inventory valuations need to be treated with discretion, since they represent notional values made by art appraisers after the fact of the artwork's creation rather than the results of actual sales. The inventory in question was, nonetheless, put together with evident care by Capecelatro's favourite artist, Domenico Gargiulo, who was also Gentileschi's sometime landscape collaborator. Its information can, therefore, be taken as accurately reflecting up-to-date market values. The lower price and slightly smaller dimensions of this work suggests that it would have been a half-length, single-figure painting – comparable with the *Penitent Magdalene* in a private collection, a painting that was originally dated to the Florentine years by R. Ward Bissell, but then resituated as an early Neapolitan painting by both Judith Mann and Roberto Contini (fig. 98).[49]

A later but relevant reference occurs in the 1718 Neapolitan inventory of Paolo Francone, marchese di Salcito. Francone's collection included a painting of *Samson* by Gentileschi that was valued at a hundred ducats and measured around 132 by 158 cm.[50] This may be identifiable with the *Samson and Delilah* now in the Intesa Sanpaolo collection which has also been dated to Gentileschi's Neapolitan period of the early to mid-1630s (fig. 99).[51]

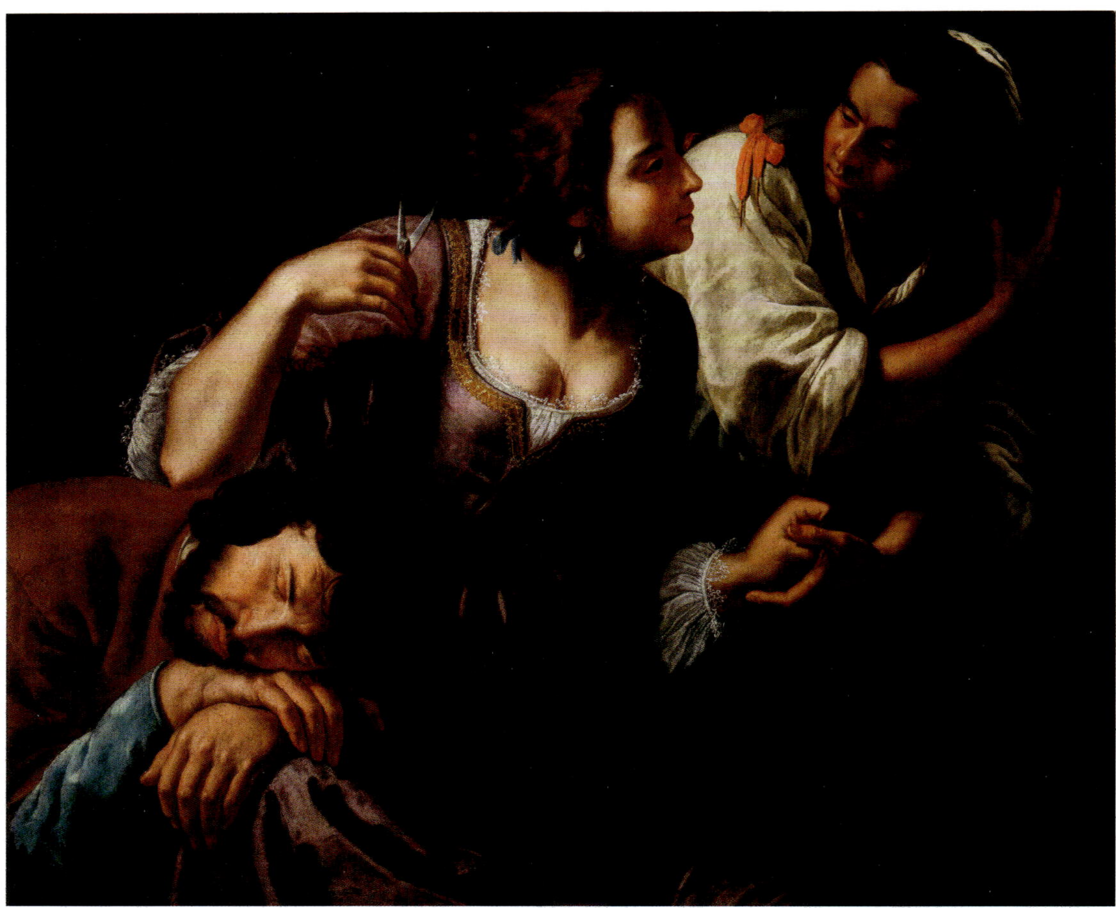

99 Artemisia Gentileschi, *Samson and Delilah*, *c.*mid-1630s, oil on canvas, 90.5 × 109.5, Collezione Intesa Sanpaolo, Gallerie d'Italia, Naples

Putting this information together allows us to recognise how Gentileschi's workshop of the 1630s would have functioned in economic terms as a calibrated range of scaled offerings distributed across at least four different price brackets. At the highest and most prestigious level were the grand gallery paintings of major dimensions that cost upwards of two hundred ducats. Then came the medium-sized paintings – like the *Samson and Delilah* – which were generally produced in a landscape format and included a limited number of mid-length or three-quarter-length figures. These were priced at around one hundred ducats. At fifty ducats or thereabouts were the single-figure paintings – like the *Saint Elisabeth of Hungary* – that could be purchased either for secular gallery spaces or devotional contexts, such as the Pisticci chapel mentioned above. Yet cheaper still were the half-length paintings of the *Magdalene* and the like, which could be had for around twenty-five ducats. Finally, there was a number of even cheaper paintings, probably in the range of ten to fifteen ducats, for bust-sized portraits or heads. An example of Gentileschi's output in this format comes in a reference to a *Head of Christ* and *Head of the Virgin* by 'Artemisia' recorded in the 1672 inventory of the collection of Davide Imperiale.[52]

Gentileschi was able to create many attendant benefits for her business by organising her workshop along these lines. In the first instance, it would have enabled her to increase her sales while helping to manage her workflow better by supplementing the deferred payments involved in commissioned work with the immediate sales generated by displaying pre-painted canvases in her workshop for immediate purchase. This would have enabled her to structure her workshop as a multi-functional space in which to do the contractual business of negotiating with clients and taking on complex commissions to be paid for in the future, while also having pre-produced work on hand to sell immediately to those with ready cash. This latter form of transaction would have often been undertaken with actual coinage – or even in the form of the barter or exchange of goods. As such, it would have fallen into the type of informal, 'grey economy' activity that would have constituted a potentially sizeable area of Gentileschi's overall business practices for which no documentation exists today.

The practice of displaying smaller and cheaper canvases in the workshop for immediate sale would have helped Gentileschi to entice those 'walk in' customers who might have had an interest in her work but who were not yet ready to commit themselves to the most complex – and expensive – aspects of her output.

It was also commonplace in Naples, during this period, for artists to deal in other artists' work.[53] If Gentileschi followed this Neapolitan practice, then we can imagine her combining her primary day-to-day activities as a painter with selling other items in the workshop that might attract her clients' collecting interests in other ways, such as frames to fit the canvases that her customers might have been interested in purchasing from her. Or it might have involved her in selling the work of other artists whose paintings she had purchased or exchanged for works of her own. Yet more specifically, it might have entailed her selling the work of her junior collaborators, such as Bernardo Cavallino, who, in turn, is known to have worked at an early stage of his career, during the 1630s, producing works to be sold on consignment from the workshop of the older and relatively more successful painter, Andrea Vaccaro.[54]

DIAMONDS AND DOWRIES: GENTILESCHI'S EARNINGS VERSUS HER COST-OF-LIVING EXPENSES

In his biography of Gentileschi's collaborator Domenico Gargiulo, De' Dominici relates a curious anecdote concerning the ultimate vanity of those artists who place an undue emphasis on the financial trappings of success.[55] In it, he speaks of Gargiulo's custom, as practised during the latter years of his greatest period of success, of eating his Sunday lunch in the company of the high-ranking Regent, Stefano Carrillo y Salsedo.[56] Gargiulo's habitually untidy, paint-spattered attire is said to have offended the aristocratic sensibilities of this refined patrician. The Regent was, accordingly, moved on one occasion to comment that Gargiulo's clothing was unbecoming to a man who had acquired such nobility from his profession. Gargiulo said nothing but returned the following week carried in a sedan and dressed in costly velvet. Carrillo noted his approval, observing that Gargiulo's bearing now brought honour upon himself and his entire profession. Gargiulo responded by throwing the clothes off his back and making a forthright pronouncement on the vanity of riches. He stated that painting was a practice akin to philosophy and that it was unbefitting of philosophers to dress in a gracious manner. He had travelled to Carrillo's palace hidden in a sedan, because he was ashamed to be seen in velvet. He was a painter, and he wished to be appreciated for his talent and not for fine clothes, since any rich, vice-ridden individual can make himself appear becoming. Gargiulo's words were said to have moved Carrillo to silence.

Gentileschi would probably have not had much time for such male posturing (which sounds, in any event, like a parable created to illustrate a general principle rather than a factually based incident). Some artists might have felt able to arrogate to themselves the ability to reject such mundane responsibilities as the maintenance of a household or the care of children (or perhaps we should say that they were free to do so in the unfettered vistas of their minds, as opposed to the more prosaic reality of their lives). Yet these were freedoms that would never have been granted to Gentileschi, even on an abstract and conceptual level. As a hard-working, fiercely independent woman artist, Gentileschi recognised the importance of maintaining a scrupulously preserved impression of elevated social bearing and refined personal appearance, as we have seen. Gentileschi's carefully constructed artistic persona would have gone hand in hand with the maintenance of an appropriate lifestyle – with servants, for example, such as she is known to have employed during the 1620s in Rome, along with other trappings of a certain level of genteel aspiration. These would have constituted, in turn, a series of carefully curated signs of her professional attainments. They functioned, in this respect, as marketing tools, advertising her professional status and reputation in a sense directly comparable with the previously discussed portraits of her produced in Rome and Venice during the 1620s. They were her professional armour, if you will, in her ongoing battle to command an appropriate level of respect – and economic reward – in a harshly unremitting and intensely competitive art world.

Some scattered references to Gentileschi's genteel mode of comporting herself during this period are found amidst the seventeenth-century English writing on Italian art. Bullen Reymes, a diplomatic courtier who visited Naples in March 1634, for example, records in his diary paying a visit to Gentileschi shortly after seeking out the brothels, as it transpired, on via Toledo in the centre of the city. He was entertained by Artemisia and her daughter, Prudenzia, who played the spinet, apparently quite well.[57] The reference to Gentileschi living close to via Toledo has been confirmed with publication in 2022 of her rental arrangements from the late 1640s to the early 1650s. These record her residing close to the Church of Santa Maria del Consiglio before then moving on to another apartment nearby, opposite the Church of Santa Maria della Mercede a Montecalvario. This second apartment was situated in a recently modernised block that has been identified as belonging to a type suitable for occupation by the upper middle classes. It was owned by Vittoria Corenzio, daughter of Belisario Corenzio (1558–1646), who had been one of the most successful painters of the previous generation. Gentileschi rented this apartment out for thirty-seven ducats a year – a medium- to upper-level annual rent in this highly sought after area of one of the world's most densely inhabited cities.[58] Finally, a further indication of the success with which Gentileschi was able to maintain an image of refined gentility during this period is also found in the observations of the late seventeenth-century English commentator Richard Graham. In an annotation to an English edition of 1695 of Charles-Alphonse Dufresnoy's *De Arte Grafica*, Graham notes that Gentileschi lived 'in great splendor' in Naples (although he cannot resist adding to this the imputation, commonly made about glamorous women, that she was as 'famous all over Europe for her Amours and Love-Intrigues, as for her talent in painting').[59]

These glittering appearances had to be accounted for in financial terms. It must have seemed maddening to Gentileschi that all the money that flowed in from her sales seemed, nonetheless, never sufficient to offset all the many obligations that followed on from her domestic and professional responsibilities. The one hundred ducats that she received for one of her mid-range paintings, for example, would have been welcome, but it could go no further than to pay for just one of the sets of earrings and necklaces that she was required to wear while entertaining her guests – a fact that can be ascertained from among the many debts incurred during her Florentine years.[60] And, of course, she had countless other commitments to deal with besides her personal appearance. Richard Spear has suggested that artists needed to be able to maintain an annual income of at least 1,000 scudi per year in order to be recognised as among the most successful practitioners of the day.[61] This correlates to the estimation made by the early seventeenth-century Roman doctor and connoisseur Giulio Mancini that the most successful painters were those who were able to earn around '4–5 scudi per day'.[62] Of course, an artist's expectations of what was sufficient in financial terms was always contingent on how much he or she could earn. The most outstandingly successful artists of the period were expected to do rather better than this – particularly those who were able to secure the most lucrative and prestigious contracts for fresco painting and other forms of high-ranking, public religious commissions. Domenichino's annual earnings at the Chapel of the Treasury of St Januarius in the cathedral in Naples, for example, have been estimated at around 2,000 scudi a year, a 'good but not exceptional income for an important artist', according to Spear.[63]

So how much money was sufficient to live on? And how little money, by contrast, was not enough to get by? The bottom line of success – at least when measured in cold, hard cash – depended on an artist's ability to live within their means. Sinking or swimming often boiled down to being able to balance earnings against the corresponding column filled with the weekly tally of outgoing living expenses. According to Filippo Baldinucci, Salvator Rosa earned the sizeable sum of 9,000 scudi during his nine-year residence in Florence, from 1640 to 1649 – an annual income of 1,000 scudi, therefore. He also notes that this proved hardly enough to live on, because of Rosa's habit of throwing elaborate parties costing some thirty to forty scudi each. Each party thus cost the same amount as a year's rent for a Florentine residence or as much as one of Rosa's own mid-level landscapes. As a result, Baldinucci remarks, when Rosa eventually decided to return to Rome from Florence, he was able to take with him only three hundred scudi in accrued savings.[64]

A yet more liberal attitude to keeping up appearances is said to have been maintained by Rubens's gifted young pupil Anthony van Dyck. Anxious to make a positive impression on polite society during his extended stay in Rome in 1622, Van Dyck is said to have presented himself at all times as 'a lord rather than a commoner'.[65] He carried out a continuous public show of always appearing 'resplendent in rich attire of suits and court dress', since, 'being by nature grand and eager to become famous, therefore in addition to his fine clothes, he adorned his head with plumes and hatbands, wore gold chains crossed on his chest, and kept a retinue of servants'. This, too, came at a cost that must have been hard to maintain as a young artist living temporarily abroad. Van Dyck, however, never chose the path of frugality. Later on, while working in London for the court of King Charles I, he is said to have run up a bill of thirty scudi a day – or around 9,000–10,000 scudi a year – on his entertainment costs alone, playing 'host to all the great personages, knights and ladies, who came daily'.

The evidence, such as it is, suggests that the relative financial success of Gentileschi's Neapolitan years enabled her to keep the wolves from the door and so to avoid the humiliation of a second round of public debt proceedings, as had occurred in Florence. But, nonetheless, she seems to have come close to economic collapse on more than one occasion. Like Rosa during the 1640s, in fact, and probably like many, if not most artists of the period, she seems to have been able to earn just enough to get by and not much more. This meant that she lacked substantial savings or any other form of financial safety net to assist her in times of particular need.

Two particularly clear instances of financial pressure during Gentileschi's later years arose as a result of her requirement to provide a dowry for her daughter. Some twelve years apart, these two instances of exceptional financial stress seem to have tested her to the limit, while also generating some innovative strategic thinking on her part, of a kind that we should perhaps have come to anticipate by now in our analysis of the business considerations of this constantly enterprising individual.

GENTILESCHI TO CASSIANO DAL POZZO IN 1637: A 'GIFT' IS PLANNED FOR THE BARBERINI TO FINANCE A DAUGHTER'S DOWRY

On 24 October 1637, Gentileschi wrote once again to her erstwhile Roman friend and supporter Cassiano dal Pozzo, this time with a rather unusual request:

> The confidence that I have always had in Your Lordship's kindness, and the now urgent matter of placing my daughter in marriage, impel me to appeal to your generosity and to ask your assistance and advice, which I trust I will obtain, as on other occasions. My Lord, to bring this marriage to conclusion, I need a small amount of money. I have kept for this purpose, since I do not have any wealth or income, some paintings measuring eleven and twelve palms each [about 290 × 316 cm]. It is my intention to offer them to Cardinals Francesco padrone and Don Antonio Barberini. However, I do not want to carry out this plan without Your Lordship's excellent advice.[66]

The letter indicates that Gentileschi's need had driven her to consider sending two unsolicited paintings to the Barberini in Rome, not simply as unencumbered 'gifts' but rather more forcefully as works whose value she hoped the Barberini would intrinsically recognise and so pay her for accordingly. The

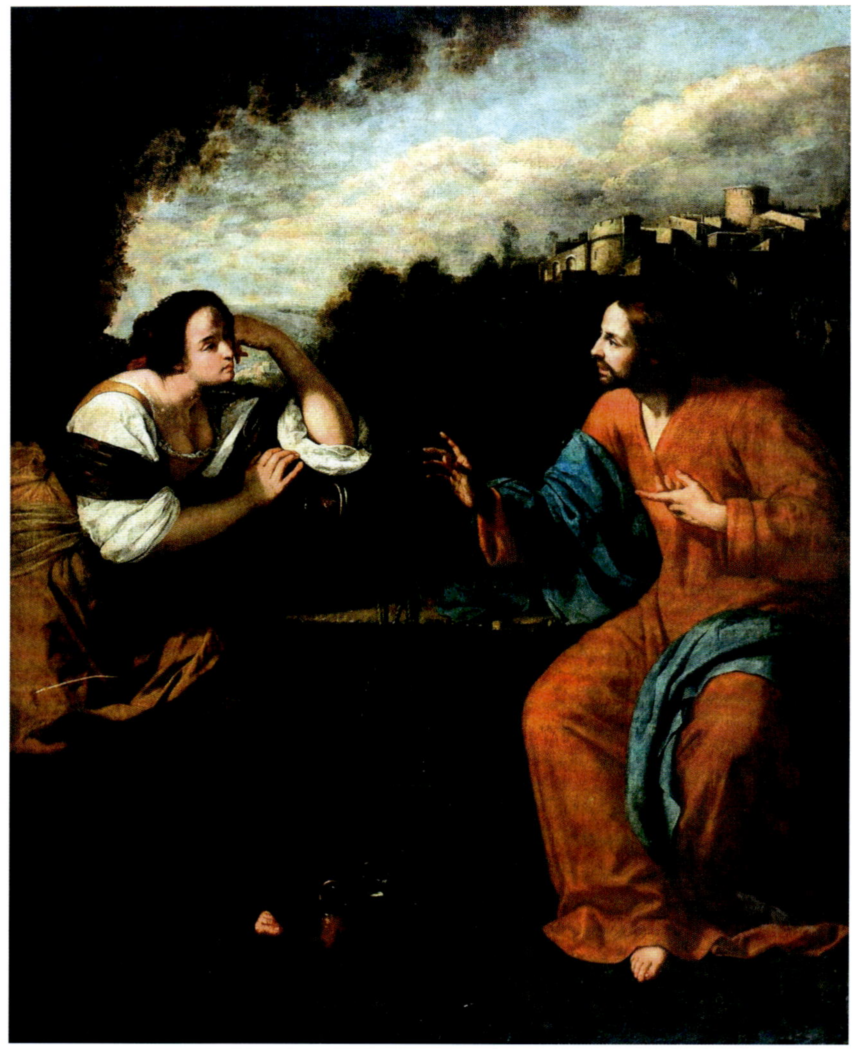

100 Artemisia Gentileschi, *Christ and the Samaritan Woman at the Well*, c.1637, oil on canvas, 267.5 × 206 cm, Palazzo Blu, Pisa, Property of the Fondazione Pisa

paintings are described in a subsequent letter as 'the Woman of Samaria with Christ and the twelve apostles, in a deep landscape, et cetera, rendered very beautifully and another painting represents St. John the Baptist in the desert'. The former painting has been identified with a painting of *Christ and the Woman of Samaria at the Well* discovered in a private collection, with its attribution being initially proposed by Luciano Arcangelo before being endorsed thereafter by a broad range of scholars (fig. 100).[67]

Gentileschi's plan seems to have formed an extension of a more common marketing ploy that she had already used on a number of occasions. This was to send unsolicited paintings from time to time as 'gifts' to important foreign dignitaries in the hope of attracting an appropriately princely recompense, or perhaps even to encourage them to patronise her work on a more formal and sustained level. In January 1635, for example, she had sent two paintings in this manner to the distinguished princely collector Francesco I d'Este, Duke of

Modena and Reggio (and she would do so again in December 1639).[68] She had also employed the same stratagem with the Medici, in order to gauge their interest in her staging a return to Florence during these same years (although their apparently tepid response to her gesture put her off this scheme).[69]

The act of cloaking a request for recompense within the guise of sending someone an unsolicited gift was a time-honoured gambit that could net significant rewards. It hinged on the idea that the recipient would be drawn into a mutually reciprocal relationship with the sender – or, at least, it did so by implication and until such time as the sender chose to reject the gift. It also created an obligation on the recipient's part to compensate the sender appropriately – to match gift with counter-gift as Guido Guerzoni has noted.[70] If the receiver was of ennobled bearing, moreover, then this set up the additional expectation that the recipient should respond with a concomitant sense of generosity and largesse. The counter-gift thus became a public declaration of the recipient's own sense of his or her liberality and munificence. The influential Roman doctor and art critic Giulio Mancini stressed the degree to which this could result in the significant inflation of an artwork's price. In his *Considerazioni sulla pittura* – a how-to guide for collectors – Mancini contrasted the simple act by 'someone of mediocre status and fortune' of purchasing an artwork by means of direct financial transaction with the more complex processes involved in 'a prince and person of respect' acquiring an artwork 'at the cost of a gift and to exchange courtesies received'. In Mancini's estimation, this often resulted in a more expensive purchase, since 'for the same painting bought from those who make a market at tens of scudi, the prince will pay hundreds, as one sees continually'.[71]

Many artists employed this strategy, including Gentileschi's own father.[72] In London, during this same period, Orazio dispatched a large and ambitious painting of *The Finding of Moses* as a diplomatic 'gift' to King Philip IV of Spain (fig. 101). The king recompensed Orazio munificently to the tune of nine hundred ducats – making this probably the most generously compensated artwork of his entire career.[73] Yet the strategy also carried certain risks. It could result in a loss of face on the sender's part if the recipient chose not to respond with appropriate generosity. At its essence, Baroque artistic gift-giving constituted a ritualised game of ceremonial etiquette. The unwritten rules of this game could result in significant moments of misalignment between a sender's expectations and those of the receiver. This was especially true in the case of artists sending gifts to aristocratic patrons, since this obviously represented an attempt on the artist's part to create an obligatory relationship of respect and recognition between two agents who remained, in other respects, considerably distant in their respective social positions. Some patrons, for example, might consider the simple acknowledgement of receipt of an artwork to be sufficient recompense in its own right. So, for example, in the 1540s, the Farnese decided that there was no need to pay Titian for a work they had commissioned, because, as Roberto Zapperi has noted, in so doing, 'Titian augmented his own prestige and also the price of his work with other buyers. There was then no need to pay him, because the compensation was implicit in the honour conferred by the most highly elevated rank of his client.'[74]

Gentileschi's gift-giving plan for the Barberini posed a risk in another sense as well. Artists electing to adopt this approach almost always chose to frame their gifts in deliberately opaque ways that left the level of remuneration entirely up to the patron. This was, indeed, one of the game's cardinal rules. Artists were expected to subordinate themselves before the patron's munificence and so allow the patron to determine the mode and scale of recompense. But the urgency of Gentileschi's need to provide for her daughter impelled her to go beyond these rules. She, accordingly, pressed Cassiano dal Pozzo to act not simply as an artistic promoter of her work to the Barberini but also to function more specifically as a kind of financial arbiter, negotiating the transaction on her behalf. In defence of her strategy, one might argue that the letter to Dal Pozzo records her speaking candidly to a friend and ally rather than to the Barberini themselves, with whom she would, no doubt, have been far more circumspect. Even so, in sending a letter of this kind to Dal Pozzo she raised the stakes of the transaction by indicating her expectation of a certain level of financial reward. Moreover, even though she herself was not addressing the Barberini in such overtly transactional terms, she was directing Dal Pozzo to do so on her behalf. This arguably crossed an unwritten line concerning an artist's need to create a smokescreen of elaborate courtesy in order to mute the self-interested tenor of the transaction. Gentileschi was arguably courting the risk of being perceived, instead, as too obvious in a situation in which she should have remained more diplomatically understated in her intentions, leaving the timing and nature of the acceptance of the gift, together with its level of financial recompense, entirely to the largesse of her patrons.

As to whether the Barberini ever supported Gentileschi financially in this manner, the evidence seems to suggest that they did not. No further mention is made of the paintings in her correspondence, and no reference to them is to be found in the Barberini inventories. On the other hand, it should be noted that the Roman associate of the Barberini, Ascanio Filomarino, is subsequently known to have owned in Naples a reduced-size variant by Gentileschi of the *St John the Baptist in the Wilderness*, so perhaps the scheme did bear some fruit.[75] Yet whether it actually netted its share of the three to four hundred scudi that one imagines Gentileschi might have wished to receive for two large gallery paintings of this size and format seems unlikely. It seems more probable, as both Spear and Arcangeli have suggested, that Gentileschi was advised not to send the works on and so was reduced to having to sell them on spec in Naples.[76]

GENTILESCHI IN 1649: A SECOND REFERENCE TO A DOWRY LEADS TO A REQUEST FOR ASSISTANCE FROM DON ANTONIO RUFFO OF MESSINA

Dowries constituted an important indication of a family's level of success. They represented one of the most significant financial obligations of the head of a household and constituted one of the biggest public declarations of financial security necessary during one's lifetime. How much, then, would a dowry of four hundred scudi – the figure suggested by Gentileschi's scheme – have represented in terms of the customary amounts put aside by parents for their daughters during this period? The answer is that it suggests a not particularly financially well-off parent, even if we begin by comparing it with the actually quite generous dowry of 1,000 scudi that was put aside for Artemisia's own marriage in 1612 by Orazio Gentileschi.

A pauper's dowry started at around twenty-five ducats. This was the amount stipulated in 1680 as the sum to be donated to the daughters of impoverished members of the Neapolitan Corporazione di Rivenditori (the guild of the Neapolitan second-hand dealers, whose ranks included artists and who also commonly sold paintings from their workshops).[77] Other, marginally more successful artists and artisans were in a position to increase this figure up to one hundred or so ducats. Thus, when Bernardo Cavallino came to marry the daughter of a local bookbinder in 1633, this was the amount that his father-in-law was able to provide for the dowry. While an obvious improvement on the base-line charity of the Rivenditori's dowries, one hundred ducats was still a very modest outlay that further corroborates the picture built up elsewhere of the relatively marginal level of financial attainment and public recognition achieved by Cavallino during his lifetime.[78]

Belisario Corenzio, on the other hand, one of the leading Neapolitan painters of the opening decades of the century, was able to manage three hundred ducats when his daughter came to marry in 1641.[79] This was more in the realm of a reasonable artisanal dowry, although it was by no means a statement of exceptional wealth. Corenzio's contemporary Bernardo Azzolino, by contrast, was able to set aside the more substantial sum of six hundred ducats as a dowry for his daughter when she married Ribera in 1618.[80] Both these amounts, however, pale into insignificance in the face of what Ribera was subsequently able to provide for his own daughter when she married a local judge of the Court of the Vicaria in 1644.[81] This fortunate child received a dowry of five thousand ducats, an extraordinarily high 'gold-standard' amount that would not be matched by other Neapolitan artists until the end of the century, when the aged Luca Giordano was able to provide his three daughters with the cumulatively higher figures of dowries worth four thousand (for each of two daughters) and seven thousand ducats (for the third) when they married in 1683, 1690 and 1704.[82]

Gentileschi's arrangements for her daughter's dowry should, therefore, be seen as equating to those of a reasonably well-off artisan rather than to what we might otherwise have expected of her. They point to the persistent tension between her ambition to be recognised as a dignified, high-ranking practitioner of her art, on the one hand, and the more prosaic reality of her ongoing financial situation, on the other. In 1649, she was again put to the test when she was called upon to provide another dowry for her daughter (this being Prudenzia's second marriage negotiation, it seems, although whether this was for an actual second marriage or – perhaps more likely – to formalise an earlier, long-standing conjugal relationship remains unclear).[83] This, in turn, precipitated a temporary economic crisis on Gentileschi's part that she describes vividly in one of her letters to her patron Don Antonio Ruffo of Messina:

> This marriage has broken me. For that reason, if there should be any opportunity for work in your city, I ask Your Most Illustrious Lordship to assist me with your usual benevolence and to keep me informed, because I need work very badly and I assure Your Most Illustrious Lordship that I am bankrupt.[84]

The extremity of Gentileschi's financial circumstances in 1649 were thus so pressing as to lead her to contemplate relocating once again. This time, she was considering a move to Sicily, in the hope of settling down with a new patron who might be able to offer her more consistent and steadily paying work than what she had been able to achieve hitherto (especially since Naples, in 1649, was still very much in the midst of a recovery from the social and economic impact of the recently concluded Revolt of Masaniello). The pressing financial needs brought about by Gentileschi's constrained economic prospects during these final years also led her to offer her patrons works at significantly reduced prices – an aspect of her last period of productivity that is discussed in the following chapter.

'IN PURSUIT OF FAME': GENTILESCHI'S LONDON SOJOURN

Gentileschi's decision in the late 1630s to roll the dice once more and leave Naples in order to travel all the way to London makes better sense when viewed against the background of her efforts to maintain an impression of genteel respectability while struggling against the reality of continual financial strain. In London, King Charles I and his consort, Queen Henrietta Maria de Bourbon (the Catholic daughter of Henry IV of France and Marie de' Medici), had been attempting to lure the leading Continental artists to the Caroline court for several years. This formed part of a broader policy to implement cultural renewal as a means of offsetting the otherwise turbulent circumstances of their reign. The policy proved only partially successful, however. Guercino, for example, elected to decline the offer on the grounds that the English climate would not suit him and, moreover, that he felt unable to work for heretics.[85] Even a more modestly ranked artist like Angelo Caroselli in Rome rejected their invitation for similar reasons.[86] For Gentileschi, by contrast, the prospect of being able to receive a regular and, it was to be hoped, munificent royal stipend after years of trading as an independent operator must have seemed like the answer to her dreams.

Another pressing motivation for Artemisia's London venture was her father's presence there – in fact, since 1626. Artemisia and Orazio had effectively gone their separate ways many years previously, following Orazio's departure from Rome in the early 1620s. They had, nevertheless, maintained at least nominal contact through the comings and goings of Gentileschi's brothers, who had shuttled back and forth between England and Italy, running various business errands for their father – and occasionally for Artemisia as well. Orazio's late career as an expatriate artist (having also worked for Queen Marie de Medici in Paris from 1624 to 1626) must have piqued Artemisia's desire to project herself as a renowned figure of international stature rather than as a mere regionalist working in a succession of Italian cities.

The prices paid to Orazio during this period were perhaps the final sweetener inclining Artemisia towards the proposal. The largesse of the English royal purse, supplemented by aristocratic patronage from the Duke of Buckingham and others, resulted in Orazio's receiving a constant flow of salaries, provisions, reimbursements for expenses and one-off sums for paintings – or so it must have seemed to Artemisia in Naples. These effectively freed Orazio of the burden of having continuously to hunt for sources of independent funding, as Artemisia had been required to do. (And yet Orazio still complained bitterly about the chaotic state of his finances, leading one to conclude that an inability to manage their personal finances constituted

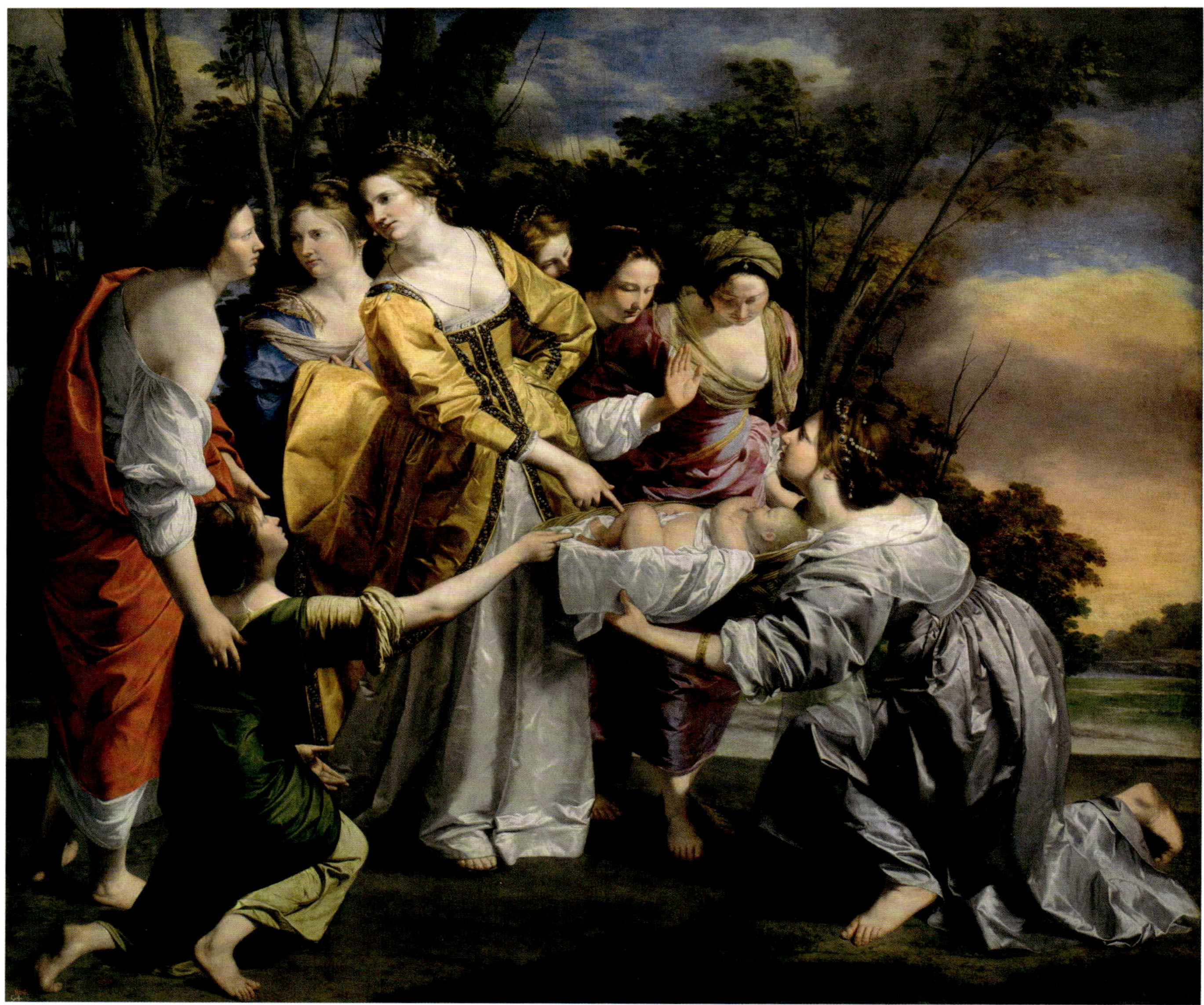

101 Orazio Gentileschi, *The Finding of Moses*, c.1629–30, oil on canvas, 242 × 281 cm, Madrid, Museo Nacional del Prado, P000147

a family trait that applied to both father and daughter.[87]) He had received a generous allowance of £500, for example, to help him set up house.[88] This was equivalent to two thousand scudi, and so the same amount as Domenichino's entire year's earnings at the Treasury of St Januarius. He was also awarded an annual stipend of £100 (equivalent to four hundred scudi), plus payments for individual works that were on a par with the more 'princely' rates awarded to Reni and Guercino. He received £100 (four hundred scudi), for example, for a painting of *Lot and his Daughters*, for which Artemisia would have been lucky to receive half as much in Naples. Orazio's position as part of the retinue of the English king and queen, moreover, gave him entrée to a broader network of other princely patrons – and to the princely amounts of money that they

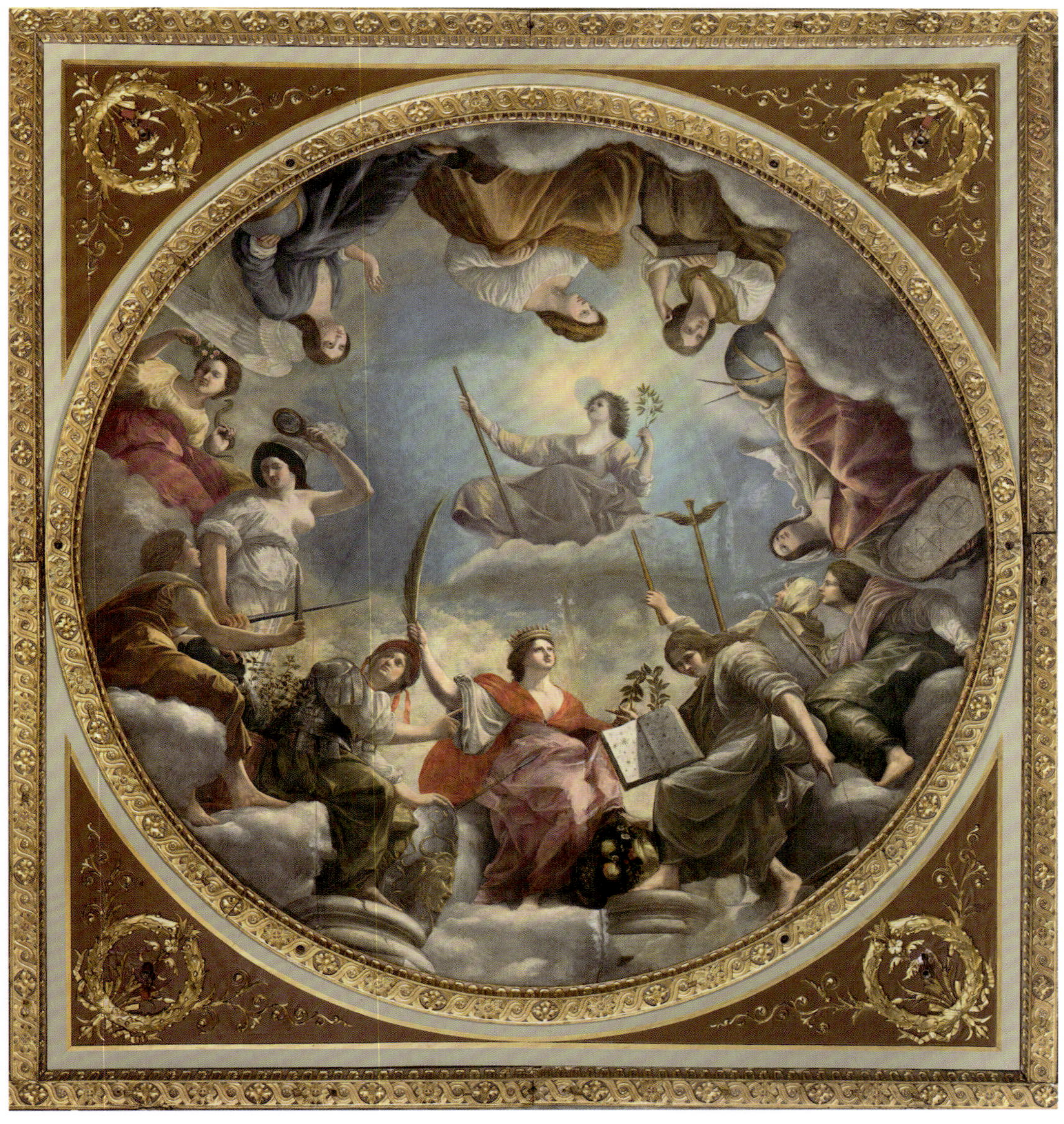

102 Orazio and Artemisia Gentileschi, central tondo, *Allegory of Peace and the Arts under the English Crown*, 1638–39, oil on canvas, Marlborough House, London (originally Queen's House, Greenwich)

were sometimes prepared to pay. The apogee of this dimension of Orazio's money-making activities came with a version of *The Finding of Moses* that he dispatched from London in 1633 to King Philip IV of Spain as a diplomatic 'gift', but for which he was still paid the very high price of 900 ducats (fig. 101; see also p. 185).[89]

By the mid-1630s, Orazio also had increasing need of Artemisia's assistance. Queen Henrietta Maria had entrusted him with the important commission to decorate the ceiling of the Queen's House at Greenwich (fig. 102). This constituted the largest and most extensive undertaking of Orazio's entire career. Taking it on represented a major challenge, given that

Orazio was then in his seventies and in failing health and had only his sons to assist him.[90] Although the invitation to Artemisia to work at the Caroline court seems to have predated this commission, it is, nonetheless, clear that the decision to award Orazio the Queen's House contract added a sense of urgency to the request.[91] After politely demurring for several years, Artemisia eventually relented and steeled herself for the arduous journey sometime in 1638.[92]

Gentileschi seems to have encountered England as not quite the land of milk and honey that she might have been otherwise led to believe. Her father, whom she had not seen for many years, was in a bad way. He would, in fact, die on 7 February 1639, less than a year after her arrival. The king and queen's ability to provide sustained patronage during these years was also significantly curtailed by the continuous distraction of a series of disastrous political misadventures. Their reign was increasingly overshadowed by a growing cycle of provincial rebellions, religious flare-ups, acts of parliamentary dissent and numerous other bitter controversies that would tip the country into the abyss of civil war in the summer of 1642. Yet Gentileschi was long gone by then. By the end of 1639, she was already working on a series of strategies to get her out of London as soon as possible. These included another letter attempting to gauge the Duke of Modena's interest in her work. The correspondence contains an unusually frank declaration of Gentileschi's sense of the importance of international fame and the reflected glamour of high-ranking, international aristocratic patronage:

> Great princes, such as Your Most Serene Highness, stimulate those creatures in pursuit of fame to improve their skills as much as possible so that they may dedicate their efforts to you and thus achieve those honourable ends that they seek. And this is precisely what is happening to me, as I am not content to be in the service of this Crown of England, from which I receive honours and singular favours. I feel I can only satisfy my ambitions by sending you this small work of mine again with my brother who is going to Italy on a commission from her Majesty the Queen, my mistress.[93]

The duke's polite but firm reply to Gentileschi's 'gift' made clear, however, that he was not interested in offering her a position. Instead, he thanked her for the work, while keeping her at arm's length by observing, 'just as from such a distance you invent ways to serve me, you will also find ways to reciprocate by involving myself in things that bring you satisfaction'.[94] She was thus forced back on her own resources. A return to Naples had become inevitable. The trail of documentary references goes cold at this point until a payment received in Naples in 1648. It is widely assumed, however, that Gentileschi returned promptly to the city that would remain her permanent base from that point onwards. Most probably, she was back in Naples by early 1640.

What might Gentileschi have learned as a result of this ultimately unsuccessful attempt to relaunch her career in a foreign territory? On the positive side, the trip had given her access to a degree of high-ranking patronage such as she had been attempting to achieve for years but had never been able to sustain. The experience seems, moreover, to have reinforced for her the importance of the image that she had cultivated of herself as an international artist working at a level above that of her immediate peers. At this stage of her career, Gentileschi evidently wished to be regarded no longer as 'just' a Neapolitan painter – or a Roman painter – or, indeed, a painter who was defined and constrained by the cultural context of whichever city she chose to live in. Instead, she aspired towards being perceived as a renowned and internationally recognised artist of distinction. It was, therefore, important for her to remind her supporters at every opportunity that her 'efforts have pleased all the greatest princes of Europe'.[95]

In positioning herself as an internationalist working for a European clientele, Gentileschi was also required to develop a modified late style that would match the more expansive, cosmopolitan predilections of this evolving client base. Her art had always been noteworthy for its ability to draw on her extensive travels to create new syntheses of often disparate artistic trends. Now, at what would become the final stage of a long and multi-faceted career, this would result in her transitioning into a late style distinguished by a yet more refined and elegant synthesis of influences.

An important stimulus to Gentileschi's thinking along these lines seems to have been her father's late style. For more than ten years, Orazio had been living the reality of a peripatetic lifestyle, moving from one foreign, aristocratic or princely court environment to the next, be it in Genoa or Turin, Paris or London. His style had, accordingly, been transforming towards what Bissell has defined as a 'hyper-real' emphasis, characterised by a 'strangely appealing blend of Caravaggio-inspired immediacy and classical purity and aloofness'.[96] The result was a form of pan-European courtly painting in which Orazio's figures become progressively more elegant in their deportment, luxurious in their attire and gracious in their actions. Bissell describes the protagonists of Orazio's *Finding of Moses* (fig. 101) as 'a tableau of aristocratic ladies before the backdrop of an English park'.[97] Artemisia would take up this aspect of Orazio's art in her own late paintings, adding to it an even more insistent emphasis on a volumetric clarity and painterly concision, together with an increased attentiveness to the dazzling effects of saturated colour and an almost statuesque treatment of figures. This final phase of her artistic evolution would result in some of the most fascinating and complex works of her career, albeit ones that continue to prove challenging to modern commentators.

CONCLUSION: 'ARTHEMISIA GENTILESCO. DONE BY HER SELF', THE LONDON *SELF-PORTRAIT AS THE ALLEGORY OF PAINTING*

Before returning to Naples, however, Gentileschi would leave behind her in London one of the masterworks of her late career. The *Self-portrait as the Allegory of Painting* (fig. 103) is occasionally identified with a canvas described by Gentileschi as 'my portrait' in a letter written in 1630 to her friend Cassiano dal Pozzo, one that she reminds him about again in 1637.[98] According to this interpretation, Dal Pozzo commissioned a self-portrait from Gentileschi in 1630. The artist then delayed its completion for a full seven years before taking it with her to London to complete, instead, for the king.[99] This hypothesis appears highly unlikely. One very much doubts that Gentileschi would have treated Dal Pozzo with such high handedness as to almost complete and then deny a painting that he had specifically requested all those years ago, particularly given his significance as one of her most trusted and influential supporters.[100] It would seem more reasonable to view the Dal Pozzo commission as being for another, earlier work.[101] The London self-portrait would then take its place as one of the many self-portraits that Gentileschi is known to have produced at various stages in her late career.

Much has been written about this painting, which was sold from the king's collection in 1649, following his execution, but was recovered during the Restoration.[102] It depicts a female painter, who appears as both a highly particularised individual – Artemisia in her mid-forties, although this identification has been challenged for a range of reasons, including the apparent age of the figure depicted[103] – and a personification of the art of painting itself. This unique combination of the general with the specific has resulted in one of the most original and distinctive paintings of the seventeenth century.

Gentileschi's ability in this canvas to combine the traditions of allegory and self-portraiture derives from the traditional linguistic convention assigning a female gender to the Latin and Italian terms for personifications. Painting is thus always a she. The identifying features of the personification of painting are also clearly spelt out in Cesare Ripa's *Iconologia*, a Baroque reference work outlining the attributes of a range of abstract and allegorical concepts. Here, Painting is described as 'a beautiful woman with full black hair, dishevelled and twisted in various ways, with arched eyebrows that show imaginative thought, the mouth covered with a cloth tied behind the ears with a chain of gold at her throat from which hangs a mask, and has written in front "imitation"'.[104] Gentileschi has omitted the mask for obvious reasons of decorum, while deftly combining the essential features of Ripa's symbolism with the trademark components of her own physiognomic iconography. Once again, the painter has depicted her own full face, long nose and the clearly defined cupid's bow of her upper lip. Most particularly, though, she has also been able to follow Ripa's text by emphasising her own conspicuous, shoulder-length, wavy hair. Her hair has, however, now been made black – in conformance with Ripa's description of

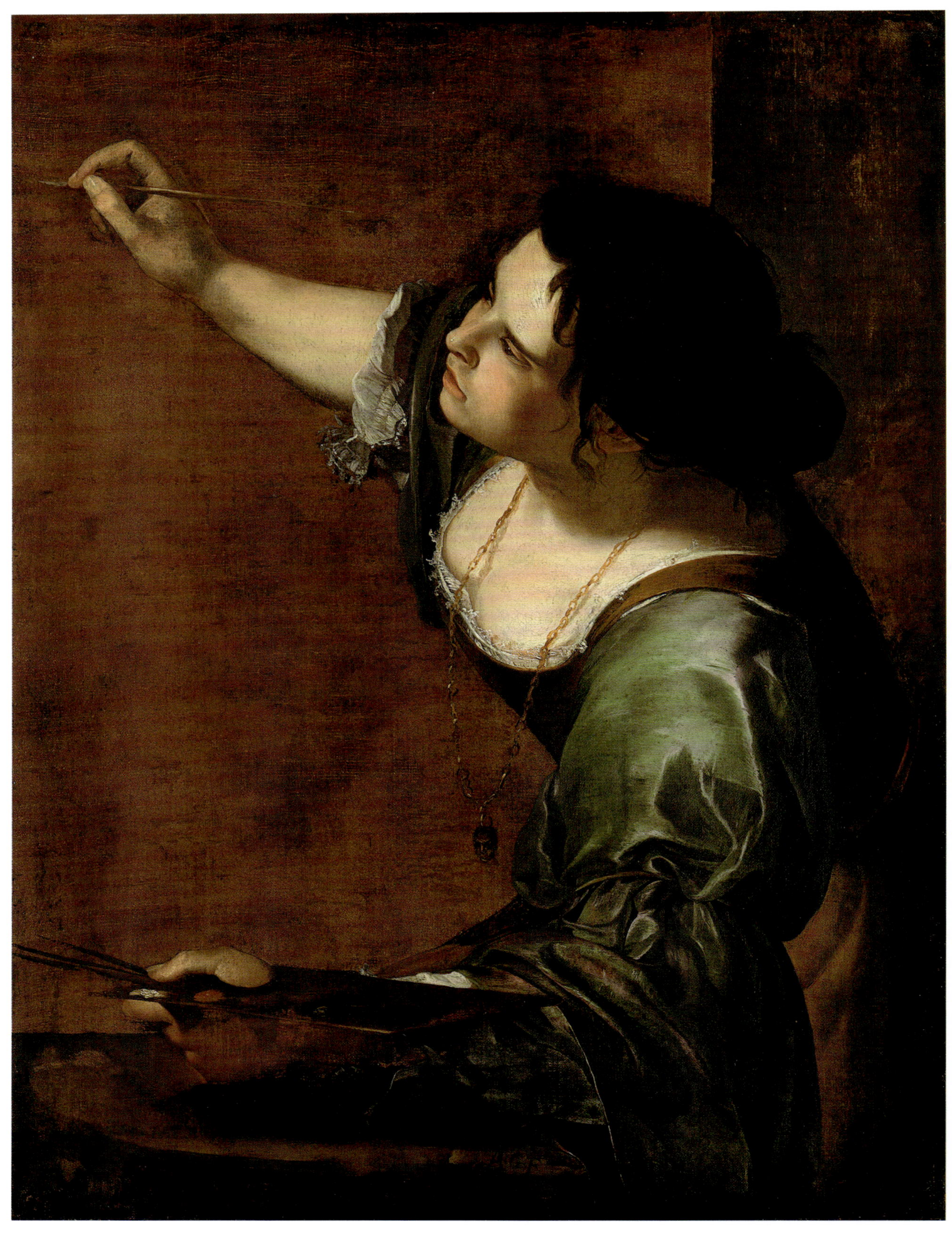

103 Artemisia Gentileschi, *Self-portrait as the Allegory of Painting (La Pittura)*, signed, c.1638–39, oil on canvas, 98.6 × 75.2 cm, The Royal Collection

Painting's 'full black hair' – and tied back in a manner that is almost identical to her appearance in the medallion of the mid-1620s (fig. 74). Gentileschi's loosely tousled hair is thus both 'natural' and, at the same time, symbolic in its correspondence to Ripa's description of the similarly dishevelled appearance of Painting's hair, which was intended to represent the 'divine frenzy' of her artistic temperament.

Artemisia/Painting is so bound up in the creative act as to have become momentarily unaware of the viewer of the canvas. This connects the *Self-portrait as the Allegory of Painting* to the role-playing, transformational self-portraits of Gentileschi's Florentine years. The painting, however, registers a far greater level of assuredness on the artist's part than those more mutable and experimental youthful essays in self-promotion. She has now evolved to such a position of artistic maturity and professional self-confidence as to feel able to frame herself as a concentrated image of idealized artistic identity without recourse to theatrical props. She no longer needs to act out some other role to merit our attention – be it a knightly warrior, gypsy minstrel, St Catherine or the Magdalene. Instead, she portrays herself playing the role of *herself*. She renders herself within the canvas as a creative individual alone in her studio, getting on with her work, while also projecting herself as the personification of the essence of painting. As a consequence, the painting joins a select group of Renaissance/Baroque self-portraits in which artists depict themselves as being so distracted by the higher calling of their art as to remain unaware of the viewer's gaze. Titian's late self-portraits – with their abstracted, side-on views and prominent gold chains – are obvious precedents in this respect.[105] The result is a portrayal of the self in which Artemisia/Painting has matured into a position of such confidence as to no longer feel the need to seek the viewer's approval of her enhanced status of dignity and bearing.

The continued appeal of the *Self-portrait as the Allegory of Painting* derives from its ability to frame its complex symbolism within a vivid evocation of the materiality of the process of painting itself. Artemisia/Painting is shown wearing a simple brown apron over her dress. She has literally rolled up her sleeves and tied them in at the elbows to get down to business. While daubing herself into existence, she leans forward against the very stone used to grind pigments. We must imagine her as just having finished the tour-de-force passage of silvery green brushwork that she has built up on her shoulder in order to evoke the iridescent effect of the shot-silk fabric of her sleeve. Now she directs her attention to the painting's uppermost corner. Her brush remains poised just above the surface of the raw, primed canvas that has been left exposed in a manner that would never have been permitted in a more conventionally conceived artwork. In making a painting that thus highlights the working methods of artistic production – elements that are usually painted over and hidden from view in the finished product – Gentileschi has created a painting about the techniques and materiality involved in the act of painting itself.

The *Self-portrait as the Allegory of Painting* derives much of its power from the sense of intimacy that it creates by granting the viewer privileged access behind the scenes of the ordinarily private area of Gentileschi's workshop. Its emphasis on the painterly process brings the public and private functions of her studio back into alignment, uniting the solitary world of the painter lost in imaginative thought with the studio's other function as a public arena for the business of commerce and self-presentation. In so doing, it transports us back to Orazio Gentileschi's original workshop, which offered Artemisia a more private domain in which to hone her skills and rehearse the innumerable drills and technical processes that enabled her to advance herself to a stage of sufficient accomplishment to be able to sign and date her first independent work. The self-portrait thus acts as a meditation on the power of art and its material processes, while also summarising Gentileschi's decades-long journey of evolving practice and professional self-realisation.

12

Naples, 1640–c.1656

GENTILESCHI'S NEAPOLITAN WORKSHOP AND THE ENDGAME OF HER FINAL YEARS

INTRODUCTION
GENTILESCHI'S PAINTINGS IN NEAPOLITAN PRIVATE COLLECTIONS

Gentileschi's ability to appeal to multiple sectors of the market for privately acquired paintings in Naples – and southern Italy more generally – is rendered clear in a table listing early primary sources (table 2, pp. 258–61). In terms of her reach into the collections of the city's most illustrious aristocratic families, for example, I have already noted the presence of her canvases in the palace of the duchi di Maddaloni (*Judith Slaying Holofernes*; see p. 152), as well as in both the urban and feudal holdings of the De Cardenas family (the *St Elisabeth of Hungary* for a chapel in Pisticci and the *Hercules and Omphale* for the family's city palace; see pp. 178–79). To these patrons can be added the D'Avalos of Naples, a prominent southern Italian dynasty whose forebears included Ferdinando Francesco d'Avalos (1489–1525), the renowned commander and victor of the Battle of Pavia in 1525. The D'Avalos collection ranked as one of the city's most magnificent, and its subsequent donation to the newly formed Italian state in 1862 remains one of the most distinguished bequests in the history of the Museo di Capodimonte.[1] The D'Avalos seem to have been particularly drawn to the sensual and luxurious aspects

FACING PAGE Artemisia Gentileschi, *Bathsheba at her Bath* (detail of fig. 115)

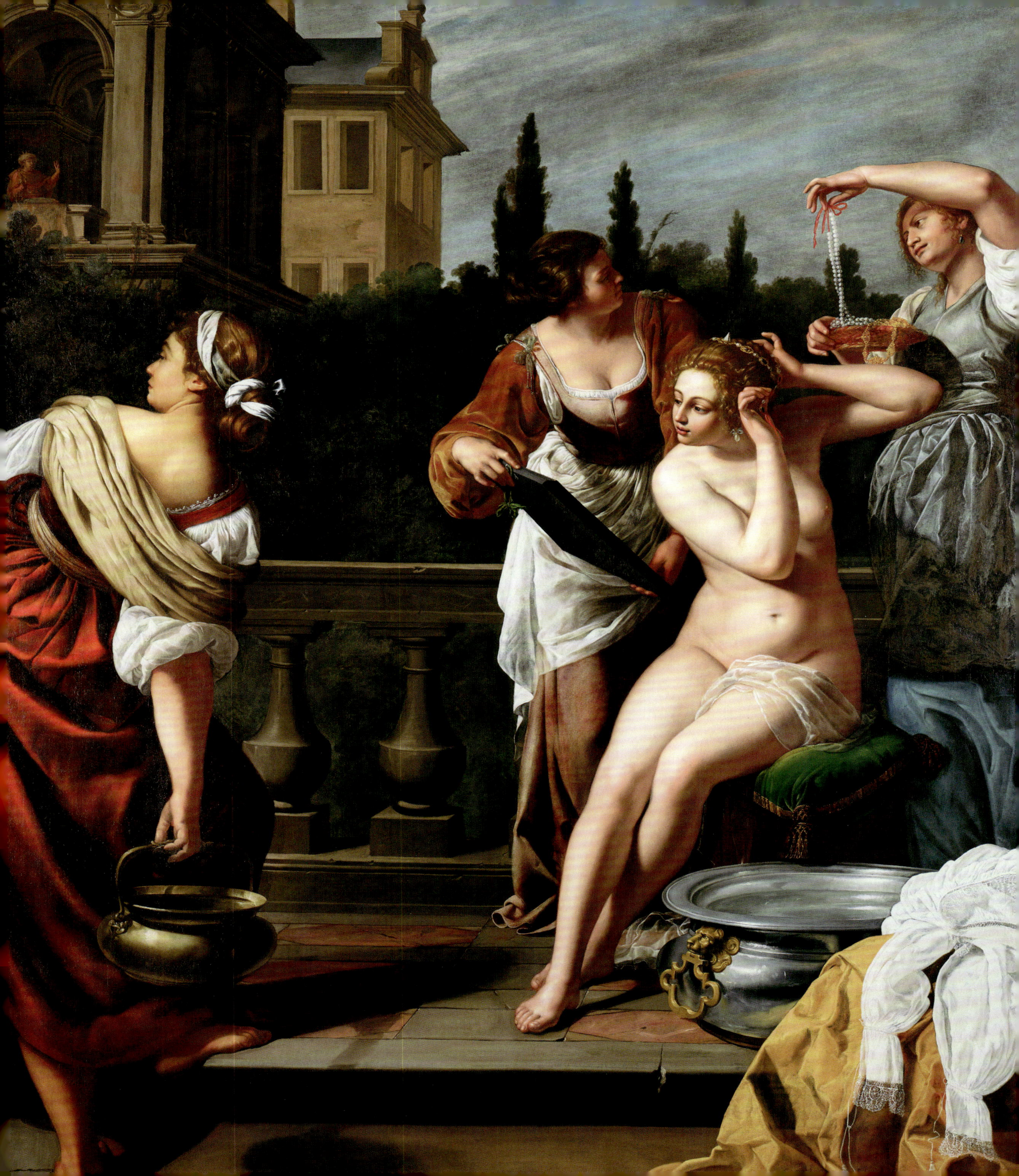

of Gentileschi's art. Besides a *Judith* (the attribution of which, however, changes in the various family inventories), they owned one of her large canvases of the *Sleeping Venus*. This they matched with other paintings of the same subject, including one by Luca Giordano that was modelled on the artist's wife (fig. 17; see p. 36).

Several key works by Gentileschi appear also in the collection of the regional baron and his consort, Conte Giangirolamo II Acquaviva d'Aragona, and Contessa Isabella Acquaviva della Rocca (niece of Ascanio Filomarino, who owned a version of Gentileschi's *John the Baptist in the Desert*).[2] The count and countess seem to have been particularly attracted to Gentileschi's associations with the culturally sophisticated traditions of recent aristocratic collecting in Rome, Florence and Venice. Their interest in such traditions formed part, in turn, of their project to foster a distinctively southern Italian neo-Renaissance court culture centered on an appreciation of the poems of Torquato Tasso, a native of Sorrento. The 1666 inventory of the Acquaviva estates at Conversano, Puglia, records two paintings by Gentileschi – a lost *Madonna* and a *Roman Charity* that has been brought to light thanks to the research of Viviana Farina (fig. 83).[3] To these can be added another rediscovered canvas, *Bathsheba at the Bath*, whose provenance can be similarly traced back to the Acquaviva (fig. 104).[4]

Gentileschi was equally adroit in attracting the patronage of the high-ranking bourgeois merchants and civil functionaries who sought to use art to signal their growing acceptance within the Neapolitan establishment. The collections of the merchants Gaspar Roomer and Ferdinand Vandeneynden belong to this category. So, too, does the collection of Davide Imperiale, a member of the Genoese mercantile colony that had traditionally dominated the city's involvement in international banking and trade.[5] Imperiale's small but distinguished collection, documented in an inventory of 1672, included two of Gentileschi's medium-sized paintings of *The Magdalene* and *Lucretia*, together with two heads of Christ and the Virgin. More notable still were Gentileschi's canvases of *The Sacrifice of Isaac* and *St Cecilia* that feature in the 1649 inventory of the collection of Vincenzo d'Andrea.[6] D'Andrea was the son of a surgeon who rose to prominence as one of the leading legal counsels during the Revolt of Masaniello in 1647–48. He provided support and advice to the leaders of the revolt, helping to moderate their punishment following the arrival of the Spanish expeditionary force. With the status quo re-established, D'Andrea was rewarded for his efforts by being appointed presidente della Sommaria and provedditore generale dell'Arsenale, before his death in 1650.

Given Gentileschi's promotion by the Venetian academies in the 1620s, it should come as no surprise to learn that she was also successful in attracting the acclamation of the Neapolitan academies, which were flourishing in the wake of the return to Naples in 1624 of the internationally renowned poet and academician Giambattista Marino.[7] Jesse Locker has highlighted the importance, in this regard, of eleven poems penned in the 1630s to early 1640s by the Neapolitan dilettante poets Girolamo Fontanella and Antonio Cappone.[8] These mention paintings by Gentileschi of *Apollo Killing the Python* and *Apollo with a Lyre*, together with a self-portrait and portraits of Fontanella and the celebrated Neapolitan singer and composer Adriana Basile (*c.*1580–1640), all of which, according to the poems, were owned by Fontanella.

A more securely documented example of the championing of Gentileschi's work by the Neapolitan literati comes in the 1647 inventory of Camillo Colonna.[9] Colonna, a friend and associate of Vincenzo d'Andrea, convened his own academy, the Accademia del Nome Romano (the Academy of the Roman Name) in an apartment that he rented within a larger palace complex owned by a fellow Roman expatriate resident in the city. Colonna's collection was neither substantial nor particularly well documented (meaning that he may have owned other works by Gentileschi besides those explicitly mentioned in the inventory). The inventory does, however, refer to a dedicated 'sala grande dove si fa l'Accademia' ('large room where the Academy is convened'). It also records four paintings 'by the hand of Artemisia'. These are described as three pictures in octagonal format (their subjects unspecified) and a large, allegorical canvas of *Hope* that would, presumably, have resembled Gentileschi's earlier allegorical painting of *Inclination* painted for the Casa Buonarroti in Florence (fig. 4). An additional point of note, and one that highlights the complex interconnections that often underpin family traditions of collecting and cultural philanthropy, is that Camillo's father was

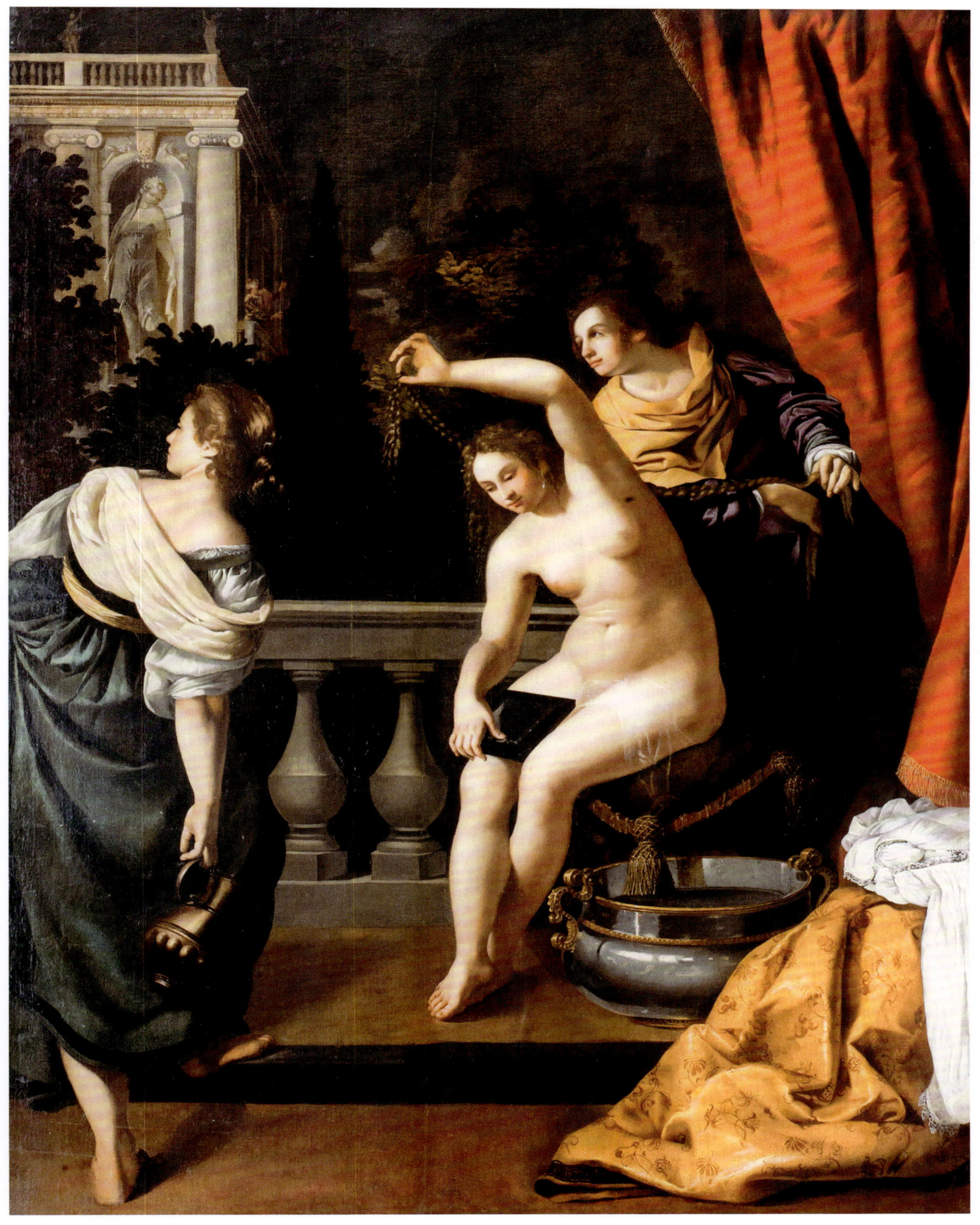

104 Artemisia Gentileschi, *Bathsheba at her Bath*, *c.*1640–45, oil on canvas, 280 × 220 cm, private collection

Marzio Colonna III, duca di Zagarolo (*c.*1570–1607). This individual had been an important patron of Caravaggio and had offered the artist protection on his estate in May 1606, following Caravaggio's flight from Rome after the death of Ranuccio Tommasoni.[10] Caravaggio produced a number of works while under Colonna's protection, including *The Ecstasy of the Magdalene*, which – in a further level of interconnection – had been an important source for Gentileschi's own painting of the same subject in the 1620s (fig. 67).

THE EXPANSION AND DIVERSIFICATION OF GENTILESCHI'S NEAPOLITAN OUTPUT AND SUBJECT MATTER

It was noted in Chapter 8 (p. 126) that one of the principal obstacles holding Gentileschi back during her mid-career period spent in Rome and Venice was the degree to which her clients seem to have typecast her as an artist who could produce a narrow range of subjects featuring female protagonists and not much else besides. Gentileschi's move to Naples, on the other hand, enabled her to overcome this professional barrier and relaunch herself as a more versatile and multi-faceted artist. Just how comprehensively she was able to achieve this significant career turnaround is made clear in a table listing the early documentary references to her later paintings, arranged according to subject matter (table 3, pp. 262–64). This incorporates some ninety paintings – twenty more, in fact, than her entire extant oeuvre. It thus provides vivid confirmation of the explosion of productivity that we now need to understand as constituting one of the defining features of Gentileschi's last twenty years of activity.

Besides the sheer number of works, another striking feature to emerge from the table is its significantly expanded range of subject matter. To be sure, Gentileschi's career mainstays remain in place. Yet the four Magdalenes and three Judiths that appear in the table, for example, are outnumbered by no fewer than five Madonnas, one Annunciation and one Head of the Virgin. This represents a major point in her career advancement, given the reluctance on the part of Gentileschi's Roman and Venetian patrons to take her seriously as a painter of altarpieces and other forms of devotional subject matter. In Naples, by contrast, Gentileschi appears to have had no difficulty in convincing her new clients of her abilities to take on a greater variety of subjects and categories.

The willingness of Gentileschi's Neapolitan clients to look beyond her obvious signature works results in the introduction into her later oeuvre of several highly distinctive and even unusual works. Two such examples are the evidently closely related variant paintings that are listed in the early eighteenth-century Neapolitan collections of the Principessa Anne-Marie Orsini and of Domenico Perrino as being by Gentileschi. These are each said to have depicted a child (possibly the Christ Child, or a more generalised putto) with his head on a pillow, asleep in a meadow and surrounded by flowers. The highly distinctive iconography of these references match an unusual painting that has been attributed to Hendrick van Somer (1602–*c.*1656), a pupil of Ribera, whose work, nevertheless, has similarities with that of Gentileschi from time to time (fig. 105).[11] As Roberto Contini has pointed out, however, the specificity of the work's iconography, in combination with its direct connection to these inventory references, seems to indicate that this painting should be re-attributed to Gentileschi's workshop, if not to the direct intervention of her hand.[12]

The greater preponderance of subjects with male protagonists also emerges as a key feature of Gentileschi's late Neapolitan years. This had represented another major imped-

105 ?Workshop of Artemisia Gentileschi, *Sleeping Christ Child*, *c.*1640s, oil on canvas, 73 × 127 cm, private collection

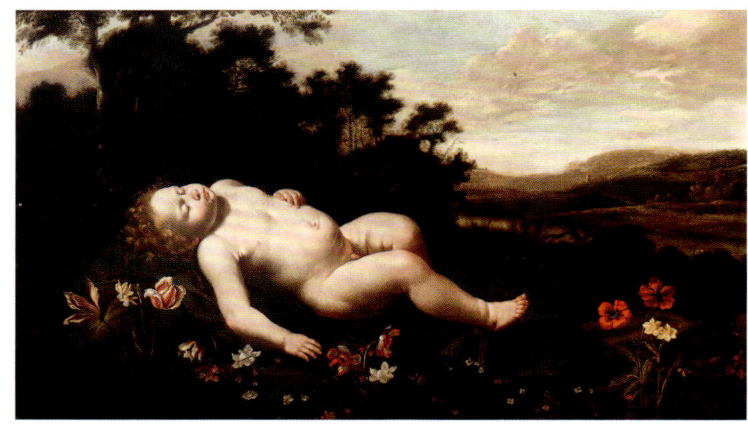

iment to her earlier career. A painting like the *Christ Blessing the Children* of 1626 (fig. 80), for example, constitutes a rarity in her oeuvre up to that point, because it depicts a man who is the protagonist of the work, rather than merely a foil to a more dominant female character. Many more of these kinds of paintings feature in the documentation for Gentileschi's Neapolitan years. One would very much like to know the original appearance, for example, of the evidently large and ambitious painting of *The Death of the First Born Sons of Egypt* listed in the early eighteenth-century collection of Nicola Pietro Carafa di San Lorenzo. Equally ambitious and in other respects unusual in Gentileschi's oeuvre is the large painting of *St Michael Vanquishing the Devil* that was viewed by De' Dominici in the collection of Dr Luigi Romeo, barone di San Luigi. So, too, the aforementioned *Apollo with a Lyre* and *Apollo Killing the Python* in the Fontanella collection provide further confirmation of Gentileschi's involvement in the production of not just sleeping Venuses and the like but also mythologies outlining the exploits of male gods and heroes, something for which there is likewise hardly any documentation prior to this period.[13]

THE CONTRIBUTION OF LANDSCAPE, ARCHITECTURE AND FIGURE SPECIALISTS TO GENTILESCHI'S NEAPOLITAN PAINTINGS

Inventories also provide occasional glimpses into the increasing contribution of Gentileschi's workshop to her Neapolitan output. The 1700 inventory of the collection of the Salernitan lawyer Fabrizio Pinto, for example, lists a small painting of the *Madonna of the Rosary with Sts Dominic and Catherine of Siena* that is said to have included figures by Gentileschi and a landscape background by Domenico Gargiulo (table 3, p. 263). This confirms the substance of De' Dominici's account of the works by Gentileschi that he had viewed in the collection of Dr Luigi Romeo:

> In the house of Dr Luigi Romeo, baron of St. Luigi, who has always professed good taste in the genre of painting . . . [there are] Two large paintings with life-sized figures depicting the stories of *Bathsheba* and *Susanna* that seem to be by the hand of Guido [but] they are by the famous Artemisia Gentileschi, with the architecture by Viviano [Codazzi] and the foliage and background view by Spadaro [the nickname for Domenico Gargiulo]. By this virtuous woman there is also a *St Michael Vanquishing Lucifer from Paradise* and a *Lot and his Daughters*, all [done] in natural scale [that is, with life-sized figures].[14]

The first two paintings have been identified with a *Bathsheba* now in the Columbus Museum of Art and with a *Susanna* sold at Sotheby's, New York, in 2022 (figs 93 and 106).[15] The *St Michael Vanquishing the Devil* remains untraced. Bissell also identifies Romeo's fourth Gentileschi as having formed part of a series with the *Bathsheba* and *Susanna* and as probably identifiable with a canvas of *Lot and His Daughters* that is now in the Toledo Museum of Art (fig. 107).[16]

De' Dominici's observation that the *Bathsheba* and *Susanna* 'seem to be by the hand of Guido' represents a form of literary shorthand, as noted above. It indicates his view that these paintings were to be highlighted as outstanding examples of a more ennobled Neapolitan artistic counter-tradition running in opposition to the realism of Caravaggio and the more harshly naturalistic traditions of southern Italian tenebrism. It is easy to appreciate why De' Dominici might have chosen to describe these canvases in these terms. With their expansive backgrounds, elegantly poised monumental figures, elaborate draperies and glittering, painterly highlights, they seem to inhabit an entirely different world from that of earlier Neapolitan Caravaggesque painting.

Gentileschi has managed in these later paintings to connect her art to a more 'progressive' series of contemporary influences. Yet she has not entirely rejected her Caravaggesque inheritance. We note, for example, the wrinkled brow and down-to-earth, quotidian appearance of the servant at the left of the *Bathsheba*. This represents a female version of a ruddy plebeian figure type that appears in the foreground of a number of Caravaggio's Neapolitan paintings (fig. 109) and is found subsequently quoted in numerous Neapolitan Caravaggesque paintings of the 1620s–40s. Gentileschi has successfully moderated this by combining it with a series of other more elegant and refined features that have been characterised by Riccardo Lattuada as rendering the *Susanna* into

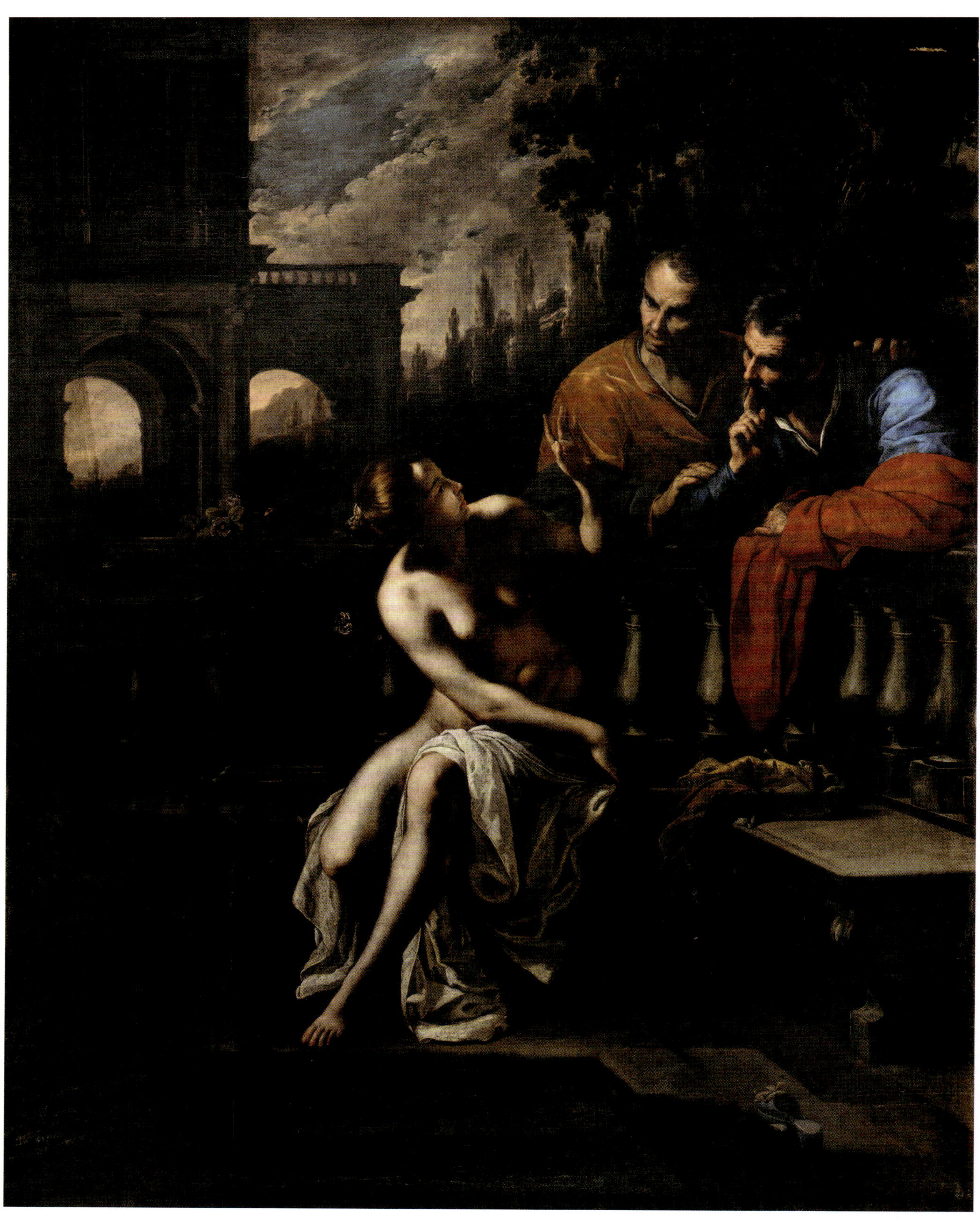

106 Artemisia Gentileschi (?with workshop assistance by Bernardo Cavallino, Viviano Codazzi and Domenico Gargiulo), *Susanna and the Elders*, c.1636–38, oil on canvas, 265 × 210 cm, sale Sotheby's, New York, 27 January 2022

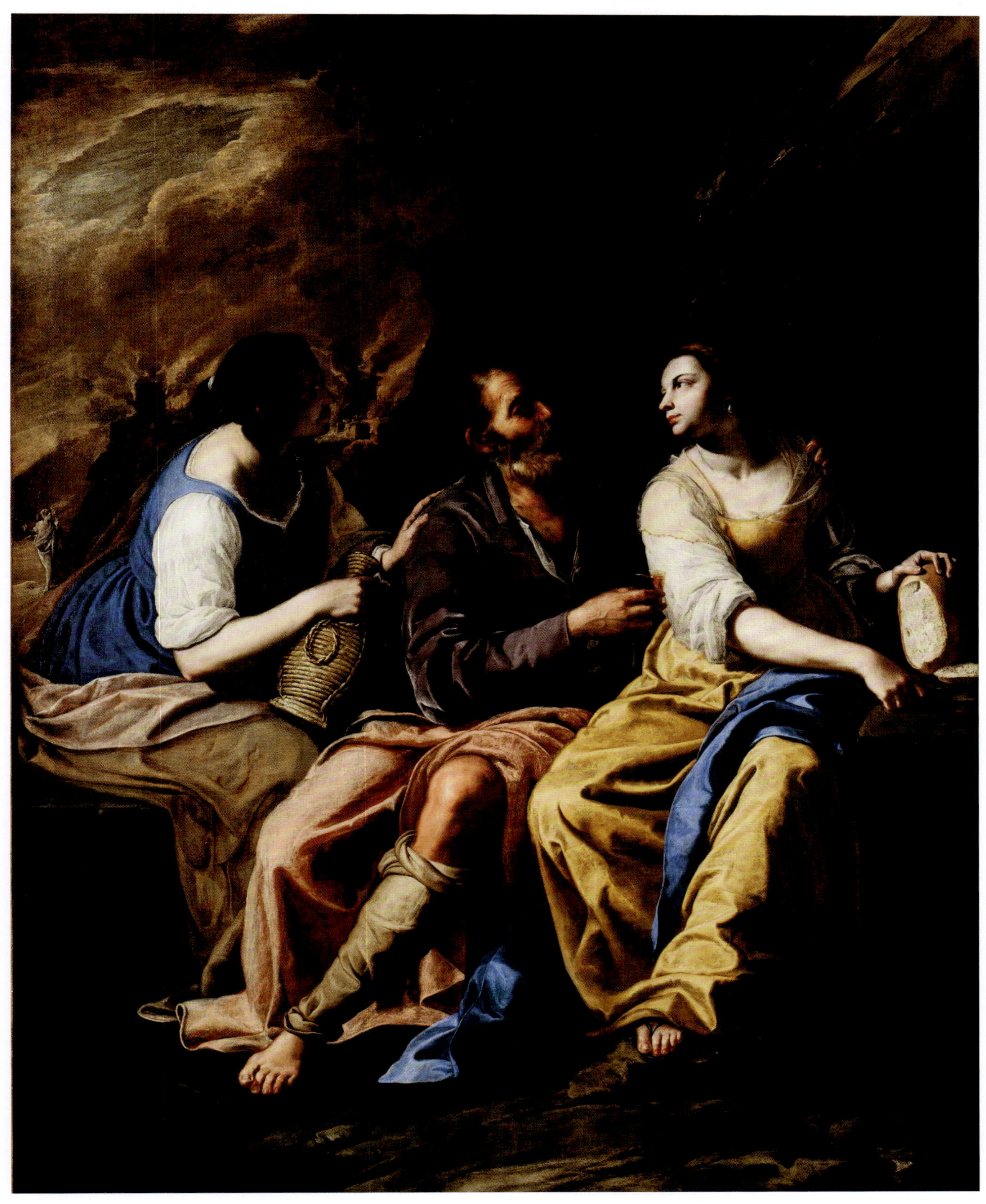

107 Artemisia Gentileschi (?with workshop assistance by Bernardo Cavallino, Domenico Gargiulo and Agostino Beltrano), *Lot and his Daughters*, c.1635–38, oil on canvas, 235 × 183 cm, Toledo Museum of Art, Toledo, Ohio, Clarence Brown Fund 1983.107

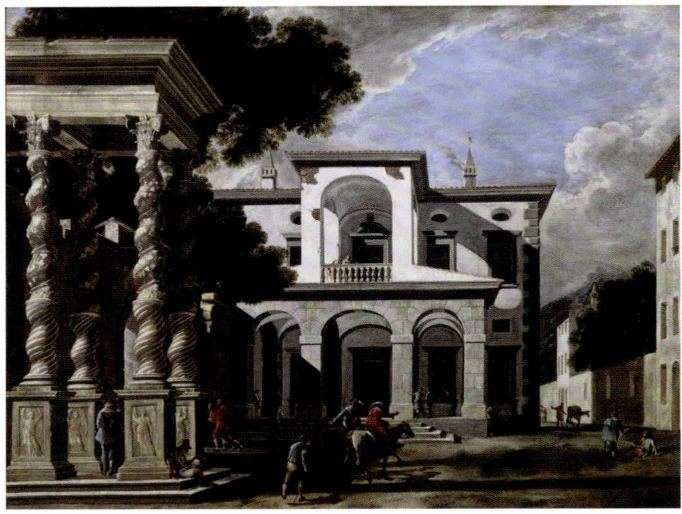

108 Viviano Codazzi and Domenico Gargiulo, *Palace with Rustic Portico, and Baldacchino with Solomonic Columns*, signed and dated 1641, oil on canvas, 130 × 160 cm, Palazzo Reale, Naples

'one of the finest accomplishments of Neapolitan painting in the first half of the seventeenth century'.[17]

A significant element adding to the *Susanna*'s Neapolitan credentials in this regard is the additional input of local specialists. Gargiulo and Codazzi's landscape and architectural background, for example, represents an important feature contributing to the painting's overall visual impression of having moved on from the shallow, dark backgrounds of earlier Neapolitan Caravaggism. Gentileschi would have probably employed these two artists as a pair to provide the landscape and architectural backgrounds of this and other paintings of the period. Gargiulo and Codazzi worked together in this way throughout the 1630s up until 1647, when Codazzi fled to Rome to escape the disturbances of the Revolt of Masaniello.[18] The partnership of the two artists spearheaded what proved to be a highly successful and even lucrative market for a new picture type in Naples – *quadratura* or architectural view painting (fig. 108).[19] These vivid depictions of urban settings enlivened by everyday contemporary figures soon became highly sought after. De' Dominici describes seeing numerous works of this kind in the local collections, and the standard catalogue of Codazzi's oeuvre lists some thirty-six examples of collaborative paintings of this type, with dozens more in the early inventories.[20]

Codazzi's and Gargiulo's architectural and landscape backgrounds in the *Bathsheba* and *Susanna* from the Romeo collection thus constitute a significant element of their more fashionably contemporary appearance. This being the case, then it is important to note Gentileschi's willingness, in these instances, to look beyond her own capabilities when seeking to upgrade her art in order to create paintings that 'seem by the hand of Guido'. Gentileschi was evidently seeking to recast her work-

109 Michelangelo Merisi da Caravaggio, *Seven Acts of Mercy*, 1606–7, oil on canvas, 390 × 260 cm, Chiesa del Pio Monte della Misericordia, Naples

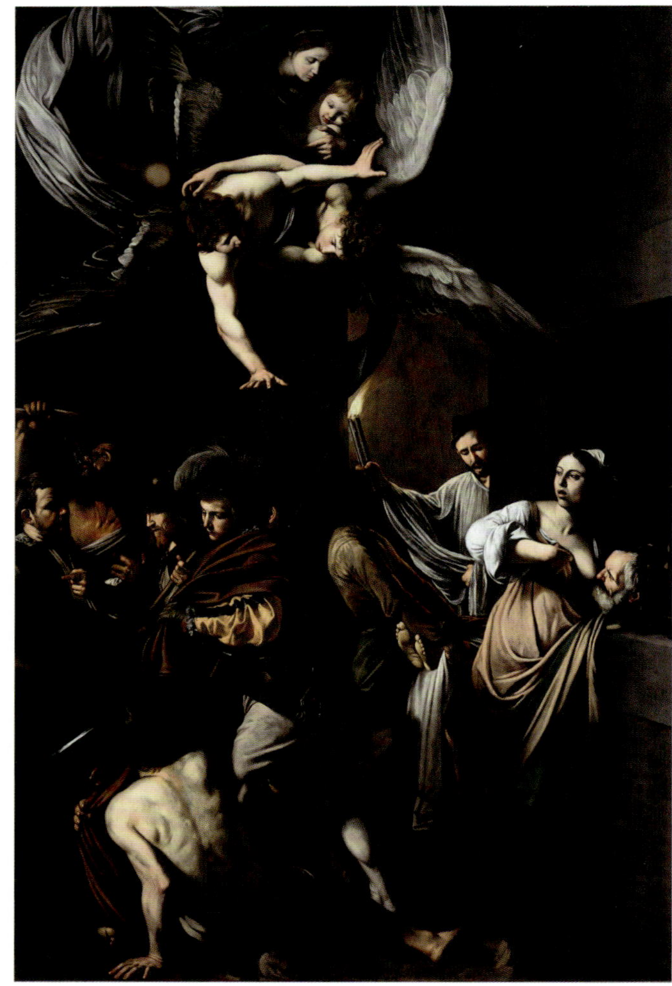

shop not only to improve its productivity but also to increase its versatility. The input of a fresh crop of specialists could help to overcome the artistic limitations that were the result of her initial training and professional background. Gentileschi had graduated from her father's workshop as an artist of exceptional talent, but she was deficient in a number of areas. These included a lack of an advanced understanding of such aspects as anatomy (especially male anatomy), foreshortening and the correct disposition of figures in perspectivally credible landscape and urban settings. Gargiulo and Codazzi were one part of Gentileschi's solution to these problems. Additional artists were also called upon to assist her in other aspects as required.

WORKSHOP INTERVENTION AND THE ISSUE OF MALE FIGURES AND MALE NUDITY IN GENTILESCHI'S NEAPOLITAN PAINTINGS

The presence in Gentileschi's late oeuvre of significant numbers of subjects involving prominent male figures would have placed additional strain on Gentileschi's capacity to meet her Neapolitan clients' requests. How could she work around her lack of training in the rendition of the male body, for example, while also finding willing participants to model for her, given the taboo against men submitting themselves to a woman's gaze for this purpose? This would have been particularly an issue for those subjects requiring various degrees of male nudity – such as the paintings of *Apollo* for Fontanella, for example. The problem would have applied also to a number of religious subjects – for example, an *Ecce Homo* for the duca di Sant'Elia. The issue of partial male nudity would have been apparent in the *John the Baptist in the Desert* painted by Gentileschi for the Barberini in 1637, a variant of which was owned also by Ascanio Filomarino.

Gentileschi's earlier solution to this problem seems to have been to clothe her male figures as much as possible. Where the subject demanded varying degrees of nakedness, however, her response seems to have been to construct the figure as a series of discrete body parts rather than present it as a convincingly modelled nude. This is the case in her signature *Judith Slaying Holofernes*, for example, where Holofernes' body reads more as an amalgam of individually conceived elements – arms, head, knees – than as a fully unified figure (fig. 29). By contrast, a later, Neapolitan painting such as *Corsica and the Satyr* reveals Gentileschi's greater degree of proficiency in the depiction of male subjects (fig. 110).[21] The shadowed and strategically covered nature of this figure, nonetheless, demonstrates her continued tentativeness in the production of convincing male nudes.

One obvious answer to this problem would have been to bring in other artists to assist her with the execution of the male figures in her Neapolitan works. A significant clue suggesting her recourse to this kind of external intervention appears once again in the inventories (table 3, p. 263). The 1700 inventory of the collection of Ferdinando d'Afflitto, principe di Scanno, includes a reference to 'Three paintings measuring 6 palmi wide and 8 palmi high with black frames and gold thread, one of St Eustace, another of David and the other of St Sebastian, and the heads are by the hand of Artemisia.'[22] Most unusually in this case, it is possible to shed further light on the commissioning of the D'Afflitto Gentileschis with reference to an independently documented bank payment published by Eduardo Nappi in 1992. In this document, dated 21 August 1631, an earlier family member named Giovanni Francesco di Afflitto, conte di Loreto, paid Gentileschi '12 ducats to make up 20 ducats that are for the price of a painting of St Sebastian of eight palmi high and six palmi wide [about 211 × 158 cm] made by her own hand and promised within eight days.'[23]

As noted above, an outlay of twenty ducats for a painting by Gentileschi would have corresponded to a single-figure composition rather than to a more expensive, multi-figure history painting. This reference, then, confirms that the three paintings by Gentileschi mentioned in the 1700 inventory of the D'Afflitto collection comprised a series of three single-figure compositions depicting a trio of male warriors of God. The canvas of St Sebastian, in particular, would have necessitated the rendition of a semi-naked male figure, the exposed torso pierced with arrows, following the traditional iconography. The inventory's important qualifier that 'the heads are by the hand of Artemisia' answers the question of whether Gentileschi would have had recourse to other, presumably male figure painters during this period.

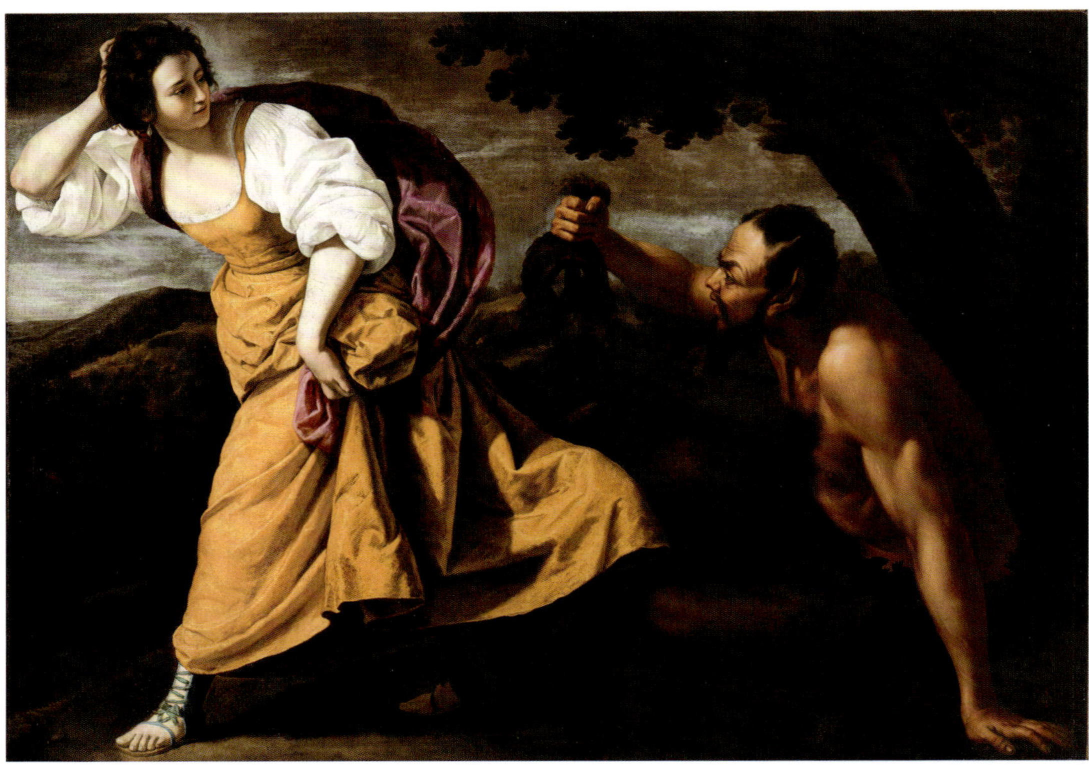

110 Artemisia Gentileschi, *Corsica and the Satyr*, signed, c.1635-40, oil on canvas, 155 × 210 cm, private collection

The inventory's inclusion of such an extremely unusual reference to Gentileschi's input being confined to the heads of the figures relates to the traditional view that faces require the most skill to complete. This area of painting will, therefore, most likely require the direct intervention of the master in order to bring the work to a satisfactory conclusion.[24] It was said of Bernini that he personally intervened to retouch only the face of Alexander on the tomb of Pope Alexander VII, leaving the remainder to be executed by the workshop, following his directions.[25] I noted above the existence of two rediscovered variants of *David with the Head of Goliath*. One – with David holding Goliath's head in his hand – was apparently the version viewed by Joachim von Sandrart in Gentileschi's studio in 1631 prior to its transferral to Giustiniani's collection, where it was inventoried in 1638. Another signed variant, on the other hand, may be one of the three paintings produced for D'Afflitto (fig. 71). If this is the case, this *David with the Head of Goliath* constitutes an important example of a work for which there is now documentary evidence confirming the contribution of Gentileschi's Neapolitan workshop to the execution of works of this kind.[26]

THE TOLEDO *LOT AND HIS DAUGHTERS* AND THE ISSUE OF CONTEMPORARY UNDERSTANDINGS OF GENTILESCHI'S NEAPOLITAN WORKSHOP

Commentators have also identified the input of a number of other, junior Neapolitan figure painters in the execution of both the female and the male figures in the ex-Romeo paintings of *Bathsheba*, *Susanna* and the *Lot and His Daughters*. In the *Bathsheba* (fig. 104), for example, Bissell has detected the likely addition of Bernardo Cavallino's hand for the figures of the two maidservants at the composition's right.[27] So, too, has Cavallino's distinctive style of depicting bearded, elderly, male figures been detected in the figures of the two elders in the *Susanna* (fig. 106).[28]

Perhaps most noteworthy of the three, however, in terms of the extent of its workshop collaboration, is the *Lot and his Daughters* (fig. 107). This painting was originally acquired for the Toledo Museum of Art in 1983 under an attribution to Cavallino. Since then, scholarly opinion has shifted in favour of a re-attribution to Gentileschi, a view that has become the consensus.[29] The question of just who else might have assisted Gentileschi in completing this work, however, remains open.

Some commentators have sought to ascribe the entire composition of the Toledo *Lot* to Gentileschi's hand alone.[30] Others have seen the hand of Gargiulo in the extensive landscape background.[31] Yet others have argued in favour of attributing the figure of Lot to Cavallino.[32] Some scholars have added to this the further qualification of viewing either Onofrio Palumbo or Agostino Beltrano (1607–1656) as responsible for the figure of Lot's daughter at the right.[33] In my own opinion, the landscape background demonstrates a subtlety and surety of execution that confirms the attribution of this section of the painting to Gargiulo. The figure of Lot's daughter at the left, on the other hand, has strong links to the kneeling maidservant at the left of the *Bathsheba* and should be attributed to Gentileschi, who should also be considered responsible for the overall composition and direction of the work. The figure of Lot, by contrast, bears the unmistakable imprint of Cavallino's hand, whereas Lot's daughter on the right, while reminiscent of the kneeling figure in Gentileschi's *Birth of St John the Baptist* (fig. 86), has a distinctive facial physiognomy that sets it apart from her direct authorship. This figure should be attributed, instead, to Agostino Beltrano, the husband of Annella de Rosa and the long-time workshop assistant to Massimo Stanzione.[34] We thus have an example of a painting that has been assembled section by section on a kind of construction-line basis, almost as if it were a jigsaw. Beginning with Gentileschi, a series of three different figure painters have each contributed a figure to the canvas while working from left to right. To this has then been added a landscape background by another specialist.[35]

The fact that scholars have been able to distinguish the presence of so many hands at work within the Toledo *Lot* and the other canvases here discussed suggests the extent to which these paintings diverge from standard Renaissance and Baroque workshop practice. There is nothing inherently unusual about artists drawing on external specialists to assist them with the execution of architectural or landscape backgrounds, for example, or still life, or even depictions of animals. These were all areas that were understood as requiring particular skill sets and could be specialisations in their own right. What is unusual, however, is the evidence of different hands at work across the paintings' principal figures in the manner just outlined. In fact, the extent to which the figures can be identified as being by distinct artistic identities is reminiscent of Giorgio Vasari's anecdote concerning the greater beauty of the angel added by the young Leonardo to Verrocchio's *Baptism of Christ* (fig. 3). Vasari's story, it will be recalled, was written as an exception that proves the rule. Contemporary readers would have been expected to recognise that what was so unusual about the anecdote was the extent to which it showed Leonardo's going wilfully against the grain of how Renaissance workshops were expected to function. The input of a junior assistant should never be allowed to stand out from the rest of the painting to the extent that it outshines the master's work – not, of course, unless the assistant happens to be Leonardo. Only in that case would it be possible to read the anecdote in a positive sense as an early intimation of Leonardo's mould-breaking genius.

Contemporary scholars will continue to debate the finer distinctions regarding the presence of different hands in Gentileschi's Neapolitan paintings. Her late Neapolitan workshop constitutes, in this respect, a fruitful avenue for future investigation. One might anticipate that further research in this area could, in fact, reveal the identities of additional Neapolitan collaborators not presently known to us.[36] But does this mean that Gentileschi's original patrons and collectors would have also been aware of these differing levels of workshop contribution when they contracted for and acquired her work? Bissell, for one, has argued in favour of this hypothesis, seeing the works as having been explicitly produced for Gentileschi's patrons to receive knowingly as collaborative works. As he puts it, 'one imagines rather an exciting partnership, a consortium that was reconstituted as the orders came in. Perhaps one of the attractions for patrons was that they were assured of a sampling of some of the best that contemporary painting in Naples had to offer, done by distinctive artists, one of them a woman, with particular specializations.'[37] Riccardo Lattuada has also championed this reading, suggesting that Gentileschi's late, collaborative paintings were produced as a kind of connoisseur's game that allowed 'an audience of expert spectators to enjoy the exercise of recognising the respective hands and their intermingling in a sophisticated puzzle'.[38]

Fascinating as this hypothesis is, I, nonetheless, feel that it needs to be rejected on the basis of the discussion above concerning contemporary understandings of workshop practice. It also seems inherently unlikely in terms of the expectations of the contemporary art market. It seems intrinsically implausible, for example, that Gentileschi would have ever thought it desirable willingly to jeopardize her most prestigious and highest paying private commissions by emphasising the contribution of junior collaborators, who would, in any event, have been utterly unknown to high-ranking patrons or, even less likely, to a foreign patron like Prince Karl Eusebius von Liechtenstein. Certainly, she never mentions any of these lesser-known artists in any of her numerous letters to actual and prospective patrons of the 1630s and 1640s. And why would she? Von Liechtenstein, for example, had paid her six hundred ducats in 1636 for three large paintings of *Bathsheba*, *Susanna* and *Lucretia* that are directly comparable with the ex-Romeo paintings. He was clearly looking for the work of prominent painters to furnish his new residence, not lesser lights with no reputation beyond their own locality. This is evident from his choice of Ribera and Gentileschi, to whom he was paying a proportionately high fee as a result. If Gentileschi had mentioned to him or his agents her intention to highlight the work of a junior artist like Cavallino, then one can imagine that this would have constituted a clear argument in favour of significantly reducing her fee. Why should Von Liechtenstein and his agents have paid two hundred ducats for a work featuring figures by Cavallino when this same artist was paid, during the same period, only seventy ducats for two large paintings of *The Annunciation* and *The Immaculate Conception*, each measuring 9 by 7 palmi (around 237 × 184 cm)?[39]

The obvious conclusion to be drawn from this is to view Gentileschi's Neapolitan workshop as a much more fluid and dynamically evolving entity than was the norm for other, more conventional workshops of the period. There was a very good reason that Gentileschi was not able to retouch the faces of Lot and one of the daughters in the Toledo painting to a degree that would have rendered the whole seamless – as should have been the case according to standard practice. This is because she was dealing with a very different kind of workforce than that used by artists presiding over more conventional workshops. Unlike Ribera or Stanzione, for example, Gentileschi did not have the luxury – or even the possibility, owing to her gender and her previous professional experience – of spending years in one place, slowly training up teenaged, male apprentices while they resided with her and learned to paint in her style. The model of a more traditional workshop was simply not available to her. She was, rather, a recently arrived, female artist – with all the professional constraints that this implied – who was faced with a sudden influx of orders for major works, with only her daughter to assist her in other respects.

In order to honour her various obligations, therefore, Gentileschi chose to augment her output by improvising a series of more or less expandable and contractable 'pop-up' workshops. This she achieved by adding to or cutting back on the number of fully matriculated junior artists – 'hired guns' in effect – that she brought in to assist her with particular compositions, according to need. She seems, in effect, to have swapped these more established, junior artists in and out of her workshop according to the varying demands of her workload – most notably when she was working on especially demanding commissions, such as the Pozzuoli paintings, but also at other times. In this context, Nicola Spinosa has highlighted a fascinating composition featuring two half-length figures that he identifies as having been produced collaboratively by Gentileschi – who painted the figure of St Agatha at the left – and Cavallino – responsible for the figure of St Peter (fig. 111). He dates the work to an early stage of their collaboration.[40] With its more reduced dimensions and smaller, half-length figures, the canvas has all the hallmarks of a trial run generated by Gentileschi to evaluate the viability of a highly

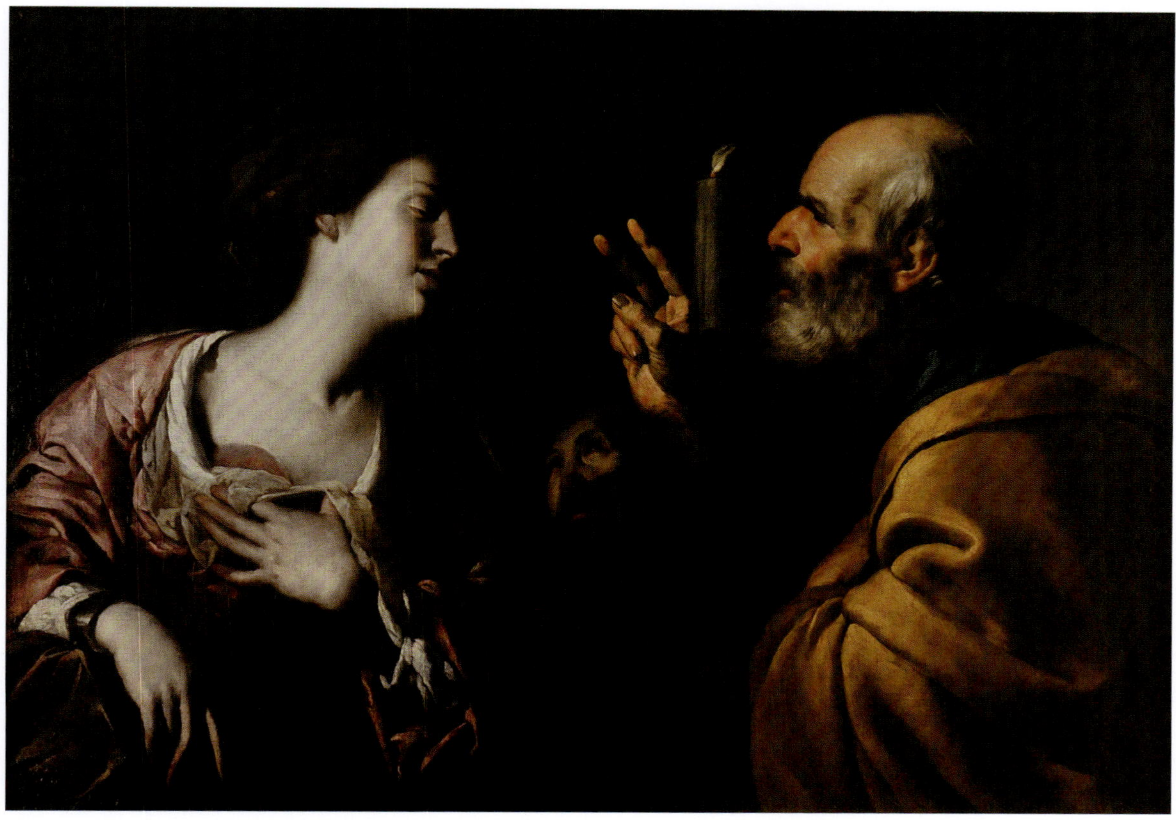

111 Bernardo Cavallino and Artemisia Gentileschi, *St Agatha Visited by St Peter in Prison*, c.mid-1630s, oil on canvas, 73 × 100.5 cm, Musée de la Faïence et des Beaux-Arts Frédéric Blandin, Nevers, inv. NP 701

unusual workshop methodology that she then developed into the progressively more elaborate and involved collaborations outlined above.

GENTILESCHI IN THE 1640S TO EARLY 1650S AND THE ISSUE OF HER LATE WORKSHOP PRODUCTION

Many chronological and biographical gaps remain to be filled in for Gentileschi's final years of activity. Following her presumed return to Naples from London at the beginning of the 1640s, the documentary record goes silent until September 1648. On that date, she is documented receiving thirty ducats from the prior of Bagnara for unspecified work.[41] This individual turns out to have been an important late contact, since he belonged to the Ruffo di Calabria clan, one of southern Italy's most illustrious aristocratic dynasties. He seems, in turn, to have recommended Gentileschi to his uncle, Don Antonio Ruffo of Messina. This was a significant break for Gentileschi, since Ruffo was at that stage assembling one of the region's most significant art collections from his palace overlooking the Straits of Messina on the north-eastern tip of Sicily. This kept him in constant correspondence with many of the leading artists of the day and with an extensive network of dealers, merchants and other commercial agents scattered throughout the major cities of Italy and beyond. As a result, Ruffo was able to create an unusually diverse and wide-ranging collection featuring such artists as Stanzione, Ribera, Guercino, Pietro da Cortona, Salvator Rosa, Mattia Preti and even Rembrandt, from whom two major late paintings were commissioned.[42]

It was during this period that Ruffo also became one of the principal patrons of Gentileschi's closing years. We know this from a trove of no fewer than thirteen letters from Gentileschi to Ruffo that were published as part of a wider study of the Ruffo family archive in 1916.[43] These show that she was still working on major commissions during her final years. In 1648, she produced for Ruffo a large and ambitious painting of *Galatea* that is described in the early documentation as measuring 8 by 10 Messinese palmi (around 211 by 264 centimetres). She then painted a companion canvas of *Diana and Actaeon*, together with two smaller pictures, a *Madonna and Child* and a self-portrait. She received 160 ducats for the *Galatea* and 230 ducats for the *Diana and Actaeon*. These were among the highest payments of her career, although they were slightly lower than the amounts paid by Ruffo to Stanzione and Ribera for otherwise comparable work (Stanzione receiving 300 ducats for a large *Judgement of Paris*, and Ribera earning 270 ducats for a similarly expansive *Pietà*).[44]

The Ruffo correspondence reveals Don Antonio Ruffo to have been one of the great connoisseurs of the day as well as one of its most tight-fisted. His preferred negotiating technique was to commission a painting and then to attempt to discount the price mid-way through its production. This he did either directly in letters to the artists concerned (Ruffo's letters being lost, so that we have only the artists' and agents' responses on record), or else through his brother, Don Flavio Ruffo, whom he used as his agent in charge of his daily business in Naples. One imagines that Gentileschi might have thus appreciated the devastatingly effective technique that was said to have been employed by Domenico Gargiulo to extract full payment from an equally niggardly patron. De' Dominici relates that a poor young artist once came to Gargiulo seeking his assistance with a patron who refused to pay the agreed amount for a commissioned portrait of the patron's wife. Outraged by this parsimony, Gargiulo took the portrait to the workshop of a local art dealer so that the dealer and the painters who attended might arbitrate on the matter. All agreed that the patron should pay the full amount of ten scudi. But still the patron refused. So Gargiulo paid the young artist twenty scudi from his own pocket. He then took the painting back to his workshop and painted in the figure of a Moorish slave lasciviously kissing and caressing the woman in the portrait. Finally, he exhibited the portrait for sale in the dealer's workshop. As might be expected, the miserly patron soon paid the full amount – plus a present for the young artist – in return for Gargiulo's promise to take back the painting and remove the offending figure of the slave.[45]

De' Dominici's account is a witty and moralising fable that highlights the ultimate victory of artistic talent over patronal parsimony. In the real world, however, and without recourse to such elaborately rhetorical strategies, Gentileschi's only means of responding to Ruffo was by a series of somewhat plaintive counter-claims. She first complained to him about the cost of her female models ('the expenses for hiring nude women are high. Believe me, Signor Don Antonio, the expenses are intolerable, because out of the fifty women who undress themselves, there is scarcely one good one'[46]). She next alluded to certain mysterious yet pressing financial obligations that she needed to fulfill ('I cannot accept a reduction, both because of the value of the painting and of my great need. Were this not so, I would give it to your Most Illustrious Lordship as a present'). She even made what might strike us today as a radically modern proposition, suggesting that a direct correlation could be drawn between the amount of money that Ruffo could pay her and the quality of the completed painting ('I can tell you for certain that the higher the price, the harder I will strive to make a painting that will please Your Most Illustrious Lordship, and that will conform to my taste and yours'[47]). In the end, however, Gentileschi had no choice but to accept Ruffo's terms, as they both knew full well. She was forced to accept graciously a reduced fee of 230 ducats for one of the most lavish and demanding works of her career, all the while entreating Ruffo for further patronage.

Gentileschi's next painting for Ruffo, the *Diana and Actaeon*, is lost. A painting by Pacecco de Rosa – another of Stanzione's pupils – might, however, offer a sense of its original appearance (fig. 112).[48] Ruffo's *Galatea*, on the other hand, is unusual in having had not one but two candidates proffered as the original work from his collection. In the early 1980s, a painting of this subject appeared on the London art market with an attribution to Bernardo Cavallino (fig. 113).[49] By the time of its acquisition in 2000 by the National Gallery of Art in Washington,

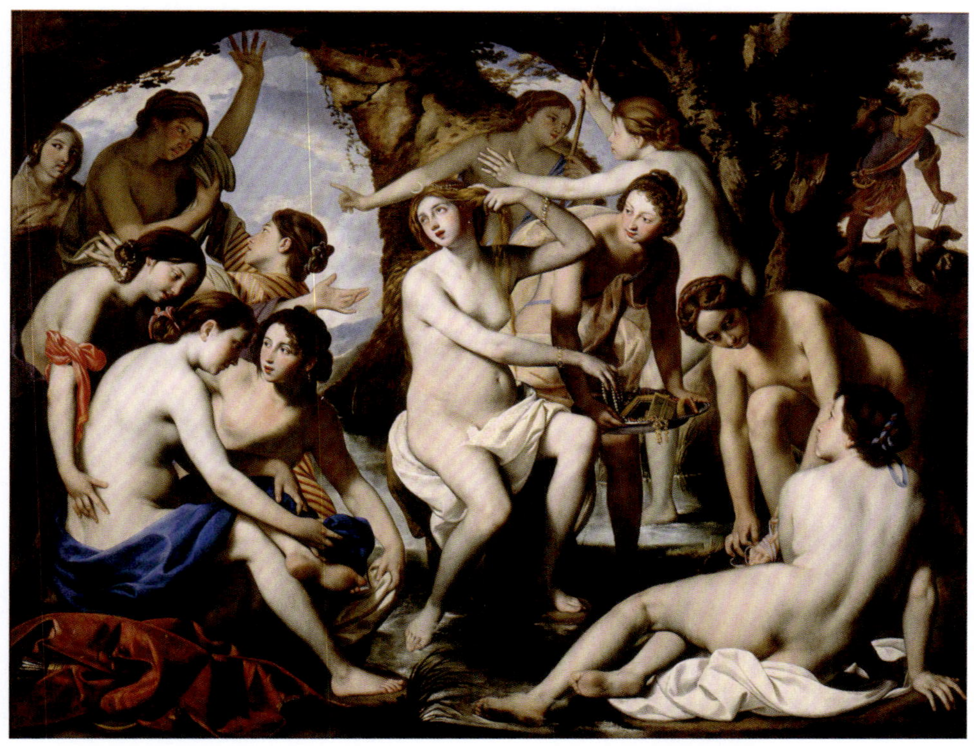

112 Pacecco de Rosa, *Diana and Actaeon*, c.1645–50, oil on canvas, 200 × 256 cm, Museo e Real Bosco di Capodimonte, Naples

however, a counter-attribution in favour of Gentileschi had gained ground, to the extent that the painting was catalogued as by her in the 1991 Casa Buonarroti exhibition, as well as in both Garrard's and Bissell's monographs.[50] Commentators – such as Bissell, Garrard, Grabski and Contini – nonetheless, continued to discern the presence of Cavallino's hand in the work. The painting was, therefore, categorised as another example of a collaborative production between Gentileschi and Cavallino. Gentileschi was perceived as responsible for the figure of Galatea and the elements of the mantle, throne, pillow and shell beneath and around Galatea, while Cavallino was judged to have painted the rest of the canvas, including most particularly its wiry male tritons. The painting's obvious connection to the early descriptions of the Ruffo *Galatea* meant that it was also generally identified as being one and the same as the Ruffo painting. Like the *Lot* and the *Susanna* from the Romeo collection, the painting was seen at that stage as constituting another prestigious commission for which Gentileschi had brought in Cavallino to paint the nude, male figures as a junior – and unacknowledged – collaborator.

In 2005, however, at the risk of unravelling such a neatly resolved consensus, I argued against this prevailing view in favour of reasserting Cavallino's sole authorship of the painting. This I argued on the basis, among other factors, of new technical information that had been provided by the National Gallery. This proved conclusively that the painting had not been cut down on the top and left sides at some point in the past, as had been suggested by those favouring the painting's identification as Ruffo's *Galatea*.[51] At no stage, therefore, did the National Gallery *Galatea* ever include the five tritons that are unequivocally listed as being present in the inventory description of Ruffo's original version. At the same time, I also connected the painting with a 1744 inventory of the collection of Carlo Arici that lists another work of this subject

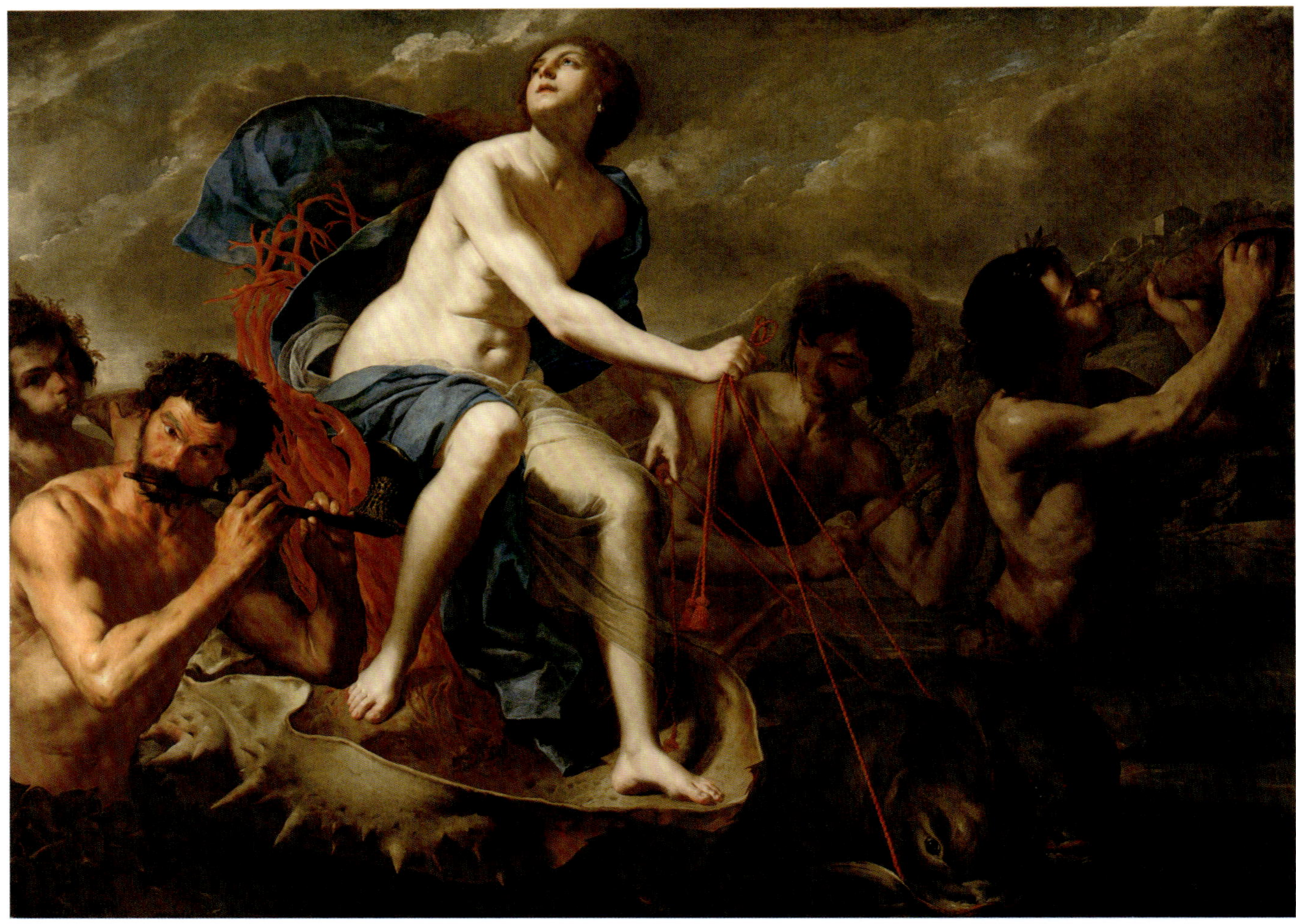

113 Bernardo Cavallino, *The Triumph of Galatea*, c.1650, oil on canvas, 148.3 × 203 cm, National Gallery of Art, Washington

and is attributed instead to Cavallino: 'A painting measuring 8 by 6 palmi [about 211 × 158 cm] where there is painted a Galatea with various putti, that travels by sea with a gilt frame in the antique manner by Bernardo Cavallino for 20 ducats.'[52] I argued that the National Gallery's *Galatea* should be regarded as an independent commission produced by Cavallino for the Arici family, while basing the work directly on Gentileschi's template in Ruffo's *Galatea*. The painting should thus be seen as providing important documentation for the way in which Gentileschi's compositions were used as models to be imitated and adapted by her assistants when pursuing their own independent commissions. This attribution and argument have subsequently gained ground, to the extent that the painting is now catalogued as a work by Cavallino on the National Gallery's website, as well as in recent exhibitions held in Naples and Rome.[53]

In 2007, there then appeared on the market another, yet larger Neapolitan Baroque painting of *Galatea* that was clearly a close relative of the National Gallery's picture (fig. 114). Originally attributed by Nicola Spinosa to Cavallino, this painting's obvious connection to Ruffo's *Galatea* meant that its attribution was also soon upgraded to that of Artemisia

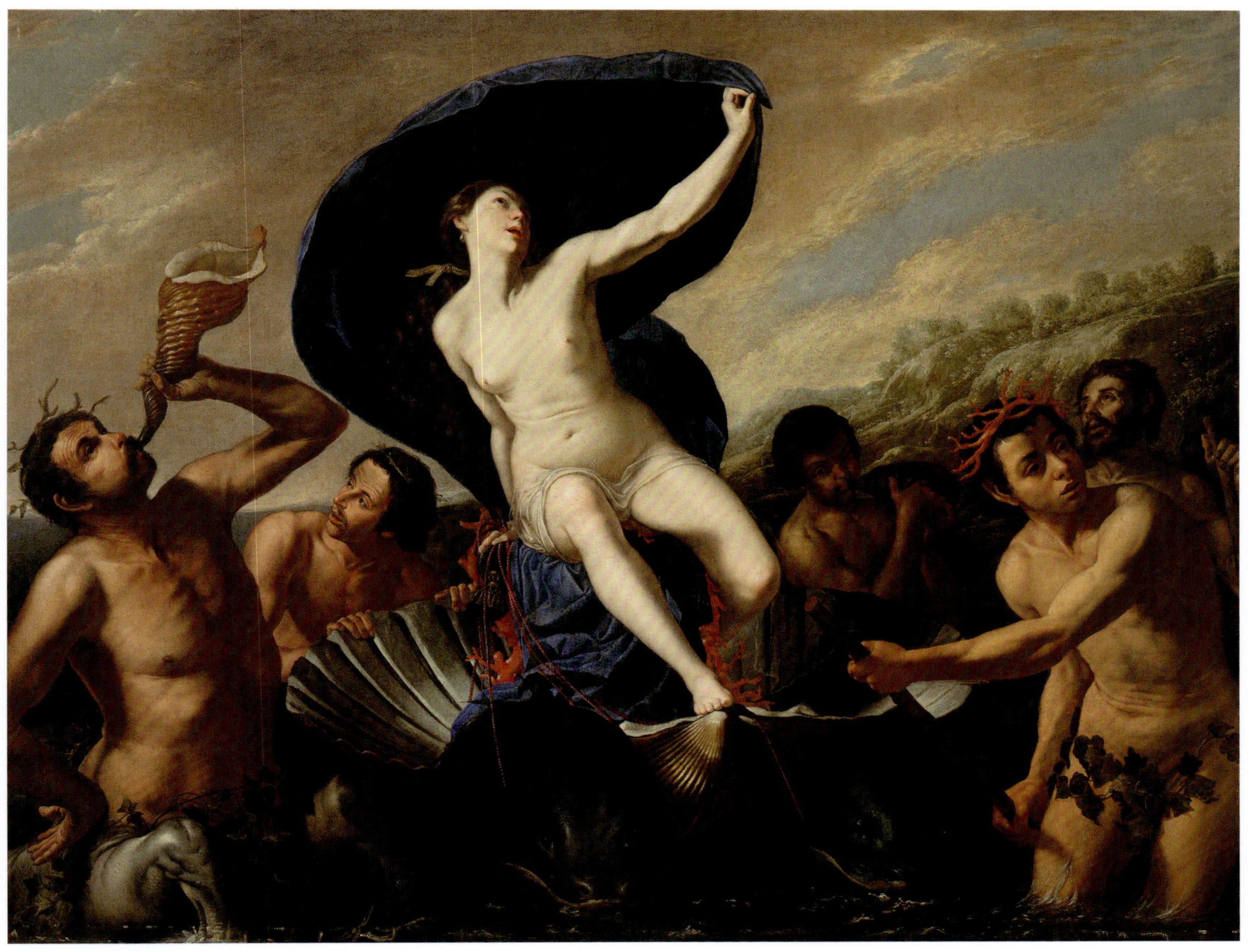

114 Attributed to Artemisia Gentileschi and Onofrio Palumbo, *The Triumph of Galatea*, c.1649–50, oil on canvas, 190 × 270 cm, Lucas Museum of Narrative Art, Los Angeles

Gentileschi herself. The only major qualification to this was that the painting was generally interpreted as an important example of the artist's collaboration with Onofrio Palumbo, a former pupil of Caracciolo, whose partnership with Gentileschi late in her career had also been recently confirmed, thanks to some new documentation published in 2005 (see below, pp. 218–21).[54] This was also the painting, incidentally, that was mentioned in the Introduction as having featured in the 2019 *Art Adorned* exhibition in advance of its sale at Christie's, New York, on 15 October 2020 and its subsequent acquisition by the Lucas Museum of Narrative Art in Los Angeles (pp. 2–5).

Commentators on the Lucas *Galatea* have argued in favour of identifying it as the work produced by Gentileschi for Ruffo.[55] This, however, cannot be the case. The inventory reference to Ruffo's *Galatea* describes it as 'Galatea seated atop a crab shell, drawn by two dolphins and accompanied by 5 tritons, measuring 8 × 10 [Messinese] palmi [about 206 × 258 cm].'[56] While the dimensions of this painting match quite well with the Ruffo inventory, the description does not. The Lucas Museum Galatea sits atop a giant scallop shell rather than the crab shell that is clearly described in the inventory. It is hard to imagine anyone confusing these two very dissimilar shell types, let alone a Baroque Sicilian surrounded on a daily basis by the sea's rich bounty. The Lucas Museum *Galatea* must, therefore, be yet another version of this evidently highly popular Gentileschian subject.

This leaves us with two possibilities. If the attribution to Gentileschi of the central figure in the Lucas *Galatea* can be sustained with reference to a greater consensus of scholars than at present, then the painting might be identifiable as another version of the subject painted by Gentileschi for another Neapolitan client, with Palumbo's unacknowledged assistance. Other, comparably large versions of *Galatea* by Gentileschi are listed, for example, in the inventories of Bernardino Belprato and Gennaro d'Andrea (table 3, pp. 262 and 263). If, on the other hand, the painting is ultimately judged to be by Palumbo's hand alone but following the direct model of Gentileschi's (still) lost prototype for Ruffo, then this painting would need to be reclassified, instead, as another example of an independent work produced by Gentileschi's assistants on the basis of her model.

The complex stylistic connections between these three paintings – one still lost and the two in American museums – confirms, in any event, the significant contemporary demand that existed for Gentileschi's compositions during her final years. There was a clear appetite among Neapolitan and southern Italian collectors of the early 1650s for 'Gentileschian' compositions that were directly based on her most popular works. This also helps to explain Gentileschi's significant impact on Neapolitan artists. In the same way that Gentileschi strengthened her Neapolitan credentials by introducing the contribution of local specialists, so, too, did her works themselves then become models for local painters to emulate.[57] Gentileschi's comprehensive integration into Neapolitan painting created a complex process of mutually enriching, cross-cultural fertilisation that benefited the works of both Gentileschi and her Neapolitan followers during this period.

THE PRICE OF TIME, I: THE 'NON-AUTOGRAPH' WORKSHOP CONTRIBUTION TO GENTILESCHI'S LATE NEAPOLITAN PAINTINGS AND THE DECLINING ECONOMIC VALUE OF HER FINAL WORKS

Gentileschi's letters to Ruffo of the late 1640s to early 1650s maintain the relentlessly upbeat tone that is a defining feature of her late correspondence. Reading them is to be brought powerfully into the presence of an indomitable spirit who would always prefer to look forwards, towards fresh professional possibilities, rather than to dwell on difficulties in the present, let alone those of the past. Nevertheless, the Ruffo correspondence does reveal the traces, as it were, of an increasing sense of strain seeping into Gentileschi's final years. This was evidently affecting her ability to function at the levels of quality and productivity that she achieved when unencumbered with anxieties.

In June 1649, for example, Gentileschi complained about a lack of job prospects, thereby implying that Ruffo should consider favouring her with more commissions. Such sentiments were readily understandable, given that Naples was still in the midst of its recovery from the catastrophic effects of the Revolt of Masaniello. And yet, in the same letter, she added somewhat contradictorily that Ruffo's nephew, Don Fabrizio Ruffo, had recently given her an order for three paintings, 'which is about all I need for now'. Complaints about her health feature more prominently in these letters than in the past. Gentileschi would turn sixty in 1653, and her forty-year career was evidently beginning to disturb her well-being. In September 1649, she admitted that the 'excessive heat and many illnesses' had delayed her work, to the extent that she was now compelled to 'try to keep well by working a little at a time'.[58] On New Year's Day 1651, she informed Ruffo that she 'spent this last Christmas in bed, as I was rather ill, and I am now still convalescing . . . as soon as I am able to paint again, you will be the first one to be served'.[59]

Gentileschi's ongoing financial concerns added an additional layer of stress to the preoccupations of these years. In March 1649, she had confessed to Ruffo that she had become 'bankrupt' as a result of having to provide a dowry for her daughter. On New Year's Day 1651, she returned to the theme by offering Ruffo two large paintings of *Perseus and Andromeda* and *Joseph and Potiphar's Wife* for the considerably reduced price of ninety scudi each. Gentileschi remarked that she had decided to discount these paintings out of a pressing need to receive money quickly, 'so that I can be treated', as she put it – so she could receive medical attention for which she could not otherwise afford to pay. Such were the special pleadings to which this internationally renowned artist was now reduced.[60]

Bissell considered these prices 'mean'. He described the tenor of these final letters as illustrating the extent to which Gentileschi had been 'pushed . . . into such straits that she had to endure cut rate fees, which in turn obviously exacerbated the situation'.[61] He would, no doubt, have considered yet more demeaning the prices cited in two subsequently published payments of 1651 and 1653. In the first, Gentileschi received 150 ducats for a series of three very large paintings of *Diana and Actaeon*, *Venus and Adonis* and 'another measuring 9 palmi [about 237 cm] of a nude figure with its accompaniment [that is, other figure/s]'.[62] In the second payment, Gentileschi was paid fifty ducats for another painting of *Susanna*. Fifty ducats represents a significantly reduced price in relation to the high-water mark of the two hundred ducats apiece that Gentileschi had received in 1636 from Von Liechtenstein for her otherwise directly comparable paintings of *Bathsheba*, *Lucretia* and *Susanna*.

Alongside these indications of a decline in the economic value of Gentileschi's last works is a certain unevenness in their execution. The precise chronology of Gentileschi's final years remains to be clarified. On the one hand, it encapsulates such consistently recognised works as *Bathsheba at her Bath* and *Tarquin and Lucretia*, both today in Potsdam (figs 115 and 116).[63] These two paintings are generally dated to the late 1640s and were almost certainly produced as part of a set of three for the Farnese of Parma. They are of exceptional quality, a point that has become more evident as a result of a recent cleaning. As I have argued elsewhere, the *Tarquin*, in particular, stands out as a summation of Gentileschi's late, internationalist style.[64] It deploys a complex array of influences and includes references to Titian, the greatest of all court painters, as well as to Giambologna's *Rape of the Sabine Women*, whose popularity was international. The result is a tour-de-force demonstration of Gentileschi's conception of a new form of cosmopolitan courtly painting. Both the *Tarquin* and the *Bathsheba* vividly document her late stylistic concern to project the figures emphatically out of their backgrounds as brightly coloured and almost statuesque presences. At the same time, they manifest an elegantly attenuated, aristocratic demeanour that seems worlds removed from the relatively raw and unconstrained realism of her early works. Judith Mann identifies the Potsdam paintings as among the 'masterworks' of Gentileschi's late career, while Bissell characterises the *Tarquin* as 'as great a tour de force of painting as Gentileschi ever achieved'.[65] To this can be added Contini's evocative appreciation of the *Tarquin* as 'a death's dance between the abundance of petrified fabrics, heedless of the force of gravity, and Neoclassical Davidian frowns: Orazio's language, thawed and seasoned with the spices and warm powders from another world'.[66]

The critical response to some of Gentileschi's other paintings from the same period, however, has not been so positive. A signed and dated *Susanna and the Elders* of 1649 has been described by Bissell as 'expressively artificial', by Contini as 'not particularly appealing' and by Mann as representing 'another Artemisia, one that comes closer to the designation "hack" than many of us who champion her work are comfortable admitting' (fig. 117).[67] To be fair, this painting is in such a compromised state of preservation as to render any judgement necessarily provisional. Yet the problems of execution to which these responses refer go beyond the work's surface to encompass the repetitive nature of its underlying composition. The *Susanna* struggles to impress as anything other than a rather unimaginative rehash of Gentileschi's earlier treatments of the subject. It has been characterised by Mann as 'reflect[ing] the somewhat uninspired regurgitation of a format and figure that Artemisia had already used several times before, one that patrons may have come to expect from her'.

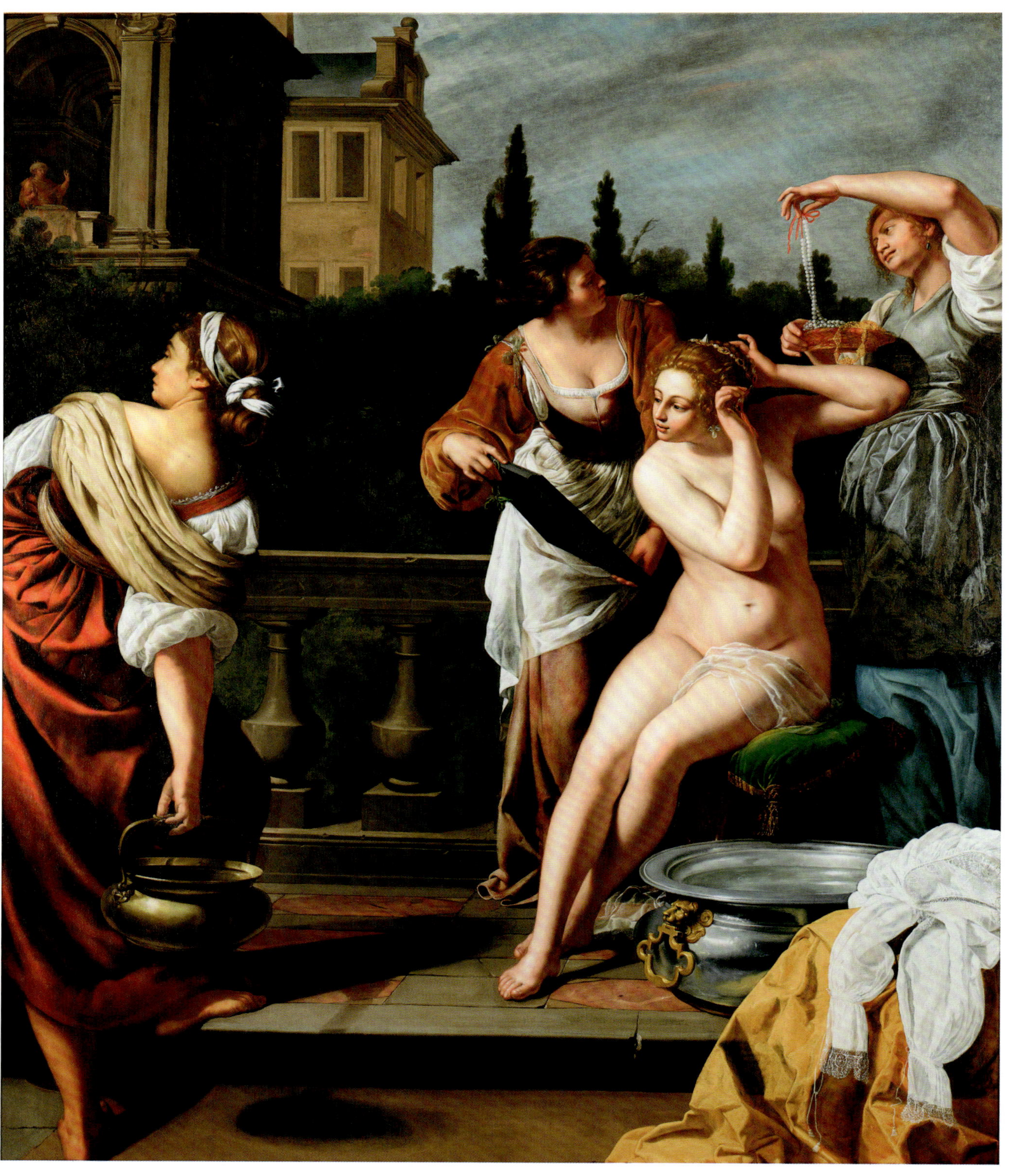

115 Artemisia Gentileschi, *Bathsheba at her Bath*, *c.*late 1640s, oil on canvas, 261 × 223 cm, Stiftung Preussische Schlösser und Gärten, Berlin-Brandenburg, inv. GKI 5392

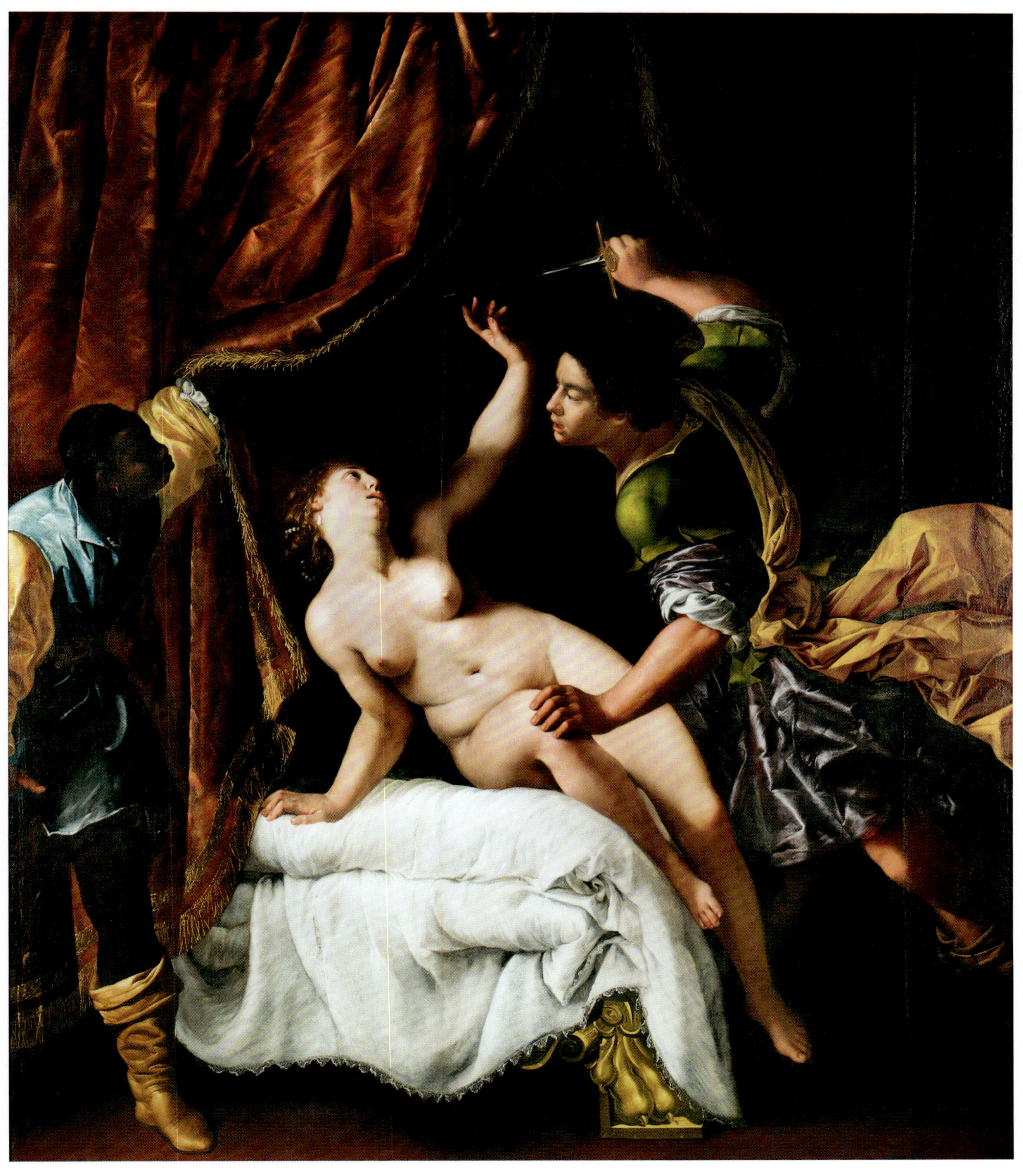

116 Artemisia Gentileschi, *Tarquin and Lucretia*, *c.* late 1640s, oil on canvas, 259 × 218 cm, Stiftung Preussische Schlösser und Gärten, Berlin-Brandenburg, inv. GKI 5389

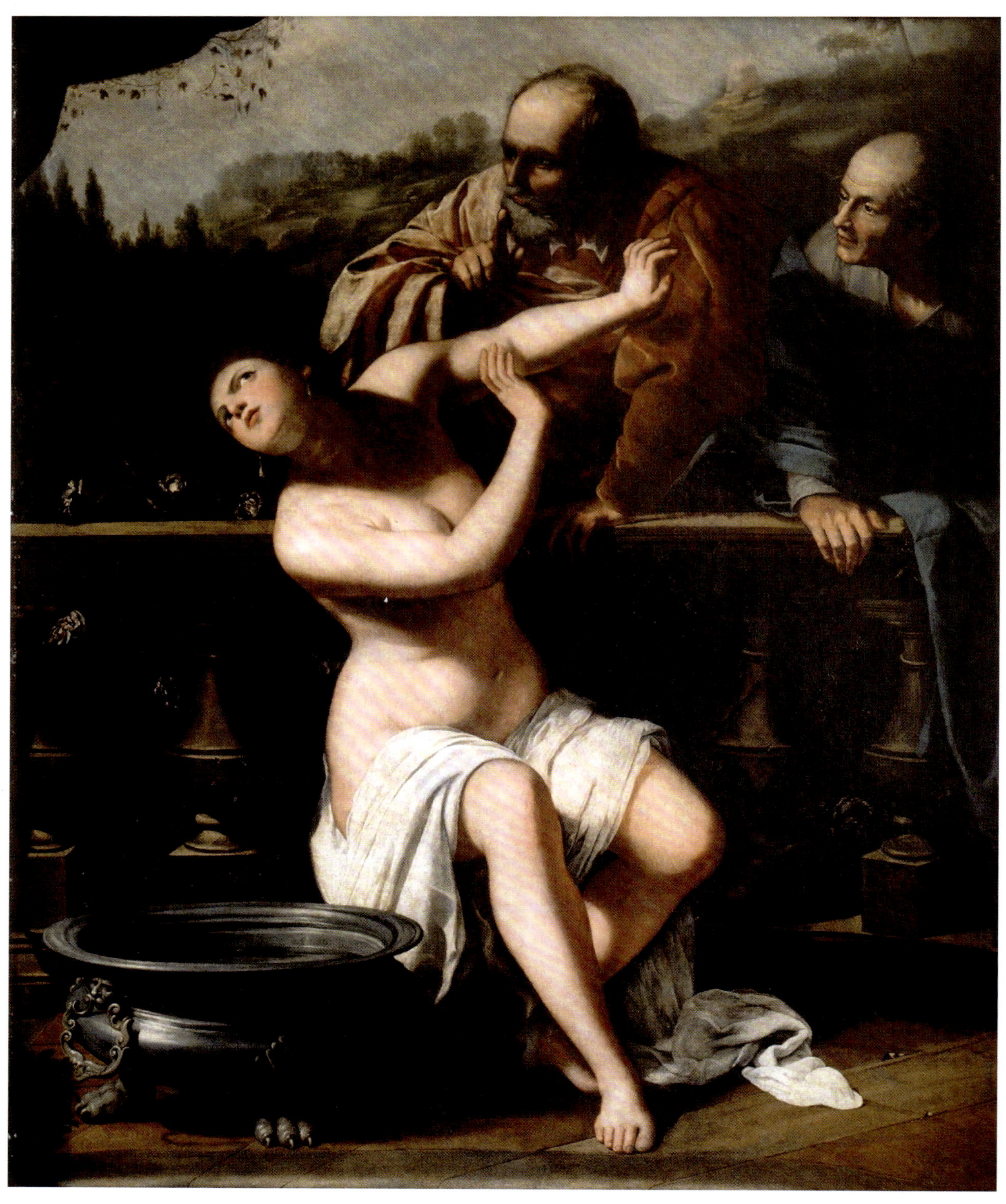

117 Artemisia Gentileschi, *Susanna and the Elders*, signed and dated 1649, oil on canvas, 206 × 167.5 cm, Moravská Galerie v Brne, Brno, inv. M246

The most common means of accounting for this drop in quality in some, at least, of Gentileschi's final Neapolitan paintings has been to assert her increased reliance on non-autograph workshop assistance.[68]

All of this points to the difficulties experienced by Gentileschi during her last years of activity. These difficulties should be easy enough to appreciate, given the inevitable challenges involved in the universal struggle to maintain momentum and professional relevance during the so-called 'third age' of an individual's career. The tendency to view an artist's late career as an almost inevitable period of decline is a topos that goes back to Vasari and beyond. Ultimately, it reflects the biological model of history that views progress in terms of its relationship to the universal life cycle of birth, youth, maturity, old age and death, followed by renewal.[69] The continued high quality of and high level of recognition afforded to Gentileschi's late output mean that we need to remain on guard against manifesting any subconscious prejudice against her last works. Nevertheless, it is clear that she grappled with major challenges during these years. There can be no doubting the increased pressures that come with age. An artist's sense of forward momentum will be unavoidably constrained by a sense of increasing competition from emerging artists and younger colleagues. So, too, will an artist at this stage of their life be almost inevitably preoccupied with the continued difficulties involved in remaining relevant in the face of a constantly changing artistic landscape.

These processes carry all before them and do not differentiate between rank or gender. In 1652, for example, Gentileschi produced her last dated painting; it was also the year of Ribera's death, aged sixty-one. This former titan of the Neapolitan art world had been progressively slowed down by his own health concerns. Nicola Spinosa has hypothetically diagnosed the debilitating illness that affected Ribera's output from the 1640s onwards as arterial hypertension with cerebral reflexions.[70] By 1651, it had brought Ribera close to bankruptcy and reduced him to writing begging letters to his long-standing patrons at the Certosa di San Martino, entreating them to send him more money so that he could complete one of his final, long-overdue works:

> While I was waiting yesterday for some relief worthy of the hand of Your Most Reverend Father, the father came bringing with him the Father Vicar's assessment of fifty ducats without which I cannot and never could conceive of a plan for the care of the household. Would to God that I did not have these anxieties. It would give me great pleasure to receive the whole sum at once. The work nevertheless progresses. Begging Your Most Reverend Father to favour me by giving the order this month to pay some other sum of money and so for this effect my son will come to visit you to pay his respects. I conclude by kissing your hands.[71]

In Gentileschi's case, her worries about health and well-being were real enough. Yet unlike Ribera's, it seems, her situation during these years was not all negative. Other factors point to a more positive and proactive continuation of her professional recognition and even to certain points of renewal at this late date. They also attest to Gentileschi's continued resilience and resourcefulness in the face of the ultimate challenge of the mounting disappointments and narrowing of horizons that inevitably accompany the final stages of one's professional activities.

In the first instance, it needs to be recognised that Gentileschi's final prices were not as demeaning as Bissell and others have suggested. Rates of between fifty and ninety ducats apiece for large paintings would not have been considered in their own time as necessarily humiliating and unexpected for a painter of Gentileschi's status. This is particularly so when they are assessed from a Neapolitan perspective rather than from the elevated heights of the Renis or Guercinos of the day. They need to be considered not so much from the extravagant prices paid to the high-flying artists active in other cities as in relation to the more hardscrabble realities of the mid-seventeenth-century Neapolitan art world. An apt point of comparison in this respect are the payments received by Andrea Vaccaro (1604–1670) during the same period. Although little known today outside specialist circles, Vaccaro was one of the foremost Neapolitan painters of the 1630s to 1660s.[72] Following initial periods spent working in the idiom of the early

Neapolitan Caravaggesque painters, Vaccaro went on to develop a highly successful, eclectic style that drew on a range of influences from Ribera, on the one hand, to Reni and Van Dyck, on the other. He was also attentive to the work of Stanzione and his circle, including Gentileschi herself, whose style and favoured subject matter he was adept at drawing upon when the need arose (fig. 118).[73]

Vaccaro's prices parallel Gentileschi's in many ways. Like Gentileschi, he was able to attract some of the highest payments of the day. In 1643, for example, he received 280 ducats for a private commission for an apparently particularly lavish and large-scale *Story of Abigail*.[74] At the same time, he was willing to accept considerably lower amounts on other occasions, particularly when working for private patrons. Thus, in 1655, he accepted 150 ducats for two large paintings, including a *Lot and his Daughters* that would have been directly comparable with Gentileschi's paintings of the same subject.[75] In 1659, he likewise received forty ducats as the total price for a privately commissioned altarpiece for a regional church in the coastal town of Vico Equense, a payment that brings to mind Gentileschi's fifty-ducat contract of 1630 for an altarpiece of St Elisabeth in Pisticci.[76] Finally, in 1660, he received 180 ducats for three paintings, *The Nativity*, *The Sacrifice of Isaac* and 'another scene from the Old Testament'. This sounds reminiscent – albeit in a more decorously religious context – of Gentileschi's 1651 payment of 150 ducats for three paintings of *Diana and Actaeon*, *Venus and Adonis* and 'a nude figure with its accompaniment'.[77] Such was the reality of the reduced yet still irrepressible Neapolitan art world of the day – particularly during the especially difficult period stretching from the time of the 1647–48 Revolt of Masaniello to the Plague of Naples of 1656 and its immediate aftermath.

118 Andrea Vaccaro, *St Mary Magdalene*, signed with monogram, c.1635–45, oil on canvas, 130 × 101 cm, Museo Nazionale di San Martino, Naples

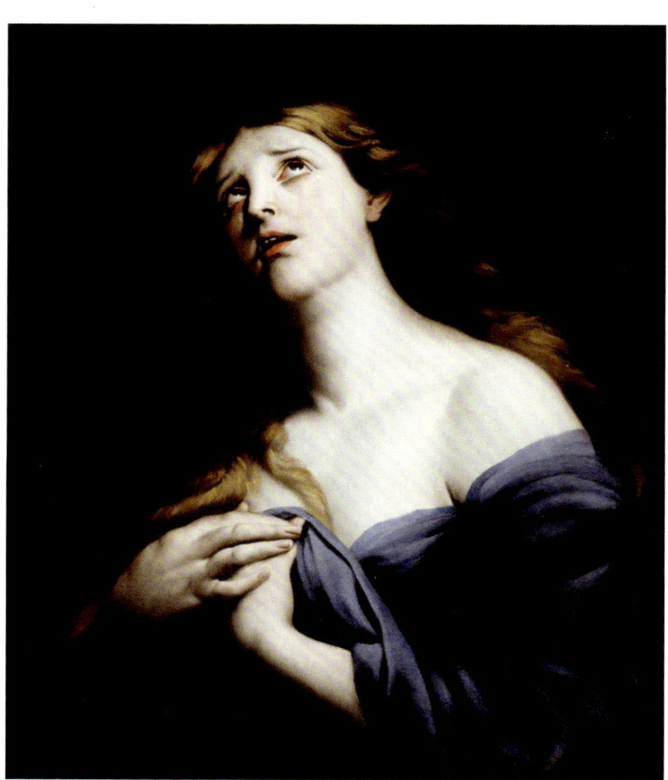

THE PRICE OF TIME, II: THE 1650S PARTNERSHIP BETWEEN GENTILESCHI AND ONOFRIO PALUMBO

Another noteworthy business strategy dating to Gentileschi's final years appears to have grown out of her attempts to counteract her concerns about her health and well-being by focusing on strengthening the quality and productivity of her workshop. Her solution to the problem seems to have centred upon the figure of Onofrio Palumbo, a talented but somewhat struggling artist whom she appears either to have brought into her workshop or to have given a more senior and prominent role than he had hitherto occupied. Palumbo's position within Gentileschi's late workshop was defined rather differently from that of a traditional assistant. He seems to have acted as a business overseer or foreman, assisting Gentileschi to complete commissions that she might not otherwise have been able to finish on her own.

Following a period spent studying under the Neapolitan Caravaggesque painter Giovanni Battista Caracciolo, Palumbo gravitated towards the circle of Stanzione during the late 1630s and from there to Gentileschi.[78] He is documented receiving independent commissions for altarpieces in 1640–41 and again in 1650.[79] In 1652, he produced one of the great statements of Neapolitan Baroque devotion, the *St Januarius* constitutes a collaborative workshop production that is directly comparable, in this sense, to some of Gentileschi's Neapolitan paintings of the late 1630s for which she employed Viviano Codazzi to contribute the architectural detailing. By the early 1650s, therefore, Palumbo was working at a level that was far

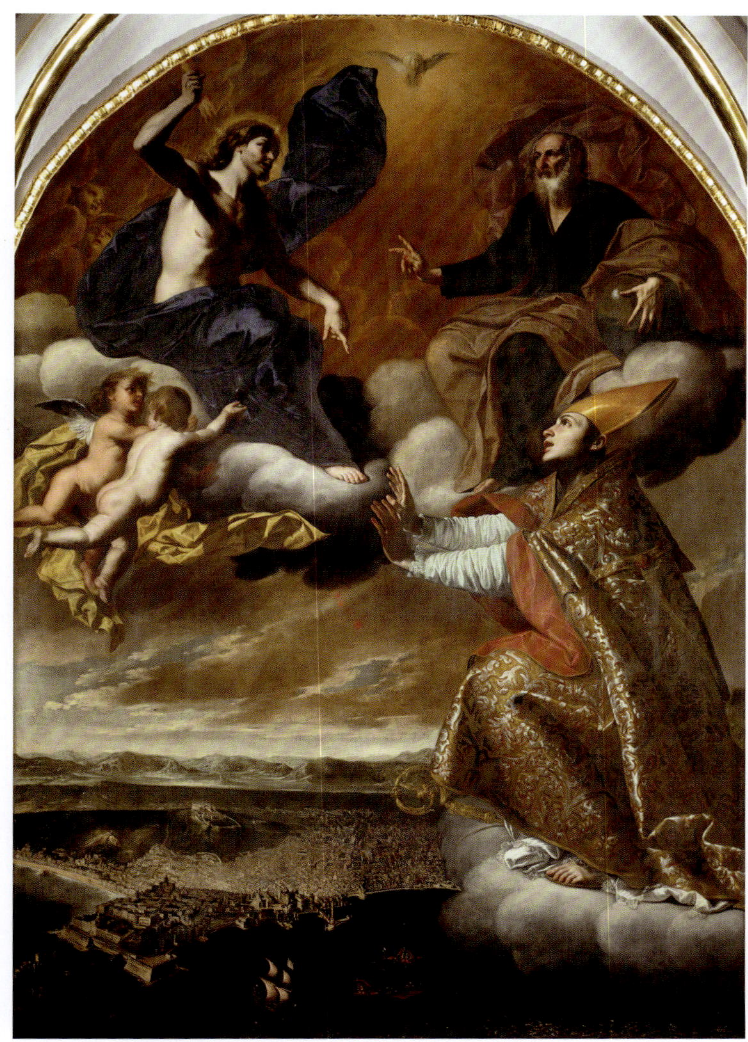

119 Onofrio Palumbo and Didier Barra, *St Januarius Interceding with the Trinity on behalf of the City of Naples*, c.1652, oil on canvas, 331 × 220 cm, Arciconfraternita della Trinità dei Pellegrini, Naples

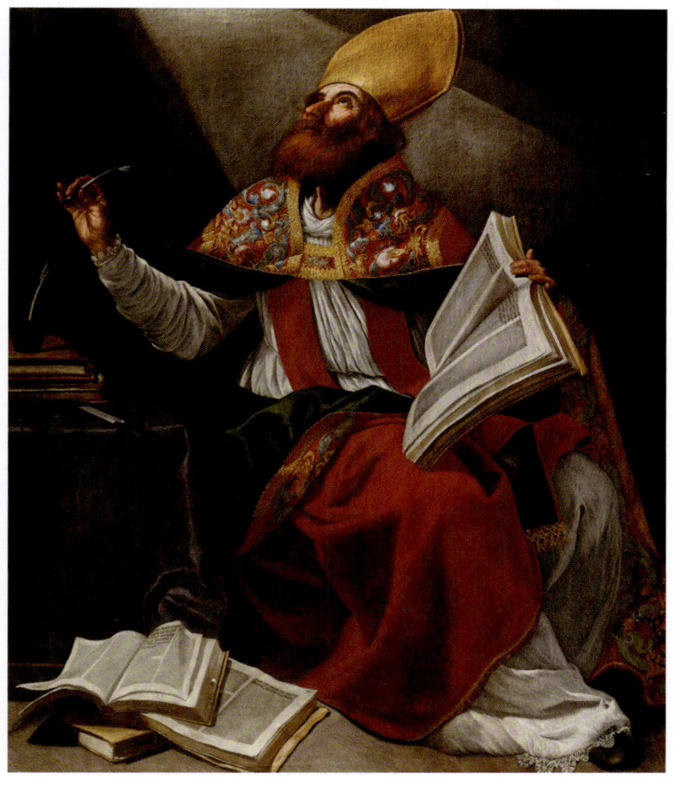

120 Onofrio Palumbo, *St Ambrose*, signed and dated 1635, oil on canvas, 150 × 124 cm, Galerie G. Sarti, Paris

Interceding with the Trinity on behalf of the City of Naples (fig. 119). This major altarpiece, produced for one of the many lay charitable institutions in Naples, shows him to have been capable of the heights of Ribera, Stanzione and Gentileschi herself when called upon to produce his most ambitious work. The painting also documents Palumbo's collaboration with the Neapolitan architectural view painter Didier Barra, who produced the detailed, map-like rendition of the city of Naples viewed from high in the sky.[80] The *St Januarius Interceding with the Trinity*

above that of a junior assistant. He had been maintaining an independent career for many years with his own workshop, involving all the professional concerns that such an undertaking would have involved. He even agreed in 1651 to take on an apprentice, whom he undertook to provide lodging for and to train for the space of five years.[81]

Yet, during these same years, this second-tier, mid-career, independent Neapolitan master also undertook to work as a kind of business partner to Gentileschi. The documents attesting to this activity were first published in 2005 by Giuseppe de Vito, Riccardo Lattuada and Eduardo Nappi. They particularly revolve around two payments dating to 1653 and 1654.[82] In the first, dated 3 January 1653, Gentileschi received a payment of fifty ducats from a certain Antonio Galise. These were said to be 'for the price of a painting of the *History of Susanna* sold by her hand'.[83] Having received the payment, Gentileschi then immediately transferred the full amount to Palumbo, a practice that is generally understood as referring to instances whereby a senior artist pays a junior assistant for subordinate work on a commission.[84]

Given that it dates to the beginning of 1653, this payment has also been tentatively associated, in turn, with a version of *Susanna and the Elders*, signed by Gentileschi and dated 1652, that was discovered in 2004 by Adelina Modesti in the deposits of the Pinacoteca Nazionale, Bologna (fig. 121).[85] Palumbo's hand has been identified as being particularly evident, once again, in the figures of the male elders in this painting. These figures share a distinctive physiognomy with that of the tritons in the Lucas Museum *Galatea* (fig. 114). The same stylistic mannerisms are also present in the male figures in Palumbo's independently produced paintings of the same period (fig. 120).[86]

The wording of the 1653 document is unusual and warrants further explanation. It records Galise's paying Gentileschi a lump sum of fifty ducats, a payment that is described as 'for the price of' the *Susanna*, rather than on account for the work ('per prezzo di', as opposed to 'in conto di', the latter being the standard wording for commissions). This suggests that the *Susanna* had been previously produced by Gentileschi and Palumbo on a speculative basis for sale on the open market.[87] This seems to have been a common practice for Gentileschi. In 1637, she had independently produced paintings of *Christ and the Woman of Samaria at the Well* and *John the Baptist*, which she had then attempted to 'gift' to the Barberini in Rome. Similarly, in 1651, she had sought to interest Ruffo in two independently produced versions of *Perseus and Andromeda* and *Joseph and Potiphar's Wife*. In this example, the painting's purchaser, Antonio Galise, was apparently operating as a walk-in customer rather than as a more traditionally defined patron. He had presumably seen the *Susanna* for sale in Gentileschi's workshop and had decided to pay the fifty ducats up front, in order to take the work 'off the shelf' from the selection of wares on display.[88]

The second document is dated 31 January 1654 and is the last dated reference for Gentileschi's life. In it, the agent Fabio Gentile pays Palumbo an on-account payment of ten ducats to go towards the cost of three paintings:

> To Fabio Gentile 10 ducats and on his behalf to Onofrio Palumbo to make up 39 ducats for three paintings which he will have to paint jointly with Artemisia Gentileschi, according to the quality and worth [that will] comply with the obligation made by the above said Artemisia with the Bank of the Monte della Pieta. And the said Onofrio will have to finish and consign the said paintings within the term of one and a half months from the 30th of the present [month].[89]

That Palumbo rather than Gentileschi was receiving the money for what was, in effect, a jointly produced private commission is extremely unusual. Palumbo was evidently being given co-responsibility for completing a commission that had been otherwise assigned to Gentileschi. Clearly, he was operating with a degree of responsibility and seniority that went far beyond that traditionally assigned to an assistant working under the aegis of a senior and experienced master painter. The document goes further in specifying the complementary roles and responsibilities for each of the two artists involved. On the one hand, even though Palumbo was being paid directly for the work, the agent making the payment still recognised Gentileschi as having oversight for the commission's legal and artistic requirements. Thus, the document stresses that the paintings should conform to the quality and excellence of an obligation that Gentileschi had made independently and for which she, rather than Palumbo, was personally responsible.

Palumbo was allocated the role of receiving the payments and of managing and completing the commission. The document identifies him as the individual liable for ensuring that the paintings were finished and delivered to the client within a month and a half of the payment. Palumbo seems, therefore, to have been operating as Gentileschi's partner or workshop manager. Gentileschi was still being recognised as the workshop's creative head, but Palumbo was assigned the equally significant role of workshop overseer, responsible for assisting her with production (even to the extent of working with her 'jointly' on the work). He was also entrusted with oversight of the project's financial and logistical aspects.

What did Palumbo gain from a partnership of this kind? In the first instance, it needs to be underlined that, for all the ongoing issues and constraints of Gentileschi's final years, she was still a highly renowned artist with a significant international clientele that far exceeded anything Palumbo might have been able to generate under his own steam. Proof of Gentileschi's continued drawing power in this respect comes in another document of 1651 which records an earlier commission negotiated also by the agent Fabio Gentile. In this document, Gentile made a down payment of forty-eight ducats towards a total price of 150 ducats that was said to be for three large mythological paintings by Gentileschi. These were to be painted for the obviously foreign patron 'Sua Maestà Cesarea dell'Imperatore'. This has been interpreted as a reference to the Holy Roman Emperor, Ferdinand III (1608–1657).[90] In 1630, Gentileschi had excused herself from being able to complete a painting for Cassiano dal Pozzo on the grounds that she was too busy working for the Spanish Infanta, Maria Anna of Spain. The Infanta was then in Naples, en route to Vienna to meet her promised spouse, at that stage the King of Hungary and Bohemia but who was to become the Holy Roman Emperor, Ferdinand III.[91] So Gentileschi's patron of 1651 was the husband of her exalted female patron back in 1630. Her international networks of high-ranking princely patrons were still effective decades later. So, too, was her recourse to sending 'gifts' to her intended international patrons in the hope of receiving something more tangible by way of recompense. In this respect, the 1651 document pointedly mentions that, while Gentileschi may hope to receive a gift for her work once it was delivered, so far as the agent, Gentile, was concerned, 150 ducats was the agreed full cost for the paintings, and he was not liable for any further payments.

CONCLUSION: THE 1652 *SUSANNA AND THE ELDERS*, GENTILESCHI'S DEATH AND THE BEGINNINGS OF HER POSTHUMOUS REDISCOVERY

The results of the mutually beneficial partnership between Gentileschi and Palumbo can be seen most clearly in the signed and dated *Susanna and the Elders* of 1652 (fig. 121). This painting, the final documented work of Gentileschi's career, is a fitting subject with which to conclude this analysis of Gentileschi's business considerations. In one sense, it maintains a clear and direct link back to her earliest documented work, the 1610 *Susanna and the Elders* produced under her father's aegis more than forty years earlier (fig. 13). And yet the 1652 canvas is much more than a mere 'uninspired regurgitation' of the 1610 composition – to borrow the above-cited criticism of the 1649 *Susanna*. The 1652 *Susanna* manifests an artistic sensibility that is entirely distinct from that of the 1610 *Susanna*. Gone is the coiled compression and earthy realism of the earlier composition; in its place is a more rhythmically developed and classically balanced arrangement of elements that exchanges the emphasis on the dominating forms of the elders for a greater focus on the complex contrapposto of the figure of Susanna herself.

Gentileschi's final Susanna maintains a carefully counterbalanced poise and elegance of form that once again enhance the sculptural qualities of the artist's late style. Roberto Contini's observation that this figure recalls the pose of the second-century C.E. *Falling Galatian* sculpture in the Grimani collection in Venice seems especially apposite in this respect.[92] The tour-de-force rendition of Susanna's drapery, moreover, further strengthens its associations with antique sculpture. Unlike the 1610 Susanna, this Susanna's nakedness has been partially covered by a soft, clinging fabric that envelops her with all the form-accentuating qualities of a Greek chiton. The differences between the gestures of the two Susannas are likewise revealing. The 1652 Susanna repudiates the two elders with a much more forthright gesture than her 1610 counterpart. She is a more convincingly assertive – even confident – protagonist than the harrowingly abject and exposed figure of the 1610 Susanna, who elicits, by contrast, a much greater

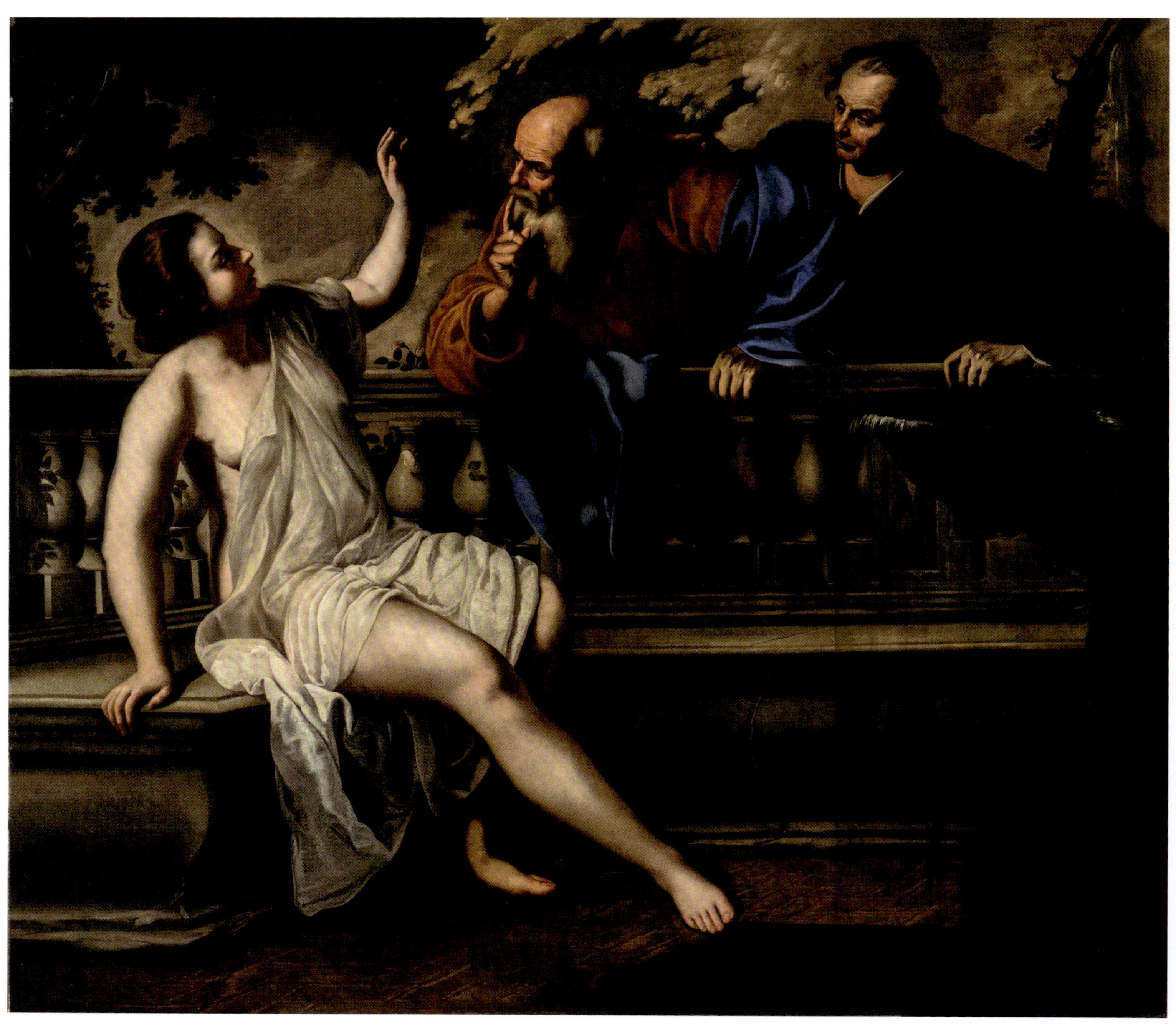

121 Artemisia Gentileschi, *Susanna and the Elders*, signed and dated 1652, oil on canvas, 200.3 × 225.6 cm, Pinacoteca Nazionale di Bologna, Polo Museale dell'Emilia Romagna, inv. 6320

sense of being physically threatened by the elders than does her older sister.

One cannot but feel that Gentileschi would have regarded the increased level of poise and assuredness in this and her other last works as a source of pride – even as a vindication of her continued relevance and success after so many years. The Gentileschi of the 1650s remained a highly sought-after artist with an international reputation and clientele. She was, moreover, still managing to operate at the upper echelons of a demanding art world some forty years after her initial successes in Rome and Florence. The art that she was producing during this ultimate phase of her artistic evolution may not have been recognisably Caravaggesque in any direct sense of the term, but one can only imagine that Gentileschi and her clients would have viewed this stage of her development as testimony to her powers of adaptation and relevance rather than as something to disparage (noting again, here, the common bias in the modern literature in favour of the earlier, Caravaggesque works). By the 1650s, the raw Caravaggism that had so inspired artists and collectors in the opening decades of the century was regarded as a distinctly antiquated, 'heritage' style. It had been superseded by multiple waves of more fashionably ascendant trends. A significant dimension of Gentileschi's achievement during these years, therefore, is her ability to adapt and revise her oeuvre in a manner that enabled her to transform her initial Caravaggesque legacy into a continuously bankable asset that remained relevant and in demand for decades on end.

Time was, nonetheless, running out for this talented and tenacious artist. In the absence of any further documentary evidence, it seems that Gentileschi died within a few years of her last *Susanna*, probably either immediately before or during the plague of 1656. The evidence suggests that she may have been buried in the Neapolitan national church of the Florentine community, San Giovanni dei Fiorentini, since early commentators claim to have seen a tomb slab there inscribed with the simple epitaph 'HEIC ARTEMISIA' ('Here lies Artemisia'). The slab is now gone, a victim first of the church's modernisation in the 1780s and then of its demolition in the 1950s.[93] If the account of her tomb is true, then this would indicate that Gentileschi was accorded in death a certain level of official commemoration by the expatriate Florentine community. It also provides further documentation of the growing tendency to use Gentileschi's first name as an instantly recognisable trademark for her persona, something that would become increasingly evident in the years following her death.

For its part, the 1652 *Susanna* somehow made its way to Florence, where it is next documented hanging in the Palazzo Medici Riccardi in the middle of the eighteenth century. At that stage owned by a cadet branch of the Medici family, the painting would help seed the beginnings of an early critical rediscovery of Gentileschi's work following a period of relative oblivion in the late seventeenth and early eighteenth centuries. The *Susanna* would find itself glowingly referred to in no fewer than three critical commentaries that were all published in the same year of 1792. Luigi Lanzi's *Storia pittorica dell'Italia* would approvingly note the 'grazia' of Gentileschi's rendition of Susanna, while Alessandro da Morrona would similarly opine that 'the Hebrew woman enjoys the gift of expressivity and a lovely demeanour. The vestment covers her with elusive pleats, and on her breast it drapes with such art, that an understanding of the nude soon appears.'[94] So, too, would the painting's owner, Averardo de' Medici, observe of this same figure that 'she is painted with mastery, delicacy and impasto quality of colouring that one could touch, I dare say, the softness of the lovely flesh with one's own hand'.[95] This early critical consensus would soon grow and even extend itself to an appreciation of the earlier works on which Gentileschi's more contemporary reputation rests. Yet this task would require the endorsement of more recent generations of keepers of the sacred flame of Gentileschi's posthumous reputation: a process of continuously evolving critical re-evaluation and re-invention, to which we shall now turn.

PAGE 225 Attributed to Artemisia Gentileschi and Onofrio Palumbo, *The Triumph of Galatea* (detail of fig. 114)

— PART V —

Resurrecting Artemisia

C.1656–THE PRESENT

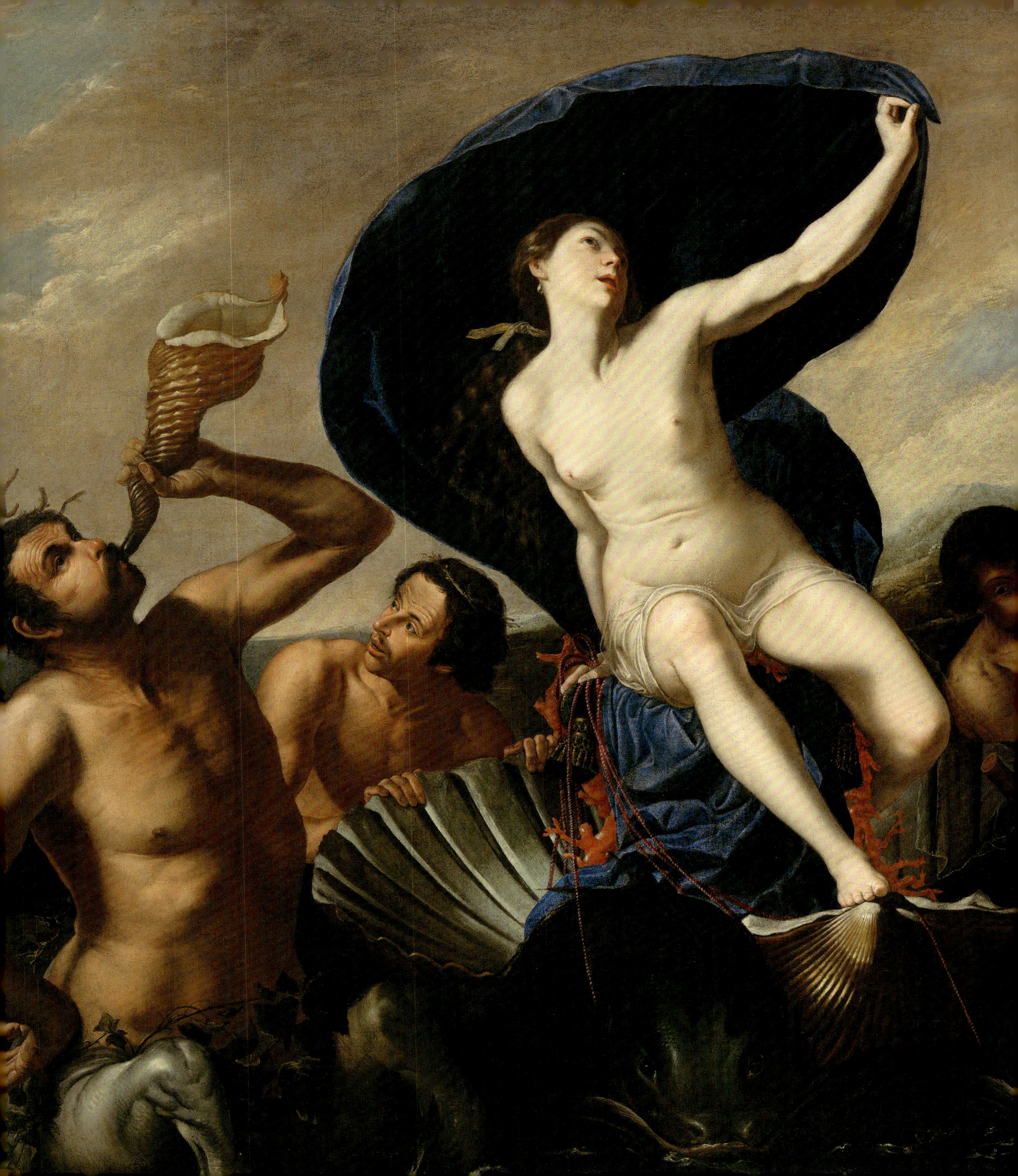

13

A Star Is Born

THE AFTERLIFE OF A 'GREAT GENIUS'

INTRODUCTION
HORROR AND DELIGHT IN THE UFFIZI

It is 2 p.m., and the conga line of visitors snaking through the final rooms of the Uffizi in Florence is beginning to flag. Having queued to pay admission before making their way up two giant flights of stairs and then down three long corridors and across forty-five galleries, they now discover that there is, in addition, a lower floor of paintings to traverse. Circulation is limited to one direction in the Uffizi. So, the museum's visitors discover also that they will have to negotiate another three corridors and dozens of additional galleries before they can reach the staircase leading to the exit via the gift shop.

Such is the dominance of the Renaissance in modern-day Florence that the Uffizi's sequencing of its magnificent Baroque collections does not occur until the very last sector of this arduous itinerary. Here, presumably in recognition of the difficulties involved in halting foot traffic at such a late stage of the visit, a concerted effort has been made to arrest the fleeing crowds. A small display of dramatic canvases devoted to knife-wielding death has been strategically placed outside the entrance to one of the final galleries (fig. 122). Caravaggio's *Sacrifice of Isaac* is given pride of place in the display, a prioritisation made especially obvious by the Uffizi's design feature of signposting its 'absolute masterpieces' by inserting giant frames into the partition walls surrounding them. It is flanked

FACING PAGE Artemisia Gentileschi, *Susanna and the Elders* (detail of fig. 121)

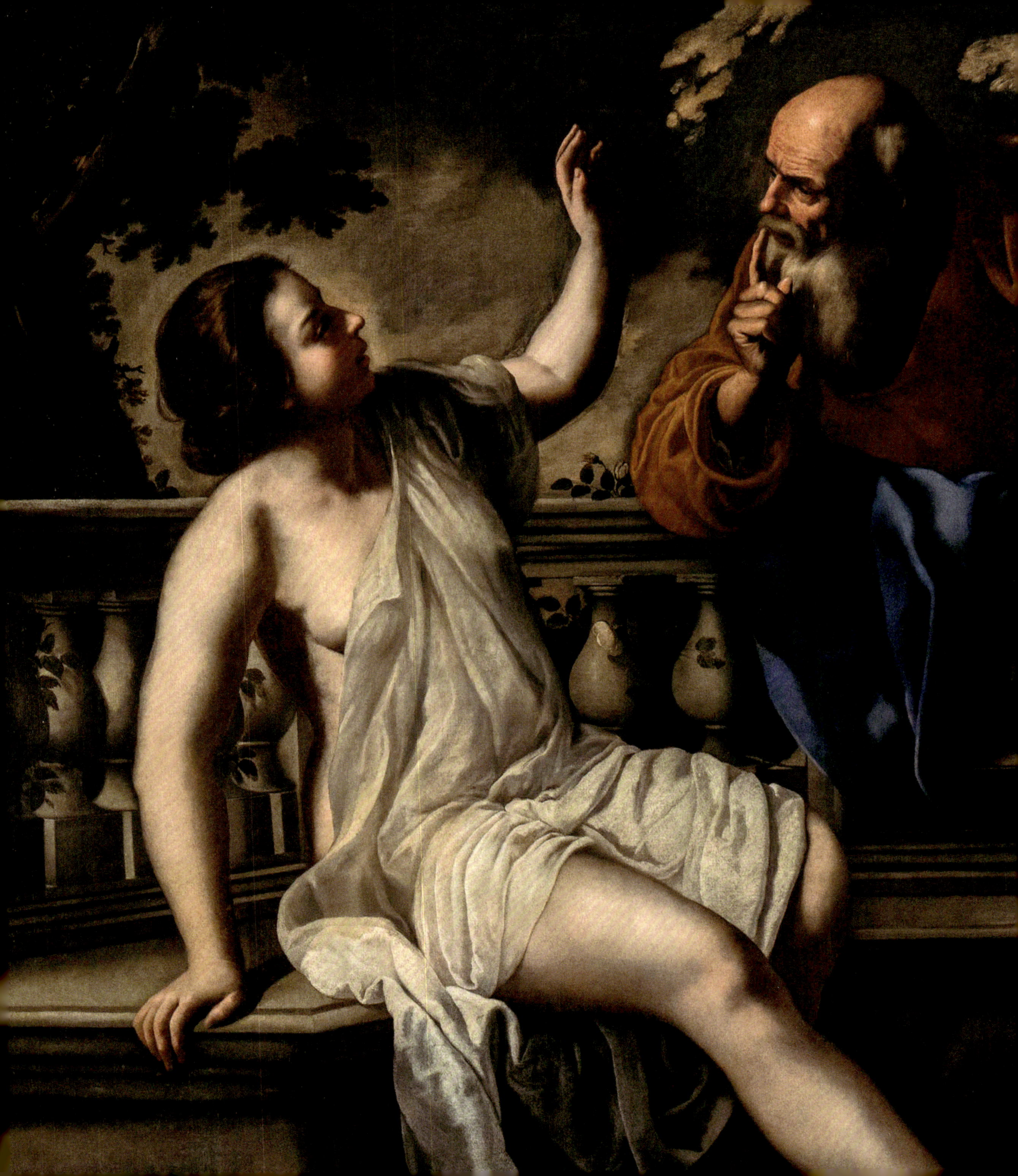

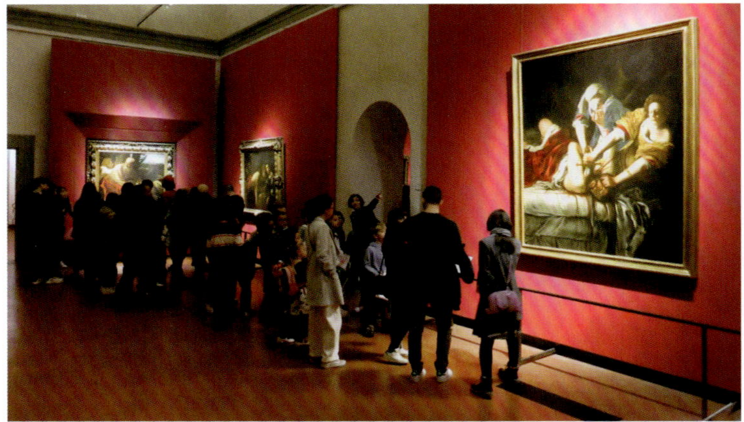

122 Exhibition view, permanent collection display, Gallery 91, Galleria degli Uffizi, Florence

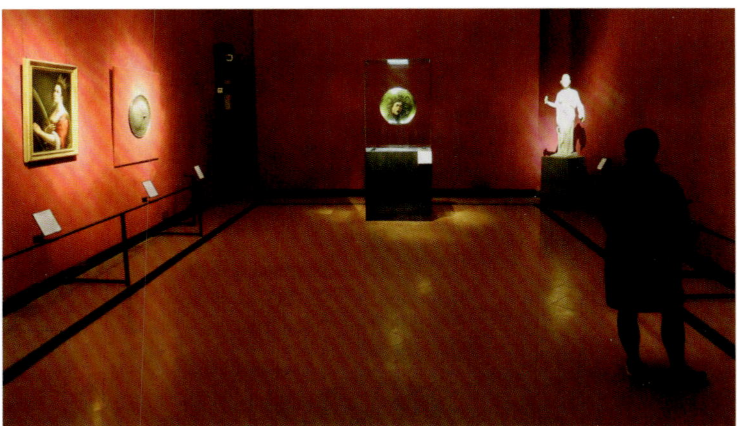

123 Exhibition view, permanent collection display, Gallery 96, Galleria degli Uffizi, Florence

by two darkly dramatic Baroque canvases: Caracciolo's *Salome with the Head of the Baptist* and Gentileschi's *Judith Slaying Holofernes* (fig. 56), both produced during the artists' respective visits to the city (see pp. 64 and 97).[1]

The gallery within highlights the dramatic impact of another Baroque tour de force of theatrical decapitation (fig. 123). Here Caravaggio's *Medusa* shield forms the centrepiece of a work-in-focus exhibition. The gallery has been arranged according to a thematic approach that is not otherwise encountered in the Uffizi's predominantly chronological and regional arrangement of its permanent collections. So, the *Medusa* sits within a small gallery surrounded by a miscellany of arms and armour, statuary and images of severed heads, disguised self-portraits, magic and the grotesque. The curators have also found space to include another of Gentileschi's key Florentine works, the *St Catherine of Alexandria* (fig. 36).

Artemisia might not be the star of this display, but the curators have, nonetheless, assigned her a dramatically prominent and arguably scene-stealing supporting role to that of Caravaggio. Yet it was not always so. Her works were left to languish in obscurity for many decades following her death. An indicative reference occurs in Marco Lastri's *Etruria pittrice* (1791–95), an important early attempt to compile a chronological overview of Tuscan painting.[2] Lastri writes positively about Gentileschi's talent, providing an important indication of the extent to which the artist's reputation was never entirely extinguished during this period. Nevertheless, the author is clear as to why Gentileschi's signature work, the Uffizi *Judith Slaying Holofernes*, had been hidden away in the past:

> Such was the horror inspired by the truncated neck of Holofernes spurting blood onto the white bed linens, and the proud posture of the heroine, that it was necessary to condemn this painting to the darkness of a corner in the Royal Gallery so that it wouldn't offend the sensibilities of our late Sovereign Maria Luisa who many times expressed her revulsion.[3]

Anna Maria Luisa de' Medici (1667–1743) was the last of the Medici family. She is justly celebrated today as the guiding force behind the 'Family Pact', a legally binding document devised to ensure that the vast accumulated cultural assets of the Medici family would remain in Florence for perpetuity. There is something especially poignant, therefore, about this visionary custodian of Florentine culture gazing upon this, the most renowned accomplishment of a distinguished artist of her own sex, before deciding to banish it to one of the most neglected corners of the gallery.

One might have anticipated that an artist's ability to create artworks with the power to arouse horror in the minds of their viewers would be viewed in positive terms. It indicates, after all, an artist's facility for creating works that can stir the emotions and overwhelm by the sheer force of their artistic vision. Giorgio Vasari famously claimed as much for Leonardo when he described Leonardo's miraculously intense painting of the severed head of the Medusa. This now-lost painting served as the direct inspiration for Caravaggio's shield of the Medusa, which was viewed, in turn, by Gentileschi in the Medici armoury.[4] (An early candidate for Leonardo's *Medusa* is included in the installation based around Caravaggio's Uffizi *Medusa*.) Jusepe de Ribera was, likewise, praised as an artist whose predilection for horror was such that it resulted in paintings that could even cause women to miscarry and whose artworks seemed literally to be painted in blood – or, as the Romantic artist and critic Théophile Gautier put it, 'You, cruel Ribera . . . you make flow in streams of blood, by way of horrible cuts, cascades of intestines.'[5] Yet it seems that horror elicited revulsion when practised by a woman. The nineteenth-century, feminist art historian Anna Jameson (1794–1860) certainly felt this way. She shared Maria Luisa's distaste of the Uffizi *Judith*, observing that she was at a loss to understand how the artist 'could coolly sit down, and day after day, hour after hour, touch after touch, dwell upon and almost realize to the eye such an abomination as this'. She also said that she viewed the painting but once, and yet she 'wished then as I do now, for the privilege of burning it to ashes'.[6]

A key turning point in the subsequent transformation of the response to the *Judith* from viscerally negative to thrillingly positive appears in an essay by Roberto Longhi in 1916. In this, the first modern reappraisal of the oeuvres of both Orazio and Artemisia Gentileschi viewed together, Longhi also evoked the concept of horror to characterise Artemisia's unique contribution to the Baroque:

> But the division between mindset and result, between civility and creation that we have already seen in Orazio is repeated in his daughter with an inevitability verging on tragic, as pictorial qualities of the highest order are lost to disgust. Indeed, who would think that upon a bed-sheet, painted with whites and cool shadows worthy of a life-size Vermeer, we would see a slaughter so brutal and ferocious as to seem painted by the hand of the executioner Lang [an infamous figure of recent memory]? Then, there is the urge to say, this is a terrible woman! How could a woman paint all this? We beg for mercy.[7]

The inherent sexism that underpins this passage has been called out on a number of occasions.[8] Longhi's reassessment of Gentileschi's talent is nonetheless more nuanced than this passage might suggest. The self-consciousness with which he revels in revulsion, for example, is clearly meant to elicit an ironic awareness in the reader's mind of the writer's conflicted admiration for the painting, an admiration that periodically threatens to break free from the passage's otherwise emphatic tone of mock disgust. The give-away here is Longhi's comment that the bed is 'worthy of Vermeer' – high praise given Vermeer's status, then as now, as the ultimate master of luminously precise, painterly observation. In 1916, however, it was still an evidently radical proposition to express admiration for a woman artist possessed of the capacity to create one of the most confrontational expressions of violence in a Caravaggesque mode. So it was that Longhi's youthful essay paved the way for the more systematic contributions of a thriving school of mid- to late twentieth-century scholarship. The concerted activity of this school of research would eventually build a new critical consensus based on a particular admiration for Artemisia's earlier Caravaggesque paintings. This would create the momentum for the artist's triumphant trans-Atlantic crossing to the New World, a passage that would, in its turn, set the seal on the global celebrity status that she enjoys today.

EARLY SCHOLARSHIP AND EXHIBITIONS OF GENTILESCHI'S WORK

The permanent-collection display at the Uffizi constitutes a classic, art-historical framing of Gentileschi in a contemporary curatorial setting. It positions her as a prominent, first-wave Caravaggesque point of comparison with the movement's father figure, Caravaggio. A fundamental point in the progression of this critical understanding was reached in a landmark exhibition that was held at the Palazzo Reale, Milan, in 1951.[9] Curated once again by Roberto Longhi, *Mostra del Caravaggio e dei Caravaggeschi* built on the numerous attributional and archival findings that had been uncovered by decades of research into Caravaggio and his followers in the years since Longhi's essay of 1916. Artemisia was, to be sure, a decidedly marginal presence in this exhibition. In particular, and in a way that would foreshadow much of the literature's emphasis from that point onwards, she was presented as a kind of one-hit wonder. Two Judiths represented her output, whereas there were a dozen paintings by her father, covering a wide range of subjects. Caravaggio, on the other hand, was allotted an unprecedented fifty-one works (albeit not all today recognised as by his hand). Typecast and marginalised though she was, Gentileschi's inclusion in this historic event was, nevertheless, fundamental in ensuring her presence at the moment that the work of the Caravaggisti emerged from neglected footnotes of Italian art to become freshly rediscovered objects of modern-day fascination.

The *Mostra del Caravaggio e dei caravaggeschi* occurred at an important juncture in the development of late twentieth-century museum culture. Its organisers were mindful of the exhibition's significance as a high-profile civic statement that proclaimed the cultural recovery of the city of Milan following the physical and emotional trauma of the recently concluded Second World War.[10] With an ambitious series of loans issued by museums from around the world and with organisational and curatorial links stretching from the Vatican to the Italian government and beyond, the exhibition signalled the moment at which post-war Italian museum exhibitions were expected to function not just as scholarly contributions to the discipline but also as major cultural events on the international calendar. The exhibition more than lived up to its promise. Four hundred thousand people filed into the Palazzo Reale to view the exhibits, making *Mostra del Caravaggio e dei Caravaggeschi* a pathbreaking forerunner of a new type of spectacular exhibition for which a specialist term did not yet exist, but for which one would soon be coined – the international blockbuster.[11]

Anyone entertaining the notion in 1951, however, that a monographic retrospective exhibition dedicated to Artemisia Gentileschi might attract comparable crowds would have been dismissed out of hand. Several key benchmarks along the path of Gentileschi's critical rehabilitation needed first to be attained. One requirement was the building up of a solid base of understanding – and consensus surrounding that understanding – in relation to the parameters of her oeuvre. This form of knowledge production has traditionally been the domain of the classic art-historical labour of love that is the catalogue raisonné. The catalogue raisonné – literally a 'reasoned catalogue' – seeks to preserve for eternity, so to speak, the definitive listing of an artist's work. It traditionally includes individually composed entries for all an artist's known oeuvre, together with works that have been lost or rejected by the author and those that are identified as remaining in doubt for reasons of attribution or provenance. An arduous and highly specialised task, it demands a sustained and concentrated field of vision that often consumes many years of research into disparate and arcane areas – private collections, archives, museum records, sales catalogues, library special collections and so on. The process of realising R. Ward Bissell's 1981 catalogue for Orazio Gentileschi, for example, stretched back to the author's 1966 Ph.D. on the artist. His subsequent work on Artemisia had an even longer period of gestation. In 1968, Bissell published important initial archival findings outlining Artemisia's chronology. Yet he did not release his catalogue raisonné until 1999.

This extended period of dedication, together with the narrowness of focus that it demands, has meant that the catalogue raisonné has itself come under critical reassessment in recent years.[12] It is now something of an endangered species in the field of scholarly publishing, a further casualty of the progressively eroding base of traditional academic publishing more generally. Nevertheless, it was for many decades regarded as fundamental to the discipline – and still is in many respects. It, accordingly, features as a staple and highly regarded fixture on the lists of all the major art-historical publishers of the post-war decades.

A number of Artemisia's colleagues were able to benefit from this process and so to become the subject of dedicated catalogues raisonnés during the latter decades of the twentieth century. A review of their publication history is, nonetheless, revealing. Caravaggio's example is atypical yet consistent with this wider process. The high level of consensus surrounding his significance is such that he has been the subject of successive waves of catalogue raisonné. Friedlander published one of the first in 1955. He was followed by Cinotti (1983), Hibbard (1985), Puglisi (1998), Spike (2001), Schütze (2009), Vodret (2009), Radini Tedeschi (2011), Pacelli (2012) and Scaletti (2017), among others. Most of the other major Italian Baroque artists, on the other hand, have had to make do with only one such release, albeit occasionally supplemented by the republication of updated, second editions. After Caravaggio, this process continued with Annibale Carracci (Posner, 1971), Bissell's previously mentioned 1981 catalogue of Orazio Gentileschi, then Domenichino (Spear, 1982), Guido Reni (Pepper, 1984, updated in 1988), Guercino (Turner and Salerno, 1988, and Stone, 1991) and, finally, Artemisia in 1999.

It would hardly be fair to blame Bissell for the belatedness of this publication relative to those of her peers, particularly given that his catalogue represents a model of its kind.[13] Its comparatively late publication, however, is one of the factors contributing to the relative uncertainty surrounding aspects of Gentileschi's oeuvre today. This is because the publication of a catalogue raisonné creates certain effects within the art industry. One of these is to stimulate the market for an artist's work. This occurs as the heightened scholarly awareness of an oeuvre that is made possible by an authoritative catalogue goes hand in hand with additional exhibitions and further publications that lead, in turn, to an increased interest by public and private collectors in securing representative examples of an artist before they disappear from the market. This has proved to be the case with Gentileschi, as noted in the Introduction in the context of her recent auction results.

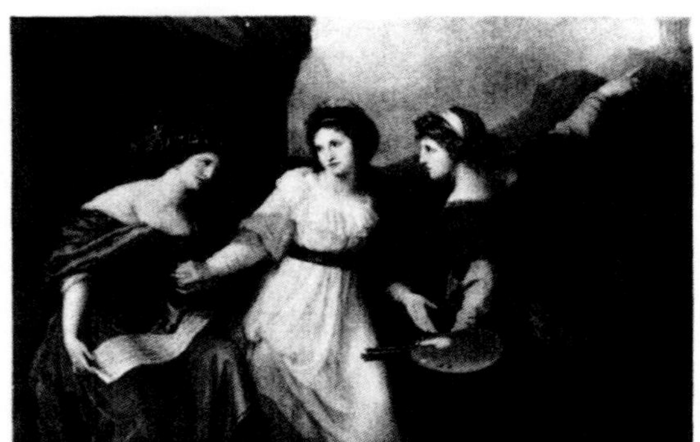

The Swiss-born Angelica Kauffmann, most of whose prolific career was spent in Italy, combines allegory with portraiture in *Angelica Hesitating between Music and Painting*, ca. 1765. Collection of R.D.G. Winn, London.

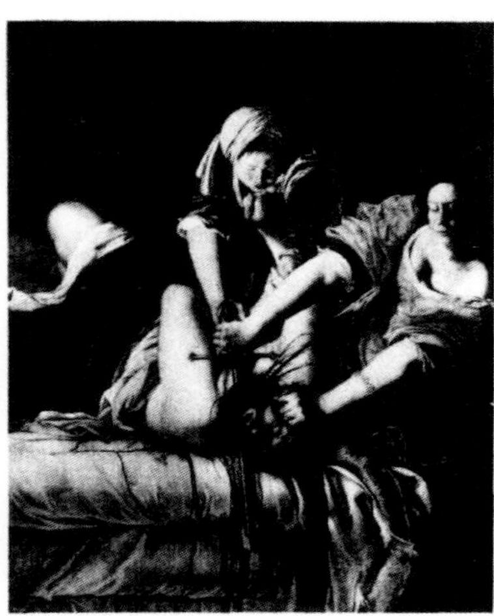

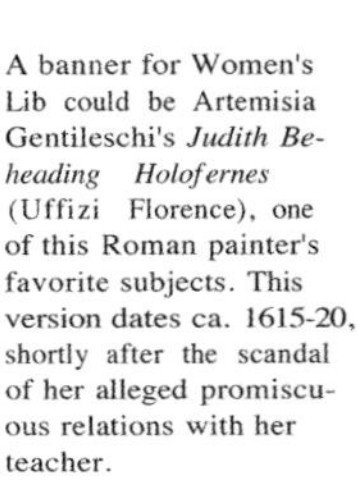

A banner for Women's Lib could be Artemisia Gentileschi's *Judith Beheading Holofernes* (Uffizi Florence), one of this Roman painter's favorite subjects. This version dates ca. 1615-20, shortly after the scandal of her alleged promiscuous relations with her teacher.

124 Linda Nochlin, 'Why Have There Been No Great Women Artists?', *ArtNews*, January 1971, p. 11

Gentileschi's reputation was also able to benefit during the 1960s and 1970s from the parallel surge of interest in her life and work that occurred as a result of her championing by the feminist movement. Gentileschi was present at the very onset of the movement's modern discourse in Linda Nochlin's pioneering essay 'Why Have There Been No Great Women Artists?' This landmark article first appeared in the January 1971 issue of *ArtNews*, which was, for the first time, devoted to the topic of 'Women's Liberation, Woman Artists and Art History'. Here Nochlin – recently appointed Professor of Art History at Vassar College – presented a prominently placed illustration of Gentileschi's Florentine *Judith* as if in response to her own rhetorical question concerning the historical bias against the recognition of 'great' female artists. The illustration's caption went further still in establishing a direct link between Gentileschi and contemporary feminist concerns (fig. 124). It did this by endorsing the artist as the literal, pre-Modern poster child for the new movement: 'A banner for Women's Lib could be Artemisia Gentileschi's *Judith Beheading Holofernes* (Uffizi, Florence)'. It then went on to underscore the topical relevance of Gentileschi's biography to the sexual politics of the day: 'This version dates ca. 1615–20, shortly after the scandal of her alleged promiscuous relations with her teacher.'[14]

In December 1976, another landmark exhibition, *Women Artists, 1550–1950*, opened at the Los Angeles County Museum of Art.[15] This exhibition had been commissioned five years earlier in response to a demand that the museum address its lack of inclusion of works by women and minority artists. Curated by Ann Sutherland Harris and Linda Nochlin, *Women Artists* would exert a major influence on feminist art theory and practice around the world. Over the course of a year it toured to four American cities, where it was hailed as the first exhibition dedicated to women artists to be presented in a western art-historical context (although, as with so many other claims to being the first, this suggestion has been subsequently disputed.[16]) It was accompanied by an intensively researched, multi-author catalogue, which was reprinted no fewer than six times between 1977 and 1984, thus establishing itself as a standard reference work on the topic for decades to come.

Women Artists canonised Artemisia – literally, in an art historical sense – by enshrining her as an especially prominent figure in a freshly minted canon of women's art history. She was accordingly presented for the first time as much more than a one-hit wonder. Unlike in the *Mostra del Caravaggio e dei Caravaggeschi* of 1951, she was represented by a generous selection of six canvases. These included not only a signature version of *Judith* but also a broad variety of examples of both Old and New Testament narratives, together with portraiture and allegory. *Women Artists* was also noteworthy for its emphasis on sourcing some of Gentileschi's largest and most physically imposing canvases then available for loan. The 1610 *Susanna and the Elders* (fig. 13), for example, measures a commanding 170 centimetres high. Likewise, the Columbus Museum's *David and Bathsheba* is an even more impressive two and half metres in height (fig. 90). In between these two reference points there was sequenced the Detroit *Judith and her Maidservant with the Head of Holofernes*, nearly two metres high (fig. 69), and, hung in close proximity, what was at that stage Gentileschi's only known full-length portrait, the 1622 *Portrait of a Gonfaloniere*, once again making an impressive showing at 208 by 128 centimetres (fig. 72).[17] This presentation formed part of a broader narrative of exceptionality that was underscored by the claims made for Gentileschi within the catalogue. The text describes her as 'mostly a series of exceptions to the rules about women and women artists' and even as 'the first woman in the history of western art to make a significant and undeniably important contribution to the art of her time'.[18]

The results of this flattering presentation can be seen in the photographic documentation of the exhibition's showing at the Brooklyn Museum (fig. 125). The imposing scale and dramatic sweep of Gentileschi's compositions provide a major focal and axial point of reference for the hanging of the exhibition's opening sequence of rooms. The *Susanna* and *Judith*, for example, have each been given their own, centrally positioned wall spaces and hung close to the floor, thereby allowing the artist to dominate the space and visually overshadow the generally smaller and more intimate works around her, such as Sophonisba Anguissola's self-portraits and Giovanna Garzoni's still lifes, which measure less than one metre high in the case of Anguissola and half a metre wide for Garzoni. As a result, and in the absence of any other candidate to perform the role of a specialist in large-format history painting, Gentileschi was cast by default as the archetypal female 'Old Master'. The emphasis on selecting a number of her grandest and most dramatic canvases thus framed her within the exhibition as the greatest – and by implication *the only* – exemplar of the canonical Female Italian Grand Manner: the female Raphael, Michelangelo and Caravaggio all rolled into one.

Other artists might have been brought in to fulfill this role. The problem was that their oeuvres – and in many cases even their identities – remained much less well understood than even Gentileschi's at that stage. In 2007, for example, paintings on this scale by Lavinia Fontana were featured in an exhibition dedicated to the work of Italian Renaissance and Baroque women artists that was held at Washington's National Museum of Women in the Arts. The expansion of scholarship on Fontana that had taken place in the intervening thirty years was emphasised on this occasion by the inclusion of such works, together with comparable works by Plautilla Nelli (1524–1588) and Orsola Caccia (1596–1676).[19] In the 1970s, by contrast, knowledge of all three artists was extremely limited. Their oeuvres, together with those of many other women artists of the period, still awaited critical rediscovery, in much the same manner that Gentileschi's art was only starting to reveal itself more fully at that stage.

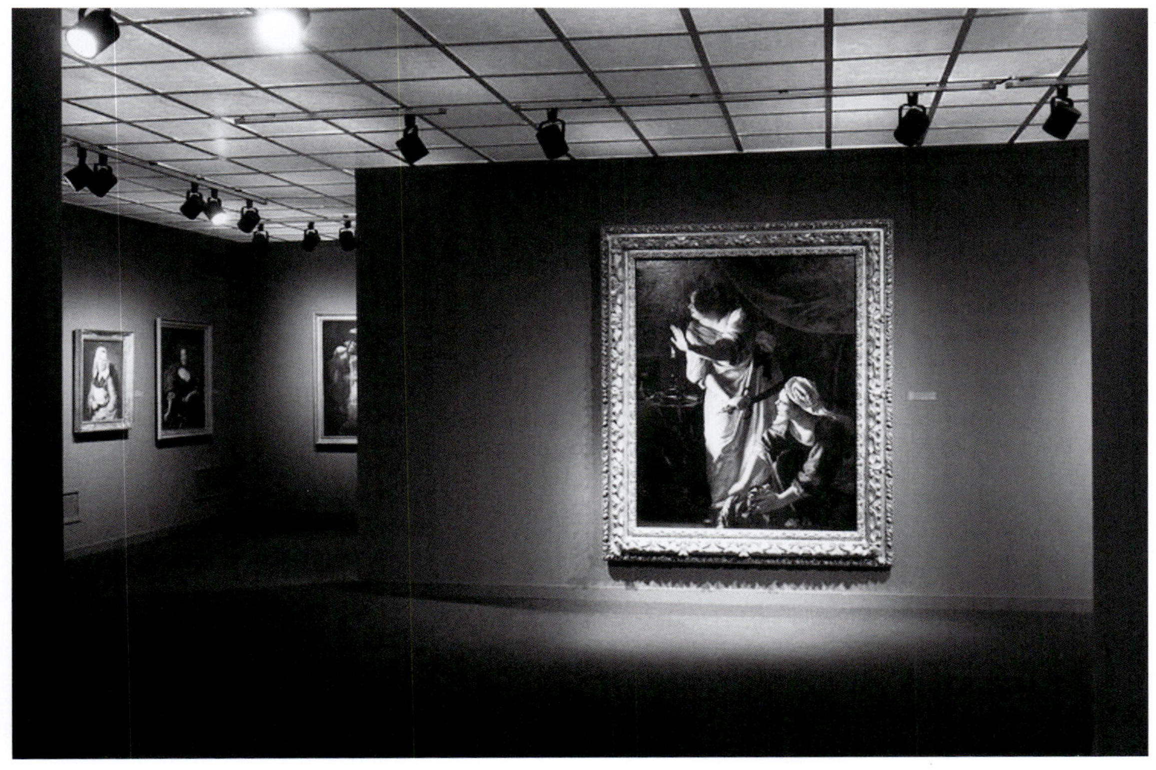

125 Exhibition view, *Women Artists: 1550–1950*, Brooklyn Museum, 1 October–27 November 1977

Another artist who fell just outside this cycle of academic rediscovery and so missed out on the opportunity of performing a comparable role in the *Women Artists* exhibition was Elisabetta Sirani. Two of Sirani's canvases were, in fact, included, and one in particular, *Porcia Wounding her Thigh* (fig. 126), while not quite on the scale of Gentileschi's larger works, is, nonetheless, directly comparable.[20] Yet, as a non-Caravaggesque follower of Guido Reni, Sirani was an evidently less popular choice than Gentileschi. In a reversal of fortune that highlights the capriciousness of fame, the formerly ascendant school of Bolognese Baroque classical artists was now judged to be of less interest to contemporary tastes than the dramatically intense compositions of the Caravaggisti. This prejudice was especially evident in the catalogue's discussion of Sirani's second work in the exhibition. In any other context this composition – a large and imposing *Magdalene* – would have made a fascinating point of comparison

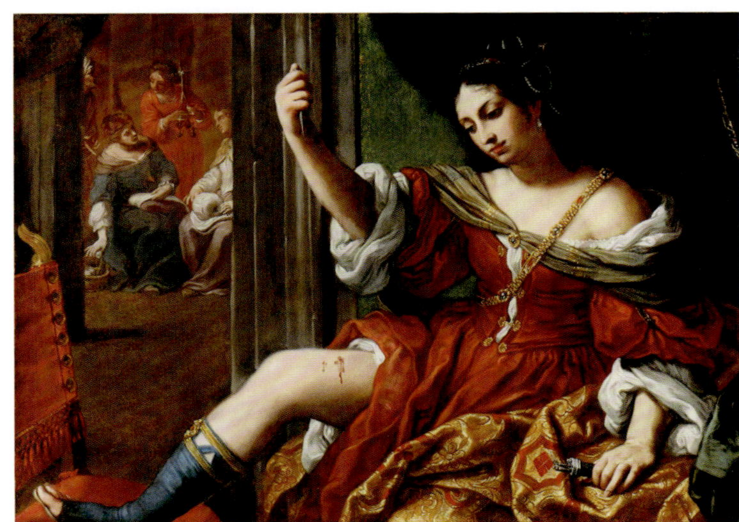

126 Elisabetta Sirani, *Porcia Wounding her Thigh*, signed and dated 1664, oil on canvas, 101 × 138 cm, Le Collezioni d'Arte e di Storia della Fondazione Cassa di Risparmio in Bologna

with Gentileschi's numerous paintings of the same subject. Yet the catalogue struggled to commend the work to the contemporary viewer. In reference to this and another version of the subject in Bologna, it noted with evident circumspection that the two paintings' 'idealized expressions directly inspired by Reni, might not be appealing. Both, however, are excellent examples of the classical spirit seen in much Italian seicento art.'[21] Sirani's time would, however, soon come. The process of her own art-historical rediscovery would occur one step after Gentileschi's, with a major exhibition dedicated to her work and the publication of a catalogue raisonné by Adelina Modesti, both occurring in 2004.[22]

A 'GREAT GENIUS' ATTENDS A FEAST OF THE GODDESSES

Gentileschi's exceptionality was also stressed in several key publications from the period. Among these was Germaine Greer's influential 1979 monograph *The Obstacle Race: The Fortunes of Women Painters and their Work*, which is arranged according to thematic and period-based chapters: 'Family', 'The Renaissance', 'Still Life and Flower Painting', and so on. Yet Gentileschi alone has been allowed to break free of this format, as if to highlight her exceptionality within the text in a structural as well as a thematic sense. She is the only artist to be given her own, whole chapter. Here she is presented triumphantly as 'The Magnificent Exception', with an opening sentence that states categorically, 'Great genius is the exception that makes the rule', and a final paragraph that begins, 'For the women of today, Artemisia represents the female equivalent of an Old Master. She is the exception to all the rules: she rejected a conventional feminine role for a revolutionary female one.'[23] So it was that this previously forgotten footnote in the history of art had now been reframed as one of the principal icons of a transformative cultural movement.

Gentileschi's canonical status within this newly erected pantheon of greatness would be yet more powerfully affirmed in the same year with the unveiling of Judy Chicago's *The Dinner Party* (fig. 127). This ambitious – and contentious – work is an enormous installation piece that takes the form of a giant, triangular table and sets out an alternative vision of the *Last Supper*. The table has been sumptuously laid out as if in preparation for a symbolic feast to be held in honour of 'mythic female characters and historic figures who have made a contribution to women's lives throughout history'.[24] The work's exhibition history constitutes a major event in its own right.[25] Following a high-profile launch at the San Francisco Museum of Modern Art on 14 March 1979, *The Dinner Party* embarked on an extended international tour for the next nine years, stopping at venues as diverse as the Edinburgh Fringe Festival and the Melbourne Exhibition Centre and attracting a combined audience of more than a million visitors along the way.[26]

The Dinner Party was especially influential in assigning to Gentileschi a highly visible place at a very select table of imagined female greatness. Presented as the 'first woman artist to make an authentically feminine work', she is placed in the company of a celestial gathering of goddesses and queens and female heroes, writers, activists and so on.[27] One of only two visual artists at the banquet (the other being Georgia O'Keeffe), Gentileschi is positioned between Queen Elizabeth I and the seventeenth-century Dutch woman of letters Anna van Schurman. Isabella d'Este is also close by – somewhat fortuitously for her sake, since she stands in for the entire tradition of enlightened female artistic patronage. Doubtless she and Gentileschi would have had much to discuss.

It was time, however, for the art historians to contribute their own, more historically based evaluations of Gentileschi's significance. The first of these was Mary D. Garrard's monograph (as opposed to a catalogue raisonné, Bissell's volume being still a decade away). Published by Princeton University Press in 1989,[28] *Artemisia Gentileschi: The Image of the Female Hero in Italian Baroque Art* has done much to confirm the artist's centrality for the teaching of early modern art history in universities around the world, and it remains a masterclass of meticulously probing scholarship. Yet it is not without its own critical issues. In particular, it proved highly influential in promulgating a vision of Gentileschi that was strongly weighted in favour of her earlier, Caravaggesque paintings over and above the works produced from the 1620s onwards. In particular, Gentileschi's late Neapolitan paintings are often criticised in judgemental terms that clash with the even-

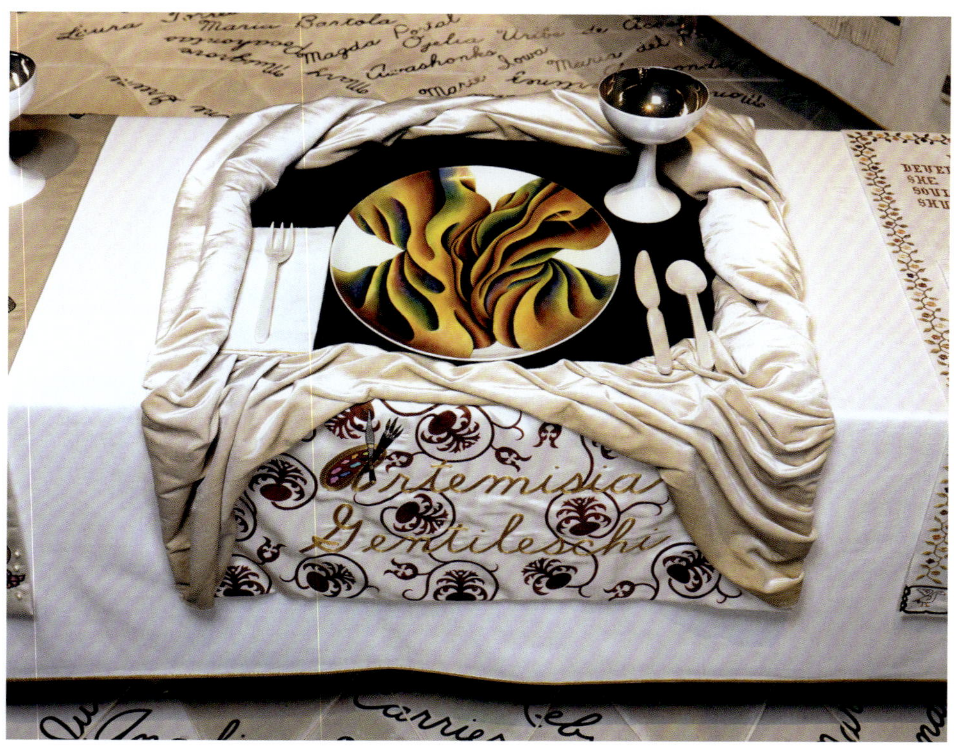

127 Judy Chicago, *The Dinner Party* (Artemisia Gentileschi place setting), 1974–79, mixed media (ceramic, porcelain, textile), Brooklyn Museum, Gift of the Elizabeth A. Sackler Foundation, 2002.10

handedness that is evident elsewhere. The book decries, for example, the 'display of stylish flesh' and 'rhetorical bombast' of the late-1640s Potsdam *Tarquin and Lucretia* – a painting that has been characterised within these pages as one of the masterworks of Gentileschi's late career (fig. 116). Garrard goes on to note that the canvas is 'merely embarrassing when judged by the standards of the Pommersfelden *Susanna* and the Genoese *Lucretia*' (two early-to-middle-period paintings of 1610 and about 1621 (figs 13 and 78)). This emphasis foreshadowed a subsequently consistent bias in the literature against Gentileschi's later works, a bias that this study has been seeking to moderate by focusing on the totality of her career.

Garrard's monograph reaffirmed the degree to which Italian Baroque art could constitute an exciting field that touched upon issues of pressing relevance to today's world as much as to its own. It, accordingly, gave rise to a flourishing school of scholarship dedicated to critical studies of the feminist and gender issues arising from the works, as well as to a more finely grained attributional discourse that would find its ultimate expression in Bissell's catalogue raisonné of 1999. Both publications also helped to stimulate the development of further exhibitions that have been held in Gentileschi's name from 1991 to the present. These exhibitions have come to constitute a major industry in their own right and have done much to convert Artemisia into one of the best-known artists of the early modern period. They have also had the effect of confirming her box-office success in terms of the canon-building processes of the modern museum. Artemisia has been repackaged and reframed in ways that have ultimately resulted in her transformation into a viable candidate for the blockbuster exhibition, which has extended its remit over the past few decades throughout Europe, the United States and beyond.

14

From the Connoisseur's Studio to the Global Blockbuster

GENTILESCHI AND THE MONOGRAPHIC RETROSPECTIVE EXHIBITION

INTRODUCTION
ARTEMISIA, 1991

In 1991, the first monographic retrospective exhibition devoted to Gentileschi was held at the Casa Buonarroti, the former Florentine residence of the Buonarroti family. It was converted into a quasi-shrine, dedicated to the memory of Michelangelo, under the aegis of the artist's great-nephew, Michelangelo Buonarroti the Younger. Gentileschi's *Inclination* of 1615–16 had made a significant contribution to the Casa Buonarroti's innovative iconographic programme (see above, p. 14 and fig. 4). At the time of its opening to the wider, modern public in 1859, the Casa Buonarroti was one of the first examples on record of a single-artist museum. It stands today, therefore, as both a priceless repository of artefacts associated with Michelangelo, as well as being a historically significant example of a very particular type of museum, one dedicated to maintaining the eternal flame of an artist's immortal reputation. As such, it represents a particularly apposite venue for the launching of what would soon grow into a thriving industry in its own right: the monographic retrospective exhibition devoted to Gentileschi's art.

FACING PAGE Exhibition view, *Artemisia Gentileschi: storia di una passione* (detail of fig. 131)

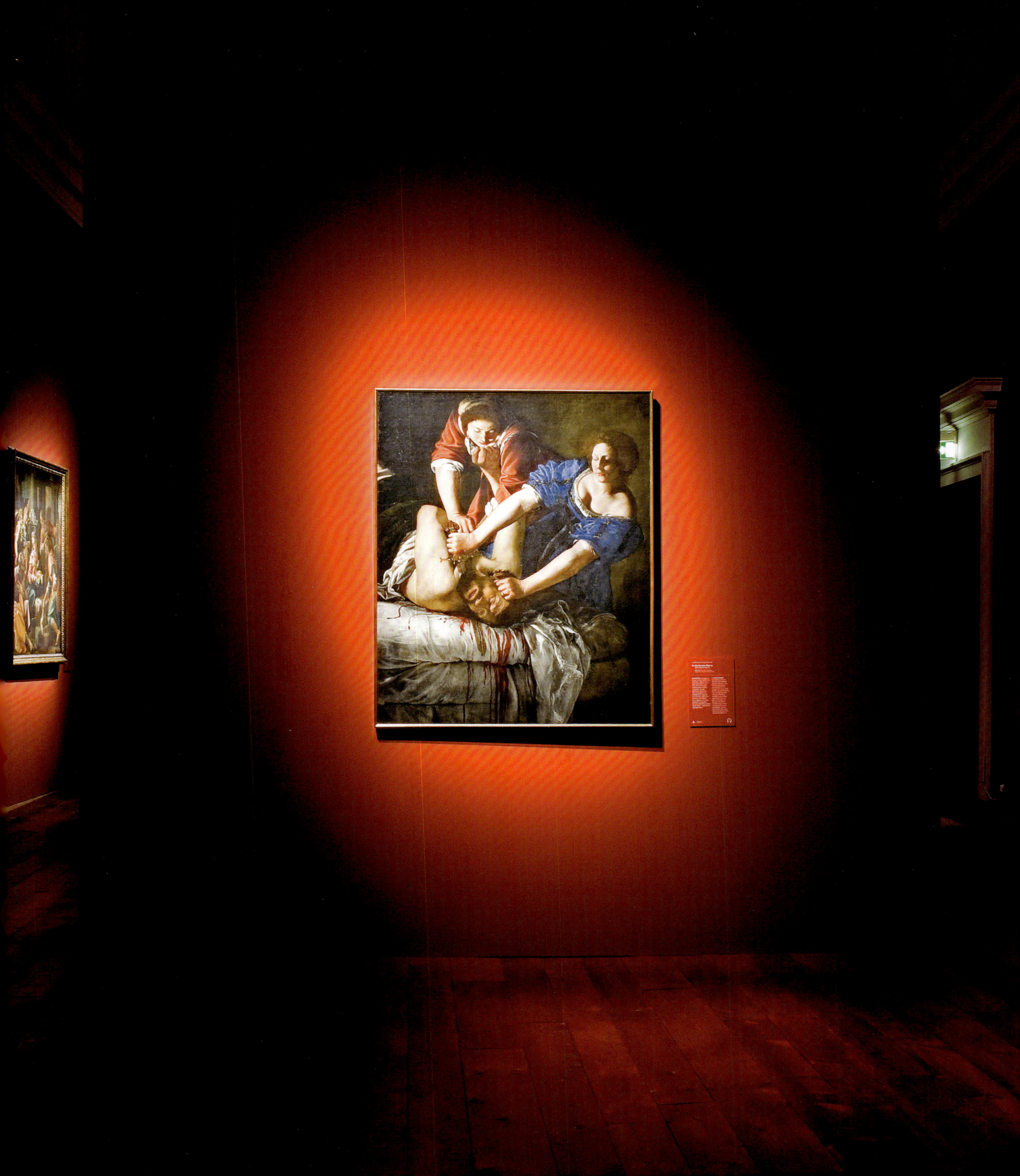

The Casa Buonarroti is an intimate, small-scale museum, with its temporary exhibition spaces comprising only four small rooms running down one side of the building's ground floor. As a venue, it is worlds removed from the monumental scale and pressing crowds that are attendant upon the Uffizi, the Accademia or any of Florence's other most visited museums. That it was the first setting for the subsequent run of exhibitions devoted to Gentileschi thus suggests that, in the early 1990s at least, the artist was still considered as a specialist topic, of interest to connoisseurs only. This state of affairs was further reflected by the relative modesty of the exhibition's scale. Its two curators, Roberto Contini and Gianni Papi, selected only twenty-seven paintings, whereas subsequent exhibitions have included up to three times that amount.

The exhibition design made a virtue of its intimacy by bringing down the level of the rooms' ceilings and directing the visitor flow with judiciously placed carpets and labels (fig. 128). The result was a concentrated selection of a widely varying group of canvases of mixed quality and attributional status. The arrangement of the first room, in particular, had the effect of submerging Gentileschi's artistic personality within a complex sequence of attributional issues as fully autograph, widely accepted works jostled for the viewer's attention alongside paintings of often highly uncertain authorship. The first painting on display, for example, diverged markedly from the kinds of signature canvases that were so much a feature of the 1976 *Women Artists* exhibition and that one might have expected to introduce an exhibition on this artist. It was, instead, a *Madonna and Child* that had been hitherto considered so tangential to the literature on the artist as to have never been previously attributed to Artemisia.[1] Here, however, it was given a central, axial position that would usually have been reserved for one of the artist's best-known works. The canvas had been included, the catalogue noted, in the hope that it 'might add some new dimensions to the Gentileschian sensations that seem to be communicated by the painting, affirming for it (possibly in the direction of Artemisia?) or rather denying them instead to another path (towards lo Spadarino? [another early follower of Caravaggio])'.[2]

This represented a bracingly speculative and open-ended curatorial methodology. It resulted in an unforgettable viewing experience that reminded viewers of the degree to which exhibitions are not the iron-clad displays of unchanging verity that they are often made out to be. They are, rather, inherently experimental enterprises that use the white cube of the gallery space as a laboratory in which to test often contentious curatorial and academic hypotheses. In particular, the Casa Buonarroti exhibition seemed to wish to emphasise the image of a youthful artist operating within a wider, 'vanguard' movement that produced a fascinating range of often challenging and innovative works that were then picked up on and further developed by other, closely related painters, all working within equally closely related artistic circles. As the first museum overview of Artemisia's work, the exhibition was, nonetheless, judged by some critics to have been perhaps *too* experimental in certain respects. As one reviewer put it, 'Unimportant or unrelated paintings are not innocuous presences in an exhibition: they can detract from the business at hand, namely the definition of a single artistic personality.'[3]

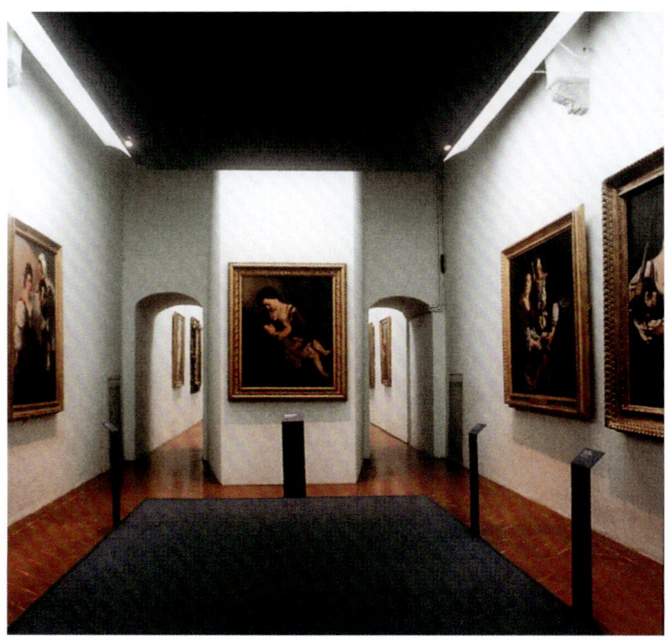

128 Exhibition view, *Artemisia*, Casa Buonarroti, Florence, 18 June–4 November 1991

The next major Gentileschi exhibition pursued a markedly different agenda. Curated by Keith Christiansen and Judith

Mann from the Metropolitan Museum of Art in New York and the St Louis Art Museum, respectively, it attempted to assemble a relatively definitive overview of the artist's work. This approach went hand in hand with a higher-profile and more complex organisational structure, in which the exhibition's costs and logistics were shared between an international consortium of major hosting institutions comprising the Palazzo Venezia in Rome and the two American museums. Gentileschi was now a trans-Atlantic touring proposition, with the exhibition opening in Rome on 15 October 2001 and concluding at St Louis nearly a year later, on 15 September 2002.

The connoisseurial complexities of Gentileschi's oeuvre had been recently highlighted by the publication of Bissell's 1999 catalogue raisonné. This allowed the curators to follow through on the suggestion that the exhibition include some 'borderline cases' to act as points of comparison with the artist's more secure works.[4] The exhibition's organisers were also able to benefit from a number of new and less well-known canvases that were just then beginning to appear on the market. So, the exhibition highlighted, for example, the *Danaë* that had been attributed to both Orazio and Artemisia and that had been recently acquired for the St Louis Art Museum following its appearance at Sotheby's, Monaco, in 1986 (fig. 22).[5]

The exhibition tended to focus on a more tightly curated selection of Artemisia's more secure canvases than had been the case in 1991. The result was the kind of authoritative and informative, mainstream art-historical exhibition that the artist's champions could only have dreamed of back in the 1970s. In the spacious, top-lit galleries of the Metropolitan Museum's installation, for example, Artemisia's canvases positively glowed as they were generously distributed along a carefully laid out itinerary of clearly differentiated spaces that led the viewer sequentially through the different stages of her career, culminating in two especially large galleries dedicated to her Florentine and Neapolitan periods (fig. 129). The exhibition was further illuminated by a lavishly produced catalogue published by the Metropolitan Museum that summarised and updated the by now substantial body of research dedicated to the artist.

And yet for all its manifest achievements, the exhibition could do no more than present an image of Artemisia that

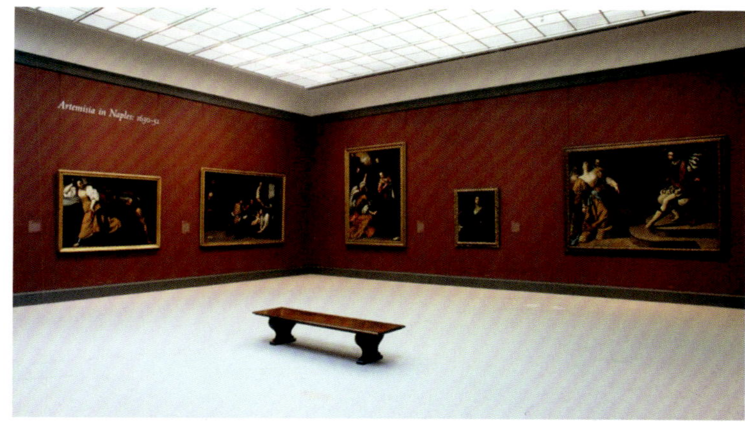

129 Exhibition view, *Orazio and Artemisia Gentileschi : Father and Daughter Painters in Baroque Italy*, The Metropolitan Museum of Art, New York, 14 February–12 May 2002

was, in its own way, only partial and in places contentious. It seemed problematic to some observers that Artemisia had at last been granted the deluxe treatment of an international touring exhibition only on the condition that her works be viewed in relation to her father's. The resulting exhibition – *Orazio and Artemisia Gentileschi: Father and Daughter Painters in Baroque Italy* – tended, by its very nature, to conflate Artemisia's career within that of Orazio's. Artemisia did not appear in the New York installation, for example, until the third room. She was, moreover, represented by a total of thirty-four paintings, whereas her father was represented by fifty. This certainly improved upon the *Mostra del Caravaggio e dei Caravaggeschi* of 1951, yet it remained the case all those years later that Artemisia was still not allowed to stand on her own two feet and in her own right in this, 'the most comprehensive display of her work ever assembled', as the Foreword notes.[6]

The cycle of Gentileschi's exhibitions seemed, by now, to have levelled out at about one every decade. So it was that in 2011 the hitherto most expansive and ambitious exhibition of her work was launched at the Palazzo Reale in Milan. This marked the artist's triumphant return to the site of her initial appearance as a peripheral figure in the 1951 *Mostra del Caravaggio e dei Caravaggeschi*. Gentileschi's canvases were now presented according to an exhibition system that had evolved to the point of virtual unrecognisability in relation to the 1951

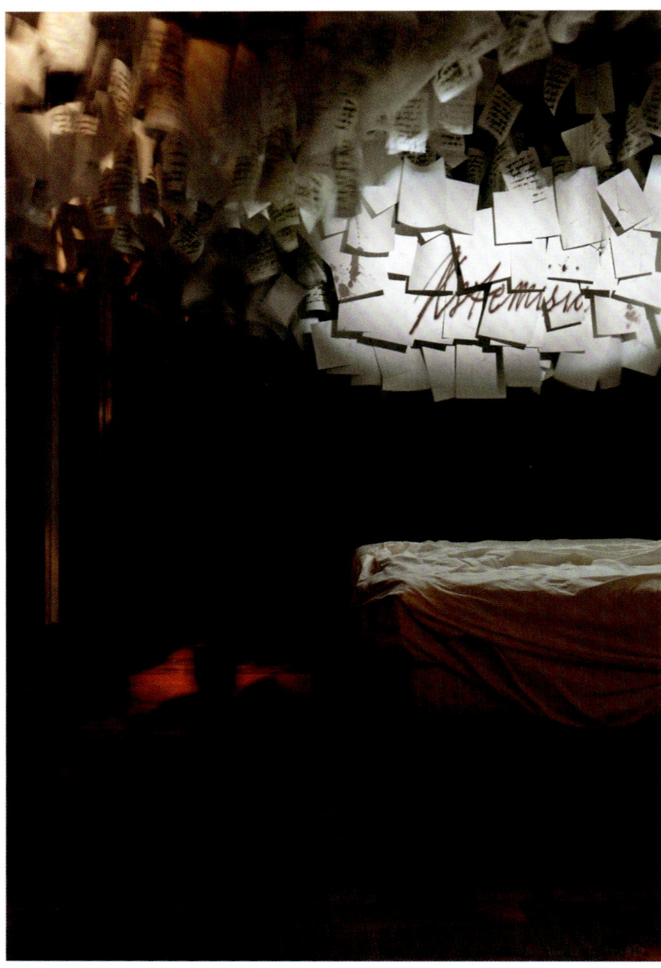

130 Exhibition view, *Artemisia Gentileschi: storia di una passione*, Palazzo Reale, Milan, 22 September 2011–29 January 2012

exhibition. For one thing, large-scale exhibition projects were now expected to function as major business ventures in their own right. Thus, the planning for *Artemisia Gentileschi: Storia di una passione* (*Artemisia Gentileschi: The Story of a Passion*) arose out of a joint public and private partnership between the Municipality of Milan, the host institution, and *24Ore Cultura*, a business organisation dedicated to developing exhibition projects as part of its wider brief to operate as 'a reference partner in the Italian culture business', as its website notes.[7]

Every exhibition needs to establish its own point of difference from what has gone before. Accordingly, *Artemisia Gentileschi: Storia di una passione*, curated by Roberto Contini and Francesco Solinas, asserted its claim to be the first exhibition to grant the artist full credit for her art in her own right. This it combined with an emphasis on the inter-personal relationships informing Gentileschi's biography. This emphasis grew, in turn, from a decision to highlight a series of recently discovered letters written by the artist to her Florentine lover, Francesco Maringhi, a discovery that revealed an entirely new dimension to Gentileschi's career and personality (see pp. 8 and 85). The media release that accompanied the launch duly noted,

> The exhibition's mission is finally to highlight the artistic greatness of this exceptional painter, whose relevance has so far been overshadowed both by the sad story of the rape of which she was a victim in 1611 and by the cumbersome figure of her father, Orazio, a famous painter but a rude and despotic individual.[8]

The prominence afforded to these new emphases was immediately evident at the exhibition's entrance. Here, the visitor was confronted with a theatrical tableau of interpretive stage machinery that had been created by the exhibition's designer, the theatre director and dramaturge Emma Dante (the work also containing a performance-art component that was activated at the exhibition launch).[9] The tableau consisted of a bed covered with crumpled, white sheets that re-enacted both the primal scene of Gentileschi's rape and its supposed re-imagining as the surface upon which Judith and her maidservant dispatch Holofernes (fig. 130). Numerous rustling letters hovered above, together with a giant projection of Artemisia's signature, as if to suggest the Kafkaesque bureaucracy of the trial proceedings as well as the primacy of Artemisia's voice, highlighted by the recently discovered trove of letters displayed nearby.

From this opening tableau, the visitor was plunged into an immersive environment made up of a series of darkened rooms lined with dramatically spot-lit canvases (fig. 131). One was reminded of just how different this intensely theatrical treatment was from the relatively neutral interiors created for the *Mostra del Caravaggio e dei Caravaggeschi* of 1951. The gilding of the paintings' frames now caught the light from out of

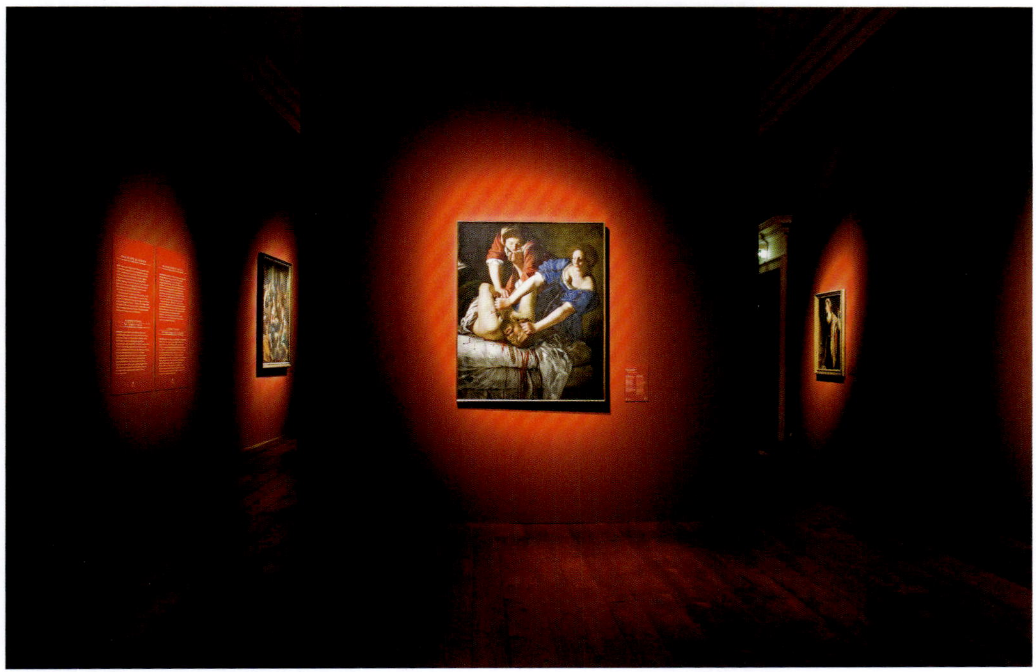

131 Exhibition view, *Artemisia Gentileschi: storia di una passione*, Palazzo Reale, Milan, 22 September 2011–29 January 2012

a penumbral darkness that was offset, in turn, by the blood-red coloration of the walls. One gallery even incorporated a series of full-length mirrors positioned alongside a grouping of Gentileschi's portraits, thereby intensifying the exhibition's emphasis on role playing and theatricality, as both the portraits and the spectators reflected back on each other in angular and distorted facets.

A number of reviewers took issue with the exhibition's 'resoundingly theatrical' design.[10] But perhaps this emphasis needs to be understood in the broader context of the kinds of logistical pressures and business imperatives underpinning twenty-first century blockbusters. One might hypothesise, for example, that the unproven nature of Gentileschi as a blockbuster proposition at this stage suggested the desirability of amplifying the theatricality of the presentational mode in order to render the viewing process as visually arresting and powerfully immersive as possible. In so doing, the exhibition planners might have hoped to create an immediately engaging visitor experience that would appeal to all audiences, not just those already familiar with the artist's work. One also senses in this exhibition the beginnings of a cross-over phenomenon taking place, as the exhibition sought to register not only its own scholarly concerns but also the growing prominence of the more accessible novelistic and cinematic treatments of Gentileschi's life. The result was an exhibition experience that jettisoned the idea of the soberly didactic installation of more traditional art exhibitions. In its place was a powerfully impactful activation of the senses that transformed the experience of visiting the Palazzo Reale into a memorable event rather than a mere lesson in art history.

The overall success of the Milan exhibition meant that Artemisia Gentileschi's reputation – her status as a museum brand in her own right – had now been confirmed. In the year that followed, a modified version of the Milan show travelled to Paris where it enjoyed a four-month stint at the Musée Maillol. Its French title – *Artemisia: pouvoir, gloire et passions d'une femme peintre* (*Artemisia: The Power, Glory and Passions of a Female Painter*) – sounded even more like a dramatic biopic than the Italian one, and its location – in another artist museum – once again reinforced the museum's function as a validator of artistic reputation.[11] By now, however, the floodgates of the Artemisian exhibition industry had swung open. From 2012 to 2020, a staggering nine exhibitions with Artemisia's name in the title were held in locations as diverse as Paris, Pisa, Moscow, Milan, Conversano, Rome, Chicago, Olomouc (Czech Republic) and, finally, London in 2020.[12]

What strikes one most about all this activity is the extent to which the strength of Artemisia Gentileschi as a museum brand has now become so well established that it is able to be either focused in on or expanded out of, depending on the project. On the one hand, Artemisia's name is now conceived as the hook upon which to hang specialised exhibition concepts that would not otherwise have been immediately identified with her. A case in point is *Artemisia e il pittori del Conte: La collezione di Giangirolamo II Acquaviva d'Aragona*. Curated by Viviana Farina and exhibited in 2018 at the church and palace of Conversano, this exhibition told the fascinating story of the cultural patronage undertaken in the 1630s–1650s by the eponymous Count Giangirolamo II Acquaviva d'Aragona and his wife, Isabella Acquaviva d'Aragona (née Filomarino) in the vital yet hitherto under-researched regional centre of Conversano, Apulia.[13] It also highlighted the significant discovery of a new late work by Artemisia, the *Roman Charity* that, unlike many other recent attributions, also has a secure provenance stretching back to the seventeenth century (fig. 83). Yet this was only one of fifty-nine exhibits, and it was the only painting by Gentileschi displayed in the exhibition. Why, then, was Gentileschi given the first word of its title? The answer, of course, is that her name was there to add accessibility and relevance to an otherwise wordy and specialised exhibition concept. It gave the exhibition immediate museological brand recognition, in other words. By drawing on her name, the exhibition organisers were able to capture the attention of anyone using the word 'Artemisia' in a Google search of exhibitions – a far greater number of hits, clearly, than would have otherwise been the case.

An alternative tendency has been to expand upon Gentileschi's name and so to supplement a limited selection of her works with related exhibits by other artists. This creates a larger pool of works out of which to construct a critical mass of display that more obviously approaches that of a major exhibition experience. An example of this method was the *Artemisia Gentileschi e il suo tempo* (*Artemisia Gentileschi and her Time*) exhibition held at the Palazzo Braschi in Rome in 2016. This exhibition, curated by Nicola Spinosa, followed the standard practice of combining a well-known master's name with the stock phrase 'The Age of' or 'and their Time'. These elastic phrases allow curators to juxtapose a restricted number of works by a major figure with a selection of exhibits by less well-known followers or contemporaries. Apart from its contextual benefits, this approach is advantageous in logistical and financial terms, since it allows exhibition planners to combine a limited number of more expensive and difficult to procure 'major' loans with a larger selection of more 'minor' – and thus easier to secure – works. Two landmark precedents for this approach were *The Age of Caravaggio* at the Metropolitan Museum of Art and the Museo di Capodimonte in 1985 and *The Age of Correggio and the Carracci* at the Metropolitan Museum of Art, the National Gallery of Art, Washington, and the Pinacoteca Nazionale, Bologna in 1986–87. *Mostra del Caravaggio e dei Caravaggeschi* of 1951 had begun the process of including Gentileschi in exhibitions as one of a host of lesser-known, 'minor' artists who had followed the blazing star of Caravaggio. Now, sixty years later, her fame had increased to the extent that she had become the central point around which entire exhibition concepts could be assembled.

This focus had an arguably distracting effect, however, on the experience of viewing *Artemisia e il suo tempo*. From a total of ninety-seven exhibits, the core grouping of thirty-one paintings attributed to Artemisia created what was, in effect, another example of a monographic retrospective of her work only five years since the one held in Milan in 2011. Yet the potential impact of this opportunity to bring together an updated overview of Gentileschi's oeuvre was diminished to a certain extent by the degree to which Artemisia's own work was at times swamped by being surrounded by dozens of contemporary variations upon her customary subjects. The effect was to cast her as almost a bystander in her own narrative as her distinctiveness as an artist was sometimes overshadowed amidst the scores of other Judiths, Lucretias and Cleopatras that crowded the walls. Sheila Barker remarked of this exhibition that it 'occasionally obscures Artemisia's personal trajectory amidst the traffic of other artists' itineraries, subordinating her timeline to the portrayal of a multi-city narrative of evolving Seicento styles'.[14]

The exhibition at the National Gallery in London in 2020, by contrast, sought to train the spotlight back onto Gentileschi's significance as an artist, alone and in her own right. Curated by Letizia Treves, it was a more tightly curated selection of thirty of Gentileschi's 'best documented, most securely attributed paintings'.[15] The result was another closely focused and authoritative overview of her works, and it was accompanied by a lavish catalogue that sought to summarise many of the key research findings from the past twenty years. Yet the exhibition's emphasis on only her 'best known [and] iconic' works resulted in an arguably somewhat essentialist presentation of the artist. It created the impression that Gentileschi – as an exhibition offering at least – was perhaps at risk of becoming over-exposed. Eve Straussman-Pflanzer picked up on this mood when she asked, in relation to a survey of exhibitions of early modern Italian women artists, 'whether the future of scholarship on Italian women artists is best served by monographic exhibitions, or by group exhibitions that introduce the public to a greater number of women artists, including those who are almost unknown, even to specialists'.[16] Her alternative – and that of the organising institutions of the Wadsworth Atheneum Museum of Art in Hartford, Conn., and the Detroit Institute of Arts – was the 2021–22 exhibition *By Her Hand: Artemisia Gentileschi and Women Artists in Italy*. The group-show methodology adopted by this last example built, in turn, on the historic legacy of *Women Artists: 1550–1950*, together with the 2007 exhibition *Italian Women Artists, from Renaissance to Baroque* and other more recent examples of its type.[17]

In considering the use of exhibitions to broadcast Gentileschi's fame in the modern era, one is struck by the degree to which each was evidently planned in reaction to what had gone before. Each constitutes, in effect, a new script, setting out a different role for Artemisia to play on the museum's global stage prior to the opening of another show at another venue. Artemisia has undertaken a long journey, in this respect, from her breakthrough appearance at the Casa Buonarroti. Her initial casting in Florence framed her as a youthful figure operating within a nascent art movement of exceptional experimentalism. From here she progressed to the larger American/Italian co-production of *Orazio and Artemisia Gentileschi*. This exhibition assigned her the part of a supporting actress, cast in the shadow of an oppressive father figure. At the Palazzo Reale, on the other hand, she was thrust into the leading role of a dramatic, diva-like figure, whose career was characterised as a struggle for autonomy carried out in the midst of a psychodrama of almost unbearable intensity. In Rome, she was then plunged into a complex production of Fellini-esque complexity that reimagined her as a peripatetic, walk-on character making her way through a crowded and rapidly evolving landscape of artistic creativity, to which she was understood as being somehow central and yet tangential at the same time. In London in 2020, she was placed front and centre once again, as the leading light of her own production. Here she was, nonetheless, restricted to a tightly curated performance of her greatest hits only.

The many unresolved elements that continue to manifest themselves in these exhibitions, the sometimes strange twists and turns that they have taken in terms of attribution and interpretation, suggest an alternative narrative that might be told about the difficulties involved in arriving at a consensus about Gentileschi. Its open-endedness points in turn to the existence of a thriving parallel industry that has developed alongside these exhibitions. This alternative dimension of Gentileschian commentary has shown itself to be remarkably unconstrained by the customary rules and restrictions of the historical process. It has flourished, instead, in often unexpected ways, by highlighting her continuing importance as a site of often freely inventive, popular imagination and wishful creativity, a distinctive additional dimension of the Artemisian industry that is the subject of the following chapter.

15

Artemisia beyond the Academy

INTRODUCTION
ANNA BANTI AND THE IMAGINARY ARTEMISIA

In the catalogue that accompanied the 1951 *Mostra del Caravaggio e dei Caravaggeschi*, Roberto Longhi included a curious reference at the end of a brief biography of Gentileschi. Readers seeking further information on the artist were referred not to an art-historical study, but to a recently released novel.[1] This had been published in 1947 by a Florentine author, translator, literary critic and art historian, who, as it transpired, was also married to Longhi. Anna Banti, the nom de plume adopted by Lucia Lopresti Longhi (1895–1985), was at that stage working alongside Longhi as the co-editor of the influential art history and literary studies periodical *Paragone*, a journal that would go on to publish numerous studies of both the Gentileschis and the Caravaggisti more generally. Banti's *Artemisia*, however, bears no resemblance to a standard art-historical text. It wilfully combines the genres of novel, biography and autobiography into a complex interleafing of contrasting points of view operating across different epochs and in a manner that Lucia Boldrini has characterized as exemplifying what she terms the 'heterobiographical I'.[2] This involves the construction of a constantly shifting narrative that adroitly interweaves the story of Gentileschi's life and career within a poignant, first-person meditation on suffering, creativity and the struggle for identity that is set against the backdrop of the ashes of the final stages of the Florentine experience of the Second World War. Translated into English in 1988,[3] *Artemisia* continues to enjoy a high regard among

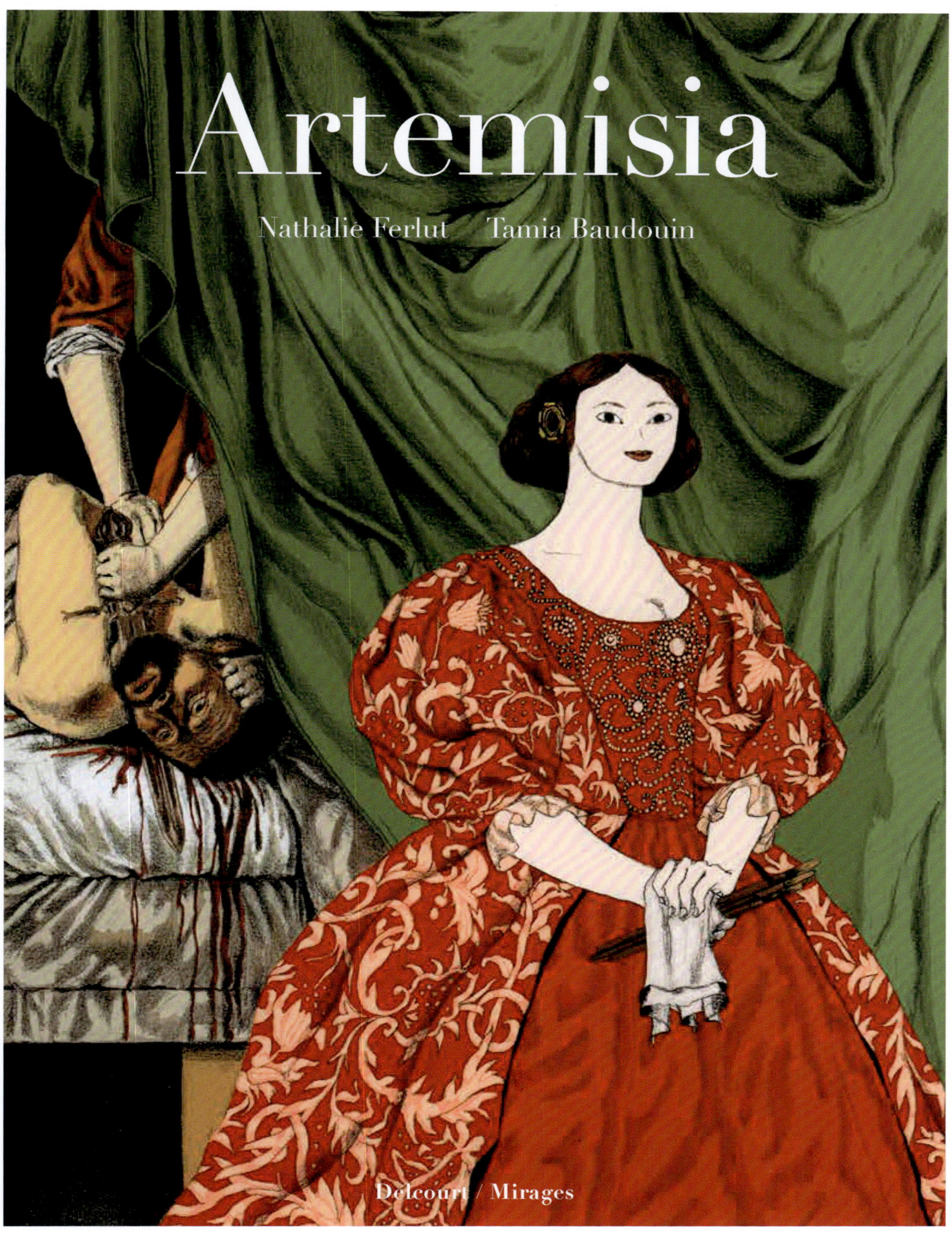

132 The cover of Nathalie Ferlut and Tamia Baudouin's novel *Artemisia*, originally published in French under the title *Artemisia*, © Editions Delcourt: Paris, 2017

readers, with Susan Sontag, for example, contributing the introduction to its 1988 English edition.[4]

Artemisia's originality lies, to a great degree, in the author's ability to mine the historical record for fascinating facts. This she then combines with a countervailing freedom to allow fresh readings into the text that would not have been possible within a more conventional, art-historical monograph. The novel's restlessly dissolving, multiple perspectives bring Artemisia constantly in and out of focus – both as an historical figure and as an elusive character within the narrative. She is, in this sense, vividly present and yet only fleetingly accessible within the pages of the text. The character of Artemisia in Banti's novel is a kind of ghost who has come to haunt the text and who manages always to slip free of the author's attempts to pin her down. At one stage, the authorial voice breaks down altogether and observes in exasperated exhaustion, 'there is no reply from Artemisia; she is immeasurably distant, light years away'.[5]

Banti's *Artemisia* is an innovative amalgamation of the traditionally distinct fields of freely associative imaginative writing with art-historical and ekphrastic literature. This works to reanimate key paintings so that they can be reimagined inhabiting an alternative dimension created for them by the author. An example is Banti's creative reinterpretation of the *Self-portrait as the Allegory of Painting* (fig. 103). Banti would have the reader reimagine this canvas as neither a self-portrait nor an allegory. Instead, it is presented in the novel as an imaginary portrait created from memory by Gentileschi in tribute to the younger Neapolitan female painter Annella de Rosa. For her part, Annella de Rosa remains, as noted in Chapter 10 (p. 152), a historically verifiable figure. Yet at the time of Banti's writing, she was even more shadowy than Gentileschi. She was known only through Bernardo de' Dominici's sensationalised, early eighteenth-century account of this young artist's early life and supposed murder at the hands of her jealous husband, himself a historically documented follower of Massimo Stanzione named Agostino Beltrano (see p. 205). In 1951, an article by Ulisse Prota Giurleo began the task of unravelling fact from fiction from this account,[6] thus initiating the painstaking – and, to this day, still far from complete – process of resurrecting Annella de Rosa from historical neglect.[7]

For Banti, the historical truth of Annella de Rosa's biography or of Gentileschi's *Self-portrait* is not as important as the deeper veracity that her novelistic method seeks to convey: 'Whether it is a self-portrait or not, a woman who paints in sixteen hundred and forty is very courageous, and this counts for Annella and for at least a hundred others, right up to the present.'[8] The novel thus presents a radically reimagined artwork standing in the place that would otherwise be occupied by the actual *Self-portrait as an Allegory of Painting*. This recasting of a known artwork into an alternative, imagined reality enables it to perform a redemptive role in the novel: to 'transform rivalry into sisterhood', as suggested by Cortney Cronberg Barko, or – as indicated by Deborah Heller – to bind Banti's narrator together with Artemisia and Annella into a conjoined creative manifestation of past and present female agency.[9]

'IT'S TRUE, IT'S TRUE, IT'S TRUE': ARTEMISIA'S FICTION AND THE RECUPERATIVE TURN

Anna Banti's *Artemisia* set in train a parallel literary tradition of often knowlingly fictionalised reimaginings of Gentileschi's life and art that has done much to spread awareness of her work beyond the limits of conventional art history. Banti herself returned to the topic in 1960 in a play, *Corte Savella*, which focused on the rape trial. This initiated a series of theatrical treatments that have been revived periodically over the course of the ensuing decades. A company currently wishing to bring Artemisia to the stage has thus no fewer than five different playscripts from which to choose. One of the most recent is Breach Productions' *It's True, It's True, It's True* of 2018, which takes as its source material a verbatim transcript of the rape-trial proceedings.[10] Yet it is the genre of historical fiction, in particular, that seems to have captured the imagination of contemporary readers seeking whatever it is that Artemisia might be said to signify today. Commencing with Maria Àngels Anglada's *Artemísia* of 1989, no fewer than a dozen novels, all devoted to her life and art, have been published over the past three decades. These attest both to the efficacy and to the mobility of Artemisia's brand as it continues to cross over from the relatively contained world of museums and art history into the publishing industry and beyond.

Biographical novels on the life and art of Gentileschi currently traverse multiple languages, formats (at least one in verse, for example) and even different categories of publishing. They thus now incorporate a growing number of Young Adult Fiction titles and even two graphic novels: Nathalie Ferlut and Tamia Baudouin's *Artemisia* of 2017 (fig. 132), and Gina Siciliano's *I Know What I Am: The Life and Times of Artemisia Gentileschi*, published by Fantagraphics in 2019.[11] An indication of the size and vitality of this burgeoning literary industry can be gauged with reference to the social cataloguing website Goodreads. Goodreads bills itself as 'the world's largest site for readers and book recommendations'. It ranks its titles according to how many 'ratings' they have received from their readers. A search in Goodreads for publications on Artemisia is revealing in this respect. First on the list is Susan Vreeland's 2002 novel, *The Passion of Artemisia*, which (at the time of writing) has garnered no fewer than 18,751 ratings, meaning that this many people have taken the time not just to read but also to rate this book for the website. Next in popularity is Alexandra Lapierre's 1998 novel, with a total of 5,515 ratings.[12]

Scholarly publications on Gentileschi, by contrast, rank considerably lower in the Goodreads ratings. Mary Garrard's 1989 monograph is by far the most popular art-historical publication, with a total of 289 ratings. By contrast, the 2001 Rome, New York and St Louis exhibition catalogue has only thirty-seven ratings, R. Ward Bissell's catalogue raisonné a mere seventeen, and only eleven ratings have been assigned to the English translation of the 2011 Milan exhibition catalogue. The greater popularity of the non-academic publications should remind us of the fundamental importance of one point that seems especially relevant to Gentileschi: more people than ever are encountering her work by way of sources that have not been sanctioned by the traditionally authoritative domains of academia and the museum. In fact, as the Goodreads tables make clear, many more people are now learning about Artemisia Gentileschi's paintings through the genre of biographical fiction than they are by studying her at university or by viewing her works in museums.

THE ARTEMISIA LITERARY INDUSTRY AND THE PROBLEM OF TRUTH

The historical novel affords writers the freedom to move beyond the limitations of what can and cannot be said in a more strictly scholarly format.[13] This has had a largely recuperative effect on the Artemisia literary industry. It has given authors the agency to fashion imagined versions of the artist's life and work that are often more dramatically framed and neatly resolved than is possible within the more cautiously provisional domain of the historical record. Accordingly, one frequently encounters in the novels attempts to 'correct' or 'improve' upon the often raggedly unresolved and even contradictory aspects of the historical record. These treatments are often rendered, moreover, in ways that are more palatable to contemporary audiences than would otherwise be admissible in the historical process.

The result is a series of novelistic images and episodes that tend to be both more dramatically neat and poetically just than the reader is ever likely to encounter within the scholarly literature. Thus, in Gina Siciliano's *I Know What I Am*, the reader encounters Artemisia painting the first version of *Judith Slaying Holofernes* with her hands still bound with bandages as a result of the torture inflicted at the recent rape trial. Similarly, in Joy McCullough's *Blood Water Paint*, the young Artemisia's prodigious skill is so powerful that her father (presented in the novel as a mediocre hack) signs her independently produced work as his own. And in Vreeland's *The Passion of Artemisia*, the artist paints the facial features of Agostino Tassi onto her depiction of Holofernes. In this way, the author renders the psychological identification of Tassi as the villain being dispatched by Judith/Artemisia as a triumphantly clear and demonstrable 'fact'. Needless to say, the extent to which Holofernes can be said to act as a surrogate in this painting for Tassi himself is a much-debated point that would never be expressed, art-historically speaking, in such definitive terms.

Yet there are limits to the degree to which these works of 'historical fiction' can deliberately depart from the strictures of historicity. This counter-gravitational pull back towards history's norms seems largely attributable to the dominance of Artemisia's own voice in the early sources. Her primary documentation has remained key to the literature since the dawn of modern art history. No fewer than six of Gentileschi's letters were included in Giovanni Bottari's foundational archival publication *Raccolta di lettere sulla pittura, scultura ed architettura* of 1757–68.[14] This was followed by Antonio Bertolotti's publication in 1876 of the rape-trial testimony, which was followed, in turn, by the publication in 1916 of Gentileschi's correspondence with Ruffo, which was then updated by the addition of yet further letters that had been published in the meantime, together with an additional transcription of the rape proceedings – all conveniently translated and brought together by Garrard in 1989. Added to this is the publication in 2011 of her letters to Maringhi.[15] As a result, Artemisia must now rank as one of the most fully documented artists of the early modern period. Any writer wishing to capture her voice can, therefore, hardly ignore, for example, her piercingly affecting strains as a seventeen-year-old repeating her claims 'over and over' during the ordeal of torture while in the presence of her abuser (the source of the 'It's true, It's true, It's true' title referred to above). Neither can one fail to acknowledge her insistent tones as an established painter standing up for the status of her art while prising money out of intransigent patrons – and so on.

The novels seem thus to be in a constant process of negotiation between the accelerating thrill of the creative impulse, on the one hand, versus the more cautious and exacting demands of historical verisimilitude, on the other. This dialectic is particularly evident in Alexandra Lapierre's *Artemisia*, which was previously noted as second only to Vreeland's novel in its popularity as a best-selling fictional account. *Artemisia* was one of the first of the current wave of novels based on Gentileschi's life and has been subsequently translated into seven languages. Lapierre views her novel as remaining faithful to the historical tradition. She sees it, in effect, as 'a narration sticking as closely to facts as possible, yet readable as fiction by non-art specialists'.[16] Documentary sources are, accordingly, continuously stressed, particularly by way of an extensive series of notes at the back of the book that refer the reader to the sources drawn on for each section, with a particular emphasis on archival references.[17]

The author's own archival research, undertaken while writing the novel, moreover, was also noteworthy. It resulted in some important findings, including new information about the rape-trial proceedings – showing, for example, that Tassi was found guilty and sentenced to banishment from Rome – together with additional information about Artemisia's husband, Pierrantonio Stiattesi. It was also Lapierre's research that was responsible for the discovery that the painting mentioned in the trial as having been stolen from Orazio Gentileschi was not Artemisia's first version of the *Judith*, as had previously been believed, but rather an early version of the subject by Orazio himself, now in Bilbao (fig. 25).[18]

On one level, therefore, Lapierre's *Artemisia* certainly meets the scholarly standards that are required of a piece of careful historical research, but, in terms of its overall framing of Artemisia's character, it is as extravagantly fictitious as anything conjured up by the likes of Baroness Orczy. This is especially noticeable in the novel's interpretation of its central theme of the ambivalent relationship between Artemisia and her father. The theatrically oppositional nature of this theme is signalled most clearly by the novel's original French subtitle: *Un duel pour l'immortalité* (*A duel for immortality*). Artemisia's entire life and career are reduced, at this level, to a daughter's titanic struggle to win her father's love and approval – a struggle that she can never hope to win, despite all her efforts. Orazio Gentileschi is framed as a constant point of reference, a source of both authority and desire that must be overcome at the same time as he must be, in an equal sense, possessed. Artemisia's struggle to control and surpass Orazio is described in this regard in tones suggesting an almost Electra-like identification with this most unforgiving of father figures: 'Secure now in her own worth, intoxicated by the certainty that she was rushing headlong towards fame at the same speed and on equal terms with him, she ardently desired to see his paintings again.'[19] Or, again, at the novel's climax, as Gentileschi paints at the primal scene of her father's deathbed:

> 'You aren't asleep?' She asked, worried by his expression. 'No. I have been observing you for a while. You are beautiful.' She blushed as if these words and that look were a reminder of old emotions. 'I want to see you. Come here.'

> He held out his arms and drew her to him. It seemed such an easy gesture, so familiar. 'God will not judge us,' he murmured. 'God refuses to choose between us.' His eyes clouded over.

While not overtly expressed as such within the novel, the apparent sub-text is that Artemisia and Orazio's intense relationship is akin to a sublimated love affair stretching boundlessly across time and place. In the novel's prologue, Lapierre even goes so far as to propose that their relationship might have involved incest: 'Artemisia and Orazio were prepared to kill in order to prove their superior talent. Both of them did much more than dream of the other's passing. Was there parricide? Incest?'[20] With its stress on the well-worn trope of the centrality to female recognition of a (literally) patriarchal system of acceptance, Lapierre's novel seems especially open in passages like these to Tina Olsin Lent's criticism of the wider Artemisia literary industry: 'By exaggerating the emotional aspects of her life they reinforce familiar ties between creativity and passion, reiterate women's creativity as exceptional and the result of male influence, as well as resonate with contemporary desires for emotional relevance and accessibility.'[21]

ARTEMISIA ON THE SCREEN

On 3 April 1998, Agnès Merlet's *Artemisia* was released to American cinemas. Pundits would presumably not have been expecting anything particularly extraordinary in terms of a public response to this film, which must have seemed like just another, relatively modest, French costume drama. This impression would have been reinforced by knowledge of the movie's budget – around US$7,000,000 – which would have further positioned it as a limited, art-house release only.[22] Yet what this film failed to recoup at the box office it certainly made up for in terms of controversy.

Merlet's *Artemisia* constitutes a particularly prominent instance of being able to gauge just how much digression from the historical record an audience might be prepared to tolerate in the name of artistic licence. The issues of this type that are raised by the film are manifold, and they tend to become more pronounced the longer one watches. Does it matter, for

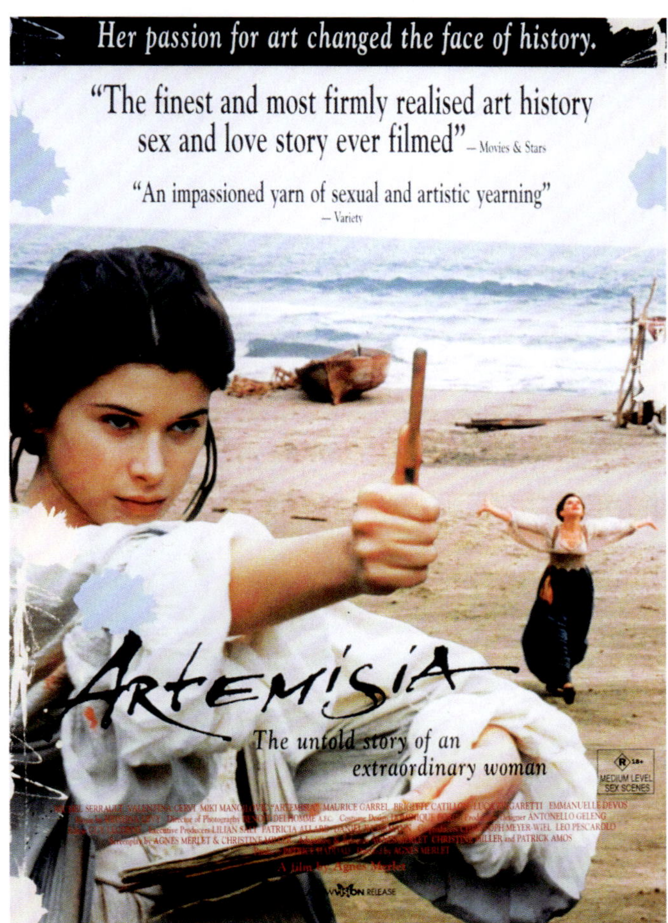

133 Promotional brochure for Agnès Merlet's *Artemisia*, 1998

example, that the actor playing the role of Artemisia bears no immediate physical resemblance to the artist's distinctive visual iconography (fig. 133)? Does it matter that the actor seems to maintain an exceptional degree of autonomy and agency such as would seem to bear little or no relationship to the much more pressurised and circumscribed conditions of Artemisia's early home environment under Orazio's care? Does it matter that Artemisia's character seems to be thoroughly preoccupied with her own personal agenda regarding sex, creativity and the getting of wisdom, to a degree that one might normally associate with a contemporary coming-of-age movie rather than what we might consider appropriate to a dramatization of this particular historical subject?

Yet more unsettling, however, is the film's treatment of Agostino Tassi's role in Artemisia's early biography. The movie portrays Tassi and Gentileschi's relationship as a loving, mutually consensual and passionate affair conducted on an initially clandestine basis by a youthful student and her middle-aged master/teacher. Tassi is depicted 'inducting' his willing student into the ways of love – a well-worn albeit highly problematic trope. (And this is also an affair, it should be further noted, that has been reinterpreted for the contemporary screen by two performers whose age difference – around twenty-four years – is even greater than that between the real Artemisia and Tassi – fifteen years.[23])

This distortion of the historical record soon brought Merlet's film into conflict with a number of Gentileschi's American supporters. In particular, it impelled Mary Garrard and Gloria Steinem to mount a public campaign against the film. They urged viewers to come to screenings armed with a 'fact sheet' denouncing the film in no uncertain terms. 'Now that you have seen the film, meet the real Artemisia Gentileschi', they wrote:

> The idea that a woman artist is the creation of a male mentor has been a persistent myth in the history of art, frequently asserted by artists and critics of the 16th and 17th centuries. So has the romanticization of violent rape, as in the rape scenes in this film, and the idea that women wish to be raped or fall in love with their rapists . . . Perhaps unwittingly, the film Artemisia taps into pervasive stereotypes about women artists in general, and it perpetuates the stigma of a primarily sexualized identity that has followed Artemisia Gentileschi from her own lifetime down.[24]

The controversy over the film acted in certain respects as a stimulus to its reception, since it helped – almost paradoxically – to increase the publicity attendant upon its US release. Yet the film's opponents were successful in forcing its US distributors to agree to retract the publicity claim that the film represented 'the true story of the first female painter in art history'.[25] The debate surrounding the film was thus arguably beneficial in that it once more highlighted the continuing power of Gentileschi's art to elicit charged, political responses from contemporary audiences.

ARTEMISIA BEYOND THE FRAME

Of all the links to have been drawn between Artemisia and other fields of art, the association between her paintings and music seems especially appropriate. Her compositions often evoke the heightened theatricality and elevated emotional tenor of opera, and many of her most memorable works depict musicians – either heavenly or earth-bound. Her *Self-portrait as a Lute Player*, for example, represents her embodiment of the musicality present in other of her artworks (fig. 37).[26]

It is perhaps surprising, then, that it was not until well into the twenty-first century that a musical treatment of Gentileschi's life made its way onto the stage. In January 2017, an opera, composed by Laura Schwendinger with a libretto by Ginger Strand, received its world premiere in New York. The opera's staging maintained a dialogue between the characters, music and paintings by means of a series of screens emitting a slideshow of Gentileschi's compositions (fig. 134). The opera was favourably reviewed by the *New York Times*, with its critic taking for granted the reader's familiarity with the artist's story: '"Artemisia" lasts just 80 minutes, but fits in big themes set to music of quivering intensity. The story of the rape is there, blended with Gentileschi's unbearably compassionate painting of the biblical character Susanna, who was ogled and shamed in her bath. But larger questions of idea and form, image and projection, sight and gaze also find nuanced and intelligent treatment.'[27] In addition to all the other crossovers featuring Gentileschi as a twenty-first century brand, music can now, therefore, be added to the list.

The New York premiere of *Artemisia* integrated opera with projected images of her compositions, which were then disseminated further through YouTube video clips. The ease with which Gentileschi's creations made the transition from physical artworks to mediated digital images projected onto the stage highlights the extent to which her imagery is now apprehended through a host of other media platforms besides those directly associated with the worlds of art history and the museum. It would, perhaps, be helpful here to look beyond the high cultural field of opera in order to cite another example of her influence upon the domain of contemporary popular culture. A search of social media using the hashtag #artemisiagentileschi will reveal some surprising results. One such discovery is Faux Machismo, a contemporary musical duo who describe themselves as a 'two piece Leeds-based stoner-witch doom-grunge band'. Faux Machismo's repertoire includes a song simply titled *Artemisia*, in which the band recast Gentileschi's most famous composition into a post-grunge, Riot grrrl expression of powerful primal disaffection (fig. 135).[28]

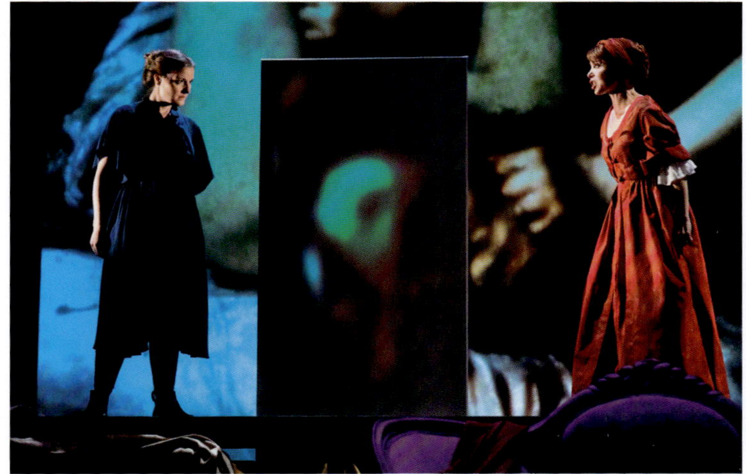

134 Still from the opera *Artemisia*, by Laura Elise Schwendinger (music) and Ginger Strand (libretto), 2019

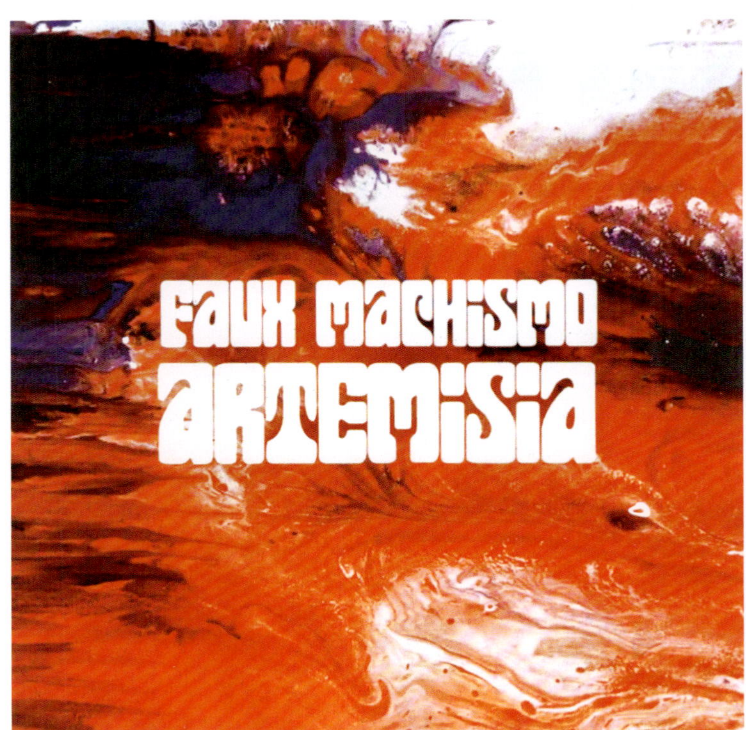

135 Faux Machismo, *Artemisia*, publicity still, 2021

These contemporary manifestations evoke the expanding parameters within which Gentileschi's influence continues to make itself felt. In this respect, Gentileschi is no longer just a painting sitting in a museum. Neither is she simply an artistic reputation that is held in place by a discourse maintained by a consensus of critics, curators, art historians and other self-appointed keepers of the sacred flame. Instead, she has now been transformed into something more fluid and mercurial. She is a hashtag, a meme, an Instagram post, a TikTok video. She moves correspondingly through a much wider – and less controllable – communicative field. One encounters Artemisia today not just in books or in galleries but also within an ever-shifting stream of observations, responses and counter-comments, all of which are being continuously replayed and recycled via the constantly evolving algorithms of social media and the internet.

This process has been given a particularly insistent impetus as a result of the #MeToo movement, which seeks to raise public awareness of sexual harassment and violence perpetuated against women by men in positions of power and authority. Gentileschi was present, for example, in September 2018, when the process informing the nomination of judges to the United States Supreme Court became yet further polarised because of the resurfacing of a number of historical allegations of rape against the then nominee. Gentileschi's name was evoked during the live transmission of the Senate enquiry surrounding this appointment, as viewers simultaneously chose to share images on Twitter of her various versions of *Judith Slaying Holofernes*.[29] In late 2021, the process was repeated

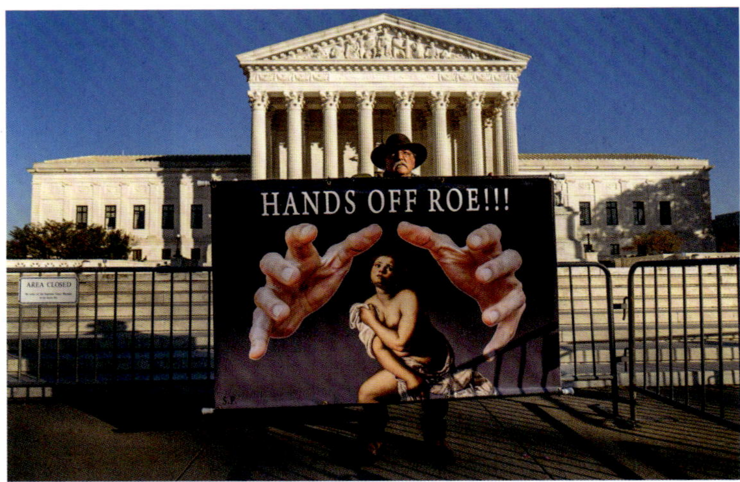

136 A protester holds a sign that reads 'Hands Off Roe!!!' outside the US Supreme Court ahead of arguments in case at the court challenging abortion laws, seen in Washington, 30 November 2021

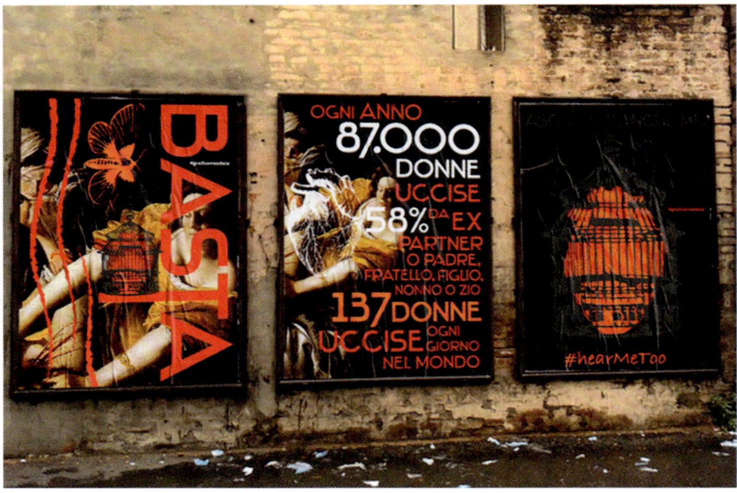

137 Sabrina Cenni, *Basta Femminicidio!*, three posters, letterpress printing on paper, screen print on paper, each 70 × 100 cm, in situ view, Rimini, May, 2019

with the use of an image of Gentileschi's 1622 *Susanna* to protest against the US Supreme Court's deliberations to curtail American abortion laws (fig. 136). Gentileschi has been cited on numerous occasions as both a precedent and a source of inspiration by many of those active in the #MeToo movement. A work by Sabrina Cenni stands out from the scores of contemporary examples that one might note in this context. It manages to recapture the still startling violence of Gentileschi's original composition by reframing it as a billboard on the streets of Rimini – this in a country with one of the most troubling records of domestic violence from across the European Union (fig. 137).[30]

CONCLUSION: ARTEMISIA UNBOUND

Artemisia has become, as they say, a household name that has come to signify much more than just art. Gentileschi's image as a trans-historical icon of creativity has, in this sense, become fused with her first name into a singular essential entity. Like other celebrity first namers – Madonna, Beyoncé, Björk, Rihanna and others – her single-name status has become synonymous with a specific set of values, outlooks and lifestyle attributes. In Artemisia's case, these have come to encompass a sense of power and drama, as well as to denote a highly distinctive personality that throws up associations of courage, independence, resoluteness, stylishness and verve. Artemisia has beome a powerful product in a literal as well as a figurative sense. She has reached a point of market recognition such that she can now be used to sell everything from canvases to exhibition concepts, to monographs, novels, movies, operas, songs, social causes and political issues – even perfume (fig. 138).

Of course, Gentileschi would have been the first to recognise the validity of this. From her audacious first act of prominently signing her 1610 demonstration piece, all the way to her last letters proclaiming her intrinsic worth as an artist, Gentileschi stands out as someone who was always especially aware of the importance of maintaining agency and control over all the complex processes involved in the marketing and selling of both herself and her work to the public. It is clear from the outset of this process that Gentileschi instinctively recognised from a very early age the importance of one fundamental truth: that she would never attain success by simply painting great artworks and then hoping for the best. Rather, her constant attentiveness to a wide range of aspects relating to the business of art meant that she remained always mindful of the necessarily contingent nature of artistic production.

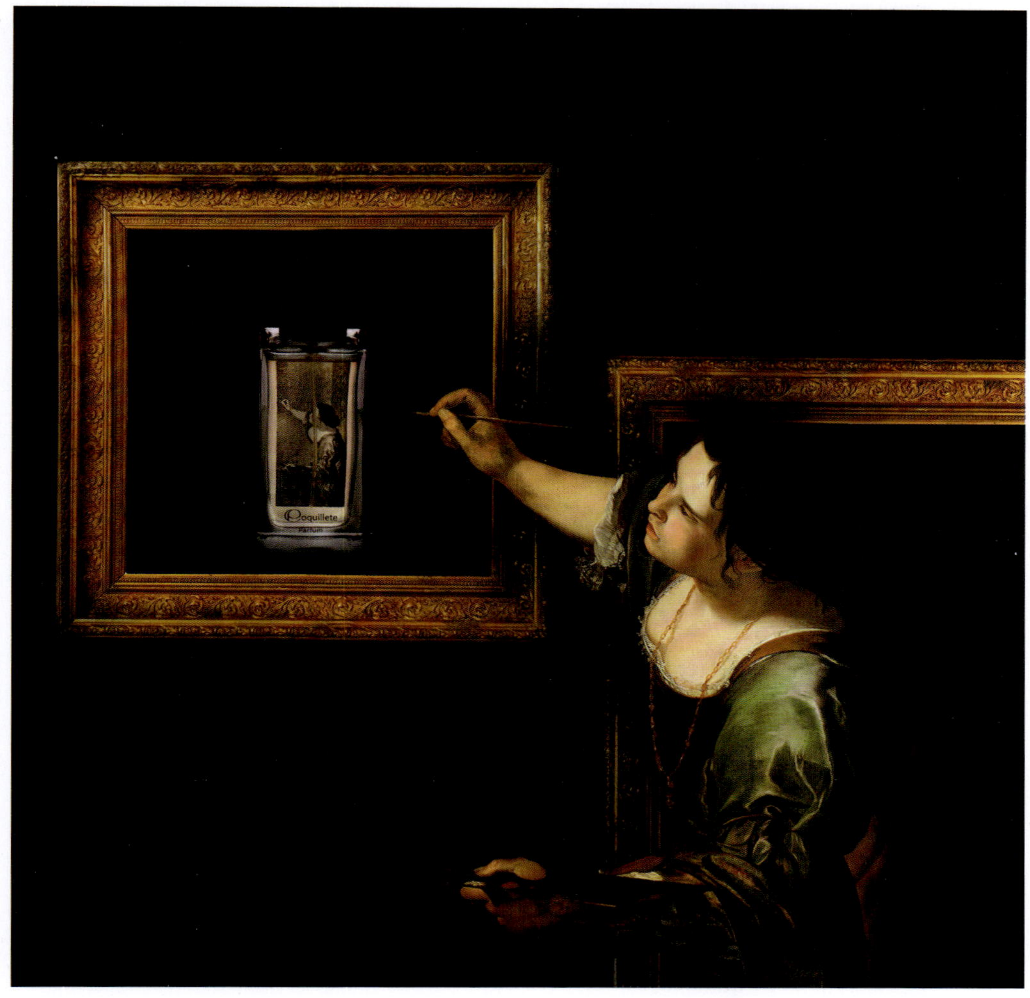

138 Advertisement for *Artemisia G.* perfume, by Coquillete Parfum, Paris

Gentileschi was among the first painters to grasp the importance of maintaining her own persona as a vital component of the transaction involved in the act of looking at art, as well as in the larger process of securing long-term recognition in the art world beyond her lifetime: the pursuit of fame and all that that entailed. In her self-portraits, whether disguised or otherwise, Gentileschi showed herself to be a true innovator in her awareness of the value of fusing her artworks and persona into a composite, singular entity. She also emerges from this study as a figure of seemingly limitless reserves of flexibility, resourcefulness and drive. Maintaining a successful career in art is a constant and relentless struggle. The Artemisia that we have been shadowing in these pages was an artistic survivor, who was always on the move, continuously evolving plans in response to an endless array of challenges and contingencies. All the documentation points to an indomitable sense of tenacity and resolve that never let up and that never allowed her the luxury of giving up and letting go. And when human frailty did, finally, slow her hand, the power and presence of the works themselves ensured that it would be only a matter of time before others would take up the task of resurrecting her reputation and so continue the process of advancing her public profile to the heights of global celebrity that she enjoys today.

To identify an artist as canonical involves a concomitant claim of ongoing artistic value that suggests that that artist's reputation might be described as being, in certain respects at least, beyond dispute. Gentileschi – Artemisia – has certainly reached that point of recognition. This represents a signal achievement. But at what stage in the long and complex development here outlined can Gentileschi be seen to have attained that goal? In truth, it is no easier to answer this question at the end of this study than it was at the outset. This is because the much-desired but always elusive quality of artistic success is a goal that tends to define itself differently, according to the varying expectations of whoever is contemplating the issue. On a basic level, we can, perhaps, conclude that this study has confirmed, once again, the essential truthfulness of the adage that success in the art world is not so much a matter of talent as it is also a product of hard work and good luck. Like many other historically significant artists, Artemisia Gentileschi seems not to have experienced much of the latter until after her death. But she certainly did match the distinctive uniqueness of her artistic vision with an equally intense attentiveness towards the cold, hard truths of the business side of art at all stages of her career.

One might identify many points in Gentileschi's career of major stress – even one might say of crisis. Many were the moments when she suffered some kind of significant limitation or setback that might have stopped other artists in their tracks. Besides the obviously detrimental nature of key aspects of her early life and professional development in her father's care, one might also cite the following existential challenges of Gentileschi's career: she might have remained content to eke out a career as an increasingly isolated Caravaggesque painter operating in a tried-and-true manner, while the taste for that kind of painting dried up and moved beyond her. But she didn't. She might have been happy staying put in one or other of the artistic centres through which she passed – in Florence, for example, or Rome, or Venice, even though they all held her back in one way or another professionally and personally. But she wasn't. She might have remained content working with the diminishing returns of a predominantly private market that did not grant her the more substantial platform of being able to pursue high-ranking public commissions. But she didn't. She might have given up towards the end of her career, when increasing health issues and financial concerns conspired to curb her productivity. But still she didn't allow herself to stop. Instead, Artemisia seems never to have flagged in her efforts to rethink and reposition herself strategically in response to the constant challenges and opportunities that she was called upon to negotiate on a daily basis. And if we add to this the intrinsic power of the paintings themselves, then we are well on the way to appreciating the complex processes that have contributed to her continued prominence in the public gaze. Gentileschi has inspired so many voices, as we have seen, all seeking to speak on her behalf. So perhaps it is fitting, instead, to stop now and to leave the final word to the artist herself:

> The works will speak for themselves. And with this I end with a most humble bow.[31]

— APPENDIX —

Tables

TABLE I: PAYMENTS TO ARTEMISIA GENTILESCHI

Date	*Amount* (*converted to ducats/scudi where relevant*)	*Subject(s)*	*Dimensions* (*converted into cm from original units of measurement where known*)	*No. of Figures*	*Purchaser*	*Source*
August 1615–August 1616	34 florins/scudi (includes extra money loaned to Gentileschi and her husband)	Allegory of Inclination	152 × 61	1	Michelangelo Buonarroti the Younger	Procacci, 1967, 13
31 July 1617	140 lire (equivalent to 20 scudi)	Judith	unspecified	1–2	Laura Corsini	Baldassari in Rome, 2016, n. 31, 33
1618	10 scudi on account down-payment	Madonna	unspecified	1	Simone Carducci on behalf of Margherita Benvenuti	Barker, 2017, doc. 14, 75
1 March 1619	150 scudi	unspecified final payment	unspecified	unspecified	Medici	Barker, 2017, doc. 7, 75
6 May 1619	50 scudi	unspecified down-payment on account for unspecified work	unspecified	unspecified	Medici	Barker, 2017, doc. 8, 75
1626–28	1467 guilij 14 baiocchi, equivalent to 146 scudi	Hercules and Omphale	large	3 or more	Philip IV	Gerard, 1982, 11
1630	4 ducats to make up 50 ducats total	St Elizabeth of Hungary, for a chapel in Pisticci, Basilicata	unspecified	1	Don Geronimo de Cardenas	Lattuada and Nappi, 2005, doc. 1, 97
1631	20 ducats	St Sebastian	158 × 210	1	Francesco d'Afflitto conte di Loreto	Nappi, 1992, 74
1636	200 ducats × 3	Bathsheba, Susanna, Lucretia	303 wide each	*c.*3–4 × 3	Pietro Gentile on behalf of Prince Karl Eusebius von Liechtenstein	Nappi, 1983, 76
1636	20 ducats to make up a total received thus far of 60 ducats, work still not finished	unspecified (?St Joseph and the Christ Child – on basis of subsequent inventory reference)	half length/not large	1–2	Bernardino Belprato, conte di Aversa	Nappi, 1983, 76
1645	20 ducats	Sacrifice of Isaac	125 × 100	3	Vincenzo d'Andrea	Abetti, 2022, 104, doc. 5, 107–8
1648	30 ducats on account	An unspecified painting	unspecified	unspecified	Fabrizio Ruffo, principe della Bagnara	Strazzullo, 1955, 44
1649	160 ducats [45 ducats for frame, acquired separately]	Galatea on a shell, with 5 tritons and 2 dolphins	211 × 264	7	Don Flavio Ruffo, on behalf of Don Antonio Ruffo of Messina	Ruffo, 1916, 48
1649–50	230 ducats	Diana and Actaeon, with 5 nymphs + 2 dogs	211 × 264	7	Don Flavio Ruffo, on behalf of Don Antonio Ruffo of Messina	Ruffo, 1916, 50
1651	90 scudi (offering price)	Perseus and Andromeda	unspecified	2	Don Antonio Ruffo of Messina	Ruffo, 1916, 53
1651	90 scudi (offering price)	Joseph and Potiphar's Wife	unspecified	2	Don Antonio Ruffo of Messina	Ruffo, 1916, 53

TABLE I (*continued . . .*)

Date	*Amount* (*converted to ducats/scudi where relevant*)	*Subject(s)*	*Dimensions* (*converted into cm from original units of measurement where known*)	*No of Figures*	*Purchaser*	*Source*
1651	48 ducats to make up 150 ducats	Diana and Actaeon, Venus and Adonis, A nude figure with accompaniment	316 (Diana and Actaeon), 263 (Venus and Adonis), 237 (A nude female figure with its accompaniment)	4 (Bath of Diana), 2 (Venus and Adonis), 2 (A nude figure and its accompaniment)	Fabio Gentile on behalf of the Holy Roman Emperor, Ferdinand III	Lattuada and Nappi, 2005, doc. 2, 97
1653	50 ducats for the total price of the painting said to have been 'sold' by the artist	Susanna and the Elders	unspecified	2–3	Antonio Galise	Lattuada and Nappi, 2005, doc. 3, 98
1654	10 ducats to make up 39 received thus far on account – payment made to Onofrio Palumbo, said to be for three paintings that he will have to paint jointly with Artemisia Gentileschi. The paintings to be completed and delivered within one and a half months of the payment	unspecified	unspecified	unspecified	Fabio Gentile	Lattuada and Nappi, 2005, doc. 6, 98

TABLE 2: REFERENCES TO PAINTINGS BY ARTEMISIA GENTILESCHI IN EARLY NEAPOLITAN AND SOUTHERN ITALIAN DOCUMENTARY SOURCES (INVENTORIES, PAYMENTS, LETTERS, BIOGRAPHIES, POEMS)

Subject(s)	*Owner*	*Dimensions (converted into cm from original units of measurement where known)*	*Date*	*Reference*
Portrait of a duchess	unspecified	unknown	1630	Garrard, 1989, 378–79
Portrait of Adriana Basile seated touching the strings of a harp	unspecified – referred to in poem by Girolamo Fontanella published in 1640	unknown	Before 1640	Lukehart, 2015, 106–7
Portrait of Girolamo Fontanella	Fontanella, Girolamo	unknown	Before 1640	Lukehart, 2015, 106
Self-portrait	unspecified – referred to in poem by Girolamo Fontanella published in 1640	unknown	Before 1640	Lukehart, 2015, 107
Self-portrait (1? 2?)	In the studio of the artist, referred to in letters to Cassiano dal Pozzo and to Don Antonio Ruffo of Messina	unknown	1630 and 1651	Garrard, 1989, 377–79; 390–94
A child/?Christ Child	Zurlo, Giacomo Capece	53 × 40	1715	Ruotolo, 1973, 151
Head of Christ	Imperiale, Davide, nobile	small	1672	Labrot, 1992, Inv. 21, item 9, 119
Christ and the Samaritan Woman	Painted for the Barberini in Rome, sold in Naples?	317 × 238	1637	Garrard, 1989, 387–88
Ecce Homo (part of a series of 8 paintings, also included 7 paintings of Angels holding the symbols of the Passion)	Palma, Francesco de, duca di S. Elia	105 × 79	1716	Labrot, 1992, Inv. 56, item 1, 284
Madonna, on copper	In studio of artist, offered to Don Antonio Ruffo of Messina	small	1651	Garrard, 1989, 399–400
Madonna	Capecelatro, Ettore, marchese di Torella	small	1655	Labrot, 1992, Inv. 16, item 35, 102
Madonna and child	Acquired by Domenico de Angelis from his brother Antonio de Martino in Naples	105 × 105	1657	Lattuada and Nappi, 2005, doc. 7, 98
Madonna	Giangerolamo II Acquaviva, conte di Conversano	unspecified	1666	Ruotolo, 1977, item 18, 73
Head of the Virgin	Imperiale, Davide, nobile	small	1672	Labrot, 1992, Inv. 21, item 9, 119
Madonna of the Rosary, with SS Dominic and Catherine of Siena, figure by Gentileschi, landscape by Gargiulo	Pinto, Fabrizio	53	1700/1701	Del Grosso and Avino, 1989, 50, 93, 142
Annunciation (attributed to Artemisia Gentileschi in a 17th-century family inventory, attributed to Agostino Beltrano in the family inventory of 1786)	Carafa, Nicola Pietro Carafa, Carafa San Lorenzo	158 × 211	1786	Ruotolo, 1974, 168
Annunciation	Quadra, Alvaro della, duca di Limatola	unspecified	1694	Getty Provenance Index, Archival Inventory I-163, page 1, item 4
St Elizabeth of Hungary, for a chapel in in Pisticci, Basilicata	Don Geronimo de Cardenas	unspecified	1630	Lattuada and Nappi, 2005, doc. 1, 97
7 paintings of Angels holding the symbols of the Passion (part of a series of 8 paintings, including a painting of Ecce Homo)	Palma, Francesco de, duca di S. Elia	105 × 79	1716	Labrot, 1992, Inv. 56, item 1, 284

TABLE 2 *(continued . . .)*

Subject(s)	*Owner*	*Dimensions (converted into cm from original units of measurement where known)*	*Date*	*Reference*
Gioseppe Giusto/St Joseph and the Christ Child	Belprato, Bernardino, conte di Anversa	unspecified	1667	Getty Provenance Index, Archival Inventory I-30, page 3, Item 0027
Gioseppe Giusto/?St Joseph and the Christ Child	Capece Piscicelli, Giovanni Battista, nobile di Seggio	large	1690	Getty Provenance Index, Archival Inventory I-245, page 9, item 25
St John the Baptist in the Desert	Painted for the Barberini in Rome, sold in Naples?	238 × 238	1637	Garrard, 1989, 387–88
St John the Baptist	Filomarino, Ascanio, duca della Torre	79 × 105	1685/1700	Labrot, 1992, Inv. 33, item 16, 161; Ruotolo, 1977, 80
St Michael overcoming the Devil	Romeo, Luigi, barone di S. Luigi	life-size figures	Before 1742	De' Dominici, 1742–45, III, 199
St Sebastian	Ruffo, Guglielmo, principe di Scilla (Calabria)	109 × 79	1748	Getty Provenance Index, Archival Inventory I-204, page 14, item 73, Bissell, 1999, cat. L83, 382
St Sebastian (head by Gentileschi)	D'Afflitto, Ferdinando, principe di Scanno (originally commissioned by Giovanni Francesco d'Afflitto, conte di Loreto, in 1631, see Nappi, 1992, 74)	211 × 158	1700	Getty Provenance Index, Archival Inventory I-24, page 2, item 16c
St Eustace (head by Gentileschi)	D'Afflitto, Ferdinando, principe di Scanno	158 × 211	1700	Getty Provenance Index, Archival Inventory I-24, page 2, item 16a
David (head by Gentileschi)	D'Afflitto, Ferdinando, principe di Scanno	158 × 211	1700	Getty Provenance Index, Archival Inventory I-24, page 2, item 16b
David	Acquired by Giovanni di Franco from Alessandro Balzamo in Naples	211 × 158	1663	Lattuada and Nappi, 2005, doc. 8, 98
David with the Head of Goliath	Viewed by Joachim von Sandrart in Gentileschi's workshop	unspecified	1631	Von Sandrart, 1675–80, II, 204
Magdalene	Capecelatro, Ettore, marchese di Torella	105 × 132	1659	Labrot, 1992, Inv. 19, item 8, 113
Magdalene	Imperiale, Davide, nobile	105 × 132	1672	Labrot, 1992, Inv. 21, item 7, 119
Magdalene	Pinto, Francesco Emanuele, principe di Ischitella	66 cm (?octagonal)	1767	Pacelli, 1979, 178
Magdalene	Acquired by Giovanni di Franco from Alessandro Balzamo in Naples	132 × 158	1663	Lattuada and Nappi, 2005, doc. 8, 98
St Catherine	In studio of artist, offered to Andrea Cioli in Florence	unknown	1635	Garrard, 1989, 375, 85–86
St Cecilia	D'Andrea, Vincenzo	53 × 79	1649	Pacelli, 1987, 145–46
St Lucy	Poliastri, Stanislao, arcivescovo di Rossano, Monsignor	105 high	1741	Labrot, 1992, Inv. 74, item 30, 403
Two paintings of holy virgins	Ciavarella, Salvatore	66	1707	Getty Provenance Index, Archival Inventory I-214, page 18, item 31
A half-length holy virgin	Pignatelli, Giovanna Battista d'Aragona, duchessa di Terranova e Monteleone	119 × 132	1723	Labrot, 1992, Inv. 61, item 322, 324
Roman Charity	Giangerolamo II Acquaviva, conte di Conversano	121 × 147	1666	Ruotolo, 1977, item 13, 73; Conversano, 2018, cat. 30, 262–66
Hope	Colonna, Camillo	large	1647	Ricciardi, 2000, 56, 60
Fortune	Orsini, Ottavio, principe di Frasso	158 × 132	1704	Labrot, 1992, Inv. 45, item 88, 228

TABLE 2 *(continued . . .)*

Subject(s)	*Owner*	*Dimensions (converted into cm from original units of measurement where known)*	*Date*	*Reference*
Circle of flowers with a child reclining in the middle	Perrino, Domenico	132 × 105	1716	Getty Provenance Index, Archival Inventory I-68, item 2
Putto sleeping with his head on a red cushion, painted on copper	Orsini, Anne-Marie de La Trémoille, principessa	158 × 237	1723	Getty Provenance Index, Archival inventory I-419, page 13v
Sacrifice of Isaac	D'Andrea, Vincenzo	105 × 79	1649	Pacelli, 1987, 145–46
Death of the First Born Sons of Egypt (attributed in a 17th-century family inventory to Francesco Antonio Giannone)	Carafa, Nicola Pietro Carafa, Carafa San Lorenzo	317 × 238	1786	Ruotolo, 1974, 167
Samson	Francone, Francesco, principe di Pietracupa	158 × 211	1718	Getty Provenance Index, Archival Inventory I-721, page 16, item 28
David and Bathsheba (one of a set of three with Susanna and the Elders and Tarquin and Lucretia)	Lorenzo Cambi and Simone Verzone on behalf of Prince Karl Eusebius von Liechtenstein	303 wide	1636	Nappi, 1983, 76
Susanna and the Elders (one of a set of three with David and Bathsheba and Tarquin and Lucretia)	Lorenzo Cambi and Simone Verzone on behalf of Prince Karl Eusebius von Liechtenstein	303 wide	1636	Nappi, 1983, 76
David and Bathsheba (probably one of a set of three with Susanna and the Elders and Lot and his Daughters)	Romeo, Luigi, barone di S. Luigi	large with life-size figures	Before 1742	De' Dominici, 1742–45, III, 198–99; Bissell, 1999, cat. 37
Susanna and the Elders (probably one of a set of three with David and Bathsheba and Lot and his Daughters)	Romeo, Luigi, barone di S. Luigi	large with life-size figures	Before 1742	De' Dominici, 1742–45, III, 198–99; Bissell, 1999, cat. 38
Susanna and the Elders	Galise, Antonio	unspecified	1653	Lattuada and Nappi, 2005, doc. 3, 98
Judith	Di Gennaro, Cesare, principe di San Martino	132 × 158	1646	Paolillo, 1985, 119
Judith	Carafa, Giuseppe, dei Duchi di Maddaloni	158 × 132	1648/1649	Labrot, 1992, Inv. 9, item 58, 77; Labrot, 1992, Inv. 11, item 2, 82
Judith (attributed to Gentileschi in 1739, subsequently reattributed to Guido Reni [1776], Bolognese school [1862] and copy after Titian [today]	D'Avalos, Gianbattista, IX marchese del Vasto	79 × 119	1739	Bugli, 2003–4, no. 131, 32
David and Abigail	Carafa, Nicola Pietro Carafa, Carafa San Lorenzo	264 × 317	1786	Ruotolo, 1974, 167
Lot and his Daughters (attributed in a 17th-century family inventory to Francesco Antonio Giannone)	Carafa, Nicola Pietro Carafa, Carafa San Lorenzo	158 × 211	1786	Ruotolo, 1974, 167
Lot and his Daughters (probably one of a set of 3 with Bathsheba and Susanna)	Romeo, Luigi, barone di S. Luigi	life-size figures	before 1742	De' Dominici, 1742-45, III, 198–99, Bissell, 1999, cat. 39

TABLE 2 *(continued . . .)*

Subject(s)	*Owner*	*Dimensions (converted into cm from original units of measurement where known)*	*Date*	*Reference*
Joseph and Potiphar's Wife	Offered for sale to Don Antonio Ruffo of Messina	211 × 264	1651	Garrard, 1989, 400–401
The Flight into Egypt, on copper	Ruffo, Antonio, principe di Scaletta	38	1678	Getty Provenance Index, Archival Inventory I-2266, page 2, Item 0007c
Hercules spinning /Hercules and Omphale	Cardenas, Carlo de, conte di Acerra, marchese di Laino	211 × 237	1699	Labrot, 1992, Inv. 42, item 75, 206.
Apollo with a lyre	Fontanella, Girolamo	unspecified	before 1640	Lukehart, 2015, 105–6
Apollo killing the Python	Fontanella, Girolamo	unspecified	before 1640	Lukehart, 2015, 106
Perseus and Andromeda	Ruffo, Don Antonio of Messina (offered to, in 1651)	unspecified	1651	Ruffo, 1916, 53
Bath of Diana with 5 nymphs and 2 dogs (also documented by payments/correspondence with Don Antonio Ruffo of Messina, 1649)	Ruffo, Antonio, principe di Scaletta	204 × 255	1678	Getty Provenance Index, Archival Inventory, I-2266, page 2, item 0007b
Diana and Actaeon	Cella, Santo Maria, duca di Frisa	343 × 211	1680	Labrot, 1992, Inv. 29, item 79, 147
Diana and Actaeon (part of a series of 3 with Venus and Adonis and 'a nude figure and its accompaniment')	Fabio Gentile on behalf of the Holy Roman Emperor, Ferdinand III	316	1651	Lattuada and Nappi, 2005, doc. 2, 97
Galatea	Belprato, Bernardino, conte di Anversa	unspecified	1667	Getty Provenance Index, Archival Inventory I-30, page 2, item 0021
Galatea pulled by 2 dolphins accompanied by 5 tritons (also documented by payments/correspondence with Don Antonio Ruffo of Messina, 1649)	Ruffo, Antonio, principe di Scaletta	204 × 255	1678	Getty Provenance Index, Archival Inventory I-2266, Page 2, Item 0007a
Galatea 'Venus on a shell drawn by various dolphins with various tritons'	D'Andrea, Gennaro	264 × 211	1710	Getty Provenance Index, Archival Inventory I-6, Page 9, item 96
Sleeping Venus	D'Avalos, Gianbattista, IX marchese del Vasto	158 × 211	1739	Bugli, 2003–4, no. 78, 31
'a nude figure and its accompaniment' (part of a series of 3 with Venus and Adonis and Diana and Actaeon)	Fabio Gentile on behalf of the Holy Roman Emperor, Ferdinand III	237	1651	Lattuada and Nappi, 2005, doc. 2, 97
Venus and Adonis (part of a series of 3 with Diana and Actaeon and 'a nude figure and its accompaniment')	Fabio Gentile on behalf of the Holy Roman Emperor, Ferdinand III	264	1651	Lattuada and Nappi, 2005, doc. 2, 97
Lucretia	Imperiale, Davide, nobile	132 × 105	1672	Labrot, 1992, Inv. 21, item 8, 119
Tarquin and Lucretia (one of a set of 3 with Susanna and Bathsheba)	Lorenzo Cambi and Simone Verzone on behalf of Prince Karl Eusebius von Liechtenstein	303 wide	1636	Nappi, 1983, 76
3 octagonal paintings of unspecified subject matter	Colonna, Camillo	small	1647	Ricciardi, 2000, 56, 60

TABLE 3: REFERENCES TO PAINTINGS BY ARTEMISIA GENTILESCHI IN EARLY NEAPOLITAN AND SOUTHERN ITALIAN INVENTORIES

Owner	*Subject(s)*	*Dimensions (converted into cm from original units of measurement where known)*	*Date*	*Reference*
Di Gennaro, Cesare, principe di San Martino	Judith	132 × 158	1646	Paolillo, 1985, 119
Colonna, Camillo	3 octagonal paintings of unspecified subject matter	small	1647	Ricciardi, 2000, 56, 60
Colonna, Camillo	Hope	large	1647	Ricciardi, 2000, 56, 60
Carafa, Giuseppe, dei Duchi di Maddaloni	Judith	158 × 132	1648/1649	Labrot, 1992, Inv. 9, item 58, 77 Labrot, 1992, Inv. 11, item 2, 82
D'Andrea, Vincenzo	Sacrifice of Isaac	105 × 79	1649	Pacelli, 1987, 145–46
D'Andrea, Vincenzo	St Cecilia	53 × 79	1649	Pacelli, 1987, 145–46
Capecelatro, Ettore, marchese di Torella	Madonna	small	1655	Labrot, 1992, Inv. 16, item 35, 102
Capecelatro, Ettore, marchese di Torella	Magdalene	105 × 132	1659	Labrot, 1992, Inv. 19, item 8, 113
Giangerolamo II Acquaviva, conte di Conversano	Roman Charity	121 × 147	1666	Ruotolo, 1977, item 13, 73; Conversano, 2018, cat. 30, 262-66
Giangerolamo II Acquaviva, conte di Conversano	Madonna	unspecified	1666	Ruotolo, 1977, item 18, 73
Belprato, Bernardino, conte di Anversa	Galatea	unspecified	1667	Getty Provenance Index, Archival Inventory I-30, Page 2, Item 0021
Belprato, Bernardino, conte di Anversa	Gioseppe Giusto/ ?St Joseph and the Christ Child	unspecified	1667	Getty Provenance Index, Archival Inventory I-30, Page 3, Item 0027
Imperiale, Davide, nobile	Magdalene	132 × 105	1672	Labrot, 1992, Inv. 21, item 7, 119
Imperiale, Davide, nobile	Lucretia	132 × 105	1672	Labrot, 1992, Inv. 21, item 8, 119
Imperiale, Davide, nobile	Head of Christ	small	1672	Labrot, 1992, Inv. 21, item 9, 119
Imperiale, Davide, nobile	Head of the Virgin	small	1672	Labrot, 1992, Inv. 21, item 9, 119
Ruffo, Antonio, principe di Scaletta	Galatea pulled by 2 dolphins accompanied by 5 tritons	204 × 255	1678	Getty Provenance Index, Archival Inventory I-2266, page 2, item 0007a
Ruffo, Antonio, principe di Scaletta	Bath of Diana with 5 nymphs and 2 dogs	204 × 255	1678	Getty Provenance Index, Archival Inventory I-2266, page 2, item 0007b
Ruffo, Antonio, principe di Scaletta	The Flight into Egypt, on copper	38	1678	Getty Provenance Index, Archival Inventory I-2266, page 2, item 0007c
Cella, Santo Maria, duca di Frisa	Diana and Actaeon	343 × 211	1680	Labrot, 1992, Inv. 29, item 79, 147
Filomarino, Ascanio, duca della Torre	St John the Baptist	79 × 105	1685/1700	Labrot, 1992, Inv. 33, item 16, 161; Ruotolo, 1977, 80
Capece Piscicelli, Giovanni Battista, nobile di Seggio	Gioseppe Giusto/ ?St Joseph and the Christ Child	large	1690	Getty Provenance Index, Archival Inventory I-245, page 9, item 25
Quadra, Alvaro della, duca di Limatola	Annunciation	unspecified	1694	Getty Provenance Index, Archival Inventory I-163, page 1, item 4

TABLE 3 *(continued . . .)*

Owner	*Subject(s)*	*Dimensions (converted into cm from original units of measurement where known)*	*Date*	*Reference*
Cardenas, Carlo de, conte di Acerra, marchese di Laino	Hercules Spinning/ Hercules and Omphale	211 × 237	1699	Labrot, 1992, Inv. 42, item 75, 206
Afflitto, Ferdinando d' Principe di Scanno	St Eustace (head by Gentileschi)	158 × 211	1700	Getty Provenance Index, Archival Inventory I-24, page 2, item 16a
Afflitto, Ferdinando d' Principe di Scanno	David (head by Gentileschi)	158 × 211	1700	Getty Provenance Index, Archival Inventory I-24, page 2, item 16b
Afflitto, Ferdinando d' Principe di Scanno	St Sebastian (head by Gentileschi)	158 × 211	1700	Getty Provenance Index, Archival Inventory I-24, page 2, item 16c
Pinto, Fabrizio	Madonna of the Rosary, figure by Gentileschi, landscape by Gargiulo	53	1700/1701	Del Grosso and Avino, 1989, 50, 93, 142
Orsini, Ottavio, principe di Frasso	Fortune	158 × 132	1704	Labrot, 1992, Inv. 45, item 88, 228
Ciavarella, Salvatore	2 paintings of holy virgins	66	1707	Getty Provenance Index, Archival Inventory I-214, page 18, item 31
D'Andrea, Gennaro	Galatea 'Venus on a shell drawn by various dolphins with various tritons'	264 × 211	1710	Getty Provenance Index, Archival Inventory I-6, page 9, item 96
Zurlo, Giacomo Capece	A baby	53 × 40	1715	Ruotolo, 1973, 151
Palma, Francesco de, duca di S. Elia	Ecce Homo	105 × 79	1716	Labrot, 1992, Inv. 56, item 1, 284
Palma, Francesco de, duca di S. Elia	7 paintings of Angels holding the symbols of the Passion	105 × 79	1716/1682	Labrot, 1992, Inv. 56, item 1, 284, and ibid., item 64, 155 where they appear in an earlier inventory of the same collection without attribution
Perrino, Domenico	Circle of flowers with a child reclining in the middle	132 × 105	1716	Getty Provenance Index, Archival Inventory I-68, page 7, item 2
Francone, Francesco, principe di Pietracupa	Samson	158 × 211	1718	Caracciolo, 1959, 37
Pignatelli, Giovanna Battista d'Aragona, duchessa di Terranova e Monteleone	A half-length holy virgin	119 × 132	1723	Labrot, 1992, Inv. 61, item 322, 324
Orsini, Anne-Marie de La Trémoille, principessa	Putto sleeping with his head on a red cushion, painted on copper	158 × 237	1723	Getty Provenance Index, Archival Inventory I-419, page 13v
D'Avalos, Gianbattista, IX marchese del Vasto	Sleeping Venus	158 × 211	1739	Bugli, 2003–4, no. 78, 31
D'Avalos, Gianbattista, IX marchese del Vasto	Judith (attributed to Gentileschi in 1739, subsequently reattributed to Guido Reni [1776], Bolognese school [1862] and copy after Titian [today]	79 × 119	1739	Bugli, 2003–4, no. 131, 32

TABLE 3 *(continued . . .)*

Owner	*Subject(s)*	*Dimensions (converted into cm from original units of measurement where known)*	*Date*	*Reference*
Poliastri, Stanislao, arcivescovo di Rossano, Monsignor	St Lucy	105 high	1741	Labrot, 1992, Inv. 74, item 30, 403
Ruffo, Guglielmo, principe di Scilla	St Sebastian	109 × 79	1748	Getty Provenance Index, Archival Inventory I-204, page 14, item 73
Pinto, Francesco Emanuele, principe di Ischitella	Magdalene	66 cm (?octagonal)	1767	Pacelli, 1979, 178
Carafa, Nicola Pietro Carafa, Carafa San Lorenzo	Annunciation (attributed to Artemisia Gentileschi in a 17th-century family inventory, attributed to Agostino Beltrano in the family inventory of 1786)	158 × 211	1786	Ruotolo, 1974, 168
Carafa, Nicola Pietro Carafa, Carafa San Lorenzo	David and Abigail	264 × 317	1786	Ruotolo, 1974, 167
Carafa, Nicola Pietro Carafa, Carafa San Lorenzo	Lot and his Daughters (attributed in a 17th-century family inventory to Francesco Antonio Giannone)	158 × 211	1786	Ruotolo, 1974, 167
Carafa, Nicola Pietro Carafa, Carafa San Lorenzo	Death of the First Born Sons of Egypt (attributed in a 17th-century family inventory to Francesco Antonio Giannone)	317 × 238	1786	Ruotolo, 1974, 167

NOTES

INTRODUCTION

1 Sharpe and da Silva 2019, n.p., and Barker 1999, 127–45, for the museological significance of the *Treasures of King Tutankhamun* exhibition

2 Attributed to Bernardo Cavallino, *Triumph of Galatea*, oil on canvas, 196.9 × 254.6 cm, sale Christie's New York, 13 April 2007, lot 91, illustrated on p. 113 of the catalogue.

3 See pp. 210–12 for further discussion.

4 The painting's exhibition history is as follows: Nicola Spinosa in Naples, 2009, cat. I.95, 196–97 (Cavallino); Spinosa in Milan, 2011, cat. 53, 254–55 (Cavallino); Spinosa in Rome, 2016, cat. 94, 278–79 (Palumbo and Gentileschi); and see further Porzio 2021, 109 (Gentileschi and Cavallino), and Naples, 2022, 42 (Gentileschi).

5 Pithers, 2019, n.p.

6 No author, 'Women in our collection', available at: https://www.nationalgallery.org.uk/paintings/women-in-our-collection.

7 Moorhead, 2020, n.p.

8 Finkel, 2021, n.p.

9 Key publications in the field include Spear, 1997; Cecchini, 2000; Fantoni, Matthews and Matthews-Grieco, 2003; Spear and Sohm, 2010; Cavazzini, 2008; Guerzoni, 2011; Marshall, 2016; and Lo Conte, 2021.

10 See, for example, the conclusions of Velthuis, 2005, 160, who notes, 'the value of an artwork does not reside in the work itself, but is, under conditions of uncertainty, produced and constantly reproduced by artists, intermediaries, and audiences, subject to numerous conventions and cultural codes of art worlds'. For a classic study of this issue, see further Grampp, 1989.

11 The chapter title, 'Becoming Artemisia', for example, draws on a phrase originally employed by Christiansen, 2004, and used thereafter by Letizia Treves in London, 2020, 122. For Christiansen, the phrase highlights the idea of Artemisia's career as a continuously evolving work in progress, while, for Treves, it foregrounds the author's view that 'it was in Florence that Artemisia found her artistic voice, becoming a painter in her own right and developing into a cultured, determined and successful individual'. My adoption of the phrase employs it as part of a broader consideration of Gentileschi's life and art as a sequence of ongoing career and reputational benchmarks. I thus trace Gentileschi's progression as, first, constituting her 'becoming' an artist in Rome, before being 'announced' as an independent master in Florence, then 'acclaimed' on a more international level in Rome and Venice, before being 'sold' more comprehensively in Naples and London. She is then, finally, 'resurrected' for new audiences in the modern to contemporary period. I should also note that I use Artemisia's first name in this text not as an authorial assertion of presumed familiarity but (a) in order to differentiate her name from that of her father, and (b) as an honorific that follows her own repeated stress upon the use of her first name as an indexical sign of her broader artistic persona.

12 Garrard 1980; Garrard, 1989; Garrard, 2001; Garrard, 2017; and Garrard, 2020.

13 For this and the price achieved for the *Danaë*, see Kuessel, 2019, n.p.

14 Villa, 2020, n.p.

15 Reyburn, 2019, n.p.

16 For a list of these works, see p. 273, n. 18.

17 Barker, 2018I; for discussion, see Chapter 1.

18 Solinas, 2011I; for discussion, see Chapter 6.

19 Lattuada and Nappi, 2005, 79–96; for discussion, see Chapter 12.

20 Barker, 2022, 78; Bianchi and Barker, forthcoming.

21 For the charge of *stuprum*, see Cohen, 2000, 59, and for the broader legal and social contexts informing rape trials in early modern Rome see further, Cohen, 1991, 169–91.

22 The Gentileschi rape-trial documents have had a complex publishing history. They were first published in reduced form by Bertolotti, 1876, 200–204, then more systematically and with additional documentation by Menzio, 1981/2004. They were then translated and published as an appendix in Garrard, 1989, 409–87, before being republished in English translation, in turn, in Barker, 2021b, 41–64. Alexandra Lapierre also analysed the rape-trial documentation, introducing some new material, which she summarises and discusses in Lapierre, 2000, 365 ff., while Patrizia Cavazzini then incorporated these findings, adding some others of her own and providing a new transcription and analysis of the documentation as a whole, in Cavazzini, 2001b, 432–44.

1 IN HER MASTER'S HOUSE

1 Vasari, 1568, 287.

2 Barolsky, 1990, passim.

3 Pon, 1996, 1015–37.

4 Florence, 1991, cat. 11, 124–28; Bissell, 1999, cat. 8, 205–8.

5 Bissell, 1999, 206–7.

6 Barker, 2018a, 416, who also allows the possibility that details of the narrative might have been provided to Bronzini by Gentileschi's associates. For further commentary, see Garrard, 2020, 31, 218; and Barker, 2022, 23–28.

7 Barker, 2018a, 415–16.

8 Barker, 2018a, n. 45, 415.

9 For the archival record relating to this individual, see Lapierre, 2000, 393–400.

10 For the Gentileschis' relocation to Florence, see further p. 57.

11 Hersey, 1993, 329. For a counter-argument to the assumption that Gentileschi's early reputation must have been negatively impacted by this early scandal, see further Cohen, 2000, 51, who notes, 'While the trial was held in camera, the proceedings themselves also might have set local tongues wagging. Gossip about Artemisia, the rape, or the court case, however, did not mean permanent damage. In early modern Rome where slander was rife, people knew enough to enjoy, but also to weigh and discard, casual talk. No other record of public contumely about the rape has been found. Neither routine gossip nor the trial itself prove Artemisia's irrevocably sullied honor. On the contrary, publicity about the adult artist depicted not a libertine, but a respectable and admired professional . . . failing evidence of an indelible blemish on her reputation, the hypothesis that she or others exploited her notoriety in the art market lacks force.'

12 Spear, 2010, 39–40.

13 For this aspect of Roman Baroque culture, see Rome, 2014–15, passim.

14 Hoogewerff, 1953, passim.

15 Garrard, 1989, 458, 478; Keith Christiansen in Rome, New York and St Louis, 2001–2, 10; Milan, 2011, 259.

16 Garrard, 1989, 485.

17 Garrard, 1989, 419.

18 The literature on the life drawing academy of the Accademia di San Luca forms part of the wider scholarship on the early history of this organisation, its statutes and leadership, organisational evolution, political contexts, disputes with other guild and professional organisations etc., for which, see Missirini, 1823; Spezzaferro, 1981, 207–79; Rossi, 1984; and the publications cited below in Lukehart, 2009; together with the publications cited below by Patrizia Cavazzini, particularly Cavazzini, 2011; and, more recently, Salvagni, 2012; and Salvagni, 2021.

19 Roccasecca, 2009, 123–59.

20 Lukehart, 2017, 36–37.

21 Lukehart, 2017, 34, 37; Cavazzini, 2008, 70–80; Cavazzini, 2009–10, 81–82.

22 For Domenichino's academy, see Spear, 1982, 1:105–7. For Sacchi's academy, see Cavazzini, 2008, 76.

23 Brooks, 2009, 235–38.

24 Lukehart, 2009, 178–80.

25 Los Angeles, 2007, cat. 13, 20 and 32.

26 Garrard, 1989, 36.

27 The first quotation is taken from the testimony of Marcantonio Coppino as cited in Cavazzini, 2001b, 434. Baglione's assessment of Gentileschi occurs in Baglione, 1642, 360. For further discussion, see Keith Christiansen in Rome, New York, St Louis, 2001–2, 4.

28 Garrard, 1989, 416.

29 Lapierre, 2000, 371, for the death certificate.

30 Judith W. Mann (2016, 14) also dates the beginning of Artemisia's apprenticeship in Orazio's workshop to around 1605–6.

31 Garrard, 1989, 463: 'io non so scrivere et poco leggere'.

32 Garrard, 1989, 483 (testimony of Bernardino de Franceschi and Nicolo Bedino) and 485 (testimony of Antinoro Bertucci).

33 For Bedino's testimony and Orazio Gentileschi's subsequent charge of perjury against him, see Lapierre, 2000, 411; Cavazzini, 2001b, 437, 441, 443. For Bedino's relationship with Tassi, see further Cavazzini, 2005, 45.

34 For a classic study of this process, see Cropper, 1984, passim.

35 Roccassecca, 2009, 127, and thereafter for discussion.

36 Goldstein, 1988, 47–48, 122–23.

37 Davis, 2009, 222–47.

38 Roccasecca, 2009, 146; Cavazzini, 2008, 66.

39 For a discussion of the dating and attribution of this painting, see Francesca Whitlum-Cooper in London, 2020, cat. 7, 130–31, with previous bibliography; and Barker, 2022, 40–41. Whitlum-Cooper and Sheila Barker follow Gianni Papi and Keith Christiansen in dating the Spada *Madonna* slightly later to Gentileschi's Florentine years of around 1613–14.

40 Gentileschi's *Jael and Sisera* and *Virgin and Child with a Rosary* (Bissell, 1999, cats 11 and 51) are both based on prints after Philips Galle and Guido Reni respectively, for which, see Bissell, 1999, 213 and fig. 71; and Rome, New York and St Louis, 2001–2, 427, fig. 147.

41 Garrard, 1989, 484.

42 Garrard, 1989, 483.

43 For Orazio Gentileschi's collaboration with Tassi on the Quirinal Palace frescoes (destroyed in the nineteenth century) and on the Casino delle Muse frescoes (still preserved), see Bissell, 1981, 27–29, and cats L-75 and 29, 222–23 and 156–58; and Rome, 2008, 30–31.

44 Artemisia refers to this portrait commission in response to questions by Agostino Tassi immediately after being subjected to the torture of the *sibille*. Garrard (1989, 463) translates the passage as 'I was asked to paint a portrait of a woman whom he said was his beloved, and I did it.' However, Cavazzini (2001a, n. 46, 293) notes that the passage should be translated in the other sense as referring to Artemisia's painting a portrait of Artigenio for his beloved. Cavazzini's reading is also supported by Bissell (1999, cat. L63, 376).

2 'RITRATTO NUDO'

1 For the reasons given above, and in full agreement with Lapierre's and Cavazzini's arguments to this effect, I would see it as inherently unlikely that Gentileschi might have assisted Orazio on the Casino delle Muse fresco commission on the Quirinal Hill (as suggested by Francesco Solinas). Had she done so, she might have become at least acquainted with the basics of fresco painting, a specialisation that is unrecorded in any form of documentation relating to her career (Garrard, 1989, 19–20; Solinas in Milan, 2011, 162; Cavazzini, 2001a, 289; Lapierre, 2000, 378).

2 For the painting's antique references, see Garrard, 1989, 196–97; and Judith W. Mann in Rome, New York and St Louis, 2001–2, cat. 51, 296–99. For a more recent re-evaluation with a renewed emphasis on the importance of the source of Santa Susanna in Rome, see Simons, 2017, 44, 49.

3 Garrard, 1989, 200. Judith W. Mann stresses the significance of the rendition of Susanna's body in similar terms: 'Nessun'altra rappresentazione contemporanea della storia di Susanna esibì una resa così credibile e accurate dell'anatomia femminile come quella del dipinto di Artemisia' (Mann, 2016, 18).

4 Mancini, 1956–57, 225, translated in Hibbard, 1983, 348.

5 Christiansen, 1986, 430–33, and passim for this aspect of Caravaggio's working practices more generally.

6 Cinotti and Dell'Acqua, 1983, cat. 150, 577.

7 For Cresenzi, see Bernstorff, 2010, passim.

8 Cavazzini, 2001a, n. 97, 294; Lapierre, 2000, 373–74.

9 For this painting, see Papi, 2007, cat. 10, figs 12–14; Portús Pérez, 2011, 56–57; Nicola Spinosa in Naples and Madrid, 2011–12, cat. 30, 166–69. Fabio Scaletti

also cites this painting, together with another related version of the subject, which he catalogues as a potential copy after Caravaggio's lost original (Koelliker collection, Milan, for which, see Scaletti, 2017, cat. D4, 202–3, and 84–86, for further discussion).

10 For Ribera's early years in Rome, see Papi, 2005, 45–56; Vannugli, 2011, 398–404; and Gianni Papi in Naples and Madrid, 2011–12, 31–60.

11 Garrard, 1989, 485.

12 Garrard, 1989, 482.

13 Rome, New York and St Louis, 2001–2, cat. 16, 94–95, with previous bibliography.

14 This section of Molli's testimony is not included in Garrard's translation. It is cited in Cavazzini, 2001b, 436, and is also translated and discussed by Keith Christiansen in Rome, New York and St Louis, 2001–2, 10.

15 Similar conclusions are reached by Keith Christiansen in Rome, New York and St Louis, 2001–2, 10–11, and Sutherland Harris, 2005, 134–37.

16 This section of Trotta's testimony is not included in Mary Garrard's translation. It is transcribed in the original Italian in Cavazzini, 2001b, 434.

17 Missirini, 1823, 70, citing item 15 of the 1596 statutes: 'Nessun studente possa far adunanze in casa, nè tener modello senza permesso del Principe'; and 83, citing item 22 of the 1607 statutes: 'Chiunque voglia esternare un suo progetto all'Accademia, lo communichi primi col capo della medesima.' For discussion, see Cavazzini, 2008, 76–77.

18 Cavazzini, 2008, n. 211, 186, citing AASL, Statuti 1607, fol. 22v.

19 Cavazzini, 2008, 77 and n. 213, 186, citing AASL, Statuti 1607, fol. 36v. This statue is quoted in more detail in Cavazzini, 2009–10, n. 66, 91: 'Concediamo licenza (. . .) di poter fare adunanze in casa, di studianti della nostra professione et servire di ignudo et vestito con conditione che non s'introduca donne ignude né vestite sotto pena di scudi dieci per ogni volta.'

20 Passeri, 1772, 285.

21 De' Dominici, 1742–45, 3:415.

22 Alpers, 1988, 31, 32, 36; and see further Harris, 2005, 142–43, who notes, 'If artists between 1500 and 1800 drew from female models, the evidence has not been preserved . . . Most of those known to me were made in the Dutch republic, mainly by Rembrandt and his pupils . . . This kind of study of the female body became regular studio practice only by the mid-nineteenth century.'

23 Washington, 1999–2000, cat. 45, 165.

24 Goldstein, 1988, 106–7, which further notes 'There is no female figure, drawn or painted, by any of the Carracci, than can be said unequivocally to have been done from a live model.'

25 Simons, 2017, 45–47.

26 Garrard, 1989, 481; Cavazzini, 2001b, 435, author's translation.

27 For discussion, see Keith Christiansen in Rome, New York and St Louis, 2001–2, 10–11, and 98; and see further Elizabeth Cropper in ibid., 274–75.

28 Boccardo, 2000, 205–6. Boccardo also hypothesises that the *Lucretia* may alternatively have come into the Gentile collection via the 1637 Genoese sale of the collection of the Duke of Alcalá, although there is no direct evidence in support of this proposal. For further discussion, see Rome, New York and St Louis, 2001–2, 97–98, 166; and Orlando, 2019, 161, 165.

29 Keith Christiansen in Rome, New York and St Louis, 2001–2, cat. 17, 97–100, with previous bibliography, where the *Cleopatra* is attributed to Orazio, and Judith W. Mann in ibid., cat. 53, 302–5, with previous bibliography, where the *Cleopatra* is attributed instead to Artemisia; and see further ibid., cat. 54, 305–8, for the *Danaë* as attributed to Artemisia. The *Cleopatra* and the *Danaë* were also both attributed to Artemisia in the London 2020 exhibition (cats 3–4, 116–23). For the *Danaë*, see further Judith W. Mann in Milan, 2011, cat. 19, 172–73; and Mann, 2017, 170, and n. 18, 185, with further bibliography.

30 Spike, 1992, 733.

31 Bissell, 2005, 22–23.

32 Papi, Bischoff and Ford, 2019, 540; and see further the comments of Letizia Treves in London, 2020, cat. 2, 115; and Angela Catalano in Rome, 2011, vol. 1, cat. VI.10, 164.

33 For Ribera's practice in this regard in Naples, see Marshall, 2016, 56–62.

34 Christiansen, 2004, 109.

35 Ibid.

36 Judith W. Mann in Milan, 2011, 172.

37 Elizabeth Cropper in Rome, New York and St Louis, 2001–2, 275.

38 Cavazzini 2001a, 290, and n. 113, 295.

39 Harris, 2005, 143.

3 'WITHOUT PEER'

1 Mann, 2009, 87.

2 Woods-Marsden, 1998, 192–93.

3 Hollanda, 1928, 15; and for discussion, see Sohm, 1995, 773–84.

4 Orazio Gentileschi to Christine de Lorraine, 3 July 1612, cit. Bissell, 1999, 1; and for further commentary, see Rome, New York, and St Louis, 2001–2, 253; Barker, 2014, 803–4. The letter is republished in Lapierre, 2000, 407–9, and Barker, 2021b, 67–74.

5 Jacobs, 1997, 3–7; 85–122; Modesti, 2014, 172–73.

6 Garrard, 1989, 141–7; Campbell, 2013, 361–79.

7 For an overview of this tradition, with a particular focus on female authorship, see Garrard, 2020, 12–68.

8 Barker, 2018a, 407–8. Bronzini's manuscript – of which Gentileschi's biography constitutes a small part – is entitled *Della dignità et della nobiltà delle donne* (*On the Dignity and Nobility of Women*) and consists of thirty-two volumes. Written largely between 1615 and 1622, it is effectively an encyclopedia outlining the history of virtuous and distinguished women through the ages.

9 For Sofonisba Anguissola's period in Spain, see Cole, 2019, 118–45; and Madrid, 2019–2020, 53–70, 139–66.

10 For Michelangelo and Anguissola, see Jacobs, 1997, 55–57; and Madrid, 2019–2020, 117–18. For the dependence of Caravaggio's *Boy Bitten by a Lizard* on Anguissola, see Mina Gregori in New York and Naples, 1985, 236, and Stefania Biancani in Washington, 2007, cat. 9, 112–13, with further bibliography.

11 Lavinia Fontana's significance in Rome as a role model for Artemisia is also highlighted by Francesco Solinas (2020, 49–50).

12 For Lavinia Fontana, see Murphy, 2003; and Madrid, 2019–2020.

13 Keith Christiansen in Rome, New York and St Louis, 2001–2, 98, also suggests that Orazio may have already been associated with Scipione Borghese during this period and that he, thus, might already have had access to Borghese's collection.

14 Lollobrigida, 2014, 67. For the rules of the Accademia di San Luca in these regards, see further Grossi and Trani, 2009, 31, 36.

15 Bissell, 1981, 6–7, and cat. 3, 134–35. For Fontana's *Stoning of St Stephen*, see Eve Straussman-Pflanzer in Hartford and Detroit, 2021–22, cat. 19, 92–93.

16 A tentative proposal to connect the Pommersfelden *Susanna* with the 1623 Ludovisi inventory was first made by Carolyn H. Wood (1992, 516). This was refuted by both Garrard (2001, 96–97, and n. 53, 151) and Mann (in Rome, New York and St Louis, 2001–2, 356 and 358), to which one might also add that Cardinal Ludovico Ludovisi (1595–1632) was only fifteen in 1610 and so too young to have been the original patron of the 1610 Pommersfelden *Susanna*.

17 For an analysis of this tradition in relation to its precedents in Giorgione, Titian and Venetian painting, and including Caravaggio, Carracci, Allori, Gentileschi etc, see Anderson, 1988, 60–69.

18 Bissell, 1981, 26.

19 Cohen, 2000, 59.

20 For a detailed analysis of the rape-trial testimony references to this painting, see Papi in Florene, 1991, 93–95; and Bissell, 1999, 198–200.

21 Pepper, 1984a, 316; Gianni Papi in Florence, 1991, 95; Lapierre, 2000, 398–99; and Papi, Bischoff and Ford, 2019, 532, for a more recent summary of these circumstances.

22 For another reading of the evidence, see Maria Cristina Terzaghi in Rome, 2021–22, 70–73.

23 Bissell, 1999, 200.

24 Garrard, 1989, 29.

25 Keith Christiansen in Rome, New York and St Louis, 2001–2, 188; and Bissell, 1999, cat. X15, 323–24, for further discussion.

26 Bissell, 1981, cat. 27, 155–56, and see further in addition to the other sources here mentioned, Judith W. Mann in Rome, 2016, cat. 18, 114–15, who also argues in favour of an attribution to Orazio Gentileschi.

27 Gianni Papi in Florence, 1991, cat. 3, 96–98.

28 Papi, Bischoff and Ford, 2019, 532–43.

29 For a more recent shift in the literature back towards an attribution in favour of Orazio Gentileschi, see Letizia Treves (in London, 2020, 110) and Patrizia Cavazzini (in Rome, 2021–22, 138).

30 See, for example, the more restrained treatment of the blood issuing from the severed head of the Baptist in Orazio Gentileschi's signed *Executioner with the Head of St John* in the Prado (Keith Christiansen in Rome, New York and St Louis, 2001–2, cat. 20, 107–9).

31 For her Capodimonte *Judith Slaying Holofernes*, see Maria Cristina Terzaghi in Rome, 2021–22, cat. III.3, 132–35, with previous bibliography.

32 Garrard, 1989, 305–13.

33 Although, see alternatively Francesca Baldassari in Rome, 2016, 134, who identifies the canvas with a documented 1617 payment of 140 lire to Artemisia from Laura Corsini (Barker, 2022, 57, also suggests that the Naples *Judith* 'may perhaps' be identifiable with the painting settlement of 31 July 1617). This argument is to be discounted, in my opinion, on two grounds: first, it neglects to take into account the evidence noted below by Christiansen concerning the likely presence of the Naples *Judith* in Orazio's workshop in Rome in around 1615–16; second, the amount mentioned in the Corsini payment document of 31 July 1617 translates into twenty ducats (Fumagalli, 2010, 173). This is too low to be identifiable as the payment for such a major undertaking as the Naples *Judith*, for which, see further p. 129 above. The Corsini payment must, therefore, refer to another lost version of *Judith*, probably a single or dual figure, half-length painting. The interpretation made by Baldassari and Barker is also questioned, for slightly different reasons, by Maria Cristina Terzaghi in Rome, 2021–22, 134.

34 Spezzaferro, 1974, 579–86; Mina Gregori in New York and Naples, 1985, cat. 74, 256–62; Michele Cuppone in Rome, 2016, cat. 1, 80–81.

35 For this tradition in relation to Caravaggio's *Judith and Holofernes* and its legacy, see Marshall, 1993, 43–52.

36 Judith W. Mann in Rome, New York and St Louis, 2001–2, 311.

37 Francesca Whitlum-Cooper in London, 2020, 124–25.

38 For the archival record relating to this individual, see p. 266, n. 9 (ch. 1).

39 Barker, 2014, 803.

40 Cavazzini, 2001a, 287–88.

41 Bissell, 1981, cat. X-1, 199–200; Rome, 2008, passim.

42 Wittkower and Wittkower, 1963, 162–64, 181–208. This classic survey of the careers of a number of artists who were also 'successful villains', such as Cellini, Caravaggio, Leone Leoni etc., also cites the example of the numerous charges brought against Agostino Tassi. During the course of this discussion, the authors describe Artemisia as 'a lascivious and precocious girl' (164), an extraordinarily chauvinist characterisation that is perhaps only partially mitigated by the fact that Artemisia was at that stage believed to have been born in 1597 rather than in 1593, as was subsequently established by Bissell's publication of her baptism records (Bissell, 1968, 153–54, and for commentary on Wittkower and Wittkhower, see further Garrard, 1989, 207).

43 Barker, 2014, 804, and Barker, 2022, 34, suggest that Orazio Gentileschi may have intended at that stage to relocate to Florence, this assertion being made on the basis of the archival finding that his brother, Aurelio Lomi, rented an apartment in the street of Borgo San Jacopo in both their names two weeks after Orazio's letter to Christine de Lorraine.

44 Bissell, 1981, 31–41; Carloni, 2001, 117–29; Fabriano, 2019, passim.

45 Bassetti's drawings are discussed by Christiansen, 2004, 101–2; Bissell, 2005, 28–30; and Patrizia Cavazzini in London, 2020, 40–41. Christiansen and Bissell argue that Bassetti must have seen the two paintings in Orazio's studio and that this indicates the continued presence of Artemisia's Naples *Judith* in Orazio's studio following her departure for Florence. Cavazzini, on the other hand, views the two drawings as forming part of a wider interest on the part of early collectors in juxtaposing the two artists' works together for comparative purposes. This suggests the alternative possibility that Bassetti might have seen the two works hanging together in a display of paintings belonging to a subsequent Roman collector, rather than in Orazio's workshop.

46 Cavazzini, 2008, 32.

47 See, for example, Solinas, 2011a, letter 12, 38–39; letter 18, 50–51, and letter 19, 52. For discussion, see Barker, 2017, n. 96, 86, who further links the source of Artemisia's and Orazio's mutual antagonism as being based around the issue of Artemisia's dowry.

48 Arizzoli, 2016, 105–14. For the difficulties of public profile experienced by women artists attached to their father's workshops more generally, see Barker, 2017, 8.

4 BIRTH, DEATH, REBIRTH

1 For Gentileschi's educational and literary development as a 'late learner', see Christiansen, 2004, 116–17; Locker, 2015, 6–8; Locker, 2017, 89–101.

2 Cropper, 2009, 195–213.

3 Barker, 2017, 65, and doc. 22, 77.

4 Cioli's letter was originally published by Orbaan (1927, 284). For discussion, see Bissell, 1968, 153–54. For Artemisia's subsequent correspondence with Cioli, then Secretary of State to Cosimo's successor, Ferdinando II de' Medici, see Garrard, 1989, 385–86.

5 Barker, 2014, 803, for example, characterises Orazio's letter as 'a somewhat maladroit attempt to gain Medici patronage for Artemisia', and in Barker, 2022, 33, it is described as falling 'on deaf ears, not only because of Orazio's uncouth, direct manner, but also because of the impropriety of the request'.

6 For an overview of the various ways in which an artist could be employed at the Italian courts during the seventeenth century, see Fumagalli and Morselli, 2014, 11–20; and for Florence more specifically, see Fumagalli, 2014, 95–136.

7 Bissell, 1968, n. 14, 154; Barker, 2017, 69, doc. 34, 79, and n. 101, 86; Barker, 2021a, 46; Barker, 2022, 3.

8 In 1624, Gentileschi is described as living in Rome with one servant and one daughter. Cropper surmised from this the death of all but one of her

children, Prudenzia (1993, 761). The letters subsequently published by Francesco Solinas in 2011 include a request from Pierantonio Stiattesi that Francesco Maringhi look after the two babies (Solinas, 2011a, 31, letter 7: Pierantonio Stiattesi to Francesco Maringhi, 12 February 1620). For the most detailed notice regarding the births and deaths of Gentileschi's children during this period, see Bissell, 1999, Appendix II, 157-62, and Lapierre, 2000, 419. For the burial of Agnola Stiattesi, who did not live long enough to be baptised, see further Barker, 2017, doc. 3, 74. The existence of this fifth child, born during Gentileschi's Florentine residence, was discovered by Barker and published in 2017, and so her name needs to be added to the earlier discussions of Gentileschi's children by Bissell and Lapierre.

9 For the archival record relating to Pierantonio Stiattesi and his Florentine family connections, see further, Lapierre, 2000, 417–19, to which should be added the important supplementary information provided by Sheila Barker (2017, 64–65; 2022, 39–43).

10 Both Cropper (1993, 761) and Lapierre (2000, 418) point out that, while it was common for Florentine families to move house periodically, it was not so usual for them to move to different districts, as was the case with the Gentileschi/Stiattesi household. For important qualifying information regarding the initial support and continuity provided by Artemisia's father-in-law, Vincenzo Stiattesi, prior to his death in 1615, see Barker, 2022, 41 and 51.

11 Solinas, 2011a, 14, 17–19, and passim.

12 Gianni Papi in Florence, 2010, 29.

13 For Medicean collecting of Caravaggesque painting, see Evelina Borea in Florence, 1970, III–X; Carofano, 2014, 22–39, 126; and Florence, 2010, passim.

14 Caracciolo's presence in Florence is documented in 1618, but he is then back in Reggio Calabria in 1619 and Naples soon thereafter, for which, see Causa, 2000, 74–79; 353–54. For Rombouts in Florence, see Papi, 1998, 26-38; and Gianni Papi in Florence, 2010, 23.

15 Gianni Papi and Mina Gregori in Florence, 2010, cats 2–3, 104–9, with previous bibliography, and see further Sebregondi, 2005, XLI–LIX.

16 Scalini, 1997, 397; Milan, 2004, 29–33.

17 Keith Sciberras and David M. Stone in Naples and London, 2004–5, 120; and see further Florence, 2010, cat. 7, 119–21.

18 Naples and London, 2004–5, cat. 8, 116–18; Florence, 2010, cat. 6, 116–18.

19 Baglione, 1642, 136, and for discussion, see Hibbard, 1983, 352.

20 Papi, 1991, 197–211; Baldassari, 2005, LXXIX–LXXXIX.

21 Cropper, 1993, n. 12, 760. Cristofano Gentileschi, nonetheless, died tragically prematurely on 6 April 1620, for which, see further p. 111 below.

22 For which, see pp. 157–58.

23 Francesca Baldassari in Rome, 2016, cat. 23, 126–27; Shearman, 1979, passim.

24 Baldinucci, 1681–1728, 3:727, and 726–28, for his discussion of the painting more generally.

25 Christiansen, 2004, 115–17.

26 Shearman, 1979, 9; Anderson, 1988, passim.

27 For an overview of this genre of portrait imagery, see Manuth, Van Leeuwen and Koldeweij, 2016; and Van Leeuwen, 2011, 109–24.

5 SELLING THE SELF

1 For visual precedents and other contemporaneous examples of the 'self-portrait en décapité' (the term is Panofsky's), see De Koomen, 2013, 191–221.

2 Tudor, 2015, 185–89; Grabes, 1982, passim.

3 Francesca Baldassari in Rome, 2016, cat. 11, 100–101.

4 Tudor, 2015, 190–91; Woods-Marsden, 1998, 201–22.

5 For Anguissola's self-portraits, see Madrid, 2019–20, 89–101; and Washington, 2007, 110–11 and 116–22. For Lavinia Fontana's *Self-portrait at the Spinet*, see Maria Teresa Cantaro in Madrid, 2019–20, cat. 8, 104–5, with previous bibliography.

6 Woods-Marsden, 1998, 192–93; Jacobs, 1997, 123–56.

7 Judith W. Mann in Rome, New York and St Louis, 2001–2, cat. 56, 320–21; Letizia Treves in London, 2020, cat. 9, 134–35.

8 Roberto Contini in Florence, 1991, cat. 16, 140–43 (Gentileschi); Bissell, 1999, cat. X-9, 314–15 (copy after Gentileschi); Judith W. Mann in Rome, New York and St Louis, 2001–2, 320 (copy after Gentileschi); Paliaga, 2011, 58 (Gentileschi).

9 Paliaga, 2011, 58–61 (Gentileschi); Francesca Baldassari in Rome, 2016, 128 (Gentileschi).

10 For an insightful overview, see Locker, 2015, 125–60.

11 Bastogi, 2010, 339, 353–54; Bastogi, 2021, 95 and n. 7, 104.

12 Gianni Papi in Florence, 2010, 30; Papi, 2011, n. 6, 847.

13 The London *Self-portrait as St Catherine of Alexandria* was dated to around 1615–17 in the National Gallery's 2020 exhibition catalogue (London, 2020, cat. 11, 140), for example, as was the Hartford *Lute Player* in the Hartford and Detroit exhibition of the following year (Hartford and Detroit, 2021–22, cat. 24, 101). This new information indicates that both works had already been completed and received by the Medici by the middle of 1615, for which, see further Nastogi, 2021, 96.

14 The *braccio fiorentino* measured around 58 cm. There are some obvious discrepancies between the measurements given in the early inventories and the actual measurements of the works registered today. Two factors, nonetheless, help to explain these: first, inventories only ever give an approximate measurement – applied more or less loosely or not depending on the circumstances – and, second, in this instance the compilers were following the standard practice of providing a rough, visually based indication of the measurement of the works with their frames included.

15 Bastogi, 2021, 95.

16 Florence, 2010, 160: 'il ritratto dell'Artemisia di sua mano che suona il liuto'.

17 Bastogi, 2010, 339: 'Dua [sic] quadri in tela con adornamenti neri filettati d'oro alti braccia 1¾ larghi braccia 1 1/3 che in uno entrovi Santa Caterina delle Ruote e nell'altro una donna con il morione che mette mano alla spada. n. 2.'

18 Florence, 2010, 30 (Papi); Bastogi, 2010, 339: 'un quadro in tela alto braccia 1¾ e largo braccia 1½ con cornice nera filettata d'oro entrovi dipinto l'Artemisia Pittrice in abito di amazzone con spada rotella e morione'.

19 Bastogi, 2021, 98: 'dipintovi fino sotto alla cintola il Ritratto della Artemisia Lomi pittrice vestita da ammazzone con spada nella destra, nudo il braccio sinistro, cimiero con penne in testa, manto giallo al braccio destro'.

20 Bastogi, 2021, 97–98.

21 Bastogi, 2021, 99: 'dipintovi fino alla cintola il Ritratto di Artemisia Lomi, rappresentante Santa Caterina delle Ruote'.

22 Papi, 2011, n. 6, 847; Bastogi, 2010, 339; Stefano Casciu in Florence, 2010, 162: 'un simile [Quadro] dipintovi Artemisia Lomi da Santa Maria Maddalena in abito giallo con una testa di morte e specchio avanti'.

23 The 1775 inventory reference to the *Conversion of the Magdalene* was first published in Bastogi, 2021, n. 12, 104: 'dipintovi figura intera sedente il Ritratto fatto di sua mano di Artemisia Lomi, rappresentante Santa Maria Magdalena scollacciata, veste gialla, destra al petto, e sinistra sul tavolino, su cui teschio di morto'.

24 Papi, 2010, 30; Bastogi, 2010, 339; Francesca Baldassari in Rome, 2016, cat. 26, 132–33.

25 For this painting, see Florence, 1983, cat. 14, 35; Haskins, 1993, 298–99; Garrard, 2001, 35 and fig. 14, 37; Hoppe, 2014, 192–93.

26 For the London *Self-portrait as St Catherine of Alexandria*, see Letizia Treves in London, 2020, cat. 11, 140–41; and Oliver Tostmann in Hartford and Detroit, 2021–22, cat. 25, 104–5, with previous bibliography.

27 See the more elaborately decorative costume worn by Caravaggio's St Catherine of Alexandria that is also sometimes cited in relation to Gentileschi's paintings of this subject (e.g., Mina Gregori in New York and Naples, 1985, cat. 72, 246–50, and 248, for the saint's 'splendid clothing' more specifically).

28 As also suggested in Keith, 2020, 95.

29 Cropper, 2001, 275.

30 For a recent discussion of Gentileschi's *St Catherine of Alexandria*, see Oliver Tostmann in Hartford and Detroit, 2021, cat. 26, 106–7, with previous bibliography.

31 Letizia Treves in London, 2020, 144.

32 Evelina Borea in Florence, 1970, 74–75; Bissell, 1999, 210.

33 New York and Naples, 1985, cat. 73, 250–55.

34 For the importance of Allori's *Judith* as a precedent and stimulus for Gentileschi's *Conversion of the Magdalene*, see further Christiansen, 2004, 115–17, which also emphasises the painting's self-conscious blurring of the boundaries between self-portraiture and the more ambiguously disguised depiction of likeness found in the disguised or historiated portrait tradition.

35 For Bellini's *Woman with a Mirror* in relation to the paragone debate, see McHam, 2008, 157–71.

36 Antonio Marchi and Francesco Floridi after Artemisia Gentileschi, *Conversion of the Magdalene*, engraving on paper, from Bardi, 1837–42, vol. 1, fig. 37.

37 For the iconography of Donatello's *Penitent Magdalene*, see Dunkelman, 2005–6, 10–13.

38 The signature shows signs of having been repainted and is located on a strip of canvas running down the left side of the painting that some scholars have read in the past as possibly constituting a later addition to the canvas. For a review of the literature on this issue and the conclusion that the canvas strip, together with the signature, are all contemporaneous with the date of creation of the work itself, see Mann, 2009, 88.

39 Harris, 1998, 116.

40 Mann, 2009, 88.

41 Ibid., 89.

42 Bastogi, 2010, 339, for this and the other points raised in this paragraph.

43 Garrard, 2020, 102–5; Letizia Treves in London, 2020, 145.

44 For a recent discussion of Gentileschi's *Self-portrait as a Lute Player*, see Oliver Tostmann in Hartford and Detroit, 2020–21, cat. 24, 101–3, with previous bibliography.

45 For this tradition, see Franklin, 2011, 128–53.

46 For this tradition in the work of Caravaggio, see Posner, 1971, 301–24. For this tradition in the work of Caravaggio's followers, see Vodret and Strinati, 2001, 112; and Celenza, 2014, 97–100.

47 Francesco Solinas in Milan, 2011, 164, who speculates, 'We have no way of knowing what kind of portrait Francesco Maria owned: a half-length figure? a reclining nude like the *Danaë* in Saint Louis?'

48 Artemisia Gentileschi to Francesco Maria Maringhi, 26 June 1620 (Solinas, 2011a, letter 31, 74).

49 Cohen, 2015, 268.

50 Locker, 2015, 136–40; Garrard, 1989, 37, 497; and for this proposal, see further Barker, 2022, 46, who concludes, 'This "Artemisia" may very well have been our painter, although it is also true that this could refer to another prominent woman at the Florentine court: Artemisia Tozzi (ca. 1590–1643), the common-born consort of Don Antonio de' Medici . . . '

51 Locker, 2015, 140.

52 Morandi, 1995, passim.

53 For Sustermans' *Portrait of Marie Madeleine of Austria, Cosimo II and Ferdinand II de' Medici*, see Florence, 1983, cat. IX, 94.

54 Britton, 2009, 13–18.

55 Barolsky, 1990, passim. For Michelangelo's portraits, see Florence, 2008; and Loh, 2015, xiv, 10–17, who stresses Michelangelo's status as 'one of the first international art celebrities in history – an artist whose legend and reputation could be matched to an instantly recognizable face produced by an industry beyond his immediate control'.

56 For example, Bissell, 1999, 328; Judith W. Mann in Rome, New York and St Louis, 2001–2, 322; Locker, 2015, 126; Francesca Baldassari in Rome, 2016, 128–29.

57 See, for example, Letizia Treves in London, 2020, 162, noting the appearance of Gentileschi's 'signature' earrings in both her portrait medal of around 1625 and in the portrait of her by Vouet.

58 See, for example, the discussions concerning the possibility that Gentileschi might have wished to reference the presence of her own features in her *Lucretia* (fig. 78), London, 2020, cat. 21, 170–73.

59 For Allori's use of his mistress, 'La Mazzafirra', as the model for the naked Magdalene (Galleria Palatina, Florence, Inv. 1890 n.2174), see Miles L. Chappell in Florence, 1984, cat. 26, 82–83. For Vouet's depiction of Virginia da Vezzo as the Magdalene in several paintings dating to the late 1620s and 1630s, see Lurie, 1993, 160–61; Candida Dreier in Potsdam, 2019, cat. 51, 206–7; and Hartford and Detroit, 2021–22, cat. 38, 130–32. For an overview of Virginia da Vezzo's career and oeuvre, see further Sara Bruno in Milan, 2021, 258–63.

60 Chapman, 1990; Indianapolis, 2006.

61 For Frida Kahlo and self-portraiture, see Grimberg, 1998, 82–104. For Cindy Sherman and portraiture and notions of self, see Moorhouse, 2019, 11–22.

62 Haskell, 1980, 142–45; London and Fort Worth, 2010, 38–40, 65–67.

63 For this, and an analysis of Rosa's career in the context of the art market more generally, see Marshall, 2017a, 367–91.

64 For this and the following painting, see London, 2010, cat. 2, 108–9; and Volpi, 2014, cat. 77, 424–25, with previous bibliography.

65 For the *St Cecilia*, see Judith W. Mann in Rome, New York and St Louis, 2001–2, cat. 63, 350–52, with previous bibliography.

66 For the Biffi inventory, see Maria Lucrezia Vicini in Cannatà and Vicini, 1992, 103: 'Due ovati piccoli con due teste rappresentante Pittura e Poesia mano di Artemisia una che ha la cornice rifatta.' For further discussion, see Papi, 1994, 198–99; Vicini, 2000, 4; Spear, 2000, 574, and n. 52, 579; Patrizia Cavazzini in Rome, New York and St Louis, 2001–2, 289, and n. 105, 294–95; Keith Christiansen in Rome, New York and St Louis, 2001–2, 104; Mann, 2005b, 52, and n. 8, 75; Cavazzini in London, 2020, 40; Francesca Whitlum-Cooper in London, 2020, 130. The Biffi inventory is also discussed in relation to Orazio Gentileschi's Spada *David Contemplating the Head of Goliath* as well as in the context of a copy after this painting in the Olomouc Museum of Art/Muzeum umění Olomouc, which is sometimes attributed as an early copy by Artemisia after Orazio (Papi, 2002, 47; Zapletalová, 2013, 253–54; and for the Olomouc Museum in relation to Artemisia, see further p. 242 below).

67 Bissell, 1999, cat. X21, 327–29; Garrard, 2001, 55–56, fig. 31, 58, and n. 76, 140; Mann, 2005b, 52, and n. 8, 75; Judith W. Mann in Milan, 2011, fig. 4, 56; Mann in Rome, 2016, fig. 1, 15 and n. 15, 21; Locker, 2015, 133–34, and n. 17, 210; Treves, 2020, 73, and n. 40, 77.

68 Ann Sutherland Harris in Washington, 2007, 55.

6 'NO LITTLE HORROR'

1 Bissell, 1999, cat. L26, 363.

2 Ibid., cat. L66, 377.

3 Barker, 2017, doc. 22, 77.

4 Bissell, 1999, cat. L-39, 369–70.

5 Solinas, 2011a, letter 6, 27.

6 For Gentileschi's subsequent paintings of *Hercules and Omphale*, see Bissell, 1999, cats L40–41, 370–71. On 20 March 1620, Pierantonio Stiattesi mentioned Artemisia's outstanding work for the Grand Duke in a letter to Francesco Maringhi in Florence (Solinas, 2011a, letter 15, 45). In the letter, he notes that the painting is nearly complete before observing, 'della Iole il cardinale Montalto ne vuole una copia' (ibid., 46). On the basis of this reference, Sheila Barker has identified the 1620 Medici *Hercules* commission as having been for *Hercules and Iole* (Barker, 2022, 70–71). However, Maringhi's letter does not explicitly connect these two references together as referring to a single work. Moreover, Francesco Solinas and Yuri Primarosa (Solinas, 2011a, n. 18, 47; Solinas, 2011b, 87; Primarosa in Milan, 2011, 270) have suggested the alternative possibility that the reference to *Iole* may be for a separate work, namely the *Jael and Sisera* of 1620.

7 Bissell, 1999, cat. L68, 377–78.

8 Although it should also be remembered that this impression has become exaggerated over time, since the composition has been cropped slightly, particularly at the top and left, as pointed out by Bissell, 1999, 198, and as further commented upon by Letizia Treves in London, 2020, 132.

9 Garrard (1989, 319) also notes this connection between Artemisia's grotesque face detail in the Judith and Caravaggio's *Head of the Medusa* shield, as does Christiansen (2004, 116) in relation to a comparison with Marinesque poetry more generally.

10 Milan, 2004, cat. 8, 102, and passim for this tradition more generally. For the Negroli workshop, see further New York, 1998, and for these shields more specifically, cats 3, 42, 68.

11 Roberto Contini in Florence, 1991, 124; Bissell, 1999, 202–3.

12 Evelina Borea (in Florence, 1970, 76) connected the Uffizi *Judith* with a 1638 Palazzo Pitti inventory reference to a painting of 'Giuditta che ammazza Oloferne'. Gianni Papi and R. Ward Bissell, however, subsequently questioned this provenance on the basis of potential discrepancies in the dimensions assigned to the inventory reference and because the painting described in the inventory carries no attribution, whereas the Uffizi *Judith* is signed at lower right (Papi in Florence, 1991, 150; Bissell, 1999, 214). On the other hand, it could be argued that the inventory's compilers may have simply missed the signature, and the inventory's dimensions, which are, in any event, approximate indications only, may have been intended to have included the frame. Borea also notes that, prior to its relining, the back of the Uffizi *Judith* used to bear a number – 574 – which is the same number as that assigned to the Pitti *Judith*, attributed at that stage to Caravaggio, when it was transferred to the Uffizi in 1774. For recent publications that follow Borea's reading of the documents, see Bastogi, 2010, 354; Francesco Solinas in Milan, 2011, 176; Francesca Baldassari in Rome, 2016, 138; and Barker, 2022, 65, who views the 1638 location of the Uffizi *Judith* in the Room of Venus at the Palazzo Pitti as part of a political programme to position the work at 'a gateway to two different ceremonial trajectories of dynastic power in Palazzo Pitti, one masculine and one feminine', which communicates, moreover, 'an image of womanly heroism [that] underscored Maria Magdalena's and Christine's dedication to protecting the grand duchy during the minority of Ferdinand II de' Medici'.

13 The Uffizi *Judith* is dated 1613–14 in London, 2020 (cat. 6, 128–29). This is too early in relation to the Naples version, in my opinion. The argument in favour of this earlier dating primarily rests on the supposedly intrinsic unlikelihood that Artemisia would have returned to a composition a number of years after its initial production: 'it is difficult to understand why she would have returned – more than eight years later – to a previous composition' (ibid, 128). However, Gentileschi modified and adapted her earlier compositions throughout her career. For the connections between Gentileschi's 1610 *Susanna and the Elders* and her 1652 version of the same subject, for example, see p. 221. For R. Ward Bissell's later dating of the Uffizi *Judith* (noted also as in agreement with Cropper), see Bissell, 1999, 214. Bissell also makes the fundamental point that the painting's 'leaps in sophistication and technical virtuosity place the Uffizi Judith several years in advance of its Naples prototype, while the presence of the Lomi surname in the signature still connects the painting to Florentine patronage'. For Garrard's similar dating, see Garrard, 1989, 51–53.

14 Bissell, 1999, 191–93; and, for the Milan copy, see further Yuri Primarosa in Milan, 2011, cat. 5, 140–41.

15 For Rosso's painting, see Gaston, 2004, 169–78.

16 Spike, 1992, 732.

17 For R. Ward Bissell's subsequent endorsement of Spike's proposal, see Bissell, 2005, 27–34.

18 Hoffrichter, 1980, 9–15.

19 Topper and Gillis, 1996, 10–13.

20 Baldinucci, 1681–1728, III, 714.

21 Barker, 2017, 60.

22 Barker, 2017, 69; Solinas, 2011b, 79–81; Barker, 2022, 67–68. As an additional motivation informing Artemisia's rushed departure from Florence at this time, Barker adds Artemisia's probable concern that Orazio might get wind of her 'financial separation' from Pierantonio Stiattesi – which she hypothesises as having occurred sometime before 1618 – and that he would then use this information as an argument for withholding payment of the second instalment of 500 Florentine scudi (plus interest) to complete the dowry of 1,000 scudi promised at the time of Artemisia's marriage.

23 Rome, New York and St Louis, 2001–2, 446; for commentary, see Solinas, 2011a, 144–46; and Solinas, 2011b, 81–82.

24 For a reading of Aremisia's departure from Florence that is in greater accord with the characterisation here presented, see Cavazzini, 2020, 41. Among other points, Cavazzini underscores the important factor that Artemisia's departure from Florence without first completing her *Hercules* for Cosimo II, after already receiving a down payment for it, represented: 'a behaviour akin to theft'.

25 Contini, 2011, 41.

26 For this painting, see Rome, 2016, cat. 34, 150–51, with previous bibliography.

27 For this painting, see Cantelli, 1983, 56 and tav. 211.

7 ROME, 1620–1627

1 For the rituals and festive activities of the Bentvueghels in Rome, see Kren, 1980, 63–80; Levine, 161–91; and Rome, 2014, passim.

2 For the opposition of the Schildersbent to the tax levied by the Accademia di San Luca, see Hughes, 1986, 52; and Lorizzo, 2003, 325–36. For other comic drawings, paintings and prints of this type, see further Rome, 2014, 144–67.

3 Susanne Baveres in Rome, 2014, 157; Cavazzini, 2020, 42.

4 See, for example, the object held by Edward Prince of Wales in Holbein's portrait now in the National Gallery of Art, Washington, D.C., for which, see Hand, 1993, 83–91.

5 Susanne Baveres in Rome, 2014, 156.

6 For Gentileschi's two Roman live-in servants, one of whom sought to bring redress for unpaid wages, see the documents summarised by Michele Nicolaci (2011, 263, entries for Lent, 1621; Lent, 1622; Lent, 1623; Lent, 1624; Lent, 1625, 15 September 1625).

7 Solinas, 2011a, 45, letter 15: Pierantonio Stiattesi to Francesco Maria Maringhi, 20 March 1620; 69–70,

letter 2: Pierantonio Stiattesi to Francesco Maria Maringhi, 30 May 1620.

8 Solinas, 2011a, 53, letter 20: Artemisia Gentileschi to Francesco Maria Maringhi, 11 April 1620. For commentary, see London, 2020, cat. 13C, 150–51; and Barker, 2022, 68.

9 Solinas, 2011a, 69–70, letter 29: Pierantonio Stiattesi to Francesco Maria Maringhi, 30 May 1620. For commentary, see London, 2020, cat. 13D, 152–53, and for the fractured relations between Artemisia and Orazio Gentileschi during this period, see Barker, 2017, n. 4, 70, and n. 96, 86; and Cavazzini, 2020, 41.

10 Judith W. Mann in Rome, New York and St Louis, 2001–2, 355; and see further Mann, 2009, 78–81.

11 Judith W. Mann in Rome, New York and St Louis, 2001–2, 355.

12 Bissell, 1999, 352, and cat. X42, 348–53, for the catalogue entry in its entirety.

13 Garrard, 1989, 204, and 202–4 for her comments on the painting in their entirety.

14 Garrard, 1989, 203.

15 Garrard, 2001, 110–11; and see further ibid., 'Collaboration or Unauthorized Alteration?', 97–113, for the argument in its entirety.

16 Christiansen, 2004, 119.

17 Christiansen, 2004, 119; Mann, 2005a, 3; Mann, 2005b, 72; Lapierre, 2005, 168; Locker, 2015, 17; Judith W. Mann in Rome, 2016, 36–37; Barker, 2022, 71.

18 Garrard, 2017, 23.

19 Wood, 1992, 515.

20 Bologna, Frankfurt and Washington, 1991–92, cat. 12, 164–65.

21 Mann, 2005b, 72.

22 Bologna, Frankfurt and Washington, 1991–92, cats 8–9, 150–53.

23 Christiansen, 2004, 119.

24 Garrard, 2001, 105.

25 See Wood, 1992, item 284, 522: 'Una Susanna Con li vecchi alta p.i 8 Cornice nere profilate e rabescate d'oro di m.o di artimitia' ('A Susanna and the Elders 8 palmi [*c.*178 cm] high with black frame [and] with golden arabesque decoration by the hand of Artemisia').

26 Judith W. Mann in Rome, New York and St Louis, 2001–2, 372, relating information provided by the Matthiesen Gallery, London.

27 Brown and Kagan, 1987, 239–40.

28 For the Seville cathedral *Penitent Magdalene*, see Bissell, 1999, cat. 16, 222–24; Judith W. Mann in Rome, New York and St Louis, 2001–2, cat. 68, 365–67; Garrard, 2001, 25–35; Christiansen, 2004, 119–20; Mann, 2005a, 3; Riccardo Lattuada in Lattuada and Nappi, 2005, 85–86; Currie et al., 2017, 226 and n. 43, 234–35; Letizia Treves in London, 2020, 187. For the *Penitent Magdalene* now in a private American collection and formerly at Tajan, Paris (sale 19 December 2001, lot 7), see Locker, 2021, where its attribution to Gentileschi was first proposed. The attribution of the Seville *Magdalene* to Gentileschi has not been universally accepted. Bissell, Garrard, Lattuada and Treves have attributed it to Gentileschi, while Christiansen and Locker have both identified it as an early copy and Mann downgraded her initial attribution after studying the painting while it was on display in the Rome, New York and St Louis exhibition of 2001–2. The issue is further complicated by the existence of additional versions, including a canvas at one stage in a private French collection that was exhibited by Richard L. Feigen and Company, New York, in 1998, and that has also been identified as either another prime version (Bissell, Garrard) or as another early copy (Mann, Christiansen, Ann Sutherland Harris, Locker).

29 Judith W. Mann in Rome, New York and St Louis, 2001–2, 365–66.

30 Bellori, 2005, 203; for discussion, see Hibbard, 1983, 51.

31 Garrard, 2017, 16–17; Papi, 2017, 147–49; Currie et al., 2017, 217–35; Letizia Treves in London, 2020, cat. 24, 182–83; Barker, 2022, 75.

32 For Caravaggio's *Ecstasy of the Magdalene*, see Scaletti, 2017, cat. D13, 220–21, and 92–97, for further discussion. For a subsequently discovered version of the subject that has been attributed to Caravaggio by Mina Gregori, see Harris, 2018, n.p.

33 Papi, 2017, 148.

34 Bissell, 1999, cat. 14, 219–20, with previous bibliography; Judith W. Mann in Rome, New York and St Louis, 2001–2, cat. 69, 368–70; Letizia Treves in London, 2020, cat. 23, 178–80.

35 Richard E. Spear in Cleveland, 1971, cat. 28, 96–97; Judith W. Mann in Rome, New York and St Louis, 2001–2, cat. 69, 368.

36 Florence, 2015.

37 For this painting, see Richard Beresford in Sydney and Melbourne, 2003–4, cat. 56, 190–91.

8 A BUSINESS EVALUATION OF GENTILESCHI'S CAREER IN THE 1620S

1 Baglione, 1642, 360.

2 See Riccardo Lattuada in Milan, 2021, cat. 5.5, 348–49, with previous bibliography; and Papi, Gillespie and Chaplin, 2020, 188–95. The painting discussed by Lattuada is likely to be the version seen by Sandrart in Gentileschi's workshop prior to its delivery to the Giustiniani collection in Rome, because both Sandrart's description and the 1638 Giustiniani inventory describe a composition in which David holds the head of Goliath in his hand. The painting illustrated in fig. 71, on the other hand, is a closely related variant – with Goliath's head resting at David's feet – which was published by Gianni Papi in 1996 on the basis of a photograph before eventually coming to light at auction in Munich in 2018. A signature and partly illegible date were discovered during cleaning, and the painting was republished in an extended study by Gianni Papi, Simon Gillespie and Tracey Chaplin (Papi, Gillespie and Chaplin, 2020, 188–95). Its attribution was further endorsed by Sheila Barker in 2022 (101 and fig. 60).

3 Sandrart, 1675–80, 204.

4 For this painting, see Francesca Whitlum-Cooper in London, 2020, cat. 14, 154–55, with previous bibliography.

5 Whitfield, 2001, 152–55; Spear, 2010, 91–95.

6 For Vincenzo Giustiani's letter of around 1620 to Teodoro Amayden, outlining his theory of painting, see Bottari, 1757–68, 6: 121–29. For translation and discussion, see Engass and Brown, 1970, 16–20. For further discussion, see Christiansen, 1986, 421–22, and Unger, 2019, 210.

7 For the critical and economic status of seventeenth-century still-life painting, see Marshall, 2017/18, 129–45.

8 For this tradition in relation to classical art theory, see Lee, 1940, 197–269.

9 Garrard, 1989, 61–62; Woods-Marsden, 1998, 192–93.

10 For the importance of this process in the parallel case study of Baroque Naples, see Marshall, 2016, 236–44.

11 For the example of the Jesuits, see Vatican City, 1990, passim.

12 Bissell, 1968, 153.

13 For a discussion of this commission, traditionally dated following De' Dominici to the mid-1620s, but then by Schütze and Willette to the early 1650s on the basis of alternative documentation, see Schütze and Willette, 1992, 41–45, and cat. D13, 261.

14 Pepper, 1984b; Turner and Salerno, 1988.

15 Spinosa, 2003; Schütze and Willette, 1992, passim.

16 Baldassari, 1995, passim.

17 Bissell, 1999, passim.

18 Works that I would place in the category of constituting more or less secure recent additions to Gentileschi's oeuvre from after Bissell's 1999 catalogue

include the following: (1) *Danaë*, oil on copper, The Saint Louis Art Museum, Saint Louis (re-attributed to Artemisia) (fig. 22); (2) *Self-portrait as St Catherine of Alexandria*, National Gallery of Art, London (fig. 35); (3) *Self-portrait as a Lute Player*, oil on canvas, Wadsworth Atheneum Museum of Art, Hartford, Conn. (fig. 37); (4) *Susanna and the Elders*, Burghley House Collections, signed and dated 1622 (re-attributed to Artemisia) (fig. 64); (5) *Mary Magdalene in Ecstasy*, Fondazione Musei Civici, Palazzo Ducale, Venice, on long-term loan from a private collection (fig. 67); (6) *Medea*, private collection (signed, Rome, 2016, cat. 37, 156–57); (7) *Lucretia*, The J. Paul Getty Museum, Los Angeles (fig. 77); (8) *Christ Blessing the Children*, Basilica di Santi Ambrogio e Carlo Borromeo al Corso, Rome (fig. 80); (9) *Cleopatra*, Fondazione Cavallini Sgarbi (Milan, 2011, cat. 20, 174–75; Milan, 2021, cat. 5.3, 347–48); (10) *David with the Head of Goliath*, private collection, signed and illegibly dated (fig. 71); (11) *Christ and the Samaritan Woman at the Well*, Palazzo Blu, Pisa, Property of the Fondazione Pisa (fig. 100); (12) *Susanna and the Elders*, Pinacoteca Nazionale, Bologna, signed and dated 1652 (fig. 121). Finally, as the book was going to press, a newly discovered late version of *Susanna and the Elders* from the British Royal Collection (13) went on display at Windsor Castle. For the scholarship informing this important new attribution, see Munz and Izat, 2023.

19 For Elisabetta Sirani's list and rates of productivity, see Morselli, 2010, 60–61; Morselli, 2020, 307–20. For Guercino's rates of productivity, see Spear in Spear and Sohm, 2010, 65.

20 The inventory is transcribed and translated in Rome, New York and St Louis, 2001–2, 446–47.

21 For De Anfora's inventory, see Marshall, 2010, 115–16.

22 Pegazzano, 1997, 131–46.

23 Fumagalli, 2010, 188 and n. 151, 327; Barker, 2017, docs. 10–14, 75; and for discussion, see Barker, 2017, 64, and n. 50, 83; and Barker, 2022, 43. Barker interprets the documentation as involving a yet more complex arrangement concerning an initial loan from Carducci of ten scudi which was subsequently converted into a commission for a painting of a Madonna to cover the debt.

24 Barker, 2017, doc. 14, 75.

25 Barker, 2017, doc. 10, 75.

26 Barker, 2017, doc. 12, 75.

27 Barker, 2017, doc. 11, 75.

28 For further discussion of Masino *merciaio* and the requirement for women to have male proxies act on their behalf, see Barker, 2017, 63–64.

29 For Laura Corsini's payment to Gentileschi, see Francesca Baldassari in Rome, 2016, n. 31, 33. For my own argument that this payment is too low to be identified with the Uffizi *Judith Slaying Holofernes*, see p. 129 above and p. 268, n. 33.

30 Wittkower and Wittkower, 1963, 34–41; Spear and Sohm, 2010, 63–65.

31 Spear, 2001–2, 339–41.

32 For Régnier's paintings in Giustiniani's collection, see Salerno, 1960, 21–27; 92–105; 135–48, 159, items I: 3, 155, 171, 173, 201, 202, 203, II: 259, 260. For Régnier's activities as painter in residence to the Giustiniani, see Lemoine, 1999/2000, 28–33.

33 Letter from Artemisia Gentileschi to Duke Francesco I d'Este, 22 May 1635, cit. Garrard, 1989, letter 7, 382; Solinas, 2011a, letter 42, 95.

34 Garrard, 1989, n. 18, 382.

35 Solinas, 2011a, letter 15, 46 and n. 18, 47. For further discussion, see Chapter 6, n. 6 above, and, for Montalto's patronage, see Granata, 2012, which confirms Montalto's sustained interest in collecting the work of female artists, including Lavinia Fontana (189) and Sofonisba Anguissola (179), whose *Self-portrait at the Easel*, now at the Muzeum-Zamek w Lancucie, Lancut, Poland (Madrid, 2019–20, cat. 5, 98–99), is identified by Granata as having been acquired by Montalto on the open market in 1592.

36 For Dal Pozzo and Artemisia, see Garrard, 1989, 84–87.

37 Lavin, 1975, 165.

38 For this painting, see Bissell, 1999, cat. 18, 225–26, with previous bibliography, plus, see further Judith W. Mann in Rome, New York and St Louis, 2001–2, cat. 70, 371–73.

39 For this letter, see Garrard, 1989, letter 5, 379–80. Mary Garrard (108–9) identifies the painting referred to in this letter as the Princeton *Sleeping Venus*, as does Judith W. Mann (in Rome, New York and St Louis, 2001–2, 372). Bissell (1999, cat. 31, 247–49), however, identifies it with another painting of *Venus Embracing Cupid*, now in a private collection in Switzerland (for this painting, see further Rome, New York and St Louis, 2001–2, cat. 82, 422–24). The attribution of this painting, however, has been less widely accepted than the Princeton *Sleeping Venus*. Garrard and Roberto Contini have both rejected its attribution to Artemisia, for example, and I also view the attribution as problematic.

40 For the Barberini as patrons of the arts, see Haskell, 1980, 24–62; and for a more recent overview, see Johannes Rösslaer in Potsdam, 2019, 87–91.

9 VENICE, 1627–1629

1 For Régnier's activities in Venice, see Zarrillo, 2017, 129–40.

2 Locker, 2015, 45–99; Locker, 2016, 43–45; Locker, 2020, 36–63; and for a further useful overview of this period with a particular emphasis on Gentileschi's interactions with the Venetian and Paduan literary academies, see Costa, 2000, 28–36.

3 The poems were originally published by Ilaria Toesca (1971); and subsequently discussed in Locker, 2015, 46–50, and Locker, 2020, 58–60.

4 Costa, 2000, 29–30; Locker, 2015, 51–53.

5 For the Neapolitan reception of Marino's *Galeria*, see Marshall, 2016, 183–84. For Marino and Caravaggio, see Cropper, 1991, 193–212. For Marino and Allori, see Christiansen, 2004, 115.

6 For this print, see Letizia Treves in London, 2020, cat. 19, 164–65.

7 London, 2020, 164.

8 Cropper, 2001, 268.

9 Garrard, 1989, 463.

10 Letizia Treves in London, 2020, cat. 18, 162–63.

11 Letizia Treves in London, 2020, cat. 17, 160–61.

12 For the association of the virtuosa with attributes of physical beauty – 'beautiful eyes, delicate hands, a lovely body, a sonorous voice, and so forth' – see Jacobs, 1997, 133 (from where the quote derives)–37.

13 Giovanni Francesco Loredan, letter to Artemisia Gentileschi, *c*.1627–28, cit. Bissell, 1999, Appendix B, 165–66: ''l mio cuor è assoggettito da maggior potenza, che della bellezza del tuo volto . . . Le ricchezze d'Amore non altro traffico, che nel tuo seno, ne' tuoi occhi, e nelle tue chiome'; and for discussion, ibid., 40–41.

14 For Vouet's portrait of Artemisia, see Roberto Contini in Biella, 2001, 151–53; Mann, 2005b, 52–53; Francesco Solinas in Milan, 2011, cat. 7, 142–43; Locker, 2015, 20–21, 129; Garrard, 2017, 11; Elizabeth Cropper in London, 2020, cat. 16, 158–59.

15 Garrard, 2017, 11.

16 Garrard, 2017, 11; Francesco Solinas in Milan, 2011, 142.

17 For the medallion, see London, 2020, fig. 46, 158.

18 For the medallion's iconography, see Roberto Contini in Biella 2001, 151–53; Garrard, 2017, 33–34; Francesco Solinas in Milan, 2011, 142.

19 Elizabeth Cropper in London, 2020, 158; Locker, 2015, 52.

20 For this painting, see Letizia Treves in London, 2020, cat. 34, 217–19.

21 Nichols, 2013, 221.

22 For Dal Pozzo's series of portraits of *uomini illustri*, see Sparti, 1992, 113–20. For the 1729 inventory reference to Vouet's portrait of Artemisia, see ibid., 238, which describes: 'Un Quadro in tela di palmi quattro Ritratto di Artemisia Gentileschi pittrice, cornice color di noce, et oro di Vouet'.

23 For this painting, see Mauro Natale in Geneva, 2004, cat. 20, 110–12; Locker, 2020, 36–63.

24 Locker, 2020, 55–56.

25 Bissell, 1999, cat. 3, 189–91; Letizia Treves in London, 2020, cat. 21, 170–73, with intervening bibliography. The painting is dated to the early 1620s in London, 2020, which also includes a helpful discussion of the issues relating to its dating (see particularly London, 2020, 173 and notes 10–11, 231).

26 Kenney, 2021, n.p.; Barker, 2022, 123 and n. 30, 133.

27 For a significant dissenting opinion, see Mary Garrard's questioning of the attribution in Garrard, 2023, 91. Another possible candidate for Gentileschi's Venetian period is a *Portrait of a Gentleman* (New Bryant Collection, for which, see Roberto Contini in Milan, 2011, cat. 24, 186–87). This has been identified as depicting the same sitter as is depicted in another print by Jérôme David after a portrait by Gentileschi which is dated to 1627 (Bissell, 1999, cat. 19, 226–27). However, it is not entirely clear that the figure shown in the painted portrait is, in fact, one and the same as the figure in the print.

28 Bissell, 1999, cat. 28, 241–44; Letizia Treves in London, 2020, cat. 25, 194–95, with intervening biography, to which should be added, Locker, 2020, 40, 51–53, and Barker, 2022, 120, 123, and n. 30, 133. Locker and Treves both date the painting to Gentileschi's Venetian period, whereas Barker dates the painting to around 1635–45.

29 For Padovanino's dependence on Veronese and points of contact with Artemisia, see Locker, 2020, 54, and Locker, 2015, 57–59, 84–86.

30 For proposed datings for the *Esther and Ahasuerus*, see Bissell, 1999, 243–44; as supplemented by Locker, 2020, 53–55; and Barker, 2022, 107–13, the latter of whom proposes a later dating of around 1639.

31 Venice, 1979–80, 123–26.

32 Bissell, 2013, 29–30; although see the more recent suggestion in D'Alessandro and Porzio, 2022, 91, that she may be the 'pintora' mentioned in Spanish diplomatic correspondence dating from 22 December 1629 to 2 March 1630 as being on her way to Naples from Venice.

33 The document was published in 2010 as part of the History of the Accademia di San Luca Project directed by the National Gallery of Art's Center for Advanced Studies in the Visual Arts.

34 For Ottavio Leoni, see Florence, 2019, passim.

35 Archivio di Stato di Roma (ASR), ASR, TNC, uff. 15, 1627, pt. 2, vol. 112, fols 707r–v, 708r–v, 709r, general meeting of painters and sculptors, 29 June 1627; available at https://www.nga.gov/content/accademia/en/documents/ASRTNCUff1516270629.html. For Michelangelo Guidi, see Ciampolini, 2012, vol. 1, no. 21.

36 Lukehart, 2009, Appendix 7D, 378.

37 On this point, see Bissell, 1999, n. 17, 404, who cites, as evidence, the fact that her name is not included in Ghezzi's 1696 list of female members of the Academy.

38 For Girolamo Gualdo's brief entry on Artemisia, see Costa, 2000, 31–34. For the very high likelihood that the still-life works referred to by Gualdo should be identified as being by Giovanna Garzoni rather than by Gentileschi, see Spear, 2001, 339; Bissell, 2013, passim; and D'Alessandro and Porzio, 2022, 92.

39 For an overview of Alcalá's patronage and collecting, see Brown and Kagan, 1987, passim; Locker, 2015, 19–23; and Marshall, 2016, 220–22, with additional bibliography.

40 For the inventory references to these paintings, see Brown and Kagan, 1987, Inv. 3, 7, and 17, 248.

41 For Alcalá's Neapolitan self-portraits by Gentileschi, see Brown and Kagan, 1987, Inv. 17 and 10, 249; and Bissell, 1999, cat. L61 and 62, 375–76.

42 The painting was initially published by Gianni Papi in 2012, with the attribution being followed by all subsequent authors (Papi, 2012, 828–31; Adriana Caprioti in Pisa, 2013, cat. 1, 39–41; Locker, 2015, 22–23; Riccardo Lattuada in Rome, 2016, cat. 67, 222–23; Amelio, 2017, unpaginated, which reproduces a photograph showing an inscription and date of 1626 that was revealed on the reverse of the canvas following conservation work undertaken in 2002–3; Rafael Japón in Naples, 2022, cat. 6, 128–29).

43 Marshall, 2016, 220–22.

44 For Oñate's viceregency, see Marshall, 2016, 230–31; 243.

45 For the documentation, see Gerard, 1982, 11.

46 For Domenichino's *Sacrifice of Isaac*, see Richard E. Spear in Rome, 1996, cat. 45, 462–63. For Reni's *Abduction of Helen*, commissioned for the Alcázar but ultimately acquired for the French royal collections, see Colantuono, 1997. For the Alcázar commission more generally, see Orso, 1986, passim.

10 'A GREAT CRY SPREAD THROUGHOUT THE CITY'

1 For the disastrous long-term consequences of this policy on the Neapolitan economy, see Calabria, 1991, passim.

2 For this painting and other contemporary depictions of the Revolt of Masaniello, see Marshall, 1998, 478–97.

3 For two classic accounts of the Revolt of Masaniello, see Burke, 1983, 3–21; and Villari, 1993.

4 Carafa's heirs had three inventories drawn up of his possessions. A number of the paintings here mentioned appear in the second listing of Carafa's belongings made in 1649. For all three inventories, see Labrot, 1992, Inv. 9, 75–78; Inv. 11, 82–83; and Inv. 12, 84–85.

5 For Gargiulo's *Execution of Don Giuseppe Carafa*, see Brigitte Daprà in Sestieri and Daprà, 1994, cat. 143, 291, with previous bibliography.

6 For contemporary accounts of the execution of Don Giuseppe Carafa, see Capecelatro, 1:56–58; and the letter of the Genoese Ambassador to Naples, 3 August 1647, in Correra, 1890, 363–64.

7 Marshall, 2016, 150–81.

8 Galasso, 1982, 46–47; De Renzi, 1867, 104–17; Strazzullo, 1957, 7–16.

9 Lattuada and Nappi, 2005, doc. 6, 98.

10 For the issue of whether Gentileschi might possibly have given birth to a second daughter during this period, see Garrard, 1989, n. 4, 391; Bissell, 1999, 157–62; Lapierre, 2000, 438; and Garrard, 2020, 63. The evidence for this derives from Gentileschi's reference in her correspondence to having to arrange a dowry for a daughter on two separate occasions: first in 1636–37, and once again in 1649. This resulted in a theory that, with Prudenzia presumably married in the late 1630s, Gentileschi might have also been compelled to arrange a dowry for a second, younger daughter, who came of age in the late 1640s and who would thus have been born sometime soon after Gentileschi's arrival in Naples. Candidates for the father of this otherwise undocumented daughter were also posited, including Gentileschi's former Florentine lover, Francesco Maringhi, who seems to have resettled in Naples sometime around this period, as well as the viceroy, the Duke of Alcalá, a suggestion speculatively advanced by Lapierre on the basis of no actual evidence. In 2022, however, documents were published establishing that 'Prudentia

Palmira Schiattese florentina' was, in fact, married in Naples on 9 February 1649 to Antonio de Napoli shortly after giving birth to a son on 3 February. Unusually for the period, the marriage was formalised at the couple's place of residence rather than a church, indicating a serious illness on Prudenzia's part. Prudenzia must, therefore, have been the subject of Gentileschi's dowry deliberations in 1649, and so too, by implication, in 1636–37. But it remains unclear as to whether this earlier marriage ever took place, or whether Prudenzia (who was thirty-two in 1649) may have first lived for some years out of wedlock with Antonio de Napoli until the birth of their son necessitated the formalisation of their relationship (D'Alessandro and Porzio, 2022, 96–99; Ruotolo, 2022, 73–74).

11 For Gentileschi's August 1630 letters to Cassiano dal Pozzo, in which she mentions these circumstances, see Garrard, 1989, 377–78; and Solinas, 2011a, letters 37–38, 85–86; and for a recent commentary, see Denunzio, 2022, 61, who suggests instead the possibility of a projected commission from Ferdinand's stepmother, Eleonora Gonzaga (1598–1655).

12 De' Dominici, 1742–45, 3:45.

13 Artemisia Gentileschi, letter to Cassiano dal Pozzo, Naples, 21 December 1630, cit. Garrard, 1989, 378–79. For commentary, see ibid.; and Solinas, 2011a, letter 39, 86–87.

14 Gentileschi mentions a duchess in her letter, whereas Isabella Filomarino (1600–1665) was a countess. A slight exaggeration of the noble ranking of her patron would be, nonetheless, in keeping with the occasionally hyperbolic tone that one encounters in Gentileschi's letters from this period. For the artistic patronage of Giangirolamo and Isabella Acquaviva, see Marshall, 2016, 193–95; and Conversano, 2018, passim.

15 For the *Roman Charity*, formerly castello di Conversano, see Viviana Farina in Conversano, 2018, cat. 30, 262–66. Farina also identifies a version of *David and Bathsheba* (Sotheby's Milan, 14–15 June 2011, lot 27, now private collection) as having the same provenance (26–27).

16 For Gentileschi's relations with Stanzione, see Schütze and Willette, 1992, 159–60. For Gentileschi's associations with the Neapolitan academies, see Locker, 2015, 102–13.

17 London, 2020, cat. 26, 198–99; Maria Cristina Terzaghi in Naples, 2022, cat. 11, 138–39.

18 Bissell, 1999, 233.

19 For the *Annunciation* in relation to Fiasella's San Giorgio *Crucifixion*, see Bissell, 1999, 233–34, with previous bibliography; and see further Barker, 2022, 85–90.

20 For an overview of Monterrey's Neapolitan patronage, see Marshall, 2016, 222–29.

21 For this series, see Schütze and Willette, 1992, 200–202, with previous bibliography. For subsequent sources, with particular reference to Gentileschi's contribution to the series, see Bissell, 1999, cat. 32, 249–56; Rome, New York and St Louis, 2001–2, cat. 77, 405–7; Andrés Úbeda de los Cobos in Milan, 2011, cat. 31, 204–5; Nicola Cleopazzo in Conversano, 2018, cat. 38, 292–93; Francesca Whitlum-Cooper in London, 2020, cat. 29, 204–6; and Mercedes Simal in Naples, 2022, 142–44. Úbeda de los Cobos proposes the slightly later date of around 1635 and argues against Vannugli's suggestion that the series was originally painted for the Ermita de San Juan. His arguments, while containing some interesting new material and proposals, include the unconvincing suggestion that Gentileschi 'used a painting she had already finished, which was then enlarged so that it could be adapted to the requests from Madrid and thus added to the Buen Retiro commission' (Milan, 2011, 204). This seems highly unlikely for two reasons: first, it clashes with the obvious care taken to co-ordinate all the elements of the cycle into a harmonious whole, and, second, Gentileschi would almost certainly not treat one of the most important commissions of her career in such a cavalier fashion as to adapt a previously completed work to make it fit this new, collaborative commission.

22 For Stanzione's contribution to the series, see Schütze and Willette, 1992, cat. A30, 200–202.

23 For the complex history of this commission, see Marshall, 2016, 34–37.

24 Guarino also paraphrased Stanzione's *Annunciation of the Birth of the Baptist* in a work produced for the Collegiata of San Michele at Solofra. For Guarino's indebtedness to the Buen Retiro series of the *Life of St John the Baptist*, see Mina Gregori in Naples, 1984, 1:304. For a more recent reappraisal, see Lattuada, 2000, cat. E50, 228–30.

25 For Cavallino's indebtedness to the series (as particularly evident in his *Meeting of Anna and Joachim at the Golden Gate*, Szépmüvézeti Múzeum, Budapest), see Cleveland and Forth Worth, 1984, 9 and 53. For Falcone's indebtedness to Gentileschi's *Birth of St John the Baptist*, see Mina Gregori in Naples, 1984, 1:304. For the similarities between Gentileschi's *Birth of St John the Baptist* and the work of the Master of the Annunciation of the Shepherds (whose work, in turn, has often been compared with that of Velázquez), see Bissell, 1999, 255.

26 Bissell, 1999, 256–59, with previous bibliography.

27 For the involvement of Stanzione and his workshop on the Pozzuoli cathedral commission, see Schütze and Willette, 1992, 210. For Monterrey's association with Martín de León y Cárdenas, Bishop of Pozzuoli, see Nicola Spinosa in Naples, 2016, 60; London, 2020, 207; and Denunzio, 2022, 67.

28 For Lanfranco's contribution to the cathedral of Pozzuoli, see Erich Schleier in Parma, Naples and Rome, 2001, cat. 98, 312–13, with previous bibliography.

29 Mina Gregori in Naples, 1984, 1:306; Garrard, 1989, 101–4; Spinosa, 2010, 306.

30 Bissell, 1999, 81.

31 Bissell, 1999, cat. 33, 256–59, with previous bibliography; Rome, New York and St Louis, 2001–2, cat. 79, 411–14; Milan, 2011, cat. 37, 218–20; Rome, 2016, cat. 76b, 240; Naples, 2022, cat. 14, 146–48.

32 For this fresco, see Spear, 1982, I, cat. 109.ix, 294.

33 The connection with Ribera is also pointed out by Nicola Spinosa in Rome, 2016, 60.

34 For artistic rivalry and competition in Vasari's *Lives*, see Clifford, 1996, 23–41; Gotlieb, 2002, 469–90; and Goffen, 2002, passim.

35 For De' Dominici's account of Gentileschi's indebtedness to Guido Reni, see further Locker, 2015, 117–18, who stresses the importance of De' Dominici's emphasis in this regard as providing the author with a means with which to highlight Gentileschi's 'bel colorito Guidesco'.

36 De' Dominici, 1742–45, 3:45: 'aveva il piacere di vederla ogni giorno dipingere, e fu il suo genio tanto soddisfatto freschezza dei bel colore usato da quella, che si propose d l'imitarlo: e con ragione, poiché ella stessa dicea aver posto ogni studio per fare acquisto del bel colorito di Guido suo maestro, che in Roma per lo Pontefice Paolo V dipingeva'.

37 De' Dominici, 1742–45, 3:34 (Life of Cavallino): 'la delicatezza de'colori'; 2:241 (Life of Palumbo): 'la dolcezza della Gentileschi'.

38 Locker, 2015, n. 109, 209, who notes the significance of the fact that De' Dominici cites Malvasia as his source for this information. This might indicate a confused recollection on De' Dominici's part, since Malvasia does not mention Gentileschi, although he does discuss Elisabetta Sirani, whom he correctly identifies as Reni's pupil.

39 Locker, 2015, 176–77, 191.

40 Getty Provenance Index, Sale Catalog Br-A2139, Lot 0167, 'The plan and new descriptive catalogue of the European Museum, King Street, St. James's Square: Instituted for the promotion of the fine arts, and the encouragement of British artists', London, February

1796, lot 167: 'Bathsheba after bathing surrounded by her female attendants is discovered by David; this beautiful picture belonged to Lord Spencer, and was always attributed to Guido, but it is in reality the most valuable work of Gentileschi'; available at https://piprod.getty.edu/starweb/pi/servlet.starweb

11 'SOLD BY HER HAND'

1 Ago, 2010, table 32, 260; and Spear and Sohm, 2010, for more detailed analyses of the population and demographic information on each of these cities during the early modern period.

2 For the importance of the *fede di credito*, see Naples, 1988, 19–26.

3 Nappi, 1983, 76.

4 For the patronage of the House of Liechtenstein, see New York, 1985, passim.

5 For Karl Eusebius von Liechtenstein and his collections, see Vienna, 2007.

6 Luzzati, 1974.

7 Waldman, 1997, 94–102.

8 Borzelli, 1939; Leone de Castris, 1991, 64.

9 Kawai, 2018, 140, 146; and, for Del Sera's activities as an agent and relations with Ribera, see Marshall, 2016, 9, 53, 254, 263.

10 Solinas, 2011a, n. 32, 47.

11 For this process, see further Marshall, 2006, 348–64.

12 Celano, 1692, 5:447. For discussion, see Marshall, 2016, 199–202.

13 Haskell, 1980, 205.

14 For Gentileschi's later Neapolitan version, *Judith and her Maidservant with the Head of Holofernes*, see Solinas, 2021, 381–93; and Maria Cristina Terzaghi in Naples, 2022, cat. 16, 150–52, both with additional previous bibliography. The issue of the autograph status of the later Capodimonte *Judith* is complicated by the fact that, besides the Capodimonte version, another almost identical version exists in the Musée des Beaux Arts de Caen (Bissell, 1999, cat. 47, 280). Both paintings are generally associated with a version of the subject in the Farnese collection that is known to have been copied by Francesco Maria Retti sometime before 1680. Terzaghi allows the possibility that the Capodimonte version might be Retti's copy, whereas Solinas identifies both works as autograph.

15 For Gentileschi's work in the Lumaga collection, see Moretti, 2005, no. A19, 38: 'Uno con Giudita che ha tagliato il capo ad Holloferne e datolo alla vechia quale lo assiuga, figura più grande del naturale, della signora Artemisia Gentileschi.' Moretti identifies this work as Gentileschi's later version of the subject now at the Musée des Beaux Arts, Caen (Bissell, 1999, cat. 47, 280). For the *Judith and Holofernes* attributed to Orazio Gentileschi in the Vandeneynden collection, see Colonna di Stigliano, 1895, 31: '60. Uno quadro di palmi 3 e 7 [*c*.79 × 184 cm] con cornice ind.ta, la Giuditta che toglie la testa ad Oloferne, m.o di Oratio Gentilesco 100 [ducats]'; and for discussion, see Bissell, 1999, 196.

16 Nappi, 1983, 78. For a discussion of the commission and the surviving paintings, see Felton, 1986, 785–89.

17 Nappi, 1990b, doc. 38, 182: 'et li altri sei ce li deve consignare ad ogni loro piacere.'

18 Besides the example cited here, see further the case of Ribera's other difficulties completing work for the Certosa di San Martino and for the protonotary of Palermo, for discussion of which see Marshall, 2016, 62–63.

19 Nappi, 1990b, doc. 36, 183: 'A Giuseppe de Rivera D.100. E per esso a Gio d'Avalos principe di Montesarchio in virtú di mandato del consigliere Andrea Marchese commessario delegato. E sono per quelli che detto Giuseppe de Rivera fe deposito sotto li 18 agosto 1632 per quelli pagare a Gio d'Avalos per tanti che detto principe li donò de caparra in conto della valuta de un quadro di S. Lorenzo da farsi per detto Giuseppe et non havendolo possuto finire per esso l'opera l'è stato fatto mandato di restituire detta somma.'

20 For Gentileschi's *Sleeping Venus* in the D'Avalos collection, see Bugli, 2004, no. 78, 31; and Marshall, 2016, 195–97, for further discussion of the D'Avalos collection.

21 For the use of 'di sua mano' in contracts, see Seymour, 1968, 1:93–105; Glasser, 1971, 73–79; Spear, 1997, 253–55; and O'Malley, 2005, 90–96.

22 For this series of paintings, see New York, 1992, cats 35–40, 112–19.

23 For the Columbus *Bathsheba*, see Bissell, 1999, cat. 37, 263–66, with previous bibliography. For subsequent references, see Lattuada, 2001, 384–85; Lattuada and Nappi, 2005, 87–89; Garrard, 2005, 109–10; Locker, 2015, 114–15; Garrard, 2017, 24; Lattuada, 2017, 187; Letizia Treves in London, 2020, cat. 33, 214–15. Most commentators follow Bissell in assigning the dating of the painting to Gentileschi's first Neapolitan period, around 1636–38, with the exception of Lattuada (2017, 187), who dates it to the mid-1640s. For the Romeo collection, see chapter 12.

24 Rome, New York and St Louis, 2001–2, 414–17. The suggestion that Cavallino may have also contributed to the Columbus *Bathsheba* was first advanced by R. Ward Bissell (1999, 85). For a more recent discussion, see London, 2020, cat. 33, 214–16.

25 For the document, see Nappi, 1983, 78. For Ribera's 1637 version of *Apollo and Marsyas*, see Denise Maria Pagano in New York, 1992, cat. 41, 118–19, with previous bibliography.

26 Haskell, 1980, 14; Garrard, 1989, n. 238, 518. For a more detailed analysis, that notes the degree to which this practice progressively lost favour over time, see Philip Sohm in Spear and Sohm, 2010, 27, and Richard E. Spear in ibid., 52–53.

27 Haskell, 1980, 14; Spear, 1994, 584, and passim.

28 Artemisia Gentileschi, letter to Don Antonio Ruffo of Messina, 30 January 1649, in Ruffo, 1916, i-ii, 48: 'Ma spero al Sig.re Idio che al aparir de quello giudicherà che non havessi in tutto il torto, et in effetto, se non era V.S. Ill.ma al quale vivo tanto aff.ta serva non mi haverei indutto a darli per li centosissanta perchè in qualunque parte io sono stata mi è stato pagato cento scudi l'una la figura tanto a Fiorenza, quanta a Venetia e quanto a Roma e a Napoli ancora quando vi erano più denari.' For the translation, see Garrard, 1989, 390.

29 Spear, 1982, 1:287; Marshall, 2016, 34–39.

30 Faraglia, 1885, 450, erroneously identified the payment evaluation as being for Ribera's *St Januarius Emerging Unscathed from the Fiery Furnace*. The wording of this document is quite clear, however, in referring to Domenichino's *Martyrdom of St Januarius*. It is also included in Spear's documents for the commission (Spear, 1982, 1:335, and cat. 109.xxiii, 298 for the altarpiece itself). Faraglia's incorrect identification of this document is, nonetheless, occasionally still repeated in more recent publications (e.g., Naples, 1992, cat. 1.91, 258).

31 Costello, 1950, n. 3, 249, n. 4, 248.

32 Bologna, Frankfurt and Washington, 1991–92, cat. 39, 262–64.

33 For discussion, see Bohn, 2011, 519; and, for the paintings themselves, see Bologna, Los Angeles and Fort Worth, 1988, cats 23–26, 220–25.

34 For further analysis, with comparative documentation, see Marshall, 2010, 128–37.

35 Marshall, 2016, xi; Marshall, 2017b, 66–68.

36 Gerard, 1982, 11; Barker, 2017, doc. 8, 75.

37 Barker, 2017, doc. 8, 75: 'A dì detto per cento cinquanta di moneta pagati a monna Artimisia Lomi pagato [a] Tommaso del Salvatico per saldo del suo conto 207 per [scudi] 150'.

38 Labrot, 1992, Inv. 42, item 75, 206. For Cavallino's *Hercules and Omphale*, see Ann Percy in Cleveland and Fort Worth, 1984–85, cat. 22, 92–93; and Spinosa, 2013, cat. A3, 403. The importance of Cavallino's

Hercules as a record of the appearance of Gentileschi's lost painting is also posited by Roberto Contini in Milan, 2011, 198. For the Beirut painting, which was severely damaged by a bomb blast on 4 August 2020, see Buchakjian, 2020, and Vartanian, 2021. The Beirut *Hercules* is further discussed and its attribution to Gentileschi endorsed by Riccardo Lattuada in Milan, 2021, 277.

39 Gérard, 1982, 11. For Domenichino's *Sacrifice of Isaac*, see further Richard E. Spear in Rome, 1996, cat. 45, 462–63.

40 Spear, 2005, 149.

41 For the prices paid to these artists and for their respective negotiating strategies, see Marshall, 2017b, 64–83.

42 Murphy, 2007, 23.

43 For this documentation, see further pp. 128-29.

44 Feci, 2018, 64–69.

45 Artemisia Gentileschi letter to Don Antonio Ruffo, 30 January 1649 and 13 November 1649, cit. and trans. Garrard, 1989, 390 and 397.

46 Lattuada and Nappi, 2005, 92.

47 Labrot, 1992, 202, and 202–13 for the inventory itself; and see further Ruotolo, 2022, 75, where, instead, Geronimo's brother, Alfonso (died 1664), is proffered as the possible patron of the *Hercules*.

48 Labrot, 1992, Inv. 19, item 8, 113, and 113–15 for the inventory itself.

49 For this painting, see Bissell, 1999, cat. 9, 208–9 (Gentileschi, c.1615–16); Judith W. Mann in Rome, New York and St Louis, 2001–2, cat. 73, 395–97 (Gentileschi, c.1630–32); Roberto Contini in Milan, 2011, cat. 28, 198–99 (Gentileschi, c.1630).

50 Caracciolo, 1959, vol. 3, item 28, 37: '27. Sansone di palmi 6 e 8 originale di Artemisia Gentileschi di valuta di ducati cento. 100'.

51 For this painting, see Bissell, 1999, cat. 35, 260–61; Roberto Contini in Milan, 2011, cat. 35, 214–15; and Giuseppe Porzio in Naples, 2022, cat. 18, 156–57. Bissell identifies the work as a copy after a lost original, whereas Contini and Porzio accept the painting as an original. The Intesa Sanpaolo *Samson* is admittedly rather smaller than the dimensions given in the Francone inventory (90.5 × 109.5 cm, as opposed to *c.*132 by 158 cm given in the inventory). But this can perhaps be accounted for by virtue of the often approximate nature of measurements given in inventories, coupled with the fact that the measurements included in inventories are often naturally somewhat larger than the modern measurements since they were measured by eye while including the frame.

52 Labrot, 1992, Inv. 21, item 9, 119: 'Due Teste, una di nostro Signore Giovine, l'altra di nostra signora della medesima Artemisia.'

53 Marshall, 2000, 15–34; Marshall, 2010, 115–16, 142–43; Marshall, 2016, 109–24.

54 Marshall, 2000, 28–29.

55 De' Dominici, 1742–45, 3:210.

56 For the collection of Stefano Carrillo y Salsedo (*c.*1618–1698) and its emphasis on the work of Domenico Gargiulo, see Ruotolo, 1973, 145–47, 151–53.

57 Lapierre, 2000, 436–37; Chaney, 1998, 111, and for further discussion, Barker, 2022, 96; and D'Alessandro and Porzio, 2022, docs 1.3 and 1.4, 94–95.

58 Abetti, 2022, 101–3, and docs 11, 13–15, 19, 108–11. For Neapolitan artists and the issue of rent, see further Marshall, 2010, 125–26.

59 Richard Graham, 'A short account of the most eminent painters', in DuFresnoy, 1695, 320.

60 In 1619 Gentileschi incurred a debt of 85 scudi from a Florentine goldsmith for 'a gold chain and a pair of golden earrings', for which, see Barker, 2017, doc. 28, 78: 'Monna Artemisia Lomi Pittora borgo ognisanti gli otene un catenazzo d'oro et un paio di orechini d'oro, pagata scudi 85.'

61 Spear, 2010, 72, 108–10.

62 Mancini, 1956–57, 1:250. For discussion, see Spear, 2010, 109.

63 Spear, 1982, 1:288.

64 Baldinucci, 1681–1728, 5:454. For discussion of Rosa's earnings during his Florentine years and prices for his paintings more generally, see Marshall, 2017a, 367–91.

65 Bellori, 2005, 216, and 218 for the subsequent quote; see further Spear, 2010, 72, for discussion.

66 Garrard, 1989, letter 13, 387–88; Solinas, 2011a, letter 49, 117: Artemisia Gentileschi to Cassiano dal Pozzo, 24 October, 1637.

67 For Gentileschi's *Christ and the Woman of Samaria at the Well*, see Luciano Arcangeli in Milan, 2011, cat. 34, 210–12; Spear, 2011, 804–5; Solinas, 2011a, n. 1, 118; Garrard, 2017, 28–29; and Barker, 2022, 95, with all writers endorsing the painting's attribution to Gentileschi.

68 For Gentileschi's paintings for the Duke of Modena, see Garrard, 1989, letters 6a and 6b, 7, 380–82; and Solinas, 2011a, letters 41–42, 94–96 (for the 1635 paintings), and 92–93 for discussion. For the 1639 paintings, see Garrard, 1989, letters 15a and 15b, 388–89; and Solinas, 2011a, letter 51, 121–22.

69 Garrard, 1989, letters 8–12, 382–87; Solinas, 2011a, letters 43–48, 104–17, esp. 101–3, 107–8 and 113, for discussion. Solinas includes an important letter (43), written by Gentileschi to Ferdinando II de Medici, that is not included in Garrard's transcription of letters.

70 Guerzoni, 2011, 134–38; and see further the references to the broader literature on gift-giving cited in Bernstorff and Kubersky-Piredda, 2013, 7–9; Guerzoni, 2011, n. 93, 201, and Findlen, 1994, n. 6, 348. For anthropological readings of the reciprocal obligations involved in Baroque ceremonial gift-giving, see also Kettering, 1988, 131–32, which emphasises the extent to which 'The euphemism of gift-giving made a patron's bestowal of benefits seem voluntary and disinterested, but in reality it was obligatory and self-interested.'

71 Mancini, 1956–57, vol. 1, 139–40.

72 For gift-giving by Baroque artists, see further Spear and Sohm, 2010, 12–13, 62–63, 77, 164, and n. 439, 313. For Orazio Gentileschi's practice of sending paintings as unsolicited diplomatic gifts to high-ranking patrons, see further the 2022 publication of documentation regarding Orazio's 1637 dispatch of a painting of a *Magdalene* from London to the Neapolitan viceroy, the Count of Monterrey. The painting had been delivered to the viceroy by Orazio's son, Francesco, who had, however, also on that occasion accepted payment of two hundred ducats for the painting. Subsequently, Artemisia Gentileschi complained to the viceroy, noting that the painting was intended as a present and demanding the payment for herself (D'Alessandro and Porzio, 2022, 91, 92, and doc. I.5, 95–96).

73 Bissell, 1981, 189, and cat. 62, 189–90; Gabriele Finaldi and Jeremy Wood in Rome, New York and St Louis, 2001–2, 238; Spear, 2005, 152.

74 Zapperi, 1990, 35; Guerzoni, 2011, 137, and n. 97, 201.

75 For Filomarino's *St John the Baptist in the Wilderness*, see Ruotolo, 1977, 80; Labrot, 1992, Inv. 33, item 16, 161; Bissell, 1999, cat. L77, 380–81. Yuri Primarosa has suggested that the *St John the Baptist* referred to in the letters may be the same painting subsequently listed in the inventory of D. Ascanio Filomarino, duca della Torre, nephew and heir of Ascanio Filomarino, Archbishop of Naples (Primarosa in Milan, 2011, 276). However, this cannot be the case, since Gentileschi clearly specifies the dimensions of the paintings produced for sale in 1637 as measuring 11 and 12 palmi (*c.*290 and 316 cm) and subsequently as 'nine palmi in height and of proportionate length' (*c.*237 cm high). The Filomarino version of *St John* is specified as measuring only 3 palmi (*c.*79 cm) and so must, therefore, have been a reduced version variant of the 1637 composition.

76 Luciano Arcangeli in Milan, 2011, 212; Spear, 2011, 805.

77 Archivio di Stato di Napoli, Cappellano Maggiore, Statuti e Congregazioni, vol. B1183, fasciolo 10, Capitoli dell'Arte di Rivenditori, 19 July 1680, statute 9. The statutes are cited and summarised in Borrelli, 1991, n. 1, 14–15.

78 For this document, see Lofano, 2014, 801–2. For the relative modesty of Cavallino's career, see Marshall, 2004, 43–45.

79 For Corenzio's daughter's dowry, see D'Addosio, 1913, 53.

80 Delfino, 1987, 79–98, New York, 1992, 232–34.

81 The marriage contract between Margarita Ribera and Giovanni Leonardo Sersale was published in New York, 1992, 247–48.

82 Nappi, 1991, docs 7–9, 165–66.

83 For the issue of whether Gentileschi might have given birth to a second daughter during her Neapolitan period, and its implications for Gentileschi's dowry planning, see p. 274, n. 10.

84 Artemisia Gentileschi to Don Antonio Ruffo of Messina, 13 March 1649, cit. Garrard, 1989, letter 17, 391; Solinas, 2011a, letter 53, 127.

85 Malvasia, 1678, 2:564.

86 Baldinucci, 1845–47, 743; for discussion see Bissell, 1981, 51.

87 For this aspect of Orazio's attitude to money, see further Spear, 2005, 152–53.

88 Gabriele Finaldi and Jeremy Wood in Rome, New York and St Louis, 2001–2, 225.

89 For the documentation for this painting, see ibid., n. 484. There is also a *Penitent Magdalene* by Orazio Gentileschi dating to the late 1620s and now at the Kunsthistorisches Museum that is sometimes identified with a note by Gerbier to the effect that Gentileschi received £300 for a 'single figure beeinge a Magdalene'. This note occurs in a list of 'Sommes of Moneys Gentilesco Hath Received' (Bissell, 1981, Appendix II, 108–9 for the list, and cat. 56, 182–83 for the *Magdalene*). However, as Bissell points out, the information contained in the list needs to be treated with caution, since the list's author, Balthasar Gerbier, was a bitter rival and enemy of Orazio during this period. Gerbier was seeking to discredit Gentileschi in a major feud during these years. It thus seems more reasonable to treat with some suspicion the quoted sum of £300 – equivalent to the astronomical sum of 1,200 scudi for a single-figure work. Gerbier's recollected version of Orazio's payments is more likely here to have been purposefully inflated as part of his wider campaign to discredit Orazio during this period.

90 Gabriele Finaldi and Jeremy Wood have argued that, with Gentileschi's sons Marco and Giulio employed for the most part as agents and go-betweens for their father, the task of assisting Orazio on this commission would have principally fallen to Francesco Gentileschi who identified himself as a painter in more formal and professional terms (Gabriele Finaldi and Jeremy Wood in Rome, New York and St Louis, 2001–2, 230; and for Francesco Gentileschi, see further Bissell, 1981, 113–17).

91 Garrard, 2020, 227 and ff. argues most forcefully in favour of the invitation for Gentileschi to work in London as having been sent independently of her father's London work commitments.

92 For the suggestion that Artemisia's relocation to London was probably timed to coincide with one of Francesco Gentileschi's trips to and from Italy on behalf of Queen Henrietta Maria in 1638–39, see Terzaghi, 2014, 38–39; Terzaghi, 2016, 70–71; and for the planning and logistics of Gentileschi's trip to London, see further Barker, 2022, 96–101, where the probable presence of Giovanna Garzoni as a co-traveller with Artemisia during the journey is added.

93 Artemisia Gentileschi to Duke Francesco I d'Este, written from London, 16 December 1639, cit. Garrard, 1989, letter 15a, 388–89; Solinas, 2011a, letter 51, 121.

94 Letter from Duke Francesco I d'Este to Artemisia Gentileschi, 16 March 1640, cit. Garrard, 1989, letter 15b, 389.

95 Artemisia Gentileschi to Duke Francesco I d'Este, written from London, 16 December 1639, cit. Garrard, 1989, letter 15a, 388–89; Solinas, 2011a, letter 51, 121.

96 Bissell, 1981, 49.

97 Ibid., 52.

98 For the references to this painting, see Gentileschi's letters to Cassiano dal Pozzo of 21 December 1630 and 24 October 1637 (Garrard, 1989, letters 4 and 13, 378–79, 387–88; Solinas, 2011a, letters 39 and 49, 86–87, 117–18).

99 Garrard, 1989, 85–86.

100 A point made also by Judith W. Mann in Rome, St Louis and New York, 2001–2, 421.

101 The self-portrait referred to in the Dal Pozzo letters is sometimes identified with another portrait, now in the Palazzo Barberini, Rome (e.g., Roberto Contini in Florence, 1991, 172–75; Bissell, 1999, 234–37; Solinas, 2011a, n. 3, 87). The attribution of this portrait to Gentileschi has, however, been disputed for many years, for which, see Judith W. Mann in Rome, New York and St Louis, 2001–2, n. 3, 421; and Candida Dreier in Potsdam, 2019, cat. 46, 196–97, who argues in favour of attributing the work to Simon Vouet; further supplemented by Yuri Primarosa in Naples, 2022, cat. 3, 120–21, who argues in favour of an attribution to Gentileschi.

102 For a helpful review of the literature up to 2001–2, see Judith W. Mann in Rome, New York and St Louis, 2001–2, cat. 81, 417–21; further supplemented by Mann, 2005b, 51–70; and Letizia Treves in London, 2020, cat. 34, 217–19.

103 The painting has been identified as a self-portrait by Michael Levey, Judith W. Mann, Lucy Whitaker and Martin Clayton (Levey, 1962, 80; Mann in Rome, New York and St Louis, 2001–2, 418; London, 2007, 301–2). Mary Garrard, by contrast, identifies the painting as an *Allegory of Painting*, reiterating more recently her position that 'though it might be based on a particular model, the figure is more plausibly a stand-in for women artists in general, a group that conspicuously includes herself' (Garrard, 2020, 222). Other commentors identifying the work as an allegory rather than a self-portrait include R. Ward Bissell, Jesse Locker and Maria Cristina Terzaghi (Bissell, 1999, cat. 42, 272–75; Locker, 2015, 131–32; Terzaghi, 2014, 32; Terzaghi, 2016, n. 17, 77). Their arguments emphasise the importance of the inventory documentation that records the original presence in the Royal Collection of two paintings by Artemisia: 'Arthemisia gentilesco. done by her self 20.000 [pounds]' and 'A Pintura A painteigne : by Arthemisia 10.00.00 [pounds]'. For the documentation of these references within the inventory of the king's collection, see further Millar, 1958–60, iii–256; and Millar, 1970–72, i–458, with the items in question occurring at Millar, 1970–72, 186 (item 5) and 191 (item 97). These authors, accordingly, argue for the original presence in the king's collection of two paintings by Artemisia: a relatively conventional and identifiable self-portrait (now lost) and an *Allegory of Painting*, which is to be identified as the painting now in the Royal Collection. Yet the evidence of the inventories does not discount the possibility that both of these paintings might have constituted 'self-portraits' and that the Hampton Court painting was recognised in its own day as having a more obviously complex and allegorical treatment.

Regarding the age of the figure depicted, some authors have expressed difficulties in reconciling the age of the figure in the Hampton Court painting with that of Artemisia in 1638–39 (Levey, 1962, 80; Richard E. Spear in Cleveland, 1971, 98–99; Millar, 1970–72, 65; Mina Gregori in Naples, 1984, 1:150; Garrard, 1989, 85–86; Bissell, 1999, 273; Terzaghi, 2014, 32). However, as Mann points out, the lack of clearly documented examples of self-portraits by Gentileschi may mean that, 'while it is clear that she produced several self-likenesses, few of them have been identified, and they seem to cover a variety of types. Indeed, we may not yet know what constitutes a proper Artemisia Gentileschi self-portrait' (Mann in Rome, New York and St Louis, 2001–2, 421). The presumed age of the figure represents no impediment either to the dating of the work to the late 1630s or to seeing the work as a self-portrait, in my opinion. It seems, moreover, perfectly reasonable to assume that Gentileschi would have preferred to portray herself in an idealized manner in terms of her age. This is also underscored by Mann (2005, 57), who points out, 'Portraitists have, however, traditionally flattered their subjects by reducing their years and a too youthful appearance does not necessarily preclude an intended likeness.'

104 Ripa, 1593, 490; trans. Rome, New York and St Louis, 2001–2, 417–18.

105 The importance of Titian's late self-portraits for the painting's conceptualisation has also been stressed by Judith W. Mann (2005, 57–59).

12 NAPLES, 1640–C.1656

1 For this collection, see Marshall, 2016, 195–97.

2 For this collection, see ibid., 193–95; and Conversano, 2018, passim.

3 Viviana Farina in Conversano, 2018, cat. 30, 262–66.

4 Ibid., 26–27; Bissell, 1999, cat. 46, 279; Nicolaci in Milan, 2011, cat. 49, 246–47.

5 For Imperiale's collection, see Labrot, 1992, Inv. 21, 118–19. For the significance of the collecting and mercantile activities of the Genoese colony in Naples, see further Marshall, 2016, 198–99.

6 Pacelli, 1987, 145–52.

7 For Marino and the Neapolitan academies, see Marshall, 2016, 183–84, with previous bibliography.

8 Locker, 2015, 100–14. Fontanella's *Nove cieli* was published in 1640, while Cappone's *Poesie liriche* was published in 1643.

9 Ricciardi, 2000, 52–60.

10 For Caravaggio's association with the Colonna and his *Ecstasy of the Magdalene*, see Calvesi, 1990, 105–64; and Berra, 2005, 310–11.

11 For this painting, see Nicola Spinosa in Naples, 2009, vol. 1, cat. 1.42, 118 (attributed to Hendrick van Somer). For Van Somer and Gentileschi, see Spinosa in Rome, 2016, 260; Giuseppe Porzio in Naples, 2022, 162–63, 180–81; and Marshall, 2016, 60–62, the latter of which includes discussion of Van Somer's *Venus and Adonis* (fig. 46, 60), which is clearly inspired by Gentileschi as well as by a composition by Van Somer's master, Jusepe de Ribera.

12 Contini, 2011, n. 2, 107.

13 Two partial exceptions are the paintings of *Hercules and Omphale* and *The Rape of Persephone* painted for the Medici (for which, see pp. 92–94), but, here again, these subjects revolve around female protagonists rather than around male characters depicted in their own right.

14 De' Dominici, 1742–45, 3:198–99: 'In casa del fu dott. Luigi Romeo, barone di S. Luigi, che ha sempre professato buon gusto in genere di pittura . . . [describes various paintings by Gargiulo and Vaccaro, before coming to] Due quadri grandi con figure al naturale, che esprimono le storie di Bersabea, e Susanna, che sembran di mano di Guido son dipinti dalla famosa Artemisia Gentileschi, e l'Architettura di Viviano, con gli arbori, e veduta dello Spadaro. Di questa virtuosa donna è eziando un S. Michele Arcangelo, che discaccia Lucifero dal Paradiso, ed un Loth con le figliuole, e tutti alla grandezza del naturale.'

15 For the Columbus *Bathsheba*, see p. 172. For the *Susanna and the Elders* (provenance, sale Sotheby's, London, 6 December 1995, lot 53, and sale Sotheby's, New York, 27 January 2022, lot 40), see Sestieri and Daprà, 1994, cat. 23, 92, with further bibliography; Bissell, 1999, cat. 38, 266–67; Judith W. Mann in Rome, New York and St Louis, 2001–2, 414 and 416; Lattuada, 2001, 384–85; Lattuada and Nappi, 2005, 88–89; Spinosa, 2010, cat. 257, 307; and Maria Cristina Terzaghi in Naples, 2022, cat. 37, 198–200.

16 For the Toledo *Lot*, see Bissell, 1999, cat. 39, 267–69, with previous bibliography. For subsequent references, see Mann, 2005a, 10 and 12 (fig. 15, 12); and Mann, 2005b, 70–71 (fig. 22, 70); Spinosa, 2013, cat. A3, 403; Locker, 2015, 114 and 116 (fig. 4.5, 116); Nicola Spinosa in Rome, 2016, cat. 88, 266–67.

17 Lattuada, 2001, 384.

18 D. Marshall, 1993, 16, who notes the additional factor of Codazzi's dissatisfaction with the recompense he was receiving from the monks of the Certosa di San Martino for whom he had been working during the previous years. For Gargiulo's collaboration with Codazzi, see further Giancarlo Sestieri in Sestieri and Daprà, 1994, 19–23.

19 D. Marshall, 1993, cat. VC 21, 96–97.

20 Ibid., passim.

21 For Gentileschi's *Corsica and the Satyr*, see Bissell, 1999, cat. 30, 245–47; Nicola Spinosa in Milan, 2011, cat. 39, 224–25; and Sheila Barker in Naples, 2022, cat. 44, 214–15.

22 Getty Provenance Index, Archival inventory I-24, page 2, item 16: 'Tre quadri di 6 larghi et 8 lunghi con cornice nera e con filetto indorato, uno con S. Eustachio e l'altro con Davide l'altro di S. Sebastiano, e le teste sono di mano di Artemisia.'

23 Nappi, 1992, 74: 'Da Gio Francesco di Afflitto, conte di Loreto, D. 12 a compimento di D. 20 per prezzo d'uno quatro di Santo Sebastiano di palmi otto alto et sei largo fatto di sua propria mano e promette consegnarlo fra otto giorni.'

24 O'Malley, 2005, 90–96, where mention is made of the examples of a 1506 contract in which Pinturicchio undertakes to provide the *disegno* and paint the heads, leaving the rest of the work to be completed by another master; a 1490 contract for Domenico Ghirlandaio to design the figures of the saints in an altarpiece but to then only paint their heads; and Signorelli's 1499 undertaking personally to paint the heads and other parts 'above the waist' for his work at Orvieto cathedral.

25 Montagu, 1989, 109, and 99–115 for 'di sua mano' and Baroque sculpture contracts.

26 For this painting, see p. 122 and p. 272, n. 2

27 The suggestion that Cavallino may have also contributed to the Columbus *Bathsheba* was first advanced by R. Ward Bissell (1999, 85). See further Lattuada, 2001, 384–85, who notes the connection but suggests that the execution of the maidservant at right is, nonetheless, by Gentileschi herself.

28 A clear comparison can be drawn between the facial type of Lot in this painting and that of St Peter in Cavallino's *St Peter* and other figures of this type (Spinosa, 2013, cat. 30, 297, cat. 102, 366–67). These highly distinctive Cavallinesque facial types share with the figure of Lot not only the general features (derived in turn from Ribera's prophets at San Martino) but also more specifically Cavallino's distinctive and repeated emphasis on the rendition of hooded eyes, which are then contrasted with a lightened and highlighted upper eyelid. Lattuada (in Lattuada and Nappi, 2005, 89) also cites this painting as a close match with the figures of the elders in the formerly Sotheby's *Susanna and the Elders* and thus as a point in favour of attributing the figures of the male elders in this painting to Cavallino's hand.

29 For the painting's earlier attributions (which have included Francesco Guarino, Antonio de Bellis and even the previously mentioned female Neapolitan painter Annella de Rosa), see Causa, 1993, n. 27, 35–36; Spinosa, 2010, cat. 255, 105–6; and Spinosa in Rome, 2016, 266.

30 For example, Stoughton, 1985, 194; Garrard, 1989, 214–17; Mann in Rome, New York and St Louis,

2001–2, 408; Letizia Treves in London, 2020, cat. 32, 212–13.

31 For example, Bissell, 1999, 268; Spinosa in Rome, 2016, 266.

32 For example, Bissell, 1999, 268–69; Spinosa, 2013, 403; Nicola Spinosa in Rome, 2016, 266.

33 Grabski, 1985, 23–40 (Beltrano); Causa, 1993, 26, and n. 27, 35–36 (Palumbo).

34 The attribution to Beltrano was originally proposed by Józef Grabski in the context of an argument in favour of attributing the entire composition to Beltrano alone (Grabski, 1985, 23–40).

35 Some commentators have sought to discern yet more subtle distinctions, attributing to Gentileschi the lower half of all three figures in the foreground and then suggesting that the other figure painters were responsible for the upper half only of the three figures in the foreground (e.g., Bissell, 1999, 268–69).

36 One wonders, for example, whether the 'Titta' Colimodio, mentioned by Artemisia in a letter to Don Antonio Ruffo of 24 July 1649 might have also been one of her occasional assistants during this period. The artistic identity of this Calabrian painter is only now beginning to come into definition, for which, see Panarello, 2011, 98–110; Pincitore, 2017, together with the additional bibliographic references cited at https://www.colimodio.it/bibliografia.html

37 Bissell, 1999, 86.

38 Lattuada, 2017, 212.

39 For the 1646 payment to Cavallino from Carlo Cioli of seventy ducats, the total price for two paintings of the *Annunciation* and *Immaculate Conception*, see Cleveland and Fort Worth, 1984–85, n. 4, 29. For Cavallino's prices more generally, see Marshall, 2004, 41–48.

40 Spinosa, 2013, cat. A1, 400–401; Nicola Spinosa in Montpellier, 2015, cat. 19, 124–25.

41 Strazzullo, 1955, 44.

42 For an overview, see Cavallino and Salerno, 2005, passim.

43 Ruffo, 1916.

44 For the prices paid to these artists and for their respective negotiating strategies, see Marshall, 2017b, 64–83.

45 De' Dominici, 1742–45, 3:206–7.

46 Artemisia Gentileschi to Don Antonio Ruffo of Messina, 12 June 1649, cit. Garrard, 1989, 393. The same claim regarding the cost of models is made in two other letters to Ruffo, both dated 13 November 1649, cit. Garrard, 1989, 397–98.

47 Artemisia Gentileschi to Don Antonio Ruffo of Messina, 23 October 1649, and 13 November 1649, cit. Garrard, 1989, 393, and 397.

48 For Pacecco de Rosa's *Diana and Actaeon*, which was also part of the D'Avalos bequest to the Museo di Capodimonte, see Pacelli, 2008, cat. 75, 340. Contini (2011, 111–12), who cites also De Rosa's *Diana and Actaeon* in the context of Gentileschi's lost painting of the same subject for Ruffo; and Giuseppe Porzio in Naples, 2022, cat. 31, 184–85.

49 For a useful early discussion of this painting, see Ann Lurie in Cleveland and Fort Worth, 1984–85, cat. 68, 186–87.

50 Grabski, 1985, 41–55; Garrard, 1989, 123–27; Roberto Contini in Florence, 1991, 76, 78, 83, n. 77, 87; Bissell, 1999, cat. 49, 287–92.

51 Marshall, 2005a, 40–44.

52 Labrot, 1992, Inv. 78, item 13, 440: 'Un quadro di palmi 8 e 6 ove è dipinta una Galatea, con varij Putti, che và per mare con cornice indorata all'antica di Bernardo Cavalliero per Docati venti D. 20.0.0.'

53 Nicola Spinosa in Naples, 2009, cat. 1.96, 198–99 (Cavallino); Spinosa, 2013, cat. 103, 368–69 (Cavallino); Spinosa in Rome, 2016, cat. 91, 272–73 (Cavallino); Barker, 2018b, 165–68 and fig. 2, 167 (Cavallino). Lattuada has also argued in favour of Cavallino's sole authorship of the painting (Lattuada and Nappi, 2005, 89, noting, 'The painting in Washington is in my view entirely by Bernardo Cavallino, whose style is so characteristic to be very distinct to that of Artemisia'). And see further Contini, 2011, 111–13, where the view ascribing the work to Cavallino alone is noted to be now 'a prevailing opinion'. Contini, nonetheless, argues that the painting should be identified as a collaboration between Cavallino and another unidentified collaborator, such as Onofrio Palumbo. To this summary of scholarly opinion should also be added the discussion by Giuseppe Porzio (in Naples, 2022, cat. 46, 222–23), who reproposes an attribution to Gentileschi, while at the same time acknowledging the degree to which the ongoing attributional debates surrounding this work 'mettono in crisi la nostra fragile connoisseurship'.

54 The painting's exhibition history is as follows: Nicola Spinosa in Naples, 2009, cat. I.95, 196–97 (Cavallino); Spinosa in Milan, 2011, cat. 53, 254–55 (Cavallino); Spinosa in Rome, 2016, cat. 94, 278–79 (Palumbo and Gentileschi).

55 See, for example, the Christie's sale catalogue at https://www.christies.com/lot/lot-artemisia-gentileschi-and-associate-the-6282019/?from=searchresults&intObjectID=6282019, together with Roberto Contini in Pisa, 2013, 25; Nicola Spinosa in Rome, 2016, 196; and Barker, 2018b, 166.

56 Ruffo, 1916, n. 1, 48: 'Galatea sopra una scorza di granchio tirata da due delfini e accompagnata da 5 tritoni palmi 8 x 10'.

57 For an insightful analysis of this issue, see Lattuada, 2017, 187–216.

58 Artemisia Gentileschi to Don Antonio Ruffo of Messina, 5 June 1649, cit. Garrard, 1989, 392; 4 September 1649, cit. Garrard, 1989, 395.

59 Artemisia Gentileschi to Don Antonio Ruffo of Messina, 4 September 1649, cit. Garrard, 1989, 395.

60 Artemisia Gentileschi to Don Antonio Ruffo of Messina, 1 January 1651, cit. Garrard, 1989, 401.

61 Bissell, 1999, 96.

62 Lattuada and Nappi, 2005, doc. 2, 97: 'et l'altro di nove palmi con una figura nuda con suo accompagnamento'.

63 For the Potsdam *Tarquin and Lucretia*, see Bissell, 1999, cat. 48b, 285–86, with previous bibliography. For subsequent references, see Judith W. Mann in Rome, New York and St Louis, 2001–2, 258–59; Marshall, 2005b, 18–24; Roberto Contini in Milan, 2011, 115; Franziska Windt in Potsdam, 2019, cat. 57, 226–27; and Denunzio, 2022, 67–70. Bissell's original proposal for dating the works to the late 1640s has been adopted by all subsequent authors, with the exception of Windt (in Potsdam, 2019), who assigns earlier dates of around 1630 (*Tarquin*) and around 1635 (*Bathsheba*) respectively, followed thereafter by Denunzio.

64 Marshall, 2005b, 18–24.

65 Judith W. Mann in Rome, New York and St Louis, 2001–2, 259; Bissell, 1999, 94.

66 Bissell, 1999, 293; Roberto Contini in Milan, 2011, 115.

67 For the Brno *Susanna*, see Bissell, 1999, cat. 50, 292–93, with previous bibliography. For subsequent references, see Roberto Contini in Milan, 2011, cat. 44, 236–37. For the cited references, see Bissell, 1999, 293; Contini in Milan, 2011, 236; Judith W. Mann, 2005a, 10.

68 See, for example, Letizia Treves in London, 2020, 222, who notes the 'only partially autograph' status of the Brno *Susanna*; and see further Lattuada, 2017, 201–5, for a perceptive analysis of the 'production-line' status of many of Gentileschi's late-Neapolitan works.

69 Sohm, 2007, Chapter 6, 'Life Cycles of Art', 131–48.

70 Nicola Spinosa in Naples, 1992, n. 20, 55.

71 Jusepe de Ribera to the Prior of the Certosa di San Martino, Naples, 23 June, 1651, cit. Faraglia, 1885–92, 673–4: 'Quando aspettavo qualche rilievo degno della mano di V.P.R.ma Hieri venne il padre e pure sequito a portare la tassa del Padre Vicario delli ducati cinquanta con li quali non ho mai possuto ne posso ultimare disegno dell'occorrenze di una Casa e Piacesse

a Dio non mi fussero li pesi che di molto gusto misaria pigliarmi tutta la summa insieme. I'opra tuttavia camina; supplicando V.R.Ma favorischi dare ordini mese paghi qualche altra summa di denaro che per tal effetto viene a ragionarnele mio figlio al quale mi rimetto con che fine le bacio le mani.' For commentary, see Marshall, 2016, 66, 102–3.

72 For Vaccaro's late-career success and competition with Giordano on the Santa Maria del Pianto commission, see Marshall, 2016, 233–34.

73 For Vaccaro's reliance on Gentileschi's female models in his paintings of the Magdalene, see further Tuck-Scala, 2003, 68. For Vaccaro's Museo di San Martino *St Mary Magdalene*, see Fernanda Capobianco in Naples, 1986, cat. 54, 90–92; and Lattuada, 2009, 96–97.

74 Nappi, 1983, 80.

75 Nappi, 1992, 109.

76 Nappi, 1990a, 164.

77 Nappi, 1992, 109.

78 For the literature on Palumbo since 1990, see Pasculli Ferrara, 1990, 201–5; Causa, 1993, 21–40; Porzio, 2006, 425–33; De Vito, 2005, 749; Pavone, 2012, 107–120; Giannattasio, 2012, 121–29; Spinosa, 2015, 379–88; Porzio, 2021, 107; Porzio, 2022, 29–36; and Porzio in Naples, 2022, 212–13.

79 Rizzo, 1984, 314–16; Rizzo, 1987, 158–59; D'Addosio, 1913, 484–85.

80 For this painting, see Spinosa, 2010, cat. 344, 360, with previous bibliography. For a review of its early documentation, see Causa, 1993, n. 41, 37. Barra was responsible for the view of Naples in a manner comparable with the way in which the architectural backgrounds to Gargiulo's paintings were contributed by Viviano Codazzi.

81 Delfino, 1987, 38. See further Porzio, 2022, n. 33, 48, who publishes additional documents citing Palumbo in 1656 and (possibly) as late as 1689.

82 De Vito, 2005, docs. 3 and 6, 98.

83 Lattuada and Nappi, 2005, doc. 3, 98: 'Ad Antonio Galise D. 50 E per lui a Artemisia Gentileschi per il prezzo d'uno quadro dell'historia di Susanna venduta di sua mano. E per lei ad Onofrio Palumbo.' See further De Vito, 2005, 749.

84 For this practice, see Marshall, 2016, 44.

85 For Modesti's contribution to the rediscovery of Gentileschi's 1652 *Susanna and the Elders*, see Modesti, 2016, 135–49. For other references to the painting, see Roberto Contini in Pisa, 2013, cat. 11, 64–66; Nicola Spinosa in Rome, 2016, cat. 95, 280–281; Letizia Treves in London, 2020, cat. 36, 222–23; and Vincenzo Sorrentino in Naples, 2022, cat. 30, 182–83. Spinosa cites Viviana Farina's suggestion that this painting might be identifiable with the version of *Susanna* recorded in Galise's payment of 3 January 1653, a suggestion also advanced by Modesti (2016, 143) and Sorrentino (in Naples, 2022, 182).

86 Compare, for example, the quizzically raised dark eyebrows and the parallel white highlights of the wrinkled forehead of the triton at the left of the Galatea with the elder at the right of the 1652 *Susanna*. The same distinctive stylistic feature is evident in Palumbo's *St Ambrose* of 1635 (fig. 120), a canvas which is securely attributable to Palumbo since it is one of a pair of paintings, the other of which is signed and dated 1635 (for which, see Nicola Spinosa in Rome, 2016, cat. 93b, 276).

87 Adelina Modesti (2016, 143) reaches the same conclusion on the basis of her reading of the document.

88 For other examples of this type of activity, see Marshall, 2000, 20, and notes 37 and 39, 31.

89 Lattuada and Nappi, 2005, doc. 5, 98.

90 For this suggestion, see Nappi and Lattuada, 2005, 92; Marshall, 2005b, 15; and Yuri Primarosa in Milan, 2011, 275.

91 For Gentileschi's letters to Cassiano dal Pozzo, dated August 1630, in which she mentions these circumstances, see Solinas, 2011a, letters 37–38, 85–86, with commentary.

92 Roberto Contini in Pisa, 2013, 29.

93 Locker, 2015, 178–80.

94 Lanzi, 1792–96, cit. Modesti, 2016, 135.

95 Averardo de Medici, 'Artemisia Gentileschi', in *Memorie istoriche di più uomini illustri pisani*, ed. Angiolo Fabroni, 4 vols, Pisa: Ranieri Prosperi, 1792, cit. Modesti, 2016, 140.

13 A STAR IS BORN

1 For Caracciolo's *Salome with the Head of the Baptist*, see Causa, 2000, cat. A52, 187; Florence, 2010, cat. 15, 140–41.

2 For discussion, see Locker, 2015, 171–74.

3 Lastri, 1791–95, vol. 2, n.p., no. LXXXIV

4 Vasari, 1550/1568, 25–26; for discussion, see Turner, 1983, 108–11.

5 Marshall, 2016, 223–25. For Ribera's *Tityus* in the context of Neapolitan still-life painting, see further Marshall, 2017–18, 140–42.

6 Jameson, 1866, 301; Jameson, 1889, 79. For discussion of Jameson's writings on Gentileschi and other early modern women artists, see Locker, 2015, 174; and Straussman-Pflanzer, 2021, 20–21.

7 Longhi, 1961, 258.

8 Benedetti, 1999, 42–44; Spear, 2000, 568–69.

9 Milan, 1951.

10 For an evaluation of the cultural and art-historical significance of this exhibition, see Aiello, 2020.

11 Barker, 1999, 127–45.

12 See, for example, the comments of Elizabeth Honig (2014, n.p.): 'Art historians have an intense love–hate relationship with their catalogs. Catalogs are condemned as involving outmoded connoisseurship rather than critical thinking, and as endowing the eye of a single individual with inordinate authority. They are too often influenced or corrupted by the demands of the art market; they become outdated as soon as the next expert produces a new catalog; and yet they are very costly to publish and to purchase.'

13 See, for example, the review by Steven Ostrow (2000, n.p.), which describes it as 'a learned and scholarly work, exemplifying traditional art history at its best'.

14 Nochlin, 1971, 1–43.

15 For discussion, see Straussman-Pflanzer, 2021, 20–24; and Jones, 2016, 8–17.

16 Eve Straussman-Pflanzer (2021, 27) cites a list of exhibitions dedicated to Italian women artists, beginning with *Old Mistresses: Women Artists of the Past*, held at the Walters Art Gallery, Baltimore, in 1972; and see further Zetterman, 2016, 15.

17 For the subsequently discovered *Portrait of a Gentleman (?Antoine de Ville)*, see Roberto Contini in Milan, 2011, cat. 24, 186–89.

18 Los Angeles, Austin, Pittsburgh and Brooklyn, 1976–77, 118.

19 Washington, 2007, 104–5, 146–47, 160–61, 216–17.

20 For a discussion of this work, see Eve Straussman-Pflanzer in Hartford and Detroit, 2021–22, cat. 43, 42–43.

21 Los Angeles, Austin, Pittsburgh and Brooklyn, 1976–77, 150.

22 Bologna, 2004; Modesti, 2004; Modesti, 2014.

23 Greer, 1979, 189, 207.

24 Chicago, n.d., sequence 17.

25 For the reception history of this work, see Los Angeles, 1996; and Gerhard, 2013.

26 https://www.judychicago.com/gallery/the-dinner-party/dp-artwork/, noting that the work toured to '16 venues in 6 countries on 3 continents to a viewing audience of over one million people'.

27 Chicago, n.d., sequence 25.

28 Garrard, 1989.

14 FROM THE CONNOISSEUR'S STUDIO TO THE GLOBAL BLOCKBUSTER

1 It is, however, certainly a significant painting in its own right, having been at one stage attributed by Roberto Longhi to Caravaggio as well as to Orazio Gentileschi. Gianni Papi (2017, 153–64, with previous bibliography) has also argued in favour of its re-attribution to Artemisia, a proposal also supported by Sheila Barker (2022, 22 and 28). For an alternative point of view in favour of an attribution to Orazio Gentileschi, see further Massimo Francucci in Rome, 2011, vol. 1, cat. VI.4, 148–49.

2 Gianni Papi in Florence, 1991, 93.

3 Spike, 1991, 732.

4 Spear, 2000, 572.

5 Rome, New York and St Louis, 2001–2.

6 Philippe de Montebello, Brent Benjamin and Claudio Strinati, Foreword, in Rome, New York and St Louis, 2001–2, viii.

7 https://www.24orecultura.com/#!/chi-siamo: 'un partner di riferimento nel business culturale italiano'.

8 No author, 2011, n.p.: 'La rassegna ha come missione quella di evidenziare finalmente la grandezza artistica di questa eccezionale pittrice la cui rilevanza è stata sin qui messa in ombra sia dalla triste vicenda dello stupro di cui fu vittima nel 1611, sia dall'ingombrante figura del padre Orazio, celeberrimo pittore ma uomo rude e accentratore.'

9 For visual documentation, see https://www.youtube.com/watch?v=bxLsX271oUo.

10 Papi, 2011, 846.

11 Paris, 2012.

12 Chicago, 2013; Olomouc, 2013; Pisa, 2013; Rome, 2016; Conversano, 2018; Moscow, 2019; Milan, 2019–20; Pisa, 2019–20; London, 2020.

13 For discussion, see Marshall, 2016, 193–95; and Conversano, 2018, with previous bibliography.

14 Barker, 2018b, 170–71.

15 McTighe, 2020, 80.

16 Straussman-Pflanzer, 2021, 24.

17 For a further noteworthy example of this exhibition methodology, see the 2021 exhibition *Le signore dell'arte: storie di donne tra '500 e '600* that was also held at the Palazzo Reale, Milan (Milan, 2021).

15 ARTEMISIA BEYOND THE ACADEMY

1 Milan, 1951, 62.

2 Boldrini, 2012, 153, 158ff.

3 Banti, 1988.

4 Susan Sontag, 'A Double Destiny', introduction to ibid., v–xx.

5 Banti, 1988, 137.

6 Prota Giurleo, 1951, 25.

7 See further De' Dominici, 1742–45, 3:98–99, 112–13; Prota Giurleo, 1951, 20, 22–25; Prota Giurleo, 1955, 30–32; Fiorillo, 1984; Novelli Radice, 1989, 147–54; Ferdinando Bologna in Naples, 1991, 136–38; Schütze and Willette, 1992, 122–23; De Vito, 1993, 129–41; Petrelli, 2008; and Giuseppe Porzio in Naples, 2022, 39–46 and cat. 47, 226–27.

8 Banti, 1988, 199.

9 Barko, 2015, 64; Heller, 2005, 6; and see further Scarparo, 2002, 372–74.

10 Banti, 1960; Clark, 1994; Caplan, 1995; Humphrey, 1996; Breach Productions, 2018.

11 Anglada, 1989; Jamis, 1990; Lapierre, 1998; Lapierre, 2000; Vreeland, 2002; Elia, 2013; Aarons-Hughes, 2016; Sacco, 2017; Ferlut and Baudouin, 2017; Connor, 2019; McCullough, 2019; Siciliano, 2019; Lafferty, 2020.

12 The data from Goodreads presented here and below has been gathered in late August 2023, during the final stages of preparing the text for press.

13 Boldrini, 2012, 119–48. For issues underlining the relationship of the genre of historical fiction to the processes of history more generally, see Mitchell and Parsons, 2012, 1–18.

14 Bottari, 1757–68.

15 Bertolotti, 1876, 183–204; Ruffo, 1916, 21ff; Garrard, 1989, 373–487; Solinas, 2011a.

16 Lapierre, 2005, 164.

17 A similar strategy is employed in Gina Siciliano's previously mentioned *I Know What I Am* (Siciliano, 2019), which includes some forty pages of notes documenting the sources used for the material contained in her graphic novel.

18 Lapierre, 2000, 398–99; and for further discussion of this painting, see pp. 50–52

19 Lapierre, 2000, 276.

20 Ibid., 6.

21 Lent, 2006, 214.

22 Krach, 1998.

23 The IMDb website gives birth dates of 13 April 1974 (Valentina Cervi) and 5 April 1950 (Predrag 'Miki' Manojlovic) respectively for the actors who played Artemisia Gentileschi and Agostino Tassi. https://www.imdb.com/name/nm0543547/?ref_=nmbio_mbio

24 Garrard and Steinem, 1998.

25 Ibid.; and see further Garrard, 2001, 121–23.

26 Milan, 2011, cat. 15, 164–65, with previous bibliography.

27 Fonseca-Wollheim, 2017, n.p. For Schwendinger's *Artemisia*, including production details, photographs, links to YouTube performance clips etc., see https://www.lauraschwendinger.com/artemisia

28 https://www.facebook.com/fauxmachismo/videos/Judith-do-it-artemisiagentileschi-judith-slaying-holofernes-fauxmachismo-leedsband/2141699749464573/

29 Steinhauer, 2018, n.p.

30 Italy ranked number one, for example, in a questionnaire of 2010 sponsored by the European Union, asking, 'How common do you think domestic violence against women is in our country?', for which, see European Commission, 2010; and see further Pianigiani, 2018.

31 Artemisia Gentileschi to Don Antonio Ruffo, 13 March 1649, cit. and trans. Garrard, 1989, 391–92.

BIBLIOGRAPHY

NO AUTHOR, 2011 No author, 'La Gentileschi a Palazzo Reale', *Il Sole 24 Ore: Domenica 24*, 18 September 2011, accessible at https://st.ilsole24ore.com/art/cultura/2011-09-17/gentileschi-palazzo-reale-144655.shtml?uuid=AagccG5D

AARONS-HUGHES, 2016 Aarons-Hughes, Rivka, *Ester and Artemisia*, New York: Less Than Three Press, 2016.

ABETTI, 2022 Abetti, Luigi, 'Appendice B: Pagamenti bancari relativi all'attività di Artemisia a Napoli', in *Artemisia Gentileschi a Napoli*, ed. Antonio Ernesto Denunzio and Giuseppe Porzio (exh. cat., Galleria d'Italia, Naples, 2022–23), Milan: Skira, 2022, pp. 101–13.

AGO, 2010 Ago, Renata, 'Five Industrious Cities', in *Painting for Profit: The Economic Lives of Seventeenth-century Italian Painters*, ed. Richard E. Spear and Philip Sohm, New Haven and London: Yale University Press, 2010, pp. 255–73.

AIELLO, 2020 Aiello, Patrizio, *Caravaggio, 1951*, Milan: Officina Libraria, 2020.

ALPERS, 1988 Alpers, Svetlana, *Rembrandt's Enterprise: The Studio and the Market*, Chicago: University of Chicago Press, 1988.

AMELIO, 2017 Amelio, Michaela, *La vera storia del dipinto di Artemisia Gentileschi 'Lasciate che i pargoli vengano a me . . . '*, privately published [Lulu Press Inc.], Rome, 2017.

ANDERSON, 1988 Anderson, Jaynie, 'The Head-hunter and Head-huntress in Italian Religious Portraiture', in *Vernacular Christianity: Essays in the Social Anthropology of Religion*, ed. Wendy James and Douglas H. Johnson, New York: Lilian Barber Press, 1988, pp. 60–69.

ANGLADA, 1989 Anglada, Maria Àngels, *Artemísia*, Barcelona: Columna, 1989.

ARIZZOLI, 2016 Arizzoli, Louise, 'Marietta Robusti in Jacopo Tintoretto's Workshop: Her Likeness and her Role as a Model for her Father', *Studi di storia dell'arte*, 27, 2016, pp. 105–14.

BAGLIONE, 1642 Baglione, Giovanni, *Le Vite de' Pittori Scultori et Architetti dal pontificato di Gregorio XIII del 1572 in fino a' tempi di Papa Urbano Ottavo nel 1642 – facsimile dell'edizione di Roma di 1642*, Rome: E. Calzone, 1935.

BALDASSARI, 1995 Baldassari, Francesca, *Carlo Dolci*, Turin: Artema, 1995.

BALDASSARI, 2005 Baldassari, Francesca, 'I pittori fiorentini a Roma dall'Anno Santo 1600 fino all'avvento del papato di Urbano VIII', in *Luce e Ombra: Caravaggismo e naturalismo nella pittura toscana del Seicento*, ed. Pierluigi Carofano (exh. cat., Centro per l'arte Otello Cirri and Museo Piaggio 'Giovanni Alberto Agnelli', Pontedera), Pisa: Felice Editore, 2005, pp. LXXIX–LXXXIX.

BALDINUCCI, 1681–1728 Baldinucci, Filippo, *Notizie dei professori del disegno da Cimabue in qua*, Florence: Santi Franchi, 1681–1728 (ed. Francesco Ranalli, Florence: Battelli, 1845–47; reprint. ed. Paola Barocchi, 7 vols, Florence: SPES, 1974–75).

BANTI, 1947 Banti, Anna, *Artemisia*, Florence: Sansoni, 1947.

BANTI, 1960 Banti, Anna, *Corte Savella*, Florence: Mondadori, 1960.

BANTI, 1988 Banti, Anna, *Artemisia*, trans. Shirley D'Ardia Caracciolo and with an introduction by Susan Sontag, Lincoln: University of Nebraska Press, 1988; first paperback printing, 1995.

BARDI, 1837–42 Bardi, Luigi, *L'Imperiale e Reale Galleria Pitti illustrata per cura di Luigi Bardi*, 4 vols, Florence: Tipografia Galileiana, 1837–42.

BARKER, 1999 Barker, Emma, 'Exhibiting the Canon: The Blockbuster Show', in *Contemporary Cultures of Display*, ed. Emma Barker, London and New Haven: Yale University Press, 1999, pp. 127–45.

BARKER, 2014 Barker, Sheila, 'A New Document Concerning Artemisia Gentileschi's Marriage', *Burlington Magazine*, 156, December 2014, pp. 803–4.

BARKER, 2016 Barker, Sheila (ed.), *Women Artists in Early Modern Italy: Careers, Fame, and Collectors*, London: Harvey Miller Publishers/London and Turnhout: Brepols, 2017.

BARKER, 2017 Barker, Sheila, 'Artemisia's Money: The Entrepreneurship of a Woman Artist in Seventeenth-Century Florence', in *Artemisia Gentileschi in a Changing Light*, ed. Sheila Barker (ed.), London: Harvey Miller Publishers/London and Turnhout: Brepols, 2017, pp. 59–88.

BARKER, 2018a Barker, Sheila, 'The First Biography of Artemisia Gentileschi: Self-Fashioning and Proto-Feminist Art History in Cristofano Bronzini's Notes on Women Artists', *Mitteilungen des Kunsthistorisches Institutes in Florenz*, 60/3, 2018, pp. 405–36.

BARKER, 2018b Barker, Sheila, review of Rome, 2016, *Early Modern Women*, 12/2, 2018, pp. 163–71.

BARKER, 2020 Barker, Sheila, 'The Muse of History: Artemisia Gentileschi's First Four Centuries of Immortal Fame', in *Artemisia*, ed. Letizia Treves (exh. cat., National Gallery, London), London: National Gallery Publications, 2020, pp. 78–89.

BARKER, 2021a Barker, Sheila, 'Art as Women's Work: The Professionalization of Women Artists in Italy, 1350–1800', in *By Her Hand: Artemisia Gentileschi and*

Women Artists in Italy, 1500–1800, ed. Eve Straussman-Pflanzer and Oliver Tostmann (exh. cat., Hartford, Conn.: Wadsworth Atheneum Museum of Art, and Detroit: Detroit Institute of Arts, 2021–22), New Haven and London: Yale University Press, 2021, pp. 43–51.

BARKER, 2021b Barker, Sheila (ed.), *Lives of Artemisia Gentileschi*, Los Angeles: J. Paul Getty Museum, 2021.

BARKER, 2022 Barker, Sheila, *Artemisia Gentileschi*, London: Lund Humphries, 2022.

BARKO, 2015 Barko, Cortney Cronberg, *Writers and Artists in Dialogue: Historical Fiction about Women Painters*, New York: Peter Lang, 2015.

BAROLSKY, 1990 Barolsky, Paul, *Michelangelo's Nose: A Myth and Its Maker*, University Park, Pa.: Penn State University Press, 1990.

BASTOGI, 2010 Bastogi, Nadia, 'Novità e riflessioni su Caravaggio e sui caravaggeschi negli archivi di Firenze/Regesto', in *Caravaggio e caravaggeschi a Firenze*, ed. Gianni Papi (exh. cat., Galleria Palatina and Galleria degli Uffizi), Florence and Livorno: Giunti and sillabe, 2010, pp. 336–65.

BASTOGI, 2021 Bastogi, Nadia, 'Novità su un Gruppo di dipinti di Artemisia Gentileschi per Cosimo II de' Medici', in *Ricerche sull'arte a Napoli in età moderna: saggi e documenti, 2020–2021*, Naples: arte'm, 2021, pp. 94–105.

BELLORI, 2005 Bellori, Giovan Pietro, *The Lives of the Modern Painters, Sculptors and Architects*, trans. Alice Sedwick Wohl, notes Hellmut Wohl, Cambridge: Cambridge University Press, 2005.

BENEDETTI, 1999 Benedetti, Laura, 'Reconstructing Artemisia: Twentieth-Century Images of a Woman Artist', *Comparative Literature*, 51/1, 1999, pp. 42–61.

BERNSTORFF, 2010 Bernstorff, Marieke von, *Agent und Maler als Akteure im Kunstbetrieb des frühen 17. Jahrhunderts: Giovan Battista Cresenzi und Bartolomeo Cavarozzi*, Munich: Hirmer, 2010.

BERNSTORFF AND KUBERSKY-PIREDDA, 2013 Bernstorff, Marieke von, and Susanne Kubersky-Piredda, 'Introduzione', in *L'arte del dono: Scambi artistici e diplomazia tra Italia e Spagna, 1550–1650. Contributi in occasione della giornata interzionale di studi, 14–15 gennaio 2008, Roma, Bibliotheca Hertziana, Istituto Max Planck per la Storia dell'Arte*, ed. Marieke von Bernstorff and Susanne Kubersky-Piredda, Milan: Silvano Editoriale S.p.A, 2013, pp. 7–11.

BERRA, 2005 Berra, Giacomo, *Il giovane Caravaggio in Lombardia, ricerche documentarie sui Merisi, gli Aratori e i Marchesi di Caravaggio*, Florence: Fondazione di Studi di Storia dell'Arte Roberto Longhi, 2005.

BERTOLOTTI, 1876 Bertolotti, Antonio, 'Agostino Tassi: Suoi scolari e compagni pittori in Roma', *Giornale di erudizione artistica*, 5, 1876, pp. 183–204.

BIANCHI AND BARKER, FORTHCOMING Bianchi, Eric and Sheila Barker, '"Upon His Visit to See My Paintings": Artemisia Gentileschi's and Pietro Della Valle's Exchanged Sonnets', *Burlington Magazine*, forthcoming.

BIELLA, 2001 *I segreti di un collezionista: Le straordinarie raccolte di Cassiano dal Pozzo (1588–1657)*, ed. Francesco Solinas (exh. cat., Museo di Territorio Biellese, Biella), Rome: De Luca, 2001.

BISSELL, 1968 Bissell, R. Ward, 'Artemisia Gentileschi: A New Documented Chronology', *Art Bulletin*, 50/2, 1968, pp. 153–68.

BISSELL, 1981 Bissell, R. Ward, *Orazio Gentileschi and the Poetic Tradition in Caravaggesque Painting*, University Park, Pa.: Penn State University Press, 1981.

BISSELL, 1999 Bissell, R. Ward, *Artemisia Gentileschi and the Authority of Art*, University Park, Pa.: Penn State University Press, 1999.

BISSELL, 2005 Bissell, R. Ward, 'Rethinking Early Artemisia', in *Artemisia Gentileschi: Taking Stock*, ed. Judith W. Mann, Turnhout: Brepols, 2005, pp. 19–38.

BISSELL, 2013 Bissell, R. Ward, 'Artemisia Gentileschi: Painter of Still Lifes?', *Source: Notes in the History of Art*, 32/2, 2013, pp. 27–34.

BOCCARDO, 2000 Boccardo, Piero, 'Un avveduto collezionista di pittura del seicento: Pietro Maria Gentile, un inventario, un Reni inedito e alcune precisazioni su altre opere e sull'esito di una quadrera Genovese', in *Studi di Storia dell'Arte in onore di Denis Mahon*, ed. Maria Grazia Bernardini, Silvia Danesi Squarzina and Claudio Strinati, Milan: Electa, 2000, pp. 205–13.

BOHN, 2011 Bohn, Babette, 'The Construction of Artistic Reputation in Seicento Bologna: Guido Reni and the Sirani', *Renaissance Studies*, 25/4, 2011, pp. 511–37.

BOLDRINI, 2012 Boldrini, Lucia, *Autobiographies of Others: Historical Subjects and Literary Fiction*, New York: Routledge, 2012.

BOLOGNA, LOS ANGELES AND FORTH WORTH, 1988–89 *Guido Reni 1575–1642* (exh. cat., Pinacoteca Nazionale di Bologna, Los Angeles County Museum of Art and Kimbell Art Museum, Fort Worth), Los Angeles: Los Angeles County Museum of Art and Nuova Alfa Editoriale, 1988.

BOLOGNA, FRANKFURT AND WASHINGTON, 1991–92 *Guercino, Master Painter of the Baroque*, ed. Denis Mahon (exh. cat., Pinacoteca Nazionale di Bologna, Schirn Kunsthalle, Frankfurt, and National Gallery of Art, Washington), Washington: National Gallery of Art, 1991–1992.

BOLOGNA, 2004 *Elisabetta Sirani 'pittrice eroina' 1638–1665*, ed. Jadranka Bentini and Vera Fortunati (exh. cat., Museo Civico Archeologico, Bologna), Bologna: Editrice Compositori, 2004.

BORRELLI, 1991 Borrelli, Gennaro, 'La borghesia napoletana della seconda metà del Seicento e la sua influenza sull'evoluzione del gusto da Barocco a Rococò', in *Ricerche sul '600 napoletano*, Milan: L&T, 1991, pp. 7–18.

BORZELLI, 1939 Borzelli, Angelo: *Un letterato minore del Cinquecento in Napoli: Alfonso Cambi Importuni*, Naples: Libreria Antiquaria, 1939.

BOTTARI, 1757–68 Bottari, Giovanni Gaetano: *Raccolta di lettere sulla pittura, scultura e architettura scritte da più celebri personaggi dei XV, XVI e XVII secoli* (Rome, 1757–68); enlarged by Stefano Ticozzi, 8 vols, Milan: G. Silvestri, 1822–25.

BREACH PRODUCTIONS, 2018 Breach Productions, *It's True, It's True, It's True*, London: Oberon Books, 2018.

BRITTON, 2009 Britton, Piers Dominic, 'Michelangelo and the "Rerum Corporis" in Vasari's "Vite": The Limits of Physiognomy', *Source: Notes in the History of Art*, 28/3, 2009, pp. 13–18.

BROOKS, 2009 Brooks, Julian, 'Florentine Artists and *Disegno* in Late Cinquecento Rome', in *The Accademia Seminars: The Accademia di San Luca in Rome, c. 1590–1635*, ed. Peter M. Lukehart, Washington: CASVA/National Gallery of Art, 2009, pp. 197–245.

BROWN AND KAGAN, 1987 Brown, Jonathan, and Richard L. Kagan, 'The Duke of Alcalá: His Collection and Its Evolution', *Art Bulletin*, 69/2, 1987, pp. 231–55.

BUCHAKJIAN, 2020 Buchakjian, Gregory, 'After the Blast: At the Sursock Palace and Museum in Beirut', *Apollo*, 3 September 2020; available at https://www.apollo-magazine.com/sursock-museum-palace-beirut-explosion/

BUGLI, 2004 Bugli, Marialuigi, 'Da Capodimonte a Palazzo Grande a Chiaia: La collezione d'Avalos "torna" nella prestigiosa dimora', in *Ricerche sul '600 napoletano: Saggi e documenti 2003–2004*, Naples: Electa, 2004, pp. 7–54.

BURKE, 1983 Burke, Peter, 'The Virgin of the Carmine and the Revolt of Masaniello', *Past and Present*, 99, 1983, pp. 3–21.

CALABRIA, 1991 Calabria, Antonio, *The Cost of Empire: The Finances of the Kingdom of Naples in the Time of Spanish Rule*, Cambridge: Cambridge University Press, 1991.

CALVESI, 1990 Calvesi, Maurizio, *La realtà di Caravaggio*, Turin: Einaudi, 1990.

CAMPBELL, 2013 Campbell, Julie D., 'The *Querelle des femmes*', in *The Ashgate Research Companion to Women and Gender in Early Modern Europe*, ed. Allyson M. Poska, Jane Couchman and Katherine A. McIver, Farnham: Ashgate, 2013, pp. 361–79.

CANNATÀ AND VICINI, 1992 Cannatà, Roberto, and Maria Lucrezia Vicini, *La Galleria di Palazzo Spada: Genesi e storia di una collezione*, Rome: Edizioni d'Europa, 1992.

CANTARO, 1989 Cantaro, Maria Teresa, *Lavinia Fontana Bolognese, 'pittora singolare', 1552–1614*, Milan: Jandi Sapi Editori, 1989.

CANTELLI, 1983 Cantelli, Giuseppe, *Repertorio della pittura Fiorentina del Seicento*, Florence: OpusLibri, 1983.

CAPECELATRO, 1850–52 Capecelatro, Don Francesco, *Diario: contenente la storia delle cose avvenute nel Reaume di Napoli negli anni 1647–50*, ed. A. Granito, 3 vols, Naples: G. Nobile, 1850–52.

CAPLAN, 1995 Caplan, Cathy, *Lapis Blue Blood Red*, New York: Playscripts inc., 1995.

CARACCIOLO, 1959 Caracciolo, Ambrogino, 'Alcuni notizie sulla famiglia Francone e l'arredamento di una casa patrizia napoletana al principio del sec. XVIII', in *Studi in onore di Riccardo Filangieri*, Naples: L'Arte Tipografica, 3 vols, 1959, vol. 3, pp. 29–50.

CARLONI, 2001 Carloni, Livia, 'Orazio Gentileschi Between Rome and the Marches', in *Orazio and Artemsia Gentileschi*, ed. Keith Christiansen and Judith W. Mann (exh. cat., Palazzo Venezia, Rome, The Metropolitan Museum of Art, New York, and St Louis Art Museum, 2001–2), New York: The Metropolitan Museum of Art, 2001, pp. 117–29.

CAROFANO, 2014 Carofano, Pierluigi, 'Il Gran Principe Ferdinando e il collezionismo di pittura caravaggesca, spigolature e riflessioni', *Valori tattili*, 3–4, 2014, pp. 22–39, 126.

CAUSA, 1993 Causa, Stefano, 'Risarcimento di Onofrio Palumbo', *Paragone*, 44/515–17, 1993, pp. 21–40.

CAUSA, 2000 Causa, Stefano, *Battistello Caracciolo: l'opera completa*, Naples: Electa, 2000.

CAVALLINO AND SALERNO, 2005 *Percorsi d'arte: tra vestigia dei Messapi, il collezionismo dei Ruffo e l'evoluzione pittorica di Mino Delle Site*, ed. Mario Alberto Pavone (exh. cat., Convento di S. Domenico, Cavallino, and Pinacoteca Provinciale, Salerno), Salerno: Graphite, 2005.

CAVAZZINI, 2001a Cavazzini, Patrizia, 'Artemisia in her Father's House', in *Orazio and Artemsia Gentileschi*, ed. Keith Christiansen and Judith W. Mann (exh. cat., Palazzo Venezia, Rome, The Metropolitan Museum of Art, New York, and St Louis Art Museum, 2001–2), New York: The Metropolitan Museum of Art, 2001, pp. 282–95.

CAVAZZINI, 2001b Cavazzini, Patrizia, 'Documents Relating to the Trial of Agostino Tassi', in *Orazio and Artemsia Gentileschi*, ed. Keith Christiansen and Judith W. Mann (exh. cat., Palazzo Venezia, Rome, The Metropolitan Museum of Art, New York, and St Louis Art Museum, 2001–2), New York: The Metropolitan Museum of Art, 2001, pp. 432–44.

CAVAZZINI, 2005 Cavazzini, Patrizia, 'Artemisia and the Other Women in Agostino Tassi's Life: Attitudes to Women's Improper Sexual Behaviour in Seventeenth-century Rome', in *Artemisia Gentileschi: Taking Stock*, ed. Judith W. Mann, Turnhout: Brepols, 2005, pp. 39–49.

CAVAZZINI, 2008 Cavazzini, Patrizia, *Painting as Business in Seventeenth-century Rome*, University Park, Pa.: Penn State University Press, 2008.

CAVAZZINI, 2009–10 Cavazzini, Patrizia, 'Accademie, autodidatti e studio dal modello nella Roma di primo seicento', *Bulletin de l'association des historiens de l'art italien*, 15–16, 2009–10, pp. 81–92.

CAVAZZINI, 2011 Cavazzini, Patrizia, 'Pittori eletti e 'bottegari' nei primi anni dell'Accademia e Compagnia di San Luca', *Rivista d'arte*, 5/1, 2011, pp. 79–96.

CAVAZZINI, 2017 Cavazzini, Patrizia, 'Success and Failure in a Violent City: Bartolomeo Manfredi, Nicolas Tournier, and Valentin de Boulogne', in *Valentin Boulogne: Beyond Caravaggio*, ed. Keith Christiansen and Annick Lemoine (exh. cat., The Metropolitan Museum of Art, New York, and the Musée du Louvre, Paris), New York: The Metropolitan Museum of Art, 2017, pp. 18–27.

CAVAZZINI, 2020 Cavazzini, Patrizia, 'Orazio and Artemisia: From "Such an Ugly Deed" to "Honours and Favours" at the English Court', in *Artemisia*, ed. Letizia Treves (exh. cat., National Gallery, London), London: National Gallery Publications, 2020, pp. 32–45.

CECCHINI, 2000 Cecchini, Isabella, *Quadri e commercio a Venezia durante il Seicento: Uno studio sul mercato dell'arte*, Venice: Marsilio Editori, 2000.

CELANO, 1692 Celano, Carlo: *Notizie del bello, dell'antico e del curioso della citta di Napoli divise dall'autore in dieci giornate per guida e comodo dei viaggiatori*, Naples, 1692 (ed. Atanasio Mozzillo et al. and repr. from the edition of 1856–60), ed. Giovan Battista Chiarini, 7 vols, Naples: Edizioni Scientifiche Italiane, 1974.

CELENZA, 2015 Celenza, Anna Harwell, 'Paesaggi sonori: Immagini della musica popolare nella Roma del Seicento', in *I bassifondi del barocco: La Roma del vizio e della miseria*, ed. Francesca Cappelletti and Annick Lemoine (exh. cat., Villa Medici, Rome, and Petit Palais, Paris), Milan: Officina Libraria, 2014, pp. 93–101.

CHANEY, 1998 Chaney, Edward, *The Evolution of the Grand Tour: Anglo-Italian Cultural Relations Since the Renaissance*, London: Frank Cass, 1998.

CHAPMAN, 1990 Chapman, H. Perry, *Rembrandt's Self Portraits: A Study in Seventeenth-century Identity*, Princeton: Princeton University Press, 1990.

CHENEY, 2015 Cheney, Liana De Girolami, 'Lavinia Fontana's Nude Minervas', *Woman's Art Journal*, 36/2, 2015, pp. 30–40.

CHICAGO, N.D. Chicago, Judy, 'The Dinner Party Project', undated typewritten description, Judy Chicago Papers, Schlesinger Library, Radcliffe Institute, Harvard University, Cambridge, Mass.; available at 'The Dinner Party. Creation. Original concept, early [written descriptions of various aspects of The Dinner Party], n.d. Sequence 17, https://iiif.lib.harvard.edu/manifests/view/drs:434775925$1i

CHICAGO, 2013 *Artemisia Gentileschi's Judith Slaying Holofernes*, ed. Eve Straussman-Pflanzer (exh. cat., Art Institute of Chicago), Chicago: Art Institute of Chicago, 2013.

CHRISTIANSEN, 1986 Christiansen, Keith, 'Caravaggio and "L'esempio davanti dal naturale"', *Art Bulletin*, 68/3, 1986, pp. 421–45.

CHRISTIANSEN, 1996 Christiansen, Keith, 'Thoughts on the Lombard Training of Caravaggio', in *Come dipingeva il Caravaggio: Atti della giornata di studio*, ed. Mina Gregori, Milan: Electa, 1996, pp. 7–28.

CHRISTIANSEN, 2004 Christiansen, Keith, 'Becoming Artemisia: Afterthoughts on the Gentileschi Exhibition', *Metropolitan Museum Journal*, 39, 2004, pp. 101–26.

CIAMPOLINI, 2012 Ciampolini, Marco, *Pittori Senesi del Seicento*, 3 vols, Siena: Nuova Immagine, 2012.

CIARDI, 2011 Ciardi, Roberto Paolo, 'The Lomi Gentileschi: A Family of Tuscan Artists Rising to the International Scenarios', in *Artemisia Gentileschi: The Story of a Passion*, ed. Roberto Contini and Francesco Solinas (exh. cat., Palazzo Reale, Milan), Milan: 24 ORE Cultura, 2011, pp. 23–35.

CINOTTI, 1983 Cinotti, Mia: *Michelangelo Merisi detto il Caravaggio: Tutte le opere*, Bergamo: Bolis, 1983.

CINOTTI AND DELL'ACQUA, 1983 Cinotti, Mia, and Gian Albert dell'Acqua, 'Michelangelo Merisi detto il Caravaggio', in *I pittori bergamaschi: Il Seicento, I*, ed. Pietro Zampetti, Bergamo: Bolis, 1983, pp. 203–641.

CLARK, 1994 Clark, Sally, *Life Without Instruction*, Vancouver: Talonbooks, 1994.

CLEVELAND, 1971 *Caravaggio and His Followers*, ed. Richard E. Spear (exh. cat., Cleveland Museum of Art), Cleveland: Cleveland Museum of Art, 1971.

CLEVELAND AND FORT WORTH, 1984–85 *Bernardo Cavallino of Naples 1616–1656*, ed. Ann Percy and Ann T. Lurie (exh. cat., Cleveland Museum of Art and Kimbell Art Museum, Fort Worth, 1984–85), Cleveland and Fort Worth: Cleveland Museum of Art and Kimbell Art Museum, 1984.

CLIFFORD, 1996 Clifford, James, 'Vasari on Competition', *The Sixteenth Century Journal*, 27/1, 1996, pp. 23–41.

COHEN, 1991 Cohen, Elizabeth Storr, 'No Longer Virgins: Self-Presentation by Young Women in Late Renaissance Rome', in *Refiguring Woman: Perspectives on Gender and the Italian Renaissance*, ed. Marilyn Migiel and Juliana Schiesari, Ithaca: Cornell University Press, 1991, pp. 169–91.

COHEN, 2000 Cohen, Elizabeth Storr, 'The Trials of Artemisia Gentileschi: A Rape as History', *The Sixteenth Century Journal*, 31/1, 2000, pp. 47–75.

COHEN, 2015 Cohen, Elizabeth Storr, 'More Trials for Artemisia Gentileschi: Her Life, Love and Letters in 1620', in *Patronage, Gender and the Arts in Early Modern Italy: Essays in Honor of Carolyn Valone*, ed. Katherine A. McIver and Cynthia Stollhans, New York: Italica Press, 2015, pp. 249–72.

COLANTUONO, 1997 Colantuono, Anthony: *Guido Reni's Abduction of Helen: The Politics and Rhetoric of Painting Seventeenth-century Europe*, Cambridge: Cambridge University Press, 1997.

COLE, 2019 Cole, Michael W., *Sofonisba's Lesson: A Renaissance Artist and Her Work*, Princeton: Princeton University Press, 2019.

COLONNA DI STIGLIANO, 1895 Colonna di Stigliano, Ferdinando, 'Inventario del Casa Colonna fatto da Luca Giordano', *Napoli Nobilissima*, 4/2, 1895, pp. 29–32.

CONNOR, 2019 Connor, Alex, *Artemisia*, Cambridge: Cranthorpe Millner Publishers, 2019.

CONTINI, 2001 Contini, Roberto, 'Artemisia Gentileschi's Florentine Inspiration', in *Orazio and Artemsia Gentileschi*, ed. Keith Christiansen and Judith W. Mann (exh. cat., Palazzo Venezia, Rome, The Metropolitan Museum of Art, New York, and St Louis Art Museum, 2001–2), New York: The Metropolitan Museum of Art, 2001, pp. 312–19.

CONTINI, 2011 Contini, Roberto, '"How Far the Intelligence and the Hand of Such a Woman Can Reach": Geography and Rank of Artemisia Gentileschi'; 'Naples, 1630s', in *Artemisia Gentileschi: The Story of a Passion*, ed. Roberto Contini and Francesco Solinas (exh. cat., Palazzo Reale, Milan), Milan: 24 ORE Cultura, 2011, pp. 36–49; 96–107.

CONVERSANO, 2000 *Paolo Finoglio e il suo tempo: Un pittore napoletano alla corte degli Acquaviva*, ed. Cosimo Damiano Fonseca (exh. cat., Pinacoteca Comunale del Castello, Conversano), Naples: Electa, 2000.

CONVERSANO, 2018 *Artemisia e i pittori del conte: La collezione di Giangirolamo II Acquaviva d'Aragona a Conversano*, ed. Viviana Farina (exh. cat., Castello e Chiesa di San Giuseppe, Conversano), Cava de' Tirreni: Areablu edizioni, 2018.

CORRERA, 1890 Correra, L., 'Inedita relazione dei tumulti napoletani del 1647', *Archivio Storico per le Province Napoletane*, 15/2, 1890, pp. 355–87.

COSTA, 2000 Costa, Patrizia, 'Artemisia Gentileschi in Venice', *Source: Notes in the History of Art*, 19/3, 2000, pp. 28–36.

COSTELLO, 1950 Costello, Jane, 'The Twelve Pictures "Ordered by Velazquez" and the Trial of Valguarnera', *Journal of the Warburg and Courtauld Institutes*, 13, 1950, pp. 237–84.

CROCE, 1954 Croce, Benedetto, 'I "lazzari"', in *Aneddoti di varia letteratura*, 4 vols, Bari: Laterza, 1954, vol. 3, pp. 198–205.

CROPPER, 1984 Cropper, Elizabeth, *The Ideal of Painting: Pietro Testa's Düsseldorf Notebook*, Princeton: Princeton University Press, 1984.

CROPPER, 1991 Cropper, Elizabeth, 'The Petrifying Art: Marino's Poetry and Caravaggio', *Metropolitan Museum Journal*, 26, 1991, pp. 193–212.

CROPPER, 1993 Cropper, Elizabeth, 'New Documents for Artemisia Gentileschi's Life in Florence', *Burlington Magazine*, 135/1088, 1993, pp. 760–61.

CROPPER, 2001 Cropper, Elizabeth, 'Life on the Edge: Artemisia Gentileschi, Famous Woman Painter', in *Orazio and Artemsia Gentileschi*, ed. Keith Christiansen and Judith W. Mann (exh. cat., Palazzo Venezia, Rome, The Metropolitan Museum of Art, New York, and St Louis Art Museum, 2001–2), New York: The Metropolitan Museum of Art, 2001, pp. 263–81.

CROPPER, 2009 Cropper, Elizabeth, 'Galileo Galilei e Artemisia Gentileschi tra storia delle idee e microstoria', in *Il cannochiale e il pennello: nuova scienza e nuova arte nell'età di Galileo*, ed. Lucia Tomasi Tongiorgi and Alessandro Tosi (exh. cat., Palazzo Blu, Pisa), Florence: Giunti, 2009, pp. 195–213.

CURRIE ET AL., 2017 Currie, Christina, Livia Depuydt-Elbaum, Valentine Henderiks, Steven Saverwyns and Ina Vanden Berghe, '*Mary Magdalene in Ecstasy* by Artemisia Gentileschi: A Technical Study', in *Artemisia Gentileschi in a Changing Light*, ed. Sheila Barker, London: Harvey Miller Publishers/London and Turnhout: Brepols, 2017, pp. 217–35.

D'ADDOSIO, 1912–13 D'Addosio, Giambattista, 'Documenti inediti di artisti napoletani del XVI e XVII secolo (I. Pittori)', *Archivio Storico per le province napoletane*, 37/4, 1912, pp. 593–616; 38/1, 1913, pp. 36–72; 38/2, 1913, pp. 232–59; 38/3, 1913, pp. 483–524; 38/4, 1913, pp. 578–83.

D'ALESSANDRO AND PORZIO, 2022 D'Alessandro, Domenico Antonio, and Giuseppe Porzio, 'Appendice A: Documenti per la biografia napoletana di Artemisia', in *Artemisia Gentileschi a Napoli*, ed. Antonio Ernesto Denunzio and Giuseppe Porzio (exh. cat., Galleria d'Italia, Naples, 2022–23), Milan: Skira, 2022, pp. 91–100.

DAVIS, 2009 Davis, Lucy, 'Renaissance Inventions: Van Eyck's Workshop as a Site of Discovery and Transformation in Jan Van Der Straet's "Nova Reperta"', *Nederlands Kunsthistorisch Jaarboek (NKJ)/Netherlands Yearbook for History of Art*, 59, 2009, pp. 222–47.

DE' DOMINICI, 1742–45 De' Dominici, Bernardo, *Vite de' pittori, scultori ed architetti napoletani*, Naples: Stamperia del Ricciardi, 3 vols, 1742–45 (facsimile edition repr. Bologna: Arnaldo Forni Editore, 1979).

DE' DOMINICI, 2003–8 De' Dominici, Bernardo, *Vite de' pittori, scultori ed architetti napoletani*, Naples: Stamperia del Ricciardi, 1742–45, critical edition with commentary, ed. Fiorella Sricchia Santoro and Andrea Zezza, 3 vols, Naples: Paparo, 2003–8.

DELFINO, 1987 Delfino, Antonio, 'Documenti inediti sui pittori del '600 tratti dall'Archivio Storico del Banco di Napoli (A.S.B.N.) e dall'Archivio Storici di Napoli (A.S.N.)', in *Ricerche sul '600 napoletano*, Milan: L&T, 1987, pp. 79–98.

DEL GROSSO AND AVINO, 1989 Del Grosso, Maria A., and Luigi Avino, *Arte e cultura nel Seicento: Il testamento e l'inventario dei beni di Fabrizio Pinto*, Salerno: Laveglia, 1989.

DE RENZI, 1867 De Renzi, Salvatore, *Napoli nell'anno 1656*, Naples: Tipografia di Domenico di Pascale, 1867.

DE VITO, 1993 De Vito, Giuseppe, 'Due postille alle "notizie" di Eduardo Nappi', in *Ricerche sul '600 napoletano*, Naples: Electa, 1993, pp. 129–41.

DE VITO, 2005 De Vito, Giuseppe, 'A Note on Gentileschi and her Collaborator, Onofrio Palumbo', *Burlington Magazine*, 147/1232, 2005, p. 749.

DENUNZIO, 2022 Denunzio, Antonio Ernesto, 'Artemisia e il potere: Qualche nota sugli incarichi degli anni napoletani', in *Artemisia Gentileschi a Napoli*, ed. Antonio Ernesto Denunzio and Giuseppe Porzio (exh. cat., Galleria d'Italia, Naples, 2022–23), Milan: Skira, 2022, pp. 61–71.

DUFRESNOY, 1695 DuFresnoy, Charles-Alphonse, *De Arte Graphica: The Art of Painting*, trans. John Dryden, with additions by Richard Graham, London: I. Heptinstall for W. Rogers, 1695.

DUNKELMAN, 2005–6 Dunkelman, Martha Levine, 'Donatello's Mary Magdalen: A Model of Courage and Survival', *Woman's Art Journal*, 26/2, 2005–6, pp. 10–13.

ELIA, 2013 Elia, Francesca, *Artemisia Gentileschi: Her Life, Her Genius, Her Due*, New York: Bettie Youngs Book Publishers, 2013.

ENGASS AND BROWN, 1970 Engass, Robert, and Jonathan Brown, *Italy and Spain: 1600–1750, Sources and Documents*, Englewood Cliffs: Prentice Hall Inc., 1970.

EUROPEAN COMMISSION European Commission, Directorate-General for Justice, Freedom and Security, *Domestic Violence Against Women: Report*, *Special Eurobarometer, no. 344*, Brussels: European Commission, 2010; available at https://europa.eu/eurobarometer/surveys/detail/816

FABRIANO, 2019 *La luce e i silenzi: Orazio Gentileschi e la pittura caravaggesca nelle Marche dei seicento*, ed. Alessandro Delpriori et al. (exh. cat., Pinacoteca Civica Bruno Molajoli, Fabriano), Ancona: Il Lavoro Editoriale, 2019.

FANTONI, MATTHEWS AND MATTHEWS-GRIECO, 2003 Fantoni, Marcello, Louisa Matthews and Sara Matthews-Grieco (eds), *The Art Market in Italy (15th–17th Centuries)/Il mercato dell'arte in Italia (sec. XV–XVII)*, Modena: Franco Cosimo Panini Editore, 2003.

FARAGLIA, 1885 AND 1892 Faraglia, Nunzio Federigo, 'Notizie di alcuni artisti che lavoravano nella Chiesa di S. Martino e nel Tesoro di S. Gennaro', *Archivio Storico per le province napoletane*, 10, 1885, pp. 435–61; 17, 1892, pp. 657–78.

FARINA, 2017 Farina, Viviana, 'Per Giuseppe di Guido alias il maestro di Fontanarosa', in *Davanti al naturale: Contributo sul movimento caravaggesco a Napoli*, ed. Gianni Papi and Francesco de Luca, Milan: Officina Libraria, 2017, pp. 85–103.

FECI, 2004 Feci, Simona, *Pesci fuor d'acqua: Donne a Roma in età moderna: diritti e patrimoni*, Rome: Viella, 2004.

FECI, 2018 Feci, Simona, 'Exceptional Women: Female Merchants and Working Women in Italy in the Early Modern Period', in *Gender, Law and Economic Well-Being in Europe from the Fifteenth to the Nineteenth Century: North Versus South?*, ed. Anna Bellavitis and Beatrice Zucca Micheletto, London: Routledge, 2018, pp. 62–76.

FELTON, 1986 Felton, Craig, 'Ribera's "Philosophers" for the Prince of Liechtenstein', *Burlington Magazine*, 128, 1986, pp. 785–89.

FERLUT AND BAUDOUIN, 2017 Ferlut, Nathalie, with illustrations by Tamia Baudouin, *Artemisia*, Paris: Delcourt, 2017.

FFOLLIOTT, 2003–4 ffolliott, Sheila, review of Rome, New York and St Louis, 2001–2, *Woman's Art Journal*, 24/2, 2003–4, pp. 53–55.

FFOLLIOTT, 2021 ffolliott, Sheila, 'Artemisia Gentileschi', in *Oxford Bibliographies in Art History*, ed. Thomas DaCosta Kauffman, New York: Oxford University Press, 2021; available at https://www.oxfordbibliographies.com/display/document/obo-9780199920105/obo-9780199920105-0164.xml#backToTop

FINDLEN, 1994 Findlen, Paula, *Possessing Nature: Museums, Collecting, and Scientific Culture in early Modern Europe*, Berkeley: University of California Press, 1994.

FINKEL, 2021 Finkel, Jori, 'Museum of Star Wars Creator George Lucas Goes on Buying Spree with International, if not Intergalactic, Focus', *Art Newspaper*, 4 October 2021; available at https://www.theartnewspaper.com/2021/10/04/lucas-museum-acquisitions

FIORILLO, 1984 Fiorillo, Ciro, 'Sei tu Annella?', *Napoli Nobilissima*, 23/5–6, 1984, pp. 208–11.

FLORENCE, 1970 *Caravaggio e caravaggeschi nelle gallerie di Firenze*, ed. Evelina Borea (exh. cat., Palazzo Pitti, Florence), Florence: Sansoni Editore, 1970.

FLORENCE, 1983 *Sustermans: Sessant'anni alla corte di Medici*, ed. Marco Chiarini (exh. cat., Palazzo Pitti, Florence), Florence: Centro Di, 1983.

FLORENCE, 1984 *Cristofano Allori, 1571–1621*, ed. Miles L. Chappell (exh. cat., Palazzo Pitti, Florence), Florence: Centro Di, 1984.

FLORENCE, 1991 *Artemisia*, ed. Roberto Contini and Gianni Papi (exh. cat., Casa Buonarroti, Florence), Rome: De Luca, 1991.

FLORENCE, 2008 *Il volto di Michelangelo*, ed. Pina Ragionieri (exh. cat., Casa Buonarroti, Florence), Florence: Mandragora, 2008.

FLORENCE, 2010 *Caravaggio e caravaggeschi a Firenze*, ed. Gianni Papi (exh. cat., Galleria Palatina, Palazzo Pitti and Galleria degli Uffizi, Florence), Florence and Livorno: Giunti and sillabe, 2010.

FLORENCE, 2015 *Gherardo delle Notti: Quadri bizzarissimi e cene allegre*, ed. Gianni Papi (exh. cat., Galleria degli Uffizi, Florence), Florence: Giunti, 2015.

FLORENCE, 2019 *Volti e storie: Ottavio Leoni (1578–1630) ritrattista nell'Accademia Colombaria e nelle raccolte Fiorentine*, ed. Piera Giovanna Tordella (exh. cat., Spazio Mostre Fondazione CR Firenze, Florence), Florence: Edizioni Polistampa, 2019.

FONSECA-WOLLHEIM, 2017 Fonseca-Wollheim, Corinna da, 'Big Piano Premieres: The Week in Classical Music', *New York Times*, 8 March 2017; available at https://www.nytimes.com/2019/03/08/arts/music/classical-music-youtube.html?searchResultPosition=8

FORGIONE, 2013 Forgione, Gianluca, 'Ancora sulla cerchia di Ribera a Napoli: proposte per Hendrick De Somer e Giovanni Ricca', *Commentari d'arte*, 19/54–55, 2013, pp. 91–97, 125.

FRANKLIN, 2011 Franklin, David, '"You Know That I Love You": Music and Youth in Caravaggio', *Caravaggio and his Followers in Rome*, ed. David Franklin and Sebastian Schütze (exh. cat., The National Gallery of Canada, Ottawa, and the Kimbell Art Museum, Fort Worth), New Haven and London: Yale University Press, 2011, pp. 128–53.

FUMAGALLI, 2010 Fumagalli, Elena, 'Florence', in *Painting for Profit: The Economic Lives of Seventeenth-century Italian Painters*, ed. Richard E. Spear and Philip Sohm, New Haven and London: Yale University Press, 2010, pp. 173–203.

FUMAGALLI, 2014 Fumagalli, Elena, 'On the Medici Payroll: At Court from Cosimo I to Ferdinando II (1540–1670)', in *The Court Artist in Seventeenth-century Italy*, ed. Elena Fumagalli and Raffaela Morselli, Rome: Kent State University European Studies, 2014, pp. 95–136.

FUMAGALLI AND MORSELLI, 2014 Fumagalli, Elena, and Raffaela Morselli, Introduction, in *The Court Artist in Seventeenth-century Italy*, ed. Elena Fumagalli and Raffaela Morselli, Rome: Kent State University European Studies, 2014, pp. 11–20.

GALASSO, 1982 Giuseppe Galasso, *Napoli spagnola dopo Masaniello: politica, cultura, società*, Florence: Sansoni, 1982.

GARRARD, 1980 Garrard, Mary D., 'Artemisia Gentileschi's Self-Portrait as the Allegory of Painting', *Art Bulletin*, 62/1, 1980, pp. 97–112.

GARRARD, 1989 Garrard, Mary D., *Artemisia Gentileschi: The Image of the Female Hero in Italian Baroque Art*, Lawrenceville: Princeton University Press, 1989.

GARRARD, 1998 Garrard, Mary D., 'Artemisia's Trial by Cinema', *Art in America*, 86/10, October 1998, pp. 65–69.

GARRARD, 2001 Garrard, Mary D., *Artemisia Gentileschi around 1622: The Shaping and Reshaping of an Artistic Identity*, Berkeley: University of California Press, 2001.

GARRARD, 2005 Garrard, Mary D., 'Artemisia's Hand', in *Artemisia Gentileschi: Taking Stock*, ed. Judith W. Mann, Turnhout: Brepols, 2005, pp. 99–120.

GARRARD, 2017 Garrard, Mary D., 'Identifying Artemisia: The Archive and the Eye', in *Artemisia Gentileschi in a Changing Light*, ed. Sheila Barker, London: Harvey Miller Publishers/Brepols, London and Turnhout, 2017, pp. 11–40.

GARRARD, 2020 Garrard, Mary D., *Artemisia Gentileschi and Feminism in Early Modern Europe*, London: Reaktion Books, 2020.

GARRARD, 2023 Garrard, Mary D., review of Barker, 2022, *Burlington Magazine*, 165, January 2023, pp. 90–91.

GARRARD AND STEINEM, 1998 Garrard, Mary D., and Gloria Steinem, 'Now That You've Seen the Film, Meet the Real Artemisia Gentileschi', reprinted in Helen Langa, 'New Film Distorts History to Create a Fictionalized and Sensationalized "Truth"'; available at https://networks.h-net.org/node/24029/pages/31480/historical-inaccuracies-artemisia

GASTON, 2004 Gaston, Vivien, 'The Prophet Armed: Macchiavelli, Savonarola and Rosso Fiorentino's *Moses Defending the Daughters of Jethro*', *Melbourne Art Journal*, 7, 2004, pp. 169–78.

GENEVA, 2004 *Cléopâtre dans le miroir de l'art occidental*, ed. Claude Ritschard (exh. cat., Musées d'Art et d'Histoire, Geneva), Milan: 5 Continents, 2004.

GERARD, 1982 Gerard, Véronique, 'Philip IV's Early Italian Commissions', *Oxford Art Journal*, 5/1, 1982, pp. 9–14.

GERHARD, 2013 Gerhard, Jane F., *The Dinner Party: Judy Chicago and the Power of Popular Feminism, 1970–2007*, Athens and London: The University of Georgia Press, 2013.

GIANNATTASIO, 2012 Giannattasio, Maria Cristina, 'Francesco Guarini, Onofrio Palumbo e la tradizione iconografica dei sette arcangeli', in *Francesco Guarini: Nuovi contributi I*, ed. Mario Alberto Pavone, Naples: Paparo Editore, 2012, pp. 121–29.

GLASSER, 1971 Glasser, Hannelore, *Artists' Contracts of the Renaissance*, New York and London: Garland, 1971.

GOFFEN, 2002 Goffen, Rona, *Renaissance Rivals: Michelangelo, Leonardo, Raphael, Titian*, London and New Haven: Yale University Press, 2002.

GOLDSTEIN, 1988 Goldstein, Carl, *Visual Fact Over Verbal Fiction: A Study of the Carracci and the Criticism, Theory and Practice of Art in Renaissance and Baroque Italy*, New York and Cambridge: Cambridge University Press, 1988.

GOTLIEB, 2002 Gotlieb, Marc, 'The Painter's Secret: Invention and Rivalry from Vasari to Balzac', *Art Bulletin*, 84/3, 2002, pp. 469–90.

GRABES, 1982 Grabes, Herbert, *The Mutable Glass: Mirror-imagery in Titles and Texts of the Middle Ages and the English Renaissance*, Cambridge: Cambridge University Press, 1982.

GRABSKI, 1985 Grabski, Józef, 'On Seicento Painting in Naples: Some Observations on Bernardo Cavallino, Artemisia Gentileschi and others', *Artibus et historiae*, 6/11, 1985, pp. 23–63.

GRAMPP, 1989 Grampp, William D., *Pricing the Priceless: Art, Artists and Economics*, New York: Basic Books, 1989.

GRANATA, 2012 Granata, Belinda, *Le passioni virtuose: collezionismo e committenze artistiche a Roma del cardinale Alessandro Peretti Montalto (1571–1623)*, Rome: Campisano, 2012.

GREER, 1979 Greer, Germaine, *The Obstacle Race: The Fortunes of Women Painters and their Work*, London: Secker and Warburg, 1979.

GRIMBERG, 1998 Grimberg, Salomon, 'Frida Kahlo: The Self as an End', in *Mirror Images: Women, Surrealism and Self-representation*, ed. Whitney Chadwick, Cambridge, Mass.: MIT Press, 1998, pp. 82–104.

GROSSI AND TRANI, 2009 Grossi, Monica, and Silvia Trani, 'From Universitas to Accademia: Notes and Reflections on the Origins and Early History of the Accademia di San Luca Based on Documents from Its Archives', in *The Accademia Seminars: The Accademia di San Luca in Rome, c. 1590–1635*, ed. Peter M. Lukehart, Washington: CASVA/National Gallery of Art, 2009, pp. 23–41.

GUERZONI, 2011 Guerzoni, Guido, *Apollo and Vulcan: The Art Markets in Italy, 1400–1700* (English translation of *Apollo e Vulcano: I mercati artistici in Italia (1400–1700)*, Venice: Marsilio Editori S.p.A., 2006), East Lansing: Michigan State University Press, 2011.

HAND, 1993 Hand, John Oliver, with the assistance of Sally E. Mansfield, *German Paintings of the Fifteenth through Seventeenth Centuries* (The Collections of the National Gallery of Art Systematic Catalogue), Washington and Cambridge: The National Gallery of Art and Cambridge University Press, 1993.

HARRIS, 1998, Harris, Ann Sutherland, 'Artemisia Gentileschi: The Literate Illiterate, or Learning From Example', in *Docere, delectare, movere: Affetti, devozione e retorica nel linguaggio artistico del primo barocco romano*, ed. Sible de Blaauw, Pieter-Matthijs Gijsbers, Sebastian Schütze, Rome: De Luca, 1998, pp. 105–20.

HARRIS, 2005 Harris, Ann Sutherland, 'Artemisia and Orazio: Drawing Conclusions', in *Artemisia Gentileschi: Taking Stock*, ed. Judith W. Mann, Turnhout: Brepols, 2005, pp. 131–46.

HARRIS, 2007 Harris, Ann Sutherland, 'Sofonisba, Lavinia, Artemisia, and Elisabetta: Thirty Years after *Women Artists, 1550–1950*', in *Italian Women Artists, from Renaissance to Baroque*, ed. Vera Fortunati, Jordana Pomeroy and Claudio Strinati (exh. cat., National Museum of Women in the Arts, Washington), Milan: Skira, 2007, pp. 41–48.

HARRIS, 2018 Harris, Gareth, 'Double Vision: Paris Show Displays Two Mary Magdalen Caravaggios', *Art Newspaper*, 14 November 2018; available at https://www.theartnewspaper.com/news/double-vision-paris-show-displays-two-mary-magdalene-caravaggios

HARTFORD AND DETROIT, 2021–22 *By Her Hand: Artemisia Gentileschi and Women Artists in Italy, 1500–1800*, ed. Eve Straussman-Pflanzer and Oliver Tostmann (exh. cat., Wadsworth Atheneum Museum of Art, Hartford, Conn., and Detroit Institute of Arts, 2021–22), New Haven and London: Yale University Press, 2021.

HASKELL, 1960 Haskell, Francis, 'Art Exhibitions in Seventeenth Century Rome', *Studi Secenteschi*, 1, 1960, pp. 102–21.

HASKELL, 1980 Haskell, Francis, *Patrons and Painters: A Study in the Relations Between Italian Art and Society in the Age of the Baroque*, rev. edn of 1963 edn, New Haven and London: Yale University Press, 1980.

HASKINS, 1993 Haskins, Susan, *Mary Magdalen: Myth and Metaphor*, London: Harper Collins, 1993.

HELLER, 2005 Heller, Deborah, 'History, Art, and Fiction: Anna Banti's Artemisia', in her, *Literary Sisterhoods: Imagining Women Artists*, Montreal and Kingston: McGill-Queen's University Press, 2005, pp. 51–67.

HERSEY, 1993 Hersey, George L., 'Female and Male Art: *Postille* to Garrard's

Artemisia Gentileschi', in *Parthenope's Splendor: Art of the Golden Age in Naples*, ed. Chenault Porter, Jeanne, and Susan S. Munshower, University Park, Pa.: Penn State University Press, 1993, pp. 322–35.

HIBBARD, 1983 Hibbard, Howard, *Caravaggio*, New York: Harper and Row, 1983.

HOFFRICHTER, 1980 Hoffrichter, Frima Fox, 'Artemisia Gentileschi's Judith and a Lost Rubens', *Rutgers Art Review*, 1, 1980, pp. 9–15.

HOLLANDA, 1928 Hollanda, Francisco de, *Four Dialogues on Painting: Rendered into English by Aubrey F.G. Bell*, London: Oxford University Press, 1928.

HONIG, 2014 Honig, Elizabeth, 'Art History and Access: The Catalogue Raisonné as Collaborative Research Site', *NANO*, special issue, *Digital Humanities, Public Humanities*, 5/2014; available at https://nanocrit.com/issues/issue5/art-history-and-access-catalogue-raisonne-collaborative-research-site

HOOGEWERFF, 1953 Hoogewerff, Goffredo J., *Via Margutta: Centro di vita artistica*, Rome: Istituto di studi Romani editore, 1953.

HOPPE, 2014 Hoppe, Ilaria, 'Engendering Pietas Austriaca: The Villa Poggio Imperiale in Florence under Maria Maddalena of Austria', in *The Habsburgs and their Courts in Europe, 1400–1700: Between Cosmopolitism and Regionalism*, ed. Herbert Karner, Ingrid Ciulisová and Bernardo J. García García, Palatium e-Publication, 2014, pp. 181–206.

HUGHES, 1986 Hughes, Anthony, '"An Academy for Doing": Academies, Status and Power in Early Modern Europe', *Oxford Art Journal*, 9/2, 1986, pp. 50–62.

HUMPHREY, 1996 Humphrey, Olga, *The Exception*, Woodstock, Ill.: Dramatic Publishing, 1996.

INDIANAPOLIS, 2006 *Rembrandt: Face to Face*, ed. Stephanie Dickey (exh. cat., Indianapolis Museum of Art), Indianapolis: Indianapolis Museum of Art, 2006.

JACOBS, 1997 Jacobs, Fredrika H., *Defining the Renaissance Virtuosa: Women Artists and the Language of Art History and Criticism*, Cambridge: Cambridge University Press, 1997.

JAMESON, 1866 Jameson, Anna, *The Diary of an Ennuyée*, Boston: Ticknor and Fields, 1866.

JAMESON, 1899 Jameson, Anna, *Characteristics of Women: Moral, Poetical, and Historical*, Boston and New York: Houghton Mifflin and Company, 1889.

JAMIS, 1990 Jamis, Rauda, *Artemisia, ou la renommée*, Paris: Presses de la Renaissance, 1990.

JONES, 2016 Jones, Amelia, 'Feminist Subjects Versus Feminist Effects: The Curating of Feminist Art (Or Is It the Feminist Curating of Art?)', *On Curating*, issue 29, *Curating in Feminist Thought*, May 2016, pp. 5–21; available at https://www.on-curating.org/issue-29-reader/feminist-subjects-versus-feminist-effects-the-curating-of-feminist-art-or-is-it-the-feminist-curating-of-art.html

KAWAI 2018 Kawai, Makiko, 'Le relazioni tra Artemisia Gentileschi e la comunità Fiorentini a Napoli/アルテミジア·ジェンティレスキとナポリのフィレンツェ人コミュニティの関係', *Mediterraneus: Annual Report of the College Mediterranistarum*, 41, 2018, 127–48.

KEITH, 2020 Keith, Larry, 'Looking at Artemisia', in *Artemisia*, ed. Letizia Treves (exh. cat., National Gallery, London), London: National Gallery Publications, 2020, pp. 90–105.

KENNEY, 2021 Kenney, Nancy, 'Getty Acquires a Striking Painting by Artemisia Gentileschi of the Roman Heroine Lucretia', *Art Newspaper*, 30 March 2021; available at https://www.theartnewspaper.com/news/getty-acquires-a-striking-painting-by-artemisia-gentileschi-of-the-roman-heroine-lucretia

KETTERING, 1988 Kettering, Sharon, 'Gift-giving and Patronage in Early Modern France', *French History*, 2/2, 1988, pp. 131–51.

KOOMEN, 2013 Koomen, Arjan R. de, 'The Self-portrait "En Décapité": Interpreting Artistic Self-insertion', in *Disembodied Heads in Medieval and Early Modern Culture*, ed. Barbara Baert, Anita Traninger, Catrien Santing, Leiden: Brill, 2013, pp. 191–221.

KRACH, 1998 Krach, Aaron, 'Art and "Artemisia": A Conversation with Agnès Merlet', *indieWire*, 8 May, 1998; available at https://www.indiewire.com/1998/05/art-and-artemisia-a-conversation-with-agnes-merlet-82870/

KREN, 1980 Kren, Thomas, 'Chi non vuol Baccho: Roeland van Laer's Burlesque Painting About Dutch Artists in Rome', *Simiolus*, 11/2, 1980, pp. 63–80.

KUESSEL, 2019 Kuessel, Christy, 'London's National Gallery bought an Orazio Gentileschi for $29 million with help from the public', *artsy.net*, 19 December 2019; available at https://www.artsy.net/news/artsy-editorial-londons-national-gallery-bought-orazio-gentileschi-painting-29-million-help-public

LABROT, 1992 Labrot, Gérard, *Collections of Paintings in Naples, 1600–1780* (Documents for the History of Collecting: Italian Inventories I, The Provenance Index of the Getty Information Institute), Munich: K. G. Saur, 1992.

LAFFERTY, 2020 Lafferty, Linda, *Fierce Dreamer: A Novel*, New York: Amazon/Lake Union Publishing, 2020.

LANZI, 1792–96 Lanzi, Luigi, *Storia pittorica della Italia, dal risorgimento delle belle arti fin presso al fine del XVIII. Secolo*, Florence, 1792–96, 5th edn, Florence: Giuseppe Molini, 1834.

LAPIERRE, 1998 Lapierre, Alexandra, *Artemisia: Un duel pour l'immortalité*, Paris: Robert Laffont, 1998.

LAPIERRE, 2000 Lapierre, Alexandra, *Artemisia: The Story of a Battle for Greatness*, London: Chatto & Windus, 2000; US edn, *Artemisia: A Novel*, New York: Grove Atlantic, 1999/2000.

LAPIERRE, 2005 Lapierre, Alexandra, 'Artemisia: Art, Facts and Fictions', in *Artemisia Gentileschi: Taking Stock*, ed. Judith W. Mann, Turnhout: Brepols, 2005, pp. 161–70.

LASTRI, 1791–95 Lastri, Marco, *L'Etruria pittrice ovvero storia della pittura Toscana dedotta dai suoi monumenti che si esibiscono in stampa dal secolo X fino al presente*, 2 vols, Florence [Niccolo Pagni and Giuseppe Bardi], 1791–95; available at https://babel.hathitrust.org/cgi/pt?id=gri.ark:/13960/t9b59518w&view=1up&seq=7

LATTUADA, 2000 Lattuada, Riccardo: *Francesco Guarino da Solofra nella pittura napoletana del Seicento (1611–1651)*, Naples: Paparo Edizioni, 2000.

LATTUADA, 2001 Lattuada, Riccardo, 'Artemisia and Naples, Naples and Artemisia', in *Orazio and Artemsia Gentileschi*, ed. Keith Christiansen and Judith W. Mann (exh. cat., Palazzo Venezia, Rome, The Metropolitan Museum of Art, New York, and St Louis Art Museum, 2001–2), New York: The Metropolitan Museum of Art, 2001, pp. 379–91.

LATTUADA AND NAPPI, 2005 Lattuada, Riccardo, and Eduardo Nappi, 'New Documents and Some Remarks on Artemisia's Production in Naples and Elsewhere', in *Artemisia Gentileschi: Taking Stock*, ed. Judith W. Mann, Turnhout: Brepols, 2005, pp. 79–96.

LATTUADA, 2009 Lattuada, Riccardo, 'I percorsi di Andrea Vaccaro (1604–1670)', in Mariaclaudia Izzo, *Nicola Vaccaro (1640–1709): Un artista a Napoli tra Barocco e Arcadia*, Todi: Tau Editrice, 2009, pp. 49–108.

LATTUADA, 2017 Lattuada, Riccardo, 'Unknown Paintings by Artemisia in Naples, and New Points Regarding her Daily Life and *Bottega*', in *Artemisia Gentileschi in a Changing Light*, ed. Sheila Barker, London: Harvey Miller Publishers/London and Turnhout: Brepols, 2017, pp. 187–216.

LAVIN, 1975 Lavin, Marilyn Aronberg, *Seventeenth-Century Barberini Documents and Inventories of Art*, New York: New York University Press, 1975.

LEE, 1940 Lee, Rensselaer W., 'Ut Pictura Poesis: The Humanistic Theory of Painting', *Art Bulletin*, 22/4, 1940, pp. 197–269.

LEMOINE, 1999–2000 Lemoine, Annick, 'Nicolas Régnier, "peintre domestique" du marquis Vincenzo Giustiniani', *Bulletin de l'Association des Historiens de l'Art Italien*, 6, 1999/2000, pp. 28–33.

LENT, 2016 Lent, Tina Olsin, '"My Heart Belongs to Daddy": The Fictionalization of Baroque Artist Artemisia Gentileschi in Contemporary Film and Novels', *Literature/Film Quarterly*, 34/3, 2006, pp. 212–18.

LEONE DE CASTRIS, 1991 Leone de Castris, Pierluigi, *La pittura del Cinquecento a Napoli 1573–1606: L'ultima maniera*, Naples: Electa, 1991.

LEVEY, 1962 Levey, Michael, 'Notes on the Royal Collection, II: Artemisia Gentileschi's "Self Portrait" at Hampton-Court', *Burlington Magazine*, 104/707, 1962, pp. 79–81.

LEVINE, 1987 Levine, David A., 'Pieter van Laer's "Artist's Tavern": An Ironic Commentary on Art', in *Hollandische Genremalerie im 17. Jahrhundert: Symposium Berlin 1984*, ed. Henning Bock and Thomas W. Gaehtgens, Berlin: Mann, 1987, pp. 161–91.

LOCKER, 2015 Locker, Jesse M., *Artemisia Gentileschi: The Language of Painting*, New Haven and London: Yale University Press, 2015.

LOCKER, 2016 Locker, Jesse M., 'Gli anni dimenticati: Artemisia Gentileschi a Venezia', in *Artemisia Gentileschi e il suo tempo*, ed. Nicola Spinosa (exh. cat., Palazzo Braschi, Rome), Milan: Skira, 2016, pp. 43–45.

LOCKER, 2017 Locker, Jesse M., 'Artemisia Gentileschi: The Literary Formation of an Unlearned Artist', in *Artemisia Gentileschi in a Changing Light*, ed. Sheila Barker, London: Harvey Miller Publishers/London and Turnhout: Brepols, 2017, pp. 89–101.

LOCKER, 2020 Locker, Jesse M., *Artemisia Gentileschi, 'A Venetian Lucretia'* (exh. cat., The Matthiesen Gallery, London), London: The Matthiesen Gallery, 2020, pp. 36–63.

LOCKER, 2021 Locker, Jesse M., 'Has a Long-lost Artemisia Finally Come to Light?', *Apollo*, 29 September 2021; available at https://www.apollo-magazine.com/artemisia-gentileschi-rediscovered-magdalene/

LO CONTE, 2021 Lo Conte, Angelo, *The Procaccini and the Business of Painting in Early Modern Milan*, London: Routledge, 2021.

LOFANO, 2014 Lofano, Francesco, 'The Marriage Contract of Bernardo Cavallino', *Burlington Magazine*, 156/December 2014, pp. 801–2.

LOH, 2015 Loh, Maria H., *Still Lives: Death, Desire, and the Portrait of the Old Master*, Princeton and Oxford: Princeton University Press, 2015.

LOLLOBRIGIDA, 2017 Lollobrigida, Consuelo, 'Women Artists in Casa Barberini: Plautilla Bricci, Maddalena Corvini, Artemisia Gentileschi, Anna Maria Vaiani, and Virginia da Vezzo', in *Artemisia Gentileschi in a Changing Light*, ed. Sheila Barker, London: Harvey Miller Publishers/London and Turnhout: Brepols, 2017, pp. 119–30.

LONDON, 2007 *The Art of Italy in the Royal Collection: Renaissance and Baroque*, ed. Lucy Whitaker and Martin Clayton, with contributions by Aislinn Loconte (exh. cat., The Queen's Gallery, London), London: Royal Collection Publications, 2007.

LONDON AND FORT WORTH, 2010 *Salvator Rosa*, ed. Helen Langdon, Xavier F. Salomon and Caterina Volpi (exh. cat., Dulwich Picture Gallery, London, and Kimbell Art Museum, Fort Worth), London: Paul Holberton, 2010.

LONDON, 2020 *Artemisia*, ed. Letizia Treves (exh. cat., National Gallery, London), London: National Gallery Publications, 2020.

LONGHI, 1916 Longhi, Roberto, 'Gentileschi padre e figlia', in *Scritti giovanili, 1912–1922*, Florence: Sansoni, 1961, pp. 219–83 (originally published in *L'arte*, 19, 1916, pp. 245–314).

LORIZZO, 2003 Lorizzo, Loredana, 'Il mercato dell'arte a Roma nel XVII secolo: "pittori bottegari" e "rivenditori di quadri" nei documenti dell'Archivio Storico dell'Accademia di San Luca', in *The Art Market in Italy (15th–17th Centuries)/Il mercato dell'arte in Italia (sec. XV–XVII)*, ed. Marcello Fantoni, Louisa Matthews and Sara Matthews-Grieco, Modena: Franco Cosimo Panini Editore, 2003, pp. 325–336.

LORIZZO, 2011 Lorizzo, Loredana, 'Un nuovo inventario dei beni di Michelangelo Cerquozzi stimato da Mario de' Fiori', *Rivista d'arte*, 5/1, 2011, pp. 283–311.

LOS ANGELES, AUSTIN, PITTSBURGH AND BROOKLYN, 1976–77 *Women Artists, 1550–1950*, ed. Linda Sutherland Harris and Linda Nochlin (exh. cat., Los Angeles County Museum of Art, The University of Texas at Austin, The Museum of Art, Carnegie Institute, Pittsburgh, and Brooklyn Museum), New York: Alfred A. Knopf, 1984.

LOS ANGELES, 1996 *Sexual Politics: Judy Chicago's Dinner Party in Feminist Art History*, ed. Amelia Jones (exh. cat., Armand Hammer Museum of Art and Cultural Center, Berkeley), Berkeley and Los Angeles: Armand Hammer Museum at UCLA and the University of California Press, 1996.

LOS ANGELES, 2007 *Taddeo and Federico Zuccaro: Artist-brothers in Renaissance Rome*, ed. Julian Brooks (exh. cat., J. Paul Getty Museum, Los Angeles), Los Angeles: J. Paul Getty Trust Publications, 2007.

LUKEHART, 2009 Lukehart, Peter M., 'Visions and Divisions in the Early History of the Accademia di San Luca', in *The Accademia Seminars: The Accademia di San Luca in Rome, c. 1590–1635*, ed. Peter M. Lukehart, Washington: CASVA/National Gallery of Art, 2009, pp. 161–95.

LUKEHART, 2017 Lukehart, Peter M., 'Life Drawing Lessons: Accademia and "accademie dal vero" at the Turn of the Seventeenth Century', in *Il disegno dal vero come pratica storica e sapere contemporaneo: L'Accademia à l'Académie*, ed. Sarah Linford (exh. cat., Museo Pietro Canonica, Rome), Rome: Editoriale Artemide, 2017, pp. 33–41.

LURIE, 1993 Lurie, Ann Tzeutschler, '"The Repentant Magdalene" by Simon Vouet', *The Bulletin of the Cleveland Museum of Art*, 80/4, 1993, pp. 158–63.

LUZZATI, 1974 Luzzati, Michele, 'Cambi', *Dizionario Biografico degli Italiani*, 17, 1974; available at https://www.treccani.it/enciclopedia/cambi_(Dizionario-Biografico)

MCCULLOUGH, 2019 McCullough, Joy, *Blood Water Paint*, New York: Penguin Books, 2019.

MCHAM, 2008 McHam, Sarah Blake, 'Reflections of Pliny in Giovanni Bellini's Woman with a Mirror', *Artibus et Historiae*, 29/58, 2008, pp. 157–71.

MCTIGHE, 2020 McTighe, Sheila, 'Role Model', review of London, 2020, *Apollo*, 192/691, 2020, pp. 80–81.

MADRID, 2019–2020 *A Tale of Two Women Painters: Sofonisba Anguissola and Lavinia Fontana*, ed. Leticia Ruiz (exh. cat. Museo Nacional del Prado, Madrid, 2019–20), Madrid: Museo Nacional del Prado, 2019.

MALVASIA, 1678 Malvasia, Carlo Cesare, *Felsina Pittrice: Vite dei pittori bolognesi*, Bologna (1678), ed. Marcella Brascaglia, 2 vols, Bologna: Edizioni ALFA, 1971.

MANCINI, 1956–57 Mancini, Giulio, *Considerazioni sulla pittura*, ed. Adriana Marucchi and Luigi Salerno, 2 vols, Rome: Accademia nazionale dei Lincei, 1956–57.

MANN, 2005a Mann, Judith W., 'Introduction: Taking Stock of Artemisia and her Symposium', in *Artemisia Gentileschi: Taking Stock*, ed. Judith W. Mann, Turnhout: Brepols, 2005, pp. 1–18.

MANN, 2005b Mann, Judith W., 'The Myth of Artemisia as Chameleon: A New Look at the London *Allegory of Painting*', in *Artemisia Gentileschi: Taking Stock*, ed. Judith W. Mann, Turnhout: Brepols, 2005, pp. 51–77.

MANN, 2009 Mann, Judith W., 'Identity Signs: Meanings and Methods in Artemisia Gentileschi's Signatures', *Renaissance Studies*, 23/1, 2009, pp. 71–107.

MANN, 2016 Mann, Judith W., 'Artemisia a Roma 1606–1613: inizi strategici e stilistici', in *Artemisia Gentileschi e il suo tempo*, ed. Nicola Spinosa (exh. cat., Palazzo Braschi, Rome), Milan: Skira, 2016, pp. 13–21.

MANN, 2017 Mann, Judith W., 'Deciphering Artemisia: Three New Narratives and How They Expand Our Understanding', in *Artemisia Gentileschi in a Changing Light*, ed. Sheila Barker, London: Harvey Miller Publishers/London and Turnhout: Brepols, 2017, pp. 167–86.

MANUTH, VAN LEEUWEN AND KOLDEWEIJ, 2016 Manuth, Volker, Rudie van Leeuwen and Jos Koldeweij (eds), *Example or Alter Ego? Aspects of the Portrait Historié in Western Art from Antiquity to the Present*, Turnhout: Brepols, 2016.

D. MARSHALL, 1993 Marshall, David Ryley, *Viviano and Niccolò Codazzi and the Baroque Architectural Fantasy*, Rome: Jandi Sapi, 1993.

MARSHALL, 1993 Marshall, Christopher R., 'Talking Heads: Physiognomy and the Grotesque in "Judith and Holofernes"', *Aedon*, 1/1, 1993, pp. 43–52.

MARSHALL, 1998 Marshall, Christopher R., '"Causa di Stravaganze": Order and Anarchy in Domenico Gargiulo's *Revolt of Masaniello*', *Art Bulletin*, 53/3, 1998, pp. 478–97.

MARSHALL, 2000 Marshall, Christopher R., '"Senza il minimo scrupolo": Artists as Dealers in Seventeenth-Century Naples', *Journal of the History of Collections*, 12/1, 2000, pp. 15–34.

MARSHALL, 2004 Marshall, Christopher R., 'Markets, Money and Artistic Manoeuvres: Bernardo Cavallino and the Grand Manner', in *'The Italians' in Australia: Studies in Renaissance and Baroque Art*, ed. David R. Marshall, Florence: Centro Di, 2004, pp. 41–48.

MARSHALL, 2005a Marshall, Christopher R., 'An Early Inventory Reference and New Technical Information for Bernardo Cavallino's "Triumph of Galatea"', *Burlington Magazine*, 147/1222, 2005, pp. 40–44.

MARSHALL, 2005b Marshall, Christopher R., 'The Spirit of Caesar in This Soul of a Woman: Artemisia Gentileschi and the Will to Succeed, 1629–54', *Melbourne Art Journal*, 8, 2005, pp. 4–27.

MARSHALL, 2006 Marshall, Christopher R., 'Dispelling Negative Perceptions: Dealers Promoting Artists in Seventeenth-Century Naples', in *Mapping Markets for Paintings in Europe and the New World, 1450–1750*, ed. Neil de Marchi and Hans J. Van Miegroet, Brussels: Brepols, 2006, pp. 348–64.

MARSHALL, 2010 Marshall, Christopher R., 'Naples', in *Painting for Profit: The Economic Lives of Seventeenth-century Italian Painters*, ed. Richard E. Spear and Philip Sohm, New Haven and London: Yale University Press, 2010, pp. 115–44.

MARSHALL, 2016 Marshall, Christopher R., *Baroque Naples and the Industry of Painting: The World in the Workbench*, New Haven and London: Yale University Press, 2016.

MARSHALL, 2017a Marshall, Christopher R., '"Per antipatia ch'have la filosofia di serrarsi ne' palazzo de' ricchi": Salvator Rosa and the quest for Ennobled Prices', in *L'iconografia dei filosofi antichi nell'arte del Seicento in Italia*, ed. Stefan Albl and Francesco Lofano, Rome: Istituto Austriaco di Studi Storici, 2017, pp. 367–91.

MARSHALL, 2017b Marshall, Christopher R., 'Prices, Payments and Career Strategies: Economic Considerations in the work of Ribera and his Contemporaries', in *Davanti al naturale: Contributo sul movimento caravaggesco a Napoli*, ed. Gianni Papi and Francesco de Luca, Milan: Officina Libraria, 2017, pp. 64–83.

MARSHALL, 2017–18 Marshall, Christopher R., '"More Beautiful than Nature Itself": The Early Commercial and Critical Fortunes of Neapolitan Baroque Still Life', *Baroque Naples: Place and Displacement, Special Issue Open Arts Journal*, issue 6, winter 2017/18, pp. 129–45.

MENZIO, 1981/2004 Menzio, Eva (ed.), with a foreword by Roland Barthes, *Artemisia Gentileschi/Agostino Tassi: atti di un processo per stupro*, Milan: Edizioni delle Donne, 1981, republished as *Lettere/Artemisia Gentileschi, precedute da Atti di un processo per stupro*, Milan: Abscondita, 2004.

MILAN, 1951 *Mostra del Caravaggio e dei caravaggeschi*, ed. Roberto Longhi (exh. cat., Palazzo Reale, Milan), Florence: Sansoni, 1951.

MILAN, 2004 *Caravaggio, la Medusa: Lo splendore degli scudi da parata del Cinquecento*, ed. Susanne E.L. Probst et al. (exh. cat., Museo Bagatti Valsecchi, Milan), Milan: Silvana Editoriale, 2004.

MILAN, 2011 *Artemisia Gentileschi: The Story of a Passion*, ed. Roberto Contini and Francesco Solinas (exh. cat., Palazzo Reale, Milan), Milan: 24 ORE Cultura, 2011.

MILAN, 2019–20 *Artemisia Gentileschi: L'Adorazione dei Magi*, ed. Nadia Righi and Roberto della Rocca (exh. cat., Chiostri di Sant'Eustorgio, Museo Diocesano, Milan, 2019–2020), Milan: Carlo Maria Martini, 2019.

MILAN, 2021 *Le signore dell'arte: storie di donne tra '500 e '600*, ed. Annamaria Bava, Gioia Mori and Alain Tapié (exh. cat., Palazzo Reale, Milan), Milan: Skira, 2021.

MILLAR, 1958–60 Millar, Oliver, 'Abraham van der Doort's Catalogue of the Collections of Charles I', *Walpole Society*, 37, 1958–60, pp. iii-256.

MILLAR, 1970–72 Millar, Oliver, 'The Inventories and Valuations of the King's Goods, 1649–51', *Walpole Society*, 43, 1970–72, pp. i–458.

MISSIRINI, 1823 Missirini, Melchiorre: *Memorie per servire alla storia della Romana Accademia di S. Luca fino alla morte di Antonio Canova*, Rome: De Romanis, 1823.

MITCHELL AND PARSONS, 2012 Mitchell, Kate, and Nicola Parsons, 'Reading the Represented Past: History and Fiction from 1700 to the Present', in *Reading Historical Fiction: The Revenant and Remembered Past*, London: Palgrave Macmillan, 2012, pp. 1–18.

MODESTI, 2004 Modesti, Adelina, *Elisabetta Sirani: Una Virtuosa del Seicento Bolognese*, Bologna: Editore Compositori, 2004.

MODESTI, 2014 Modesti, Adelina, *Elisabetta Sirani 'Virtuosa': Women's Cultural Production in Early Modern Bologna*, Turnhout: Brepols, 2014.

MODESTI, 2016 Modesti, Adelina, 'A Newly Discovered Late Work by Artemisia Gentileschi: *Susanna and the Elders* of 1652', in *Women Artists in Early Modern Italy: Careers, Fame and Collectors*, ed.Sheila Barker, Turnhout: Brepols/Harvey Miller Publishers, 2016, pp. 135–49.

MONTPELLIER, 2015 *L'âge d'or de la peinture â Naples de Ribera a Giordano*, ed. Michel Hilaire and Nicola Spinosa (exh. cat., Musée Fabre, Montpellier), Paris: Lienart éditions, 2015.

MONTAGU, 1989 Montagu, Jennifer, *Roman Baroque Sculpture: The Industry of Art*, New Haven and London: Yale University Press, 1989.

MOORHEAD, 2020 Moorhead, Joanna, 'National Gallery hopes Artemisia exhibition will inspire public to "get through the Covid crisis"', *Art Newspaper*, 29 September 2020; available at https://www.theartnewspaper.com/news/national-gallery-hopes-artemisia-exhibition-will-inspire-public-to-get-through-the-covid-crisis

MOORHOUSE, 2019 Moorhouse, Paul, 'Cindy Sherman's Personae', in *Cindy Sherman*, ed. Paul Moorhouse (exh. cat., National Portrait Gallery, London, 2019), London: National Portrait Gallery, 2019, pp. 11–22.

MORANDI, 1995 Morandi, Clarissa: *Ritratti Medicei del Seicento*, Florence: Arnaud, 1995.

MORETTI, 2005 Moretti, Lina, 'La raccolta Lumaga: Giovanni Andrea Lumaga', *Ricerche sul '600 napoletano, Saggi e documenti 2005, rubrica per Luca Giordano*, Naples: Electa, 2005, pp. 27–64.

MORSELLI, 2010 Morselli, Raffaella, 'Bologna', in *Painting for Profit: The Economic Lives of Seventeenth-century Italian Painters*, ed. Richard E. Spear and Philip Sohm, New Haven and London: Yale University Press, 2010, pp. 145–71.

MORSELLI, 2020 Morselli, Raffaella, 'Il diario di lavoro di Elisabetta Sirani e la gestione familiare dei suoi profitti', in *Amica veritas: Studi di storia dell'arte in onore di Claudio Strinati*, ed. Antonio Vannugli, Rome: Edizioni Quasar, 2020, pp. 307–20.

MOSCOW, 2019 *Kartiny iz sobranij Muzeja i Korolevskogo parka Kapodimonte, Neapol' i GMII im. A.S. Puškina*, ed. Viktorija Markova and Džejms P. Anno (exh. cat., The Pushkin State Museum of Fine Arts, Moscow), Moscow, 2019.

MUNZ AND IZAT, 2023 Munz, Niko and Adelaide Izat, 'Artemisia Gentileschi's "Susanna and the Elders" Painted for Henrietta Maria', *Burlington Magazine*, 165/1447, October, 2023, pp. 105–-73.

MURPHY, 2003 Murphy, Caroline P., *Lavinia Fontana: A Painter and her Patrons in Sixteenth-century Bologna*, New Haven and London: Yale University Press, 2003.

MURPHY, 2007 Murphy, Caroline P., 'The Economics of the Woman Artist', in *Italian Women Artists, from Renaissance to Baroque*, ed. Vera Fortunati, Jordana Pomeroy and Claudio Strinati (exh. cat., National Museum of Women in the Arts, Washington), Milan: Skira, 2007, pp. 23–30.

NAPLES, 1984 *Civiltà del Seicento a Napoli*, ed. Raffaello Causa et al. (exh. cat., Museo di Capodimonte and Museo Diego Aragona Pignatelli Cortes, Naples), 2 vols, Naples: Electa, 1984.

NAPLES, 1986 Museo Nazionale di San Martino, *Il Quarto del Priore*, ed. Luciana Arbace et al. (coll. cat.), Naples: Sergio Civita Editore, 1986.

NAPLES, 1988 No author [Research Department and the Historical Department of Banco di Napoli], *The Historical Archive of Banco di Napoli*, Naples: Francesco Giannini & Figli, 1988.

NAPLES, 1991 *Battistello Caracciolo e il primo naturalismo a Napoli*, ed. Ferdinando Bologna (exh. cat., Castel Sant'Elmo, Naples), Naples: Electa, 1991.

NAPLES, 1992 *Jusepe de Ribera, 1591–1652*, ed. Alfonso E. Peréz Sanchéz and Nicola Spinosa (exh. cat., Castel Sant'Elmo, Certosa di San Martino and Cappella del Tesoro di San Gennaro, Naples), Naples: Electa, 1992.

NAPLES AND LONDON, 2004–5 *Caravaggio: The Final Years*, ed. Silvia Cassani and Maria Sapio (exh. cat., Museo di Capodimonte, Naples, and National Gallery, London, 2004–5), Naples: Electa, 2004.

NAPLES, 2009 *Ritorno al barocco: da Caravaggio a Vanvitelli*, ed. Nicola Spinosa (exh. cat., Museo di Capodimonte, Certosa e Museo di San Martino, Castel Sant' Elmo, Museo Pignatelli, Museo Duca di Martina and Palazzo Reale, Naples), 2 vols, Naples: arte'm, 2009–10.

NAPLES AND MADRID, 2011–12 *Il giovane Ribera tra Roma, Parma e Napoli, 1608–1624*, ed. José Milicua, Javier Portus and Nicola Spinosa (exh. cat., Museo di Capodimonte, Naples, and Museo Nacional del Prado, Madrid, 2011–12), Naples: arte'm, 2011.

NAPLES, 2022 *Artemisia Gentileschi a Napoli*, ed. Antonio Ernesto Denunzio and Giuseppe Porzio (exh. cat., Galleria d'Italia, Naples, 2022–23), Milan: Skira, 2022.

NAPPI, 1983 Nappi, Eduardo, 'Pittori del '600 a Napoli: Notizie inedite dai documenti dell'Archivio Storico del Banco di Napoli', in *Ricerche sul '600 napoletano: Saggi vari*, Milan: L&T, 1983, pp. 73–80.

NAPPI, 1990a Nappi, Eduardo, 'La chiesa di Sant'Eframo Vecchio in Napoli', *Studi e ricerche francescane*, 19, 1990, pp. 117–84.

NAPPI, 1990b Nappi, Eduardo, 'Un regesto di documenti editi ed inediti, tratti prevalentemente dall'Archivio Storico del Banco di Napoli, riguardanti Giuseppe Ribera e una conferma della presenza a Napoli nel novembre 1630 di Velázquez', in *Ricerche sul '600 napoletano*, Milan: L&T, 1990, pp. 177–86.

NAPPI, 1991 Nappi, Eduardo, 'Momenti della vita di Luca Giordano nei documenti dell'Archivio Storico del Banco di Napoli', in *Ricerche sul '600 napoletano*, Milan: L&T, 1991, pp. 157–182.

NAPPI, 1992 Nappi, Eduardo (ed.), *Ricerche sul '600 napoletano: Catalogo delle pubblicazioni edite dal 1883 al 1990, riguardanti le opere di architetti, pittori, scultori, marmorari ed intagliatori per i secoli XVI e XVII, pagate tramite gli antichi banchi pubblici napoletani*, Milan: L&T, 1992.

NEW YORK, 1985 *Liechtenstein: The Princely Collections*, ed. Kathleen Howard (exh. cat., The Metropolitan Museum of Art, New York), New York: The Metropolitan Museum of Art, 1985.

NEW YORK AND NAPLES, 1985 *The Age of Caravaggio*, ed. Mina Gregori (exh. cat., The Metropolitan Museum of Art, New York, and Museo Nazionale di Capodimonte, Naples), New York and Milan: The Metropolitan Museum of Art and Electa, 1985.

NEW YORK, 1992 *Jusepe de Ribera, 1591–1652*, ed. Alfonso E. Pérez Sánchez and Nicola Spinosa (exh. cat., The Metropolitan Museum of Art, New York), New York: The Metropolitan Museum of Art, 1992.

NEW YORK, 1998 *Heroic Armor of the Italian Renaissance: Filippo Negroli and His Contemporaries*, ed. Stuart W. Phyrr, José-A. Godoy and Silvio Leydi (exh. cat., The Metropolitan Museum of Art, New York), New York: The Metropolitan Museum of Art, 1998.

NICHOLS, 2013 Nichols, Tom, 'The Master as Monument: Titian and his Images', *Artibus et Historiae*, 67/34, 2013, pp. 219–38.

NICOLACI, 2011 Nicolaci, Michele, 'Appendix I: Biographical Conspectus of Artemisia Lomi Gentileschi (Rome 1593 – Naples after 1654)', in *Artemisia Gentileschi: The Story of a Passion*, ed. Roberto Contini and Francesco Solinas (exh. cat., Palazzo Reale, Milan), Milan: 24 ORE Cultura, 2011, pp. 258–69.

NOCHLIN, 1971 Nochlin, Linda, 'Why Have There Been No Great Women Artists?', *ArtNews*, January 1971, pp. 1–43.

NOVELLI RADICE, 1989 Novelli Radice, Magda, 'Una traccia per Annella de Rosa', *Napoli Nobilissima*, 28/1–6, 1989, pp. 147–54.

OLOMOUC, 2013 *Artemisia Gentileschi, David rozjímající nad Goliášovou hlavou*, ed. Marie Dočekalová (exh. cat., Muzeum umění Olomouc), Olomouc: Muzeum umění Olomouc, 2013.

O'MALLEY, 2005 O'Malley, Michelle, *The Business of Art: Contracts and the Commissioning Process in Renaissance Italy*, New Haven and London: Yale University Press, 2005.

ORBAAN, 1927 Orbaan, Johannes A., 'Florentijnsche Gegevens IV', *Oud Holland*, 44, 1927, pp. 280–84.

ORLANDO, 2019 Orlando, Anna, 'I Gentileschi a Genova: Dati certi e incerti per Orazio, Artemisia, Francesco e Giulio', in *Caravaggio e i Genovesi*, ed. Anna Orlando (exh. cat., Palazzo della Meridiana, Genoa) Genoa: Sagep Editori, 2019, pp. 150–73.

ORSO, 1986 Orso, Steven N.: *Philip IV and the Decoration of the Alcázar of Madrid*, Princeton: Princeton University Press, 1986.

OSTROW, 2000 Ostrow, Steven F., review of Bissell, 1999, *CAA.reviews*, 19 January 2000; available at http://www.caareviews.org/reviews/157

PACELLI, 1979 Pacelli, Vincenzo, 'La collezione di Francesco Emanuele Pinto, Principe di Ischitella', *Storia dell'arte*, 35/37, 1979, pp. 165–204.

PACELLI, 1987 Pacelli, Vincenzo, 'La Quadreria di Vincenzo D'Andrea guirista e rivoluzionario, da un inventario del 1649', in *Ricerche sul '600 napoletano*, Milan: L&T, 1987, pp. 145–52.

PACELLI, 2008 Pacelli, Vincenzo, *Giovan Francesco de Rosa detto Pacecco de Rosa, 1607–1656*, Naples: paparo edizioni, 2008.

PACELLI, 2012 Pacelli, Vincenzo (ed.), *Caravaggio tra arte e scienza*, Naples: Paparo, 2012.

PALIAGA, 2011 Paliaga, Franco, 'Una "Santa Caterina" di Artemisia Gentileschi', *Storia dell'arte*, 129, 2011, pp. 57–63.

PANARELLO, 2011/2014 Panarello, Mario, 'Documenti inediti sulla vita dei pittori Francesco Antonio e Giovan Battista Colimodio da Orsomarso', *Esperide*, 4/7–8, 2011 [published 2014], pp. 98–110.

PAOLILLO, 1985 Paolillo, Ciro, 'Un inventario dei beni del principe di San Martino redatto da Filippo Vitale ed Andrea Abate', in *Ricerche sul '600 napoletano*, Milan: L&T, 1985, pp. 113–32.

PAPI, 1991, Papi, Gianni, 'Nuove considerazioni sul naturalismo caravaggesco a Firenze', *Artemisia*, ed. Roberto Contini and Gianni Papi (exh. cat., Casa Buonarroti, Florence), Rome: De Luca, 1991, pp. 197–211.

PAPI, 1998, Papi, Gianni, 'Sul soggiorno fiorentino di Theodor Rombouts', *Paragone*, 49/577, 1998, pp. 26–38.

PAPI, 1994, Papi, Gianni, 'Artemisia, senza dimora conosciuta', *Paragone*, 45/529-531-533, 1994, pp. 197–202.

PAPI, 2002 Papi, Gianni, 'Il "David" Spada di Orazio Gentileschi, opera di collaborazione', *Paragone*, 53/46, 2002, pp. 43–48.

PAPI, 2005 Papi, Gianni, 'Ribera a Roma: Dopo Caravaggio una seconda rivoluzione', in *Caravaggio e l'Europa: il movimento caravaggesco internazionale da Caravaggio a Mattia Preti*, ed. Vittorio Sgarbi et al. (exh. cat., Palazzo Reale, Milan, and Liechtenstein Museum, Vienna, 2005–6), Milan: Skira editore, 2005, pp. 45–56.

PAPI, 2007 Papi, Gianni: *Ribera a Roma*, Cremona: Edizioni dei Soncino, 2007.

PAPI, 2011 Papi, Gianni, review of Milan, 2011, *Burlington Magazine*, 153/1305, December, 2011, pp. 846–47.

PAPI, 2012 Papi, Gianni, 'Artemisia Gentileschi's "Suffer the Little Children to Come Unto Me"', *Burlington Magazine*, 154/1317, December, 2012, pp. 828–31.

PAPI, 2017 Papi, Gianni, '*Mary Magdalene in Ecstasy* and the *Madonna of the Svezzamento*: Two Masterpieces by Artemisia', in *Artemisia Gentileschi in a Changing Light*, ed. Sheila Barker, London: Harvey Miller Publishers/London and Turnhout: Brepols, 2017, pp. 147–66.

PAPI, BISCHOFF AND FORD, 2019 Papi, Gianni, Nina Gram Bischoff and Thierry Ford, 'Orazio and Artemisia Gentileschi and "Judith and her Maidservant" in Oslo', *Burlington Magazine*, 161/1396, 2019, pp. 532–43.

PAPI, GILLESPIE AND CHAPLIN, 2020 Papi, Gianni, Simon Gillespie and Tracey Chaplin, 'A "David and Goliath" by Artemisia Gentileschi Rediscovered', *Burlington Magazine*, 162/1404, 2020, pp. 188–95.

PARIS, 2012 *Artemisia: pouvoir, gloire et passions d'une femme peintre*, ed. Roberto Ciardi, Roberto Contini and Francesco Solinas (exh. cat., Musée Maillol, Paris), Paris: Gallimard, 2012.

PARMA, NAPLES AND ROME, 2001 *Giovanni Lanfranco: Un pittore barocco tra Parma, Roma e Napoli*, ed. Erich Schleier (exh. cat., Reggia di Colorno, Parma, Castel Sant'Elmo, Naples and Palazzo Venezia, Rome) Naples: Electa, 2001.

PASCULLI FERRARA, 1990 Pasculli Ferrara, Mimma [Domenica], 'Precisazioni cronologiche su Onofrio Palumbo', in *Ricerche sul '600 napoletano*, Milan: L&T, 1990, pp. 201–5.

PASSERI, 1772 Passeri, Giovanni Battista, *Vite de' Pittori, Scultori et Architetti che hanno lavorato in Rome, morti dal 1641 fino al 1673*, Rome, 1772, reissued with notes by Jacob Hess, Leipzig and Vienna: Verlag Heinrich Keller/Verlag Antonio Schroll & Co., 1934.

PAVONE, 2012 Pavone, Mario Alberto, 'Onofrio Palumbo e Francesco Guarini: due percorsi paralleli', in *Francesco Guarini: Nuovi contributi I*, ed. Mario Alberto Pavone, Naples: Paparo Editore, 2012, pp. 107–20

PEGAZZANO, 1997 Pegazzano, Donatella, 'Documenti per Tommaso Salini', *Paragone*, 48/571–73, 1997, pp. 131–46.

PEPPER, 1984a Pepper, D. Stephen, 'Baroque Paintings at Colnaghi's, New York', *Burlington Magazine*, 126/974, 1984, pp. 313–16.

PEPPER, 1984b Pepper, D. Stephen, *Guido Reni: A Complete Catalogue of his Works with an Introductory Text*, Oxford: Phaidon, 1984.

PETRELLI, 2008 Petrelli, Flavia, 'Una luce su Diana de Rosa nota in arte come Annella', in *Ricerche sul '600 napoletano: Saggi e documenti 2008*, Naples: Electa, 2009, pp. 87–92.

PIANIGIANI, 2018 Pianigiani, Gaia, 'For Italy's Abused Women, a Legal Labyrinth Compounds the Wounds', *New York Times*, 11 August 2018; available at https://www.nytimes.com/2018/08/11/world/europe/italy-abused-women.html?auth=login-email&login=email

PINCITORE, 2017 Pincitore, Alberto, *Giovanni Battista Colimodio: Vita e opere di un pittore del Seicento*, Rossano: Ferrari editore, 2017.

PISA, 2013 *Artemisia, la musa Clio e gli anni napoletani*, ed. Roberto Contini and Francesco Solinas (exh. cat., Palazzo Blu, Pisa), Rome: De Luca, 2013.

PISA, 2019–20 *Simon Vouet e il ritratto di Artemisia*, exh. [without catalogue], Palazzo Blu, Pisa, 2019–20.

PITHERS, 2019 Pithers, Ellie 'Couture Comes To Christie's With An Extravagant Dolce & Gabbana Exhibition', *Vogue*, London, 23 November 2019; available at https://www.vogue.co.uk/news/article/dolce-gabbana-couture-christies-exhibition-2019

PON, 1996 Pon, Lisa, 'Michelangelo's Lives: Sixteenth-century Books by Vasari, Condivi and Others', *The Sixteenth Century Journal*, 27/4, 1996, pp. 1015–37.

PORTÚS PÉREZ, 2011 Portús Pérez, Javier, *Ribera*, Barcelona: Ediciones Poligrafa, 2011.

PORZIO, 2006 Porzio, Giuseppe, 'Appunti sul catalogo di Onofrio Palumbo', in *Ottant'anni di un Maestro: Omaggio a Ferdinando Bologna*, ed. Francesco Abbate, Naples: Paparo, 2006, pp. 425–33.

PORZIO, 2014 Porzio, Giuseppe, *La scuola di Ribera: Giovanni Dò, Bartolomeo Passante, Enrico Fiammingo*, Naples: arte'm, 2014.

PORZIO, 2015 Porzio, Giuseppe, 'Novità e conferme per Antonio de Bellis', *Bolletino d'arte*, 100/25, 2015, pp. 101–10.

PORZIO, 2021 Porzio, Giuseppe, 'Artemisia a Napoli: Nuovi dipinti, vecchie questioni', in *Ricerche sull'arte a Napoli in età moderna: saggi e documenti, 2020–2021*, Naples: arte,m, 2021, pp. 106–23.

PORZIO, 2022 Porzio, Giuseppe, 'Artemisia a Napoli: Novità, problemi, prospettive', in *Artemisia Gentileschi a Napoli*, ed. Antonio Ernesto Denunzio and Giuseppe

Porzio (exh. cat., Galleria d'Italia, Naples, 2022–23), Milan: Skira, 2022, pp. 27–49.

POSNER, 1971 Posner, Donald, 'Caravaggio's Homo-erotic Early Works', *The Art Quarterly*, 34, 1971, pp. 301–24.

POTSDAM, 2019 *Baroque Pathways: The National Galleries Barberini Corsini in Rome*, ed. Ortrud Westheider and Michael Philipp (exh. cat., Museum Barberini, Potsdam), Munich, London and New York: Prestel, 2019.

PROCACCI, 1967 Procacci, Ugo (ed.), *La casa Buonarroti a Firenze*, Milan: Electa, 1967.

PROTA GIURLEO, 1951 Prota Giurleo, Ulisse, 'Un complesso familiare di artisti napoletani del secolo XVII', *Napoli: Rivista Municipale*, 2/7–8, 1951, pp. 19–32.

PROTA GIURLEO, 1955 Prota Giurleo, Ulisse, 'Notizie su Massimo Stanzione e sul presunto manoscritto falsificato dal De Dominici', *Napoli: Rivista Municipale*, 81/11, 1955, pp. 17–32.

PUGLISI, 1998 Puglisi, Catherine R., *Caravaggio*, London: Phaidon, 1998.

RADINI TEDESCHI, 2011 Radini Tedeschi, Daniele, *Caravaggio: Il corpus filologico completo indagato attraverso simboli e ideali*, Rome: La Rosa dei Venti, 2011.

REYBURN, 2019 Reyburn, Scott, 'Jeff Koons "Rabbit" Sets Auction Record for Most Expensive Work by Living Artist', *New York Times*, 15 May 2019; available at https://advance.lexis.com/api/document?collection=news&id=urn:contentItem:5W46-DFW1-DXY4-X0HK-00000-00&context=1516831

RICCIARDI, 2000 Ricciardi, Emilio, 'Collezionisti del XVII secolo in Napoli: Santi Francucci e Camillo Colonna', *Ricerche sul '600 napoletano, 2000*, Naples: Electa, 2001, pp. 52–60.

RIPA, 1593 Ripa, Cesare, *Iconologia; overro Descrittione dell'imagini universali cavati dall'antichità, et da altri luoghi*, Rome, 1593, reprinted Venice: Presso Cristoforo Tomasini, 1645.

RIZZO, 1984 Rizzo, Vincenzo, 'Documenti su Cavallino, Corenzio, De Matteis, Giordano, Lanfranco, Solimena, Stanzione, Zamperi ed altri, del 1636 al 1715', in *Seicento napoletano: Arte, Costume, Ambiente*, Milan: Edizioni di Comunità, 1984, pp. 314–33.

RIZZO, 1987 Rizzo, Vincenzo, 'Altre notizie su pittori, scultori ed architetti napoletani del Seicento (dai documenti dell Archivio Storico del Banco di Napoli)', *Ricerche sul '600 napoletano*, Milan: L&T, 1987, pp. 153–75.

ROCCASECCA, 2009 Roccasecca, Pietro, 'Teaching in the Studio of the "Accademia del Disegno dei pittori, scultori e architetti di Roma" (1594–1636)', in *The Accademia Seminars: The Accademia di San Luca in Rome, c. 1590–1635*, ed.Peter M. Lukehart, Washington: CASVA/National Gallery of Art, 2009, pp. 123–59.

RÖTTGEN, 2002 Röttgen, Herwarth, *Il Cavalier Giuseppe Cesari d'Arpino: Un grande pittore nella spendore della fama e nell'inconstanza della fortuna*, Rome: Ugo Bozzi Editore, 2002.

ROME, 1996 *Domenichino, 1581–1641*, ed. Richard E. Spear et al. (exh. cat., Palazzo Venezia, Rome, 1996–97), Milan: Electa, 1996.

ROME, NEW YORK AND ST LOUIS, 2001–2 *Orazio and Artemsia Gentileschi*, ed. Keith Christiansen and Judith W. Mann (exh. cat., Palazzo Venezia, Rome, The Metropolitan Museum of Art, New York, and St Louis Art Museum, 2001–2), New York: The Metropolitan Museum of Art, 2001.

ROME, 2008 *Agostino Tassi (1578–164): Un paesaggista tra immaginario e realtà*, ed. Patrizia Cavazzini (exh. cat., Palazzo di Venezia, Rome), Rome: Iride per il terzo millennio, 2008.

ROME, 2011 *Roma al tempo di Caravaggio, 1600–1630*, ed. Rossella Vodret (exh. cat., Museo Nazionale di Palazzo Venezia, Rome), 2 vols, Milan: Skira, 2011.

ROME, 2014–15 *I bassifondi del barocco: La Roma del vizio e della miseria*, ed. Francesca Cappelletti and Annick Lemoine (exh. cat., Villa Medici, Rome, and Petit Palais, Paris), Milan: Officina Libraria, 2014.

ROME, 2016 *Artemisia Gentileschi e il suo tempo*, ed. Nicola Spinosa (exh. cat., Palazzo Braschi, Rome), Milan: Skira, 2016.

ROME, 2021–22 *Caravaggio e Artemisia: La sfida di 'Giuditta'. Violenza e seduzione nella pittura tra Cinquecento e Seicento*, ed. Maria Cristina Terzaghi (exh. cat., Galleria Nazionale d'Arte Antica di Palazzo Barberini, Rome, 2021–22), Rome: Officina Libraria, 2021.

ROSSI, 1984 Rossi, Sergio, 'La Compagnia di San Luca nel Cinquecento e la sua evoluzione in accademia', in *Ricerche per la storia religiosa di Roma*, 5: *Le confraternite romane, esperienza religiosa, società, committenza artistica*, Rome: Edizioni di Storia e Letteratura, 1984, pp. 367–94.

RUFFO, 1916 Ruffo, Vincenzo, 'Galleria Ruffo nel secolo XVII in Messina (con lettere di pittori ed altri documenti inediti)', *Bollettino d'arte*, 1916, 1–2, pp. 21–64; 3–4, pp. 95–128; 5–6, pp. 165–92; 7–8, pp. 237–56; 9–10, pp. 284–320; 11–12, pp. 369–88.

RUOTOLO, 1973 Ruotolo, Renato, 'Collezioni e mecenati napoletani del XVII secolo', *Napoli Nobilissima*, 12/3, 1973, pp. 118–19; 12/4, 1973, pp. 145–53.

RUOTOLO, 1974 Ruotolo, Renato, 'La raccolta Carafa di S. Lorenzo', *Napoli Nobilissima*, 13/5, 1974, pp. 161–68.

RUOTOLO, 1977 Ruotolo, Renato, 'Aspetti del collezionismo napoletano: il Cardinale Filomarino', *Antologia di Belle Arti*, 1, 1977, pp. 71–82.

RUOTOLO, 2022 Ruotolo, Renato, 'Artemisia e i suoi collezionisti a Napoli: Precisazioni e note biografiche', *Artemisia Gentileschi a Napoli*, ed. Antonio Ernesto Denunzio and Giuseppe Porzio (exh. cat., Galleria d'Italia, Naples, 2022–23), Milan: Skira, 2022, pp. 73–78.

SACCO, 2017 Sacco, Bruno, *Artemisia e gli occhi del diavolo*, Naples: Kairòs Edizioni, 2017.

SALERNO, 1960 Salerno, Luigi, 'The Picture Gallery of Vincenzo Giustiniani', *Burlington Magazine*, 102/682, 1960, pp. 21–27; 102/684, 1960, pp. 92–105; 102/685, 1960, pp. 135–48, 159.

SALERNO, 1988 Salerno, Luigi, with scientific consultation from Denis Mahon, *I dipinti del Guercino*, Rome: Ugo Bozzi, 1988.

SALVAGNI, 2012 Salvagni, Isabella, *Da Univeritas ad Academia: La corporazione dei Pittori nella chiesa di san Luca a Roma, 1478–1588*, Rome: Campisano Editore, 2012.

SALVAGNI, 2021 Salvagni, Isabella, *Da Univeritas ad Academia*, 2: *La fondazione dell'Accademia de i Pittori e Scultori di Roma nella chiesa dei santi Luca e Martina, 1588–1705*, Rome: Società Romana di Storia Patria, 2021.

SANDRART, 1675–80 Sandrart, Joachim von, *Joachim von Sandrart: Teutsche Academie der Bau-, Bild-, und Mahlerey-Künste*, Nuremberg, 1675–80, scholarly annotated online edn, ed. T. Kirchner, A. Nova, C. Blüm, A. Schreurs and T. Wübbema, 2008–12; available at http://ta.sandrart.net/en/info/citation/ accessed 1 July 2017.

SCALETTI, 2017 Scaletti, Fabio, *Caravaggio: Catalogo ragionato delle opere autografe, attribuite e controverse*, Naples: artstudiopaparo, 2017.

SCALINI, 1997 Scalini, Mario, 'L'armeria europea e orientale', in *Magnificenza alla Corte dei Medici: Arte a Firenze alla fine del Cinquecento* (exh. cat. Palazzo Pitti, Florence, 1997–98), Florence: Electa, 1997, pp. 396–98.

SCARPARO, 2002 Scarparo, Susanna, '"Artemisia": The Invention of a "Real" Woman', *Italica*, 79/3, 2002, pp. 363–78.

SCAVIZZI AND DE VITO, 2012 Scavizzi, Giuseppe, and Giuseppe de Vito, *Luca Giordano giovane, 1650–1664*, Naples: arte'm, 2012.

SCHÜTZE AND WILLETTE, 1992 Schütze, Sebastian, and Thomas C. Willette, *Massimo Stanzione: L'opera completa*, Naples: Electa, 1992.

SCHÜTZE, 2009 Schütze, Sebastian, *Caravaggio: The Complete Works*, Cologne: Taschen, 2009.

SEBREGONDI, 2005 Sebregondi, Ludovica, 'Caravaggio e la Toscana', in *Luce e Ombra: Caravaggismo e naturalismo nella pittura toscana del Seicento*, ed. Pierluigi Carofano (exh. cat., Centro per l'arte Otello Cirri and Museo Piaggio 'Giovanni Alberto Agnelli', Pontedera, 2005), Pisa: Felice Editore, 2005, pp. XLI–LIX.

SESTIERI AND DAPRA, 1994 Sestieri, Giancarlo, and Brigitte Daprà, *Domenico Gargiulo detto Micco Spadaro: Paesaggista e 'cronista' napoletano*, Milan and Rome: Jandi Sapi, 1994.

SEYMOUR, 1968 Seymour, Charles, '"Fatto di sua mano": Another Look at the Fonte Gaia Fragments in London and New York', in *Festschrift Ulrich Middeldorf*, ed. Ante Middeldorf Kosegarten, 2 vols, Berlin: de Gruyter, 1968, vol. 1, pp. 93–105.

SHARPE AND DA SILVA, 2019 Sharpe, Emily, and José da Silva, 'Art's most popular: Here are 2018's most visited shows and museums', *Art Newspaper*, 24 March 2019; available at https://www.theartnewspaper.com/analysis/fashion-provides-winning-formula

SHEARMAN, 1979 Shearman, John, 'Cristofano Allori's Judith', *Burlington Magazine*, 121/910, 1979, pp. 3–10.

SICILIANO, 2019 Siciliano, Gina, *I Know What I Am: The Life and Times of Artemisia Gentileschi*, Seattle: Fantagraphics, 2019.

SIMONS, 2017 Simons, Patricia, 'Artemisia Gentileschi's *Susanna and the Elders* (1610) in the Context of Counter Reformation Rome', in *Artemisia Gentileschi in a Changing Light*, ed. Sheila Barker, London: Harvey Miller Publishers/ London and Turnhout: Brepols, 2017, pp. 41–57.

SOHM, 1995 Sohm, Philip, 'Gendered Style in Italian Art Criticism from Michelangelo to Malvasia', *Renaissance Quarterly*, 48, 1995, pp. 759–808.

SOHM, 2007 Sohm, Philip, *The Artist Grows Old: The Aging of Art and Artists in Italy, 1500–1800*, New Haven and London: Yale University Press, 2007.

SOLINAS, 2011a Solinas, Francesco (ed.), *Lettere di Artemisia*, Rome: De Luca Editori d'Arte, 2011.

SOLINAS, 2011b Solinas, Francesco, 'Return to Rome, 1620–27', in *Artemisia Gentileschi: The Story of a Passion*, ed. Roberto Contini and Francesco Solinas (exh. cat., Palazzo Reale, Milan), Milan: 24 ORE Cultura, 2011, pp. 79–95.

SOLINAS, 2020 Solinas, Francesco, '"Bella, pulita e senza macchia": Artemisia and her Letters', in *Artemisia*, ed. Letizia Treves (exh. cat., National Gallery, London), London: National Gallery Publications, 2020, pp. 46–63.

SOLINAS, 2021 Solinas, Francesco, 'Artemisia Gentileschi a Napoli: *Giuditta e la fantesca nella tenda d'Oloferne* del Musée de la Castre a Cannes', in *Close Reading: Kunsthistorische Interpretationen vom Mittelalter bis in die Moderne*, ed. Stefan Albl, Berthold Hub and Anna Frasca-Rath, Berlin, Boston: De Gruyter, 2021, pp. 381–93.

SONTAG, 1995 Sontag, Susan, 'A Double Destiny', Introduction, in Anna Banti, *Artemisia*, Lincoln: University of Nebraska Press, 1995.

SPARTI, 1992 Sparti, Donatella, *La collezioni dal Pozzo: Storia di una famiglia e del suo museo nella Roma seicentesca*, Modena: Franco Cosimo Panini Editore, 1992.

SPEAR, 1982 Spear, Richard E., *Domenichino*, 2 vols, New Haven and London: Yale University Press, 1982.

SPEAR, 1994 Spear, Richard E., 'Guercino's "Prix-Fixe": Observations on Studio Practices and Art Marketing in Emilia', *Burlington Magazine*, 136/1098, 1994, pp. 592–602.

SPEAR, 1997 Spear, Richard E., *The 'Divine' Guido: Religion: Sex, Money, and Art in the World of Guido Reni*, New Haven and London: Yale University Press, 1997.

SPEAR, 2000 Spear, Richard E., 'Artemisia Gentileschi: Ten Years of Fact and Fiction', *Art Bulletin*, 82/3, 2000, pp. 568–79.

SPEAR, 2001 Spear, Richard E., '"I have made up my mind to take a short trip to Rome"', in *Orazio and Artemsia Gentileschi*, ed. Keith Christiansen and Judith W. Mann (exh. cat., Palazzo Venezia, Rome, The Metropolitan Museum of Art, New York, and St Louis Art Museum, 2001–2), New York: The Metropolitan Museum of Art, 2001, pp. 335–43.

SPEAR, 2005 Spear, Richard E., 'Money Matters: The Gentileschi's Finances', in *Artemisia Gentileschi: Taking Stock*, ed. Judith W. Mann, Turnhout: Brepols, 2005, pp. 147–59.

SPEAR, 2010 Spear, Richard E., 'Rome', in *Painting for Profit: The Economic Lives of Seventeenth-century Italian Painters*, ed. Richard E. Spear and Philip Sohm, New Haven and London: Yale University Press, 2010, pp. 33–113.

SPEAR, 2011 Spear, Richard E., 'Artemisia Gentileschi's "Christ and the Woman of Samaria"', *Burlington Magazine*, 153/1305, 2011, pp. 804–5.

SPEAR AND SOHM, 2010 Spear, Richard E. and Philip Sohm (eds), *Painting for Profit: The Economic Lives of Seventeenth-century Italian Painters*, New Haven and London: Yale University Press, 2010.

SPEZZAFERRO, 1974 Spezzaferro, Luigi, 'The Documentary Findings: Ottavio Costa as a Patron of Caravaggio', *Burlington Magazine*, 116/859, 1974, pp. 579–86.

SPEZZAFERRO, 1981 Spezzaferro, Luigi, 'Il recupero del Rinascimento', in *Storia dell'arte italiana*, ed. Giulio Bollati, Paolo Fossati and Federico Zeri, vol. 6, part 1, Turin: Giulio Einaudi editore, pp. 185–279.

SPIKE, 1992 Spike, John T., review of Florence, 1991, *Burlington Magazine*, 134/1067, 1992, pp. 732–734.

SPIKE, 2001 Spike, John T., *Caravaggio*, New York and London: Abbeville, 2001.

SPINOSA, 1995 Spinosa, Nicola, 'Aggiunte a Hendrick van Somer, "alias" Enrico Fiammingo', in *Napoli, l'Europa: Ricerche di Storia dell'Arte in onore di Ferdinando Bologna*, ed. Francesco Abbate and Fiorella Sricchia Santoro, Catanzano: Merdiana Libri, 1995, pp. 223–30.

SPINOSA, 2003 Spinosa, Nicola, *Ribera: L'opera completa*, Naples: Electa, 2003.

SPINOSA, 2010 Spinosa, Nicola, *Pittura del seicento a Napoli: Da Caravaggio a Massimo Stanzione*, Naples: arte'm, 2010.

SPINOSA, 2013 Spinosa, Nicola, *Grazia e tenerezza 'in posa': Bernardo Cavallino e il suo tempo 1616–1656*, Rome: Ugo Bozzi editore, 2013.

SPINOSA, 2015 Spinosa, Nicola, 'Artemisia Gentileschi e Onofrio Palumbo: insieme o "separati"', in *Una vita per la storia dell'arte: Scritti in memoria di Maurizio Marini*, ed. Pietro di Loreto, Rome: Etgraphiaei, 2015 pp. 379–88.

STEINHAUER, 2018 Jillian Steinhauer, 'Female Artists Delete Rape's "Heroic" Underpinnings', *New York Times*, 16 October 2018; available at https://www.nytimes.com/2018/10/16/arts/design/review-the-un-heroic-act-sexual-violence.html

STONE, 1991 Stone, David M., *Guercino: Catalogo complete dei dipinti*, Florence: Cantini, 1991.

STOUGHTON, 1985 Stoughon, Michael, review of Cleveland and Fort Worth, 1984–85, *Burlington Magazine*, 127, 1985, pp. 193–94.

STRAUSSMAN-PFLANZER, 2021 Straussman-Pflanzer, Eve, 'Why Have There Been No Exhibitions of Early Modern Women Artists in Hartford or Detroit', in *By Her Hand: Artemisia Gentileschi and Women Artists in Italy, 1500–1800*, ed. Eve Straussman-Pflanzer and Oliver Tostmann (exh. cat., Wadsworth Atheneum

Museum of Art, Hartford, Conn., and Detroit Institute of Arts, 2021–22), New Haven and London: Yale University Press, 2021, pp. 16–29.

STRAZZULLO, 1955 Strazzullo, Franco, *Documenti inediti per la storia dell'arte a Napoli (pittori)*, Naples: *Il Fuidoro*, 1955.

STRAZZULLO, 1957 Strazzullo, Franco, 'La peste del 1656 a Napoli', *Il Fuidoro*, 4/1–2, 1957, pp. 7–16.

SYDNEY AND MELBOURNE, 2003–4 *Darkness and Light: Caravaggio and his World*, ed. Edmund Capon et al. (exh. cat., Art Gallery of New South Wales, Sydney, and National Gallery of Victoria, Melbourne, 2003–4), Sydney: Art Gallery of New South Wales, 2004.

TERZAGHI, 2014 Terzaghi, Maria Cristina, 'Notes on Artemisia in London', in Giuseppe Porzio and Maria Cristina Terzaghi, *Artemisia Gentileschi, Cleopatra* (exh. cat., Galerie G. Sarti, Paris), Paris: Galerie G. Sarti, 2014, pp. 31–45.

TERZAGHI, 2016 Terzaghi, Maria Cristina, 'Artemisia Gentileschi a Londra', in *Artemisia Gentileschi e il suo tempo*, ed. Nicola Spinosa (exh. cat., Palazzo Braschi, Rome), Milan: Skira, 2016, pp. 69–77.

TOESCA, 1971 Toesca, Ilaria, 'Versi in lode di Artemisia Gentileschi', *Paragone*, 22/251, 1971, pp. 89–92.

TOPPER AND GILLIS, 1996 Topper, David, and Cynthia Gillis, 'Trajectories of Blood: Artemisia Gentileschi and Galileo's Parabolic Path', *Woman's Art Journal*, 17/1, 1996, pp. 10–13.

TREVES, 2020 Treves, Letizia, 'Artemisia Portraying Herself', in *Artemisia*, ed. Letizia Treves (exh. cat., National Gallery, London), London: National Gallery Publications, 2020, pp. 64–77.

TUCK-SCALA, 2003 Tuck-Scala, Anna K., 'The Documented Paintings and Life of Andrea Vaccaro (1604–1670)', Ph.D. dissertation, The Pennsylvania State University, 2003.

TUDOR, Tudor, Faye, '"Gazing in hir glasse of vaineglorie": Negotiating Vanity', in *The Senses in Early Modern England, 1558–1660*, ed. Simon Smith, Jackie Watson and Amy Kenny, Manchester: Manchester University Press, 2015, pp. 185–200.

TURNER AND SALERNO, 2017 Turner, Nicholas, and Luigi Salerno, *The Paintings of Guercino: A Revised and Expanded Catalogue Raisonné*, Rome: Ugo Bozzi Editore, 2017.

TURNER, 1983 Turner, Richard, 'Words and Pictures: The Birth and Death of Leonardo's Medusa', *Arte Lombarda*, 66/3, 1983, pp. 103–11.

UNGER, 2019 Unger, Daniel M., *Redefining Eclecticism in Early Modern Bolognese Painting: Ideology, Practice, and Criticism*, Amsterdam: Amsterdam University Press, 2019.

VAN LEEUWEN, 2011 Van Leeuwen, Rudie, 'The Portrait Historié in Religious Context and its Condemnation', in *Pokerfaced: Flemish and Dutch Baroque Faces Unveiled*, ed. Katlijne Van der Stighelen, Hannelore Magnus and Bert Watteeuw, Brepols: Turnhout, 2011 (Museum at the Crossroads, 19), pp. 109–24.

VANNUGLI, 2011 Vannugli, Antonio, 'Two New Attributions to Ribera', *Burlington Magazine*, 153, June 2011, pp. 398–404.

VARTANIAN, 2021 Vartanian, Vrag, 'Art Historian May Have Discovered Two Artemisia Gentileschi Paintings in Beirut', *Hyperallergic*, 9 June 2021; available at https://hyperallergic.com/652364/consensus-grows-about-sursock-palace-artemisia-gentileschi-paintings-and-gregory-buchakjian-research-after-beirut-explosion/

VASARI, 1568 Vasari, Giorgio, *The Lives of the Artists*, Florence, 1668, trans. Julia Conaway Bondanella and Peter Bondanella, Oxford: Oxford University Press, 1991.

VASARI, 1550/1568 Vasari, Giorgio, *Le vite de' più eccellenti pittori scultori e architettori nelle redazioni del 1550 e 1568*, ed. Rosanna Bettarini and Paola Barocchi, 8 vols, Florence: Sansoni Editore, 1966–87.

VATICAN CITY, 1990 *Saint, Site and Sacred Strategy: Ignatius, Rome and Jesuit Urbanism*, ed. Thomas M. Lucas (exh. cat., Biblioteca Apostolica Vaticana), Vatican City: Biblioteca Apostolica Vaticana, 1990.

VELTHUIS, 2005 Velthuis, Olav, *Talking Prices: Symbolic Meanings of Prices on the Market for Contemporary Art*, Princeton: Princeton University Press, 2005.

VENICE, 1979–80 *Venezia e la Peste, 1348–1797* (exh. cat., Palazzo Ducale, Venice, 1979–80), Venice: Marsilio Editori, 1980.

VICINI, 2000 Vicini, Maria Lucrezia, *Orazio e Artemisia Gentileschi alla Galleria Spada: padre e figlia a confronto*, Rome: Arti Grafiche Tilligraf, 2000.

VIENNA, 2007 *Fürst Karl Eusebius von Liechtenstein, 1611–1684: Erbe und Bewahrer in schwerer Zeit*, ed. Herbert Haupt (exh. cat., Liechtenstein Museum, Vienna), Munich: Prestel, 2007.

VILLA, 2020 Villa, Angelica, 'New branding for old masters: why a seemingly forgotten collecting category is on the rise', *ARTnews*, 8 October 2020; available at https://www.artnews.com/art-news/market/old-masters-collecting-category-popular-1234572443/

VILLARI, 1993 Villari, Rosario, trans. James Newell, *The Revolt of Naples*, English translation of *La rivolta antispagnola a Napoli: Le origini (1585–1647)*, Bari: Editori Laterza, 1967, with the additional afterwords, 'Masaniello: Contemporary and Recent Interpretations', and 'Naples and the Contemporaneous Revolutions: Some Points of Convergence', Cambridge: Polity Press, 1993.

VODRET, 2009 Vodret, Rossella, *Caravaggio, l'opera completa*, Milan: Silvana editoriale, 2009.

VODRET AND STRINATI, 2001 Vodret, Rossella, and Claudio Strinati, 'Painted Music: "A New and Affecting Manner"' in *The Genius of Rome 1592–1623*, ed. Beverley Louise Brown (exh. cat., Royal Academy of Arts, London), London: Royal Academy, 2001, pp. 92–115.

VOLPI, 2014 Volpi, Caterina, *Salvator Rosa (1615–1673): 'pittore famoso'*, Rome: Ugo Bozzi, 2014.

VREELAND, 2002 Vreeland, Susan, *The Passion of Artemisia*, New York: Penguin Books, 2002.

WALDMAN, 1997 Waldman, Louis Alexander, 'Bronzino's Uffizi "Pietà" and the Cambi Chapel in S. Trinita, Florence', *Burlington Magazine*, 139/1127, 1997, pp. 94–102.

WASHINGTON, 1999–2000 *The Drawings of Annibale Carracci*, ed. Daniele Benati et al. (exh. cat., National Gallery of Art, Washington, 1999–2000), Washington: National Gallery of Art, 1999.

WASHINGTON, 2007 *Italian Women Artists, from Renaissance to Baroque*, ed. Vera Fortunati, Jordana Pomeroy and Claudio Strinati (exh. cat., National Museum of Women in the Arts, Washington), Milan: Skira, 2007.

WHITFIELD, 2001 Whitfield, Clovis, 'Portraiture: From the "Simple Portrait" to the "Resemblance Parlante"', in *The Genius of Rome 1592–1623*, ed. Beverley Louise Brown (exh. cat., Royal Academy of Arts, London), London: Royal Academy, 2001, pp. 140–71.

WITTKOWER AND WITTKOWER, 1963 Wittkower, Rudolf, and Margot Wittkower, *Born Under Saturn: The Character and Conduct of Artists, a Documented History From Antiquity to the French Revolution*, New York: W.W. Norton, 1963.

WOOD, 1992 Wood, Carolyn H., 'The Ludovisi Collection of Paintings in 1623', *Burlington Magazine*, 134/1073, 1992, pp. 515–23.

WOODS-MARSDEN, 1998 Woods-Marsden, Joanna, *Renaissance Self-portraiture: The Visual Construction of Identity and the Social Status of the Artist*, New Haven and London: Yale University Press, 1998.

ZAPLETALOVÁ, 2013 Zapletalová, Jana, 'Artemisia Gentileschi: A Newly Attributed Painting', *Arte Cristiana*, 877, 2013, pp. 251–58.

ZAPPERI, 1990 Zapperi, Roberto, *Tiziano, Paolo III e i suoi nipoti: Nepotismo e ritratto di Stato*, Turin: Bollati Boringhieri, 1990.

ZARRILLO, 2017 Zarrillo, Taryn Marie, 'Complimentary Activities: Marco Boschini, Paolo del Sera and Niccolò Renieri as Merchants, Collectors and Painters in Seicento Venice', in *Early Modern Merchants as Collectors*, ed. Christina M. Anderson, London and New York: Routledge, 2017, pp. 129–40.

ZETTERMAN, 2016 Zetterman, Eve, 'Curatorial Strategies on the Art Scene During the Feminist Movement: Los Angeles in the 1970s', in *Curating Differently: Feminisms, Exhibitions and Curatorial Spaces*, ed. Jessica Sjöholm Skrubbe, Newcastle: Cambridge Scholars Publishing, 2016, pp. 1–28.

INDEX

'AG' refers to Artemisia Gentileschi. Page numbers in *italic* indicate illustrations.

ACKNOWLEDGEMENTS

One hot afternoon in August 1991, I expectantly made my way as a young student to the Casa Buonarroti, Florence. On display was the first retrospective exhibition dedicated to Artemisia Gentileschi. I remember the experience as being both energising and challenging. Each canvas seemed to project out of its gilded frame as an insistent exclamation mark that was also, at one and the same time, a puzzling interrogative. Now, as I reach my own exclamation point along an immensely rewarding journey, I find that these words can still be used to describe my response to the topic of Artemisia Gentileschi and all that she has come to represent.

Thanks are due in the first instance to the legions of dedicated scholars whose persistent and probing research has done so much to shed light on a topic that was, until not so long ago, considered to be highly specialised and of limited interest only. I have endeavoured to acknowledge the myriad ways that this diverse and committed community has contributed to our knowledge of all things Gentileschian. But if I have neglected to acknowledge appropriately any author's contribution, I sincerely beg their pardon in advance: it is an omission of oversight rather than of intentional design. I am intensely grateful also to the anonymous reviewers of the manuscript. Their generous and perceptive reading of my work pressed me to reconsider and reconceptualise many aspects of the text. The finished work has benefited greatly from their input. Any errors that do remain, however, are mine alone.

I have been able to enjoy an ongoing dialogue of lively discussions and exchanges of ideas with many others working in the area. They are too numerous to mention – but I, nonetheless, feel impelled to thank at least some of them by name: Jesse Locker, Riccardo Lattuada, Gianni Papi, Sebastian Schütze, Giuseppe Porzio, Gianluca Forgione, Viviana Farina, Gregory Buchakjian, Charles Dempsey, Gabriele Finaldi, David Jaffé, Francesco Lofano and Nicholas Penny. I was also fortunate enough to be able to enjoy a period of extended time working on what became one of the strands leading into this project at the Center for Advanced Study in the Visual Arts at the National Gallery of Art, Washington, D.C., under the lively and supportive guidance of Peter M. Lukehart and Elizabeth Cropper.

Art-market research forms a particular focus of this study, and, in this respect, I benefited greatly from my association with professors Hans van Miegroet and Neil de Marchi of Duke University. My participation in their project 'Mapping Markets for Paintings in Europe' gave me entrée into an expanded, inter-disciplinary field of researchers that I found extraordinarily beneficial to my work, and a follow-up fellowship at Duke University cemented my deep respect and gratitude for their ongoing generosity and support. I was also lucky enough to be able to collaborate with Richard E. Spear and Philip Sohm on their 'Economic Lives of Italian Baroque Painters' project, subsequently published by Yale University Press.

At Princeton University Press, special thanks are owed to Michelle Komie for her unwavering support of this project. Sincere thanks are due also to Gillian Malpass for her early championing of the manuscript and for her adroit copy-editing and deft and handsome design of the published work. Thanks are due also to Jane Brown from the Visual Cultures Resource Centre of the University of Melbourne for providing specialist assistance with the photographs. I also remain immensely grateful to the fundamental support provided by the staff of the Bibliotheca Hertziana, Rome, the Kunsthistorishes Institut, Florence, and my own research library, the Baillieu Library at the University of Melbourne.

Extended periods of research leave and acquisitions funding for this project were generously made available by the University of Melbourne. Research for this book was further supported by grants from the University of Melbourne Faculty of Arts Special Studies Program and the Small Grant Program of the Australian Research Council, for which I am also most grateful. Finally, though, I must thank Jane, Laura and Dominic, for their continuing love and companionship and for their willingness to accompany me yet further down the road towards the point of resolution – wherever it may lie – towards which all our endeavours must ultimately aspire.

PHOTOGRAPHY AND COPYRIGHT CREDITS

© Accademia Nazionale di San Luca, Rome, Bridgeman Images: 34
Alamy: 44
Alamy, Andrew Harnik/AP: 136
© Amministrazione Doria Pamphilj, s.r.l., DeAgostini Picture Library/Photo Scala, Florence: 66
© Archivio Fotografico Museo Nacional del Prado, Madrid: 85, 86, 97, 101
Archivio Patrimonio Artistico Intesa San Paolo, Pedicini fotografi: 99
Arciconfraternita della Trinità dei Pellegrini, Naples, Pedicini fotografi: 119
Art Gallery of New South Wales, Sydney: 70
ArtNews, January 1971: 124
Author: 122, 123
Basilica di San Carlo Borromeo al Corso, La Venerabile Arciconfraternita dei Santi Ambrogio e Carlo, Rome, Alamy: 80
Brooklyn Museum Archives, Records of the Department of Photography: 125
Courtesy of The Burghley House Collection, Bridgeman Images: 64
Cappella del Tesoro di San Gennaro, Naples Cathedral, Pedicini fotografi: 89, 94
Image © Casa Buonarroti, Florence: 128
Casa Buonarroti, Florence, Fine Art Images/Archivi Alinari, Firenze: 4
Catedral de Sevilla, Seville, Alamy: 65
Catello collection, Naples, Pedicini fotografi: 87
Cathedral Basilica San Procolo martire, Diocese of Pozzuoli, Naples, Pedicini fotografi: 88
Chiesa del Pio Monte della Misericordia, Naples, Pedicini fotografi: 109
© Christie's, London, Alamy: 1
Collezioni Comunali d'Arte Bologna, Alamy: 72
© Columbus Museum of Art, Columbus, Ohio: 90
Courtesy of Coquillete Parfum, Paris: 138
Detroit Institute of Arts: 10, 21, 42, 48, 69
Etro Collection, Alamy: 21
Etro Collection, Mondadori Portfolio/Bridgeman Images: 78
Exhibition Design: DWA Design Studio, Frederik De Wachter + Alberto Artesani, Photo, Helenio Barbetta: 130, 131
Courtesy of Faux Machismo: 135
Fondazione di Studi di Storia dell'Arte Roberto Longhi, Scala Archives: 33
Fondazione Musei Civici, Palazzo Ducale, Venice, on long-term loan from a private collection, Alamy: 67
Courtesy of the Fondazione Torino Musei—Museo Civico d'Arte Antica e Palazzo Madama, Turin, Alamy: 16
Courtesy of Galerie G. Sarti, Paris: 120
The Getty Research Institute, Los Angeles: 6, 9
Image © Guerrilla Girls, courtesy guerrillagirls.com: 2
Indianapolis Museum of Art: 93
The J. Paul Getty Museum, Los Angeles: 5, 77
© Judy Chicago, Photo courtesy of Judy Chicago/Art Resource, NY: 127
Kunsthistorisches Museum, Vienna, Photo Austrian Archives/Scala, Florence: 43
Laura Elise Schwendinger, Photo, Vivian Sachs: 134
Le Collezioni d'Arte e di Storia della Fondazione Cassa di Risparmio in Bologna, Alamy: 126
Lucas Museum of Narrative Art, Los Angeles, Photo © Christie's Images/Bridgeman Images: 114
Image © The Metropolitan Museum of Art, New York: 129

The Metropolitan Museum of Art, New York: 23, 58, 59, 79
Courtesy of the Ministero per i Beni e delle Attività Culturali e del Turismo, Galleria degli Uffizi, Florence, Photo Scala, Florence: 3
Galleria Borghese, Photo Scala, Florence: 20, 24
Galleria degli Uffizi, Florence, Archivi Alinari, Firenze: 19, 56
Galleria degli Uffizi, Florence, Bridgeman Images: 61
Galleria degli Uffizi, Florence, Finsiel/Alinari Archives/Bridgeman Images: 60
Galleria degli Uffizi, Florence, Finsiel/Archivi Alinari, Firenze: 47
Galleria degli Uffizi, Florence, Photo Scala, Florence: 31, 36, 55
Galleria Nazionale d'Arte Antica di Palazzo Barberini, Photo Scala, Florence: 30
Galleria Palatina, Palazzo Pitti, Archivi Alinari, Firenze: 8
Galleria Palatina, Palazzo Pitti, Fine Art Images/Archivi Alinari, Firenze: 40
Galleria Palatina, Palazzo Pitti, Florence, Archivi Alinari, Firenze: 52
Galleria Palatina, Palazzo Pitti, Raffaello Benini/Archivi Alinari, Firenze: 41
Galleria Spada, Rome, Photo © Stefano Baldini/Bridgeman Images: 11
Galleria Spada, Rome, Photo Scala, Florence: 81
Museo e Real Bosco di Capodimonte, Naples, Archivi Alinari, Firenze: 29
Museo e Real Bosco di Capodimonte, Naples, Pedicini fotografi: 17, 84, 91
Museo Nazionale del Bargello, Florence, Finsiel/Archivi Alinari, Firenze: 53
Museo Nazionale di San Martino, Naples, Photo Scala, Florence: 82
Museo Nazionale di San Martino, Pedicini fotografi: 118
Pinacoteca Nazionale di Bologna, Bridgeman Images: 12
Pinacoteca Nazionale di Bologna, Polo Museale dell'Emilia Romagna, Photo © Fine Art Images/Bridgeman Images: 121
Rallaello Bencini, Archivi Alinari, Firenze: 32
Moravská Galerie v Brne, Brno, Alamy: 117
Münzkabinett, Staatliche Museen zu Berlin, BPK Bildagentur für Kunst, Kultur und Geschichte, Berlin: 74
Musée de la Faïence et des Beaux-Arts, 'Frédéric Blandin', Nevers: 111
Musée des Beaux-Arts de Marseille, Bridgeman Images: 68
Musée du Louvre, Département des Arts Graphiques, Archivi Alinari, Firenze: 18
Musées Royaux des Beaux-Arts de Belgique, Brussels, RKD Netherlands Institute for Art History: 62, 63
Museo de Bellas Artes de Bilbao: 25, 27
Museo dell'Opera del Duomo, Florence, Photo Scala, Florence: 45
Nathalie Ferlut and Tamia Baudouin/Editions Delcourt: Paris, 2017: 132
© The National Gallery, London: 35, 49
National Gallery of Art, Washington: 113
National Gallery of Ireland, Dublin: 14
The National Museum of Art, Architecture and Design, Oslo © Nasjonalgalleriet, Oslo, Fine Art Images/Archivi Alinari, Firenze: 26, 28
The National Museum of Art, Architecture and Design, Oslo, on loan from a private collection: 39
The National Museum of Western Art, Tokyo, Bridgeman Images: 95
Palazzo Blu, Pisa, Property of the Fondazione Pisa, Alamy: 76, 100
Palazzo Reale, Naples, Pedicini fotografi: 108
Private collection, Alamy: 104
Private collection, courtesy of the owner/Gianni Papi: 71
Private collection, courtesy of the owner/Viviana Farina: 83
Private collection, Pedicini fotografi: 105, 110
Private collection USA, Bridgeman Images: 38
Promotional brochure, Agnès Merlet, *Artemisia*, 1998: 133
Quadreria dell'Arcivescovado, Milan, Mondadori Portfolio/Electa/ Sergio Anelli/Bridgeman Images: 54
Raffaello Bencini/ Archivi Alinari, Firenze: 46
Rita R. R. and Marc A. Seidner collection, Los Angeles, Alamy: 98
Royal Academy of Arts, London: 57
The Royal Collection Trust, © His Majesty King Charles III: 102, 103
Courtesy of Sabrina Cenni: 137
© The Saint Louis Art Museum: 22
© The San Diego Museum of Art: 15
Schloss Weißenstein, Pommersfelden, Archivi Alinari, Firenze: 13
Schloss Weißenstein, Pommersfelden, Fine Art Images/Archivi Alinari, Firenze: 7
Photograph courtesy of Sotheby's, Inc. © 2023: 106
Stiftung Preussische Schlösser und Gärten, Berlin-Brandenburg: 115, 116
Sursock-Cochrane Palace, Beirut, Gregory Buchakjian/Roderick Cochrane: 96
Toledo Museum of Art, Toledo, Ohio, Photo Richard Goodbody Inc., New York: 107
© The Trustees of the British Museum, London: 73, 75
© Wadsworth Atheneum Museum of Art, Hartford, Connecticut: 37, 50
Whereabouts unknown, Alamy: 51

Published by Princeton University Press, 41 William Street, Princeton, New Jersey 08540

In the United Kingdom: Princeton University Press, 99 Banbury Road, Oxford OX2 6JX

press.princeton.edu

FRONT JACKET IMAGE Artemisia Gentileschi, *Self-portrait as St Catherine of Alexandria*, *c.*1615–17, oil on canvas, 71.4 × 69 cm, Bought with the support of the American Friends of the National Gallery, the National Gallery Trust, Art Fund (through the legacy of Sir Denis Mahon), Lord and Lady Sassoon, Lady Getty, Hannah Rothschild CBE and other donors including those who wish to remain anonymous, 2018 (detail of fig. 35). © The National Gallery, London

BACK JACKET IMAGE Artemisia Gentileschi, *Self-portrait as the Allegory of Painting (La Pittura)*, signed, *c.*1638–39, oil on canvas, 98.6 × 75.2 cm, The Royal Collection (detail of fig. 103). Royal Collection Trust / © His Majesty King Charles III 2024

FRONTISPIECE Artemisia Gentileschi, *Self-portrait as the Allegory of Painting (La Pittura)* (detail of fig. 103)

LIBRARY OF CONGRESS CATALOGING-IN-PUBLICATION DATA

Names: Marshall, Christopher R., author.
Title: Artemisia Gentileschi and the business of art / Christopher R. Marshall.
Description: Princeton : Princeton University Press, [2024] | Includes bibliographical references and index.
Identifiers: LCCN 2023044720 (print) | LCCN 2023044721 (ebook) | ISBN 9780691253886 (hardback) | ISBN 9780691258010 (ebook)
Subjects: LCSH: Gentileschi, Artemisia, 1593-1652 or 1653. | Gentileschi, Artemisia, 1593-1652 or 1653--Appreciation. | Painters--Italy--Economic conditions--17th century. | Painting--Economic aspects--History. | BISAC: ART / History / Baroque & Rococo | SOCIAL SCIENCE / Feminism & Feminist Theory
Classification: LCC ND623.G364 M37 2024 (print) | LCC ND623.G364 (ebook)
| DDC 759.5 [B]--dc23/eng/20231212
LC record available at https://lccn.loc.gov/2023044720
LC ebook record available at https://lccn.loc.gov/2023044721

British Library Cataloging-in-Publication Data is available

Designed by Gillian Malpass
This book has been composed in Van Dijck MT Std and Rialto Grande Df
Printed on acid-free paper. ∞
Printed in Italy
10 9 8 7 6 5 4 3 2 1